DULLES

BOOKS BY LEONARD MOSLEY

DUEL FOR KILIMANJARO
THE LAST DAYS OF THE BRITISH RAJ
THE GLORIOUS FAULT: The Life of Lord Curzon
THE CAT AND THE MICE: A German Spy in Cairo
REPORT FROM GERMANY, 1945
GIDEON GOES TO WAR: A Biography of Orde Wingate
DOWNSTREAM, 1939
CASTLEROSSE: The Life of a Bon Vivant
SO FAR SO GOOD: A Fragment of Autobiography
HAILE SELASSIE: The Conquering Lion
FACES FROM THE FIRE: Biography of Sir Archibald McIndoe
HIROHITO: Emperor of Japan
ON BORROWED TIME: How World War II Began
THE BATTLE OF BRITAIN
BACKS TO THE WALL: London in World War II
POWER PLAY: Oil in the Middle East
THE REICH MARSHAL: A Biography of Hermann Goering
LINDBERGH: A Biography

NOVELS
SO I KILLED HER
NO MORE REMAINS
WAR LORD
EACH HAD A SONG
THE SEDUCTIVE MIRROR

DULLES:

*A Biography of Eleanor, Allen,
and John Foster Dulles
and Their Family Network*

by Leonard Mosley

The Dial Press/James Wade
New York 1978

Published by
The Dial Press/James Wade
1 Dag Hammarskjold Plaza
New York, N.Y. 10017

Grateful acknowledgment is made to the following for permission to reprint previously
published material:

Excerpts from *The Secret Surrender* by Allen Dulles. Copyright © 1966 by Harper & Row
  Publishers, Inc. By permission of the publishers.
Excerpts from *Secrets, Spies and Scholars* by Ray S. Cline (Washington, D.C.: Acropolis
  Books, 1976)
Excerpt from *The Devil and John Foster Dulles* by Townsend Hoopes (Boston: Atlantic,
  Little, Brown, 1973)
Excerpts from *The Craft of Intelligence* by Allen Dulles (New York: Harper & Row, 1963)
Excerpts from *Germany's Underground* by Allen Dulles (New York: The Macmillan Com-
  pany, 1947)
Excerpts from *War or Peace?* by John Foster Dulles (New York: The Macmillan Company,
  1950)
Excerpts from *My Silent War* by Kim Philby (London: McGibbon & Kee Ltd., 1968)
Excerpts from *Baker Street Irregular* by Bickham Sweet-Escott (London: Methuen & Co.
  Ltd., 1965)
Excerpt from *Go East Young Man* by William O. Douglas (New York: Random House,
  1974)

Library of Congress Cataloging in Publication Data

Mosley, Leonard, 1913–
  Dulles.

  Bibliography: p.
  Includes index.
  1. Dulles family. 2. Dulles, John Foster, 1888–1959. 3. Dulles, Eleanor Lansing,
1896–
4. Dulles, Allen Welsh, 1893–1969. 5. Statesmen—
United States—Biography. 6. Economists—United
States—Biography. 7. United States. Central
Intelligence Agency—Officials and employees—Biography.
8. United States—Foreign relations—20th century.
I. Title.
E748.D87M67   973.9′092′2 [2]   77–19042
ISBN 0-8037-1744-X

Manufactured in the United States of America

Design by Francesca Belanger

Acknowledgments

At the end of this book will be found a bibliographical essay giving in full detail all the archives, documents, authorities, and other sources I have consulted during my study of the lives and background of John Foster, Allen Welsh, and Eleanor Lansing Dulles. Here I would simply like to express my gratitude to those who went out of their way to be particularly helpful to me in the course of my researches.

I am especially grateful, first of all, to Eleanor Lansing Dulles herself. Both at her home in Washington, D.C., and at my home in the south of France, she gave me many hours of her time and filled them with endlessly fascinating stories about her brothers and herself. In the spring of 1976 she came to my house at St. Paul de Vence from Germany, where she had been an honored guest of the Bonn government at their Bicentennial Salute to the United States. The weather was unseasonably chilly but she bathed four times a day in the family pool and obviously relished the icy water. On June 1, 1976, we lunched together at a portside restaurant at Villefranche-sur-Mer and she beamed happily across the sea and mountains of the Côte d'Azur, which she had last seen in 1918, on leave from the Western Front during World War I.

"I can't think of a nicer way to celebrate my birthday," she said. She was eighty-one that day.

Many were the friends, acquaintances, and former colleagues of Foster and Allen Dulles who spared me time, and their names will be found in the bibliographical essay. But several went beyond the call of duty by not simply talking or providing documentation, but also suggesting new avenues of approach and new sources of information. In this category I would single out Mr. Walter Pforzheimer, former legislative counsel of the CIA and later its chief archivist, and one of the world's greatest authorities on the history of espionage: I shall long remember my visits to his private archives at Watergate, and his abrasive and entertaining comments on the great figures of politics and intelligence he has known. I must also thank Mr. Lawrence Houston, former general counsel of the CIA, for enabling me to gain access to the Allen Welsh Dulles Papers at Princeton University, where I was already studying the John Foster Dulles Papers.

Both Mr. William Bundy, editor of *Foreign Affairs,* and his brother, Mr. McGeorge Bundy, president of the Ford Foundation, talked to me at some length of their own associations with the Dulles brothers and gave me useful leads to new informants. Two statesmen-turned-academics, Robert Bowie of Harvard and Dean Rusk at the University of Georgia, cut into busy schedules to dig into their memories and submit to questioning about their association with Foster Dulles at crucial moments in his career. Robert Amory, former deputy director of the CIA, deserves mention for the entertaining nature of his lunch-time conversation as well as the quality of his information.

Perhaps the most enlightening and thoughtful analysis of what life was like in the CIA under Allen Dulles came from Richard Bissell, Jr., for whom covert action and clandestine collection were obviously never the fascinating game which Allen found them. In his quiet, cultivated way, Bissell threw a grim and baleful light on the nature of the business. So in a rather more rueful manner did another former hunter in the espionage jungle, Mr. Howard Roman, whose wry references to the bizarre CIA safaris of the 1950s made them sound totally unlike the daredevil adventures that Allen Dulles relished.

Mr. Christopher Dobson, whose knowledge of terrorist and underground activities in the Middle East is acute, was kind enough to lend me tapes of some of his talks with Arab leaders, and they revealed some fascinating details of CIA activities in Egypt and the Gulf. He has my warm thanks.

One to whom time was most precious of all, the late Earl of Avon ᾿ (better known as Anthony Eden), allowed me to steal some of it during the last summer of his life, in August 1976. I saw him at his home in Wiltshire, and though he knew quite well he was dying, he had taken the trouble to prepare elaborate notes for our meeting. We talked at great length about the traumatic autumn twenty years earlier when, as Prime Minister, he led Britain in the Suez adventure and clashed with Foster Dulles and Dwight D. Eisenhower. He was as vigorous and vehement as ever in defense of his actions, as bitter as ever over the manner in which he believed Foster Dulles had misled him.

Finally, I would like to thank H. A. R. (Kim) Philby for taking the trouble to write me from Moscow and give me what might be called the KGB view of Allen and Foster Dulles, the CIA, and the Eisenhower administration. When I first met Philby, he was a member of the British SIS (Secret Intelligence Service) and neither I nor anyone else guessed that he was in fact working for the Russians, and had been since the days of the Spanish Civil War. After he defected to Moscow in 1963, some mutual friends kept contact with him, and it was through one of them that I got into touch with him while researching this book. I sent him a questionnaire but did not expect an answer. Then, around Christmas time 1976, the following letter arrived:

> Dear Mr. Mosley,—I have just returned to Moscow after a long trip, and was not a little surprised to find your letter and questionnaire awaiting me. Of course, I know you by reputation. I had the pleasure some years ago of reading your *Curzon* which still adorns my shelves, and have read reviews of *Lindbergh.*
>
> I would like to earn a copy of your latest work by answering your questionnaire, but I am afraid I must ask you for a little more time. I found a mountain of work awaiting me on my return, and it will be two or three weeks before I can deal with your questions in the serious manner which they deserve.
>
> Of the people you mention, I can claim to have known reasonably well Allen Dulles, Bedell Smith, Frank Wisner and Kim Roosevelt. I may have met any or all of the others but, if so, only so casually that they have slipped my memory. I never met JFD [John Foster Dulles], whose legacy (I hope) we have finally put behind us! You have found a fascinating subject . . .
>
> With best wishes. Yours sincerely
> H A R Philby.

His answers to my questionnaire followed in February 1977, and a clarification of some statements he made at that time, plus replies to some further questions, were received the following April. Readers interested in assessing the character of Kim Philby, whose wit, percipience, and urbane charm even his enemies acknowledge, might find it useful to study the correspondence, which is printed as an appendix.

One last word. This book could not have been researched or written without the aid and comfort of the constant companion, fellow researcher, and joy of my life. My *remerciements* to her above all.

Contents

Acknowledgments vii

PROLOGUE *The Man Upstairs* 3

CHAPTER ONE *Cradle Marks* 13

CHAPTER TWO *Breaking Out* 28

CHAPTER THREE *Trio Abroad* 44

CHAPTER FOUR *Foster Father* 63

CHAPTER FIVE *Mixed Marriage* 84

CHAPTER SIX *Enter Wild Bill* 101

CHAPTER SEVEN *"Pontificating American!"* 116

CHAPTER EIGHT *Swiss Role* 131

CHAPTER NINE *Dumbarton Acorns* 150

CHAPTER TEN *Frustration* 166

CHAPTER ELEVEN *Sunrise* 174

CHAPTER TWELVE *"Lucky Rear"* 189

CHAPTER THIRTEEN *Thwarted* 214

CHAPTER FOURTEEN *Call to Battle* 237

CHAPTER FIFTEEN *The Gospel According to Luke* 253

CHAPTER SIXTEEN *Beetle Juice* 268

CHAPTER SEVENTEEN *All Aboard* 287

CHAPTER EIGHTEEN *Bread and Circuses* 302

CHAPTER NINETEEN *Double Deals* 318

Contents

CHAPTER TWENTY   *Double Agents*   342

CHAPTER TWENTY-ONE   *Spy in the Sky*   363

CHAPTER TWENTY-TWO   *Nile Boil*   379

CHAPTER TWENTY-THREE   *Not Worth a Dam*   393

CHAPTER TWENTY-FOUR   *"A Very Sloppy Performance"*   408

CHAPTER TWENTY-FIVE   *Spies in the Stratosphere*   426

CHAPTER TWENTY-SIX   *Final Call*   439

CHAPTER TWENTY-SEVEN   *Nose in the Trough*   450

CHAPTER TWENTY-EIGHT   *Siempre Fidel*   464

CHAPTER TWENTY-NINE   *Such Other Functions*   475

Envoi   484

APPENDIX: *Letters from a Spy*   487

Source Notes   499

Index   519

DULLES

PROLOGUE

The Man Upstairs

The guests had been summoned for the evening of December 24, 1968, and those among them who were parents with young children, Christmas stockings still to be filled, were not the only ones who had come reluctantly. It had been a week in Washington for festive parties on the embassy party circuit, departmental boozeups, clubs, college and congressional reunions. Ahead lay the interminable family dinners, rowdy ballgames and circus outings with the kids, and the raucous roundelays of the approaching New Year weekend. Christmas Eve should have been a chance to stay home and take a breather.

But except for those who had already left for the Caribbean, Palm Springs, or the ski slopes, no one had refused the invitation, and there was a large turnout at the house on Q Street, in Georgetown. Mrs. Clover Dulles, the hostess of the evening, looked around the crowded rooms with the complacent expression of one who feels the party is going well. There were times when Clover Dulles could look, in the words of a friend, like "a terrified doe just before the hunter plugs her right between the eyes," but for the moment the tension lines in her face had relaxed and she seemed to be floating on air. Years ago she had been a hauntingly lovely young woman, and the smile she wore now was a reminder of it, lighting her features with a rejuvenating glow.

This household had a reputation in Washington for giving good, even lavish parties, and this one was certainly up to standard. Clover's husband sometimes told colleagues that his wife had no sense of money and that she was inclined to spend it like water—"just wastes it on useless things." At least on this occasion the expenditure had gone on good drink and excellent food (superbly prepared by a Guatemalan cook, Natalia, the household treasure), and even the most hesitant guests were beginning to be glad they had come. All of them were friends, and most of them were distinguished in their fields. There was a senator and a congressman, an admiral and an Air Force general, a sprinkling of State Department and Foreign Service officials, a Briton and a German with vague-sounding jobs at their embassies who were almost certainly members of their countries' intelligence services. But most of the guests were senior officers and former officers of the CIA and their wives. No surprise in that. The host of the evening (even if he was nowhere to be seen) was Allen Dulles, and though he had not been director of the Central Intelligence Agency since President Kennedy had sacked him in 1962, his was still a name to be rolled over the tongue wherever intelligence men gathered. When he summoned them to his house, even if it was Christmas Eve, and even if he did it through an invitation from his wife, they canceled other engagements to be there.

But where was Allen Dulles? He had the reputation of being a great partygoer, as everyone in Washington knew, normally never missing a convivial assembly of interesting people—especially if it included some pretty and intelligent women—and certainly not his own. One of those present this evening was Jeanie Houston, wife of the general counsel of the CIA, a tall, long-legged, elegant blonde with a sharp wit and loads of charm, and she alone would have made Allen's evening worthwhile. "Where's Allen?" she had asked Clover when she arrived. "Upstairs," Clover said briefly, and moved on.

Jeanie Houston was used to her hostess's vagueness. But she found it hard to believe that such an impeccably polite man as Allen Dulles would fail to be on time for his own party, and she was disturbed. She waited until her husband, Lawrence Reid Houston, had greeted his friends and been given his drink, and then she went over to him.

"Larry," she whispered, "I'm worried. I think you should go upstairs and find out what's happening to Allen."

It would be an exaggeration to say that the name Dulles no longer meant anything in Washington in 1968, but certainly most of the *éclat* had gone out of it. A decade earlier it had been a name that appeared almost daily in newspaper headlines. In most of the chancelleries of

Europe and Asia it was uttered like an incantation or muttered like an imprecation every morning, and probably several times each day, by presidents, prime ministers, and chairmen of political committees.

During all but the final months of the Eisenhower era it was the Dulles family which managed and manipulated the foreign affairs of the United States, and, in consequence, decidedly influenced the policies of the rest of the world. John Foster Dulles was at the peak of his powers, a Secretary of State so powerful and implacable that no government in what was then fervently referred to as the Free World would have dared to take a decision of international importance without first getting his nod of approval. There were those who had tried to proceed without it, and lived to rue the day.

In Europe the cockpit of East and West conflict was West Berlin, and its affairs were controlled from Washington by Eleanor Lansing Dulles, John Foster's "little sister," as he patronizingly called her. She ran the Berlin desk at State from 1952 to 1959.

But it was through Allen Welsh Dulles, the younger brother, that the family consolidated its control over the external policies of the United States. Allen was the romantic and adventurous member of the family, with a reputation both as a successful secret agent and a not-so-secret swinger (in the days before either the word or the habit had become accepted). A hero of the undercover war against Hitler in World War II, he had relapsed into private life as a junior partner in his brother's law firm in the early postwar years, and wilted on the vine. The cold war had brought him back to intelligence and back to life, for the essence of his life was espionage. When Eisenhower became President and his brother Secretary of State, Allen Welsh Dulles had reached the summit of his career (if not the apogee of his ambitions), and became, in the opinion of many, one of the three or four most powerful men in the United States.

As director of Central Intelligence he controlled an enterprise far richer and more pervasive in its espionage activities than anything ever achieved by the Abwehr in Nazi Germany, the KGB in Russia, or SIS in Britain. He ran it almost entirely free from congressional control, he dispensed an annual budget of around $97 million,* for which he needed to give only the most general accounting, and he was capable

*The figure for 1950.

5

at his sole discretion of sending agents into action against any nation, ally or enemy, neutral or potential foe. In the 1950s he was the all-powerful spymaster, not simply with his agents operating in every country on the globe, but with his own scientists, economists, agronomists, meteorologists, psychiatrists, and medical specialists. He ran his own planes, he recruited his own soldiers, and he initiated his own military campaigns.

Ilya Ehrenburg, the tireless Soviet propagandist, once dubbed him the most dangerous man in the world, far more dangerous than his brother, the Secretary of State, and wrote in *Isvestia* that if he ever succeeded in getting into heaven, he would "be found mining the clouds, shooting up the stars and slaughtering the angels." Allen Dulles was delighted. Not only did the "enemy" put him a notch higher in importance than his brother; the quotation also made an apt introduction for the speeches and lectures he was beginning to give about his espionage adventures and his work as director of the CIA.

In many ways he was a much darker, more ruthless and unscrupulous man than his brother, and certainly his heart was stonier than that of his sister, Eleanor; but on the other hand he could be a more cheerful, worldly, witty person than either of them. Women adored him. He was an ever popular feature of the cocktail party circuit, and welcome at any embassy dinner table in town, guaranteed to make the evening sparkle. He was good in salons, back parlors, and political caucus rooms. He got on well with senators and congressmen. The legislators were, in fact, almost wholly fond of him. They remembered the day he came before them for confirmation as CIA director, because the morning before a photograph had appeared in the newspapers of Allen Dulles bent sorrowfully yet proudly over the prostrate form of his only son, desperately wounded and just shipped back from Korea. There were tears in the eyes of some of them as they listened to him, in closed executive session,* talking so earnestly about the problems of the nation and the world and giving no indication of his own heart-breaking burden.

These were great days for all the Dulles clan, but it was obvious that Allen was the one who relished them most. He had never felt more buoyant about his own future. It was not that he had ambitions beyond

*The official account is still not on available record.

6

the CIA, for what was the need so long as the CIA continued to flourish and expand, and he along with it? He was fully aware of the nature and potential of his power, and he was quick to resent any criticism of the way he employed it. "Do you realize my responsibilities?" he once heatedly asked his sister. "I have to send people out to get killed. Who else in this country in peacetime has the right to do that? It is not something I take lightly." To his colleagues he hinted that they all had responsibilities which would grow with the years, and they must all measure up to them. What role did he see for himself in the future? Whatever it was, the prospect did not seem to daunt him at all.

And then, in 1959, after six good years, things went terribly wrong.

That was the year in which John Foster Dulles died. Allen Dulles's attitude toward his older brother had always been ambivalent, a mixture of admiration and condescension, of affection tinged with envy and frequent resentment. But when John Foster died, he was grief-stricken. He felt as if a beam had been torn out of the edifice of his life; as indeed it had. He shared the pride of the family when President Eisenhower ordered for his dead Secretary of State a funeral of almost presidential proportions, and statesmen came in from all parts of the world to pay tribute. Even the aged German chancellor, Konrad Adenauer, flew in from Bonn to pay his respects. There could not have been many, outside his family circle, who had loved John Foster Dulles —respect, fear, tolerance, or loathing were the dominant emotions he had engendered—but the men who marched in the solemn procession and the congregation which packed Washington Cathedral felt the need to pay a tribute to his stature and importance. The lavishness of the ceremonials would not be seen again in the nation's capital until the funeral of John F. Kennedy.

Allen Dulles had sometimes envied his brother because, by the simple fact of seniority, Foster had enjoyed the privileges of the older son of the family, and got there first to the opportunities that were going. Allen often felt he could have exploited them more brilliantly. It was not that he was cleverer than John Foster. Eleanor Dulles once said, "Foster had a better brain than both of us," and Allen had never disagreed with that. But it was what you did with your brain and the kind of life you allowed it to shape that mattered, and he never had any doubt that his life had been freer and more adventurous than that of his brother.

7

But had it been independent of him? Where would he have been without Foster's help?

He was not long in discovering the answers to that. Even in the final years of the Eisenhower administration things changed. The new Secretary of State was Christian Herter, a man with whom he had previously exchanged jokes about their mutual aches and pains. (Allen Dulles suffered from gout, Herter from crippling arthritis. "Yours is the disease of self-indulgence," Herter would say. "Mine stems from the rheumatism of my pioneering ancestors, who labored in the damp and the cold." "Nonsense, we both get our afflictions from our poxy forbears," Allen would reply.) Now the relationship subtly changed, and questions were asked, from the State Department and the White House, which had never before required an answer. The CIA remained his personal domain, yet he began to realize how much his late brother had been a protective buttress as well as a benevolent partner in his activities. This discovery was something of a shock.

By the time President John F. Kennedy took office, there were those in the Agency who would say that Allen Dulles was a changed man. He seemed to have lost his self-assurance. This man who had masterminded a hundred major coups, who had outwitted Khrushchev, manipulated foreign governments, toppled dictators, now seemed to be touched with doubts about his own future role and that of the CIA.

It could not have happened to him at a more inappropriate moment, because the new administration was not sympathetic to doubters. In public, the President lauded Allen Dulles as a public servant of inestimable value, but in private he sent his brother Bobby around to snoop and find out what was going on. "We got the feeling there were people in the Justice Department, the FBI, and on Pennsylvania Avenue who were waiting for something to go wrong," one man in the Agency recalled.

What did go blatantly wrong was the Bay of Pigs. Kennedy publicly took the blame for that débâcle, but Washington knew that it was Allen Welsh Dulles who had initiated the misadventure, and allowed it to be carried out so ineptly.

The debris of the disaster was swept under the carpet, where it still crackles uncomfortably each time anyone treads over the old ground. That Allen Dulles was not swept away with it was due more to a momentary need to keep up appearances than any desire to keep him around. The President's brother was sent to tell him he could take his own time resigning, provided he was not there for longer than twelve months. Allen Dulles made a recommendation about his successor. It was ignored and another man chosen.

Suddenly all was over. It was a shabby end to a remarkable career, and the worst of it was the sudden obscurity. No one knows the head of KGB, and most other nations' spy chiefs jealously preserve their anonymity, but Allen Dulles had deliberately chosen the limelight in which to work out his career as an espionage agent. Even during World War II, as the OSS station chief in Switzerland, he had put a plaque with his name on it beside his door, and always thereafter he had kept himself in the public eye. "One of my own guiding principles in intelligence work," he wrote, "was . . . not to make a mystery of what is a matter of common knowledge or obvious to friend and foe alike." So he had appeared and spoken in public as the CIA's chief; people recognized him when they saw his picture in the newspapers, and pointed him out when he went to film premieres, big fights, baseball games, and presidential dinners.

Now he was a nobody, a slightly bent figure with bushy eyebrows and a droopy moustache, shuffling around in an unpressed suit and carpet slippers. Friends had watched him diminishing after his resignation in 1962, and worried about him. In 1964 he had made a temporary comeback by sitting on the Warren Commission investigating the assassination of the President who had dismissed him, and there would be repercussions over that in the years to come. Then, with the aid of a collaborator, he had started writing the story of some of his espionage activities in World War II, and compiling anthologies of fictional spy stories. People reacted when they saw his name on the bookshelves, remembering him as the man who had built the General Motors of American intelligence, and his books were quite popular.

But it was a measure of his eclipse that even at a party in his own house, on this night before Christmas 1968, seven years after his dismissal, only a few of his close friends noticed that he wasn't out there with his guests, flirting with the pretty women.

Larry Houston came down the stairs and walked into the living room, aware as he passed them that Clover Dulles and his wife were watching him, but determined to ignore them for the moment. Once in Greece during the bloody civil war that raged in the wake of World War II, when the OSS was deeply involved on the side of the anti-Communists, Houston had been present when they fished the body of one of his agents, also one of his closest friends, out of Salonika Harbor. The young American, an ex-flier who had fought and been shot up over Bataan, had been tied up with barbed wire and tossed into the water to struggle and drown. Houston's face seemed expressionless as he looked down at the mangled body of his friend. "Hell, you'd never have guessed that he cared," another ex-OSS man said later, "unless you knew that when Larry was boiling inside a pulse started beating in his left temple."

The pulse was beating now, and Jeanie Houston noticed it.

Houston was looking for someone in the crowd, and when he sighted him he went across, cut him out of the group, edged him into the hall and up the stairs. The man was Jim Hunt, a veteran member of the CIA and one of Allen Dulles's oldest friends. Some CIA members who had never belonged to Allen Dulles's charmed inner circle when he was at the Agency referred derisively to Jim Hunt as a playboy. Certainly he was very rich and went around with that fine free careless attitude which sometimes seems to go with people who don't have to worry about paying the bills or the mortgage. It was true that he was in the CIA for the fun of it, because he liked the risks and the zestful feeling it gave him that there was still a war on and he was in there still fighting.

But Hunt was also a serious and effective member of the Agency. If he had belonged to a French political party, he would have been called a "militant." He was a catalyst. He felt that the CIA should be an activist organization. He had operated for and campaigned with Allen Dulles on many a delicate mission, and he worshipped the ground his ex-chief walked on.

When the two men reached the bedroom and went inside, Hunt took one look at the man lying underneath the covers and said: "Christ!" Allen Dulles's face was drained of blood and had a yellow translucent look. His hair and moustaches were wet with sweat and he was obviously in pain, half-choking as if he could not swallow.

"He's sick, all right," Houston said.

"God almighty, he's not just sick, he's in trouble," Hunt said. "We've got to do something. Why hasn't she called a doctor?"

A voice from behind them said: "He saw the doctor this morning. It's a touch of flu. He'll be all right. He has these spells." Clover Dulles had followed them upstairs.

"The hell with spells," Hunt said. "What we need to do is get him to a hospital." To Houston, gesturing to the hubbub they could hear faintly from the party down below: "Let's get those people out of here. Tell them Allen's ill. I'm going to call an ambulance."

Houston went down to tell the guests to drink up and go. The hubbub died down to a whisper, then people began to creep away. Hunt picked up the telephone and started giving orders. Clover Dulles hovered around, looking sad, helpless, uncertain, as she often had during her lifetime with Allen Dulles.

Presently the ambulance appeared, and two male nurses came into the bedroom with a stretcher. Allen Dulles was aware of what was happening now, and though he could not speak he shook his head violently.

The Dulles family had a dislike of stretchers. Once when John Foster Dulles was in agony and about to be taken to a hospital for an operation, he too had been approached by stretcher bearers and had angrily waved them away. Instead, he had staggered to the head of the stairs, painfully squatted on the top step, and then bumped his way down on his rump, stair by stair, to the bottom.

Now Allen Dulles swung himself so that he was sitting on the edge of the bed. He tried to stand up, failed, tried again, and failed again. Watching him, Larry Houston was reminded of a story Allen was fond of telling about the German delegate at Versailles after World War I when the Peace Treaty was handed to him. He didn't rise when the Allied delegates came over to him but stayed in his seat, and a murmur swept through the hall and people got angry, because they thought the German was being insolent.

"He wasn't insolent that day," Allen said. "He couldn't stand up because he was so affected by emotion, poor fellow. He was just plain frightened and he couldn't stand on his legs. I was sitting there not more than thirty or forty feet from him, and the fellow couldn't get up under the weight of the treaty."

Houston and Hunt went over and helped Allen Dulles to his feet; then the nurses took over and half-carried him down the stairs. Clover climbed into the ambulance with him. Jeanie Houston came running

11

after her with her coat and hat, for it was cold outside, but it was too late. The ambulance was on its way.

On Christmas morning Clover Dulles telephoned Howard Roman, who collaborated with Allen on his books, and asked him if he could come over at once to the house on Q Street. She seemed in great distress, and Roman presumed she was worried about Allen. But that did not prove to be her principal anxiety. She had come back from the hospital in the early hours of the morning, she said, and because she was cold she had decided to take a hot bath. She had gone into the bathroom and turned on the taps good and strong, then went back into her bedroom while the tub was filling.

"Then I forgot about it," she said. "I didn't think about it again until this morning." She added, "There's quite a mess."

As Roman discovered when he got to the house on Q Street, mess was a mild word for what had happened. The water had flooded over the ceilings of at least four rooms, and there was plaster everywhere, over furniture and Christmas decorations. There was imminent danger that the ceilings would come down, 2 tons of them. Somehow, Roman managed to dig out an agent of the Hartford Insurance Company, who took one look and gulped with panic. Once he had heard how the disaster happened, he quickly made it plain that he and his company would be most reluctant to foot the bill for what was obviously going to be a highly expensive repair job.

Clover Dulles didn't seem to be too worried about that. What she kept saying to the agent was: "I just want it done. But remember, under no circumstances must you say anything about this to my husband. At all costs, I don't want him to know what happened."

When the agent had gone, Roman said to her: "You realize Allen will find out all about it when he comes out of the hospital?"

"I know," she said miserably, her eyes welling with tears as she looked at the dreadful debris all around her.

But he did not come out of the hospital, and he never did find out about the flood.

CHAPTER ONE

Cradle Marks

There were those in the Dulles family who wondered, later on, whether it was a mistake to tell Allen the secret of his birth, on the grounds that he brooded about it and the knowledge affected his nature. There were others who thought the mistake was in making such a melodramatic fuss, especially the silly business of having them all swear it would never be revealed beyond the family circle.

For what was there to hide? Simply that when Edith Foster Dulles took to her bed for the birth of her third child on the night of April 6, 1893, it proved to be a long and agonizing accouchement, and when the baby was eventually delivered the following morning it was seen that there was something wrong. It was a boy and he had a club foot.

Edith's husband, the Reverend Allen Macy Dulles, was the pastor of the Presbyterian church in Watertown, New York. He had the reputation of being an enlightened clergyman. Later on he would defy threats of ouster from the synod of his church because he had cast doubt on the virgin birth and because he actually dared to conduct the ceremony of remarriage of a divorcée (though the nuptials took place in his home rather than in his church). Despite the fact that he was far from being a liberal in the permissive sense of the term—he believed in heaven and hell, the divine will, and the wages of sin—he was known never to have turned a sinner away from his door, or failed to give him or her sympathy and understanding.

Nevertheless, he seemed to find something dark and shameful in the fact that his second son had been born with a club foot, and as soon as it was physically possible the boy was taken secretly to Syracuse and there operated on to rectify the deformity. Only then were relatives,

13

friends, and members of the church invited to the baptism of Allen Welsh Dulles.

There were two more children born to Edith Dulles after Allen, making five in all, three girls and two boys; as they grew old enough to understand, they were all told about the club foot and gave a pledge that they would never mention it beyond the confines of the family. Foster and Margaret, the two oldest, were told by their father; later, Foster was given the task of passing the family secret on to the two youngest, Eleanor and Nataline. But before that happened Allie, as the family called him, had been informed, shortly after his sixth birthday.

He came in one day after several hours of swimming and boating on Lake Ontario, at Henderson, where his maternal grandparents had a summer cottage, and complained of a dull ache in his left foot. A mustard bath was made up for him. While he steeped the aching foot in the hot water, feeling the pain seep away, the reason for it was explained to him. Foster was there. He was ten years old, studying the classics and already prematurely sententious. He said gravely: "You must regard it as your Achilles' heel."

Allie seemed to take the news lightly, and soon was his old self, apparently as happy-go-lucky as ever. But a couple of years later he changed. That was the year, 1901, when both Foster and Margaret caught typhoid from swallowing the water of the Black River, which was used in Watertown's mills. The manse was hushed and the curtains drawn as the doctors fought and the Reverend Dulles prayed to God to spare the two children.

Hand in hand, Allie and Eleanor peered through the blinds at the awesome spectacle of their older brother, pink with fever, being lowered like a lobster into a bath of ice to bring his temperature down. One day Allie crept into Margaret's room to look at his sister and fled in terror at the sight of her, all her golden curls gone, as bald as an egg. Eleanor found him curled up in a dark corner of an outhouse, shaking with emotion, and the two of them sobbed in each other's arms, appalled at the ugliness of the world into which they were growing.

Not many months later Margaret's curls had grown again, but it was a long time before Foster completely recovered. He was too weak to walk, had to be carried everywhere, and looked like a bag of bones.

This traumatic experience seemed to have had its effect on Allie.

14

There were periods when he was Eleanor's joyful companion as they played on the dockside or hunted in the woods. He was already studying history and philosophy, in the hope, one suspects, of catching up with Foster, who had long since become knowledgeable in both, and Allie loved to show off before his sister, reeling off dates or declaiming Shakespeare. But then without warning his temper would turn from sunny to thunderous. He would round on Eleanor, and rant and rave at her in a black rage. Its intensity could be devastating, so that she fled his presence. From then on, she said later:

"Ours was always a fluctuating relationship, ranging all the way from rebellion and anger to a passionate desire for approval. My changing moods and his strong reactions to them throughout our lives brought pain and pleasure. His charm was irresistible and his intensity of rage, his emotions, when he objected to something, was often overwhelming."

Not many people were aware of this tougher side. Eleanor Dulles later learned to avoid it by staying away from him, sometimes for months at a time, for her love for her brother was strong and she wished to avoid "the stress and furore which he stirred in me."

While she was a child at home, of course, it was impossible for her to separate herself from Allie when he was in one of his moods, and this sometimes caused her great anguish. But there were compensations. One day, for instance, when she was five years old, he came to her and confided to her that he had written a book. Gravely, he handed over to her a wad of over a hundred pages of careful schoolboy script with a large title in red letters over the first page: "THE BOER WAR: A History" by Allen Welsh Dulles.

Allie had listened in to dinner conversations at home and at his grandparents' house at Henderson about the war that was then going on in South Africa between the Boer settlers and the British. Sentiment in the United States was almost overwhelmingly on the side of the Boers—except, curiously enough, in the Dulles household—and the English, the target of charges of imperialism and international skulduggery of a kind that the United States would come to know a half century later, were being widely vilified. At the age of eight, Allen Dulles had become a convinced and perfervid pro-Boer and had poured out his feelings in a screed of some six thousand words which, for his age, had been remarkably well researched.

15

Eleanor read it through without understanding much of its nature or significance, but when she mentioned it later to her parents, they took and read the manuscript with great pleasure and pride, even though they disagreed with its sentiments. Edith Dulles took it with her to her parents' house at Henderson, and proudly handed it over to her father, who, at that time, was Secretary of State to President Benjamin Harrison. The Secretary was equally impressed, and asked if he might keep the manuscript for a while. The reason why became apparent later when he reappeared with a booklet which he had had printed privately. The Secretary of State himself wrote a preface (albeit anonymously) in which he remarked:

> The author of this history, who is eight years old, has been since the war began in South Africa an ardent admirer and partisan of the Boers, and this in spite of the fact that all his immediate family favor the British cause. The reported suffering of the Boer women and children in the African concentration camps and the destitution of the Boer prisoners in the Bermudas aroused his sympathy and the desire to do something to relieve their condition. Two months ago he determined to write a history of the war with the avowed purpose of sending the money, which he should receive from its sale, to the Boer Relief Committee for the benefit of these sufferers. Since that time he has industriously gathered his facts, and day after day for nearly two months he has written out what he has read and heard together with his own opinions and conclusions. . . . The humane purpose for which this book is written and the perseverance and originality of the author will commend it to all readers of history. Washington, D.C. March 15, 1902.

As Secretary Foster pointed out, Allie's text was "entirely free from suggestion or correction in regard to subject, language or arrangement," and its message was forthright:

"The Boers want peace," Allie wrote, "but England has to have the gold and so she goes around fighting all the little countries but she never dares to fight eather [sic] China or Russia . . . I hope that the Boers will win for the Boers are in the wright and the British are in the wrong in the War."

With the exception of Foster, who dubbed it "a wrong-headed and infantile effort," the family glowed with pride at the literary genius in the family. The booklet was assiduously circulated by the Secretary's friends in Washington and New York, and resulted in contributions of several hundred dollars to Boer relief.*

For a time his reputation as an author seemed to blow away some of the turbulence in Allie's character, but Eleanor was still wary of him, never quite knowing what to expect. One day about a year later, she, Allie, and their baby sister Nataline were playing on the dockside at Henderson, the two older children skimming rocks on the water, the small tot trying to emulate and impress them by chucking ever bigger rocks over the side. Finally Nataline picked one so big that when she staggered to the edge of the dock she toppled into the water with it, and down she plunged beneath the surface, still clinging to the rock. Eventually she came up again, her pink dress billowing around her like a balloon, the wind picking at it and driving her away from the shore.

Even at nine and a half, Allen Dulles was a strong swimmer, and to have jumped in and rescued his baby sister was well within his capacity. To Eleanor's astonishment, he remained on the dock and watched Nataline drifting away before the wind. Only when she began to cry for help did he join in, and their mother came rushing down to see what was amiss. It was a period when Edith Dulles, as the children well knew, was in ill-health and suffering agonizing migraines, but without hesitation she plunged into the water, scooped up her child, and brought her ashore. Allie stood immobile on the dockside, just watching. Both he and Eleanor got a beating with a hairbrush from their father that evening for discomfiting their mother and not exercising sufficient vigilance over the safety of their sister.

As the years passed, the more cheerful side of Allen Dulles began to prevail, but there were lapses. At one period he went through a Byronic phase, exaggerating his limp as he walked through the woods on one of the islands in the lake, loudly spouting verses in Greek and threatening to risk drowning by swimming back through the choppy waters to the mainland. He and Foster had found a wounded crow, and Allie tended its injured wing and tamed it. For a while afterwards he took the crow everywhere with him. One Sunday he was missing when the family marched through the town to the church for the morning service, but shortly after the first hymn had been sung the congrega-

*Shortly after Allen Dulles became director of the CIA in 1953, the Agency reprinted the booklet in an edition of several hundred copies.

tion was astonished (and the Reverend Dulles infuriated) to see Allen limping down the aisle to the family pews, his pet crow cawing softly on his shoulder.

Later on, when he became a victim of gout—and the affliction hit him quite early—it was always in his left foot that the first symptoms came. For the rest of his life, each time the pain stabbed him, he was sharply reminded of the malformation with which he had been born.

John Foster Dulles was four years older than Allen, seven years older than Eleanor, and very much their privileged superior.

For all Allen's precocity, it was Foster upon whom Edith Dulles focused most of her hopes, as well as her affection. As if to put a special benison on him, she had moved into her parents' home in Washington when she was in the final stages of her pregnancy, and it was there that Foster was born on February 25, 1888. Her father was John Watson Foster, Secretary of State in the Harrison administration, and a personage of great influence in both the Republican Party and the business and banking world. Edith Dulles was a hard-driving woman, who was too fond of her less worldly husband to prod him beyond his comfortable life on the middle rungs of the Presbyterian Church, but she stored up her latent energies on behalf of her son. Her ambitions for him had developed along with the fetus in her womb, and as soon as it was confirmed that her baby was indeed a boy, she began planning the training for him that would bring him a political career in keeping with the family name. There was never any doubt what she would call her son. He was christened John Foster after her father.

Almost from the time he could walk and talk, John Foster Dulles found himself thrown into the company of men who mattered in the government and management of the affairs of the United States. The Reverend Dulles was a clergyman of modest means and a self-sufficient man who had never asked, and never wanted his wife to ask, for financial help from his powerful in-laws. But in the winter and spring Edith was often in Washington visiting them, and in summer she sometimes saw more of them than she did of her hardworking husband. After leaving the State Department, John W. Foster joined the boards of several rich and powerful Wall Street corporations. He had built himself a lodge and several simple guest cottages at Henderson, New York, on Lake Ontario, and important guests—senators, big banking magnates, statesmen, like William Howard Taft, John W. Davis, Andrew Carnegie, and Bernard Baruch—came to stay with him for the fishing. Henderson was near enough to Watertown for Edith to drive over in a horse and buggy with the children, and she spent much of her summer there. Allie and the others were considered too young; but Foster, though still in his teens, was always taken along on the fishing parties, no matter how distinguished the guests, and he was generally considered by all of them as a most serious and promising young man. He greatly admired his grandfather and sat at his feet, imbibing his political wisdom.

Unlike Allie, Foster never seemed precocious because he always seemed so much older than his years. Knowledge seemed to come naturally to him. He was quoting the philosophy of William James at the age of ten, but a few years later he had turned from pragmatism to behaviorism. Eleanor, who has always had a love of jewelry, had seen a hatpin with a bright blue stone in a store in Watertown and saved up to buy it, but when she got enough money together she found that the pin had been sold. She sobbed bitterly. Foster came upon her while she was crying and after learning why, said loftily: "You are not crying because you're sad, you are sad because you are crying."

It was a remark that gave her no comfort. Thanks to her brothers, she was not to have much comfort in the Dulles household. Around about the age of twelve, she went through a phase when she had many aches and pains. Foster, who had no sympathy for any kind of weakness, mental, moral, or physical, made a sign which read: "Eleanor has a——ache." Where the blank was he inserted a hook, and on this he gave her a model ear, nose, eye, head, leg, arm, and trunk to hang on it according to her latest dolor.

"Then you won't have to tell us all about it," he said.

It was not discovered until quite late that Eleanor had only about 30 percent normal sight, and until her eyes were tested and she was fitted with glasses she had a trying and often frightening time, always tumbling over things. The boys were inclined to put obstacles in her way and jeer at her when she fell over them, or throw her a ball and laugh when she grappled desperately with thin air in a vain attempt to catch it. They caused her a great deal of unhappiness, but her love for them was such that she could not be angry with them for long, only envy them and wish to be like them.

"My brothers were the paragons I both wanted to imitate and at times to destroy," she said later.

It was when "outsiders" tried to play tricks with her that her temper boiled over. One such "outsider" was Uncle Bert, who was often to be found at the summer parties at Henderson. Robert M. Lansing was a young and ambitious lawyer who had married one of John W. Foster's daughters, Edith's sister, Eleanor, chiefly, Washington gossips said, for the inside track it gave him with his influential father-in-law.* The boys liked him because he treated them as grownups and regaled them with saucy Washington scandals and juicy political rumors, and Foster in particular bent an avid ear toward him because he knew him to be a highly successful lawyer; it was in the direction of the law that his own ambitions were turning from 1908 onward.

But if Uncle Bert flattered the boys, all he did with Eleanor was tease. He was always pointing out wondrous butterflies or birds which, with her blurred sight, she could not see, and which, in fact, as the boys told her afterwards, were not there. She had a small friend named Mandy, daughter of one of the black servants, with whom she would sit around and read or talk, trying to convey to the less privileged child some of the knowledge she was being fed by her governess. One day Lansing brought a large black rag doll, dressed in a smock like Mandy's, and put it in a darkish corner of the hall, then hid until Eleanor came along. He listened with delight as she prattled away to the doll in the belief that it was her friend, until one of his chuckles disturbed her. She reached across to grasp Mandy's hand and shrieked at contact with a lump of cloth. It was not until 1918 in Paris that she forgave Uncle Bert for the mockery of her infirmity.

Somehow, though there were five children, it was always as a triad that Eleanor, Allen, and Foster Dulles spent the formative years in Watertown and Henderson, and this grouping was something that would continue throughout their lives, each of them symbiotically feeding on the other emotionally, professionally, and politically. There were times when they would hate one or the other, when they would try to break away from each other's orbit or influence, but they always

*He later became Secretary of State in the Wilson administration.

came back together again, for better or for worse, in triumph and in tragedy.

That Foster was the strong personality and leader in the trio there was never any doubt. Eleanor acknowledged him because he belonged to the male sex, although she would come increasingly to doubt the automatic superiority of men as the years went on. Allen reluctantly accepted him as the arbiter of the group because he was older, stronger, more assertive.

It was Foster who was first allowed to drive the family car, though he was only fifteen (Allen had to wait until he was seventeen). It was Foster who was given the first sailing boat ever to be seen on that part of Lake Ontario, a present from his grandfather, and it was he who had the first lessons in fishing and shooting from Will Stevens, their handyman and friend. On the Fourth of July it was Foster who was allowed to go down to the water with the men and help set off the firework display, while Allen had to stay on the porch of the house with the women; though he was permitted to supervise the lighting of candles inside paper balloons, which were released and sent drifting across the waters.

But, almost paternally, as if apologizing for his seniority, Foster would sometimes let them take the tiller of his cherished Boat No. 5, as his open sailing dinghy was called, and he was meticulous in passing on his lessons in the handling of rod and gun. Margaret was delicate and Nataline too young, but the other three trained themselves to be tough, and matched themselves against each other in tests of their stamina and durability. Whenever they were out in Foster's boat, they were expected to dive over the side for a swim, no matter what the weather, so long as the temperature of the water—which Foster carefully took with his thermometer—was over 50 degrees. In fact it was not too much of an ordeal, for the Reverend Dulles routinely ordained cold showers for each of them every morning and it was not until they were grownups that any of them knew what it was like to have a hot bath.

Neither of the other two could stay in the lake as long as Foster could, nor did they, though both strong swimmers, ever equal his record of swimming there and back across Henderson Harbor, a 5-mile swim. What they never even attempted to compete with was his appetite, which was always a matter of wonder, even in the family.

"I believe Foster as a growing boy ate more than almost any human being I have ever known," Eleanor said later. "He'd just run through everything from raw tomatoes and raw onions, soup, steak or chops, potatoes and ear after ear of corn, and then fish, maybe cucumbers, maybe another vegetable, and then two or three kinds of pie. Then, quite often, a little fruit, doughnuts, and coffee. During those meals I can see my grandfather, when he was with us on a shore dinner, with his luxuriant Franz Josef-type sidewhiskers, sitting on a rustic table or on a log reminiscing about the Civil War or his early days as a diplomat in Mexico, Russia, Europe, and China. Foster rarely chipped in with a question. He was too busy listening—and eating."

What Allie could beat Foster at was fishing, for he proved to be much more wily and effective with a line. He had paid close heed to a local verse about fishing in the lake which went:

> When the wind is in the North
> Then the fisherman goes not forth.
> When the wind is in the East
> Then the fish they bite the least.
> When the wind is in the South
> It blows the bait in the fish's mouth.
> When the wind is in the West
> Then the fishes bite the best.

He not only knew the best days but also the best places to go to catch the tasty bass which inhabited these waters.

"The way you catch bass," he said later, "you wait until the mouth is at the right angle, and then you hit him, but you don't hit him too hard. It's difficult to judge the angle because the bass is in twenty feet of water. It's a disgrace if you let the fish swallow the bait, so you catch them way down on the insides, and it's very unpleasant getting the hook out. What you do is catch them in the upper lip or the lower lip, where it doesn't hurt at all, and you pull him in and he fights much better that way."

It was very much like counter-espionage work, he used to say later on, when you are trying to tempt a wily enemy spy to walk into a trap.

"If it's a very still day," he went on, "you may want to troll a little bit. You try to find out where the fish are, and gently you slip an anchor. Part of the skill is finding where those fish are. The reason you take a boat and pay the boatman a great deal is you get a man who over the years knows where the fish are. You guard with the greatest secrecy the bearings which give you your position, because in many cases there is below, where you can't see it, a rock where the fish concentrate, and you want to be right over that rock, so you've got to get your position within a few feet, allowing for the wind and so forth.

"So, finding the fish, hooking the fish and playing the fish—you don't want to just haul the fish right in—it'll break away from you. You don't want to let the fish jump if you can help it, because he'll shake the hook loose when he gets in the air. So you've got to try to keep him from jumping. You draw him in and tire him, until he's almost glad to be caught in the net. It requires a lot of patience."

Foster had patience, plenty of it. But where he went wrong was in his choice of where to fish. He would pick a spot, drop his anchor, and put out his line, convinced that this was the right place to be. Why? Because he had chosen it.

"The fish didn't always agree with him," Allen said. "He never did learn that sometimes you have to see it from their point of view."

In other ways, however, Foster was indeed a paragon of a boy, almost infuriatingly perfect in the eyes of his brother and sister. They loved him and admired him, but sometimes they compared themselves with him and despaired over their imperfections. He never lost his temper, like Allie. He never complained of an ache or a pain, like Eleanor. He was such a fervent Christian and so generously strong of purpose that he often made the other two feel sinful and guilty in their weaknesses. He already had adopted a rigid code by which he had decided to direct his life.

"He thought people ought to be able to order their lives in a decent way," Eleanor said later, "but he recognized that some people are weak. He didn't expect his friends or his family to be weak, but he knew there were a lot of people who were extremely vulnerable. I think he was very tolerant as soon as he put them in the class where they almost couldn't expect to do better."

Like his father, Foster considered himself a man of the world, in no sense rigid or priggish. During this period of his development the Dulles household employed a very pretty and happy-go-lucky girl as a living-in maid. Soon the son of a local farmer was climbing the tall tree outside her attic window and spending romantic nights in her room. When this fact was discovered, the Reverend Dulles refused to be shocked, but he did decide that perhaps it would be best if the girl were returned to the protection of her family.

He sighed as he watched her climb into the family car.

"So pretty," he said, "it's almost a pity she isn't a professional."

It was a remark of which Foster would not have disapproved. You had to keep your eyes open, keep your sense of humor, and accept things the way they were. And above all not be bigoted.

Nevertheless, his younger brother and sister were not eager to lay bare their own fallibilities to their brother's cool and tolerant eye.

What particularly awed them both was not just his confident outlook on the imperfect world around him, but also the prodigious, almost encyclopedic knowledge he seemed to have absorbed from his lessons at Watertown High School and his omnivorous reading at home. He knew the Bible by heart. He read all the classics: Spenser, Shakespeare, Thackeray, Scott, Dickens, and was making his way through Voltaire, Molière, and La Fontaine in the original French. By the time he was sixteen his parents and his grandfather decided that only a university could teach him more, and he was enrolled at Princeton.

It is a long time ago and memories are difficult to check, but it seems almost certain that during his sophomore year Foster's self-confidence was shattered and the invulnerable citadel he considered himself to be breached by an emotion of a kind he had never experienced before. He developed a schoolboy "crush," for he was still only sixteen, on one of his fellow students, a wild-eyed rebel two years older than himself. The feeling was more than returned. It was an exhilarating experience until the moment when he discovered from his adored older partner that male relationships can also have their physical side. To a young man who had, so far, only once embarrassedly bussed a girl at a party, it was a devastating and shocking revelation of what he knew from his Bible to be a shame and a sin. He conveyed his sense of degradation with such effect that the fellow student walked out of his room and left the college.

Foster would never talk about the experience later, but he did say to his sister:

"I went to college too young. I shouldn't have gone to college that young. It would have been better if I had waited a year . . . I was very unsophisticated and unprepared."

Eleanor added: "He spoke with real feeling as if he had had some difficult experiences in his first year, his second year at Princeton . . . some things that were almost humiliating for him."

In her view, it had a profound effect upon him.

"I think it is possible that Foster began to develop a feeling about human relations which explains a little bit about what most people thought was his reserve, his sense that you were vulnerable if you opened up too readily. . . . There wasn't anything in his precollege experience that would have made him cautious that way, so I'm inclined to attribute it to his experience in his early months at Princeton."

He seemed to have been shocked by his own vulnerability, and resolved to overcome it. Those who were close to Foster later surmised that this was a critical turning point in his life when he took measures to shape his future image before the world. Filled with an almost precognitive realization of what he must become, an outwardly autonomous being proudly self-contained and self-sure, he was aware inside himself of the loneliness that would inevitably go with it. Near the end of his life he opened up his mind to one of his personal aides and revealed some of the painful sense of isolation, of apartness, which is part of the life style of an outwardly arrogant, inwardly-directed man. He said to William Macomber:

"You know all my life I've been able to make people like me, and I would have preferred to have people like me. As Secretary of State I could have conducted myself in this office in a way that people would have liked me. But unfortunately the times that I dealt with were times when sternness, firmness, resoluteness were the qualities that were required."

Macomber commented: "I guess he knew he was a respected figure but, at least until the end of his life, not a beloved figure."

It was as if, in those formative years at Princeton, he was making his personal dispositions in anticipation of the challenges to come. And young as he was, one senses that he was aware that self-sufficiency might bring him the respect and even the grudging admiration of his fellow men, but would also put him, isolated, on a very lonely pinnacle.

But whatever decisions were made by Foster at this time, he kept them to himself. By the end of his stay at Princeton, he gave every sign of having recovered from any doubts that may have troubled him. He joined no clubs because, he said later, they would have distracted him from his educative pursuits,* but he was elected to Phi Beta Kappa, majored in philosophy, and did a paper on pragmatism. His thesis was on "The Theory of Judgment." It won him the Chancellor Green Mental Science Fellowship, which brought with it a year's scholarship to the Sorbonne in Paris and study under the Nobel Prize-winning French philosopher, Henri Bergson.

He stood second at Princeton in the class of 1908 and gave the valedictory speech at the graduation ceremonies in that year. Then he departed for Paris to work under Bergson.

Allen followed him to Princeton in 1910 and did not do nearly so well. There were rows with his father in the manse at Auburn, New York (to which the family had now moved) when he was accused of taking life too lightly, of spending too much time running after girls, of neglecting his courses for parties and outings. The Reverend Dulles was appalled when Allen assured him that it would be all right when the examinations came along. He would put on steam in the last weeks and make up for lost time. What sort of attitude was that? Did he think that an education was just a question of last-minute learning, of cramming facts just to regurgitate them mindlessly? Why did he not follow Foster's example and apply himself, work hard and abandon frivolity for honest toil? He might not have Foster's brain, but at least he could imitate his dedicated application.

Allen walked out in one of his black rages. Feeling that this was an occasion when his sister was unlikely to give him any comfort—he knew Eleanor disapproved of his lighthearted attitude to work—he contacted instead a young woman named Janet Avery, whose family lived in Auburn. In the next few weeks he dated Janet regularly. He must have been aware that his brother Foster had already begun seeing Janet and had several times expressed his approval of her. Allen may well have had the idea of diminishing his paragon brother by stealing his girl away from him. But if that was his intention, he did not go through with it. He found Janet a dull girl, with none of the sparkle, zest, and worldliness he was coming to demand from female compan-

*Though he did join the Cottage Club after he became a successful lawyer.

ions. He retired to the sidelines and allowed Foster to take the field again, no doubt cherishing to himself the smug feeling: "I could have if I'd wanted to."

As for his exams, he was as good as he had promised. Like Foster, he majored in philosophy. Like Foster he did an essay on pragmatism, and he too won a prize—a cash prize large enough to pay for a passage to India.

He had begun to find the family pressures too much for him, and he was only too aware that everyone was measuring him against Foster. He needed to get away and show them that he had his special qualities too.

CHAPTER TWO

Breaking Out

If Janet Avery had ever entertained any serious thoughts about Allen, they were quickly dissipated when John Foster Dulles reappeared on the scene in the spring of 1911. She had not seen much of him during the previous months because he had been living with his grandparents in Washington while studying law. Now he came back to Auburn and may well have sensed that he had a rival for Janet's favors, and his own brother at that, of whose dash and charm he was only too well aware.

With the kind of self-confidence or arrogance which was to awe his friends and anger his critics from now on, Foster calmly balanced his priorities and decided that things had better be settled once and for all. He had not yet qualified for the bar and he did not have a job, or a prospect of one, but it was clear to him that Janet had better be secured before his brother or anyone else could get a rope around her. He made a date with her to go canoeing in Auburn on the day he took his bar exams in Buffalo, answered just enough questions to satisfy himself that he had passed, and took the train back to Auburn and his rendezvous. It was while they were canoeing on Owasco Lake that he asked Janet to marry him, and she accepted at once.

That same night Foster casually mentioned to his parents that he had become engaged. They were surprised, if not exactly astonished. They knew their son well enough by now to realize that he would never take a girl out more than twice unless he had serious intentions toward her. And in spite of his lack of prospects, it never occurred to them to raise any objections. They were only too well aware that Foster always knew exactly what he was doing in life, and that he was unlikely to cause them or anyone attached to him any anxiety, financial or otherwise. Unsettled though his future might seem, they were confident that he was a good catch for any girl, and that Janet Avery was lucky to have got him. Consequently, they were by no means pleased when they heard that the Avery family were not exactly overjoyed at the news their daughter had brought them, and they were even more nettled when it was reported that the Averys were rushing around trying to find out more about this young man who had, as far as they were concerned, swept their beloved girl off her feet. Who was he? What were his prospects? Was he worthy of being admitted into their family circle? Annoyed, the Reverend Dulles paced the floor of his study, exclaiming: "Well fancy! The idea of anybody not realizing what Foster is like!"

The Averys did not really need to worry about Foster. When the bar results came out, it was seen that he had passed all his exams, as he knew he would. Immediately after the list was published he applied for a post at the law firm in New York which, he had been assured, was the most important of its kind in the nation, Sullivan & Cromwell of Wall Street. He was confident that his qualifications were more than adequate even for such a prestigious firm, and he thought the list impressive as he wrote it out: an already good working knowledge of general and international law, an excellent knowledge of French, good Spanish, adequate German, a perfect scholastic record at Princeton and the Washington Law School, and a course at the Sorbonne.*

He was considerably put out when he heard that, far from finding his record notable, the partners at Sullivan & Cromwell thought it quite commonplace. In those days Princeton had strong ties to the South and was still a provincial college for would-be clergymen, Washington Law School did not have much standing in New York, and any tourist could enrol for a summer course at the Sorbonne. Sullivan & Cromwell tersely pointed out that they had the pick of the cream of the crop from Harvard and Yale, and that many of their entrants had postgraduate degrees from Oxford, Cambridge, and Heidelberg.

Foster, rebuffed but far from crushed, enlisted his grandfather's

---

*He had done a course at the Sorbonne in between Princeton and law school while on a trip to Paris with his family in the summer of 1910, when he was twenty-two. Allen (then fifteen) was enrolled in the École Alsaciènne at the same time. It was while they were in Paris that Foster met Janet Avery for the first time as a pigtailed schoolgirl doing a finishing course in Paris at Madame Marti's Academy.

help, and word was whispered in the ears of the partners that they could well be in danger of overlooking a potential legal genius. Did they not know that young John Foster Dulles, while still in college, had been ex-Secretary John Foster's chief assistant at the International Peace Conference at The Hague and had played an important role in bringing the delegates together?* Would they like to see a list of the distinguished senators, bankers, foreign statesmen who considered him a most brilliant and promising young man?

The partners changed their minds and opened the doors of Sullivan & Cromwell to him. He rushed round to see his fiancée and happily told her: "Just you wait. In a year or two, I'll be hiring young men myself. I'll be a partner in the firm too!"

Janet Avery was sure he would, if he said so. She had by now quite decided that in accepting Foster she had linked herself with the man of her dreams, that there would never be any other man in the world to match him, and she did not change that opinion for the rest of her life. Many years later, when Eleanor Dulles told her that she was writing a book about Foster, and that she hoped Janet wouldn't mind if she described him "warts and all," Janet said coldly: "What warts? Foster was perfect."

She was a pretty girl of the kind that, in those days, would have been called "a chocolate box beauty." The word Eleanor Dulles used about her was "exquisite." She was "very dainty, beautifully dressed and good looking, rather on the fragile side." She had dark hair, very bright eyes, and a slender figure.

"Foster always liked objets d'art," Eleanor said later, "and Janet was that to him."

Allen had found her dull, and a lot of people were to share that opinion of her in the years to come. Once in the 1950s, when a meeting of the South East Asia Treaty Organization foreign ministers was being held in Bangkok, their wives accompanied them and they were asked what could be done to entertain them while their husbands conferred. Clarissa Eden, wife of Anthony Eden (later the Earl of Avon), the British delegate, expressed a wish to see the temples of

---

*The participating nations had neglected to decide their order of precedence for courtesy calls on one another, and were each waiting for the others to make the first move. Deadlock, until John Foster Dulles had the inspiration of seeing that all calling cards were delivered simultaneously. He took them round himself.

Angkor Wat, in neighboring Cambodia, and Janet Dulles said she would go along too. Clarissa walked through the magnificent ruins with mounting excitement, but increasingly became aware of Janet's glum face and unresponsive attitude. When they reached the hotel beside the ruins and went into a bathroom to wash up, Janet's face lit up for the first time. Looking down at the washbasin, she cried: "Why, Pear's soap! Isn't that wonderful? How did they know that my favorite soap is Pear's? Isn't that really wonderful?"

There would be scores of stories like it from many a wife in many a capital. Yet John Foster Dulles found her both an adorable and a fascinating young woman, and she kept him constantly entertained.

"She didn't have what I'd call a good education, but it was pretty good for the times," Eleanor Dulles said later. "Janet was very well read, better read than practically anyone I knew. She read books. By and large her taste was discriminating. Proust and all the classical French literature. Of course, French literature is quite educating in lots of ways, both in philosophy and in customs and morals and habits and world outlook. But she had a real feeling for it and Foster did too. I think that is one of the things that appealed to him. You can imagine him in Auburn, working hard and then he sees this girl with whom he can talk about Paris, the world and literature, and philosophy, and she is good to look at. And of course, once having fallen in love with her, he never fell out of love with her."

They were married in Auburn in 1912, and departed for a honeymoon in the Catskills which can hardly have been the idyll that a young bride expected. Foster had recently made one of his first overseas missions for Sullivan & Cromwell, to British Guyana, and had there contracted such a serious bout of malaria that he had nearly died. A heavy dosage of quinine had left him extremely weak, his sight impaired, an optic nerve in his eye damaged and jumping.*

Sullivan & Cromwell upped his weekly salary to $100. His grandfather, John Foster, intended to leave $20,000 apiece to his grandchildren when he died. He liked Janet, approved of the marriage, and let Foster know that he could commence drawing on the $20,000 immediately in furtherance of his career. It was the beginning of a marriage

*The tic in his eye disappeared in later years, but at certain moments his eye tended to water copiously. Cynical French and British statesmen called the phenomenon "Foster's crocodile tears."

about which, later on, Foster's admirers would say: "They were made for each other," and his detractors would say: "They deserve each other."

One thing was certain. Foster thought Janet was wonderful and would henceforth do anything for her—"anything to save her pain, anything to give her pleasure."

This did not change Allen's opinion that she was, nevertheless, an extremely dull young woman, and he was a lucky man to have eluded her.

In any case, Allen was restless and in no mood for collecting appendages of any kind, including a wife. By 1912 his sister remembers him as a tall, rangy, amiable young man with the beginnings of a moustache, a "dream of a smile," and a Ho-Ho-Ho laugh whose resonance and spontaneity made everyone want to laugh along with him. His black moods aside, he could be a charmer. Princeton had smoothed the edges off his early education at Watertown and Auburn high schools, and he was worldly and sophisticated in manner and conversation. Like Foster, he spoke reasonably good French for his age, and he had learned wine and food lore while at Princeton. But he was well aware that there was a large world around him waiting to be discovered, and he would never be ready to settle down until he had seen it all.

Foster left with his bride for New York, and the trio split up for a time. Allen spent part of the 1912 vacation coaching Eleanor through her entrance exams for Bryn Mawr ("He talked to me about Greece and Rome and brought them alive for me"), but shortly after graduation he used his prize money to buy a ticket for India, via Spain and the Middle East, and set off for Allahabad, in the Central Provinces, where he had been promised a job at the agricultural college which had been opened there by an American professor, Sam Higginbotham.

"It wasn't the job that mattered," he said later. "I had no intention of spending my life as a teacher. But it was a way to see the world, and that was what I wanted most to do at that time."

His appetite for travel had been whetted by the family visits to Switzerland and France, but always on those occasions Foster had been with him, a restrictive influence, and he had felt no freedom, no independence. Once when they were staying on Lake Geneva, Foster had announced that he was joining a party to climb one of the Alps, the

Dent du Midi, but when Allen asked to be allowed to go along he was refused.

"It was considered that I was too young to make the grade [he was fifteen] and I was not allowed to accompany him. It was a great disappointment. It was always my ambition to climb that mountain, but they wouldn't let me go."

He added: "I didn't take it out on Foster. It wasn't his fault, exactly."

They were staying at the time with the Herzog family in Lausanne, to learn French, and both of them were smitten by the blond daughter of the family, Helene, who was encouraged by her parents to go around with the two young men and see that they spoke nothing but French. She was seventeen and soon showed that she was attracted by Allen's changeable nature, his raffish, rather rapscallion air, and his evident strong feelings toward her. Foster on the other hand was dour and unforthcoming. In fact he was not happy in the Herzog household, chiefly because his appetite was still prodigious and he was constantly hungry, since the family meals were quite inadequate to satisfy his needs.

One day he came across Allen and Helene giggling in a corner over the girl's mispronunciation of the American slang Allen was teaching her in lieu of speaking French. Ignoring Allen, he loftily addressed himself to Helene, wondering how a grown-up young woman could spend so much time playing frivolous games with someone who, after all, was still a schoolboy. Helene was abashed, Allen humiliated. The rapport between them was ruptured from then on by the two-year gulf between boyhood and young womanhood . . .

Well, now Foster was no longer around to spike his guns, and he was free. All India awaited.

In India, as Eleanor later disdainfully remarked, Allen became "a sahib with five Hindu servants and people pulling punkahs back and forth." She felt that "all those houris, Indian maidens, and clerks" gave him a taste for the easy life, and that from then on "there was hardly a time when he didn't have someone to fetch and carry for him."

It wasn't a completely fair summation of his sojourn in Allahabad. Even though he did have servants ("And who didn't? Even servants have servants in India"), he worked hard teaching English to the students, and learned a great deal himself. He became fluent in Hindi and

learned Sanskrit. He mixed easily with the Indians and soon discovered that, although World War I had begun and the streets were full
of marching Sepoys, Sikhs, and Mahrattis off to the fighting in Europe,
not all the young men and women he met believed that Britain's
struggle was their struggle. A lively independence movement was already in being in Allahabad, and unknown to the British authorities he
attended several meetings and listened to impassioned speeches
against the arrogant British Raj.

In this way he was introduced to a well-known local lawyer, Motilal
Nehru, and came to know his family, including his eldest son, Jawaharlal, and one of his daughters, Vijaya Lakshmi. Jawaharlal he found a
rather patronizing young man (he was just back from England, where
he had been to Harrow and Cambridge), who seemed destined for a
place in the British Indian hierarchy rather than fame as the rebel who
would lead the nation to freedom from the British. On the other hand,
his younger sister, Vijaya Lakshmi, was already an emancipated and
fervent apostle of freedom for Indian women and independence for
the Indian people, though still only fourteen years old. She was no
ordinary schoolgirl, and he did not treat her like one.*

From India Allen made his way into China, picking up teaching posts
in Shanghai, Canton, and Peking, and from there moved through the
Far East and across the Pacific back to the United States. He arrived
back home in 1915, having circumnavigated the globe. He was twenty-
two years old and had all the self-confidence of a young man who has
seen the world.

Only what was he going to do for a living?

Another Princetonian, Woodrow Wilson, had been elected President of the United States in 1912, and the Dulles brothers regarded
it almost as a family coup. Wilson had been one of Foster's professors
and he had continued to give an occasional lecture even after assuming
the presidency, during Allen's stay. Eleanor shared their admiration
for his high-minded principles and lofty aspirations, and fervently
agreed with his determination to keep the United States out of the
disastrous war that had started in Europe.

What gave them all a sense of family participation in the administra-

*When, in 1953, as Mrs. Pandit, she became the first woman president of the United
Nations General Assembly, he sent her a note of felicitation. "Allahabad 1914," it said.

tion was the fact that their Uncle Bert was a vital part of it. The Secretary of State under Wilson was William Jennings Bryan, but the most powerful and important personality in the State Department was undoubtedly Robert M. Lansing, its chief counsellor. Bryan owed his appointment as Secretary principally to Wilson's gratitude to him for having procured him the Democratic nomination in 1912. Bryan knew next to nothing about foreign affairs, was an avowed pacifist and a determined proponent of absolute impartiality toward the warring nations in Europe.

That was all right so long as the Wilson régime genuinely remained aloof from the conflict and treated each belligerent with equal justice. It soon became apparent to Bryan that, in fact, his chief counsellor had no intention of exercising impartiality and that the more exigent the British became in demanding, for instance, control of the seas, the right to board neutral vessels, even the right to search United States ships at sea, the more Robert Lansing was ready to give way to them. While having no brief for the German government, Bryan contended that this was leaning over backwards toward the British and edging the United States dangerously toward involvement in the war on the Allied side.

He was quite right. Lansing, while taking a public stance of strict impartiality, even of camouflaging his real feelings by issuing stern criticisms of British attacks on U.S. neutrality, was in fact doing his best to further Allied interests against Germany in any way he could. As he wrote later in his memoirs:

"In dealing with the British Government there was always in my mind the conviction that we would ultimately become an ally of Great Britain, and that it would not do, therefore, to let our controversies reach a point where diplomatic correspondence gave place to action."

Prodded into protesting against British high-handedness, he produced long and complicated notes designed equally to appease public opinion at home and yet refrain from interfering with British actions.

"The notes that were sent," he wrote later, "were long and exhaustive treatises which opened up new subjects for discussion rather than closing them in controversy. . . . It was done with deliberate purpose. It ensured continuance of the controversies and left the questions unsettled."

Bryan protested to President Wilson at the meager results Lansing was securing from the British in his protests against their blockade, and was assured by his chief that all would be taken care of, that a firm stand would be adopted. The British blockade tightened. American ships bound for German and neutral ports in Europe were boarded by British naval patrols and steered into British ports for examination. By the beginning of 1915, freedom of the seas had come to an end and the Royal Navy decided where any ship, particularly any American ship, could sail.

It was a situation Bryan was reluctant to swallow, but he was prepared to do so as long as the United States continued to protest and to make its position clear. What he was not ready to stomach were what he considered even more blatant breaches of U.S. neutrality, namely, the loading of armed British ships in American harbors with weapons of war and other military supplies. He discovered that the Wall Street banking firm of J. P. Morgan and Co. had raised a loan of $1,100,-453,950 for the purchase of material for the Allies, and planned to ship it to the United Kingdom in armed British ships.

Among the vessels chosen was the Cunard liner *Lusitania.* This ship had, in fact, been registered as a vessel of war and fitted with guns after the outbreak of hostilities between Great Britain and Germany; nevertheless, she continued to make the transatlantic passage between Liverpool and New York and back, and advertised herself in American newspapers as a normal passenger ship. German intelligence services in the United States and spies aboard the *Lusitania* herself reported to their embassy in Washington that the *Lusitania* was armed, and that military supplies and guns, munitions, ordinance, and so on, were being loaded aboard her. This information was in turn conveyed to the State Department and turned over to Counsellor Lansing. He ignored it.

The German Embassy then formally asked the U.S. authorities to dissuade any American citizen from sailing in the British ship, on the grounds that she was a vessel of war and liable to attack by German armed ships or submarines. At the same time, advertisements were placed in leading U.S. newspapers (financed by the Germans) warning potential passengers of the risks they ran.

To Bryan's astonishment, neither Lansing nor the President himself was prepared to accede to the German request, choosing instead to regard it as a blatant attempt to intimidate the U.S. government. And though Lansing was only too well aware of the nature of the British liner's cargo, and equally cognizant of the fact that she was armed, he took the public stance that she was a harmless passenger vessel whose rights of passage should under no circumstances be interfered with by the Germans. When, on May 7, 1915, the *Lusitania* was attacked by a German U-boat off Ireland, torpedoed, and sunk with the loss of 1,198 lives, including those of 128 American citizens, he persuaded President Wilson to protest vehemently to the German government against a "wanton attack on an innocent vessel," and drummed up public opinion against the cold-blooded murderers of Americans going about their lawful occasions.

Bryan resigned his post as Secretary of State in disgust. Robert M. Lansing took his place. Foster had some doubts about Uncle Bert's legal position *vis-à-vis* the *Lusitania*'s voyage and the subsequent protest to Germany. Allen thought it was all part of "a devious method of getting us into a war we will have to fight in the end." Eleanor came down from Bryn Mawr to stay with her grandfather and, meeting her uncle at dinner, blurted out: "Why don't you just declare war and have done with it?" All of them were aware that he had manipulated the facts and was continuing to do so,* and it did nothing to improve their opinion of his probity. But it had to be faced that they were all extremely fond of his wife, their Aunt Eleanor, and after all he was now Secretary of State. The prestige of his new position rubbed off on all of them. So none of them told him he was a liar and a cheat to his face, though Eleanor confesses that she was tempted to do so.

In a way, Allen Dulles had reason to be grateful both to the *Lusitania* and to his uncle, because through the first he found a vocation and through the second he got a job.

One of the reasons why Robert M. Lansing knew exactly how flagrantly the British were breaching the United States neutrality laws was because he had become close friends with the two chief British agents in charge of the operation, Sir Courtney Bennett and Captain Alex Gaunt. Both were spies operating under the intelligence network run from London by the legendary Admiral Sir Reginald Hall of the British Admiralty. Lansing became particularly fond of Gaunt, and

---

*He also succeeded in rigging the subsequent inquiry so that the truth about the *Lusitania*'s voyage was suppressed and relatives of U.S. citizens lost aboard her were cheated of adequate compensation.

brought him frequently to Henderson Harbor or to meetings in New York, when they would all go off to football games together. Gaunt, a gregarious type, obviously very fond of Americans, made no bones about the fact that he was an espionage agent, and would keep Allen entranced for hours with stories of his prewar missions into Germany and eastern Europe. So closely did Lansing work with Gaunt that he even introduced him to American special agents and ordered one of them, Bruce Bielaski, to cooperate with Gaunt and turn over to him the information he had uncovered about German espionage activity in the United States. Bielaski, who was chief of the investigative division of the Department of Justice, was just as much an intelligence operative as Gaunt, but for Allen Dulles he somehow lacked the *éclat* of the urbane, elegant Englishman.

Robert Lansing was something of a snob, and so pro-English that he even took elocution lessons to perfect the English accent he was cultivating. Allen got a lot of quiet amusement listening to his uncle torturing his vocal cords in an effort to imitate Gaunt's easy but unmistakably Oxford accent. He thought Gaunt was one of the most exciting men he had ever met, and he made up his mind that one of these days he would become an intelligence operative just like him—except for the accent, of course.

In the meantime, there was the matter of settling down to doing some work and earning some money. Unlike his brother, he did not have access to the legacy his grandfather was planning to leave him, and the small allowance he was getting from his father did not get him very far. "Allen always had extravagant tastes," Eleanor said drily, and girls, food, theaters, tennis club subscriptions were all expensive. While he was staying with his grandfather in Washington some time in 1915, a family council of war discussed what Allen was going to do. Finally, Robert Lansing (this was before he became Secretary) said: "Why don't you come into the State Department? We need young men in the diplomatic service. If you can pass the Department exams, I think I could get you a post overseas."

Allen was not particularly enamored of the idea, since he thought most diplomats were stuffy, but he said he thought it might be fun to take the Department exam just to see if he could pass it. He did not have much trouble in doing so. At the beginning of 1916 he agreed to accept a job in the Foreign Service, and left shortly afterwards for his first posting, as third secretary in the U.S. Embassy to the Austro-Hungarian Empire in Vienna.

It was marvelous to be overseas again, and it seemed like the start of a great and glamorous adventure. But the day after his arrival in the Austrian capital, the U.S. ambassador, Penfield, called him in to welcome him aboard, and after a routine peptalk, said: "Oh, by the way, Dulles, when you go out, would you please take my suit to the cleaners?"

There was a heavy pause, then Allen said: "Sir, I may be your third secretary, but I am not your valet."

He turned on his heel and walked out, deciding that bootlicking would get him nowhere. He was depressed. Was this what he had joined the Foreign Service for, to be an errand boy? What future lay ahead of him? Was he going to turn into a Foreign Service hack, a stuffed shirt like Penfield? What did he have to do to become the American equivalent of his dashing hero, Captain Alex Gaunt?

As it turned out, he didn't have to do anything. The United States government did it for him. On April 6, 1917, America declared war on Germany and the Austro-Hungarian Empire. When the U.S. Embassy packed up to leave Vienna, Allen Dulles had already been posted to the American Legation in Berne, in neutral Switzerland.

When he asked what his function would be at the legation, no one at first seemed to know. The whole place was in chaos, snowed under with new arrivals as the legation endeavored to face up to the new responsibilities it would have now that the United States was involved in the war. When he asked to see the U.S. minister, his new boss, he was told that he was too busy reading up about the origins of the war. Finally, the harassed first secretary, Hugh Wilson, said:

"I guess the best thing for you to do is take charge of intelligence. Keep your eyes open. This place is swarming with spies. And write me a weekly report."

Allen Dulles swallowed, his throat dry with excitement and joy.

"Dear Father," he wrote home that May,

here am I in Switzerland again after all these years, and who do you think I saw last weekend? The Herzog Family!!! The Legation here is undergoing an upheaval to meet the new situation of war, and all is turmoil, with folks falling over each other and no elbow room anywhere. . . . As for me, I am one of the many cogs in the wheel, and I cannot tell you much about what I do. Except that it has to do with Intelligence!

He must also have been tempted to have Uncle Bert pass the word to his friend Captain Gaunt that he was now a fellow member of the brotherhood.

When the announcement came that the United States had entered the war, Eleanor Dulles rushed down to Washington to see Uncle Bert and ask him what she could do to help. He laughed at her, saying that war was serious and no business of young women. The best thing she could do was go back home to New York and start sewing socks for soldiers.

Eleanor was furious. She was about to graduate from Bryn Mawr and her ideas of women's place in the scheme of things, far from orthodox even before she went to college, had burgeoned under the tutelage of one of her mentors, Professor Susan Kingsbury. If war had not come, she had had ambitions to go out into the world of business and industry and match her talents against those of the male sex. She was already convinced that when it came to brains and enterprise, if not brawn, she could more than measure up to any man who came along to challenge her.

She was a bright, eager, attractive girl whose thick glasses, perched on the middle of a sensitive nose, gave her a look of frailty that was soon belied by the forthrightness of her views and conversation and the firmness of her handshake. She could hardly have grown up in the company of two sturdy brothers without learning to handle herself. She came alive in boats and could handle a skittish sailing dinghy in the worst of the storms that swept Lake Ontario. As a swimmer she did not have Foster's endurance or Allen's speed in the water, but like them both, she was impervious to cold and could swim for hours in the choppiest waters. Up at Henderson she could swing an ax with the best of the boys, and could handle a gun and a fishing line; but around the campfire in the evening, her pretty face pink in the light of the flames, she sang sentimental songs in a pleasant soprano and looked like an angel.

Foster believed in God and the teachings of the scriptures and never had any doubts about religion. Allen, it sometimes seemed to Eleanor, was a believer because it gave him such a delicious sense of sin when he transgressed the Ten Commandments. She was the skeptic of the family. She never talked about it to her parents, who would have been shocked, but she had long since decided that there was far too much mumbo-jumbo about the Church, and if God there was, then he was sometimes extremely backward, hard-nosed, and unintelligent.

What she did believe in passionately were human relationships, and she set great store by them. At Bryn Mawr she had been through some fumbling lesbian encounters which had not by any means shocked her, had, in fact, given her some comfort in her moments of loneliness, but had proved to be otherwise frustrating. She came from a heterosexual family, and she knew that true warmth would only touch her heart when she cleaved to a member of the opposite sex. But if there was someone out there who was going to make the contact, so far she had not found him. In 1917 she was twenty-two years old, and there was something offputting in her manner, perhaps the formidable catholicity of her knowledge and conversation, her sheer intellectual ability, which seemed to discourage the young men in whose company she found herself.

In any case, now that there was a war on she decided the time was temporarily past for worrying about men. She wanted to get in on the conflict, and fretted that Allen was ahead of her, already involved, even if on the neutral sidelines. The more she thought about it, and the more she read the war news in the newspapers, the more eager she became to get herself to France and see what war was actually like, instead of merely reading about it.

For one moment, fearing that her parents would disapprove, she considered scraping all her savings together and running off to Europe without informing them. Finally she decided that this would be unnecessarily cruel, and asked them if they had any objection to her going to Paris, where she hoped to get a job working with one of the welfare groups that were being organized. She had made up her mind that if they opposed her, she would go anyway, but to her delight they responded that they thought it was a wonderful idea. Her father gave her $1,000 as an emergency fund, and two days after graduating from Bryn Mawr Eleanor sailed for France.

She shared a cabin on the steamer going over with Henrietta Ely, the extrovert daughter of a well-known Philadelphia family. Henrietta was a great traveler and a great talker. Between 1914 and 1916 she had journeyed extensively through Russia, Austria, and Germany, and she talked at great length about her adventures to one of her fellow passengers, a taciturn Frenchman who turned out to be the Minister of Education in Paris. Henrietta's lively stories did not so much entertain him as arouse his suspicions, which he passed on to the authorities the moment the liner docked at Bordeaux.

The result was that the two young women were escorted ashore by the French police and confined in a small hotel with no explanation of why they were being held. Their passports and money were confiscated, and they were forbidden to leave the hotel, or to telephone or telegraph. After two days a young man from the U.S. Consulate came to visit them, and Eleanor, furious at being held, never one to neglect an influential name when it might help, pointed out to him that her uncle was Robert M. Lansing and would he get her out fast. The young man was unimpressed, and doubted whether it would help. He seemed to share the French conviction that the two young women were dangerous spies.

It was a week before Eleanor, increasingly frustrated, fearful that she would never see Paris after all, dredged up a name from her memory of someone who might help. She remembered that a man she had once met at her grandfather's house, Woods Bliss, was counsellor at the Paris Embassy. When she told the young consul to telephone him, he reluctantly agreed to do so.

"My God," said Woods Bliss, "don't you realize who she is? That's the Secretary's niece. You'd better get her out fast. She could get your hide."

Shortly afterwards, the French arrived, profuse with apologies. Eleanor Dulles finally reached Paris on June 4, 1917, and was among the cheering crowds on the pavement of the rue de Rivoli when the first American troops marched through Paris on their way to the front. By that time she was dressed in a uniform (though it was strictly unofficial) and she felt like a veteran, especially later that day when a passing doughboy saluted her. Soon she would be under fire, which was more than her brothers would ever be able to say.

On the day the United States declared war on Germany, John Foster Dulles was in Central America on a mission for the government. Once more Uncle Bert had come to the aid of one of his in-laws. With hostilities about to begin, the administration needed assurance from Costa Rica and Nicaragua, whose territories lay athwart Panama and the Canal, that they would align their policies with those of the United States once war began; and that they, as well as the Panamanian government, would restrain pro-German elements and hunt down spies and potential saboteurs who might interfere with the passage of military supplies through the Canal.

It was a mission that would have to be carried out with tact and delicacy, for the Central American powers were touchy about U.S. interference and full of *amour propre.* Lansing sent the name of his nephew through to the President, pointing out that despite the relationship there was no nepotism involved, since Foster Dulles had already carried out a successful mission for Sullivan & Cromwell in Panama and Guyana, and that his firm was, in fact, the legal adviser of the Panamanian government. He would know whom to see and what to say.

He did indeed, and carried out his mission with quiet efficiency. When he got back to Washington, he immediately volunteered for combat service in the U.S. Army but was turned down for what would always be a family curse: defective eyesight. Instead, the Army gave him a direct commission as captain and posted him as a lawyer to the War Industries Board superintending shipments to neutral nations.

As it turned out, that would prove to be much more useful for his future career. For, among other things, it brought him under the eye of one of the most influential men of the day, Bernard Baruch.

It bothered Foster that he would never know what it was like to take part in a battle. Janet Dulles was later to say: "After all, you can always find people to do the fighting. It's the men who do the thinking in wartime who are in short supply."

But Foster did not agree. He did not feel guilty about not being "over there," but he was an intensely patriotic citizen and he was genuinely regretful that a physical infirmity should have kept him not only from the duty of every good American—to fight for his country —but also, he felt, from a rewarding and enriching personal experience.

CHAPTER THREE

Trio Abroad

The U.S. special envoy and minister plenipotentiary to the Swiss government in 1917 was the Hon. Pleasant Alexander Stovall. A Southern gentleman of the old school, who wore striped pants, a Prince Albert coat, and pince-nez, he looked so much like a dignitary of a Fifth Avenue church that one day, when he introduced himself to a young American by saying: "I'm the American minister," the other shot out his hand and replied: "Pleased to meet you, parson."

In fact Minister Stovall back home in Georgia was proprietor of the Savannah *Press.* He was an old friend and supporter of President Wilson and his was a political appointment, made before the war began, when the legation at Berne was more interested in trade in cuckoo clocks and cowbells than the more sinister traffickings of war. Stovall, who knew next to nothing about foreign affairs, was there principally for the tourism, and left most of the running of the legation to a couple of regular Foreign Service secretaries and a small, locally recruited staff.

The war itself and America's entry into it had changed all that. Around the minister's coattails, much to his confusion and bewilderment, now swirled a whirlwind of activity, and a whole host of reinforcements had arrived from the United States and the shuttered embassies of German-controlled Europe—new secretaries, press counsellors, propagandists, cypher experts, and the like.

As the late Robert Murphy has pointed out,* Switzerland functioned in World War I rather like the United Nations does today, as a neutral

*Murphy worked in the Berne Legation as a code clerk in 1917–18.

ground on which belligerents from both sides could operate, even meet, talk peace, make deals. It was also the stamping ground of a large number of ethnic groups, Czechs, Slovaks, Slavs, and Croats, hoping to return to independent countries once the Austro-Hungarian Empire was defeated and broken up. Among its exile leaders were the Czechs Jan Masaryk and Edouard Beneš, and, most important of all, Vladimir Ilich Lenin, waiting the call in Zurich to return to Russia and take over from the crumbling czarist régime.

Though the American Legation in Berne was a humming hive of activity when Allen Dulles got there at the end of March 1917, it unfortunately was not much good at making honey. So far as security and intelligence were concerned, its members were amateurish in their methods and sometimes innocent to the point of naïveté in their political judgment. It so happened that many of the exiles, looking to the "enlightened" sympathy of President Wilson and the backing of their compatriots in the United States, kept in close touch with the Berne Legation, and often brought intelligence from their underground cells in the occupied countries, all of which was of great value to the Allies. Masaryk was a particularly good source of information, but on at least two occasions his agents were compromised and arrested by the Germans and the Austrians owing to the carelessness of Americans in Berne. On the first occasion, a message in which the agent's name was used was sent in a code which, as they should have known, was in possession of the Germans, since it had been left behind in the closed American Consulate in Leipzig after war with Germany began. On the second occasion a Czech girl employed by the legation and allowed free run of the code room was discovered to be a German spy. It was one of the British agents operating in Berne who contacted Allen Dulles shortly after he assumed his duties as intelligence officer and produced proof for him that the girl, who had a young brother and sister in Prague, was being blackmailed by the Austrians into cooperating with them. The Briton maintained that he had already warned the Americans twice that there was a spy in their midst, but no action had been taken. As a result, he said, at least two Czech agents had been identified by the girl, arrested, and shot, and a prominent Austrian working for the British had been compromised.

Like several other young men in the legation, Allen Dulles had taken the Czech employee out on dates and had found her a pleasant companion. He now had the melancholy task of delivering her to the British, who wanted her for reasons of their own. He took her out to dinner and walked her home afterwards through the Old Town, where, at the corner of the Nydegg Church, two men were waiting.

"I never heard what happened to her," he said later. "It was my first lesson in intelligence. Never be certain that someone is not betraying you, just because you like and trust them. Anyone, but anyone, can be blackmailed. And it is often the most patriotic citizen who is turned into a traitor and betrays the cause he loves."

His own career in espionage had got off to a somewhat mixed start, thanks to his carelessness and lack of zeal. One incident was to become famous in CIA annals in later years, especially since it involved none other than Lenin himself.

Vladimir Ilich Lenin, the Bolshevik leader, while living in exile in Switzerland, had established a liaison with the American consul in Zurich, James C. McNally, to whom he occasionally passed on information reaching him from his comrades inside Russia. It was a much more accurate picture of the chaotic state of the régime than the Allies were getting from their own sources in Petrograd, but not much notice of it was taken in Washington and some of it Berne did not even bother to send on. They considered Lenin to be a red revolutionary who could not possibly be telling them the truth. In any case, what conceivable impact could he have on the situation in Russia, since he was immobilized in Switzerland, separated from his homeland by Germany and Austria, a solid mass of enemy territory?

What was more, Lenin was passing his information through McNally, and the American consul himself was suspect. McNally's daughter had married a young German naval officer before war began, and she and her husband were now in Berlin, where he was working at the Admiralty. It turned out that though his son-in-law was now an enemy alien, the consul was still keeping in touch with him through Germans arriving in Switzerland from Berlin. In fact, McNally's son-in-law had been persuaded by his wife to send naval information through to her father (she thought it would help in her husband's rehabilitation after the war), and this in turn the consul relayed to General Pershing at U.S. headquarters in France. He was later thanked for his "valuable help."

The Americans in Berne did not seem to be aware of this. All they knew was that Consul McNally had been denounced by a busybody living in Zurich, Dr. Herbert Field, for "consorting with the enemy," and Minister Stovall was taking the accusation so seriously that he was considering packing off McNally back to the United States.*

In the circumstances, Lenin's value either as an informant or as a future leader of the Russian people was hardly appreciated for its true worth in Berne, and Allen Dulles was certainly not told to regard him as a vital cog in the machinery of espionage he was now operating. Though that was no excuse for what followed.

On April 11, 1917, he was duty officer at the legation, most of the personnel and all of the senior officials having left for the afternoon. The telephone rang and Allen Dulles answered it. A voice speaking in German with a heavy accent announced that this was Vladimir Ilich Lenin. Lenin, who seemed to be laboring under a heavy emotion, explained that he would be arriving in Berne in the late afternoon and must at all costs speak to someone in the legation.

Allen, who had a date with a girl within the hour, crisply informed him that by that time the legation would be closed, and that Mr. Lenin had better come in the following morning.

"Tomorrow," said the voice, rising in excitement, "will be too late. I must talk to someone this afternoon. It is most important. I must see someone."

Just another of those unstable émigrés, Allen decided. What could he possibly tell him that could not wait until tomorrow? That the czar had been overthrown and the Russian revolutionaries had taken over? It was in all the newspapers. And for the moment, anyway, what did it matter who was in power in Russia so long as they remained allies and went on fighting the Germans? What possible influence could an exile like Lenin have on the situation, stuck as he was in Switzerland, unable to get home?

He said firmly: "I'm sorry, it will have to be tomorrow. Ten o'clock tomorrow, when the office opens."

At ten o'clock the following morning, Vladimir Ilich Lenin had already left Switzerland and was on his way back to Russia by train, his passage facilitated by the Germans, who wanted him and his comrades to take Russia out of the war. Lenin arrived in Petrograd at the Finland

---

*He was subsequently sent back in disgrace, and dismissed from the Foreign Service. The injustice was never satisfactorily cleared up.

Station on April 17, 1917, and immediately ordered peace negotiations with the Germans to begin. It was news of this startling decision that the Russian leader had undoubtedly planned to reveal to the Americans, for passing on to President Wilson, whom he was known to admire. Allen Dulles had snubbed him in favor of a date with a girl.

In later years, after he became director of the CIA, Allen used to cite the incident as a cautionary tale to new recruits to the Agency, warning them never to repeat his folly and neglect a lead, no matter how inconvenient, in favor of a personal engagement. In his CIA lectures he always said that his date was to play tennis with a pretty girl. In fact, it was a much more serious rendezvous than that. The girl was Helene Herzog, daughter of the family with whom he and Foster had studied French in Lausanne before the war. Then she had succumbed to Foster's scorn and rejected Allen because he was a fifteen-year-old schoolboy. He was now old enough to be taken seriously.

But though Allen mentioned to his family that he had seen Helene, he never did reveal to anyone whether the meeting turned out to be worth rebuffing the Father of the Russian Revolution.

What is certain is that he learned his lesson, and never neglected an émigré again. In fact, from then on he spent much time in the company of Czech, Slav, Moravian, Bothnian, and Serbian groups operating on neutral Swiss ground, and for the two Czech leaders, Jan Masaryk and Edouard Beneš, he conceived a great devotion and admiration. His firm belief in their crusade for an independent Czechoslovakia was to have a considerable influence on him—and through him on the shape of postwar Europe, for Allen Dulles would be one of the men who drew the new lines on the maps when the war was over.

There was another encounter in Switzerland which was to have repercussions upon his future, and that was with the meddlesome Dr. Herbert Field in Zurich. Dr. Field was the American who had virtually ruined the U.S. consul, James C. McNally, by denouncing him to the legation, and Allen Dulles decided he had better make contact with him. Field obviously kept his eyes and ears open, and seemed to have no compunction about tattling of the activities of his compatriots. He might well prove to be a fertile source of intelligence.

To his astonishment, Dr. Field proved to be quite the opposite from the usual nark or sneak or squealer upon whom intelligence agencies, like the police, rely for a great number of their leads. Field, a New

England Quaker, educated at Harvard, married to an Englishwoman and father of four children, had settled in Zurich to run the Concilium Bibliographicum, an international institute devoted to the compilation of a full bibliography of scientific research in all parts of the world. With the outbreak of war, he had branched out into charitable activities and was the head of a lively Quaker relief organization which ran food relief programs for the starving populations of war-torn Europe. He was regarded by everyone as a great and good man, an ardent pacifist who deplored the war and had no malice toward either side engaged in it.

How could such a man come to denounce a fellow American simply because he was preserving contact with his daughter and his German son-in-law? Even if McNally had been engaged in activities more sinister than that (and there is no evidence whatsoever that he did so), how could a Quaker of Dr. Field's character take an action which he must have known would ruin the consul's career? The answers to those questions have never been forthcoming, and it is unlikely now that they ever will be. Certainly, to judge by his reports, there is no evidence that Allen Dulles asked for or received an explanation. He was simply interested in Field as a source, and when he asked about that the answer he got was a dusty one. The Quaker quietly informed him that he was not ready to compromise his position in neutral Switzerland by working for U.S. intelligence. But he was pleasant and welcoming, and he invited his fellow American to stay for lunch.

It was then that Allen met the rest of the Field family, Mrs. Nina Field and their two sons and two daughters. It was the eldest son whom Dulles would always remember as he saw him that day, a gangling pale boy, twelve years old, who, when he asked him what he wanted to do in life, replied solemnly: "Bring peace to the world."

His name was Noel—Noel Field. Thirty years later it would be making headlines in all the newspapers and causing Allen Dulles perhaps more trouble than any other spy in the course of his career.

The German armies began their great offensive on the Western Front in June 1918, and pushed as far as the outer defenses of Paris. For the first time the French capital came under shellfire, because the Germans had wheeled up their secret weapon of World War I, and began bombarding the city with the great railway gun subsequently dubbed Big Bertha. Eleanor Dulles had already learned what it was like to be bombed, because German airships were attacking Paris frequently at this time. She had stood in the streets to watch the sinister cigar shapes slipping serenely through the cloud-flecked, moonlit skies, and cheered wildly when one of them, caught in the searchlights, was punctured by an antiaircraft shell, flamed, crumpled, and fell like a meteor in slow motion somewhere over by the Bois de Boulogne.

The airship bombs had done quite a bit of damage in the outer suburbs and several had even dropped right inside the city itself, but Eleanor had found the raids exciting rather than frightening. Being in the streets when one was in progress was rather like being a bit player in a well-written, action-packed drama. There was so much going on all around: the distant noise of ambulance and police-van klaxons, the faint sewing-machine putt-putt-putt of the airship's engines up there in the black sky, the sudden whooshing roar of a night-fighter plane diving on a target that usually turned out to be a cloud, the groping fingers of the searchlights, the crump of the bombs, the baleful flicker of fire from burning buildings. It set the heart beating faster, and she noticed that she was not the only one who was aroused and stimulated when a raid was going on, and somehow rather serene and sated after it was over.

The shelling from Big Bertha was something else again. The missiles seemed to come out of nowhere, and you never knew where they were going to land. As Londoners would do in World War II when the V-2 rockets hit the city, the Parisians said to each other: "If you hear them land, you know they've missed you."

The damage the shelling did was heavy but uncoordinated. Anything might be hit, a munitions factory, an orphanage, a hospital, an open park. There was something of almost cosmic indifference or terrifying randomness about the shelling, and no one was excited or stimulated by it, only thankful when it ceased for the day.

While Parisians cowered under the bombardment, knowing that their fate was being decided by the great battle raging on the Marne, Eleanor Dulles was working in the slums of the city among refugee families from the devastated towns and villages over which the armies had fought and bled since 1914. She was part of a team of volunteer workers that had been organized by a redoubtable young American woman, Mrs. Ernest Shurtleff, wife of a pastor from Boston. They brought food and clothing for the refugees, washed babies, bandaged wounds and sores, scrubbed floors, tended the sick. The French government was too busy panicking over the imminent threat to the city to bother about the streams of refugees flowing in from the battlefields, and made few efforts to house or care for them. Inevitably, they were crammed into the poorer areas of the city, and left to fend for themselves. Some were so shell-shocked that they were little more than walking wounded, women listless, children whimpering with terror.

Eleanor's "beat" was a dark, forbidding slum just beyond Montparnasse, an area of tall tenements, narrow streets, alleyways, and dark corridors lit only by guttering gaslamps or sometimes not at all. It was a district where cheap prostitution was a local industry, and pimps (mostly deserters from the army) hung around in the shadows, protecting their properties, sizing up new prospects. Mrs. Shurtleff had given each of the girls a small rubber truncheon and a whistle as protection against molestation, but in fact they never needed either. It was as if their work was recognized and a truce declared, and they were allowed to move around freely. What Eleanor found much more terrifying than the pimps were the bugs in the houses, the lice on the children, and the stench of urine and excrement. It took her many months to learn to live with the conditions in which she had to work, and sometimes she had to creep away into a corner and vomit. When Big Bertha began firing, and they descended for safety to the stinking black cellars beneath the tenements, it was an ordeal to sit in the darkness and listen to the squeak of the rats, the moaning of the children, and feel the bugs in the chill cellar searching for the warmth of your body and a meal on your blood. It was then that she came to bless the indefatigable cheerfulness of the whores, who, when spirits had reached their nadir, would start to sing, sentimental songs, obscene songs, soldiers' songs, anything to drive the despair and terror away.

As the Battle of the Marne reached its climax, Eleanor wrote a letter home to her parents (on June 6, 1918) from an address which sounds appropriate in the circumstances (Place d'Enfert-Rochereau, Paris 14):

> Tuesday we began following the offensive anxiously, but it was not until Wednesday night that we realized the grave threat to Paris. Our days began and ended in the cellars and were punctuated by the cannon

at irregular intervals. (We still hear that people in America think it is a joke that we go down to the cellars. It may be funny but we do.) Friday night we first saw how things were going. It is always a little hard to tell from the papers here. . . . Saturday there was the funniest feeling in the air. At the conference we spoke in a different way of the people who had left without their packages of clothes, of the people in the path of the offensive, and sort of looked around and wondered where we would meet next. . . . On Sunday, the last chance, Mrs. Shurtleff got her trunks off. The station was not crowded when we went down early, but there was a steady stream of people and trunks leaving. . . .

She was writing to her parents to reassure them, not to alarm them, and there is a resolute note of cheerfulness about her narrative. She went on:

Others have gone but I don't think any of our Committee will leave. The rest of us are strong and husky. We felt that the imminent crisis was over Sunday. Things seem to have stabilized. I guess we have a little time of waiting. We've taken it half as a joke our preparations to leave. We are sure to get plenty of warning and of time. Most of us have our little bundles done up and we have a good deal of money on our persons. Mrs. Shurtleff feels we should each have about four hundred dollars with us. Do not worry if and when you get this, you find things exciting. . . . None of us will be obstinate about staying if it comes to anything serious, we don't want to.

She had celebrated her twenty-third birthday (June 1, 1918) during a long, double air raid by both Zeppelins and planes, and later Big Bertha joined in.

"And then at night," she wrote,

there was another raid. With the heavy defensive barrage, there has been some damage which is very impressive but not very serious. On the whole, the realization of what was going on out there on the Marne, it made it the most exciting day I have lived, probably. Mrs. Shurtleff had me over to celebrate and I also spent the night with her as well as Sunday night. Refugees have been pouring in. Some from Soissons told me how the Americans evacuated them under gas fire when their friends were dropping dead around them in the street. Some of the workers up there have come back with exciting tales. Some of them had ten minutes warning to get out, and saw the German airship advance guard before

52

they left. For the last two nights there have been no raids. This is also a sign that things are letting up for a while. . . .

The Battle of the Marne had failed. The Germans would make another big push that summer as Ludendorff tried desperately to end the deadlock, but the American divisions were now taking over everywhere from the decimated and exhausted British and French, and the tides of war were turning. The ghastly death toll would continue to mount, but in truth the war was coming to an end.

It was while peace rumors were running through Paris that Eleanor Dulles heard that her application to go to the front to work with refugees in the battle areas had been accepted. She got her orders to leave on November 9, when it was known that peace was imminent, and her friends all urged her to stay behind in Paris and celebrate with them. She was tempted, but duty and her conscience prevailed. After all, no matter what was signed at the peace table, the war was not over for the refugees, and she felt she must go where she was needed. So on November 11, 1918, the day on which World War I officially ended, she wrote home from somewhere near Château-Thierry:

> Dear Mother: What a day! But I can write only about my own little doings, for I've not been in Paris since eight o'clock this morning and have not received news about the signing of the Armistice, and know little except the Kaiser is supposed to be in Holland.
>
> I am *very* sorry I could not be in Paris. It seems rather a pity to leave just today when, I suppose, there were all kinds of rejoicing there, but it did not seem possible to change my plans for a personal desire like that, and after all I have certainly had a thrilling time myself today. . . .
>
> Never has the Gare de l'Est seemed more full of fine-looking soldiers of all the armies—and it was wonderful to feel that they were not going out to be killed any more. When we changed trains at Château Thierry many people said the Armistice had been signed, but we were not sure. We could see the results of the fighting, though we did not have time to go about the town at all. The station and the houses along the line were pretty badly knocked about. . . . All the way up we saw little gun emplacements, shell holes in the fields, stone walls knocked to pieces at places where there had evidently been hard resistance, little groups of graves. . . .

She finished her journey by truck at a village called Mareuil-le-Port, where about fifty families were living, amid the rolling hills of the Marne. The town sat on a main military road and had been badly shelled, but a small *équipe* of American volunteers had established themselves in the less damaged houses and in the *mairie,* from which they carried out their relief work.

> All day the guns have been booming around us in celebration, and they're still going tonight. They rang the *mairie* bell till they broke the rope. And the children in school have been shouting the *Marseillaise.* We have felt like shouting ourselves but have not yet been a big enough crowd to do it. It is impossible to realize, and yet I think already we feel differently about everything. . . . Now I shall go to bed and I shall never know what queer things I may have written, but I must say that it is all that I hoped here and more, and that I am a thousand times glad that I came. . . . It's great to be here. Lots of love, Eleanor.

Foster Dulles still genuinely regretted that his eyesight had kept him from taking a physical role in the combat in Europe, and as some compensation he labored prodigiously both in Washington and New York at his job in the Commerce Department, where he dealt with the intricacies of neutral shipping and supplies. It was a complicated job deciding how to keep such disparate areas as Holland, Scandinavia, and the whole of South America supplied with food and raw materials and at the same time make sure that none of it was passed on for reshipment to Germany or to German blockade-runners. He handled it well and impressed his superiors. The result was that he made some powerful contacts on Capitol Hill and in Wall Street who would prove good sponsors for him in his future career in the law.

He and Janet had already started a family. First John (1913) then Lillias (1914) and Avery (1918) were born. They were handed over to the care of a nanny, and would never really make any serious inroads on the time which Foster and Janet spent together, for neither of them would have allowed that to happen. They had grown into an intensely self-sufficient couple, and though it would be too strong to suggest that their children were an intrusion, they were certainly never permitted to interfere with the closely knit association that their parents had formed. Already wherever Foster went Janet went too, and it would be so throughout their lifetime. The children took second place to Foster, and had to learn to accept it as a family condition.

Foster and Janet were attending Sunday morning service at the Presbyterian Church in Washington* when they heard the news that President Woodrow Wilson would personally lead the United States Delegation to the treaty negotiations at Versailles. Next day Foster Dulles hastened round to see Uncle Bert at the State Department and ask to be taken along. His personal ambitions had never really been put on one side even during the war, and now they were instantly revived. He felt that the cachet of being a member of the peace delegation would put the final touch to his wartime career and launch him into the postwar world with a sparkle to his name.

To his astonishment and mortification, Uncle Bert reacted with the utmost reluctance to the prospect of having him aboard. Robert M. Lansing had not had a comfortable war at all. Solidly successful though many of his wartime measures had been, he had seen his relationship with his President going steadily downhill as other influences came into play in the White House. The rift between the two men had come when Lansing objected to Wilson's decision to make the journey to Paris as head of the American delegation. Lansing no doubt had his own selfish reasons for his opposition, since he had pictured himself as the American delegation leader and dreamed of returning from successful negotiations at Versailles—the world restored by his patient efforts to peace and sanity—to a Washington that would acclaim his achievements and see him as prime presidential material for the election in 1920. But, to be fair, Lansing also had more altruistic and much more valid reasons for opposing the President's plan. He saw the forthcoming Versailles Conference as an occasion where wile, guile, and maneuver would be much more important than high ideals and lofty aspirations. Neither the position of the presidency nor the character of the President himself were made for the realpolitik that would prevail. President Wilson would be the only head of state there, forced to come down to the market place and argue and bargain with prime ministers and premiers. And since these ministers would include Lloyd George for Great Britain and Clemenceau for France, both masters of

---

*Their main church, of which Foster was an elder, was the Park Avenue Presbyterian Church of New York, which was later merged with the Brick Church. It had some famous and influential members.

political intrigue, Wilson would find himself outflanked and out-maneuvered on every important occasion. Far better for the Secretary of State to take over the game and start dealing the cards . . .

Woodrow Wilson was deeply offended at Lansing's opposition, and more than willing to listen to his advisers in the White House (Colonel House in particular) who whispered that the Secretary of State wanted the glory for himself. The President really had no idea what sort of a situation he was going to find himself in when he got to Versailles. He was in a euphoric mood, firmly convinced that his famous Fourteen Points had brought this terrible war to an end, and that now the nations, both Allied and enemy, would sit down at the same table and rationally and reasonably put the world back to rights. This would be not so much a meeting of the victors and the vanquished as a meeting of minds resolved on peace, decency, and human understanding. And he, astride his Fourteen Points, would lead mankind back to sanity.

In the circumstances, Lansing must have considered himself lucky to be going with the delegation, so fierce was the heat blowing toward him from the White House. Taking his nephew along would only heap coals of fire upon his head. He curtly told Foster that it was out of the question.

Luckily for Foster, there were other ways. The head of the War Industries Board in Washington had been the statesman and banker Bernard Baruch, and Foster's activities had come under his aegis. He had been impressed by the young lawyer's clear-mindedness and organizing ability, and when President Wilson made Baruch one of his chief counsellors at Versailles, Baruch selected Foster as his assistant.

It was to prove a rewarding relationship. Shortly after the delegation reached Paris, Baruch was appointed chief U.S. representative to the Reparations Commission, which would decide how much Germany and the Entente powers must pay in money, material, and land for having lost the war. He left many of the discussions to his deputy, as did the British and French representatives, and Foster Dulles thus came into contact with two of the keenest and most far-seeing economic specialists in Europe, John Maynard Keynes of Britain and Jean Monnet of France. While their elders squabbled over blood and revenge (Lloyd George and Clemenceau, as Keynes remarked, were out to squeeze the Germans like lemons "until the pips squeak"), these three matched wits and minds and found themselves close together in their outlook on the future of the world.

Sensing that this was a historic occasion, which the family must under no circumstances miss, the Dulles clan made a point of foregathering at the Versailles Conference. Secretary of State Robert M. Lansing had brought his wife, Aunt Eleanor, along with him, and two of his sisters were part of the delegation staff. Foster naturally refused to leave Janet behind. Allen came in from the legation at Berne, having succeeded in getting himself made a member of the Boundary Commission, which had already started the task of redrawing the map of Europe. Eleanor Dulles came in every three weeks or so from the Marne. The American delegation was housed in the Hotel Crillon, next door to the U.S. Embassy and overlooking the Place de la Concorde. Uncle Bert and Aunt Eleanor had the rose-pink royal suite on the corner, with a splendid view of the Place and the Champs Élysées, along which the processions of the victorious delegations passed.

All the clan except Foster and Janet (who were still on their way across the Atlantic) gathered on the balcony of the suite the day President Wilson drove ceremoniously into Paris. The great French crowd greeted him with such fervent rapture that they all found themselves cheering and weeping in shared excitement and pride. Never had an American President been so popular with the French as Woodrow Wilson was that day. It was the last time. After that everything would go downhill.

Already on that day there was one member of the clan who had little reason to be happy. Robert M. Lansing's strained relations with the President had grown worse on the voyage across the Atlantic, when it had become apparent that Wilson had no intention of taking his Secretary of State's advice on anything, and planned to be his own Secretary during the conference. Colonel House, his chief adviser, had the presidential ear and made sure that Lansing never got a word in. The way in which he was being sidetracked and snubbed soon became the gossip of the corridors at Versailles, but, as Eleanor Dulles said, "Uncle Bert was a very controlled man and I don't think he ever expressed what he was feeling."

For the United States and particularly for Woodrow Wilson it was soon a time of disillusion. The President tried to temper the Allies' vengeful greed for retribution. When he failed, he sulked in his chambers, appalled at the short-sightedness of the politicians, unwilling to sit down at a table and do battle with them, insulted by their disdain for his lofty ideals.

As the political wolfpack tore into the rump of defeated Germany, Foster Dulles and J. M. Keynes found themselves increasingly in agreement over the folly of exacting too heavy a toll from the vanquished and helpless Germans. Their opposition to the reparations program being spelled out at Versailles was economic rather than sentimental. They realized that Germany simply could not pay the huge forfeits being demanded of her without causing starvation at home, thus sowing the seeds of unrest on what could be the breeding ground of future war. They saw the danger clearly and made their views known, but no one among the Allies was willing to listen to them.

Eleanor Dulles used to come into Paris during the conferences from her welfare work in the battle-torn villages along the Marne; it was like another world. The winter of 1918–19 was a cold and bitter one along the Western Front, and the lot of the peasants whose homes, farms, and livestock had been destroyed by war was tragic enough to make any young girl despair.

"I was pretty young, twenty-three," she said later, "but in a spotty way I was aware of what was going on during the Treaty preparations in Paris. I argued with Foster about reparations. Like the peasants, I didn't see why the Huns shouldn't pay. I said, 'Look, these peasants have lost their cows and their horses and their sheep. Why can't we go into Germany and drive their cows and their horses and their sheep into France?' Well you see how unsophisticated I was. But Foster was very patient with me. He tried to explain. He said, 'You don't gain wealth by transferring wealth. That wouldn't work. It would just impoverish the Germans and confuse the situation. You've got to be constructive, build up one without depriving the other.'"

She met Keynes with her brother and they sat late in sidewalk cafés arguing hotly, she passionately pleading for her miserable peasants and inveighing against the hated Hun, the young men coolly and calmly stressing the sheer impracticability of a policy of revenge, the dire results it could produce in the years to come. Then, when she came back for another visit, Keynes was no longer in Paris. He had resigned and gone home in disgust. He went back to England to write the book that was to bring him fame, *The Economic Consequences of the Peace,* with its condign condemnation of Allied policies at Versailles.

"Some people thought Foster should have resigned too," Eleanor said later, "but he felt, I think correctly, that to stay and keep on fighting against the extreme views that were prevailing meant that he could do more than if he resigned and went home. Now Keynes looks like a hero, and he did write that very interesting book. But at the time he did not affect the Versailles Treaty clauses in any shape or manner."

Did Foster, by staying on and fighting?

"Yes, he did," Eleanor said. "He influenced the bill against Germany. Not enough, maybe. But he did write a long memorandum pointing out the danger of what was going on, and he was commended for it by President Wilson. He laid the groundwork for the later Dawes Plan and Young Plan. But it was Keynes, by his brilliant writing, who got the kudos."

There was one person who would certainly have been shattered if Foster had resigned and gone home. Janet Dulles was having a ball in Paris. It was her first experience of being the wife of a delegate at an important international occasion, and she relished every moment of the luncheons, outings, banquets, and ceremonials which the French government laid on for the Allied representatives. She would certainly have been reluctant to miss any single moment of it, though Foster's word would always be law as far as she was concerned, and she would have obediently packed her bags and followed him home had he decided that resignation was the action to take.

As it was, he immediately accepted a request from the President not only to stay on the job but to prolong his stay beyond the period for which he had been engaged. Unlike his Uncle Bert, he had won approval from all sides of the American delegation for his percipience, his dedication, and his refusal to be influenced by French and British blandishments to soften his opposition to their policies. One of the Americans who was particularly impressed with him was Thomas W. Lamont, whose law firm in New York handled the affairs of the J. P. Morgan banking organization. He offered Foster a job in the firm when he got back to New York.

Foster said he would think it over. The next day he thanked Lamont for the offer, which was a tempting one, but turned him down. He did not tell Sullivan & Cromwell of the offer or his refusal until he returned to the United States.

With all his troubles, there must have been times when Uncle Bert longed to be alone with his wife; but some member of the Dulles family was always around the Secretarial Suite in the Crillon, using it as a meeting place, an eating place, or, in the case of Eleanor Dulles, as somewhere she could take a bath and find a bed. She would creep in from the battle area, filthy, cold, and hungry, peel off the layers of sweaters and thick socks she wore to ward off the chills of northern France, and lower her chilblained feet and tired body into Uncle Bert's huge pink sunken bath, then crawl into his bed and fall asleep. He would leave her there until morning and share his wife's bedroom instead.

"I don't know what the servants thought," Eleanor said later, "when they brought his breakfast in the morning and found me in his bed."

Allen Dulles would sometimes arrive to pick up his sister and take her to one of the parties he was always attending in various parts of Paris, for he was a popular young man and seemed to have loads of friends, many of them adoring young women. She did not, however, get to all the parties, nor did she get to meet the girl who became his particular companion at this time. Paris had become an open city so far as the Americans were concerned, its female population filled with a spirit of giving, and some of the places where they gathered and the parties they gave were not exactly the kind a young man would take his sister to. As to the girl, the evidence differs as to who she was and where she came from. Some say that she was a famous Parisian *cocotte* named Jacqueline Forzane, but this seems unlikely. Forzane went in for English or Irish milords* rather than American third secretaries, and was, in any case, reputed to be in England about this time. Another story had it that Allen had become besotted with a girl who worked in the notorious Parisian brothel, the Sphynx, and that he had bought her out and installed her in an apartment in Montparnasse. The source for this story was said to be the late General (then Lieutenant) Walter Bedell Smith, who later became Allen's boss in the CIA, and who was

*The Irish peer, Viscount Castlerosse, was one of her wartime lovers.

said to have met the young secretary and his girl at the Sphynx while on leave from the U.S. Army.

Some CIA sources have even embellished this tale with a piquant additional detail, that the girl became pregnant and Allen wished to marry her, but was persuaded by Foster to pay her off instead. There are no records, family or otherwise, to corroborate any of this. They are the inevitable rumors bound to attach themselves to a young man who made no secret of the fact that he was extremely fond of women, and felt glum and lonely when he was unattached.

So far as his work at the Peace Conference was concerned, he had cause for satisfaction.

"Foster was working on reparations and I was mostly concerned with boundaries," he said later. "I was a member of the Czechoslovak Boundary Commission. I don't know that I deserve any great credit for the shape of the country I produced in Czechoslovakia. It looked something like a banana lying across the map there in Central Europe."

His two companions on the Czechoslovak sector of the Boundary Commission were a Frenchman, Jules Cambon, one of the two famous banking brothers, and a fellow American, Charles Seymour, later president of Yale. All three were determined to make the new state into a geographically viable one, and so, in addition to Bohemia and Moravia, they drew a red line over a considerable chunk of German-speaking territory known as the Sudetenland. The Czechs were in the minority there, but the plains and rolling hills gave Bohemia and its capital, Prague, a hinterland where any future German attack could be held.

"I sometimes wonder whether we weren't a little too free with the red pencil," Allen said later. "Those were the days when we were full of a spirit of generosity toward the new nations of Europe."*

He was as sharply aware as his brother that the conference was turning sour, and felt sorry for President Wilson.

"When he came he was the arbiter of Europe," Allen Dulles said later. "But come a few months later, when he had opposed the French idea of the Rhine as a boundary, the incorporation of the Rhineland

---

*It was over the Sudetenland that Adolf Hitler created the Munich Crisis of 1938 which subsequently led to World War II.

and so forth and so on, when he had to turn down the French boundary ambitions *vis-à-vis* Germany and elsewhere, the Italian ones on Fiume . . . everyone rounded on the President. It just shows you that popularity is a very ephemeral matter, and national ambitions, national greed, if not satisfied, can make everyone just turn on a man who is really their saviour."

He shared with his brother the sneaking feeling that the Germans had been cheated.

"We had sold the armistice conditions and the Fourteen Points, and the Germans had surrendered in the very sincere belief that Wilson would carry them out, that these were Wilson's views and he would carry them out. Well, they weren't carried out too well, at least not the way the Germans had interpreted them."

In the fall of 1919 Allen was posted to the U.S. Delegation in Berlin, and Foster joined him there a few weeks later for a short stay. It was the time of the Kapp Putsch, when three thousand ex-officers and NCOs of the German army marched on the capital and tried (and failed) to wrest the government from the Communists. Groups of dissident army officers were forming up into private armies. Adolf Hitler was still to be heard from, but there was rancor in the air and the bitter sense of injustice which Foster had predicted at Versailles. Everywhere the brothers went they heard Germans angrily declaring that they hadn't really been licked in the war, that they could have fought on, that Wilson had cheated them.

The experience was to condition the thinking of both men in the decades to come.

CHAPTER FOUR

Foster Father

First Eleanor and then Foster arrived back in the United States in the fall of 1919, and they were a source of envy to their friends and of pride to their parents, for they had added cubits to their stature as a result of their experiences in Europe.

Foster reported back to Sullivan & Cromwell, and at his first meeting with Royall Victor, the senior partner, quietly revealed the offer which Thomas B. Lamont had made to him in Paris, adding that he had, of course, turned it down. Victor was impressed. Most young lawyers he knew would have used the offer to negotiate a raise in salary and an advancement in the firm. He consulted his two most senior partners, Alfred Jaritzky and Henry Hill Pierce, and they mutually agreed to reward Foster's loyalty by giving him rather more than he would probably have gained by parlaying the bid from the rival firm. He was made a junior partner and awarded a substantial increase in salary.

Henceforward, he worked very closely with Royall Victor, participating in a number of complicated cases, notably the corporate reorganizations of the American Oil Company and the Chicago and Indiana Railway Company; he also played a leading role in the proxy fight for control of the Remington Typewriter Company, which thereafter became one of Sullivan & Cromwell's most faithful clients.

Foster was thirty years old, and already his contemporaries were beginning to regard him as one of the most promising young corporate lawyers in Wall Street.

Allen's return to the United States was only temporary. He came back in 1920 from Berlin and Vienna, where he had served on the Control Commissions, for both leave and reassignment. His future was by no means so sure or so promising as that of his brother, but for the moment he was not worrying about that. If his observations in Berlin had made him anxious about the future of postwar Europe, he had found compensations in Vienna. True, there was want and starvation in the Austrian capital which was, if anything, even more devastating to experience than in Germany, but somehow the Austrians seemed to bear their defeat and the privations that went with it with less anger and bitterness than he had experienced in Berlin. In any case, he had always had a great love affair with Vienna, stemming from his first posting there in 1917. There were many old friends to search out among the remnants of the old Austro-Hungarian court, and the largesse he brought with him in the shape of substantial American rations of food and drink did nothing to diminish the warmth of his welcome. Many a count and, particularly, many a countess owed their survival to his ministrations, and were not stinting in their gratitude.

He confided to his sister that in spite of the miseries all around him, Vienna had been "endless fun." Now he was back to relax before his next assignment, which was not likely to prove so entertaining. Rumor had it that he was being posted to Constantinople, where the Turks were in the middle of a revolution, and social occasions were going to be in short supply. So were pretty women. So, while he waited, he was accepting every invitation to a party that came along, and relishing every moment of them.

In the summer of 1920 he relished one in particular. In mid-July he rushed into the drawing room of his parents' home in Auburn, a wide smile on his sunburned face, and announced that he was in love.

"I have met the most wonderful girl in the world," he told his father, mother, and sister. "She has knocked me sideways. I've never known anything like it. I can't wait until you meet her."

"Bring her in," said Eleanor. She was a little skeptical. She had seen it happen in Paris, and she knew how Allen was about girls.

It turned out that the girl of his dreams had gone home to *her* parents to tell them there was a young man in her life.

"We've decided to be very restrained," Allen said. "We are not announcing our engagement until next Sunday."

Her name was Clover Todd. Her father was a professor at Columbia University and the family was reputed, in Janet Dulles's words, to be *très snob.* Allen had been for the weekend at Thousand Islands at the house of one of Janet's relatives, and Clover had walked into his vision like a revelation. She was slim, palely beautiful, with an ethereal quality that both awed and enchanted him.

"I've never met anyone like her before," he told his sister. "She makes other girls seem—earthy."

Eleanor, who would always follow her brother's amorous adventures with a tolerant eye, wondered how long this one would last. She doubted whether the girl would live up to Allen's rapturous description. They seldom did. They were usually much more practical—and earthy—than he seemed to think, and once the rose-pink film had dropped from his eyes, and the first flush of passion faded, he lost his enthusiasm and passed on to the next pretty face and well-turned leg.

But when Eleanor met her the following weekend, Clover Todd proved to be indeed something special, and everyone was delighted with her. She had a lovely fresh quality, a dazzling smile, an eagerness to please, and she had them all laughing when she recounted the shock she had created in her family when she told them she had fallen in love with Allen Dulles. Allen *Who?* They had never heard of him or his family. Professor Todd hastened to his reference books and looked him up.

"My God," he said, "he's an author. Why didn't you say he was an author?"

Clover, whose only clue to Allen's profession was that he had mentioned he was in the State Department, looked dismayed. Her father pointed to the reference book. *Allen Dulles,* it said, *The Boer War: A History.* Then he looked again and saw the date: 1902.

"He must be an old man," he said. "Don't tell me you want to marry an old man?"

"Oh no," Clover had cried. "He's not all that old. He told me. He's twenty-seven."

Professor Todd checked the reference book and made a hasty calculation.

"But he can't be," he spluttered. "He can't have written this book when he was *eight years old*! Why, I didn't write my first book until I was thirty-two!"

Her eyes were sparkling and her cheeks flushed as she told them the story, and Allen put his arm around her and hugged her. She had won them over at the first meeting, and he was proud of her. He was all for taking her off and marrying her at once.

But he came from a clergyman's family and the Todds were snobs. It was not until three months later, on October 16, 1920, that the ceremony actually took place. As they sped away on their honeymoon, Foster said to Eleanor: "I have never seen Allie so happy. We will never have to worry about him again."

Eleanor reflected that Foster didn't really know his brother at all.

When Allen had burst in to announce his discovery of Clover, Eleanor Dulles had been on the point of telling her parents about her first summer as a working girl; after the interruption she never did get back to it.

They probably would not have grasped what she had to tell them anyway, because she had spent the summer of 1920 working in a steel factory, and how could she convey to them the excitement of it—the noise, the heat, the smell of the great mill? Her old professor at Bryn Mawr, Dr. Anne Bezanson, working with Dr. Susan Kingsbury, had started a course in industrial management during the war to help persuade women to take the place of the men who had been called up. The course had gone on after the war was over, because Professor Kingsbury believed that women would only throw off the shackles that bound them to the kitchen when they went into the factories and learned to work on the benches. Through that experience, they would rise to become executives and learn to work beside and in charge of men.

She had offered Eleanor a fellowship, and it was eagerly accepted.

The course had a practical side. "You went into factories one day a week," Eleanor said later. "I went to the Atlantic Refining Company, and I went to the J. R. Scott Company, which was an executive-control time and motion study in Philadelphia. Then in the summer each of us was put out to factories for four months. I went to the American Tube and Stamping Company in Bridgeport, Connecticut. I worked both in the office and on the punch presses and assembly lines—dirty, noisy, dusty, dark, exciting and chaotic. They paid me twelve dollars a week."

The experience gave her a taste for working in industry, and when the course ended she informed her parents that she was off to New York to find a job. They let her go without a murmur. They were well aware that her experiences in France had changed her. She had cut her hair. She wore silk stockings. She smoked cigarettes in public, and, unlike her brother Foster, across whose lips a swearword would never pass, she had even been heard to say "Damn." Allen laughed when he heard what she planned to do and said he never thought they would have a "modern woman" in the family. Foster was shocked and said, rather reluctantly, that if she insisted on going through with her mad project she had better come and stay with Janet and the family in New York.

Eleanor refused, instinctively feeling that Janet wouldn't like it. It was only some years later she discovered how right she had been. Working at the New York Public Library on some research, she stayed with Foster and Janet for several weeks. Janet suggested that Eleanor should come in and see her each morning before she set off for the Library; so Eleanor would knock on the bedroom door and talk to her for a few minutes while Janet combed her long hair before the mirror. Then one day, Foster came to her, very angry.

"If you ever interrupt my wife again while she is combing her hair," he said, "you will have to leave this house."

Janet had never given any indication that she found Eleanor's presence trying, but had complained to her husband. For him her word was law. He had stopped speaking to his eldest sister, Margaret, because Janet found her husband, the Reverend Deane Edwards, a trial. He was a rigidly puritanical clergyman who neither smoked nor drank, and was apt to pontificate.

Instead of the creature comforts of Foster's home, Eleanor found herself a cold-water flat on Staten Island and started looking around for a job. Business was bad and work was hard to find. Eventually she found a job as an employment clerk at Glen and Company, in Long Island City, where they assembled and packed hairnets.

"It was horrible," she said later. "It wasn't dirty or noisy like the steel mill, and it wasn't as exciting as a steel mill. I interviewed about a hundred girls every Monday and about fifty every Tuesday and about thirty every Wednesday. The rate of turnover was fantastic. There were three hundred girls and five men for the heavy work, and fifty or sixty of them would be gone by the first payday. Their pay was twelve dollars a week and they lost the three dollars which was held back from them, but they never protested, they just disappeared."

The hairnets were made from human hair imported from Hong Kong and were sold to Sears, Roebuck, and the big stores.

"The owner of the factory never came out there, he just sat in New York and took the money," Eleanor said. "The manager was a very sharp type. I told him I could increase production, so I worked out an incentive scheme whereby for a fifty percent increase in production they could make thirty-forty percent more in wages. It was a sliding scale, and it worked. The girls really began to put out. They got very much interested in their work, and the good ones were soon earning sixteen dollars and more a week."

To her astonishment, the manager didn't like it.

"I'm not going to have those girls thinking they are good," he said. "I'm going to get rid of the good girls. I think it's bad for the spirit of the shop to have some of them think they're really efficient. They're just factory girls. I don't pay them to get above themselves. I'm going to clean them out."

He deliberately slowed down supplies and made things awkward for the smarter girls, so they just lost spirit and left. Eleanor Dulles was depressed by the way working girls were victimized, by the whole status of working women. To make her salary go further, she had started sharing a room with a girl who worked in the Ivory Soap factory, and so began meeting the women from there. They too worked in parlous conditions, and were treated like cattle, or worse.

"Each Christmas there was a party at the hairnet factory," Eleanor said, "and I happened to mention it once when I met Janet. She was very impressed. She had starry-eyed ideas of what went on in factories in those days. She said she would like to come to the party, and I had to make excuses, say that outsiders weren't invited. Because I knew what the Christmas party was like. Men came out from the New York office and brought large amounts of liquor, and they sat around in whatever little storeroom or remote part of the plant there was and gave themselves a good time. Very few men went out of the factory alone that night. It got a little rough. Janet would have died of shock."

By the time she had spent a year working in New York, she decided that if there wasn't much hope for the girls on the factory floor, neither were the prospects very bright for college girls who wanted to climb up higher.

"I came to the conclusion, which I think was valid at the time," she said, "that unless you had influence, power, or an absolute ruthless determination, you couldn't get anywhere in industry if you were a woman. I didn't have influence, I didn't have money, I didn't have power, so there was no future for me. Some of the girls I knew from Bryn Mawr had gone into retail selling and they were doing well, but I didn't want that. I wanted to get into heavy industry, and I found that women weren't wanted there. They were hard days for the female sex."

Reluctantly, she threw up her job with the hairnet factory and went back to Bryn Mawr, where she was asked to teach economics. It transformed her life. After six months, she scraped together her meager savings and sailed for England. There she enrolled at the London School of Economics, where she studied under Beveridge, took tea with Sidney and Beatrice Webb, and rubbed shoulders with Laski, Westemar, Rowley, Robson, Hobhouse, Tawney, and Dalton, all either famous or about-to-become famous authorities of the day.

She was alive with ideas, but hadn't yet pinned down what she wanted to do. She studied for a time at the British Museum, with a mad plan in her mind to write an epic poem about the Russian Revolution. She did a work study of the exploited men and women of the London slums, who, in appalling dark rooms in Stepney, Poplar, and the East India Docks, sewed buttons, turned suits, made artificial flowers for a few pennies a dozen. (The project was directed by Felix Morley,* who later became editor of the Washington *Post.*) She walked through the English Lake District and bicycled through Cornwall.

She went off to Germany with a party of friends just in time to hear the shots resounding through Munich in the wake of Adolf Hitler's 1923 Beerhall Putsch. She was hounded out of a village near Berchtesgaden and called a whore because she was wearing plus fours and boots. She was involved in a riot in Vienna.

In 1924 Eleanor returned to the United States and went to Radcliffe, where she proposed a thesis for her doctorate that was at once ac-

*Brother of Christopher Morley.

cepted, and she got a grant to go with it. She had thought long and hard, and had concluded that if she was going to make a name for herself in economics, she must do it by both surprising and impressing her contemporaries. Why not take the subject that was preoccupying the whole of Europe in the 1920s, and driving masses of ordinary people to suicide and death by starvation: runaway inflation? And why not do it by scientifically studying how it was happening?

When her brother Foster asked her what the subject of her thesis would be, she said: "It will be called The French Franc. I am writing a study of a major country's currency under siege."

Foster snorted. "Far too big a subject for you," he said. "It's like trying to cross the Atlantic in a rowing boat."

She was back in Paris toward the end of 1925, and took a room in Montmartre, No. 10 rue du Grandcharme, with no running water, a screen, a basin, and floorboards you could see through into the entrance hall below. ("I was always dropping my pencil through them," she said.) She studied at the Bank of France and the offices of the *Journal Officiel,* and haunted the corridors of the Paris Bourse. She worked in one of Montmartre's favored artists' cafés, the Rotunda, preferring it to the Dôme because the Dôme had round tables and the Rotunda square ones, so that one's papers didn't fall off. There she wrote her thesis.

And there, in late June 1926, she met the great love of her life.

It was the most devastating thing that had ever happened to her. She was a practical young woman, and she tried not to get panicky about it. But the more she let the situation develop, the more she realized that this was real, that he was like no other man she had ever met, and that she was hopelessly and irrevocably in love. It was about this time that she heard from home that not only would her parents be visiting Paris that summer but Foster and Janet were coming, too.

Hers was a WASP family if ever there was one. How was she going to tell them that the man in her life was a Jew? And how would they behave when they met him?

To Allen Welsh Dulles the 1920s were what he was later to call "my Slough of Despond." He was over thirty years of age and, professionally, life was going sour on him. It seemed a long, long time ago since he had run the intelligence operations in Berne, and even longer since he had dreamed of being a superspy like Captain Alex Gaunt; nothing now coming his way convinced him he would ever make a career in intelligence. It was true that some private organizations were working to get a peacetime intelligence service going, but officially the United States government simply refused to see the necessity for an efficiently run security service. Not only did the administration agree with Henry L. Stimson's frigid attitude to counter-espionage ("Gentlemen don't read each other's mail"), but didn't think it mattered, anyway.

There had been moments after the end of World War I when Allen's hopes had been high, for himself if not for the world. In Berlin and Vienna in 1919 and in Turkey in 1920 he had watched new leaders and new nations emerging, and he had seen a career ahead of him as a watchdog for America amid the chaos and confusion, feeding back to Washington the information that would keep both government and people alert to the way the postwar world was shaping. He wrote voluminous reports about political leaders and the new movements they were creating. He did studies of Kemal Ataturk, the new dictator of Turkey. He wrote about French and British rivalries in the Near East and completed a paper about Arab nationalism and the problems of Syria, Iraq, and Palestine. When he came home he opened a filing cabinet in the State Department one day and found his reports stacked in a corner, laden with dust. Obviously no one had ever bothered to read them.

From 1922 to 1926 he was head of the Near Eastern Department of State, and from a personal point of view it was a rewarding assignment. He went back to Turkey to talk to Ataturk. He visited Palestine and formed an acquaintanceship with Chaim Weizmann that was to grow in later years. He got to know such Arab leaders as King Feisal of Iraq and Abdullah of Transjordan, and renewed an association (during a visit to London) with T. E. Lawrence whom he had first met at Versailles.

He was a delegate to the Conference on Arms Traffic at Geneva in 1925 and back for the Disarmament Conference the following year. (Foster was there too on both occasions. From now on, when the American authorities looked for names to pick for the big international conferences, one or other of the brothers, and usually both, were

71

drawn out of the file.) Clover had started a family and their first daughter, Clover Todd, was born in 1922. Another girl, Joan (1923) and a son, Allen Macy (1930), followed in the next few years, and since Clover was a more devoted mother than Janet Dulles, she often stayed home with her family during Allen's trips. It did not inhibit him. He was the gregarious type, rarely without friends to call on no matter what capital he was visiting, and he was already in the process of compiling a list of international contacts that would one day be the wonder of the CIA. Politicians, bankers, businessmen—and their wives, daughters, sisters, and girlfriends—kept him fed with all the local gossip and provided the raw material for a succession of informative memoranda which he sent back to Washington. This time they were read but no one acted on them. They pleaded for a relaxation of the rigid anti-armament clauses of the Versailles Treaty, to allow the more liberal elements in German democratic government to build some sort of defensive force, thus cutting the ground from under the feet of the militant Fascist elements that were backing secret and illegal rearmament. He condemned French policies in the Levant and British policies in Palestine and Egypt.

Allen's reports had absolutely no effect upon State Department or administration policy. His Uncle Bert, who might have been badgered into persuading someone to read and act on them, had long since been thrown out of office by President Wilson. Wilson had in turn been succeeded by Harding and Calvin Coolidge. It was the low point of what Allen Nevins would later call "the most unreasonable, irresponsible and repulsive decade in American history," and few cared what went on beyond the United States because they were too busy at home making money and spending it.

Allen Dulles was not the rebellious type. He was already what he would remain for the rest of his life, a staunch member of the Republican Party, convinced that things would work out provided you didn't meddle with them too much. Unlike some members of the State Department who felt equally frustrated, he was not tempted to join the Communist Party or toy with socialism and vote (secretly) for way-out candidates at elections. His beliefs were solidly based on the status quo so far as government was concerned, and though he sympathized with those who sometimes kicked out, he had no desire to do so himself.* But he was unhappy with the sheer plodding unimaginative bureaucracy to which he had become attached, and he saw no happy future for himself in it.

Things might have been easier for him to bear had he been able to keep up with his contemporaries, who all around him were getting rich. Foster was a constant reminder of how prosperous were the times for those in private enterprise. Every year his standard of living seemed to grow in stature. He had now branched out and bought himself a second home, at Cold Spring Harbor, on Long Island's north shore, for himself and his family. They would go there at weekends throughout the year from their home on East 91st Street, and spend much of the summer there, boating, playing tennis, giving dinner parties and receptions for lawyers, politicians, and big businessmen. Foster never stinted himself or his guests when it came to food and drink, and Allen particularly envied him his cellar.

His own salary at State was $8,000 a year, and a small inheritance from his grandfather brought him in another $600. It was nowhere near enough for the needs of himself and his family, and he had bills outstanding all over Washington. He had been unlucky with his investments and was up to his ears at his brokers, and Clover (darling Clover) seemed to have no idea of the value of money. He loved her dearly, as he continued to insist, but she *was* a bit casual sometimes, the way she went on. Only too often he came home to find the servant hadn't been paid, no food had been bought, the light and gas bills were overdue, and she had spent her week's housekeeping allowance on a dress or a coat or a gadget she had left in a bus.

He was learning that he had to be careful in his treatment of Clover. She was temperamental and unpredictable. She never lost her temper, as Allen often did with her (when she curled into a womblike ball while he ranted at her), but would wait until it was all over and then slip quietly out of the house. At first he didn't worry about it, simply waited

---

*One newcomer to the State Department in the postwar years was Noel Field, whom Allen had last met at his father's home in Zürich in 1918. Field was already lashing out against the system in Washington and was turning—though Allen did not know it at the time—to communism. One day Allen ran into him demonstrating with a mixed bunch of blacks and whites against a segregated theater show which he and Clover were attending. Noel Field asked him to join the demonstration. He crisply refused. On the other hand, he did not report Field's extracurricular activities to State.

for her to come back, when he intended to apologize and have a splendid reconciliation. He knew she couldn't have gone far away, because she had walked out into the rain without taking hat, coat, or even her purse.

But then the telephone would ring, and it was Janet in New York. Her tone was supercilious as she exclaimed, with many a tinkling chuckle, that Clover was with her, goodness knows how she'd got there, seems she had bummed her fare from a man she had met at the railroad station, and borrowed 10 cents for a phone call from Travelers' Aid when she'd reached New York. Of course, they were giving the poor child a bed for the night and making sure she had a ticket and boarded the train tomorrow. Janet was most kind and understanding, and assured him she knew how it was with young marrieds, even if she and Foster never had such upsets.

Allen thanked her profusely—and could have cheerfully strangled her. He could have strangled Clover too had she been there at that moment; but when she did get back, slim, pale, woefully lovely, those large eyes liquid with sorrow, he scooped her up in his arms and vowed never to be such a cad again. Until the next time.

The first time she caught him straying with another woman was at a tennis party at his brother's house at Cold Spring Harbor. He believed he had been admirably discreet until a few days later, when a bill arrived from Cartier's. He burst in on Clover, waving it in his hand. She was wearing a simple, very beautiful, emerald on a gold chain around her neck. It was her *compensation,* she told him, calmly. Each time she found him playing around with another woman, he was going to pay for it. And, she promised him, it would always be expensive.

On his salary from the State Department, it would also be disastrous. Something would have to be done—about the job, he meant, not the indiscretions.

No one would ever call Allen Dulles a lazy man. Over the months, in addition to his duties at State, he had been studying for his bar examinations at George Washington University, Foster's old school. He attended evening classes, found the whole thing an easy ride, and passed without much difficulty. He had imagined that being a lawyer might give him additional clout in the Foreign Service, but when the next posting came along, a Grade 2 job in China, the salary stayed at

$8,000 a year. China was tempting because the country and people had always fascinated him and he would have liked to go back, but on that scale of pay he would be bankrupt in a year. He went to Foster for advice.

Foster was in a good position to help, because in prestige he had gone up considerably in the world. He had won international attention among lawyers and statesmen in 1923–24, when, at the request of J. P. Morgan, he had been retained as special counsel to the Dawes Committee. This was a body which had been formed by Secretary Charles Evans Hughes to try to get some order into the postwar reparations problem. As Foster, Keynes, and Monnet had predicted, the whole thing was in a mess. The Germans had proved unable to pay the huge debts which the victorious British and French had piled upon them. President Coolidge had urged the two Allies to go easy on the Germans, but since he was, at the same time, demanding that they pay back their own debts to the United States, they were in no mood to do that.

Foster came up with a proposal that was adopted in 1924 and became the so-called Dawes Plan, whereby the United States lent money to Germany, which in turn paid off the British and French, who then paid back the United States. Financially speaking, it was a mad sort of merry-go-round, but it gave the statesmen a breathing space. Foster would have preferred to have forged an agreement to limit reparations to a fixed sum, but settled for the best solution he could get through. His efforts were widely recognized and praised.

His growing reputation did him no harm at Sullivan & Cromwell, where the situation was changing rapidly in the boardroom. In 1925, Alfred Jaritzky died suddenly. The following year, the senior partner, Royall Victor, set off in his boat from Oyster Bay to sail round the point to Cold Spring Harbor and a visit to the Dulles household. He never arrived. Though only in his early forties, he was suddenly felled by a massive heart attack and died before he could reach land.

Who would take over the firm? The third most senior partner, Henry Hill Pierce, had been a sick man for several years. Confronted by the sudden demise of his two colleagues, he firmly made it clear that he was not going to be saddled with all the responsibilities of the firm and announced his retirement. One of his last suggestions before leaving his office was to recommend that rather than go outside the firm for a replacement at the top, they should promote the ablest junior in the organization.

No one had any doubt who that was. John Foster Dulles was appointed senior partner of Sullivan & Cromwell in 1926, with Edward Green, Eustace Seligman, and Wilbur Cummings as his senior assistants. He was thirty-eight years old and chief of one of the most famous law firms in the world, a role that would normally have taken him a lifetime to fill. He had made it to the top in only six years since returning from Europe. It was a phenomenal rise, but no one suggested he was incapable of filling it. His prowess as an international lawyer was already recognized.

It was a measure of Foster's self-confidence that when Allen came to him and posed his problem, the solution seemed to him simple. All he had to do was give up the Foreign Service and join Sullivan & Cromwell. This was nepotism of a high order. It was difficult for the most brilliant young lawyers from the top schools to get into Sullivan & Cromwell, let alone latecomers like Allen, who had qualified through a night-school course at a college with no great reputation in those days.

A few months earlier Foster had interviewed an applicant with a promising legal record from Columbia Law School, and had turned him down as not being quite up to the standard required by a top Wall Street law firm. His name was William O. Douglas.* Allen was hardly in Douglas's class, legally speaking, but then neither was Douglas the brother of the head of the firm.

Allen went back to Washington and handed in his resignation from the Foreign Service, then told Clover she had better start preparing to move the family to New York. He was not particularly happy about the decision he had made. The law struck him as being a stuffy profession, and Sullivan & Cromwell the most rigid and hidebound of legal firms. ("Sanctimonious" was the word William O. Douglas used to describe

---

*Who later became Justice of the Supreme Court. Douglas always subsequently maintained that it was he who had turned down Sullivan & Cromwell. "I saw John Foster Dulles and decided against him," he wrote later, "because he was so pontifical. He made it appear that the greatest favor he could do to a young lawyer was to hire him. He seemed to me like a high churchman out to exploit someone. In fact, I was so struck by Dulles' pomposity that when he helped me on with my coat, as I was leaving the office, I turned and gave him a quarter tip."

the atmosphere that clung to its Wall Street offices.) But, as he discovered in the next few months, there were compensations. It was a long time before he was allowed by his brother to handle cases of his own, and even when he did so it was understood in the offices that he must always be supported by an experienced lawyer when he was working on the background to a case; but, in any case, his value to Sullivan & Cromwell was never measured in terms of his deep legal knowledge or forensic skill.

"Where he was an asset to the firm," said one of his fellow lawyers later, "was in his ability to bring in business to Sullivan & Cromwell. He was a great customers' man. He loved the life in New York, and you began to see him everywhere, particularly where the tycoons, the company presidents, or their wives gather—opening nights at the Metropolitan Opera, charity balls, club dinners, squash sessions at the New York Athletic Club, tennis parties. He was a good tennis player and he knew when to lose. If he was playing with a tycoon's wife, he made certain they would win. But if the tycoon himself was in the opposite court, he'd keep the game ding-donging along until practically the final volley, when Allen would fumble and flub. That way the tycoon felt marvelous, having won a hard-fought game, and his wife didn't feel too bad either—after all, it wasn't her fault they'd lost—and both felt benevolent toward Allen. Such a good loser he was, too."

Sullivan & Cromwell could be generous with expenses when new clients were in prospect, but as his legal knowhow improved, there were more substantial compensations. He successfully saw through a complicated case for the United Fruit Company over leases. He believed with his brother that the German government should be allowed some measure of rearmament, and when the Allies persisted in forbidding it, he connived with one of the company's clients, du Pont, to get munitions through export controls and into Germany. By 1930 Foster and his fellow partners were persuaded that Allen had won his legal spurs; he was promoted to a junior partner, with a commensurate raise in salary. His life style grew with his bank balance, and so did his share folio. He bought into International Nickel, the American Bank Note Company, and Babcock & Wilcox, all firms of which Foster was a director, and he also became possessor of a block of shares from a grateful United Fruit Company. He raised a loan with Sullivan & Cromwell to buy a house on Long Island at Lloyd Neck, a short distance away from his brother's house at Cold Spring Harbor, and soon was a popular figure at the weekend house parties along the north shore. Foster eschewed the Island's feverish social round as being too light-minded for his taste, but Allen thrived on it. On a summer's evening at an Oyster Bay cocktail party, dressed in blazer and slacks and just in from tennis, he might have walked right out of Scott Fitzgerald. But he wasn't frivolous, even if he was catholic in his social taste. Both sexes found him attractive because he was both charming and cultivated. He took a box at the opera, admittedly for the contacts it gave him, but unlike many of his fellow boxholders, he preferred *Figaro* to *Bohème* and knew the score of *Così fan Tutte.*

At last he had enough money to begin laying down a cellar which, he hoped, would rival Foster's collection of Moselles, hocks, and clarets. It never did, "but I soon had a better line in Havanas," he said later, "even if I never equaled those I used to steal later on from Eleanor."

It was a far cry from his youthful ambition to control the intelligence services of the nation. All he could do now was keep in touch with those elements who were persisting in trying to build up a foreign security service for the nation, and this he did on his travels abroad on official government business or on frequent trips to Washington. But intelligence for the moment was no longer in the mainstream of his life. The romantic past was over and done with. He had had his fling as a spy. He still believed that the country would not be safe until a prestigious intelligence service, manned by first-class brains, was officially backed so that the enemies of the state could be watched on their home ground, and the nation warned of crises in prospect. He was certain that the day would come when such an organization would become respectable and attract the top talents once more. Then America would begin expertly reading its neighbors' mail again, gentlemanly or not.

But that was not his affair now. In any case, he consoled himself, he wouldn't have been able to afford a job in espionage any more, even if it hadn't become a dead-end and infra-dig job. His standard of living was too high. Clover was increasingly demonstrating that she didn't understand the value of money, except that it was something to be spent. And there was the additional expense of raising and educating his family.

It was a time to count blessings, and to be grateful to Foster, and Sullivan & Cromwell, from whom all blessings flowed.

When some of his friends around this time speculated about the future of John Foster Dulles, the general consensus was that he would end up as a Justice of the United States Supreme Court, though no one seemed to feel that he would make Chief Justice. He lacked the suppleness of mind for that, they thought.

He had passed his fortieth birthday and had reached a sort of plateau in his career. If he never climbed any higher, it seemed to most of his contemporaries that he had made a success of himself. He was respected by his solid and affluent contemporaries. He was envied by young lawyers. He gave the appearance of being well satisfied with his own progress and position, and not expectant of much more.

In fact, he was by no means satisfied, and the attitude he adopted was one meant to conceal from the outside world the ambitions that still consumed him. He had two grandfathers and an uncle who had been distinguished statesmen, whose names would go down in the history of the United States, and he was determined that one day he would emulate and perhaps even surpass them.

"I expect great things from you, Foster," his grandfather, John Foster, had said before he died, and nothing that he spoke would ever go unheeded in his grandson's lifetime. Being the senior partner in a great law firm and rising one day to be a Justice of the Supreme Court was not enough. Even becoming the Secretary of State was not exactly the summit of his ambitions, because Uncle Bert had attained that position—and he knew himself to be a better man than Uncle Bert. His goal went beyond that, above any other statesman in the nation, and one day he was convinced he would reach it.

It was just a question of working quietly, and waiting, a matter of patience, and Foster Dulles was a very patient man. He would always be content to wait, for the fulfillment of an ambition, the maturing of a plan, the squaring of an account.

Meanwhile, at Sullivan & Cromwell he gave every outward sign of being content with his lot. He had a comfortable home on East 91st

Street in New York, a house at Cold Spring Harbor, on Long Island, and a yacht which he loved to sail across Lake Ontario and the St. Lawrence into the Atlantic. He was as strong and as healthy as a bull, with a hide as tough as a rhinoceros (whose poor eyesight he also shared). His clients were some of the most distinguished organizations in the United States, Germany, and France, and he did well by them, for he read his briefs, was adroit in court, and gave good advice. He was an elder of the fashionable Brick Church in Manhattan. He traveled widely on the continent, was received with respect, listened to with attention. He still loved food, but demanded the highest quality nowadays, and had developed a taste for good wines and liqueurs to go with it. His guests came to his table not just for the fare but also for the conversation, which was usually political but always absorbing. He loved Wagner and standard classical literature, particularly by French authors, whom he always read in the original language. He liked women—in their place, which was in the home, working for a man. He was an archetypical solid Eastern establishment figure of his time, in fact, with his two feet on the ground and his head turned in the right direction.

"He knew that if he wasn't right in his opinions on life, he was as right as he could be, and as right as most people he knew," his sister said later. "He had few doubts. He was sure of himself in everything he did. He knew he was a good lawyer. He knew he was a good sailor. He knew he was a good husband."

What he was not was a good father to his three children. And that was curious because his brother and sister, Allen and Eleanor, had long since found him a satisfactory father figure. His children had other feelings. It seemed to them that the most important elements in their father's life were, first, his wife, Janet, then his work, and then his brother and sister. Only last in line came his three children, John, Lillias, and Avery.

"But of course he paid attention to his children," his sister said. "He taught them to sail, he taught them to play Ping-Pong, he taught them to fish. He didn't mess around with bedtime stories and things like that, but he was a good father in the serious things that he thought would help them."

Then she added: "But I do think the children may have felt that these other things he was absorbed in, and this tremendous drive he had in his work, left them a little on the sidelines."

It was curious that he should treat them so coolly, because he sometimes confessed to his brother and sister that he hoped to see a Dulles dynasty established in the history books one day. Only he said it as if he had their children in mind rather than his own.

"You have the best chance of carrying on the family heritage," he once said to Eleanor's son. It was a revelation of how much his own children had ceased to figure in his scheme of things. John, his eldest son, he had given up early. He had been a happy-go-lucky schoolboy until the age of twelve, when suddenly something seemed to go wrong with him. He took to mooning around the house, remote and brooding. He became touchy, oversensitive, and highly emotional, none of which was an approved attitude around the Dulles household. Sometimes he would be badgered into playing a game of backgammon or checkers, but when he lost he burst into tears. His father was shocked.

"Foster couldn't understand this," Eleanor said. "In the first place you didn't lose. Well, somebody had to lose. *But nobody cried."*

His attitude toward his daughter was curious. She was to grow up to be an attractive woman, but as a child she was not exactly an angel in appearance or manner, and as a girl she was difficult to approach. He was slightly alarmed when she showed signs of wishing to emulate her Aunt Eleanor and make a career for herself. Half-jokingly, half-seriously, he set out to prevent it.

"He didn't want her to learn anything," Eleanor said, "except maybe the feminine charms which he thought she lacked. He sent her to a school in Paris where there was little danger of her getting any particular or serious knowledge, just a smattering of art and culture and so on."

He was quite disappointed when she came home and said she wanted to go on to college. Janet hadn't gone to college. Why should his daughter? It made women bossy, gadabout, assertive—like Eleanor.

He was mollified when Lillias agreed to go to Bennington, because he thought that was a "safe" college where they abjured serious matters and concentrated on the frivolous. What he didn't know was that about the time Lillias went there, Bennington was getting ideas (above its station, Foster would have said) and you could actually learn things there, if you really wanted to.

81

"The trouble with Foster and his daughter was he wanted her to be like Janet," said Eleanor, "and Lillias wasn't like Janet. And I think Lillias probably felt that in not being like Janet maybe she wasn't fitting into the picture Foster had of her. I don't know about his relations with her other than what I've told you. There was never anything that jarred on you, and there was always an atmosphere of humor and friendliness in the house. I never heard anyone say an angry word or be disagreeable to anyone. Humanly, you would have expected a little bit more irritation, but there wasn't."

When Lillias later on married Edward Hinshaw, son of one of Foster's public relations men whom both he and Janet decided was "unsuitable," since he was neither dynamic nor successful, it was almost a comfort to Foster because it confirmed his inner conviction that his daughter had tried to shape her life the wrong way, and would have been far happier and more successful had she modeled herself on her mother. Of course he did not say any of this to his daughter or anyone else except his wife, but Janet was not so reticent, and soon the family knew how Foster felt about his daughter's "failure."

"But, as I say, it was all very civilized, well handled," Eleanor said, "and I thought the wedding was charming."

The youngest son, Avery, now a pillar of the Roman Catholic Church, looks back on his childhood and remembers no lack of contact between himself and his father (though he is much more reticent about his mother).

"I would think it was completely false," he said later, "to suggest that there was no rapport in our household between children and parents. We were a very closely knit family and there was a great deal of interaction. He was very much of a family man and he liked to come home and play games, whether it was Ping-Pong or bridge or tennis or backgammon or conversation, and so forth. We really did do things together a great deal, considering how busy he was . . . The idea that there was any alienation between the generations seems to me to be entirely wrong."

But when Avery Dulles came to take the most important decision of his life, and one that profoundly affected his father's plans for his future, he did not tell him beforehand. He decided to become first a Roman Catholic and then a priest of the Church, and knew only too well what a shock that would be to his solidly Protestant family.

"They were a little startled, I suppose," he said later. "But it was a kind of personal decision which I felt I had to make on my own."

Once more Foster was very civilized about it, although the family remembers that Janet got "extremely emotional."

"They tried to make the best of it," Avery said. "My father looked upon freedom of conscience as a sacred value. While he no doubt regretted I chose to exercise freedom in that way, he recognized that as far as I was concerned it was a moral imperative, and he respected that and appreciated it."

Long before that happened, the Foster Dulles household had split into levels, and no denial by Father Avery can convince the rest of the family that there was no gulf between the generations. The children were thrown increasingly upon each other and their own resources, well aware that they would have to resolve their childhood crises together, with no help from their parents. Janet was wrapped up in Foster and had no time for them. Foster was absorbed in his work, and his unspoken ambitions.

"His work was very important to him," Eleanor said, "and he felt a real sense of obligation toward colleagues and subordinates. He couldn't neglect them for his children."

When someone once questioned the order of his priorities, he said, in exasperation: "Being the head of a law firm is not that easy. I am responsible for the lives and careers of a hundred young lawyers. I've got to take it seriously."

"He was very considerate of other people," Avery said.

CHAPTER FIVE

Mixed Marriage

The long thesis which Eleanor Dulles had laboriously copied out on the rectangular tables of the Rotunda in Montparnasse won her a doctorate from Radcliffe in 1926, and was published shortly afterwards under the title of *The French Franc.* It was a study of a currency under the pressures of postwar inflation, and its approach was bold and fresh, its conclusions percipient. It not only gained her the respect of some of the world's better known economists but elicited a letter from the most famous of them, John Maynard Keynes himself. He wrote her: "Congratulations. Yours is the best book on monetary inflation that I know."

It would have been nice to rest for a spell on her laurels, but she had problems on her hands. One was financial. Brilliant though she might be at economics, she had proved herself a babe-in-the-woods so far as the stock market was concerned, and she had come a cropper, most of her savings, including her grandfather's legacy, being wiped out in the Wall Street crash. She needed a job and was considerably relieved when Radcliffe and Harvard eventually came up with a joint fellowship, worth $1,500 plus living expenses and secretarial help, to go back to Europe and write a study of the vexed question of Germany's crippling hangover debts from World War I and the Bank of International Settlements which had been set up to handle them.

It was a big subject for a comparatively new economist to handle, but she counted on help from her brothers in securing the contacts she would need. Both of them were now involved in Europe on official missions to which they had been seconded from Sullivan & Cromwell. She was confident that both could help open many doors for her.

84

But it was another problem that was causing her most anguish, and her brothers were the last persons in the world who could help her solve it. What was she going to do about the man in her life?

She had first met David Blondheim at a party in Montparnasse to which she had been taken by a young man named Jake, whom she was seeing frequently at this time. Jake came from Kansas City and was working on the Paris edition of the Chicago *Tribune.* He was good clean fun and she liked him, but then one night this older man came around. His dark eyes were so large behind his thick glasses that she realized he must be even more myopic than she was. He sat next to her and said hardly a word. When she thought about that meeting later on, all she could bring to mind were those dark eyes, thick glasses, and brooding features which were unmistakably Jewish.

From then on she became increasingly aware of his presence. The first time they were alone together he asked her if she realized he was Jewish, and she laughed. He did not laugh back. She became gradually aware that his Jewishness was the most intense thing in his life, both his pride and his burden.

He had been born and brought up in Baltimore, the second son and third child of Orthodox Jews. His father had immigrated from Frankfurt, in Germany, and had gone to work in the Baltimore garment industry, which was practically the monopoly of the Jews. He had allowed America to make little change in his life style, stayed poor and rigidly attached to the strict rules of his sect. His insistence that his three children obey all the laws of Orthodoxy had made their early life a burden. They had grown up constantly aware of the gap between them and the ordinary children with whom they mixed, who never allowed them to forget that they were strange and "different."

Only David had finally decided to break the religious bonds that bound him. He told his shocked and scandalized family that he no longer believed in Jahveh or the codes by which his father, his mother, and his brother and sister lived. Amid the wailing of his family, who put on ritual sackcloth and ashes, he departed to make his own way in the world.

He may have broken with Orthodoxy but he remained fundamentally Jewish in his culture, work, and outlook. Until Eleanor Dulles came into his life, he had thought of little else but the Jews, their history, ancestry, tradition, culture, and literature. He had collected a

85

number of fellowships from Johns Hopkins and other universities and had come to Europe to do studies of the Talmud and make glossaries of the ancient words and phrases of the great Hebrew writers. He was a natural linguist who knew modern and ancient Hebrew, spoke perfect French, German, Italian, and Spanish, and was fluent in at least another twenty languages and dialects. He had combed every corner of Europe in search of ancient manuscripts, and thought nothing of using up a year to track down a single word to its most archaic origins in some flaking document hidden in an obscure Balkan synagogue. The depth of his researches made Eleanor feel ashamed, and her own efforts puny in comparison.

One night David Blondheim told her something about himself that made her heart miss a beat. While still living at home with his family, he said, he had allowed his father to produce a bride for him, a good, Orthodox Jewish girl. On his part, it had been a loveless marriage, and as soon as he broke away from his religious ties he had divorced her. But there had been a child, a son, and although the family had tried to hide him away, sometimes, through the kindness of his sister, he had seen him playing in the streets of the Baltimore ghetto. Eleanor soon realized that the only thing which really hurt David about the separation from his family was the fact that it had cost him his son. He had paid a high price for his freedom.

As they looked at each other across the tables of the small Latin Quarter bistros where they were now meeting, the candlelight flickering on their thick glasses, they were well aware of the bizarre nature of their situation. David Blondheim was over forty, Eleanor Dulles in her thirties, and they were supposedly independent as well as grown-up people. But they were only too conscious of the pressures bearing down on their relationship.

Upbringing, background, tradition, religion—and, above all, *families* —oppressed them. It was still within David Blondheim's power to return to the bosom of Abraham, confess his sins, and regain his son. But if he married a goy, he would never be forgiven and his name would be forever expunged from the family tablets. As for Eleanor's family, how would the Reverend Dulles react? What would Foster— and Janet—say if she told them she proposed to marry a divorced father who was also a Jew? Why, no one in the family had even married a Catholic.

They realized only too well that their situation had an absurd side to it, for what was more ridiculous than the dilemma of a middle-aged Romeo and a mature Juliet? It was painful and real to them, just the same, and Eleanor in particular agonized over what to do about it.

To think things out, she took a slow boat to Turkey from Marseilles and joined her sister, Nataline, who was working as a nurse in Istanbul; but when she got back, David was waiting outside the door of her Parisian garret, and they walked in together, hand in hand. They made up their minds. They would become engaged to be married.

Then the Reverend Dulles and his wife arrived in Paris for a holiday, and as they drove from the station together she casually announced: "By the way, I'm engaged." She was appalled at the shock she had given her father by the lightheartedness of her announcement, and realized that nothing that she told him about her fiancé would relieve it. The questions began. What were his religious views? Well, he wasn't exactly an atheist, but he was no longer very religious and he was certainly a very fine man. Yes, but what was his background? Then she told them.

They all dined that night together at the Trianon Palace Hotel in Versailles, and David put on a tuxedo to please her. But it was a painful occasion, nevertheless. Her fiancé was the only person at ease. He talked freely and fascinatingly, and her father later on drew Eleanor aside to tell her she had found herself a most interesting and cultivated man, a real scholar. But she could see that he was distressed. Her mother had told her earlier on that the Reverend Dulles was a very sick man, and it hurt her to know that she had added a mental worry to his physical pain.

It was then that she probably made up her mind. She would live with David but she would not marry him. Not for the time being, anyway, not while her father was alive.

Allen laughed when he heard the news that Eleanor was living in sin. "Good for you. I admire your independence," he told her. But he never did ask her to introduce him to her lover.

Foster and Janet met David when they came to Paris, and Foster afterwards told her he also thought he was "a very fine man." But he was relieved to hear that she did not propose to marry him. They showed no sign of shock when she said she was going to live with him, but obviously considered it the best way out of a delicate situation.

When they came back to America, they took care to invite David as well as Eleanor to dinner at the house on 91st Street, but only for intimate private parties.

Eleanor was far from convinced that it was a satisfactory solution to the situation. She would much sooner have been married. And in any case, what if she decided to have a baby? To hell with David's family or her own, she was certainly not going to produce a bastard.

It was not only through David Blondheim that the Jews had begun to make an impact on the attitudes of Allen and Foster Dulles. Both brothers spent large amounts of time in Germany, where Sullivan & Cromwell had considerable interests,* during the early thirties, and both were only too conscious of the rise of the National Socialists. It was while working with the American delegation to Berlin during the so-called Standstill Agreement (a temporary moratorium on Germany's reparation debts) that Allen met Fritz Thyssen, the Ruhr industrialist. Thyssen had recently secretly joined the Nazi Party and contributed 50 million marks to its funds (he doubled it later), so he was in a position to demand and get visiting privileges with the leader, Adolf Hitler. He took Allen along to a meeting at Party headquarters in Berlin and brought him into Hitler's presence, where he was given a lecture on the blindness of Americans to the evils of Jewish international finance. Allen replied that it had been the British and the French who had been squeezing the German people since 1919, and had he made a mistake—were Lloyd George and Georges Clemenceau both Jews? Thyssen hastily explained to Hitler that Dulles was making a joke, and the Führer laughed.

"He had a laugh louder than Foster's," Allen said afterwards. "I always thought my brother brayed like a donkey when he was amused, but I now know he sounds like a turtle dove compared with Hitler."

But he missed nothing of what was going on in Germany, and he was both depressed and alarmed. Sullivan & Cromwell had offices in Hamburg and Berlin, and some good friends among their German-Jewish clients who told Allen of the pressures that were growing on them. When the Nazis closed in on them, they hoped Sullivan & Cromwell

*They represented several provincial governments, some large industrial combines, a number of big American companies with interests in the Reich, and some rich individuals.

88

would come to their aid. He promised that all the resources of both the U.S. government and the law firm would be exerted on their behalf. When the Nazis eventually came to power in 1933 and the persecutions of the Jews began, he was among those who prodded the State Department to take action. And so far as Sullivan & Cromwell was concerned, he pointed out to his brother that many of their most powerful clients were now either provincial states controlled by the Nazis or German industries whose chiefs had financed the Party and helped to bring it to power. It was true that some of the American clients whom they represented in Germany showed no concern at all about the savage political changes that were taking place. Such firms as the Remington Typewriter Company, Standard Oil, and General Motors had made no complaints. On the other hand, he knew from his own personal contacts that the du Ponts—and they were extremely powerful clients—did not like the Nazis at all and were growing restive. In the circumstances, was it not both politically unwise as well as distasteful to go on operating in Germany and representing these people?

John Foster Dulles knew all about the Nazis in Germany and the persecution of the Jews, because Eleanor had been bombarding him with dire forecasts for some time. She had made several trips to Berlin herself (leaving David Blondheim behind in Paris or in Baltimore), and had been appalled at the way in which anti-Semitism was spreading like a scourge through the nation. She had traveled with a fellow American, Nancy Wertheimer, who was working for the Foreign Policy Association and happened to be Jewish. Together they went to Party headquarters for a scheduled interview with Joseph Goebbels, the Nazis' chief spokesman, but never reached him. Sighting Nancy, a crowd of Party workers surrounded her, shouting: "Are you Jewish?"

"I'm American," she replied.

"But are you Jewish, are you Jewish?" they continued shouting, beginning to jostle her.

Eleanor decided it was no place to linger; grabbing Nancy's hand she began pulling her out of the office into the street, where they were followed by whistling and booing Nazis. She was indignant and revolted by the incident, and by the humiliation of the Jews she saw all round her in Berlin. But when she came back to America and warned her brother of these happenings, he said he had seen them himself but thought them the temporary (if regrettable) by-products of a much more important and fundamental change in the power structure of Europe. In a speech at Princeton in March 1936, he seemed to suggest that what was happening in Germany and Italy was all part of the inevitable struggle between the new "dynamic" nations and the "static" nations like England and France, and that Americans must adjust themselves to the changes that were coming. He added that although "distasteful," the Nazi revolution in Germany represented a change that it would be better to accept rather than go to war to stop, and that if everyone yielded gracefully, then Hitler, National Socialism, and its excesses would prove to be a passing phase.

Many of his friends in Wall Street, as well as Allen, Eleanor, and some of his partners, were astonished at his complacency over what was happening. John J. McCloy,* a fellow lawyer, expressed puzzlement over Foster's ambivalent attitude to the Nazis.

"I rather gathered the impression that he was not particularly concerned about it," he said. "His disposition to settle all disputes without resorting to violence rather influenced him in rationalizing this Hitler movement."

In any case, Foster still believed that Britain, France, and the United States had committed such enormous injustices at Versailles that "they must be paid for," and Adolf Hitler was one of the bills they would have to accept and meet. He deprecated Eleanor's "working herself up" over the persecution of the Jews, and was even more scathing over President Roosevelt's denunciations of Nazi excesses, which he characterized as "drumming up mass emotionalism."

"I don't think he realized in the mid-thirties that the Jewish question was the major question in Germany," Eleanor said later. "He told me that he had been in Berlin and talked to Warburg and Melchior there, two Jewish banker friends of his. He said they had made motions to him to indicate that even in a closed room with the windows shut and nobody else present, they were afraid that trucks outside were picking up what they were saying. They indicated to him that they felt absolutely no freedom any longer in Germany."

But when she asked him what he was going to do about it, he said: "There's nothing that a person like me can do except, probably, to

*Who became U.S. high commissioner in Germany after World War II.

keep away from them. They're safer if I keep away."

But Allen and one or two other members of the Sullivan & Cromwell staff were convinced that just keeping away from their Jewish clients in Germany—turning their backs on them, in fact—was a cowardly way to tackle the problem. Something much more drastic would have to be done. Otherwise, Foster was warned, Sullivan & Cromwell would begin to get the reputation on Wall Street of being pro-Nazi and anti-Jewish.

Foster was outraged. "How could anyone think we were anti-Jewish?" he asked angrily. "Do you realize that Sullivan & Cromwell is the first big law firm, big non-Jewish law firm, to have a Jewish partner?"

It was true that Eustace Seligman had been made a partner in the firm during the régime of Foster Dulles's predecessors, and though he was for a time referred to snidely on Wall Street as "S & C's token Jew," that epithet lost its sting later on, when more Jewish members of the staff rose through the ranks and were given partnership status. No one at Sullivan & Cromwell suggested that Foster was showing any bias or antipathy toward the Jews by preferring to ignore what was being done to them in Germany; but they were shocked by what they felt was his lack of feeling and sensitivity, and his cold-bloodedness in allowing business with his German (now Nazi) clients to go on as usual, simply because they were highly profitable.

A movement began among the staff to persuade him to close down Sullivan & Cromwell's operations in Germany as an expression of distaste for Nazi methods. Foster was angry when he heard about it, and extremely hurt when he realized that his brother Allen was one of those who believed that all relations with Germany should be severed. At a stormy meeting of the partners Foster vehemently defended his policy of leaving well enough alone, and stressed the financial loss the firm would suffer if it abandoned its German clients.

"What will our American clients think, those whose interests we represent in Germany, if we desert them?" he asked. "It will do great harm to our prestige in the United States."

He was thinking particularly of a favorite client, the Remington Typewriter Company, on behalf of whose German interests he had fought several court battles. Allen pointed out that Sullivan & Cromwell were more likely to lose prestige with some of their clients by staying in Germany than by getting out. It so happened that he had authority for what he was saying. He had maintained close contact with du Pont ever since 1925, when, as a member of the State Department and later, he had winked at du Pont's illegal dealings with German arms manufacturers and persuaded the Senate to overlook them too. His efforts had been rewarded and he was now a shareholder in some of the companies. He therefore knew that du Pont, unwilling to help the Nazi rearmament program, was preparing to withdraw its German operations.

"It might be better for us to leave Germany before du Pont leaves us," he said.

For the first time since he had assumed the post of senior partner in Sullivan & Cromwell, Foster Dulles seems to have sensed that he was in danger of losing his control of the firm. He was firmly convinced that his policy of neutrality toward the Nazis was the correct one, that what they did inside their own country was no concern of an American law firm. He argued long, eloquently, and persuasively in favor of leaving things be, but when he looked around the table and saw the hostile, rebellious faces, and realized that even his own brother for once was emotionally concerned and determinedly against him, he abruptly changed his direction. It would not be the last occasion in his lifetime that he would do so.

"So be it," he said. "Who is in favor of our closing down our operation in Germany?" He looked around at the upraised hands. "Then that is decided." A pause. "The vote is unanimous."

The office in Hamburg and the branch in the Esplanade Hotel in Berlin were closed, and the bookings for the semiannual trip which Foster and Janet normally took to Germany were canceled. The atmosphere in the office was much happier once it was done, and Foster gave no outward sign that he regretted it. In fact, it was a wise move to have taken. As Allen said later: "You couldn't practice law there [under the Nazis]. People came to you asking how to evade the law, not how to respect the law. When that happens, you can't be much of a lawyer."

But Foster's attitude reminded both him and his sister of the difference between them and their older brother. Eleanor would always be a highly emotional, keyed-up person, with partisan ideas that she would defend to the death. Allen was a creature of impulse and instinct, willing to go out on a limb for something he believed in. But they sensed in their brother a chilling capacity to be completely dispassionate, to reduce even the most anguishing problem to a question of expediency.

For Eleanor the implications of the row at Sullivan & Cromwell came only at second hand, through Clover (who was very indignant about the whole business), as well as through Eustace Seligman's daughter, who was her friend. But she had already gone through her own experience of Foster's cool inhumanity toward matters of deep personal concern, and she had been wounded.

Her concern was, of course, her relationship with David Blondheim. Their affair was now five years old, and it had often been rough going for both of them. "It was all on account of psyche and emotion, we were both rather high strung," is how Eleanor described it later. There had been months in Paris when they had known the peak of happiness that was fulfillment for both of them. There were long separations which made their mutual need deeper, while he was poking around in some dusty cellar in Rumania and she was researching in Basle.* But there were also the bitter times back home in the United States, when they both seem to have decided that a love that could be open in Europe must be clandestine here. David was working in Baltimore and regularly seeing his brother and sister, but could not bear to tell them he was living with a goy. Eleanor was teaching at Philadelphia and afraid she would lose her job (they needed the money) if it was known she was living in sin—with a Jew. They met, hole-in-the-corner, at obscure bars and restaurants in Philadelphia and crept away for "illicit" weekends. It was a stormy time when they lashed out and hurt each other badly.

It could not go on. But then the Reverend Dulles died in 1931, and Eleanor decided that the time to marry had come. She had plans, though she did not confide them to David. She wrote a letter to tell Foster that she would be marrying shortly. She did not ask for, or expect, his approval, but neither did she anticipate the reply he subsequently sent her.

There is now no record of exactly what Foster Dulles wrote to his sister, because she tore up his letter and burned it. One gathers that

*The result of her studies, a book on *The Bank of International Settlements,* was published in 1930.

it was couched in his most coldly rational and insensitive terms. Did she realize what she was doing in marrying a Jew? Had she reckoned with the complications it would make in her life? She was beginning to carve a career for herself in economics and in teaching. Academically, socially, it would be disastrous. The whole thrust of the letter was: *Go on living with him if you wish, but don't marry him.*

Thinking back on it over the years, Eleanor Dulles is now ready to forgive her brother.

"I think Foster felt he had to protect me," she said. "And he did it in a way in which, if we hadn't really had a good deal of respect for each other, might have been very painful."

She did not feel that there was any anti-Semitism involved in his feelings. She interpreted it in the sense that he was, as usual, trying to be the practical member of the family, trying to make her accept things as they were, as he saw them in New York, where they were always saying: "We can't have too many Jews in this club," or, "We can't have too many Jews in this firm." She must learn to live with certain things just as she lived with the climate; it was almost as if he were saying: "I don't think you should go to live in Gabon, because the climate is so terrible."

Only this wasn't the weather and this wasn't Gabon, it was the man she loved, and he was well aware that she loved him. She destroyed the letter and decided that she would not reply to it, waited for a few days until her emotions had calmed down, then wrote to Janet instead. If she and Foster were so worried about her decision to marry, she said, then it was quite clear that henceforward she must go her own way, and they need not bother about her any more. She did not add, because it went without saying, that this would leave a great gap in her life, that she loved, admired, and needed the friendship and counsel of her brother; only her need to stabilize her relationship with David was stronger.

Janet did not reply, and nothing was ever said about the matter again. Eleanor Lansing Dulles and David Blondheim were married quietly on December 9, 1932, in Washington, D.C. No relatives were present from either family.

As far as Foster's attitude was concerned, it was as if nothing had changed. The letter might never have been written. He was as ready as ever to give his sister help and advice.

94

David Blondheim's brother informed David (through a third party) that he never wished to see him again, that he had wiped his name from the slate, that he had ceased to exist as a member of the Blondheim family. Eleanor noted that her husband was deeply distressed at this news, and went on worrying about it.

She began to work at ways of compensating him for the loss of his family. In the summer of 1934, she got confirmation that she was pregnant, and prayed that she would produce a son for David. But she did not tell him about it—yet.

For Allen Dulles, Foster's attitude toward Germany was beginning to be a matter of concern. He could not understand how his brother could be so complacent about the way things were going. The row over the German office of Sullivan & Cromwell was in some ways a milestone in their political, though not their familial, relationship. For a time, at least, their thinking diverged sharply, especially over what was happening in Europe. Allen Dulles's antennae had become sensitized by his experiences in Europe in World War I, and all the indications they brought him as he traveled abroad or talked to statesmen, diplomats, or newsmen warned him that the advent of Adolf Hitler was not only evil in itself but would mean war, and that it would be a war in which the United States would inevitably be involved.

This was a conviction that profoundly irritated Foster. He saw no reason why the United States should participate in any European quarrel, and he did not believe that Europe need go to war either. Often on weekends at Cold Spring Harbor the two brothers would foregather for dinner and a game of chess, but now chess was abandoned for argument, in which Clover, passionately in support of Allen's contentions, and young Avery Dulles, who was very much a disciple of his father's position, would join.

It was a curious spectacle, and Avery remembers being very "conscious of the difference in temperament between my father and his brother." He had always considered his Uncle Allen to be a light, rather frivolous man, unconcerned with anything but his own selfish needs and demands. He once summed up the difference in temperament between the two men by saying:

"When my father dropped his napkin at table, he always rescued it before the servant could pick it up. Allen waited for it to be restored to him. 'What's the use of having servants,' he used to say, 'if they can't pick up your napkin for you?' "

But in these heated discussions, it was Allen who displayed deep emotion and concern over what was happening in Germany and his heartfelt belief that no man could stand aside in the face of Adolf Hitler's persecution of his minorities and threats against his neighbors. And it was Foster, the proud Christian churchman, who preached caution, impartiality, and a careful policy of wait-and-see. Everything would settle down so long as people stayed calm and reasonable.

Infuriated by such complacency, Allen angrily shouted at his brother: "How can you call yourself a Christian and ignore what is happening in Germany? Why don't you go over and see what is happening there? It is terrible."

In fact, Foster Dulles had long been intrigued by Hitler and would have liked to go to Germany to meet him and listen to him speaking. He envied his brother his encounter with the Nazi leader. Increasingly in recent months, his mind had been turning toward politics, for the time had come, he had decided, to do something about his ambition to become more than the senior partner of Sullivan & Cromwell. He had begun giving lectures and speeches on subjects other than law, edging further and further into the realms of international politics, the fight to keep the peace. He had found a platform in the World Council of Churches and had spoken at several conferences sponsored by this organization, but felt that perhaps his delivery, the way he assembled his message, lacked a certain compulsion.

"He was very interested in the techniques of capturing the interests of the electorate," said his son, Avery. "He believed, in other words, in expediency but only as subordinate to principle. He saw in Hitler the example of a person who could capture the enthusiasm of the people as a demagogue . . ."

It would be interesting to see the successful demagogue at work, and when Foster sailed for Europe in 1937—taking Janet, as usual, and Avery with him—he had a plan to make a side trip to Germany. But at the last moment he decided against it, perhaps feeling that the possibilities for embarrassment outweighed the opportunities for demagogic instruction.

The main purpose of his visit was to preside over a seminar in Paris on "Peaceful Change" at which a number of politicians, economists, and intellectuals had come together to discuss how grievances in Europe, specifically those of Germany and Italy, might be resolved without resort to conflict. The proceedings bogged down into a series of denunciations of National Socialism and fascism which, Foster believed, were irrelevant to the purpose of the discussions, and Avery felt that he was "rather dissatisfied with the results. He felt the people attending were not able to rise above their nationalistic self-interest and prejudices."

He went across the Channel to a meeting of the World Council of Churches at Oxford, where, he found, passions were more muted and a readiness to seek solutions rather than pronounce denunciations was the keynote of the proceedings. He was much impressed both by the sincerity of his fellow Christians and by the effectiveness of the World Council as a platform for international pronouncements which secured considerable attention at home. From that time onward his interest in and participation in the Council's work never flagged.

Foster's trip to Europe did nothing to change his attitude toward what was happening over there, and in his arguments with Allen he would continue to deplore the excesses of National Socialism but insist that the good sense and stability of the Germans themselves would take care of it. Coming back on the boat he scribbled away at a book that had been formulating in his mind, which he described as "the result of much thinking and study since the Paris Peace Conference of 1919." It was far from being an apologia for Hitler, but he did blame Franco-British selfishness and greed at the end of World War I for the threatening climate of 1937 and the crises of 1938–39.

The book, a densely argued, rather remote plea for the creation of an international body to control what was happening in the world, was published at the beginning of 1939 under the title *War, Peace and Change.* Among its recommendations was one to promote "such alteration of the international status quo as may seem necessary to prevent the growth of powerful forces emotionally committed to exaggerated and drastic change." It was a euphemistic way of describing what Germany was already doing in Europe, and since it was written at a time when the Nazis were grabbing Austria and the Sudetenland and beginning a campaign of racial discrimination and terror, it sounded like nothing more than a verbal slap on the wrist for Hitler and his gang. The book stressed the "inevitability" of change in the world, and made no reference to the human anguish and suffering involved nor any condemnation of the Nazi creed.

Allen hated the book, and was riled by his brother's increasing tendency, as the international situation got rougher, to preach at him and chide him for being emotional. Foster could always find a quotation from the Bible to justify the standpoint he had taken, and his brother seethed at his own inability to reply in kind and show up the casuistic nature of the extracts from the Gospel that were thrown at him.

"[Father] was somewhat selective in his reading of the New Testament," said Avery later, "but he did read it frequently and he got themes from it which he felt harmonized with his own philosophy of life. He took things from the Sermon on the Mount like 'Seek first the Kingdom of God,' and he interpreted the texts in a pragmatic way, saying that if you are devoted to the moral law you will succeed, your efforts will be crowned with temporal success. . . . He felt it necessary to have a moral vision and faith, and be convinced that what you are doing and saying is objectively right, and not just a matter of expediency."

It was maddening for Allen to be told by Foster that he was selfish in being so concerned about Nazism and the fate of the Jews, which was only a passing phase. What he should be thinking about was the future, of what Avery called "ultimates rather than proximates."

"But can't you see, this is happening *now*," Allen would reply in exasperation. "We must do something."

Avery Dulles said: "In 1938–39, my father and Allen got about as far apart in their assessment of foreign policy as they ever did. My uncle was strongly interventionist, and my father was non-interventionist— I don't think isolationist would be the right term to describe his attitude."

Foster refused to call himself an isolationist too, but once war broke out in Europe in 1939 there was little doubt about where he stood. His indifference toward the British and the French was noticeable in most of the speeches he began making at this time, and there was never any condemnation of the Nazis. "Dynamic" was a word increasingly employed by him to describe the nature of democracy's enemies, and Allen squirmed each time he used it.

"I dislike isolation," Foster declared, in a speech to the YMCA of

Detroit on October 29, 1939, "but I prefer it to identification with a senseless repetition of the cyclical struggle between the dynamic and the static forces of the world. [I see] neither in the underlying causes of the war, nor its long range objectives, any reason for the United States becoming a participant in the war. Were we to act now, it would be to reaffirm an international order which by its very nature is self-destructive and a breeder of violent revolt."

He scoffed at Britain's complaints that the Nazis were aggressors and treaty-breakers, and declared:

"The tragedy is that we seem to have learned nothing. I hear the same talk about 'sanctity of treaties,' 'law and order,' 'resisting aggression,' and 'enforcement of morality.' Such phrases have always been the stock in trade of those who have vested interests which they want to preserve against those in revolt against a rigid system."

Change was coming, he insisted, and, as Henri Bergson had taught him when he studied under the Nobel Prize–winner at the Sorbonne in 1910, "change is the ultimate fact to which we must become accustomed."

A near neighbor of both the Dulles brothers on Long Island was Charles A. Lindbergh (he had a house at Lloyd Neck), who was just beginning his strident campaign on behalf of America First. Allen and Clover were on visiting terms with the flier and his wife until their viewpoints polarized and it was no longer possible to have a comfortable evening together. For some reason, the Lindberghs and the Foster Dulleses were not so closely acquainted, although their opinions of the war and its protagonists were much more closely matched. But Foster generally approved of the America First campaign,* and after a speech Lindbergh made in November 1939, he wrote to him:

> I am very glad you spoke as you did. I do not agree with everything that you said, but I do agree with the result, and I feel that there is grave danger that, under the influence of emotion, we will decide upon a national policy which is quite the reverse of what we had more or less agreed upon when we were thinking clearly.

Foster had definitely decided that this was not America's war, and not his either. Neither politically nor morally did he see any justification for it, nor, in his own case, did he see any advantage accruing to

*Though he always strenuously denied ever contributing to it.

himself from any participation in it. If he did not lend his support to the America First campaign, he certainly made it clear that he would strenuously oppose any attempt by President Roosevelt to involve the United States in the conflict and would throw his weight behind any Republican candidate capable of sabotaging the President's schemes.

He had a readymade one, he believed, in the person of Thomas E. Dewey, the up-and-coming New York attorney, who was being groomed by New York State Republicans as Roosevelt's opponent in the presidential elections of 1940. Dewey was firmly against any involvement in the war, and Dewey was something of a Dulles protégé. He came to Foster as a fount of wisdom on all matters of foreign policy and hearkened well to what he was told.

Foster called in his brother in December 1939 to tell him that Dewey would be nominated, was capable of overthrowing Roosevelt, and was dedicated to destroying the socialistic evils of the New Deal. Would Allen support him in the efforts to procure the Republican ticket for Dewey?

It was a difficult position in which Allen Dulles found himself. It was true that he was a registered Republican, true that he shared the family's dislike for Roosevelt and his administration. On the other hand, he warmly approved all the moves FDR was making to back Britain in the war, and he had let it be known to his Democrat friends that he was bipartisan on foreign policy and with them in every effort they were making to aid Britain, even up to and including intervention.

How could he square this with a promise to campaign for Thomas Dewey, whose election, he was well aware, though it would please Foster, Adolf Hitler, and the America Firsters, might well doom Britain to defeat in the war in Europe?

CHAPTER SIX

Enter Wild Bill

The Republican Convention of 1940 was held in Philadelphia and Foster, Allen, and Eleanor Dulles were all there to see their candidate nominated. Most of the pundits as well as the satraps of the party seemed reasonably confident that Thomas E. Dewey would emerge with the Republican ticket in his pocket. He had a nationwide reputation as the fighting district attorney who had fearlessly done battle with the gangsters of New York. He had edged out Robert A. Taft in the primaries. Though no isolationist, he was firmly in favor of a hands-off policy toward Europe and a stern opponent of the meddling interventionists of the Roosevelt New Deal. If he won the nomination, his supporters anticipated that he would fight a hard-hitting campaign against the incumbent President, and not least at the way Roosevelt was cutting corners around the Constitution in his eagerness to give the Allies all the help they could get in Europe.

There were those among Dewey's backers who did not hesitate to use the word "impeachment" in their condemnation of Roosevelt's tactics; they were confident that there were votes to be won, and the White House gained, from the kind of accurate revelations Dewey could make about the Rooseveltian maneuvers behind America's back.

Allen and Eleanor had their particular personal reasons for feeling gloomy, whether Dewey succeeded or not, but Foster Dulles arrived at the convention supremely confident not only about the outcome but about his own future. Politically, it looked as if things were beginning to come his way at last. It was not simply that he believed Dewey would win the nomination. He was sure, if the right tactics were adopted, Dewey would knock out Roosevelt just as squarely as he had smashed the racketeers of New York. His own political apotheosis would automatically follow.

Foster Dulles had known Thomas Dewey since the early 1930s, and they had become firm friends and mutual admirers in 1937. At that time, before Dewey's rise to fame and the headlines, Foster had grown convinced that he was an attorney of first-class quality and decided that his talents would fill a gap in Sullivan & Cromwell's roster of lawyers. He offered him a partnership in the firm.

It was a moment when Dewey's fortunes were low and his prospects uncertain. He was about to accept when, abruptly, his situation changed. A staunch and active Republican, he was offered the post of district attorney of New York in return for services rendered, and his progression seemed certain from that moment on. But he had not forgotten Foster Dulles's offer and would never cease to be grateful to him. An association began in which Foster became the younger lawyer's mentor, grooming him and advising him on international law and international politics. It was very much as an echo of Foster's views and pronouncements that Dewey had gone forward as a candidate for the nomination, and if the day came next November when he was elected President, it seemed certain that the older man would receive his substantial reward as a member of the new administration.

For Allen Dulles there would be rewards, too, no doubt, though on a lesser scale of importance, but the contemplation of them filled him with no joy whatsoever. In many ways, he was ashamed of himself. In many ways Clover was right when she declared, in an unusual gesture of independence: "I don't care what the rest of the family are going to do. I shall vote for Roosevelt next November. He is doing what I believe is right for the United States!"

Allen would never bring himself to vote the Democratic ticket, but he might have supported a Republican who came closer to his political feelings, who was in favor of a bipartisan policy so far as the war in Europe was concerned. There was one such candidate in the field, a dark horse, true, but one who shared Allen's belief in the evil of Nazism, the justice of Britain's cause, and the necessity for the United States to take risks in supporting her. That character was a comparative newcomer named Wendell Willkie, and for all Foster's contempt of him, Allen would rather have been on his side.

Instead he was backing Dewey, the man who reflected Foster's ideas about the war and was equally determined to avoid any involvement. For Allen it had meant not just a sacrifice of his principles but also the abandonment of some of his friends. A number of them, Democrats and Republicans alike, all members of pro-Allied bodies like the Century Group and William Allen White's Committee to Win the War by Aiding the Allies, were sponsoring a proposal to have the U.S. government lease laid-up U.S. destroyers to the Royal Navy to help the fight against German U-boats in the Atlantic. One of the chief sponsors was a friend and fellow lawyer, Dean Acheson, who had been loaned to the administration as chairman of the Attorney General's Committee on Administrative Procedure from his Washington law firm, Covington, Burling, Rublee, Acheson and Shorb.

Acheson was pushing the President hard to turn the destroyers over to the British, but Roosevelt hesitated, inhibited by a law which insisted that the destroyers must first be certified as nonessential to U.S. national defense, and the Congress satisfied on that point. Acheson had started canvassing his fellow members of the pro-Allied groups for help in persuading the President to turn over the ships, and had promised Roosevelt he would find a legal excuse for circumventing Congress if he would only sign on the dotted line.

To spur him on, he had come up with the idea of writing a letter to *The New York Times* pointing out that the sale (or lease) of the destroyers could legally be fitted into the framework of the prevailing laws on the transfer of weapons to belligerent powers, and spelling out how. He had already secured the support of two other well-known lawyers, C. C. Burlingham and Thomas Thatcher, both leading lights of the New York bar, to sign along with him. He needed a fourth name and approached Allen, who read the text and promised to append his signature.

But when the letter came round to Sullivan & Cromwell and Foster heard about it, he was appalled, even more so when he realized that it was about to appear in *The New York Times.** He sent for his brother and told him that under no circumstances was he to sign the letter. Its appearance with Allen's name attached would be of considerable embarrassment to Dewey, for the knowledge that one of his supporters and brother of his chief adviser on foreign policy was urging the sale

---

*Acheson had approached a Yale classmate, Charles Merz, who was editor of the *Times* editorial page, and received a promise from him that the letter would run.

of destroyers to Britain would seriously undermine his nonintervention stand.

Allen sent the letter back unsigned. Acheson, who had promised Merz there would be four signatures, had to fall back on his law partner, George Rublee, to fill in the gap left by Allen's withdrawal. He never did talk to Allen himself about it afterwards, but he did express his views to family and friends later about how much he felt Allen's lack of courage diminished him. William Bundy, who later became Acheson's son-in-law, said:

"There was this old thing how Allen declined to go along in a letter in 1940 about the destroyers-bases deal that Dean Acheson had worked out with C. C. Burlingham and others. I know that Dean always took a very poor view of Allen not having signed. He was a strong interventionist by then, but I think he had the feeling that Foster and the German clients of the firm had pulled his coat tails. At any rate, Dean felt that Allen in 1940 had not been stout under pressure."

Allen Dulles must have been well aware of how his friends felt about him. In no sense could he have shared his brother's euphoria over the prospect of Dewey's nomination.

Among other members of the family in the Dewey camp was Foster's younger son, Avery. He had just passed his twenty-first birthday and would be eligible to vote when the presidential election came around. Although, as he explained later, Dewey was "never one of my heroes," he had accepted when his father offered him a job at campaign headquarters as a researcher during the primaries. He too was at Philadelphia rooting for Dewey's victory.

It was quite a family party. Janet was there, of course; Foster never went anywhere without her. Allen's wife, Clover, took time out from her three children to look in on the proceedings, mostly, one suspects, to assure herself that things were not going according to Foster's plan —which they weren't.

Eleanor brought her son, David, for a visit to give him the smell of the political arena in which, she hoped, he would one day perform himself. He was five years old.

Eleanor Lansing Dulles in 1940 was a very different woman from the shiny-eyed romantic who, eight years earlier, had defied the family and the conventions of her class to marry the son of an Orthodox Jew.

It had gone so well for them to begin with. David Blondheim's studies and glossaries of the Talmud had been published and welcomed by Hebrew scholars as important contributions to the history and under-standing of Jewish religious writing. Eleanor Lansing Dulles's books on currency, banking, and the politics of lending had gone into the academic libraries, and she was acknowledged as a brilliant if erratic exponent of modern economic thinking. And David and Eleanor Blondheim working in concert together had embarked on a project that promised them years of happy professional collaboration: the completion of a dictionary of the French language, which, once they and the committees working under them got started, they proposed to present to the Académie Française as an American contribution to French philological scholarship.

But then things had begun to go terribly wrong. It was as if the seemingly inexorable march of Nazism in Europe, spreading brutish anti-Semitism in its path, stirred a feeling of guilt in David Blondheim. In abandoning his Orthodox faith, in his marriage outside the Jewish religion, he seemed to feel he had forsaken his people in the hour when all Jews should be ready to stand together and be counted.

Always a moody man, subject to fits of irascibility, he now began to lapse into periods of acute depression, and soon he was obsessed with his guilt, able to think of nothing but the fate of his people and the conviction that he had betrayed them. What finally crushed his spirit was the news from Eleanor which she had believed would lift him up and give him something to live for: in the spring of 1934 she at last revealed that she was pregnant with their child. Instead, it broke him. He could not bear the prospect, it seemed, of being father to a baby in whose body Gentile blood would be mingled with his own, a con-stant living reminder of how he had turned his back on his people. He could not even bear to see it born. And so, in an ironic precurse of the fate of millions of his fellow Jews a decade later, he killed himself by putting his head in a gas oven—in September 1934, shortly before the baby was due.

It was a cruel blow to have dealt the woman who had dearly loved him and had always been ready to make any sacrifice to stay with him. Eleanor Dulles was not the kind of person to contemplate suicide herself—the Dulles family always believed that pain was something you should learn to endure—but there were moments after the birth of her posthumous son (born on October 6, 1934) when she moiled in the depths of despair, and her brothers worried over her condition.

This was one of the times when John Foster Dulles showed himself to be more than just a father figure. He took things in hand and dealt firmly with the consequences of his sister's dolorous situation. First of all, the tragedy must be hushed up, and he took steps to see that that was done. Then he told Eleanor she must rid herself of her married name, on the grounds that every time she wrote it or heard it she would be stabbed with the memory of her dead husband, Blondheim. It was no good as a name for an academic, anyway. She had no objection; she had never used her married name professionally, in any case, except in collaboration with David. So the motions were gone through and the name Blondheim officially wiped out of the Dulles family record.* It was not, of course, so easy to wipe David out of her memory, or to heal the wound his suicide had inflicted on her.

But now he was six years dead the scar only twitched occasionally, when some reminder rubbed against it. It would not be true to say that the tragedy had changed Eleanor Dulles's nature; it had not made her less bold, less ready to accept a challenge, less eager to make her way in the world. But it had certainly made her tougher and more invulnerable. There were now two children in her family (she had adopted a daughter, Ann, as a playmate for David), and she was determined to show that she was more than capable of being their breadwinner. Loans from the family and the sale of some of David's books had tided her over her initial depression, but in 1940 she was fighting fit again and earning her living. Men who worked with her were learning that she asked no quarter of them nor gave any. She showed a certain skepticism toward them, and they sensed that she was probing them for their weaknesses.

"She's a hard lady," a male colleague in the State Department later said of her. She would never be that, and would always remain the most human member of the Dulles family. But she wore armor plating now when she moved in the world of men.

Thomas E. Dewey, in Eleanor Dulles's view, was not really of presidential caliber. Not in 1940, anyway. He simply did not have the

---

*At the same time, her son's name was officially changed to David Dulles. Eleanor told him of her action when he was old enough to understand and said he could change it back to Blondheim any time he wished. He has retained the name of Dulles.

strength, the experience, or the outlook for the job. But if his election meant that her brother Foster joined the administration in Washington, then that would balance things out. So she was for him, and would vote for him. *If* he got the nomination.

It took six ballots to decide, and with each one John Foster Dulles watched his hopes fading. The most powerful wing of the Republican Party was on the side of Thomas E. Dewey, but no amount of backroom bargaining could help him once the trend of the voting began to emerge. For once in a way, the grass roots had taken over the convention from the Big Boys, and the man they were behind was an Indiana lawyer named Wendell Willkie who stood for all the things Foster Dulles loathed. He was a turncoat Democrat who still saw many good qualities in Roosevelt's New Deal. He wrote articles and made speeches in which he talked about "We, the people."* He was unequivocally in favor of supporting the British in their fight against Nazism, and no nonsense about "impartiality" or nonintervention.

As the packed galleries began chanting: "We want Willkie," and the inevitability of Dewey's defeat became apparent, Foster put on the bland face which he assumed for the outside world in time of crisis and got ready to congratulate the winner. He did not promise him support, for their positions were really too far apart; if he voted for Willkie in 1940, it can only have been token loyalty to the Republicans and to register his loathing of Franklin D. Roosevelt.

For Foster it *was* a considerable setback, but not one that he allowed to humiliate him or shatter his hopes. He had no doubt whatsoever that the wrong man had been chosen, and he did not propose to alter his policies or attitudes in any way simply because the Republican Party was now committed to the British side in the war. None of his positions had lost any of their validity, he believed, and Wendell Willkie's openly expressed abhorrence of Adolf Hitler and National Socialism was pure emotionalism, poor statesmanship. It played into the hands of the Democrats.

When Allen Dulles returned to his hotel after the final vote, a hand clapped him on the back as he threaded his way through the crowded

*Though he was, in fact, a well-strapped stock market operator later referred to by the Democrats as "the barefoot boy from Wall Street."

lobby and a voice said: "Let's go into the bar and talk."

The speaker was a Wall Street lawyer and fellow member of the New York Republican delegation named William J. Donovan. To Allen's surprise, he seemed by no means downhearted at the cavalier manner in which the party's Eastern establishment had been outvoted by "middle Americans." With an open grin on his face, he pointed out that Willkie's nomination would considerably simplify America's situation with regard to the war in Europe. Since both candidates shared a common viewpoint and advocated a similar policy, it was now all but certain that the incumbent President would be confirmed in the White House for a third term. The inevitable would follow. He knew the way Franklin D. Roosevelt's mind was working, and he saw the way the world political situation was developing. One way or another, by deliberate intervention, or by some sort of incident too grave to be overlooked, the United States was going to be involved in the war.

"We'll be in it before the end of 1941," he said, confidently, "and when we are, there are certain preparations which should already have been made. That's where you come in."

General William Joseph Donovan was fifty-seven years old in 1940, but looked ten years younger despite his cropped gray hair. A short, pugnacious little man, full of Irish charm, he was known by his nickname of "Wild Bill" Donovan because of his audacious exploits in World War I, when he had risen from private to the rank of colonel in the famous Fighting Irish 69th Division, and won a congressional medal of honor for conspicuous valor and leadership in battle.

Since that time Donovan had added considerable color to his already gaudy reputation. He had made himself a millionaire on Wall Street as a corporation lawyer. He had sallied into politics and fought to be Republican governor of New York against the entrenched Democrat, Herbert Lehman. It was a hard-headed campaign but, Lehman subsequently declared, one of the cleanest he had ever experienced. In 1933, however, the Republicans were in eclipse as the New Deal took over the country, and Lehman won hands down.

But law and politics were not Donovan's only preoccupations. He was also fascinated by war and the threat to the democratic world posed by the rise of fascism in Europe. All through the 1930s he had been traveling the world, getting himself a close-up view of the excesses of the new ideologies. He was in Ethiopia when Mussolini's armies drove south from Eritrea in 1936 and expelled Emperor Haile Selassie from his mountain kingdom. He managed to get to the front line in Spain (on the Franco side) during the Civil War of 1936–37 and saw Hitler's Nazi infiltrators, the crack Condor Legion, fighting with the Spanish right-wing forces to overthrow the legally established Spanish government.

By the time World War II had begun in Europe, Donovan was one of the few Americans to sense that here was the beginning of a global conflict, and that the United States would be in danger if it failed to realize that the nature of this one would be very different from any other war mankind had known.

Donovan, though a Republican, had always had close relations with Franklin D. Roosevelt. They shared a mutual friend in John Lord O'Brien, a powerful figure in upstate New York and a welcome visitor to the White House from the days of Woodrow Wilson. He was on close terms with and a trusted adviser to Roosevelt. It was he who had brought Donovan into his Buffalo law firm, and it was he who had recommended him to the President. Since before World War II began, Donovan and Roosevelt had discussed what it would mean for America once the war started, and had begun drawing up plans.

Until the Republican Convention, Donovan had refrained from too public a declaration of his pro-Allied standpoint; but now he told Allen he would soon be coming out into the open. He also revealed to him that he had just returned from Europe, where he had been on a secret mission for the President. He had been in Britain to talk to Winston Churchill and examine the situation in the wake of the fall of France and the evacuation of the British armies from Dunkirk, and he had brought the answers to a series of specific questions the President had given him. Would England continue to fight on alone against Hitler, as Churchill had promised? And did the British have the means to do so? If they did go on fighting, what aid could America give to help them most effectively?

Donovan had come back buoyed up by his talks with the British leaders in London. Britain would fight on, no matter how thin her chances of beating the Germans. He had proposed a series of measures to the President whereby America could make these chances much less slim, and they had been accepted.* In the meantime he was making preparations of his own for the emergency he was certain the United States would soon be facing.

"While in Britain he also made a study of the organization and techniques of British intelligence," Allen wrote later. "He was convinced that America's military planning and its whole national strategy would depend on intelligence as never before and that the American intelligence setup should be completely revamped."

It was this project that was uppermost in Donovan's mind, and with the tacit support of the President he was already drawing up plans for an intelligence setup that would meet the needs of the times. But he needed men to help him who knew what intelligence was all about and how it worked, and who could adapt themselves to the methods that the Nazis were now using in their campaign to conquer the world. He was an old friend of the Dulles family (his own family came from Buffalo) and had been on visiting terms since boyhood. He was well aware of Allen's World War I record as an espionage agent in Switzerland and Vienna.

Now he wanted to know whether Allen would join him—when the time came—in the new kind of intelligence war that was looming.

"When do you want me to start?" Allen asked.

"As soon as the election's over," Donovan said. "I'll call you."

It took longer than that.

The election came out just as Donovan had forecast. Wendell Willkie took only eight states, and Franklin D. Roosevelt was back in the White House for an unprecedented third term.

On December 1, 1940, the President called Donovan down to Washington and gave him a second mission, this time to make a strategic appreciation of the economic, political, and military prospects in the Mediterranean area. Donovan was away for three and a half months. He traveled from Gibraltar to Cairo and the Levant, from North Africa to Italy, Greece, and Vichy France, sizing up Great Britain's situation and calculating her chances of holding on to her Middle Eastern bastions.

He returned more than ever confident of the British capacity to

*They were later incorporated in the Lend-Lease Act.

survive, and once he had turned in his report he took to both the media
and the stump to make sure the American public realized the truth of
the war situation.

"Our orientation has been wrong," he declared in a speech in Philadelphia. "We have been talking of aid to Britain as if Britain were a
beggar at the gate, whereas, in point of fact, Britain has been our shield
behind which we can pull up our socks, tie our shoelaces and get
ready."

He also pointed out that the British were, to some extent, America's
laboratory where new experiments in warfare were being tried out, and
he had come back brimming with new ideas about running an intelligence service, and about the use of psychological, political, and guerilla warfare and sabotage.

"Donovan saw all these instruments as part of an integrated whole,"
Allen Dulles wrote later,

> and he presented [to the President] a plan for an organization which
> would create and direct them. His report included a special section on
> what he had found out about British commandos during his Mediterra-
> nean trip. He pointed out that the Imperial General Staff had made its
> first task after Dunkirk the creation of a special force of British guerillas
> and, against this background, urged the President to apply like princi-
> ples to the American position. It would take at least two years, he es-
> timated, to raise, train and equip armies that would be necessary to
> defeat the Germans in a straight fight. Meanwhile, America must prepare
> to employ the techniques of unconventional warfare.

But for Roosevelt this was going too far too fast. America was not
even in the war yet, and opposition to any preparations for such an
eventuality had, if anything, grown stronger in the United States. Allen
Dulles noted that his brother Foster spent less and less time in the
office at Sullivan & Cromwell now and more and more on speechmak-
ing, in which he warned the public against the "warmongers" Churchill and Roosevelt. Audiences were giving him an attentive hearing. In
the Middle West the America First campaign was attracting hundreds
of new members, all pledged to keep the United States out of the war.

It was no moment for putting Donovan in charge of what would be
dubbed a private army. Instead, on July 11, 1941, the President created
what was called the Office of Coordinator of Information (COI) with

111

Donovan as its chief. The duties of the Coordinator were "to collect and analyze all information and data which bear on national security; to correlate such information and data and to make it available to the President, and to such departments and officials of the Government as the President may determine."

Donovan took some comfort from the fact that the terms of his appointment allowed the COI to engage in "such supplementary activities as may facilitate the securing of information, important for national security," and he resolved to interpret this authority in the broadest possible terms. But from the start the organization was circumscribed by opposition from the State Department (where it had reluctantly been given an office in Washington), from the armed forces (which had their own, highly inefficient intelligence formations), and most vehemently from the FBI. J. Edgar Hoover saw in Donovan a dangerous rival, and his attitude toward the COI and its offspring, the OSS, was so ruthlessly antagonistic that Donovan ruefully remarked on one occasion: "The Abwehr gets better treatment from the FBI than we do."

Certainly Hoover persecuted the COI with much more zeal, infiltrating agents into the organization and doing his damndest to sabotage its activities. The most notorious case was when COI operators, through an anti-Franco attaché, gained access to the code room of the Spanish Embassy in Washington. Several visits were made by a team of safebreakers and code experts. But the FBI found out about it and sent agents in cars to surround the embassy and set off their sirens. Donovan's men had to retreat, their work half-finished.

Complaints were made to the White House, and Hoover promised not to do it again. But in return he exacted a pledge that the COI would never, in future, engage in any clandestine activities on United States territory.* It was and would remain the FBI's exclusive turf so far as intelligence and security were concerned.

The COI was far from being the all-inclusive covert organization that Donovan had visualized. So long as America remained uninvolved in the war, it lacked drive and purpose and many of the recruits who had come in at the Coordinator's request found themselves only too often doing nothing amid a frenzy of purposeless chaos. They included

*He demanded, and got, a similar pledge with regard to South America, but this was subsequently ignored by OSS operatives.

several dozen lawyers of Donovan's professional acquaintance and some highly prominent and extremely rich presidents and chairmen of prominent companies, so many of them, in fact, that someone slyly remarked that "Donovan is staffing the COI with future clients to keep them out of the draft."

Those who were not trying to sabotage his efforts were skeptical of his chances of building up a worthwhile organization.

"There's plenty of noise on the landing, but when are they coming downstairs?" asked one British agent, impatient to get to work and collaborate with the Americans. Fortunately, Donovan remained supremely confident that the COI had a splendid future. As one of his staff remarked: "Whenever he looked at an acorn he saw an oak tree growing."

Allen Dulles was more cautious. He had to be. He simply could not afford to answer Donovan's call so long as the United States stayed neutral. He needed the money he was earning at Sullivan & Cromwell, and he was anxious to avoid a family quarrel with Foster, who persisted in believing that America should not and would not intervene in the war. Foster had made it clear to his staff that he would not encourage them to leave for so-called patriotic purposes until U.S. interests were vitally engaged, and though he too was a friend of Donovan's, he had several times expressed the opinion that Wild Bill was an appropriate description; he was running a "crackpot" organization that was already doing great harm by creating "war hysteria" in the country through its propaganda arm.* When Donovan suggested that Allen should meet and talk with the President, he turned him down for fear of offending Foster. But at Donovan's behest, Allen maintained a quiet connection with members of British intelligence units operating more or less openly in New York, and he kept his ears open when foreign clients came to Sullivan & Cromwell, or when he went to Washington diplomatic parties.

It was not until after Pearl Harbor and America's official entry into the war that Allen "came aboard" as a member of the staff of COI. Then, in 1942, he was made head of the New York office in Room 3663

---

*The COI at this time also had control of a propaganda department under Robert Sherwood, though this was later detached and turned into the Office of War Information (OWI).

of the International Building at Rockefeller Center, and soon built up a staff of experts on German and European affairs which included such fellow lawyers as Arthur Goldberg, as well as a number of German émigrés and refugees from the Nazis. He also maintained a close liaison with the British Security Commission (BSC), a British intelligence outfit that operated out of the same building and was headed by a clever, hard-eyed Canadian named William Stephenson. "He had much to teach me," Allen said later, "and I picked his brains."

The German émigrés who now swarmed into the Rockefeller Center came from all parts of the political spectrum. There were the rightwingers like Baron Wolfgang zu Pulitz, a former Nazi diplomat, and Gottfried Treviranus, a bemonocled Prussian; men of the center like ex-Chancellor Heinrich Bruening; and leftwingers such as Dr. Karl Frank. It was the leftwingers who attracted the unfavorable attention of the FBI, and Edgar Hoover was soon complaining to the President that Allen Dulles was hiring "a bunch of Bolsheviks." The resultant fuss was such that he had to disband the committee of émigrés which he had formed to advise and inform him.

This did not mollify Hoover, who seemed to believe, for some time afterwards, that Allen had secret Communist leanings, and marked down the whole of the Dulles family as "internationalists" (whatever that was supposed to mean) with too many foreign, particularly German, connections.

Donovan's plan for Allen's future was that he would eventually accompany David Bruce to London, where they would open an office that would work closely with British intelligence. But Allen had other ideas. He had no intention of working with Bruce, amiable and expert though he might be, nor of being subordinate to anyone once he was out of America. London, he believed, was the last place for a good intelligence man to get stuck, with half the generals in the army looking over your shoulder.

He was confident that the most effective center from which an active agent should operate was in a neutral country. It should be a country on the enemy's doorstep, with good communications across the frontier. It had to be far enough away from Washington to allow its station chief freedom to use his own initiative. And it should be one that he knew like the back of his hand.

For Allen Dulles, that meant Switzerland. Nazi Germany was its nearest neighbor, and traffic between the two countries was dense. He made it plain to Donovan that, when posting time came, that was where he wished to go.

Switzerland. It would be just like old times—only more so.

CHAPTER SEVEN

"Pontificating American!"

Ironically enough, it was John Foster Dulles who got to wartime Europe first, several months ahead of Allen. He flew to London in July 1942 with a number of Republican senators, his avowed intention being to find out what plans the British were making for a just and lasting peace once the war was over. He received a dusty answer, and it did nothing to improve his opinion of America's Ally.

For Foster, now that the United States was in the war, had pretty well decided to ignore the sweat, blood, and pain that would be involved in winning it. He had no doubt whatsoever that it would be won, thanks to American power. But the means were no concern of his. All he hoped for, as he said in his speeches and writings, was that the nation, while fighting, would build up the religious faith which alone could make victory possible, "a faith so profound that we too will feel that we have a mission to spread it throughout the world."

He felt that the American people were "cynical and disillusioned," and believed that only a profound spiritual awakening and a concentration on the future of mankind *after* the war was over would provide them with a target to aim for while the fighting was going on. He had become chairman of an organization called Commission for a Just and Durable Peace, and despite the fact that its membership included some distinguished thinkers and theologians (among them Reinhold Niebuhr) he dominated its proceedings and ran it practically as a one-man show. Foster made it clear that he had dedicated himself to seeing that World War II did not end as World War I had done, with greed and vengeance as the motivations of the victors. The postwar nations should meet, he declared, with their minds concentrated on the thoughts that Christ expressed: "humility, repentance, avoidance of personal hatreds and hypocrisies, recognition of the personal supremacy of God rather than the state."

President Roosevelt and the British prime minister, Winston Churchill, had met at sea on September 18, 1941, and from their talks had emerged a statement of their views of the world called the Atlantic Charter. For Foster and his colleagues, it was a far from satisfactory document, too securely cemented in big power concepts. Foster Dulles had not forgotten that it was his idol, President Wilson, who had conceived the idea of the League of Nations, only to have its efficacy destroyed by America's refusal to join it. Now he preached the need for a replacement organization, this one with the United States as an enthusiastic member but with small nations given an equal say with the big powers in the management of its affairs and the world.

How did the British feel about such a body? What plans were they making to readjust the world once the war was over? It was to discover the answers to those questions that he flew to London in July 1942. He fully expected to have a long talk with Prime Minister Churchill about them.

Foster may not have known it, but it so happened that Churchill had proposed during his talks with Roosevelt that a reference should be made in the Atlantic Charter to the creation of an international body to control the postwar world, which in turn had been rebuffed by the President.

But that was in 1941, before America was in the war, and the British premier, anxious to stress the purity of Britain's reasons for fighting, was appealing to American idealism. By July 1942, the United States was his Ally, and he had other things on his mind. If the mood in the United States in that first half-year of war was down in the dumps, people in Britain were close to despair, because everything was going wrong.

The British had just come through the nightly attacks on their cities by Nazi bombers which was now known as the Blitz. It had been a painful ordeal, costly in lives and matériel, though it had also not been without its moments of high drama, terrifying and exhilarating at the same time.

Now the bombing was temporarily over, while Hitler turned his army and air forces against Russia. And somehow the British found the lull harder to bear than the bombs, for they had nothing to think about but the parlousness of their position. German U-boats were winning the Battle of the Atlantic, and the food and supplies the United States were sending over only too often went down to feed the fishes. The rations on which Britons were living (and few were the people who got more) were extremely meager, barely enough to keep a body together. Nobody had seen an orange or a banana for months, and wouldn't do so until after the war. The people were ragged because shoes and clothing were on "points," and a whole book for a year would only buy one suit.

It was a dull, frustrating, depressing life, with not even an air raid warning to enliven it; what made it worse was that the war news from abroad was uniformly bad. The British bastion in the Western Desert, Tobruk, fell in June 1942; Egypt, the Suez Canal, and the lifeline to India were threatened by Rommel's advancing armies in North Africa. Sebastopol, the great Russian port in the Crimea, fell to the Nazis on July 2, 1942, after a siege lasting two hundred and fifty days. The U.S. Navy was doing badly against the Japanese in the Pacific.

Morale was so bad and moroseness so widespread that even Churchill's prestige—and maybe his leadership—was threatened. On June 24, a Tory MP, Sir John Wardlaw-Milne, proposed a motion of censure against his own government for its conduct of the war, and made it clear that the target of his criticism was Churchill. It was debated on July 1, 1942, amid a great deal of acrimony, and though Churchill easily won a vote of confidence he did so only because Wardlaw-Milne presented a poorly argued case against him.

The extracts from the debates did nothing to lift British spirits. Nor did the sight of U.S. soldiers around Britain make people feel happier, since these were early days, the Americans were still training, and seemed to have lots of leave. It was not exactly anti-Americanism that was in the air, but a vague feeling of resentment. A London woman, in a report she made to an opinion-gathering organization (Mass Observation), wrote that summer:

> John, by no means pro-American in the ordinary way, is the only person I've come across yet with anything but curses for the Americans over here. It is really extraordinary what a passion of dislike everyone seems to feel for them. I suppose their pay, so enormously higher than

that of our own fighting men, is at the bottom of it: that and the amount of time off they get and their double rations-plus, and in general the vast superiority of their clothing and feeding allowances and their accommodation. . . . Even with John it's not a matter of any liking, but merely the conscientious refusal to give way to dislike because he feels that to do so is playing Hitler's game. As it is, of course—but how can one help resenting the full-fed, candy-pampered, gum-chewing swagger of our "invaders"?

It was into a London where rancor, misery, hunger, and hopelessness hung around the people like a miasma that John Foster Dulles arrived in June 1942. He was not pleased by the quality of his reception, and insensitive to the prevailing mood. He had understood that the Archbishop of Canterbury and a number of leading Anglican clergymen would give him time, but it turned out that, like Churchill, they were too heavily occupied with the war and general morale.

Foster was at first irritated and then indignant at the complete lack of interest that the British government showed not only in his own presence, but in postwar planning. He could not discover whether the British had any plans or not. He could not find anyone of political importance who was willing to listen to his own.*

In the end, much to his annoyance, he was forced to solicit the aid of the U.S. ambassador, John G. Winant, in getting him appointments with political figures. Churchill was too deeply involved in his own personal political crisis to spare him time, but his deputy prime minister, Clement Attlee, and the Minister of Labor, the tough and pugnacious Ernest Bevin, agreed to see him. Attlee and Bevin were both Socialists** who might have been expected to welcome a discussion on the shaping of the postwar world. But Foster seems to have found them hardly worth his time, wrapped up as they were in the day-to-day problems of running the war. In any case, their ideas and his were unlikely to coincide.

He was mollified somewhat when the dashing *jeune premier* of the Churchill cabinet, Foreign Minister Anthony Eden, asked him to a luncheon at his apartment in the Foreign Office and switched on his famous charm for the benefit of the American visitor, at the same time

*Though he did meet and talk with both Arnold Toynbee and Barbara Ward.

**Elections had been banned for the duration of the war, and Churchill's government was a coalition of the three main parties, Tories, Socialists, and Liberals.

allowing Foster to expatiate at length on his ideas for world government and European federation. In the report which he later wrote for the Federal Council of Churches, Foster remarked that Eden had done little but lend him an ear.

"What else could I do?" Eden said later. "His proposals were not exactly concrete, and we had other things on our mind—survival, for example. But it would have been impolite not to listen."

Eden found John Foster Dulles harmless—at that time, anyway. One of the senior Foreign Office officials who was also present, Sir Alexander Cadogan, was much more restive and wrote in his diary that night (July 13, 1942):

"J.F.D. the woolliest type of useless pontificating American . . . Heaven help us!"

Foster flew back to the United States at the end of July 1942, and reported that the British did not seem to be interested in postwar planning, but were too absorbed in their own interests and "exaggerated nationalism." He produced his report for the Federal Council of Churches, then threw himself into a project which had been occupying his time ever since the publication of the Atlantic Charter: his own blueprint for the reshaping of the world once the war was over. His idea was to turn the Charter into a "beneficent reality" by stripping away the big power conceptions on which it was based and replacing them with a more egalitarian sharing of world government. The plan went through many stages and was eventually published as a manifesto called *Six Pillars of Peace.* As such it was backed by the Federal Council of Churches, which organized an intensive campaign to promote public interest in it.

The campaign included lobbying in Congress, and this was so successful that four senators, spurred on by Dulles and his committee, introduced a motion into the Senate* calling for U.S. endorsement of a postwar peace organization.

It was the work of a man genuinely concerned to see that the mistakes of the victors after World War I were not repeated, and that this time the United States would play its part in the remaking of the war-torn world. All the same, John Foster Dulles was by no means

*It was known as the B2H2 Resolution, after its sponsors, Senators Ball, Burton, Hatch, and Hill.

disinterested in the political dividends attached to his humanitarian activities, and he did not fail to keep his friend and protégé, Thomas E. Dewey, closely informed of what he was about.

It was not until June 13, 1942, that President Roosevelt finally signed the order which turned the COI into the OSS and put William J. Donovan's organization ostensibly under the jurisdiction of the Joint Chiefs of Staff, but in reality under the control of no one but himself.

As it was newly constituted, the Office of Strategic Services had all the powers Donovan insisted it needed to become the new-style intelligence operation which the wartime situation demanded. Not only was it authorized to collect and analyze intelligence; it was also empowered "to plan and operate such special services as may be directed by the United States Joint Chiefs of Staff."

Allen Dulles wrote later:

> With this Donovan's blueprint for the coordination of strategic intelligence collection with secret operations was realized. "Special services" in intelligence terms meant unconventional warfare, commandos, support of partisans and guerillas and the exploitation by covert means of all the weaknesses of Mussolini's and Hitler's empires. . . . An intelligence organization had been created for the first time in the United States which brought together under one roof the work of intelligence collection and counterespionage, with the support of underground resistance activities, sabotage and almost anything else in aid of our national effort that the regular armed forces were not equipped to do.

The stroke of the President's pen did not unleash the OSS into any immediately spectacular operations, and for a time it seemed that all the official blessing had done was to increase business at OSS recruiting sessions and chaos in its administration. Among the early applicants for a job with the agency was Charles A. Lindbergh, his isolationist stance abandoned now that the United States was at war. Donovan saw him on January 4, 1942, and must have been aware that President Roosevelt, still resentful of Lindbergh's antiwar campaign, had banned him from any official role in the armed forces or its ancillaries.* But,

*Though, of course, Roosevelt's antipathy to Lindbergh dated back long before this —to the early days of the New Deal, when Lindbergh had challenged and beaten him on air mail contracts.

as Lindbergh later remarked, "Donovan was very pleasant" and "said he would be glad to have me provided it would be satisfactory to the President."

There was, of course, no chance of that. Lindbergh comforted himself over Donovan's polite rebuff by remarking that "He did not leave me with a feeling of enthusiasm for joining his operation," and added: "I hear it is full of politics, ballyhoo, and controversy."

If by controversy he meant hostility, he was certainly right. Though OSS was now a part of the U.S. war machine, it was still regarded with hot suspicion and resentment by the older government agencies in Washington, whose attitude toward it ranged from antipathy to sabotage.

The State Department was particularly obstructive. Word had reached Mrs. Ruth Shipley, the formidable lady who ran the U.S. Passport Office—without whose personal benison supposedly free Americans could not leave their native shores—that the OSS was a rival to the Foreign Service and was "not to be helped." So when operatives assigned to sensitive countries overseas collected their passports, they found that they had been stamped "OSS." Mrs. Shipley was going to make it clear to all and sundry, including the enemy, that American spies were abroad.

Donovan complained to the President and an order was sent down curbing the Passport Office's bile. So State changed its tactics. One day Jimmy Murphy, Donovan's secretary, telephoned Bickham Sweet-Escott, the British intelligence service's liaison officer in Washington, to say that at long last OSS was getting one of their men into Vichy France, something they had been trying to do for months.

"This could be done only if their representative were to be given the cover of vice-consul," wrote Sweet-Escott later.

> That morning the State Department had told them that they had at last obtained the consent of the Vichy Government to the arrangement. The man whom the OSS wished to send was a certain Nicol Smith. He was to leave for Vichy via Lisbon in a day or two. Colonel Donovan was anxious that we should make every use of him that we could without compromising his cover.

The British were delighted. It would solve a lot of their problems (getting money to their agents in France, for example) if they could use

Nicol Smith's services. Sweet-Escott cabled London to have an intelligence chief meet Nicol Smith in Lisbon and fill him in on British requirements.

"The next day Jimmy Murphy telephoned me to say they had some serious news for me, and would I come over," Sweet-Escott wrote.

> He was exceedingly sorry to say that they had found out the night before that, in asking the Vichy embassy in Washington for permission to send Nicol Smith to Vichy as vice-consul, the State Department had carefully explained that he would not, of course, be a real vice-consul at all. In fact they had as good as told the Vichy embassy that Nicol Smith would use his appointment as a cover for something else. Obviously it would be highly dangerous for any of our people to approach him, and I had better undo anything I had done.

Admiral William Leahy, the U.S. ambassador in Vichy, was only one of America's envoys who strenuously objected to having OSS men on their staff.

"General Donovan accused me of interfering with his work," Leahy said later. "I told him that the diplomatic service was *my* business."

J. Edgar Hoover and the FBI also remained intensely suspicious of Donovan's organization, despite the agreement by the OSS to cease any intelligence activities on U.S. soil, and a close watch was kept on the Agency's operatives and their relatives to see that they did not step out of line.

One day in the summer of 1942, Bill Donovan called Allen Dulles down to Washington and asked him whether he knew that his sister, Eleanor, was being "gumshoed" by agents of the FBI.

It seemed (Donovan said) that Eleanor Dulles was having regular meetings, three times each week, at obscure Washington bars and suburban restaurants with a certain Polish teacher named Michael "X." He had discovered that during recent weeks both she and the man she was meeting were under the close surveillance of the FBI.

Donovan asked Allen whether he knew the Pole in question, and showed him a photograph of the man sitting with Eleanor in a restaurant. Allen glanced at it with some distaste, shook his head, and said he had never seen the man in his life.

"Will you ask her about him?" asked Donovan.

"Not on your life," replied Allen. "If Eleanor wanted me to know

123

about him, she'd tell me. But I can say this—if Eleanor's meeting him regularly, he's all right."

Donovan made a noncommittal sound and dropped the subject, but a few weeks later, after a Joint Chiefs of Staff meeting in Washington, he and Allen went off to lunch together, and as they sat over coffee, Donovan said:

"Remember the Pole we talked about? The one your sister's been seeing?" A pause. "Strange you've never met him. They've been having those meetings for five years now—three times a week, every Tuesday, Saturday, and Sunday."

Allen said, shortly: "I told you before, what Eleanor does is her own affair. She's a grown-up person. She can be trusted."

Donovan grinned. "Hoover and the FBI don't think so. Knowing your sister has just cost her Polish friend a job. With the FBI, what's more."

He went on to explain that Michael "X" was a fluent Russian speaker and expert on Polish and Soviet affairs, and knowing that the FBI were short of specialists in their Russian sector he had applied for a job. He had come through all the written and oral tests that the Bureau gave him with flying colors. But then the check on his background had begun, and almost at once the FBI's invigilators had turned up some piquant information.

Michael "X" had gone on a trip to Europe just before the outbreak of World War II and had got stuck there when hostilities began. He found it difficult to secure a reentry permit into the United States, and had finally sent a cable to Eleanor Dulles appealing for her help. She had guaranteed him with the State Department and he had been allowed to return.

With this information in their possession, the FBI began to tail both Michael "X" and Eleanor Dulles, and in this way discovered their regular trysts. Hoover being Hoover ("a moralistic bastard," Donovan called him), he had turned down the Pole for the job.

When Allen asked him how he knew all this, Donovan grinned and said: "When the FBI infiltrated us and pulled that stunt at the Spanish Embassy, I thought that's a game two can play. I've had our men inside the Bureau for months."

He added that being turned down by the FBI was practically a recommendation in his eyes. Moreover, he agreed with Allen—if Eleanor was so stuck on the man, he must be all right. So he had called him into OSS headquarters, ran some tests on him, and hired him.

"We need Russian analysts more than Hoover does," he said. "The FBI don't know what they've missed."

Michael "X" stayed in the Agency until the end of World War II. He and Eleanor Dulles continued their thrice-weekly rendezvous for another fourteen years, and during the whole of that time she mentioned not a word about him to her brothers or her family.

Allen Dulles never did tell her that he knew all about it. Nor mention it to his brother, Foster.

It would have been hypocritical of Allen to chide his sister on her clandestine meetings, for he indulged in quite a few of his own, not all of them on behalf of the OSS.

"There were at least a hundred women in love with Allen at one time or another," Eleanor said later, "and some of them didn't even get to close quarters with him."

But many of them did, and he was never a man to fight off an attractive woman. The march of time had by no means diminished his charm or the magnetism of his personality. His conversation was witty, urbane, never wounding, and he had a smile that warmed the heart. There was something about him that made men like him and, at social gatherings, drew every woman in his direction. He found it difficult to resist the evident pleasure they took in his company, and over the years he had indulged in everything from mild flirtations to serious affairs with a multifarious gallery of women. His appeal was wide-ranging; empty-headed blondes as well as serious career women seemed to be equally vulnerable to it.

"Were you Allen Dulles's mistress?" an American writer once asked the English author, Rebecca West.

"Alas, no," she replied, "but I wish I had been."

Clover had long since grown accustomed to the hints from kind friends of Allen's latest transgressions, and was well aware that most of them regarded her as far too longsuffering in not doing something drastic about it. She had long since abandoned the ploy of going to Cartier every time he tricked her. It had only been a gesture, anyway, for she wasn't the kind of woman who salved her misery by making her husband pay; and the acrid quarrels which broke out when she up-

125

braided him for his unfaithfulness both frightened and exhausted her, sometimes made her feel suicidal. She had taken to consulting psychiatrists in an effort to assuage her pain, and had been urged to seek comfort by finding the rationale for Allen's behavior: the tensions of his job in the clandestine world of espionage, tensions which manifested themselves increasingly in attacks of painful gout in his reshaped left foot. He was simply seeking masculine reassurance, she was told.

She accepted that, but did not find that it made it easier to bear, or her own loneliness less acute. Often she would disappear for days, or wander around the house in such evident distress that her young family would become agonizingly aware of it.

Of the two girls and a boy in the Allen Dulles family now, none was more sensitively aware of the strain on his mother's nerves, and the tension in her relations with his father, than her schoolboy son, Allen Macy. He was an introspective child, and he missed nothing of what was going on in the household. He brooded over it.

Relations between Allen and Clover Dulles had reached one of the critical stages in 1942, and it was just as well that he was on the point of departure. Clover had no illusions over what would happen when he reached Switzerland. She knew that he would find someone there who would assuage any loneliness he might feel, but at least there wouldn't be friends around to tell her about it, and it wouldn't be happening on her own doorstep. She told her close confidantes that she loved him as deeply as she had always done, and that, despite everything, she realized that he still loved her too ("He just can't help it, I know," she said). But it was better for him to get away. Her nerves couldn't stand it any more.

Allen Dulles left for Switzerland on November 2, 1942, and was lucky to make it. He only just avoided landing in the hands of the Gestapo instead.

He was well aware that Operation Torch, the Allied invasion of the Vichy-controlled territories in North Africa, was due to begin in the first week or ten days of November, and that it was vital for him to reach Switzerland before it happened. The only route to Switzerland for an American at that stage of the war was by flying to Lisbon, and then traveling overland through Portugal, Spain, and Vichy France to Geneva.

"We estimated in Washington that as soon as the landings in Africa took place the Nazis would move immediately to occupy all of Vichy France," he wrote later. "The military necessity for them to control the French ports on the Mediterranean would be urgent. Toulon could not be left to the French Navy."

Unfortunately, his departure had been several times delayed, not least by the deliberate procrastination of the State Department, which objected to having a spy posing as a diplomat attached to the U.S. Legation in Berne. They persisted in arguing about his position and status, until it was finally agreed that he should be given the anomolous-sounding title of Assistant to the Minister. It took time, and Mrs. Shipley did not hurry either.

As the Catalina flying boat bumped its way over a stormy Atlantic Ocean, Allen was uneasily aware that he had not many hours in which to get under the wire before the Germans closed in on Unoccupied France. Those hours ticked away to no good purpose whatsoever in the Azores, where the plane was held up by the weather. By the time he landed in Lisbon he knew that the Anglo-American convoys must already be on their way to North Africa, and as he descended from the train at Port Bou, the last Spanish station on the frontier with France, the ships were sailing into the Mediterranean.

He had picked up some old Swiss acquaintances on the train journey across Spain, and was lunching with them in a Port Bou bistro when the Swiss diplomatic courier joined them. He brought news that the Allied invasion had begun. A German occupation of Vichy France* could be expected to begin at any moment.

A more prudent character would have paused before going on. It was true that he was traveling with a diplomatic passport, but the Nazis were not likely to find that an obstruction to his arrest. They knew who he was. He carried compromising papers, and they would soon realize that he had valuable information to impart to them, not least about the anti-Nazi operations he had masterminded in New York. It was not a pleasant prospect.

On the other hand, Allen Dulles was superstitious about trains, and firmly believed that nothing disastrous could happen to him when he was on a rail journey. Once, in 1920, while taking a State Department

*The Nazis already controlled Paris and the northern half of the country.

diplomatic bag to Berlin, he had stepped off the train at Cologne while it made its usual ten-minute halt, and took a stroll along the platform, leaving his baggage and the diplomatic pouch locked in his compartment. He had turned from buying a newspaper to see the train on its way out of the station, taking with it not only his luggage but his career in the State Department. Five minutes later the train was back; it had merely gone into a siding to take on extra carriages. After that, he decided that trains were lucky for him.

So, early next morning he crossed the frontier into France and boarded the train for Switzerland. While it waited in the station, a crowd of Frenchmen gathered around his carriage and began to cheer him, shouting: "Vive les États Unis!" They had heard the news of the North African landings and seemed to believe that they would be imminently followed by an Allied landing in France herself, and that Allen Dulles was an American emissary come to arrange their arrival. He did nothing to disabuse them, and was glad when the train at length took off on its journey.

He had decided that if he saw any evidence of Nazi controls at the towns through which he passed, he would slip off the train and disappear into the countryside, hoping to contact the French Resistance and be passed by them into Switzerland. But it was not until Annemasse, the last station in France before the Swiss frontier, that he ran into any difficulty. All passengers had to disembark there for a passport examination before being allowed to proceed.

"I found that a person in civilian dress, obviously a German, was supervising the work of the French border officials," he wrote later.

> I had been told in Washington that there would probably be a Gestapo agent at this frontier. I was the only one among the passengers who failed to pass muster.* The Gestapo man carefully put down in his notebook the particulars of my passport, and a few minutes later a French gendarme explained to me that an order had just been received from Vichy to detain all Americans and British presenting themselves at the frontier and to report all such cases to Marshal Pétain directly.

Allen summoned up his best French** and made an impassioned plea to the gendarme to be allowed through, invoking the shades of

*But see pp. 129–30.
**He spoke excellent French and German, though with a strong American accent.

Lafayette and Pershing, and the undying nature of Franco-American amity. To no avail. He was left to pace the platform, miserably aware that he was being watched, and that it would be next to impossible to slip away.

"Finally, around noon," he went on,

> when it was about time for the train to leave for Geneva, the gendarme came up to me, hurriedly motioned for me to get on the train and whispered to me, "Allez passez. Vous voyez que notre collaboration n'est que symbolique." (Go ahead. You see our cooperation with the Nazis is only symbolic.) The Gestapo man was nowhere to be seen. Later I learned that every day, promptly at noon, he went down the street to the nearest pub and had his drink of beer and his lunch. . . . The French authorities had gone through the motions of phoning Vichy, as they had been ordered to do. But once the Gestapo man had left his post for his noon siesta, they were free to act on their own.

Fifteen minutes later he was over the frontier and safe on the soil of neutral Switzerland. The next day the German army took over Annemasse station and the frontier post beyond.

"I had crossed the French border into Switzerland legally," Allen Dulles wrote. "I was one of the last Americans to do so until the liberation of France."

He reported to the U.S. Legation in Berne and then began taking up his contacts, old and new. The war had entered a tricky political phase, and there was much to do.

Allen Dulles felt like a hunting dog let loose in the woods again, after too long under leash in the kennels.

By one of those curious coincidences that were to figure often in their association, a fellow American well known to Allen Dulles had also been aboard the train which had brought him to Annemasse. But the other man took care that Dulles did not see him. At that moment it could have caused him too many complications.

The second American was Noel Field, whom Allen had met as a twelve-year-old boy in Zurich with his father, Dr. Herbert Field, in 1918. Their paths had crossed many times since, in the State Department in Washington, at the League of Nations in Geneva, at disarmament conferences in Paris.

Noel Field was traveling with his wife, and they too were desperately anxious to make it to Switzerland before the frontier gates clanged shut. They had come up from Marseilles and had kept one step ahead of the Gestapo all the way. They had quite a bit to hide and no diplomatic passports to protect them if they were caught. So at Annemasse they had not waited for their passport checks but mingled with the local French travelers and hurried with them into the town. There they stayed until nightfall in a small inn.

Noel Field knew this part of France like the stubble on his chin. He had walked over most of the border country with his father when he was a schoolboy. In the past year he had passed this way often, in his role as a courier traveling between Marseilles and Geneva; and he was well known to local officials.

After darkness had fallen, Field and his wife, Herta, climbed into a car and set off for the frontier. They later reported that they were followed for part of the way by another car, which flashed its lights at them and repeatedly tried to pass on the sinuous mountain road. Was it the Gestapo? They did not stop at the French frontier post at Collonges to find out, but raced on through to the Swiss station 50 meters further on. Once the officials had checked them through, they drove quietly through the placid Swiss countryside into Geneva.

It was not until two months later that Noel Field picked up the telephone and called Allen Dulles in Berne, to make his presence known, and to offer his services.

Twenty-four years earlier, Allen had asked the wide-eyed schoolboy what he wanted to do when he grew up, and had heard his reply:

"Bring peace to the world."

That was still Noel Field's mission in life. But, as Allen Dulles would now discover, he had begun to adopt some queer methods of achieving it.

CHAPTER EIGHT

Swiss Role

Forty-eight hours after Allen Dulles's arrival in Berne, the ring snapped shut around Switzerland, from now on a neutral oasis in a hostile desert. Nazi Germany and Italy between them controlled all the frontiers with Switzerland, including those of Austria and France as well as their own, and except by hazardous clandestine means there was no longer any way in or out for Americans, British, or their Allies.

In some ways it was a spymaster's dream. Even the ubiquitous Wild Bill Donovan, who had a habit of turning up on the ramparts of his intelligence kingdom, to prod, harry, and take part, could not get at his station chief in Berne except by cable contact or scrambled telephone conversations. With no one to look over his shoulder, Allen Dulles was free to recruit his own staff, make his own dispositions, initiate his own operations with the comforting knowledge that he could stall or parry any criticism of his actions until they were faits accomplis. One of the reasons why he had been desperately anxious to avoid capture by the Gestapo on his way across France was that he was carrying with him, in addition to some of the esoteric devices of espionage, a banker's draft for more than $1 million with which to finance his activities. Since he hated above all things the need to keep track of the money in his pocket, the knowledge that he was temporarily cut off from OSS accountants gave him a particularly heady sense of freedom.

He had reported to the U.S. Legation on his arrival in Berne and found a couple of resident intelligence operatives and a secretary waiting for him at an office a few doors down the street. He resolved to do business, however, from more anonymous quarters, and rented a comfortable, spacious apartment at Herrengasse 23, in the old quarter of the town. From the window he could look across the cobbled streets to a corner of the cathedral, the same corner where, one night in 1918, he had delivered a pretty girl spy for the Germans into the hands of British intelligence.

"Between my apartment and the river below," he wrote later, "grew vineyards which afforded an ideal covered approach for visitors who did not wish to be seen entering my front door on the Herrengasse. From the terrace above I had an inspiring view of the whole stretch of the Bernese Alps."

It was not long before the visitors started arriving at his door. Shortly after he had installed himself, the *Journal de Génève,* alerted by a tipster in the Swiss customs, printed an item announcing that "a personal representative of President Roosevelt" had arrived at the U.S. Legation for "special duties" of an unspecified nature, and this well and truly blew his cover. Allen Dulles was not particularly perturbed.

"It had the result of bringing to my door," he wrote later,

> purveyors of information, volunteers and adventurers of every sort, professional and amateur spies, good and bad. Donovan's operating principle was not to have his senior representatives try to go deep underground, on the very reasonable premise that it was futile and that it was better to let people know you were in the business of intelligence and tell them where they could find you. The unsolicited Swiss newspaper item put this principle into practise in short order, though not exactly in the terms I would have chosen for myself.

On the other hand, it aroused the ire of members of the British intelligence network operating out of Switzerland. They had already been warned that an OSS representative was about to appear among them, and they now became convinced that he was a publicity hound whose appetite for headlines would expose all of them. He must be fended off.

The British operation in Switzerland was directed from London by a short-tempered, anti-American colonel named Claud Dansey, and his local chief was a count of the Holy Roman Empire, Vanden Huyvel. They had made some good contacts inside Nazi Germany and were producing some remarkable information (though they proved inefficient at analyzing and interpreting it), and they were determined that no amateur death-or-glory boy from America was going to get his clumsy hands entangled with their network. On Dansey's instructions, Count Vanden Huyvel was told to pay lip service to Anglo-American cooperation but to hold back on any real aid to the newcomer, "and above all keep his nose away from our files."

The first meeting of the count with his American counterpart should have demonstrated to him that Allen Dulles was anything but a go-go Yank of the Jimmy Cagney school, and the reciprocal luncheon which Allen gave him at the Herrengasse should have shown him that the American served better food, superior wines, and could more than match him in the depth, knowledge, and sophistication of his conversation. But there was no rapport, and Allen Dulles was quick to realize it. Quite obviously, the British were not prepared to give or to receive his help; once he had got over the initial shock, he accepted the situation as a challenge.

When word got around to some of the less arrogantly chauvinistic British of the way he was being treated, some of them approached him with offers of unofficial help. He declined them with thanks. And that was a pity. Because one of them, Edge Leslie of M16, had *he* been invited to lunch at the Herrengasse apartment, would undoubtedly have recognized Allen Dulles's newly appointed housekeeper-cook. She had once worked for him, and she not only produced superb meals and kept a meticulously clean household, but also made a few extra francs as a petty spy for the Nazi Legation.

Allen Dulles's isolation from America had its drawbacks as well as its advantages. Being cut off from his headquarters in Washington meant that he could not gather around him the expert advisers and willing spies to back the operations which he now proceeded to plan. The principal mission with which he had been charged by Donovan was to penetrate the Nazi Reich and discover the extent and efficiency of German opposition to Hitler. Rumors of incipient revolt were circulating in neutral capitals. Approaches had been made to both the Americans and the British by emissaries claiming to represent powerful elements in the German army seeking backing for anti-Hitler plots and conditions for an armistice.

How genuine were these approaches? Admittedly, a number of them were deliberate attempts by the Gestapo to entrap the Allies for propaganda purposes. The British, in the early days of the war, had fallen for one such plot and seen two of their key intelligence men kidnapped by the SS at Venlo, Holland, and taken into Germany to be paraded before the world press. But though they were anxious not to be taken for another such ride, they must have been well aware that some of the approaches they were now getting were quite sincere. The British had cracked the code by which the Abwehr, the German secret intelligence service, communicated with its agents, and they knew that its chief, Admiral Canaris, had become increasingly disenchanted with the Nazis and was ready to connive at an uprising in conjunction with disillusioned members of the German army. Some of the emissaries spoke in the name of men so powerful that their complots might deliver Hitler's head on a charger and the rendition of the Reich (under agreed terms) to the Allies.

But which ones? It has been suggested in recent years that the British were continually and deliberately confused over which were the fake and which were the true peaceseekers by the British intelligence agent who was in charge of reading the Abwehr code. He was H. A. R. (Kim) Philby, who later proved to be a Soviet agent working inside M16 headquarters in London for the KGB. His Russian masters were obviously anxious to prevent any peace overtures from elements inside Germany made through the Allies, especially ones which attached armistice conditions concerning the penetration of Germany by the Red Army.

Philby's manipulations may have helped to muddy the waters, but undoubtedly what stopped the British in their tracks whenever they were confronted by a peace emissary was the precondition which each one attached to their proposals: that the British and Americans, in return for Germany's surrender, would guarantee to protect the Reich from a Soviet army occupation and to eliminate the Russians from any part in the discussion of peace terms. The British attitude was strongly reinforced when President Roosevelt and Prime Minister Winston Churchill met at Casablanca in January 1943, and pledged themselves to make no separate peace and accept no less than what they termed Unconditional Surrender. So far as Allied intelligence services were concerned, rarely has a major decision caused more difficulties for station agents in the field. At a moment when everywhere the Axis

134

showed signs of cracking up, when there was a chance of making some sort of a deal to halt the slaughter, the Unconditional Surrender clause became the great inhibition. The British, in particular, received the sternest warnings from London instructing them to talk with no one who was not prepared to discuss outright surrender, with no conditions attached. Washington was no less exigent, but Allen Dulles was a long way away, and prepared to be more flexible. But he did say later: "I think we could have cut the war short by several months and maybe a year if there hadn't been that decision at Casablanca."*

Count Vanden Huyvel warned Allen Dulles at their first meeting to beware of all overtures, whether from visiting Germans or resident émigrés in Switzerland, inferring that not a single one was to be trusted. Any idea that there was a genuine peace movement in Germany capable of mounting a plot to overthrow Hitler was "either balderdash or bluff."

"Personally," the count added, "I kick the fellows out of the office the moment I've milked them of any information they can give me. And I take that with a damned big pinch of salt, too."

British skepticism did not daunt Allen, but it did make him realize the urgency of building up his own independent organization of knowledgeable agents, if he was to make contacts with the Germans, and distinguish the genuine from the phonies, the influential from the simply sincere. He was well aware of the vital importance of his Berne assignment. He was in charge of an espionage organization which, though admittedly in need of overhaul, had tentacles that stretched all the way through Nazi-occupied Europe from Germany herself to Austria, Yugoslavia, Hungary, and Rumania. He was in communication with agents in every one of those countries, and the information he might extract from them could well shape the course of the war— and how to end it. What he lacked was help inside Switzerland, for he had brought no staff who were able or even willing to give him aid. Instead, he let it be known among his fellow Americans working in the

---

*Later on, Allen received a rather happier story about Casablanca from one of his informants in Berlin. A Nazi agent in Spain got wind of the conference and alerted the Abwehr in a cable saying: CHURCHILL AND ROOSEVELT MEETING CASABLANCA IN JANUARY, and suggesting a Luftwaffe raid on the conference. Unfortunately the Abwehr, aware that their agent was a Spaniard, thought he was simply using his native language when he specified Casablanca and translated it as *casa blanca*—White House. What was the fellow thinking about, suggesting they try to make a raid on *Washington*?

country that he was in the market for their services, and would appreciate any help, information, or contacts they could give him.

"I borrowed a few aides from among the American officials already stationed in Switzerland whose original assignments had become more or less outdated now that Switzerland was isolated," he wrote later.

> But most of those who worked closely with me during the ensuing years of my stay in Switzerland I found among Americans who had been living privately in Switzerland for various reasons, or who had been stranded by the sudden closing of the frontier. Some had had jobs with the sadly dying League of Nations at Geneva. Some had been in Switzerland for their health. Some had simply been caught there while traveling, overtaken by the unexpected events of the war and the Nazi occupation of Vichy France.

One of the first recruits to breeze into Allen Dulles's office was, in fact, not an American at all but an Austrian citizen named Kurt Grimm. If the character had been invented in those days, Herr Grimm could have been compared to Mr. Magoo. He huffed and puffed with the same peacock sense of self-importance, had the same fruity voice and myopic look. But his appearance and manner were deceptive, and Allen Dulles was shrewd enough to realize it. Grimm bitterly loathed the Nazis and had not forgiven them for occupying his native Austria and suborning her people; yet his manner belied his convictions to such good effect that he was completely trusted, and maintained close connections not only with Vienna but with all parts of Germany and the Balkans.

He produced a letter smuggled out of prison from the Austrian ex-Chancellor, Kurt von Schuschnigg, together with a list of Austrian anti-Nazis willing to act as informants for the Americans inside the Reich. If he was genuine (and Allen Dulles suspected that he was genuine, but resolved to check) he would be an invaluable pipeline into enemy territory. He had no ax to grind. He was not stating preconditions. All he asked was that he might help in defeating the Nazis and setting his country free. He had friends in high places, and Dulles sensed that, with luck, he might one day produce something really important.

His instincts were right. Later in the spring of 1943 Kurt Grimm sent him a message that a courier was on his way from Vienna with important documents, and asked for a rendezvous. A meeting was arranged at a safehouse in Zurich, and there a delighted Herr Grimm, puffing with pride like a pouter pigeon, introduced him to a tall, handsome, sunburned young man named Fritz Molden. Molden, an expert skier and climber, had just made a hazardous journey through the mountains, dodging Nazi ski patrols, from Austria into Switzerland.

He had brought with him documents smuggled to Vienna from north Germany by Austrian scientists working on secret projects for the Nazis. There were plans of the island of Peenemünde, in the Baltic Sea, and photographs of the camouflaged factories which had been operating there for the past few months. They were turning out the V-1 and V-2 rockets with which Hitler planned to begin bombarding London later in the year.

This was a coup of prime importance, and Allen Dulles lost no time in getting the news to David Bruce, his OSS counterpart in London. Rumors had been widespread that Hitler was readying a secret weapon with which he would turn the tides of war, and Allied strategists suspected that rockets were what he was building. But this was the first indication of where they were being built. Bruce, in turn, handed on the information to a grateful Winston Churchill, and the British premier, well aware of the threat to civilian morale if London came under rocket bombardment, ordered the RAF to take action without delay. Peenemünde was subjected to heavy raids throughout August 1943, and the havoc wreaked on the rocket factories was heavy enough to interrupt Hitler's program. Rocket attacks on London, planned for that autumn, had to be postponed until the following summer, when they were too late to save Germany from inexorable defeat.

Churchill asked Bruce to send his thanks and felicitations to Allen Dulles in Berne. Allen, pleased with the bravery and enterprise of the Austrians, attracted by the vitality and optimism of the young courier from Vienna, took Fritz Molden back with him to Berne. There he installed him for a time in his apartment in the Herrengasse, and saw that he was served all the good food and drink that were unavailable in heavily rationed Vienna. His admiration for Molden grew as he got to know him better. As a result, the young Austrian made several trips between Vienna and Switzerland in the next eighteen months—and a friendship began that was to last a lifetime.*

Hard on Kurt Grimm's heels came other recruits. The American rector of Geneva University, Dr. William Rappard, volunteered for service and clandestinely brought forward a young intellectual named Adam von Trott zu Solz, a former Rhodes scholar, now working in the German Foreign Service, who represented a group of anti-Nazi professionals in Germany. He pleaded with Dulles** to aid his fellow conspirators before, in despair, they turned to the Russians for help.

Another who came forward was a naturalized American of German parentage named Gero von Schulz Gaevernitz, a highly persuasive and potent opponent of the Hitler régime. His father, who now lived in Switzerland, had once been a member of the legislature of the Weimar Republic, but had fled when Hitler took over, fearful for the safety of his Jewish wife. Young Gaevernitz had already established close connections with the anti-Nazi underground, and he quickly lined them up for Dulles's inspection.

One was a huge, bespectacled Prussian, 6 feet 6 in his elastic-sided boots, named Hans Berndt Gisevius, who was down in the Swiss diplomatic lists as a member of the German Consulate in Zurich, but was in reality an agent of the Abwehr. His manners were stiff, his uniform the striped pants, black coat, and stiff white collar of the German Foreign Office, and he seemed to be full of a sense of *amour propre,* an unlikely looking rebel against the rulers of his country. The British had, in fact, already dismissed him as a contact on the grounds of a murky Nazi past and the fact that he flew into a rage every time Vanden Huyvel asked him to filch documents out of the German Consulate.

"I will not demean myself by being a common thief, stealing trivia from office filing cabinets," he told Allen Dulles, "but I will give you a list of every general in Germany who wishes to see Hitler dead, and I will help you communicate with them. In the meantime, I will tell you when my friends are planning to assassinate the Fuehrer."

He named a date: March 13, 1943, and said that on that day an explosive device would be placed in Hitler's personal plane when he

---

*Molden subsequently met and married Allen Dulles's elder daughter, Joan, but they were later divorced. Molden now lives with a new wife and family in Vienna, where he is a publisher.

**Through one of his aides. Dulles did not actually meet him.

flew from Berlin to his forward headquarters in Poland. Would Dulles promise the support of President Roosevelt and the United States for the conspirators in the putsch that would follow?

"How do I know you can be trusted?" Allen asked.

For answer Gisevius pulled a black notebook out of his pocket and began to read from it. To the American's astonishment, what he read were the texts of a number of cables which the OSS office in Berne had sent to Washington and London during the past few weeks. They were not operational messages, for which Allen had a code of his own, but situation reports sent in one of the U.S. Legation codes giving the OSS view of the political situations in Germany and Italy. One of them made the shrewd forecast (a good example of Allen's percipience) that Count Ciano would join in the revolt against his father-in-law, Mussolini, the Italian Fascist leader, when the time came to strike.

Gisevius pointed out that the B-Dienst Group cipher experts had broken the American code, and that this particular message had been shown to Hitler himself, who had immediately ordered a copy forwarded to Mussolini.

Allen Dulles was impressed, and convinced of Gisevius's sincerity. In the spy game you don't tell your enemy you have broken his code unless you are willing to join him.

He did not tell Gisevius that the code was not his operational one, and, in fact, from then on he used it solely for sending messages which he was anxious for the Germans to read. But he did promise to forward the tenor of their conversation to Washington, and meanwhile waited with some impatience for March 13.

As it turned out, the plot misfired. The device failed to go off in Hitler's plane. A further attempt at the end of March also fizzled out. Allen Dulles was not impressed by the expertise of the anti-Nazi conspirators, and he reflected wryly that there was an ironic touch to the code name he had given to them in his messages to Donovan: The Breakers. They had a bull-in-a-china-shop quality about them; increasingly, as time went on, they were prone to smash up everything except the object they were setting out to crush.

For the moment, however, it suited his purposes. After the declarations at Casablanca, Donovan had warned him to beware of making deals with anyone in Germany. So long as the anti-Nazi underground was not producing, he did not need to do so. He simply encouraged them to plot and plan, and spread the anti-Nazi word around, and made any promises of aid strictly contingent on results.

In the meantime, he had an excellent go-between in Hans Gisevius, and they arranged to meet each time the German came back from a mission in Berlin. He would usually wait until after darkness (though neutral, Switzerland had imposed a blackout on all her cities), then come into the Herrengasse apartment through the vineyard by the back entrance. One night, during a rainstorm, he came to the apartment wearing an old Tyrolean hunting hat.

Allen Dulles's housekeeper was usually dismissed in the early evening, before his visitors arrived, but on this occasion she came back for a mislaid scarf and saw Gisevius arriving. After he had passed into Dulles's firelit study, she took his hat away to the kitchen to dry it, and noted the initials inside it: H.B.G. She reported to the German Legation next day that her American boss had received and spent a long time talking to a giant German whose initials were H.B.G.

When Gisevius called in at the German Legation in Berne two days later, two senior members of the legation staff, who had already seen the housekeeper's report (but had luckily not yet reported it to the Gestapo), were waiting for him.

"[They] took him aside and accused him of having contact with me," Allen reported later.

> He was equal to the assault. Fixing the senior of them with his eyes, he sternly remarked that he had, in fact, been dining with me, that I was one of his chief sources of Intelligence about Allied affairs and that if they ever mentioned it to anyone, he would see to it that they were immediately removed from the diplomatic service. He added that his contacts with me were known only to Admiral Canaris and at the highest levels of the German Government. They humbly apologized to my friend and, as far as I know, they kept their mouths shut.

Allen later repeated the story to CIA recruits as an object lesson from which all concerned learned something: "I that my cook was a spy; my German contact that he should remove his initials from his hat; and all of us that attack is the best defense and that if Agent A is working with Agent B, one sometimes never knows until the day of judgment who, after all, is deceiving whom."

In World War I Allen Dulles's telltale cook might have suffered the same drastic fate as the pretty spy he had turned over to the British; but in World War II there were easier ways of handling petty informers. If diplomats on either side suspected they had a spy on their staff, they simply called up the Swiss police, who quietly arrested the suspect and lodged him or her in jail for the duration. That was where the Herrengasse cook spent the rest of the war.

Espionage would never cease to be a romantic profession so far as Allen Dulles was concerned, and life in Berne during 1943–45 fulfilled all his expectations. The cloak-and-dagger element of his daily life in a country stuffed with spies and counterspies, secret police, émigrés and exiles, saboteurs, professional assassins, *agents provocateurs* and *provocatrices,* Fascists and anti-Fascists, Nazis and anti-Nazis, Communists and anti-Communists, all intriguing against each other, appealed to his sense of the theatrical. It was all a great game and he relished every moment of it.

Shortly after his arrival in Berne he was asked to meet a couple of distinguished Italian liberals living in Switzerland, through whom anti-Fascist partisans in northern Italy maintained contact with the outside world. The couple were extremely anxious that their activities remain secret, and though Allen Dulles was confident that both Fascist and Nazi secret police were aware of their work, he consented to a clandestine meeting. He was given a rendezvous in the cemetery of a small village overlooking the lake of Lugano, where he was told to find a certain grave. He arrived in pouring rain, carrying a wreath, and was delighted when a darkly beautiful but considerably soaked woman in mourning clothes came out from behind a mausoleum and said, dramatically: "I am Countess de Grubelli."

"And I," he said, "am very wet. Let's find an inn and get ourselves dry."

By the time they got back to Geneva they were considerably better acquainted; shortly thereafter, the need for secrecy forgotten, the countess was throwing parties for him and introducing him to Swiss society.

It was through the Grubellis that the OSS became involved in an operation which, though it had little effect upon the course of the war, strongly appealed to Allen Dulles's penchant for melodramatic gestures of a James Bondish character. Though Washington and London

141

were still hesitant about how far to go in helping the Hitler opposition in Germany, they had no such inhibitions so far as aid to the Italian partisans were concerned. Dulles was urged to give all help possible in arms, money, and information. For the moment, that was not as easy as Donovan imagined. Germany was still fighting hard, the war was far from over, and the Swiss, anxious not to offend Berlin and bring Nazi troops across their frontiers, remained strictly neutral, frowning on any overt activity on behalf of the Italian partisans.

It was true that Allen Dulles's code was a secure one and that neither the Swiss nor the Germans had succeeded in cracking it.* But he could trust only two code clerks, and their capacity, as well as the cable, was limited. Messages had to be brief. There was a scrambled radio telephone by which he could talk to London and Washington, but he was aware that the Swiss were listening in on that, and he had to restrain any tendency toward confidential revelations.

"I once had the experience at a dinner party of having a high Swiss official repeat with a smile a remark to me which I had just made in a telephone conversation with Washington," he reported later. "Knowing that the Swiss listened to my talks with headquarters, I usually managed to include a few remarks in my reports which I wanted the Swiss to hear."

But one afternoon, when the svelte Italian countess had come with a request for aid for her friends across the border, and was given a dissertation on the difficulties of the situation, she said smoothly: "Why can't we smuggle in supplies through Campione?"

Allen Dulles had forgotten Campione. It was an enclave of Italian territory, some 8 square miles in area, on the shores of Lake Lugano, entirely surrounded by land and water under Swiss control. In peacetime it was notable for a gambling casino chiefly patronized by the Swiss, whose laws do not allow gambling. Two hundred and fifty yards of Swiss territory on the landward side of Campione separated it from Fascist Italy proper, and by the time Allen Dulles had studied a large-scale map of the area an idea was born in his mind. The countess had suggested smuggling supplies through Campione, but why not do more than that? Why not take over the whole place and use it as a base for OSS operations into Italy? It was well known that Campione's

*He had his own code name, too: Battle Cloud.

population of six hundred was enthusiastically anti-Fascist, and the six carabinieri who represented Mussolini's régime in the territory were hardly likely to risk their necks if the population rose in revolt.

Preparations were made all through the autumn of 1943. The following January, on a dark night under the cover of a snowstorm, an OSS team slipped out of the yacht harbor of Lugano town in a small boat containing arms for twenty men and a supply of hand grenades. Partisans were waiting on the Campione shore to take over. It was a bloodless revolution, the carabinieri surrendering without a fight. The next day the whole population gathered in the town square to proclaim their allegiance to the Italian régime in south Italy, now working with the Allies.

The OSS immediately set up a radio station in Campione, opened up a training camp for guerilla warfare, established an arms dump, and began ferrying anti-Nazi partisans to and fro across the 250 yards of Swiss territory into Fascist Italy.

There was only one trouble. The citizens of Campione, by making themselves independent of Italy, had lost their financial subventions from the Fascists and faced dire economic consequences. Allen Dulles had a solution for that. He suggested that the territory start issuing its own stamps, which, in the circumstances, were likely to become collectors' items. He arranged with a Swiss firm to have the stamps printed (and paid for with OSS money), and told the Campione citizens to start writing and posting letters to the stamp dealers of the world. It turned out to be a thriving industry.

Accompanied by the countess, he paid a visit to Campione shortly after its revolution. He was received with a banquet, speeches, toasts to the United States, and an offer to have his likeness put on one of the Campione stamps. He cited his need for anonymity, and suggested that they might use the head of George Washington instead.

It was a busy life.

One of the women who swam in and out of it at this time was a tempestuous Italian named Mrs. Wally Castelbarco, who had been working as a courier with the partisans in northern Italy, and was passionately devoted to the Italian leader, Feruccio Parri. For Parri and for Italy she was prepared to sacrifice her life or anything else she had to give, and the fraught situations from which she had extricated herself while passing through the Nazi lines in Italy had required all the courage, guile, ruthlessness, wit, and downright female sexuality that she possessed in abundance.

Feruccio Parri she loved, but Allen Dulles fascinated her. One day, watching him at work, tugging at the strings of his network in his study in the Herrengasse, she said: "You know, in some ways, *caro,* you remind me of my father. You may not have his Italian panache, but you would have made a great conductor."

Her father was the famous maestro, Arturo Toscanini, and her comparison apt. It was a vast clandestine orchestra Allen Dulles was now conducting: a wave of his baton controlled players all the way across Europe from the Balkans to Berlin. They were not yet playing Wagner's *Twilight of the Gods,* but they were tuning up for it.

Allen Dulles had once told his sister that he would tip his hat to the devil himself if it would help him get a clearer picture of conditions in hell, and among the turbulent elements with whom he was now dealing in occupied Europe were quite a few evil, as well as sincerely motivated, men. He was filtering money into France not only to the resistance fighters of General de Gaulle's Free French guerillas* but also to the anti-Gaullist factions of his arch-rival, General Giraud. He was in close contact with the pro-royalist forces of Badoglio and Ciano in Italy, while at the same time blandly assuring Mrs. Castelbarco and her Socialist friends that he despised King Victor Emmanuele's decadent régime and would have nothing to do with it. He was playing both sides against the middle in Yugoslavia, where he was in touch with both Tito and Mihailovic's agents, not yet having decided which side to back.

In Germany he had quietly let it be known that not even Nazis would be turned away from his door if they had something to sell worth buying.

As conditions began to crumble inside the Nazi Reich (it was the time of the fall of Stalingrad, of the Allied armies' advance in Italy), the rats showed signs of wanting to quit, and some of them were big ones. Early in 1943 one of the smoothest rodents in the pack turned up in Switzerland, and made an arrangement to meet Dulles under elaborate conditions of secrecy. The plan at first had been to rendezvous on a remote mountain ski run near the village of Les Diablerets,

*A move to which Gaullists in London strongly objected, describing OSS money as "impure and corrupting."

but Allen Dulles was suffering from a bad attack of gout in his left foot and was in no condition for winter sports, and they finally had their first conversation in a car parked on a lane close to the border with Liechtenstein.

The Nazi emissary was no stranger. His name was Prince Egon Maximilian von Hohenlohe, and Allen Dulles had first met him when he was a junior attaché in the U.S. Embassy in Vienna in 1916. After World War I, von Hohenlohe had several times visited the United States and was a frequent visitor to both the Dulles brothers' houses on Long Island. A Sudeten German, married to a rich member of the Spanish royal family, he traveled now on a Liechtenstein passport— which opened the world's frontiers to him as a German passport could not—and was as suave and entertaining as ever.

He had become the great apologist for the Nazis and a charming deprecator of the "wild men" of the régime. The obscenities of National Socialism diminished as he explained them away as the excesses of the extremists, nothing that a few evictions and good house cleaning at Party headquarters could not clear up. He was a delightful if unmitigated scoundrel, and at their second meeting—in a Liechtenstein château—he showed that he had lost none of his flair for superb wines and excellent food. Allen Dulles, despite his gout, found it impossible to resist them; that he was able to resist von Hohenlohe himself is more probable.

The prince revealed that he came as a representative of the Gestapo, hinting that he had received his instructions directly from Heinrich Himmler, the head of that sinister organization. In fact, he was acting on behalf of Himmler's second-in-command, Walter Schellenberg, and he came with a proposition: If the Gestapo leader and his henchmen organized a revolt against Adolf Hitler, and toppled the Nazi leader, would the Allied governments treat with Heinrich Himmler as his legitimate successor? With the exception of frontier adjustments in Poland and Czechoslovakia, would the Allies accept the status quo in Europe; and would they make a separate peace, eliminating the Soviet Union from all or any part of the discussions?

Allen Dulles never talked to his sister about the von Hohenlohe negotiations, and the relevant documents referring to the conversations are still embargoed by the CIA archivists at Langley. Von Hohenlohe's own transcript of the talks was seized by the Russians after the war and subsequently leaked to two pro-Communist writers, who used them to try to prove that Allen was anti-Semitic and quite ready for an accommodation with the Nazis.

The Hohenlohe transcript, as revealed by Moscow,* quoted Allen as saying that:

> He was fed up with listening all the time to outdated politicians, émigrés and prejudiced Jews. In his view, a peace had to be made in Europe in the preservation of which all concerned would have a real interest. There must not again be a division into victor and vanquished, that is, contented and discontented; never again must nations like Germany be driven by want and injustice to desperate experiments and heroism. The German state must continue to exist as a factor of order and progress; there could be no question of its partition or the separation of Austria.

The document went on to infer that Allen "seemed to attach little importance" to the Czech question, though "at the same time he felt it necessary to support a cordon sanitaire against Bolshevism and pan-Slavism through the eastward enlargement of Poland and the preservation of Rumania and a strong Hungary." He recognized Germany's right to be Europe's most important industrial nation, and, according to von Hohenlohe, while having "scant sympathy" for Soviet Russia, he did not "reject National Socialism in its basic ideas and deeds," but added that "with all respect to the historical importance of Adolf Hitler and his work, it was hardly conceivable that the Anglo-Saxons' worked-up public opinion could accept Hitler as unchallenged master of Greater Germany."

Could Allen possibly have made such statements? It seems unlikely that even in the circumstances in which these conversations were held, he would have referred to Adolf Hitler in such terms. His loathing for him was deep. Otherwise, it seems unlikely that the Soviet Union would have to do much "doctoring" of the documents, for he could well have made all the remarks attributed to him. He was giving a supposedly sympathetic ear to an old friend from the past, one who had now come to him with the startling news that even the second most

---

*CIA sources have always maintained that the Communists "doctored" the document.

powerful man in Hitler's Reich was turning against the Führer and planning to overthrow him.

Should he have dissuaded him by reminding von Hohenlohe that the Allies had pledged themselves to accept nothing but Unconditional Surrender? Should he have nipped Himmler's hopes—and troublemaking capacity—in the bud by saying that in no circumstances would the Allies deal with such a bloodthirsty monster? It was a time when anything that would hasten the end of Hitler's Germany was to be encouraged. That was why Allen Dulles and the OSS were in Berne, the main purpose of his mission. He was there to encourage the destruction of National Socialism; if the Nazis were willing to help destroy it themselves, who was he to discourage them?

As if to give the lie to those who would later accuse him of being an instinctive pro-Nazi, Allen Dulles almost simultaneously with his von Hohenlohe conversations was entering into a deep liaison with the Communist underground cell in Switzerland, and establishing contact with the red anti-Nazi movement in Germany itself. His go-between during these negotiations was Noel Field, who had presented himself one evening at the apartment in the Herrengasse and volunteered the information that he was in touch both with red Party leaders in Switzerland (where Communists were officially banned) and with the couriers who came in regularly from the red cells in Berlin, Munich, the Ruhr, and Hamburg.

Field explained that he had got to know the Communist leaders during his work among Spanish refugees in Vichy France in 1940–42, where he had directed the Unitarian Service Committee's charity mission. He was now European director of the Unitarian Committee in Geneva, and had kept up his Communist contacts; he thus had a pipeline into secret Socialist and trade union circles in Germany, with which the reds were now working.

Field pointed out that the red German émigrés he was meeting were extremely bitter at the treatment they had received from Russia, since they had been abandoned to their fate the moment Moscow had signed the Nazi-Soviet Pact in 1939. Left to fend for themselves, hunted down by the Gestapo in Germany, half of them had ended up in concentration camps, the rest left to rot in Switzerland, without funds, food, or encouragement. Yet they had still reestablished their connections with the workers in the Reich, and would be received as conquering heroes when the time came for them to return.

Here was a chance, Field said, for the OSS to wean them away from Russia and make use of their reputations and influence once the Reich was liberated. All that was necessary was to make use of their contacts, encourage them, give them funds with which to finance their underground work.

Allen Dulles was impressed by Noel Field's sincerity. He asked him a point-blank question: Are you a Communist yourself? He got a point-blank reply: *No, I am simply a man of peace, as always.*

In fact, Noel Field was lying. He, his wife Herta, and their foster daughter, Erika, had all been card-carrying members of the Communist Party for several years, and all were extremely loyal servants of the Soviet Union. If Noel's object was still to bring peace to the world, it was a Soviet world he was working for.

But Allen Dulles believed him. He dug into his secret funds, gave him $5,000 to hand over to the leaders of the red cells in Geneva and Zurich, and told him to come back a week later for $5,000 more. In return, he asked for a full report on Communist, Socialist, and trade union illegal activities in the Ruhr.

Noel Field thanked him gravely, and pocketed the money. There was just one more thing. Would Dulles please make sure that no word of his work for the OSS reached his parent service, the Unitarian Church, in New York? They would be extremely embarrassed if they discovered he was collaborating with an intelligence organization.

Allen Dulles was now working with the German generals and Admiral Canaris's Abwehr through Hans Gisevius. He was in touch with Church leaders in Germany through the World Council of Churches in Geneva. He was talking to German liberals through the idealistic Adam von Trott zu Solz. He was encouraging Himmler's Gestapo to overthrow Hitler. He was financing Communist anti-Nazis by way of Noel Field. This was the larger part of his work, but there were other projects: sending spies to Hungary and Rumania, watching the situation in Yugoslavia, organizing sabotage teams in Occupied France, treating with the Italian royalists, ferrying men and supplies to the Italian Socialist partisans, and keeping his eyes on the German, Italian,

Margaret, Eleanor, Allen Welsh, and John Foster Dulles spent much of their childhood on the waters of Lake Ontario, near their homes at Henderson and Auburn,
N.Y. Here they are aboard a homemade raft on Henderson Bay.

(Dulles family photo.)

The Reverend and Mrs. Allen Macy Dulles' five children photographed on February 25, 1900, the twelfth birthday of the eldest child, John Foster Dulles. *Left to right*: John Foster, Margaret, Allen Welsh, Eleanor, and Nataline. (*Dulles family photo.*)

When Allen Dulles was eight years old he wrote a booklet about the Boer War and 30,000 copies were printed and sold on behalf of Boer War victims. The booklet was later reprinted by the CIA. The original was published in 1902; the title page and first page of Chapter One from the CIA reprint are shown here, with Allen Dulles' schoolboy spelling left intact.

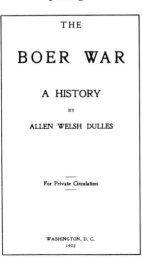

THE

BOER WAR

A HISTORY

BY

ALLEN WELSH DULLES

———
For Private Circulation
———

WASHINGTON, D. C.
1902

THE BOER WAR.
———

CHAPTER I.

THE BOERS AND BRITISH IN SOUTH AFRICA.

In the year 1652 the Boers landed on Cape of Good Hope, Finding no people but a few Indians which they had to fight before they could have the land to themselves, but as soon as they had conquered the Indians they set to work to build towns and houses. But the smallpox got among the Dutch so there was room for the new commers; but after a little the Dutch found that there was some gold at a place called Johannesburg.

In 1806 Britain sent trupes which were defeated by the dutch and they took Cape town. But in the year 1814 Britain paid a large sum of six millions to restore Cape town and some other South African land. I think if Britain had known sooner

John Foster Dulles at Princeton in 1907, aged nineteen. (*Dulles family photo.*)

The wedding reception of John Foster and Janet (Avery) Dulles at Auburn, N.Y., June 26, 1912. (*Dulles family photo.*)

John Foster Dulles in Army uniform during World War I. (*Dulles family photo.*)

Childhood picture of Eleanor Lansing Dulles.
(*Dulles family photo.*)

Eleanor Dulles, in charge of the Berlin desk at the State Department, greets
Chancellor Konrad Adenauer of Germany on an official visit to the U.S.

(U.S. government photo.)

Facing page: December 9, 1932. Eleanor Dulles photographed on her wedding
day in Washington, D.C., at 14th and F Streets.   *(Dulles family photo.)*

Eleanor Dulles with Willy
Brandt of Germany.
(U.S. government photo.)

Eleanor Dulles photo-
graphed at the Taj Mahal,
India, during a State
Department trip around
the world in 1960. She was
in severe pain and had an
abdominal operation shortly
after this picture was taken.
(Dulles family photo.)

Eleanor and Allen Dulles, retired Director of the CIA, pictured at a reception in Washington following publication of one of her books in 1965. (*Dulles family photo.*)

John Foster Dulles shown with his wife, Janet, listening in New York to the returns in the election for the U.S. Senate in 1949. He was defeated by the Democratic candidate, Herbert Lehman.

Facing page: In his bipartisan role, Dulles was assigned by President Truman and Dean Acheson to draw up a Japanese peace treaty and secure Allied agreement to it. Here Japanese Prime Minister Yoshida is shown signing the treaty in San Francisco in September, 1951. Looking on are (*left to right*) Senator Alexander Wiley, Dulles, and Acheson. Many considered this the finest achievement of Dulles' diplomatic career. (*Wide World photo.*)

John Foster Dulles with MacArthur in Tokyo, January 25, 1951. Dulles was on a Far East tour as the Republican bipartisan member of Dean Acheson's team at the State Department. (*U.S. Army photo.*)

General William J. ("Wild Bill") Donovan, Director of OSS during World War II.   (*U.S. Army photo.*)

Allen Welsh Dulles in Berne,
Switzerland, 1942, shortly after
arriving to head the OSS office
in the neutral capital.
 (Comet Photo Agency, Zurich.)

Noel Field, the man in-between.
 (CIA photo.)

Mary Bancroft, close friend
and collaborator with Allen
Dulles in Switzerland,
1942–45. She also introduced
Clover Dulles to Jungian
psychiatry and handled the
problems of Eleanor's
children when she was in
Austria after the war.
*(Photo copyright © 1978 by
Mary Bancroft.)*

Major Max Waibel (*left*), go-between in the negotiations for the German surrender,
pictured with Professor Max Husmann and Baron Luigi Parilli, two others who
played a part in the negotiations.   *(Dulles family papers.)*

Allen Welsh Dulles with his German-American assistant, Gero von S. Gaevernitz, in Switzerland in the spring of 1945, just after Dulles had been approached by Nazi envoys with an offer to surrender the German armies in Northern Italy.

(Dulles family papers, Princeton University.)

The villa at Ascona, Lake Maggiore, Switzerland, where Allen Dulles met with General Karl Wolff, Commander-in-Chief of the Nazi SS armies in Italy. While the surrender negotiations went on, Allen's wife, Clover, was kept marooned on the lake for eight hours. *(Dulles family papers.)*

A Czech radio operator, cover-named "Wally" and attached to OSS in Switzerland, volunteered to go to SS headquarters in Italy to maintain communications between Dulles and General Wolff. This photograph, taken by Wolff's aide, shows "Wally" operating in Bolzano. *(Dulles family papers.)*

Soviet, British, French (Gaullist and anti-Gaullist) espionage services in Switzerland.

A busy life indeed. But it did not prevent him from enjoying a considerable social life. And it did not prevent him from pursuing his favorite occupation, the female sex. There was a new woman in his life. She was rich, she was beautiful, she was forthright, she was highly intelligent, she was liberal—and she was American.

Allen Dulles had never met anyone quite like her before.

CHAPTER NINE

Dumbarton Acorns

They were tall, strong in muscle and thigh, and tough as old boots so
far as cold water and pain were concerned; but the Dulles brothers and
their sister were prone to an extraordinary number of illnesses in their
lifetime, and physical crises were apt to confront them at the most
fraught moments of their lives. Allen Dulles was only too often immobilized by crippling attacks of gout when he had decisions to make,
agents to meet, vital appointments to keep. Eleanor was subject to
dizzy spells, and later on was downed by an agonizing internal attack
while in the Himalayas on a mission for the State Department, in need
of urgent attention and 1,000 miles from the nearest surgeon.

In 1944 it was Foster who was hammered off his feet by an unexpected malaise which could not have happened at a worse time in his
career. This was the year when the Allied armies swarmed across the
English Channel and, at long last, set their feet again on the soil of
occupied Europe. The war was far from being over, but the long hard
bloody slog to Berlin had begun.

In the United States it was also election year, with Franklin D. Roosevelt presenting himself as Democratic candidate for an unprecedented
fourth term as President. His Republican opponent, as almost in 1940,
was Thomas E. Dewey, with John Foster Dulles once more as his
adviser behind the scenes.

More than ever it was going to be difficult to shift Franklin D.
Roosevelt out of the White House, because the way many Americans
felt about him at the moment he could almost have asked for a presidential mandate for life. His popularity was riding on the crest of a

it could have a vital effect upon the presidential vote, and upon Dewey's future and his own. He was determined to go, danger or not.

In the end, Dewey lent him one of the most comfortable limousines from the New York State stable (he was still governor of New York at this time), and he made the journey by road. Nevertheless it was far from being an easy trip, and the doctor traveling with Foster and Janet kept an anxious eye on him until the moment when he reached a friend's house in Georgetown and crawled up the stairs to bed, to rest there before the meeting.

In those wartime days gasoline was rationed. Drew Pearson, writing his column a few days later, sourly remarked that Foster Dulles's "comfortable" journey had been made at the cost of the blood of American soldiers, who were desperately short of gasoline in Europe. Eleanor Dulles remembered that as her brother read this item it was one of the few occasions when he was close to tears, cast down by the injustices of the world.

The Dulles family never let physical pain or disability interfere with their work, and Foster felt that his wits were sharpened by the throbbing agony from his ankle. He was shown the background documents to the Dumbarton Oaks agreement by Cordell Hull, to reassure him that the Democratic administration had made its position clear over the United Nations, and would join no big power clique to rule the postwar world. At the same time, Foster quickly divined that the Secretary of State (obviously under orders from the wily, election-conscious FDR) wished to earn dividends from his gesture by securing from Foster a bipartisan agreement to eschew campaign controversy over postwar foreign policy. Foster was too smart to fall into that trap. His candidate was aiming for the votes of the ethnic minorities, particularly the Poles, and Dewey planned to make an issue of the way the Russians were drawing a ring, if not a noose, around the small nations of eastern Europe as they advanced westward.

So Foster Dulles refused to have any bipartisan pledge included in the communiqué issued after the meeting except with regard to joint approval of the creation of a United Nations, and the two men privately agreed that neither candidate would make an issue of whether the new international body would have the power to mount a peacekeeping army. Dewey later claimed that Roosevelt broke this agreement.

"[He] said in a very deft way," the Republican candidate said later, "that the town hall didn't have any power unless it had a policeman, thereby satisfying a great many people who felt that there should be a United Nations army, about which I had a good many reservations. I have been proved right, and he won the election."

FDR would have won it anyway. There was never any chance of a Republican victory. But Dewey probably got more votes than he would have done without Foster Dulles's adroit intervention in Washington and his masterly handling of preelection strategy. It won him the admiration of many senior members of the party, particularly Senator Arthur Vandenberg and his old World War I mentor, Bernard Baruch.

After the conference was over, Foster went into hospital for an operation, a complicated and delicate affair which consisted of crushing the nerves behind his ankle. It got rid of the clot and the phlebitis, but it left him even more subject to another of the family complaints, gout.

Allen Dulles heard about his brother's operation early in September, while attending a meeting with Wild Bill Donovan at a French guerilla headquarters in central France. He managed to send him a get-well telegram. It seems likely that the thought also passed through his mind that now Foster, too, had his Achilles' heel.

The reason for Allen Dulles's presence in France was that he was en route to London and Washington to report on his first year as the OSS station chief in Berne. It had been quite a year, full of excitements, and it had been crowned by one of the greatest coups in the history of intelligence, the recruitment of the perfect spy.

Fritz Kolbe was his name, and he was an official of the Foreign Office in Berlin. Unlike most of the men and women who betray their countries to the espionage services of the enemy, this man was not interested in money, was not trying to get away from his wife or to escape the consequences of a crime. He had no sense of grievance except one: that the Nazis were in control of his beloved Germany, and he wanted them out. At one time he had believed that the anti-Nazi conspirators for whom Hans Gisevius was working, Admiral Canaris and the German generals, would overthrow Hitler and bring decency back to his country. But on closer examination of the men in the conspiracy, he had come to the conclusion that it would never succeed, that the generals had the will but not the know-how.

As early as 1941, Fritz Kolbe had decided that the only way Germany was going to get rid of the Nazis was by having them lose the war, but it was not until 1943 that his determination crystalized and he decided to devote his life to the task of helping to ensure Germany's defeat by feeding vital information to the Allies that would tip the balance in their favor.

Fritz Kolbe was stubby, bald-headed, a practicing Roman Catholic, forty-one years old in 1943. His job in the Foreign Office in Berlin was to screen and distribute to appropriate departments all messages between the German armies and the Foreign Office, and between the Foreign Office and its diplomatic posts abroad. He saw all information sent out to military and air attachés about military operations; and their return messages, including operational information from Tokyo about Japanese army and air force plans, were also routed through him.

He was trusted by his superiors, and he was mobile. He was frequently sent out of Germany on missions abroad, and he often came to Switzerland, carrying confidential messages for the legation and the clandestine services. What his Nazi masters did not know was that he carefully copied out every piece of information he thought of importance to the Allies, then had it microfilmed.

In the summer of 1943, Fritz Kolbe arrived in Berne on one of his regular missions, but this time determined that he was going to cast the die and mortgage his future. With his briefcase under his arm, he slipped into the British Legation in Berne and asked to see the military attaché. He was eventually shown into the office of an assistant, and told the callow young lieutenant that he had just arrived from Berlin and had information to convey. The assistant listened with growing skepticism, disappeared into a back office to consult, and subsequently came back and showed Kolbe the door. He had been told that the man was either a crank or a crook or an *agent provocateur,* and to throw him out.

Kolbe then looked up the name of the head of chancery of the British Legation and went to see him at his private address. He still had his briefcase with him, but he was not asked to open it. He was once more politely told to be on his way. The British simply could not believe he was genuine, and suspected that they were being asked to walk into a clumsy trap.

155

It was then that he decided to go to the Americans. Unwilling to risk another personal rebuff, Kolbe this time picked an intermediary. He had a friend, an anti-Nazi émigré doctor whom he trusted, and he sent him to the OWI office of the U.S. Legation in Berne, where he was seen by an OSS operative who happened to be an American of German-Jewish extraction and again an extremely skeptical type.* Nevertheless, after he had heard the doctor's story, he passed on a message to Allen Dulles and a rendezvous was fixed.

Years later, emotion would choke in Allen's throat as he recalled that meeting. Kolbe, picked up by an emissary after a mass in the Roman Catholic church, was taken through the vineyard to the Herrengasse apartment under cover of the blackout, and shown into Allen Dulles's study, where the American, sprawled in a leather armchair, was awaiting him. The German was asked to sit down and chose the only stiff-backed chair in the room, sitting well forward, his blue eyes staring directly into Allen's face. His briefcase, bulging at the pleats, sat squarely on his knees. His first words, as Allen Dulles later recalled them, were:

"I want to see Germany defeated in this war. It is the only way to save my country. I think I can help in securing that defeat. I am an official of the German Foreign Office and I see all the telegrams that pass through the Department. I have copies of them in this briefcase. I brought them into Switzerland in the diplomatic bag, and I am willing to turn them over to you. There are more where these come from."

He spoke in accented English and his words had obviously been carefully rehearsed. But there was something about the quality of the man, a sort of burning sincerity glowing from him, that drove suspicion and skepticism out of Allen Dulles from the start. He said later that he knew instinctively, right away, that this man was genuine. He asked if he could see the contents of the briefcase.

The German took a small key attached to his watch chain, turned it in the briefcase lock, and then upturned it, spilling the contents onto the desk by the window. There were typed documents. There were pages of handwriting. There were rolls of microfilms. Allen rose, picked up a typed sheet at random, and read it. It was a report from the German General Staff about the strategic plans for the utilization

*Gerald Mayer.

of V-weapons against England, the flying bombs and the rockets that would soon be proclaimed as Hitler's Secret Weapon. He picked up another. It was the military attaché's report from Tokyo of the Japanese army's plans for an offensive in Burma, complete with troop dispositions and targets.

Allen Dulles was excited, astounded, elated. There were scores of documents.

"You can keep them for a few days and make copies of them," Kolbe said. "Your experts will need to study them to make sure they are genuine." He added, staring into Allen Dulles's eyes: "They are genuine, I can assure you."

Allen said: "What are your terms?"

"I have none," the German replied. Then, with quiet vehemence: "I simply want to see Hitler and those other men dead, and Germany free."

So it had begun.

The first batch of documents proved to be a treasure trove of such vital information that the experts checked and rechecked; each time they came to the conclusion that there could be no doubt about it, these were genuine. The military information was encoded and forwarded to Washington, where Donovan rushed it to the Chiefs of Staff and copies to the British intelligence service. It was there that a cold eye of skepticism and disbelief was turned in Allen Dulles's direction, which threatened to ruin the whole enterprise.

In London, Colonel Claud Dansey, promoted to assistant chief of M16, and the man who controlled British intelligence services in Switzerland, took one look at the documents and scoffed in derision. One fellow member of M16 reported him as saying that "it was clearly impossible that Dulles could have pulled off this spectacular scoop under his nose. Therefore he had not. The stuff was obviously a plant, and Dulles had fallen for it like a ton of bricks." His colleagues cautioned him to be wary of such downright condemnation, and hinted that he should await verification measures which were in process before expressing himself so forthrightly. Dansey snorted that he refused to let Dulles and the OSS "run riot all over Switzerland, fouling up the whole intelligence field. Heaven knew what damage they wouldn't do. Such matters had to be handled only by officers with experience of the pitfalls that beset the unwary. For all he knew, OSS, if egged on in this way, could blow the whole of his network in a matter of days."

Dansey called in the chief of his counter-espionage section, Felix Henry Cowgill, and ordered him to disprove the documents at once and lay bare their spurious nature. Cowgill passed on the task to an energetic member of his department who had more reasons than just patriotic ones for hoping the messages were genuine. His name was H. A. R. (Kim) Philby. Philby shared Dulles's instinctive feeling that Fritz Kolbe was a genuine anti-Nazi and that his documents were authentic. He decided to send some of them for checking to a branch of the British government Code and Cipher School, which, thanks to the Ultra machine, was already "reading" a number of German military messages. He directed them to the attention of Commander Alastair Denniston, who handled enemy diplomatic messages.

"I chose for his scrutiny," Philby wrote later

> a striking series of telegrams from the German military attaché in Tokyo to the German General Staff which had been transmitted through diplomatic channels. They contained detailed statements of the Japanese Order of Battle and assessments of future Japanese intentions. There were about a dozen in all and, if genuine, they were clearly of highest importance.

Denniston telephoned Philby two days later, his voice full of excitement, to say that three of the telegrams exactly matched those already deciphered through Ultra, and the others had enabled his cryptographers to speed up their reading of the German diplomatic code.

"Could I get him more?" wrote Philby.

> I could indeed, and began to feed the stuff in to Denniston as fast as he could absorb it. When about a third of the material had passed through his hands with a steadily increasing tally of matches, and never a suggestion of anything phony, I felt that I had no choice but to circulate the documents as genuine. . . . The reaction of the service departments was immediate. Army, Navy and Air Force—all three howled for more. The Foreign Office was more sedate, but also very polite. I asked all sections concerned to get written evaluations of the material from their departments. I also asked Denniston for a minute explaining the cryptographic reasons for supposing the documents to be genuine. I needed all the ammunition I could get for the inevitable and imminent confrontation with Dansey.

Dansey, of course, was furious. Even though he now admitted the authenticity of the material, he could not stomach the idea that this had been achieved by Allen Dulles and the OSS, both of whom he loathed more than ever. But to that, Philby innocently explained that he had not circulated the documents as coming from the OSS. As far as the British services were concerned, this was a British coup. He cunningly inferred that Dansey himself, as controller of the SIS in Switzerland, would probably be given the credit for it. Dansey was mollified.

"Carry on," he told Philby. "You're not such a fool as I thought."

In Berne, Allen Dulles shrugged his shoulders ruefully when he heard about it. If the British chose to hog the credit, there was nothing he could do. It was no time for a quarrel between Allies. In any case, Washington knew the truth. And what was more, the operation was far from over. Fritz Kolbe had only just begun, and there were new revelations coming.

Allen arranged a code name for Kolbe in his cables to Washington. He called him "George Wood" after an old family friend of his parents. He also arranged a means of communicating with Kolbe in Germany if and when it was necessary to get in touch with him there (because sometimes weeks passed between his visits to Switzerland). He told Kolbe he must take a girlfriend in Switzerland.

The German was shocked. He was obviously not a character for sexual peccadilloes, which he considered frivolous and sinful, especially at this grave stage in the war. But Allen reassured him. The girl would simply be a "cover" for their communications. He introduced him to a young Swiss girl who was, in fact, a member of the staff of the World Council of Churches in Geneva but also an undercover agent for the OSS. Her nationality and her work enabled her to mix with both Allied and German citizens, and her friendship with Kolbe seemed to be nothing more than a wartime companionship with no sinister overtones. When Kolbe went back to Berlin he sent the girl postcards, and she returned them; not often but enough to indicate that the friendship was ongoing. But when Allen Dulles wanted Kolbe to come to Switzerland, he had the girl write a card from Montreux or Lugano or Zurich: "Missing you. Wish you were here. Emmy." Once, when he urgently needed military information about the Japanese, Emmy sent a postcard from the Jungfrau and wrote on it, as Allen Dulles later recalled, "that a friend of hers in Zurich had a shop which formerly sold Japanese toys, but had run out of them and couldn't import them because of wartime restrictions; in view of the close relations between Germany and Japan, couldn't he help her out by suggesting where in Germany she could buy Japanese toys for her shop?" Kolbe got the point and included a batch of military telegrams from Japan in his next shipment of documents.

Allen continued to be astonished by the wealth of information which his dedicated spy produced for him. He warned the Allies of the first shipments of V-1 flying bombs to their stations in the Pas de Calais, Holland, and Belgium. He delivered plans of the V-2 rocket missiles. He produced the minutes of the meetings of Hitler's inner council. He handed over marked maps and reports pinpointing the targets of Allied bombing raids and detailing the damage done, in life, property, and morale.

From the British point of view (and the OSS was meticulously continuing to hand over copies of all Kolbe's messages to the SIS), the spy's most sensational revelation was that the Germans had planted an agent in the British Embassy in Ankara, Turkey. This was Elyesa Bazna, known to the Nazis by the code name Cicero, who had been hired as a valet by the ambassador, Sir Hugh Knatchbull-Hugessen, and took the opportunity while pressing the envoy's pants to extract the keys and combination to the embassy safe.

There have been some suggestions in recent years that Cicero's presence in the Ankara Embassy was known all along to British intelligence, and that he was deliberately fed genuine information in order to impress the Nazis with the mounting might of the Allied forces gathered against them. It may be so, but as one who knew Knatchbull-Hugessen reasonably well and was a frequent visitor to the Ankara Embassy during World War II, the author will remain skeptical of that. Whatever is now being said, the fact remains that Cicero, as a result of his burglarizing activities, was able to inform the Germans of conferences and plans for the invasion of Europe and of the code name (Overlord) for the forthcoming operation—far too valuable secrets, one would have thought, to give away in return for their fright effect on the enemy. It was certainly not the way to overawe Adolf Hitler.

Whatever the truth may be, SIS reacted with panic haste the moment Allen Dulles informed his opposite number in Berne that a cuckoo had been nesting in the British Embassy in Turkey. Security men were rushed to Ankara to change the lock and the combination of the safe. Sir Hugh and senior officials of the embassy were ordered to dismiss all their servants,* and start anew, a command which dissolved one of the counsellors into floods of tears. He had a quartet of small boys— dressed like manikin caliphs in jeweled turbans and bright baggy silk pants, angelic smiles on their rubicund faces—who waited at table and saw to his wants, and he loved them dearly. His protests were in vain. He was given a middle-aged chauffeur-valet of British nationality and stolid rectitude.

By the spring of 1944, Fritz Kolbe had turned over no less than twelve hundred documents and microfilms either to Allen Dulles or, by arrangement, to an OSS agent in Stockholm. They not only included a wealth of military and economic information, but also painted a picture of a Nazi Reich rumbling and reverberating with the portents of disaster.

Leafing through the piles of diplomatic situation reports which Nazi envoys were now pouring into Berlin, Allen Dulles decided to write a sitrep of his own, to give Washington some idea of what was happening in Germany. In April 1944, he sent the following telegram to Donovan:

> Sincerely regret that you cannot at this time see Wood's [Kolbe's] material as it stands without condensation or abridgement. In some four hundred pages, dealing with the internal maneuvering of German diplomatic policy for the past two months, a picture of imminent doom and final downfall is presented. Into a tormented General Headquarters and a half-dead Foreign Office stream the lamentations of a score of diplomatic posts. It is a scene wherein haggard Secret Service and diplomatic agents are doing their best to cope with the defeatism and desertion of flatly defiant satellites and allies and recalcitrant neutrals. . . . The final death-bed contortions of a putrefied Nazi diplomacy are pictured in these telegrams. The reader is carried from one extreme of emotion to the other as he examines these messages and sees the cruelty exhibited by the Germans in their final swansong of brutality toward the people so irrevocably and pitifully enmeshed by the Gestapo after half a decade of futile struggles, and yet at the same time sees also the absurdity of the

---

*Cicero had resigned some time before, to live a fat, full life on the £300,000 which the Germans paid him for the secrets he had purloined. His standard of living collapsed catastrophically when it was discovered that he had been paid in forged currency.

161

dilemma which now confronts this diplomacy both within and outside of *Festung Europa.*

He had never felt happier with his role of spymaster than he did at this moment. Rarely in the history of intelligence can one man have had so many lines into the enemy camp, and so deftly controlled them. Kolbe's microfilms told him what the Nazis were thinking and planning; Hans Gisevius kept him in touch with the Breakers, the anti-Nazi plotters who were planning Hitler's downfall. Between them they were providing him with a ringside seat—and a controlling interest—in a drama of cataclysmic proportions. And the climax was approaching. In April 1944, he sent another cable to Donovan:

> The end of the war in Europe is definitely in sight. In this crisis the resistance group in Germany, headed by Goerdeler and General Beck, state that they are now willing and ready to endeavor to initiate action for the removal of Hitler and the overthrow of the Nazis . . .

And then, suddenly, Allen was faced by a crisis that threatened to disrupt his smooth-running organization. On a trip to Switzerland in May 1944, at a meeting in a safehouse in Zurich, Kolbe announced that he was fed up with being a spy, and wanted to be a hero instead. The time for action had arrived, he said. He had decided to throw in his lot with the anti-Hitler conspirators and join the plot, timed for the following July, to assassinate Hitler and take over Germany. He was now convinced that the plotters had improved their expertise, and that this time they would succeed.

Allen Dulles was aghast. The last thing he wanted Fritz Kolbe to do was involve himself in this fraught and dangerous enterprise. Conspirators were two a penny in Germany now, but Kolbe was worth his weight in diamonds—so long as he stayed in his job and continued to bring in the documents. He did not argue that the anti-Hitler plot was too hazardous an undertaking for Kolbe to join, because the German was obviously in a do-or-die mood and filled with a need to sacrifice himself. But he did try to reason with him, saying that what he planned to do was rather like an ace pilot of the air force suddenly deciding that he must go out and fight with the infantry. It was a sheer waste of skill and experience.

Kolbe was not convinced. Fortunately for Allen, it happened that the German's "cover" girlfriend, Emmy, was present at the meeting. She

162

had been listening quietly to the argument going on between the two men. At last she spoke, to the German: "Does that mean you will not be coming to Switzerland again?"

"Not until it is all over," he said.

She began to cry. Kolbe looked at her with great distress, watching the tears roll down her pretty face. There was a long silence, broken only by Emmy's sobs, until at last Kolbe sighed, turned to Dulles, and said: "Perhaps I will make one or two more trips before I finally decide."

Allen was relieved. He could hardly have told Kolbe that he had just received a message from Washington warning him that he should promise no help to the conspirators whether their project was successful or not. The anti-Nazi leaders were still maintaining that once they had succeeded in wresting Germany from Hitler's control, they would surrender only to the British and the Americans, and would refuse to treat with the Russians. They even expected help from the Western Allies in preventing the Red Army from taking over Germany, and Dulles knew they would not get it. Roosevelt and Churchill had made it clear that there would be no split, no separate peace, only Unconditional Surrender.

So the conspirators would be on their own, and Allen Dulles feared for them.

He was quite right. The bomb that Count Claus Schenk von Stauffenberg carried in his briefcase into the Führer's bunker on July 20, 1944, failed to kill Hitler, and, in fact, built up the myth of his omnipotence when he went on the radio later to tell the German people he was still alive and in command. The conspirators made a botch of their communications network, and ordered their followers to rise up at a moment when they should have been warning them to go to ground. They were rounded up and hung by the flesh on meathooks, strangled with chicken wire, shot in the stomach and left to die in rat-ridden cells. Their relatives were massacred, their friends persecuted, and a terror spread through Germany that was the worst Europe had known since the French Revolution.

One of the few to escape was Hans Gisevius. His name was known to the Gestapo as a top member of the conspiracy, and a manhunt began throughout Germany to find him and bring him before one of the kangaroo courts that were now quickly being set up. He went to cover in a safehouse which Fritz Kolbe had set up not far from the Swiss frontier, and it was Kolbe again who brought to him from Berne in the winter of 1944 the false papers which Allen Dulles had had forged in London. They included a Gestapo passport that enabled Gisevius to pass over to Switzerland in the first weeks of 1945.* He, Kolbe, and Allen dined together in the Herrengasse to celebrate his deliverance.

Watching them as he sipped his brandy, Allen reflected that if it hadn't been for Emmy's tears, he would have lost both of them. Now they would live to spy and to conspire another day.

Despite the failure of the July 20 plot, Allen Dulles had reason to be proud of his record; when a telegram arrived from Washington from Donovan summoning him home for consultations, he had grounds for believing that he was in for some sort of reward. A promotion, maybe. He had heard that David Bruce, who ran the OSS's operations from London, was changing jobs. At this stage in the war, he would not mind leaving Berne for London and taking over, provided certain personal arrangements could be made. London controlled the whole of the European operation of the OSS, from the United Kingdom and the Iberian Peninsula to Turkey, and it was the most important station outside headquarters in Washington.

The Allied sweeps across France, from the English Channel and the Mediterranean, had opened up a corridor to the Swiss border and ended two years of isolation. In September 1944, Allen Dulles motored to a Free French guerilla headquarters near Lyon, where he had been told a plane would be waiting for him to fly to London, en route for the United States.

To his surprise, when he reached the guerilla camp, Wild Bill Donovan was there. He explained that he had been on a tour of the OSS units operating in France, but although a remarkable campaign called Operation JEDBURGH, involving fifty American and British officers, was then in progress in German-occupied France, Dulles suspected that Donovan was principally there to meet him.

*While Gisevius was in hiding in Germany, Allen Dulles spread the rumor that he had managed to escape into Switzerland, and a Gestapo murder squad was sent to search him out and kill him. The OSS tipped off the Swiss police, who arrested the assassins and imprisoned them for the duration.

He realized why the same evening when Donovan drew him aside and told him that though Bruce wanted to leave his London post, Donovan had persuaded him to stay on until the end of the hostilities in Europe.

"I didn't want anyone to be unhappy over David's replacement," Donovan said. "There are lots of guys shooting for the job, good guys, with marvelous records—the best men we've got. But they can't see that it isn't the sort of job they're suited for. Just because they're brilliant station chiefs doesn't mean they can handle London—all that administration. Nearly all of them are lousy administrators. They could foul things up at a vital stage in the war." A pause and then: "So I'm ordering David to stay on, just as I'm asking you to do the same. God knows what would happen if we had a change in Berne at this juncture. We just can't afford to lose you."

Allen got the message: he was to stay where he was and not start any lobbying for promotion when he got to Washington. He had the feeling that his chief was just a little jealous of his achievements in Switzerland, and rather envious of the eventful life he had been leading.

They flew off to London together, old friends reunited after two years. In the British capital they were drinking together in the bar of the Savoy Hotel when the first of the V-2 rockets, Hitler's ultimate secret weapon, exploded in the City. In the next few days, Allen noted that many a Briton who had gone through the Blitz with a stiff upper lip was terrified by the new bombardment. It came out of nowhere, without warning, a sort of cosmic horror against which there was no defense. One could almost feel London's millions cringing with fear as they gazed up into the empty sky.

It was just as well that he had been able to turn over the secrets of Peenemünde to the British, so that they could bomb the rocket factories and delay production. If this bombardment had come eight months earlier . . .

He flew on to Washington, arriving there in mid-September 1944.

CHAPTER TEN

Frustration

————————— ◆◆◆◆ —————————

Washington had changed. When Allen Dulles left it in 1942, it had still not geared itself up for war, was still something of a Southern town, lazy, complacent, an annex of administrators apart from the industrial life of the nation. Now it was bustling, alive, full of self-importance, its streets, offices, hotels packed with purposeful men in uniform and brisk, pretty girls. And the mood was optimistic, with a feeling in the air that the war was all but over, a glorious future ahead.

Allen found that his brother and sister only partly shared that optimism, though for disparate reasons. Foster seemed unconcerned that his candidate, Thomas Dewey, was inevitably going to lose the forthcoming presidential election. That was a foregone conclusion; there was no likelihood of unseating Franklin D. Roosevelt, the "architect of victory," as he sarcastically called him. But the polls were promising and the auguries good for 1948. Meanwhile, his own reputation had risen—and not simply in the Republican Party. He was becoming widely known in the nation as a spokesman for the reshaping of the postwar world, to make it more just for ordinary men and women, more equal for small nations, less pressured by bureaucracy at home, less politically manipulated by the big powers abroad.

And that was where he was worried. Did Roosevelt really care about these things? He confided to his brother and sister that he had no faith in Roosevelt's sincerity, and added, to Allen's considerable amazement—for his experience in Europe was teaching him better—that he had more faith in the goodwill of Stalin and the Russians than he did in the Democratic President of the United States. As Dewey himself was later to remark, it was a period when John Foster Dulles was adopting "a very high-minded approach." He added: "I wouldn't say he was naïve, but he was certainly idealistic."

Not all that idealistic, however, in Eleanor's view. She knew that her elder brother was in the process of writing a memorandum about Germany's role in the postwar world, and though she had few illusions about Germany herself, Foster's plans went far beyond her own for the disposition of the Reich. He appeared to have joined Morgenthau (though he never consulted him) and the "squeeze Germany until the pips squeak" brigade, and, in direct contrast to his attitude toward Germany after World War I, was now in favor of "cutting it down to manageable size." He proposed that Germany should be carved up, that the Rhineland be given to France, southern Germany and Bavaria to Austria, East Prussia to Poland to compensate her for any inroads on her territory Russia might make in the postwar readjustments. Germany was to be left a small nation of Prussians, incapable of ever becoming a belligerent nation again.

It was a solution certainly in keeping with American mood at that moment, but hardly one that a supposedly high-minded idealist would have been expected to adopt.*

Eleanor found it ironic that her brother should distrust Roosevelt because he feared he would not be tough enough toward Germany; her suspicions of the President were based on misgivings of a quite contrary nature. Sometime before her reunion with Allen, in the summer of 1944, she was working in the State Department and had been coopted as a member of what was called the German Committee. It had been organized to work out a plan of how to deal with the Reich, in strictly practical ways, once it was defeated and occupied.

"The committee was divided into the soft-heads and the hard-heads," she said later. "I was a hard-head. I had no reason to love Germany, after all. But on the other hand, I knew what had happened after World War I and I didn't want to see that start again."

She had little time, however, for one or two members of the committee whose hearts, she found, were already bleeding for the Germans.

"We had one dope on the committee," she said, "and he wrote a paper that although we had fought a terrible war, we must forget it, and only remember that the Germans are human beings and what

*The memorandum was never published and Foster Dulles never referred to it in later years, but it is to be found in his papers at Princeton University.

good would it do to make them suffer. We must feed and nurture and help them. Well, I thought this was going too far. Anyway, it was irrelevant. We were writing a report on practical plans, not making a play for German sympathy, and I thought the paper shouldn't have gone into our final report. But it did. And when it got to the White House and Roosevelt read it through, he drew a line around one of these sentimental phrases and said: 'Let them eat soup.' Then he sent it to Morgenthau and said: 'These people in the State Department are a bunch of saps.' And Morgenthau started drawing up his plan for the complete pastoralization of Germany."

No, she at least did not share Foster's view that Roosevelt was going to be too lenient with the Germans. She told Allen that the President was in a vengeful mood, and cited the note which he had written the previous August in which he had said: "The German people as a whole must have it driven home to them that the whole nation has been engaged in a lawless conspiracy against the decencies of modern civilization."

She feared that any reasonable plan for Germany's postwar role in Europe would be blocked by the President, that he was ready to carve up the Reich and hand it over to the Russians as compensation for their sufferings.

"I think if Roosevelt hadn't died," she said later, "it would have been difficult to get any kind of German program on course."

She might have added that if Dewey had won the 1944 election, Germany might have fared even worse, for Foster would have been his Secretary of State, and *his* plans for the Reich went far beyond the Morgenthau plan for the country's pastoralization. He wanted it all but wiped off the map.

The two brothers and their sister got together often while Allen was in Washington and, as usual, when they argued about the future their exchanges of ideas were heated, but stimulating and refreshing. They struck sparks off each other as no one else did. They admired each other anew, and were confirmed in their feeling that there was no one quite like them.

The election campaign was in full swing. But Foster managed to give a family party before Allen left to go back to Europe. Foster's sons, John and Avery, were away at the war and his daughter Lillias was with her family, but Eleanor brought her two children, and Clover was there with her three. Clover was aglow, and for once on the same waveband as everyone there, even listening to Janet's steady and unremitting praise of Foster.

She was happy because Allen had promised that as soon as arrangements could be made, she would follow him to Switzerland. Neither of them had really changed. Clover could be as vague and as infuriating as ever, and even during his short stay in Washington there were times when he couldn't lay his hands on her.

"You're like a firefly, always zipping around," he complained.

"Oh," she said, delighted. "Do I light up? Can you see me in the dark?"

She had heard the gossip about Allen's amorous activities in Switzerland, having ruefully discovered that even war doesn't stop scandal from spreading, but she didn't care. She knew he was glad to see her, knew that he had missed her—enough to want her with him now that it was once more possible, despite all the other arrangements he had made in Switzerland. She would face all that when she got there; or maybe not face it.

Foster looked across at them and smiled benevolently, more, Eleanor thought, as she watched, like a father figure than ever.

It was a break of less than two months, but by the time Allen Dulles got back to Berne in the beginning of November 1944, things had changed. All the OSS operatives who couldn't get into Switzerland while the Germans and Italians ringed it round now came swarming in, and there were many new faces, and new departments to accommodate them.

There were labor experts to liaise with the underground trade unionists in Germany. There were Slav experts to help untangle the complicated guerilla situation in Yugoslavia and the Balkans. There were cipher experts, code breakers, safebreakers, muscle men, dedicated émigrés of every shape, size, and both sexes, radiomen, telephone tappers. There were Soviet experts and scholars, second-generation Ukranians, Kazaks, Georgians, and Armenians. Mrs. Shipley in the Passport Office must have been working overtime, and the Swiss government had been lavish and unquestioning with visas, an indication of how conditions were changing. Allen Dulles guessed that quite a few of the new recruits would turn out to be four flushers and crooks (which indeed proved to be so), but there would certainly be no lack of manpower from now on.

There was one compensation. His own staff stayed tightly knit and intact, a personal entourage he appreciated and trusted. It included Mary Bancroft, to whom he had become especially attached.

Mary Bancroft. He had met her shortly after his arrival in Switzerland at some sort of social gathering, a tall, fresh-faced, handsome brunette who strode across the crowded room like some latter-day Queen Boadicea, cutting a swathe through the people who did not matter in her purposeful path toward him. She knew who he was. She knew why he was there. She supposed, she said, with a touch of scorn in her voice, that he had come to scheme the overthrow of the Nazis in order to make Germany safe again for the Junkers and the Prussians.

"And for Sullivan and Cromwell, of course," she added.

She was the Boston-born daughter of the publisher of the *Wall Street Journal,* twice married, twice divorced, mother of a small daughter by her first husband. She had come to Switzerland in 1935 with the second husband, a Swiss banker, but had sloughed him off in favor of a less physical relationship with the Swiss philosopher and psychologist, C. G. Jung. From him she had imbibed wisdom and self-knowledge which had, if anything, increased her qualities of forthrightness, outspokenness, and a hatred of sham and self-delusion. She said what she thought, believing in the long run that complete honesty, even if it hurt, was best. She believed that "love and power are mutually exclusive," and once wrote her view of power in these words:

> The other day in the zoo, the keeper of the camels wanted to give M.J. [her daughter] two little kittens to bring home, for unless he found someone to take them away, the director of the zoo would give them— still living, though doped—to the "big birds." Now if you take birds as a symbol of thoughts and ideas—as they are taken by so many primitive cultures and by analysts in dreams—and raise them to be "big birds"— i.e. "big ideas"—and take the kittens as symbols of feelings and the human heart—you get what as I see it is going on all the time. The key to the situation is the role of the keeper. Whose side is he on? In this instance he was for the kittens against the birds. I see you, Harry, as a kind of keeper. And naturally I get all wrought up when I feel you are on the side of the birds—particularly the big birds.

The "Harry" she was referring to was Henry M. Luce, founder and editor-in-chief of *Time* magazine, with whom she later formed a close attachment, but she often addressed similar sentiments to Allen Dulles. She could make him wince.

Mary Bancroft was potently attractive, she was generous, as eager to give as she was to receive, but her complete frankness made her hard to take, and only strong men could take her. Allen Dulles had decided that he was strong enough. He had brought her into OSS—where her contacts, her percipience, her knowledge of Switzerland and Germany made her invaluable—but also into his private life, and sometimes it was as devastating as one of those plunges into the ice-cold water of Lake Ontario on a late spring morning. But once you got over the shock, it was wondrously refreshing.

Professionally, he had come back to a frustrating period. He and his chief aide, Gero von Gaevernitz, had several schemes going for making contact with elements inside Germany whose efforts or influence might help shorten the war. One was the creation of a Generals' Committee of captured German staff officers who would get messages through, by radio and other means, to their colleagues still fighting and persuade them to accept honorable surrender. The Generals' Committee would be the Western Allies' reply to a similar movement that had been formed among Nazi POW officers captured in Russia after the fall of Stalingrad. The plan received the support of General Bradley, C-in-C of the 6th U.S. Army, but Washington rejected it on the grounds that it would make Moscow suspicious of American intentions. They were still being inhibited on every side by the Roosevelt-Churchill policy of Unconditional Surrender.

Fritz Kolbe turned up with a proposal which sounded promising: an uprising of young student-soldiers in Berlin, under the banner of a resuscitated Social Democratic Party, to take over the capital and hold it until the Americans and British arrived. This too was rejected because it would suggest that the West was trying to get to Berlin before the Soviets—which was, indeed, the intention of the plan.

Noel Field had come in with another promising scheme. He proposed the recruitment of a Workers' Committee among the German émigrés now gathered in camps in liberated France and their dispatch to Germany with the advancing Allied armies, to make contact with their confrères in the Ruhr and other industrial areas, and prevent Nazi sabotage of the factories. Many of the émigrés had fought in Spain, he pointed out, and he knew them well.

Allen Dulles sent him to Paris with a recommendation that the scheme should be launched, and asked the Americans there to cooperate. But what Noel Field had not told Dulles was that his plan was to recruit mainly Communist émigrés, so that, once in Germany, the Party would have cadres installed and ready to take over. Without U.S. or British sponsorship, they would otherwise not be able to get back into the Reich.

The OSS analyst in Paris who interviewed Field saw through him at once and reported to his chief that the American was a phoney.

"What struck me most was Field's self-righteous stupidity," the analyst recalled later. "He was a Quaker Communist, filled with smugness and sacrifice, and not a very intelligent man."

But neither the analyst (Arthur Schlesinger, Jr.) nor his chief (Philip Norton) mentioned anything of Field's political loyalties in their report to Washington, nor in their playback to Allen Dulles. Instead, they rejected the American's plan on purely administrative grounds. So in Allen Dulles's eyes Noel Field continued to be what he said he was, a politically unattached idealist who happened to have plenty of Socialist and Communist friends. When Field's foster daughter, Erika Gläser, took a job as secretary-interpreter to Gerhard van Arkel, one of the OSS labor and union experts now attached to his staff, Allen signed her character reference.

Field could have told him that Erika was a member of the underground Communist Party of Switzerland, and that she had taken the post with instructions to report back to the Party on the OSS's negotiations with the workers' movement in Germany. But he kept silent; later on Allen Dulles would remember that.

So all these various schemes had come to nothing. Though the war was coming to an end, the fighting and the killing went on, and he had the feeling that, if it weren't for politics, there was much he could do to prevent the slaughter. From his neutral observation post, he was acutely conscious that many powerful Germans, Nazis among them, were now anxious to make a deal and bring the agonizing struggle to a halt. Envoys and emissaries flitted back and forth across the frontier: a consul returning from Berlin to his post in Lugano, bringing with him a message from Schellenberg, the Gestapo's number two official;

a cardinal from Milan with an offer from the German armies in Italy and a message for the Pope in Rome;* an approach purporting to come from General Rundstedt, the commander of the Western Front. Opportunities for negotiation floated in the murky air, but the Allies, fearful of Stalin's wrath, were afraid to grasp them.

Allen Dulles's mood was close to despair. He was suffering from a bad dose of gout and forced to limp around in his carpet slippers. His loud laugh no longer pierced the padded walls of his study in the Herrengasse, but his wrath when any of his subordinates went wrong was terrible. Mary Bancroft was fascinated by these manifestations of his acute distress. Though she did not know about the club foot episode, her Jungian sense of divination must have told her there was a deep-rooted reason why it was always his left foot that swelled and agonized him whenever things went wrong. She did what she could to comfort him, for she agreed that it was monstrous that men should continue to die when offers of peace were available. If there was a chance of halting the slaughter, she felt it should be explored—though not, of course, at the cost of preserving the Nazis in power.

It was at this nadir of his wartime career that the Swiss came to his rescue. On February 25, 1945, "a particularly cold and sunless day," as Allen Dulles later recalled, Major Max Waibel of Swiss military intelligence sent a message to him asking for an urgent meeting.

*The Vatican and southern Italy were, by this time, in Allied hands whereas northern Italy was still controlled by the Nazis.

CHAPTER ELEVEN

Sunrise

———————◆—▰▰▰—◆———————

Throughout the war the Swiss government had followed an even-handed policy toward the activities of the Germans and the Allies inside its country, except that, to adapt George Orwell, it had sometimes been more even-handed toward the one rather than the other, according to the way the tide of the war was flowing.

It was definitely the Allies' turn to be favored in the spring of 1945, and not simply because they were now certain to win. How soon they won, and what the Germans did before they lost, was the urgent concern of the Swiss now.

They were particularly anxious that the battle in northern Italy should be brought to a conclusion as speedily as possible, before the port of Genoa, through which land-locked Switzerland received most of her supplies, was completely wrecked. And they dreaded a long-drawn-out slogging match between the two armies which would, inevitably, end with a German retreat, for that would mean the escaping troops would try to take refuge in Switzerland, where they already had all the refugees they could handle.

Max Waibel was the intelligence chief whom the Swiss government had assigned to handle liaison with the activities of Allied espionage services in the country,* and Allen Dulles had grown to like the slim, bespectacled, highly cultivated officer. "I put my confidence in Waibel and never had occasion to regret it," he wrote later.

As a result of Waibel's message, Gero von Gaevernitz, Allen, and

*One of his fellow officers liaised with the Germans. They obviously compared notes, but did not appear to pass on their mutual knowledge to either of the belligerents.

Waibel all had dinner together the following evening at a restaurant near Lake Lucerne, and after eating "some excellent trout" and drinking a good hock, the Swiss said he had something to say which he thought might interest the Americans. That day he had been in communication with an Italian and a Swiss, and he believed what they had told him should be followed up.

Allen was disappointed. "It was just another peace feeler from the Italian front," he thought. "I must admit that my immediate reaction was not enthusiastic. This approach had many of the earmarks of earlier feelings from Italian industrialists who were concerned about the German scorched-earth policy."*

Reluctantly, mainly to please Waibel, he agreed to see the two men. He was even more skeptical when they told him that they were in contact with the SS armies in northern Italy and their commander-in-chief, General Karl Wolff, and that he wished to talk surrender. Would Dulles agree to meet one of Wolff's representatives—in Switzerland? The spy chief shrugged his shoulders. What had he to lose? Waibel arranged a password by which the Italian and the Swiss contacts would indicate when they were ready to produce the German spokesman, and they departed back to Nazi-occupied Italy. Allen never expected to see them again.

"But we were wrong," he wrote later.

> Only five days had passed since the meeting when we had an urgent call from Waibel. Parilli [the Italian go-between] had returned to Switzerland. Not only that; with him were two Waffen SS officers, Colonel Eugen Dollmann and Captain Guido Zimmer, from Milan. Waibel had quietly arranged for their admission to Switzerland and would find safe quarters for them in Lugano. Their presence in Switzerland could be kept a secret. They would have to return to Italy in a few days. The rest was up to us.

Could this approach really be taken seriously? The SS forces were reputed to be the most dedicated Nazis of them all, with every officer personally pledged in allegiance to the Führer. It was hard to believe they were ready to give in rather than expire heroically on the bat-

---

*The Nazis were threatening to destroy everything, factories, churches, art treasures, as they retreated.

tlefield. Was it a trick? How could their sincerity be tested?

It was while running these thoughts through his mind that Allen Dulles had an inspiration.

It so happened that a few weeks earlier Feruccio Parri, the Italian partisan leader, and Antonio Usmiani, one of his lieutenants and also a frequent agent on OSS missions into northern Italy, had been captured by the Gestapo. Parri's arrest, in particular, had caused considerable distress in partisan circles, and several attempts had been made to rescue him, all of them abortive, one of them resulting in the capture of two more partisans. Mrs. Wally Castelbarco had come to plead with Allen Dulles to do something for her beloved Parri, whom she knew was being tortured, whose imminent execution she feared. Allen found it hard to resist the tears and anguish of this powerfully attractive young woman, but he had been able to promise her nothing. What could he do?

But now he saw a way. He called in a young member of his staff, Paul Blum, and instructed him to get down to Lugano and talk to the two SS men. Blum was an American Jew who was not likely to take things at their face value, especially when dealing with Nazis. Shown into the presence of Colonel Dollmann and Captain Zimmer by the Italian go-between,* Blum swallowed hard and faced his first decision. Dollmann was holding out his hand. Should he shake it? Swiftly he made up his mind.

"If I am willing to speak to a man and want to get his candid views," was how he rationalized it later, "I see no point in refusing him my hand."

He shook hands with the black-haired, Italian-looking SS colonel and his blond, clean-cut assistant. They began to speak in French, in which all were fluent, but it was mostly Dollmann who led the conversation. Almost immediately he asked whether the Allies would be willing to treat with Heinrich Himmler if he supported a separate action for peace in northern Italy. Blum, who knew the Americans and British would never negotiate with the butcher of the Gestapo, answered at once, in English: "Not a Chinaman's chance."

Then Dollmann, who almost seemed pleased at this reply, asked what would happen if his chief, General Wolff, came personally to

---

*The meeting took place in the private dining room of a Lugano restaurant normally reserved for weekly meetings of the Rotary Club.

Switzerland to negotiate the surrender of all SS troops in northern Italy (and maybe the whole of the German armed forces there). Would Allen Dulles see him?

"Before the meeting," Allen reported later, "I had told Paul that, if we were to continue the conversations with the German emissaries, we should have to have concrete evidence both of their seriousness and of their authority. I had given Paul a slip of paper . . ."

Paul Blum now pulled it from his pocket. On it were the names of the two captured partisans, Parri and Usmiani. By this time Allen knew that Parri was in the hands of a particularly brutish Gestapo unit in a maximum security jail in Verona, while Usmiani had been transferred to Turin. Through Blum, he presented his conditions.

> I proposed, therefore, that General Wolff, if he wanted to see me, should give evidence of the seriousness of his intentions by releasing these two prisoners to me in Switzerland. In asking for Parri I realized that I was asking for probably the most important Italian prisoner the SS held. . . . I knew that in asking for his release I was asking for something that would be very difficult for Wolff to do, and in fact I was putting the stakes high—almost too high, as it later turned out. Yet if these men could be released, the seriousness of General Wolff's intentions would be amply demonstrated. Also, I had deliberately chosen two men who were imprisoned in different places in Italy to test out the extent of Wolff's authority.

Dollmann was shocked by the demand, but, after swallowing hard, agreed to do everything in his power to meet it. He said he would report back in a few days.

When Blum got back to Berne and described what had happened, Allen Dulles began to think he had asked too much. But Blum wasn't so certain. He had been deeply impressed by Dollmann's sense of purpose, the grave urgency of his manner.

"Anyway," Allen decided, "if we had called the German's bluff and put an end to proceedings which were not serious, I need have no regrets; and at least I had done what I could to free Parri, who had bravely fought Hitler in Italy."

It would also show the lovely Castelbarco (when he eventually came to tell her about it) that he had tried to save her leader.

It was on March 4, 1945, that Dollmann, Zimmer, and the Italian go-between passed back into Nazi-controlled Italy on their way to report to General Wolff. On March 8, an SS car drove up to the Swiss frontier at Chiasso; a captain stepped out, went to the military guard, and gave a password. It was Zimmer. One of Major Waibel's representatives was called, and more passwords were exchanged. Then Zimmer said:

"I have two men here for you. Please take them to Mr. Allen Dulles with the compliments of General Wolff."

Two men climbed out of the car and, in a semi daze, walked tentatively across the last yards of Italian territory into Switzerland, glancing back apprehensively as if fearing a last-minute bullet in the back, when the SS car revved its engine, turned, and went back down the road.

Feruccio Parri and Antonio Usmiani were free. In no uncertain fashion, General Wolff had demonstrated that he was "serious."

Two hours later the SS car arrived once more at the Chiasso frontier post, and four men descended this time. They were all in civilian clothes, and, after an exchange of passwords, they were allowed onto Swiss soil. The first across the line was Captain Zimmer. Following him came Colonel Dollmann. Then, walking together, an SS adjutant, Sturmbannführer Wenner, accompanied a tall, bronzed, blue-eyed man with thin blond hair and a formidable hawklike nose.

This was Heinrich Himmler's senior representative in Italy and commander-in-chief of all SS forces, General Karl Wolff himself, come to talk surrender on neutral soil with Allen Dulles.

So far Allen Dulles had kept his negotiations with the Germans secret from everyone, including Washington. As he wrote later:

> An intelligence officer in the field is supposed to keep his home office informed of what he is doing. That is quite true, but with some reservations, as he may overdo it. If, for example, he tells too much or asks too often for instructions, he is likely to get some he doesn't relish, and, what is worse, he may well find headquarters trying to take over the whole conduct of the operation.

In any case, as he put it, he "had no desire to stir up exaggerated hopes in Washington that we were about to engineer a German surrender, or to create the impression that we were engaged in any kind of high-level negotiations requiring policy decisions in Washington."

But after several hours of conversation with General Wolff before a roaring log fire in the study of the Herrengasse apartment,* he decided that both the U.S. government and Allied Army Headquarters at Caserta, Italy, should be informed of the way the talks were going. For not only was General Wolff showing himself eager for a deal, but the proposals he made included further gestures to demonstrate the sincerity of his demand for a cessation of hostilities. He promised to issue a declaration, signed by all principal army officers in Italy, setting forth the uselessness of the struggle, and calling upon the army to dissociate itself from Hitler and Himmler, the declaration to be reinforced by radio and leaflet action to get the message to both soldiers and people.

In addition he said that just as he had released Parri and Usmiani to show his goodwill, he would now:

1. Discontinue active warfare against the Italian partisans;
2. Release to Switzerland several hundred Jews interned at Bolzano;
3. Assume full responsibility for the safety of 350 American and British POWs at Mantua, of whom 150 were in hospital and 200 in a camp on the outskirts of the town;
4. Facilitate the return to northern Italy of Italian officers in Germany who might be useful in keeping order during the post-hostility period.

Allen cabled details of Wolff's suggestions, and there was an immediate reaction from Allied Headquarters. Two high officers, one American (Major General Lyman L. Lemnitzer) and one British (Major General Terence S. Airey) flew in from Caserta to talk to General Wolff. He had gone back to Italy by the time they arrived, but he returned some days later, and they were at once impressed by his earnestness of purpose. They reported back to Caserta that they believed a deal could be made.

They also told Dulles that the operation had now been given a code name, SUNRISE, and that Moscow had been informed of Wolff's ap-

---

*"I have always tried to have important meetings around a fireplace," Allen wrote later. "There is some subtle influence in a wood fire which makes people feel at ease and less inhibited in their conversation; and if you are asked a question you are in no hurry to answer, you can stir up the fire and study the patterns the flames make until you have shaped your answer. If I needed more time to answer, I always had my pipe handy to fill and light."

proach and the fact that they were talking. Allen was delighted. He was glad Stalin had been informed, since he could not now be accused of having gone behind Russia's back in starting talks with the Germans in Italy. As for Allied Command at Caserta, there the atmosphere was joyful, optimistic. American, British, Canadian, and Polish troops were being marshaled ready for the last big push against the Nazi armies in northern Italy. It would be a battle fought over difficult terrain against desperate, well-positioned, highly trained soldiers. No one was looking forward to it, for it was estimated that Allied loss of life would be extremely heavy. If thousands of lives could be saved through SUNRISE, then let there be a benison on its chances of success.

But at this point things began to go wrong. In Germany, Heinrich Himmler got wind of Wolff's surrender moves, and threatened to arrest his wife and family and hold them hostage against Wolff's continued loyalty to the Führer. From Moscow, Stalin cabled a bitter message to Franklin D. Roosevelt accusing him and Winston Churchill of going behind Russia's back and trying to sign a separate peace with the Germans. The American President, by this time gravely ill, sent an appeasing message to Moscow. That was on the morning of April 12, 1945. It was his last communication with the Russian dictator.

For days Allen Dulles had been walking on air, convinced that he was on the brink of the greatest coup of his career. He had never felt fitter. All trace of gout seemed to have vanished from his system, and he was buoyed up by a sense of well-being.

On the night of April 12, he came into the apartment in the Herrengasse from a late dinner in the town to find a message awaiting him. Franklin D. Roosevelt was dead. Almost at once he felt an agonizing stab of pain in his left ankle. Next morning it was worse. All through the next few days, the pain grew and grew.

There had been some personal and domestic problems in the middle of the negotiations, but these he had managed with comparative ease. Clover was now with him. She had arrived from America by way of liberated France and erupted into his life at the beginning of the SUNRISE talks, but Mary Bancroft was swiftly on the scene to take over. She sized up Clover as a prime case for Jungian therapy and introduced her to one of the master's disciples, who began the first of many therapy sessions (which eventually lasted several years) in which he probed into the recesses of her mind for fears, faults, grievances, and resentments.

Clover was grateful. She was well aware of the close relationship between Mary Bancroft and her husband, but far from bearing any grudge or hatred toward the other woman, she established a close and loving rapport with her, and, in moments of crisis, clung to her.

But in the nature of things, Mary Bancroft could not always be there. She was an integral part of the OSS team and had work to do, contacts to meet, missions to prepare, reports to write. In between her therapy sessions, Allen Dulles could hardly confine Clover to the house. Nevertheless, he was extremely anxious that she should not wander off in her aimless fashion, to be picked up by some German or Italian agent, or by a newsman, and persuaded to talk about her husband's activities. He was by no means sure of her discretion. When Mary Bancroft was away, or otherwise engaged, he did his best to ensure that Clover was around where he could keep an eye on her.

At one point in the SUNRISE negotiations, an important meeting was arranged to which General Wolff and other German officers would be coming with new proposals. No word of the rendezvous must leak out, and so Gero von Gaevernitz fixed the conference at the house of his brother-in-law, on a large private estate overlooking the lake at Ascona, just across the frontier from Italy. Here they would be well sheltered from prying eyes.

Allen had told Clover nothing of the negotiations that were in progress, and she was unaware of the fact that he was having meetings with a higher officer of the Nazi armies. Nevertheless, he decided that he dare not risk leaving her behind in Berne on this occasion, particularly since she was in a very restless mood, and he finally decided to take her with him to Ascona. Frau Waibel, wife of the Swiss intelligence chief, was also asked along and the pretense was made that they were all off on a family outing.

They had only been in Ascona for a short time when a call came for Major Waibel to tell him that the Germans had arrived at the Swiss frontier and were on their way. Allen had decided that it would be dangerous if Clover caught sight of his visitors, so Frau Waibel was hastily summoned and told to take Mrs. Dulles out rowing on the lake, and to keep her out there until a signal came from the shore that it was safe to return.

Frau Waibel spoke only German, a language Clover did not speak at all, but the Swiss was a nice little friendly woman, and it was a pleasant, sunny day. They were helped into the rowing boat, and with Frau Waibel valiantly pulling on the oars, they set out across the lake. Everyone expected the meeting to be over in an hour, when the ladies would be recalled and they would all have a jolly al fresco lunch.

Unfortunately, General Wolff brought news of complications in the arrangements he had been making on the other side of the frontier, and plans had to be made, contingencies discussed. Instead of taking an hour, the meeting dragged on. Lunch and drinks were brought in and the discussions continued. Every so often Waibel glanced through the French windows of the big house to the lake, and noticed that the rowing boat had come close in to shore, looking for a sign; but then, seeing none, had swung round and made back toward the middle of the lake.

Two hours passed. The sun went in and a scud of wind and rain flurried the lake's surface. Waibel remembered that Clover had been dressed only in a pair of white tennis shorts and a shirt. He glanced across at Allen Dulles, and wondered whether to say something. But the American was absorbed in his deep discussions. The Swiss realized that he was not giving a moment's thought to his wife, and would not care to be reminded of her at this moment. Four hours. The sun came out again, hot now. There was no shade on the lake. Several times the rowing boat had come close to shore, but then, being a good Swiss wife, and seeing no sign, Frau Waibel had dutifully swung the boat around. Waibel wondered what the American woman was saying to her at such moments. It was just as well that his wife did not understand English.

It was not until nearly six hours later that the Germans finally departed. Waibel immediately ran on to the terrace to a pole facing the waterfront and hoisted the Swiss flag, signaling his wife to return. Almost immediately, the small boat turned for the shore.

As they came up the steps Frau Waibel, a sturdy, imperturbable woman, was smiling valiantly, but Clover was in tears and on the verge of collapse, her legs and arms red and blistered, her hair awry. She had been alternately chilled and sunburned, she was hungry and thirsty, and she was angry.

But the moment Allen Dulles saw her approaching, he rushed forward.

"What on earth kept you out there?" he asked reproachfully. And then, putting his arms around her in a loving embrace: "I missed you."

He had had a little trouble, too, with the Italians. Feruccio Parri, the partisan leader, was immensely grateful to Dulles for having secured his release and "broke into tears and flung his arms around me," he reported later. But the first thing the Italian asked was to be allowed to return to his partisan troops in northern Italy, and when Allen told him he must remain in Switzerland for the time being and tell no one he was there, he was immediately suspicious. Had Allen Dulles consented to do a deal with the Germans at the expense of the partisans, in order to secure his release? If so, he would rather renounce it. He did not wish to be free if it meant that the struggle against the Germans was to be halted. He would rather give himself up to the Gestapo and let the fight go on.

With some difficulty, Allen Dulles convinced him that his comrades were not being betrayed, and persuaded him to stay, along with Usmiani, in a Zurich medical clinic in the strictest secrecy. But when the negotiations dragged on, he brought Parri to Berne and installed him in the apartment in the Herrengasse. It was necessary to keep an eye on the Italian, too.

A few days later, Mrs. Wally Castelbarco arrived at the Herrengasse, and she was in great emotional distress. No one, of course, had been told of Parri's release, and so far as the Italian partisans were concerned he was still a prisoner of the Gestapo in Verona. Toscanini's daughter feared for him. If he was still alive, he must be going through hell at the hands of the Nazi beasts. She pleaded with Allen Dulles—in the name of their own close relationship—to do everything he could to get Parri rescued. Like some real-life Tosca, she beseeched him to help.

Should he tell her that Parri was safe, that he was, in fact, elsewhere in the very apartment where she was laying bare her heart, that if he opened two doors they could be reunited?

It did not even occur to Allen Dulles. He knew his priorities. As he wrote later, with the sangfroid of which he was eminently capable on occasion:

> The very day she came to me to beg me to do something to rescue Parri, he was in the next room. It was hard for me to keep a straight face as I assured my eloquent and persuasive visitor that I was doing everything I could to save her friend. Later when the war was over I had quite a time of it explaining my deception.

Mrs. Castelbarco left the Herrengasse still not knowing whether her beloved Parri was alive or dead.

Neither her distress nor Clover's worried Allen overmuch. He was far more concerned with what was happening to SUNRISE.

Mary Bancroft had told Allen Dulles that his gout was psychosomatic, and it was true that it came upon him mostly when he was deeply worried and great crises were looming. To that extent, his gout was precognitive, too, for it often hit him *before* rather than during or after an emergency, as if to warn him that disaster was approaching. He had been smitten with his latest (and worst) attack on April 12, 1945, the day that Franklin D. Roosevelt died. Eight days later, under the new presidency of Harry S Truman, the blow fell. On April 20 there arrived from Washington an urgent top-secret cable:

> JCS [Joint Chiefs of Staff] DIRECT THAT OSS BREAK OFF ALL CONTACT WITH GERMAN EMISSARIES AT ONCE. DULLES IS THEREFORE INSTRUCTED TO DISCONTINUE IMMEDIATELY ALL SUCH CONTACTS.
>
> CCS [Combined Chiefs of Staff] HAVE APPROVED MESSAGE TO [Field Marshal Sir Harold] ALEXANDER [Commander-in-Chief, Allied Forces in Italy] STATING THAT IT IS CLEAR TO THEM THAT GERMAN COMMANDER IN CHIEF IN ITALY DOES NOT INTEND TO SURRENDER HIS FORCES AT THIS TIME ON ACCEPTABLE TERMS. ACCORDINGLY, ESPECIALLY IN VIEW OF COMPLICATIONS WHICH HAVE ARISEN WITH THE RUSSIANS, THE U.S. AND BRITISH GOVERNMENTS HAVE DECIDED OSS SHOULD BREAK OFF CONTACTS; THAT JCS ARE SO INSTRUCTING OSS; THAT THE WHOLE MATTER IS TO BE REGARDED AS CLOSED AND THAT RUSSIANS BE INFORMED. . . .

It could not have come at a worse moment from the point of view of the SUNRISE negotiations. For, contrary to what the Combined Chiefs of Staff professed to believe, the Germans were now on the brink of surrendering without making any terms whatsoever. Allen Dulles had even planted an OSS radio operator inside SS headquarters in Milan, where, with the connivance of General Wolff, he would send and receive messages.* The Nazi gauleiter of the Tyrol, Franz Hofer, had expressed willingness to hand over his administration to the Allies. Other high officers were falling into line.

Why had Truman ordered the Combined Chiefs of Staff to break things off at such a vital moment, just before the dreaded last battle was due to begin, when so many lives could be saved? Could it be sabotage? A report had reached him that the German High Command in Milan had been approached by a mysterious officer in British army uniform, who urged them to ignore SUNRISE and begin direct negotiations with the British authorities. But when Allen Dulles queried this, the British were able to show that they were working in closest cooperation with the Americans, and knew nothing of the strange emissary. Could he have been a Russian agent in disguise, seeking to disrupt the negotiations and trying to drive a wedge between the United States and Great Britain?

On the morning of April 23, 1945, the telephone rang in the Herrengasse. It was Waibel, the Swiss intelligence officer, on the line.

"He had astounding news," Allen Dulles recalled later.

> General Wolff, his adjutant, Major Wenner, and one of Vietinghoff's high staff officers, Lt. Col. Viktor von Schweinitz, were on their way to Switzerland.** They were coming to surrender . . . Wolff and Schweinitz were ready to go to Caserta immediately to arrange for the capitulation of all the German forces, Wehrmacht and SS, in North Italy. They proposed an immediate meeting with me in Lucerne to arrange the details of the trip to Allied headquarters. And I was under the strictest military orders to have no dealings with them!

Allen, by this time racked by his madly painful bout of gout, which had now crept up his left leg from the ankle to the knee, sent an SOS to Allied Headquarters. Would they get him off the hook and allow him to continue talking? Caserta in turn signaled Washington. But Truman, less than two weeks in office, was stumbling in the dark. During

---

*He was a private in the Free Czech Army who, like many of his comrades, had adopted a nom-de-guerre to protect his relatives at home. He was known as Wally.

**General Heinrich von Vietinghoff was Commander-in-Chief, German Army Group C, in Italy.

his time as Vice-President to Roosevelt, he had been deliberately kept away from all details of U.S. secret operations. He had been given no background briefings. It was impossible for him to catch up in so short a period with all the underground operations that had been taking place. He was desperately afraid of putting a foot wrong, especially with Josef Stalin, and, as a result, was determined to take no chances which might fatally damage postwar relations with the USSR. He refused to allow the Joint Chiefs to rescue Dulles from his dilemma.

All they could do was suggest to him that perhaps the Swiss might like to take a hand instead, and conduct the negotiations for him, keeping him in touch with what was going on. Allen Dulles hit the roof when he was handed the suggestion, and snapped several of his pipes in two in his gout-fired rage. But eventually he called Waibel and passed on the suggestion. The Swiss intelligence officer knew full well that his government would never consent to breach its determined neutrality by engaging in peace negotiations on behalf of one of the belligerents. He would be in trouble himself for even listening to such a proposal. On the other hand, he had grown close to Allen Dulles, his heart was in the peace negotiations, and he dearly wanted to see an end to the costly and increasingly cruel and bloodthirsty war in north Italy.

He agreed to meet the Germans and start the talks, without revealing to them that Dulles was forbidden to see them or deal with them. It was a droll situation, one to make the Swiss government blench with horror had they known about it.

While Waibel sounded out the German emissaries, Allen made his painful way to Lucerne. By the time he reached there, the pain from his gout was practically insupportable. He had never known such agony. Even the famous Dulles capacity for endurance was tried beyond its limits, and the flashes of pain in his ankle and knee were now so distracting that they prevented him from thinking calmly about the crisis with which he was confronted. Gaevernitz, who had accompanied his chief and was suffering mentally with him, could finally bear it no longer and took it upon himself to call in a doctor. The doctor made some tests, then injected Allen with a heavy dose of morphine. It deadened the pain but did nothing to lull his growing sense of unease.

For one thing, the Germans were beginning to panic. They were increasingly suspicious of Allen Dulles's absence, and suspected they had walked into an Allied trap. Meanwhile, in Italy the Allies had launched their big push against the German lines, and had won a heavy slogging match south of the River Po and around Bologna. Wolff questioned whether he was being held in Switzerland because the Allies wanted him away from his troops during the battle. But if the push was really on and there were no longer any hopes of a peaceful surrender, then he must get back—and not just for the sake of the German troops. He pointed out that Hitler had given an order for the destruction of all the great industrial complexes in north Italy, as well as the port installations at Genoa, and it would be carried out once the German armies were forced to retreat. Only he and General Vietinghoff could prevent it.

All this Waibel conveyed to Allen Dulles in his hideout in Lucerne. In turn, he sent repeated messages to Caserta asking for guidance.

"Two more days passed and there were still no instructions from Washington or Caserta," Allen reported later. "Time was running out. Every few hours the impatient German envoys at Waibel's villa would inquire whether we had any word. Probably never in all history had plenipotentiaries, desiring to surrender a great army, received so strange a reception."

On April 25, 1945, General Wolff decided he could wait no longer, and took the train from Lucerne back to the Italian frontier. On April 27, Truman got a grip on himself, and reversed his preceding order. He instructed Alexander to send a plane to pick up the German envoys and bring them to Caserta to sign the surrender. A Russian representative would be invited to witness the ceremony.

It was too late to intercept Wolff, but at noon on April 28 Field Marshal Alexander's plane arrived at Annecy—just over the Swiss border in France—picked up two of the Germans, Major Wenner and Colonel Schweinitz, and flew them to Caserta. By this time they also carried authority to surrender the Italian Fascist armies in Italy as well. And Wolff, back in Italy, was seeing that his troops committed no acts of sabotage while waiting to hand over their arms.

There was many an incident between the signing in Caserta and the return of peace to the Italian north, but to all intents and purposes it was over.

Allen Dulles had been invited to Caserta as an honored guest, to see the last act performed in what had been a fraught and intensely dramatic operation. He refused the invitation, on the grounds that "my presence at the surrender ceremony might well have been discovered by the press and have blown the security of the operation we had so carefully preserved up to this point." In fact, he did not go because he did not relish the thought of having to hobble on his gouty leg (or be carried) into the signing chamber.

And that was a curious thing. The moment the plane took off for Caserta with the German envoys, and news of their departure was signaled to Allen Dulles back in Berne, something seemed to happen to him. He had been without morphine for more than twelve hours, but the pain did not come back. He stood up and found he could walk without limping. The attack was over.

And so was Operation SUNRISE. Though no thanks to Harry S Truman or Josef Stalin.

CHAPTER TWELVE

"Lucky Rear"

John Foster Dulles was fifty-seven when World War II ended in 1945, and he had still not reached the status achieved by his grandfather and his uncle, both of whom had been Secretaries of State well before that age. It was disappointing, but he was a man of patience and conviction, and his eyes, heart, and mind were focused on 1948, the year he believed would see the fulfillment of his ambitions, or at least part of them.

He was still a pillar of the Republican Party—as he always would be —and his political wagon was firmly hitched to the future of Thomas E. Dewey, the party's favored candidate for the next presidential election. Could there be any doubt that he would win? This time he would be fighting not against an incumbent President cunningly cashing in on the wartime sentiments of the people, but against a nonentity who was in danger of making a fumbling mess of the problems of the peace. No one, least of all Roosevelt, would have chosen him as Vice-President had they imagined that Harry S Truman would ever succeed to the highest office in the land. Like many another contemptuous member of the GOP, Foster Dulles often referred to Truman as "that shirt salesman from Kansas City,"* and feared for the future of the nation and the postwar world if they remained in his hands. Fortunately, that was extremely unlikely. The year 1948 would, he was sure, see the United States back in the hands of experienced statesmen, and the affairs of the world under the control of one who understood its problems.

*Later on, Truman sarcastically called Foster Dulles "that fella from Wall Street."

189

In the meantime, it could hardly be said that Foster Dulles was at loose ends or frustrated. If he was not yet a popular or recognizable personality in the United States, he was certainly known and respected by his peers for his wisdom, sagacity, and political know-how. He remained senior partner of Sullivan & Cromwell and was consulted on all its cases. He was head of the Carnegie Endowment for International Peace, a trustee of the Rockefeller Foundation and of the Union Theological Seminary. He was also a delegate to most of the major conferences which now began in Moscow, London, and Paris as the Allies set out to reshape the postwar world. Under the Roosevelt administration, the President, aware of his need for congressional backing for his postwar plans, had reluctantly agreed to a measure of bipartisanship in the conduct of foreign affairs. In return for their congressional support, the Republicans were to be consulted on major decisions and given a place at the meetings of the big powers.

It gave no pleasure whatsoever to Roosevelt when the GOP nominated John Foster Dulles as its foreign policy spokesman, and one of the President's last acts before he died was to try to prevent Dulles from having a place at the San Francisco Conference which brought the United Nations into being. Senator Vandenberg and his old friend, Bernard Baruch, persuaded him to put his personal antipathies aside, and the President finally agreed to endorse Foster Dulles's appointment. He recognized an ultimatum even when it was sugar-coated, and he gave in, but it left a sour taste.

Some of the Democratic representatives at San Francisco were soon experiencing a similar distaste, for they had their first experience of what would soon be recognized as a most effective ploy of John Foster Dulles at major conferences. He turned out to be a prime manipulator of the press, and an expert leaker of news calculated to redound to his own credit and that of his party.

The two official spokesmen of the U.S. Delegation were Adlai Stevenson and Edward Stettinius. At a formal meeting of all their members, they had agreed not in any circumstances to leak to the press anything about what was going on behind the scenes during the creation of the United Nations, but to wait until concrete decisions had been made. Foster voted for this decision.

"But every day," a member of the delegation said later, "Foster would go out into the corridors of the St. Francis Hotel, where the

190

delegation was staying, and would meet newspapermen and leak to them details of what had been discussed during the day. But he would always leak it from a Republican slant, and lay emphasis on his own constructive part in the discussions. This used to infuriate the Democrats, and particularly Adlai Stevenson, who complained very bitterly about it."

The delegate added, cynically: "They had not yet learned what others subsequently did, that whenever you had Foster in on bipartisan policy, you had to have a Democrat with a Democratic leak to counterbalance the Republican leak which Foster would already have made, otherwise you would be cheated out of the next day's headline."

When James R. Byrnes was appointed Secretary of State by President Truman, Foster hardly needed to leak his views. He simply leaned on the Secretary and pressured him into accepting his standpoint. Byrnes, one of the more mediocre appointments of the Truman administration, had little or no experience of foreign affairs and was naïve in his dealings with the Russians. He was also extremely anxious to come back from his first big challenge as Secretary with some sort of an agreement. This was the foreign ministers' meeting in London in 1945, at which Byrnes, Molotov, Bevin, and Bidault were the chief representatives.

After three weeks of often acrimonious discussion, the Russians proved adamant in pressing their policies. One day Byrnes called Foster Dulles to his room and said: "Well, pardner, we've pushed these babies about as far as they'll go, and I think we'd better start thinking about a compromise."

Foster, who hated being called "pardner" by a man with whom he had most reluctantly joined forces, icily replied that if such was his view, "I feel compelled as a bipartisan representative of this delegation to go back to Washington on the first plane out and make a public pronouncement on the radio to the country of my views of what I consider to be a disastrous move on your part." In the strongest language, he made it clear that a complete break was better than any compromise.

Byrnes took the hint from him and stood firm. The assembled newsmen did not need to be told why.

Under the aegis of Secretary of State George C. Marshall, appointed to succeed Byrnes in 1946, the situation was somewhat different. Foster had genuinely admired General Marshall's performance during World War II and thought him one of the giants of the wartime administration, a master military strategist. The two men met for the first time in Berlin just before the Moscow Conference of 1947, at which an attempt would be made to forge an agreement over Germany with the Russians and iron out a peace treaty with Austria. Eleanor Dulles had been called to Berlin by her brother to brief him privately on the Austrian situation, and they met at the U.S. guesthouse overlooking the lake, the Wannsee, on the edge of the city.

What Eleanor did not know until she got there was that Secretary Marshall was also expected. General Marshall wanted to get Dulles's views on the world situation before the Moscow Conference began, and had made the gesture of fixing a private meeting. Was it a measure of his admiration for Foster Dulles's qualities as a foreign policy expert, or was it the polite deference of a man who believed (as did so many others at the time) that Dulles would be Secretary of State himself under Dewey after the next election?

Eleanor was struck by the contrast between the two men. Foster seemed to dwarf the general, his broad, slightly hunched shoulders towering over him as they strolled along the verandah overlooking the Wannsee.

"It was late afternoon and the sun was setting on the lake," Eleanor said later. "I remember Foster and I were having tea and highballs. . . . We were talking when Marshall was announced. I stayed a little, then left. I always have a vision of the two men standing together. It was interesting to me. Here were two great figures from American life, and I could see that they were both scared of each other, both nervous of the encounter. I felt it very definitely in Foster and I felt it a little bit in Marshall."

Marshall was a man with whom few (if any) dared to become intimate. Even President Truman always called him "General Marshall," never "George," and always remained somewhat in awe of him. But in Foster Dulles's case, the awe, if any, diminished as he saw him at work as Secretary. The two men had obviously measured each other up, and after this first encounter they always afterwards treated each other with great circumspection. Once they got to Moscow, Marshall's deference to Dulles was noticed by all the delegates, and resented by some, and Foster Dulles in turn went out of his way never to give the

192

Secretary a moment's embarrassment. But he closely studied Marshall's methods of dealing with the Russians, and though he never said so until he got home (and then only in private), he was severely critical of them. He felt that General Marshall lacked background, suppleness, and inspiration in his dealings with the Soviet government, and that nothing in his military experience had equipped him for the elaborate poker-cum-chess games which negotiations with the Russians inevitably became. He never let a word or hint of his feelings come out either in Moscow or when he got home. But he confided to his brother and sister that "Marshall will certainly never go down in history as one of the great Secretaries." That opinion was more than confirmed by his subsequent experiences.

But if he respected his chief and even praised him while he was in Moscow, Foster was less gentle with other members of the delegation, nor did he by any means abandon leaking as a means of getting his name in the newspapers. The American delegation to the Moscow Conference included some considerable talents among its members, such as General Lucius Clay, military governor of the U.S. Zone in Germany; General Mark Clark, U.S. military governor of Austria; Robert C. Murphy; General Walter Bedell Smith, the U.S. ambassador to the USSR; Ben Cohen; and a brilliant Russian expert, Charles (Chip) Bohlen, as spokesman. Plus, of course, John Foster Dulles.

Arrangements for the conference were chaotic. There was no adequate room at the U.S. Embassy for all the delegates and their staff. Stenographic help was scarce, and desks had to be set up in the billiard alley and any odd corner. The Russians organized the meetings in large windy ballrooms, and liked to meet very late at night, with much vodka and caviare. As for the American delegates themselves, "There were a lot of prima donnas there, squabbling around Secretary Marshall for attention," one delegate* remembers. "Most heated was General Clay, who kept clashing with General Mark Clark."

General Mark Clark was, in the meantime, feuding with Foster Dulles, and soon he was not the only one.

Each day, after the sessions with the Russians, Chip Bohlen would foregather with Secretary Marshall to iron out exactly what should be said to the newsmen at the evening press conference. Foster Dulles,

*Ambassador H. Freeman Matthews.

however, did not feel any confidence in Bohlen's talents and believed that his own viewpoint on what was going on should be known to the newsmen, because only then, he considered, could some sense be brought out of the contention and confusion.

"Every day Foster Dulles would give a conference which clashed with the official one given by Chip Bohlen," Matthews said. "This dual press conference caused confusion. Mr. Dulles would have one viewpoint which he would express and Bohlen would have another. This caused some amusement, some irritation. It was irregular to hold a separate press conference and it was done without agreement. Chip was rather irritated by the unauthorized competition."

He complained to Marshall, but the Secretary refused to challenge Dulles's right to give his views to the correspondents. In any case, he had nothing personal to complain about. If Foster Dulles always slanted his news to give his own part in the discussions due (and often, in Bohlen's view, undue) weight, he also never failed to praise the brilliance and steadfastness of his chief.

Mark Clark was particularly furious, because Foster often expounded upon Austrian problems, which were his bailiwick. He knew Eleanor had been up to Berlin to talk to Foster, and had evidently primed him. He called his staff together and told them that if any one of them even said so much as a word to Dulles, they would be sent home at once.

Most of the other delegates simply shrugged their shoulders fatalistically at Dulles's ploys, but the U.S. ambassador, General Walter Bedell Smith, watching it all from the sidelines, could not resist taking a rise out of the bipartisan delegate one day. He gave an official lunch to the U.S. Delegation, at which talk at the table turned to the antics of the terrible Vishinski, the Russian delegate, who was at his brilliantly infuriating best during the conference, his verbosity pouring out like ectoplasm, able to switch from vitriol to honey with the turn of a phrase or the wave of a hand.

One of the lunch guests wondered aloud what position Vishinski would have had if he had lived and worked in the United States.

"Why," said Bedell Smith, "there's no doubt about it. He would have been senior partner at Sullivan and Cromwell."

Everybody turned to look at Foster Dulles. He laughed, "but with a slightly pained look," the delegate recalled.

It was the first but certainly not the last time that Chip Bohlen and the Democratic Party were upstaged at important conferences by the mental agility, dexterous maneuvring, and sheer guile of their redoubtable Republican colleague. Paul Nitze (a Democrat and a State Department adviser) remembers another big power meeting with the Russians, in 1948–49, after the crisis over Berlin and the Russian blockade of the Free City. The Russians had stipulated that there must be a four power consultation as the price for their lifting the blockade, and the Allies agreed.

"We had an initial staff conference in Paris [in December 1948] to prepare for that Palais Rose conference," Nitze said. "Chip Bohlen was masterminding the political aspects of it. I was masterminding the economic aspects of it. . . . And at the first staff meeting Chip was asked to brief the entire group—there were about twenty of us, I guess— about the political aspects and I to brief them on the economic aspects of the problem."

When they had finished, comments were asked for. The only delegate who spoke up was Foster Dulles.

"Foster said he deeply disagreed with what we had to say, and he asked the minutes to record that the positions we were advocating were excessively tough and did not sufficiently take into account the interests of the Soviet Union. Our chief at the table, Dean Acheson, said: 'Of course, Foster, if you would like to have the minutes so read, we will see that they are so read.' And then we went in to the initial session with the Russians."

On this occasion too Vishinski was the chief Russian delegate. Ernest Bevin represented Great Britain, Robert Schuman, France, and Dean Acheson was there for the United States.

"On the first go-around," said Nitze, "it became clear that Ernie Bevin wanted to take the middle position between the U.S. and the Soviet position. Schuman leaned more to supporting Acheson but didn't want to get out too far in that direction. Then Vishinski made his presentation. That presentation was completely outrageous."

The moment the delegates got down to discussing arrangements for Berlin, the Russian insisted that the Soviet Union have a veto on all personnel appointments in the city. *All appointments?* Bevin asked, incredulously. *All,* said Vishinski, with finality. *Even the appointment of a guard at the Fine Arts Museum?* asked Bevin. *Even that,* said the Russian.

Otherwise, the Germans might try to appoint some dreadful person like Mayor Reuther.

"At that point, Bevin got really annoyed," said Nitze, "and said he couldn't see how we could work anything out if the Russians insisted on having a veto on everything, including the most minute personnel appointments. So he switched sides and became as adamant as Acheson, and Ernie was wholly on Acheson's side from that moment on."

Foster Dulles had, of course, been sitting in on all these exchanges, and the expression on his face must have been something to see. After the conference was over, he approached Dean Acheson.

"Dean, do you remember my request that the minutes record my dissent from the Bohlen-Nitze briefing?"

"Yes," said Acheson, "and it was so done."

"Well," said Dulles, "I'd like to have that excised."

His objections were expunged from the record.

But it didn't end there. When the delegation got back to Washington, there was an article in *The New York Times* by its Washington correspondent, James (Scotty) Reston, in which Reston stressed that it had been John Foster Dulles who had put backbone into the U.S. Delegation. If it hadn't been for his presence, Reston maintained, the administration would have taken a very wishy-washy attitude toward the Russians. But Dulles's consistent firmness had saved the day.

Scotty Reston was Paul Nitze's next-door neighbor in Washington. When next they saw each other over the garden hedge, Nitze said: "For God's sake, Scotty, where on earth did you get that nonsense?"

Scotty replied: "Where else? When Dulles got back to New York from the Palais Rose conference, he called some of us and gave us a press briefing about it. Off the record, of course. This was Foster's version of exactly how it went."

But Foster Dulles's attendance at these postwar conferences was not simply to keep his name before press, politicians, and public. He was watching and learning about the Russians, about America's Allies, about the behavior around the table of his colleagues and their adversaries, squirreling up the knowledge against the day when he too would lead a delegation to a big power meeting.

"At some of those long encounters with the Soviets, full of wind and rain and very little sunshine," one delegate recalled, "it was sometimes hard to keep up your concentration. But not even the most boring session ever caught Foster napping. He sat there, a huge bear of a man, absolutely still except for those flinty eyes darting from one to the other as they spoke, or reacted. You were always conscious of his presence."

That he was indeed missing nothing became apparent later on, when, during one of the despondent sloughs in his career, Foster wrote an account of his observations of the international scene in the first few years after the end of the war. Published under the title *War or Peace* in 1950,* it contained some shrewd portraits of the protagonists and a neat gift for setting a scene. As for instance a Kremlin dinner during the 1947 conference in Russia:

> Mr. Molotov gave a welcoming dinner in honor of the other delegates. He sat in the middle of a narrow table. At his right sat Mr. Bevin (the British delegate), and at his left Secretary Marshall. Immediately opposite him sat Mr. Bidault (the French delegate). The attitude of Mr. Molotov toward Mr. Bevin and Secretary Marshall was formally correct. Toward Mr. Bidault he was effusive. Mr. Bidault responded in kind. They repeatedly toasted each other. They leaned nearer and nearer, until it almost seemed that they would fall into each other's arms. That typified French-Soviet relations as the conference began.

Of Ernest Bevin, he wrote a description which his British colleagues recognized as accurate and felicitous:

> Mr. Bevin was bluff and hearty, easily angered and quickly repentant of his anger. Mr. Molotov treated him as a banderillo treats a bull, planting darts that would arouse him to an outburst—from which he rapidly reacted in a manner implying a tendency to make concessions.

And of Molotov:

> [He] conducted himself with an adroitness which has seldom been equalled in diplomacy. [It was] a remarkable performance. His techniques, different in each case, were carried out with extraordinary skill. I have seen in action all the great international statesmen of this century, beginning with those who met at the Hague Peace Conference of 1907. I have never seen personal diplomatic skill at so high a degree of perfection as Mr. Molotov's at that session.

*It was reissued in 1957.

Foster relished the prospect of one day crossing swords with him.

The Moscow Conference of 1947 was an important way station in Foster Dulles's road to an understanding of the policies and plans of Stalinist Russia. It was his first real encounter with the intransigence of Stalinism, and with the unswerving determination of the Soviet government to remake the world in its own image; but it would be another year or more before he fully understood the implications of the Russian attitude. He wrote of the 1947 conference:

> To those of us who were there [it was] like a streak of lightning that suddenly illumined a dark and stormy scene. We saw as never before the magnitude of the task of saving Europe for Western civilization. We saw the need of economic and moral support and the need of a program that would be both comprehensive and creative.

For a time he would continue to insist that an accommodation with Russia was possible, and maintain that American policy was too maladroit. When George Marshall, flying home from Moscow, conceived the idea of the aid plan which subsequently bore his name, Foster Dulles was one of the first to support it. Credit for putting it into a form that would be acceptable to Congress goes, of course, to Senator Arthur H. Vandenberg, then chairman of the Foreign Relations Committee, who rewrote the legislation and worked unremittingly to get it past the House. There are those who believe that the great scheme which did so much to save the world from starvation in the grim period after World War II could have been better named the Vandenberg Plan than the Marshall Plan.

Foster believed that the British Foreign Secretary, Ernest Bevin, a solid, downright trade union and Labor Party leader, also deserved the highest praise for getting the Plan to work in Europe, and in later years gave him more credit for its success than Marshall himself.

"Foster always gave the principal credit for the Marshall Plan to Ernie Bevin," Eleanor Dulles said later. "Secretary Marshall threw a wild forward pass, and Bevin grabbed it out of the empty air and ran with it."

It was Bevin who suggested that the aid from the Marshall Plan should be extended across the board to all nations which had been involved in the war and had suffered from its ravages, the defeated as well as the victorious, and that it should be open to the Soviet Union and its satellites too. This was reluctantly accepted by Vandenberg, who knew how difficult it was going to be to persuade Congress to send money and supplies to the Soviet bloc; but Foster Dulles enthusiastically supported Bevin and promised to back up Vandenberg by lobbying his fellow Republicans, arguing that an aid program would considerably soften the rigidity of the Russians.

He was considerably shocked when Stalin not only refused to have any part of the Plan but forbade his east European satellites to participate in it. It was Foster's second experience (the first had been in Moscow itself) of Soviet hostility and stubbornness, and, like Bevin, he did not quite understand it. Why was Stalin refusing such a munificent goodwill offer? Why was he so suspicious of American intentions?

Foster Dulles was still convinced that the Russians could be reasoned with, on other things, perhaps, even if they were determined to look the Marshall Plan gift horse in the mouth. It was only slowly that he began changing his mind about them, and for at least another year he went on considering them rather like protagonists in one of his court cases, to be bested or convinced by argument and maneuvered into a reasonable settlement. It was not until the Palais Rose Conference of 1949—when even Bevin, who had been brought up to think of the Russians as the saviours of the working class, was repeatedly and brutally snubbed—that he became resigned to the fact that there was something baleful about Stalinism, and realized that the Kremlin's basic ill will, its morose determination to repulse every gesture and avoid concluding even just and equitable settlements, turned goodwill gestures from the United States into signs of weakness.

"He did not want to be anti-Soviet," his sister maintained. "It was the Soviets who made him so."

The growing doubts Foster had formed about the qualities of General George C. Marshall as Secretary of State, as he had watched him at work in Moscow and London, were confirmed in the fall of 1948 when a U.S. Delegation arrived in Paris for a session of the newly formed United Nations. The General Assembly was to meet in the Palais de Chaillot. Two items on the agenda were of particular importance to the United States, and both of them concerned the new State of Israel. The first was a proposal that the so-called Bernadotte Plan for the partition of the old state of Palestine into an Israeli and an Arab sector should be accepted by the Assembly.

The Bernadotte Plan had been drawn up by the United Nations envoy to Palestine, Count Folk Bernadotte, a Swede, and the Israelis, fresh from a victory in their war of independence, did not like it at all. It laid down boundaries for their new nation far narrower than those they had won in battle, and would award them frontiers, they believed, that would expose them to constant danger of attack and partition by their Arab neighbors.

The other proposal was to vote on Israel's formal application for admission to the United Nations.

Secretary Marshall led the U.S. Delegation. Foster Dulles had been appointed his deputy, an appointment made not simply because he was the Republican Party's bipartisan representative but because the 1948 presidential election was now drawing near, and if it went the way everyone (except Truman) thought it would, Foster would be Secretary of State in the new Republican administration. The other delegates were Eleanor Roosevelt, FDR's widow; Ben Cohen, an old legal adviser to the Roosevelt administration; and a young Democratic lawyer from Georgia, Dean Rusk.

To Foster's astonishment, when the U.S. Delegation met privately to discuss their attitude at the General Assembly, Secretary Marshall made it clear that he was (a) in favor of accepting the Bernadotte Plan for the partition of Palestine, and (b) against the immediate admission of Israel to United Nations membership. Foster intervened at once and argued long and eloquently against both these decisions. He pointed out that Israel had just fought and won, against mighty odds, a war of independence which had not only demonstrated the moral and spiritual strength of the Israeli people but had amply proved their right to have a country of their own, and one, moreover, whose borders should be viable and safe from attack.

Eleanor Roosevelt spoke up to say that Foster Dulles had her full support; she was followed by Ben Cohen, with a reinforcement of the argument for a rejection of the Bernadotte Plan and the support of Israeli entry into the United Nations. But then came Dean Rusk to stress his entire agreement with Marshall. His strong advocacy of a policy of extreme caution toward Israel was backed by a succession of statements from service members of the delegation, all of whom were pro-Bernadotte and lukewarm toward the Israeli state.

It was thereupon agreed that U.S. policy would follow the lines suggested by Secretary Marshall, and future meetings were scheduled to discuss ways and means of carrying it out. Foster Dulles was so convinced that the wrong decisions had been taken that, he later confessed, he did not even bother to attend many of these working meetings.

The Israeli chances of getting the votes they wanted looked dim. They were certainly not brightened when news reached Paris from Tel Aviv that Count Bernadotte had been assassinated by Irgun terrorists. When the Assembly met for the opening ceremonies in the Palais de Chaillot, the Swedish delegation filed in dressed in black. Everyone turned to look at the gallery where Abba Eban and Moshe Shertok (later Sharett), the Israeli representatives, were sitting. Black was the color of their prospects, too.

And then the wind suddenly changed. For some days there had been rumblings from Germany about a crisis with the Russians over access to Berlin, and now the emergency had come. Berlin was blockaded. Secretary Marshall was called urgently back to Washington. John Foster Dulles immediately found himself in command of the U.S. Delegation.

The downcast Israelis, who had been tipped off about the hard-line U.S. policy toward them favored by Marshall, revived and at once asked for an interview with Dulles. He saw Eban and Shertok in his suite at the Hotel Crillon and made it clear to them that he fully sympathized with Israel's desire to work out her own destiny. He explained that he was in a difficult, not to say ambivalent, position because Truman had appointed him deputy to what was a Democratic delegation, even though he was adviser to the Republican candidate at the forthcoming election. But he assured them that he would do his best to *influence* the delegation to take the right steps to aid Israel gain the independent status and respect she had so richly earned.

He did too. Israeli historians have no doubt whatsoever that it was mainly due to John Foster Dulles's influence on the delegation he now headed and U.S. pressure on other delegations that the Bernadotte Plan was defeated in the General Assembly and Israel's membership in the United Nations eventually confirmed. His attitude toward Israel was to harden in the years to come, but the help he gave the new nation at a critical moment in its development has never been forgotten.

During one of the early London conferences, in 1947, Foster was reunited with his son, Avery, whom he had not seen since the young man had gone off to join the Navy halfway through World War II. Now he was personnel officer with the Mediterranean Fleet in Naples.

"I suddenly got a cable from COMNAVEU [Commander of Naval Forces, Europe] in London to report there at once for temporary duty," Avery recalled later. "That was all it said. I was worried that I was about to be reprimanded because I'd done something wrong in my work as personnel officer, and I could not figure out what papers I should take with me."

When he reached London on a three-day pass, he discovered that he had to report to the Conference of Foreign Ministers.

"My father had gotten word to the naval people that he'd like to see me, and they had brought me to London for several days. I stayed at Claridges with my parents. I met Averill Harriman, who was our ambassador at the time, but I didn't meet Bevin, alas, because I knew he was always a great support to my father."

During their reunion, short though it was, Foster tried to see as much as he could of his son by taking him to all the opening meetings and all the receptions. At Claridges he introduced Avery to that redoubtable American, Lady Astor, who promptly said: "Do you mean you came all the way from Naples and you didn't bring any fruit with you?"

"I didn't realize you were short of fresh fruit," Avery said.

"That's the trouble with you Americans," Lady Astor retorted, sharply. "They feed you so well, you never find out how the ordinary people live. We haven't seen oranges around here for years."

Foster was so evidently happy at seeing his son again and was obviously so deeply involved in the proceedings of the conference that Avery did not have the heart to tell him that he was on the verge of taking a vital decision, one likely to make a convulsive change in his life style.

Four years earlier, in 1941, while still in law school at Harvard, Avery had taken the decision to become a Roman Catholic.

"I wrote home that I was going to do this," he said later. "I think they were surprised. The background was very Protestant, you know. My father's father had been a Presbyterian minister and theology professor. So my parents called me and asked me to come down to New York and talk about it, and I did. I took the train down, and we talked about it for a whole evening, but there wasn't much to be said."

Foster had tried hard to understand, Janet (one suspects) less so. It was a matter of religious feeling, Avery thought. He confessed that he never really knew whether his mother had any religious feelings, though he said later that he doubted it.

"She was reticent in the extreme, anyway," he said. "She maintained a church membership but she never gave any indications of a strong religious faith."

So for her Avery's decision to espouse Roman Catholicism was perhaps more cataclysmic than it was for Foster, "whose piety was very simple but very solid." He had "got used to the idea as time went on," and by the time he met his son in London he seemed completely reconciled to his different religion.

But what would he say to Avery's new decision? Avery had decided to take his conversion one step further, and become a priest of the Church. It meant the shattering of his father's last hope that one of his sons would one day follow in his footsteps, become a lawyer and maybe a statesman, and found a Dulles dynasty. He had long since given up his other son, John, who had cut away from the family and dropped out of college.* Now the cleverest and keenest of his brood was taking a step that would end all the worldly ambitions his father cherished for him.

This was no moment to shatter his illusions. Avery decided to keep his decision to himself until a more appropriate point, when his father would have the time to consider it and accept it with goodwill. He admired, loved, and respected his father and was anxious to have his understanding, unwilling to cause him distress at a moment of pressure. So father and son enjoyed three days together with nothing contentious or disturbing to come between them—except, of course, the abortive four power conference, for which Foster had to keep breaking away every now and then.

*In fact, John had dropped out of college because he hated studying law. But later, when he found an interest in engineering, he went back—to Arizona this time—and took his degree. He subsequently became a successful mining engineer.

*   *   *

By a strange coincidence, at the same time that Foster was seeing his son again in London, Eleanor was having her own reunion with her two children. The meeting took place in Switzerland, and it was even more joyful because, until a short time before they met, Eleanor did not know whether her son and daughter were in America or Europe, sick or well, happy or miserable.

David Dulles was ten years old, and his stepsister, Ann, was seven when their mother decided, in 1945, that she just had to get involved in the remolding of postwar Europe. Aside from sitting on the German Committee, Eleanor Dulles had had a frustrating war in Washington. It had been spent working for exacting bosses in the State Department and the Department of Commerce, and she was exasperated with carrying out tasks which she considered well beneath her capabilities. It was a moment when the role of women in American government was developing rapidly because of the war, but the State Department in general and her chiefs in particular did not seem to have heard about it. The State Department was still predominantly, proudly masculine, and at least one of her superiors—though a brilliant administrator—was a bullying and unrepentant male chauvinist pig. She was still as ambitious as ever, and still dreamed of having a department, or an ambassadorship, before she was too much older; but she was also well aware that she was never going to get anywhere so long as she remained in her present job.

Then one day the telephone rang and a voice said: "How would you like to go to Vienna?"

It was Jacob Erhard. A Brooklyn-born Foreign Service officer, who had once served as U.S. consul in Hamburg and as an attaché under Ambassador Joseph Kennedy in London, Erhard had just been appointed political adviser to the U.S. military delegation to Austria. General Mark Clark would be the American representative on the Four Power Occupation Commission, and it would be Erhard's job to keep him on the right lines when dealing with the Austrians, the Allies, and particularly the Russians.

It turned out that Erhard had been dining with a professor at Princeton and lamenting his inability to find a good, fresh-minded economist to join him as a financial expert on Austrian problems, and the professor said: "Why don't you get that gal who wrote *The French Franc*? She knows all about sticky postwar problems."

Now he was offering Eleanor Dulles the job, and she grabbed it with both hands. She rented her house. She warned the children that she was taking them out of school. Then she went to Ruth Shipley at the Passport Office and asked for passports for herself, for David, and for Ann.

The formidable Mrs. Shipley looked at her as if she was mad and said: "Nothing doing, Mrs. Dulles. You can't take the children with you."

"I'm not going without my children," Eleanor said.

"Then you're not going," said Mrs. Shipley.

That was in February 1945. For the next six weeks, Eleanor Dulles pulled every string she knew in an effort to wrest passports for her children out of Mrs. Shipley's office. But to no avail.

"She was a tartar and a despot," Eleanor said later. "It was a harrowing experience. We were booked six times on the ship for Lisbon. We would be all dressed up and packed, and waiting in the house, and the people in the Passport Office would telephone and say, 'We'll let you know the moment she changes her mind.' We'd go off to the station and call them, and they would say: 'It hasn't come through.' So we'd go back and unpack, and the children would go back to school."

Mrs. Shipley had a point. A devastating war was just ending. Nobody was taking children to Europe. But then, Eleanor wasn't nobody. She was a Dulles—and the Dulleses broke the rules.

This went on until April. Soon Eleanor's struggle to prize passports out of Mrs. Shipley for herself and her children became the talk of diplomatic Washington, and everyone watched the battle royal between the two women. What finally turned it in Eleanor's favor was a neat psychological ploy by two of her friends and admirers, Lord Lothian, the British ambassador, and Hans Brugmann, the Swiss ambassador. Both of them offered to give her authorized visas on their official notepaper (Mrs. Shipley had confiscated Eleanor's passport*), allowing her and her family to land in their countries.

On hearing this, Mrs. Shipley relented and issued passports allowing

*She rightly suspected that Eleanor and her children would have sailed without permission had she not done so.

them all to go to London. They sailed in April 1945, aboard a Liberty ship, *The Marine Fox,* in a convoy of sixty ships. Joan Dulles, Allen's daughter, just graduated from Radcliffe, accompanied them. She was officially listed as nanny to David and Ann, but was really going along for the ride.

In London, Eleanor was confident that she would have no trouble getting her children across the Channel and into Austria, but she reckoned without Mrs. Shipley, who had been to see the State Department to make sure the Dulles children stayed in England. Just before Eleanor was due to sail from Dover, she got a call from the embassy. They had received a cable from the State Department signed by Edward Stettinius, then Assistant Secretary of State, saying: UNDER NO CONDITIONS ARE THE DULLES CHILDREN TO LEAVE LONDON.

"I've got my ticket, I've got my plans, what will happen if I go anyway?" Eleanor asked.

"I'll be fired," said the man at the embassy.

She was under orders to report urgently to the U.S. Delegation, which was now waiting in Italy to go into Austria.

"I talked about my problem to a very peculiar man who was head of the Austrian rear echelon in London," she said, "and he said: 'You've got to go. Otherwise I'm going to report you as being delinquent in duty.' When I said I would stay with my children for the time being, he threatened to cable the State Department that I was being insubordinate. Well, I decided I'd have to go, otherwise I might get recalled for misbehavior, and that was the last thing I wanted. Besides, that dope at rear echelon convinced me that I really was urgently needed. I finally persuaded my niece Joan to take her title seriously for the time being and become governess to my children in London until I could do something about them. Then I took off."

In fact, the U.S. mission in Austria was kept hanging around in Italy awaiting permission to proceed north, and it was weeks before they set up a full headquarters in Vienna. Meantime, she heard nothing from London. There were no letters, no telegrams, nothing. It was months before she would learn what had happened to her children. Meanwhile she had no idea when she would see them again, or where.

In the fall of 1945 Eleanor Dulles, Dixie Davis (General Mark Clark's secretary), and four other women attached to the military mission

206

drove into Vienna from Salzburg. General Clark had commandeered a couple of bullet-proof cars, one of which had once belonged to Adolf Hitler, the other to Benito Mussolini, and provided them with a motor-cycle escort for their drive through Russian-occupied territory. When they were stopped at the demarcation line by red soldiers and asked for their papers, their escort airily described them as "General Clark's girls." The grim faces broke into smiles and the sentries saluted the general's catholicity in the choice of his female company.

But Eleanor was at once cast down by the gloomy state of Vienna and the quiet desperation of its people. Red troops in the city were still flexing their muscles, and there was much looting, drunkenness, and violence. The civilian population was living on a ration of 1,200 calories a day, and people were dying of starvation.

"You could see them crumpling in the street," Eleanor said later, "and though I knew that the Austrians had mostly brought it on themselves, I couldn't say with Roosevelt: 'Let them eat soup.' They would do anything for food. A woman came to see me with a nice silver tray and asked me to buy it from her, for a couple of cartons of cigarettes. I looked it over and gave her $400 for it, and she burst into tears. I was offered a house and a car for the canned food I had been allowed to bring into Austria from the Post Exchange in Italy."

She had met a young Viennese Quaker girl in Philadelphia before the war when she was teaching, and now she decided to look her up. It was well that she did, for the girl was almost dead from malnutrition. Eleanor started to give her food, and soon she was dividing her own military rations in half and giving them to needy people she met.

One day, after the Quaker girl had partially recovered, she brought two friends round to see Eleanor Dulles. She had found Eleanor a place to live, she said.

"It turned out to be a Viennese palace just close to the Ring," Eleanor said later, "with forty-eight rooms, a ballroom, lots of salons, terraces, courtyards, and gardens planted with lilac trees. The two people turned out to be the Winkelbauers, who owned it. They asked me to take it over, and I went to see General Keyes and he agreed to requisition it for me. I then told the Winkelbauers that I didn't really need all this space, and that they could have half of it and stay on there. They were delighted, of course, because they could keep an eye on their things—they had some treasures. Then I told them I'd pay them

207

—and this was very unusual—$200 a month into an account in Switzer-land. Nobody in the occupation forces paid anything. You just took. But I couldn't do that. Anyway, I thought I was richer than I was. I wasn't paying any income tax—you could defer it when you went overseas. It was only when I came home . . ."

The palace was a providential find because it was ideal for parties and receptions, and Eleanor was the only woman in the U.S. mission with the hostess experience (and the rank) to give them. It was an ironic touch to the situation in Vienna that, amid all the chaos, misery, and want, a considerable social life was going on with the Austrians. Over the frontier the Germans, officially, at least, were being treated like lepers by the occupying powers, but the Austrians were different. For reasons which were not exactly valid, the assumption had long ago been made by the Allies that the Austrians had been victims rather than villains during World War II, unwilling partners of the Nazis, forced to fight alongside of them, and therefore not to be punished as severely. The policy was not to treat them over-tenderly, but at least to recognize them as human beings and mix with them freely.

Right from the start a Provisional Government had been organized and recognized by the four powers, but Eleanor soon discovered that though Allied officers were more than willing to give parties for the old Austro-Hungarian aristocrats and the pretty young women who floated around the capital, no one had yet invited the government as such to any reception. She decided she would change all that.

"I could invite anybody in the Provisional Government on a day's notice," she said. "They always came—because of the food. They were hungry. Then they got to like me, and they began to come anyway. In that way I got into close and friendly relations with everyone in the government from Chancellor Figl down, with the Minister of Finance, the Minister of Reconstruction, the head of the National Bank, the whole outfit."

The winter of 1945–6 was a bad one in Europe for victors and vanquished alike. Rations were down to a minimum in Britain, there were desperate shortages in France, and in Germany large numbers of people were dying of starvation. In Austria the situation was equally grim. It was bitterly cold and there were no warm clothes to be had. Food, raw cotton, coal were all down to minimum stocks. What touched Eleanor's heart, but infuriated her at the same time, was the almost fatalistic cheerfulness with which the Viennese coped with their situation. Or rather did not cope. There was nothing dramatic about the way in which they crumpled up on the streets, or lay back and died in their beds. Those who knew members of the occupation forces got help from military rations. In the back streets scores of Harry Limes hovered in doorways, selling off food or desperately needed medical supplies for old family heirlooms and bits of jewelry. But for the bulk of the population, shivering in their bombed-out and unheated tenements, there was only one thing to do.

"They just faded away—smiling," Eleanor said.

She knew that the U.S. Army in Germany and in other parts of Europe was sitting on enormous quantities of raw materials, which had been shipped over in case the war went on. It kept on coming in and stayed there, on the docks, waiting for someone to call for it.

"I decided I had to wangle some of it out of the Army," Eleanor said. "Finally I called General Clay's chief supply officer in Frankfurt and proposed a deal to him."

She knew he was an old cavalry officer and that there was many another cavalry corps veteran among the American occupation forces in Germany. So she asked the colonel for shipments of food and raw materials, and said she would repay in kind.

"What kind?" he asked.

"How about horses?" she said. "Lippizaner and other thoroughbred horses, the same horses they use in the Spanish Riding School here in Vienna."

"Wow," said the colonel. "How many supplies do you need?"

She had a hundred horses ready for the deal. The Austrians were so desperate that the food distribution office had sent out an order that they be killed for food, but the officials in charge of them just couldn't bear to kill them, or contemplate eating them, they were such beautiful horses.

She told the colonel in Frankfurt to send down a trainload of cabbages and potatoes for the Austrians, and she would ship twenty horses back in payment. Twenty horses a trainload, that would be the going rate.

"I went to Frankfurt with the first shipment," she said. "I'd been cut off in Vienna and no one could tell me what had happened to my children. I'd cabled Ambassador Winant in London and Ambassador

Kirk in Rome to try to get news, and they hadn't even answered. I figured I might get better communications in Frankfurt."

She was right. The first thing she did when she got to army headquarters was pick up a telephone and ask for "Lucky Rear." She knew this was the code name of her brother's OSS headquarters in Switzerland, and took a chance it had not changed now he had moved into Germany. She got through at once. She knew she wasn't supposed to use Allen's code name, but she decided that this was an emergency, and she demanded to speak to Battle Cloud. Allen's voice came on the line.

"Where are my children?" she asked.

"For heaven's sake, Eleanor," he roared back, "don't you know better than to call me about a thing like that? They're in Switzerland, of course. Where else would they be?"

Allen, who ruthlessly cut through regulations like a knife through butter, had fixed everything, and his daughter Joan and Eleanor's two children had arrived in Switzerland within a week of her departure from London. From the moment of their arrival, the supremely efficient Mary Bancroft had taken them in hand (Clover being too busy with her Jungian therapy), escorting them on a tour of the lakes and mountains, seeing them into schools, making sure that they wrote weekly letters to their mother. Unfortunately, owing to communication foul-ups between Switzerland and the occupied zones in Austria, none of the letters had arrived.

Eleanor took a few days off to go and see them in Zurich and catch up with their adventures—David had fallen and badly gashed his face, Ann had set fire to their hotel room in London—and then she went back to the grim, gray, starving people of Vienna.

Her feelings were ambivalent about the Austrian people, particularly the men. She thought they were feckless and frivolous, far too liable to accept tragedy and injustice with a shrug of the shoulders. They were in the hands of four conquerors whose behavior toward them ranged from the casually callous to the downright brutish. Their womenfolk were still being raped by the licentious Russian soldiery, their houses looted, their factories stripped and carted away. It infuriated her that they accepted it all with such dull resignation. They seemed to have no hopes for themselves, no plans for the future.

It is difficult to know what other attitude they could have taken at the time. The Red Army was in no mood to accept criticism of its behavior, and the Americans, British, and French were not likely to have taken Austria's side in any conflict with their erstwhile wartime ally. But Eleanor Dulles still writhed not so much at Austrian helplessness as at the fatalism with which the people accepted their situation.

"By this time I felt like a lawyer with a new client. I was working for the Austrians now," she said, "and I had to do what I could for them, get them galvanized."

She was aware that the Russians were stripping whole factories throughout Austria—as they were in their zone in Germany—and though she knew it was rough on the Austrians, she accepted that it was rough justice. The Russians had had their own factories leveled to the ground by the Germans and Austrians. They needed to get their people working again. So she did not complain when they said the Austrians must compensate them in machinery, tools, and material. Had she not suggested the same thing to Foster in France at the end of World War I?

But then she made a tour of the country, and everywhere, in railroad sidings, she found cars loaded with machinery and parts rusting away. They had been there for months, never having got beyond the frontier, left to rot.

"We had a meeting with the British, the French, and the Russians in Vienna," she said. "The Russians insisted that the Austrians were Nazis, and therefore they could seize their industries. They charged us with not pursuing war criminals harshly enough. We quoted the 1943 agreement we had made in Moscow under which it had been agreed that the Austrians would receive special treatment. So then the Russians changed their tack. They kept trying to insist that certain Austrian properties they were taking over were in fact German. 'This man sold his property willingly to the Germans,' they said about one Jewish house. He had in fact sold a property worth half a million dollars for two thousand dollars, but the Russians wanted it. We insisted it wasn't a willing operation if you sold something for less than two or three percent of its value. This man had sold in fear for his life. We managed to show that he had signed the documents while in jail, but they insisted that he *had* sold it and it was now German, and therefore Nazi and seizable. The relations with the Russians in Vienna were very uneasy. It was really the beginning of the cold war."

In 1947, the moment the Marshall Plan was announced, Eleanor Dulles called in the Austrian ministers of Finance and Reconstruction and told them it was their opportunity to get themselves organized. The Plan was not just confined to the Allied nations. Anyone in Europe could participate, Russia, her satellites, Austria.

"I told the ministers that they had to get themselves geared up, so that they could go to Paris in a couple of weeks and tell the Marshall Plan Committee what they needed," she said. "The trouble was, they didn't know what they needed. They gave that old shrug of the shoulders. They had been so long under the thumb of the Germans that they had lost all initiative. So I got the old census figures and found out what they had imported way back, and I fiddled around with them, so much cotton, so much coal, so many machinery tools, etc. Then I handed them the list. They went down it and started criticizing the figures and correcting them. That was the way I tricked them into setting up a program, and by the time I sent two of them off to Paris they had drawn up a pretty good bill of particulars."

Altogether, thanks to Eleanor Dulles, Austria received well over $1 million in Marshall Plan aid, and, because she had moved so swiftly, was among the first countries to get it. The money and materials built new factories, mended roads, repaired housing and schools. They even built new ski lifts and refurbished winter sports resorts in the Tyrol after Eleanor had convinced the Marshall Plan controllers that tourism was an essential Austrian industry. The only application she could not drive through was a grant to restart the Opera in Vienna.

"Congress said it was frivolous," she said. "We tried to explain that the Opera was a kind of kingpin of the tourist industry, but they wouldn't have it. In the end, it was the Russians who got the Vienna Opera going again. They gave them a large grant. Considering what they had done to the Austrians, I found that ironic."

But it was Eleanor Dulles who pulled and pushed, bullied and finally put Austria back on her feet again. It was a remarkable achievement for one woman. The Austrians were grateful and have never forgotten her efforts on their behalf.

She stayed on in Vienna as financial adviser to the U.S. Occupation Mission until 1948. By that time she was considered by many Austrians to be saviour of their country. When she was eventually recalled to

Washington in that year, the Austrian government gave her a farewell dinner to which all the diplomatic corps, the military commanders, and the whole of the Austrian cabinet came. After the meal and the speeches, there was an orchestra for dancing.

Eleanor was due to leave early by car the following morning, so at 11:30 she declared it was time to go. She was asked for one last dance. A signal was given to the orchestra, which struck up to the strains of *The Blue Danube*. An American general swung her out onto the floor.

Then one by one, every single one of the male guests cut in and danced a round with her, the generals, the ambassadors, the ministers, until finally Chancellor Figl took over. He danced her once round the ballroom, and then, still dancing, out of the door, past an applauding line of guests, to her waiting car.

Two days later, she was driving across France en route to Paris when she turned on the car radio. The results of the 1948 presidential election were coming in. She was amused and then finally annoyed with the French, because they kept reporting that the wrong man was winning.

"How clumsy the French are," she said out loud. "They don't know the difference between Truman and Dewey. Don't they realize that Dewey is the man who's going to win?"

CHAPTER THIRTEEN

Thwarted

For nearly a year, everyone had been treating John Foster Dulles as if he were the next Secretary of State. But now the obvious hadn't happened, and all the polls and predictions had proved wrong. Harry Truman had won; Thomas Dewey was resoundingly defeated. Where did that leave Foster?

Eleanor Dulles drove into Paris on the late afternoon of November 4, 1948, and parked her car on the forefront of the U.S. Embassy, at the corner of the Place de la Concorde. She put her pet poodle, Daisy, which she had brought with her from Vienna, on a leash and took her for a short stroll through the gardens of the Champs Élysées. Then she crossed the road to the Hotel Crillon and walked into the elevator. Foster was in Paris with Secretary Marshall at yet another conference, and Janet was with him. They had taken the same suite in the hotel, on the first floor, that Uncle Robert Lansing had used during the Versailles Conference after World War I, from the balcony of which they had waved and cheered at the arrival of President Wilson.

Just before the doors closed a woman came into the elevator, and Eleanor recognized her as Eleanor Roosevelt, widow of the wartime President. Mrs. Roosevelt flashed a broad, happy smile and said, gaily: "Isn't the election wonderful?"

It was only then that Eleanor Dulles realized the French radio commentators hadn't been so stupid after all, and that the Democrats had won.

When she got to the Dulles suite and knocked on the door, Janet opened it.

"She was marvelously dressed in a beautiful evening gown," Eleanor said. "Foster was in a tuxedo. They knew I was coming, but they had a dinner engagement that night, and they couldn't get out of it."

She asked them if what she had heard about the election was true, and they sadly assured her that it was. Foster explained that he and Janet had an evening before them which they were not exactly relishing. The Philippines foreign minister, Carlos Romulo, anxious to ingratiate himself with the incoming (as he thought) Republican administration, had arranged a "victory" banquet for Mr. and Mrs. Dulles. It would now have the atmosphere of a wake. Nevertheless, it had not occurred to Foster to duck the engagement, and Eleanor admired him for that.

But she grieved for him. She knew how much the election had meant to him, and tears came into her eyes as he jokingly repeated the remark he had made to CBS correspondent David Schoenbrun earlier in the day: "You see before you the former future Secretary of State."

He had already sent a cable to Dewey:

"Am deeply disappointed. Your campaign had dignity and elevation and was in the best American tradition. I am rather frightened by the influences which prevented it from succeeding."

In fact, the only influences that had prevented it from succeeding were arrogance and lack of initiative, as one of Dewey's principal aides later confessed. While Foster Dulles had played the bipartisan observer at the big power meetings, his brother, Allen, had come back to the United States from his OSS operations in Europe to help in getting Dewey elected. Like Foster, he had a vested interest in the outcome.

He set up an office in the Roosevelt Hotel in New York with a small staff to help him. His chief aide was McGeorge Bundy.*

"Dewey's view was that if he made no mistakes he would win," Bundy said later. "So we sat around making sure he would make no mistakes. And I think we succeeded, but in fact that wasn't the way it went. We wrote a lot of drafts and sometimes they were used and sometimes not. Then we spent an unconscionable time, I am afraid, interviewing lots of people whom we thought would make good ambassadors. There was this assumption that if nobody rocked the boat, Dewey would be the next President."

*Now president of the Ford Foundation.

When the results began to come in, and it was obvious that he was losing, Bundy was impressed by the way Dewey took it.

"I must say it was a terrible shock," Bundy said, "although maybe not to Allen. He was a very resilient man. And Dewey was never better than the morning after. He came around and thanked everybody and was much more warm than he had been at any time during the campaign. I think we deserved the suffering we got, because there had been a certain overconfidence. It was an expensive lesson."

Resilient or not, Allen was hit by an attack of gout when the results came in.

"He was very brave with the pain, very gallant about it," Bundy remembered. "It hurts like hell, you know, but he stayed very cheerful."

Allen retreated to his house on Long Island to nurse his gout. Foster came back from Paris. Both of them reappeared at the office on Wall Street and resumed reading briefs at Sullivan & Cromwell. But both of them had now tasted fruits that were sweeter than the law, and Wall Street was only a place to mark time before setting off in search of new political orchards. But which crop should they tackle this time?

So far as Foster was concerned, Thomas E. Dewey had a temporary answer. Defeated presidential candidate though he might be, he was still governor of New York, and in that capacity he possessed the perquisites of his office. One of them was the right to make appointments to fill Congress or Senate seats vacated by resignation, death, or other reasons. In the summer of 1949, Senator Robert F. Wagner, on the grounds of ill-health, resigned his seat in the U.S. Senate, and Governor Dewey decided to contact Foster Dulles and ask him to take over the seat.

Foster and Janet were on holiday in their cabin on Duck Island, off the shores of Lake Ontario, when the island lighthouse keeper came across with a radio message. Could he call Governor Dewey at once? There was no telephone and the lake was whipped by a stiff summer storm, so that it was not until the next day that he reached the mainland and called the governor. To begin with, he was not enthusiastic. Wagner's term had only six weeks to run, and to make Dewey's offer worthwhile meant consenting to run for election for a further four-year term in the fall. Did he really want that? He had always visualized his political progress and apotheosis through presidential selection rather than public acclamation at the polls.

Dewey thought Foster was "a little scandalized by the whole idea, frankly," but the governor still considered him his political mentor and "a great American," and believed he "would make a great contribution even if he were only there for six weeks."

So an agreement was made that Foster wouldn't have to run in the fall, and Dewey sent his name through to Washington. On July 8, 1949, Foster resigned from Sullivan & Cromwell and, on the same day, was sworn in as a member of the Senate. He thought of it to begin with as a dutiful chore, but he was soon relishing every moment of it.

Not that his fellow senators received him with the respect he might reasonably have expected. After all, he was a bipartisan figure with considerable experience of foreign affairs. Nevertheless, he was asked to play no part in the work of Senate committees concerned with external policy, and was instead, as a very junior senator, appointed to the District Committee (which looks after the affairs of the District of Columbia) and the Post Office Committee.

"Junior senators get all the worst chores," Paul Nitze, who had many dealings with the Senate at that time, said. "He had real difficulty with his fellow Republicans. He was kind of excluded from the club. In those days the Senate was like a club with lots of subclubs in it, and he was an outsider, rather humiliated, and not given much influence at all during the period he was there."

A junior senator is expected to keep his mouth shut for at least a year, but within three days of his first appearance on Capitol Hill, on July 8, 1949, the ratification of the North Atlantic Treaty Organization (NATO) came up. Foster decided to thumb his nose at convention and speak in its favor. It was a good speech and it was praised by most reasonable men in the Senate. But it won absolutely no approval at all from Republican isolationists, who, headed by Senator Taft, were leading a drive to avoid any further military ties with Europe. He was soon conscious of the cool winds of party criticism blowing in his direction. Not for the first or the last time, Senator Vandenberg, the Republican leader in the Senate, came to his rescue. Yet again, as he had done ever since 1945, Vandenberg was struggling with his recalcitrant members, cajoling and persuading them to accept measures that went against their political grain, because he personally felt they were good for the

217

nation. He told Foster that his speech about NATO had been a good one, but that work would have to be done in altering the bill to meet Republican objections if it was ever to get through the Senate and the House. Would Foster help him redraft it and make it read less threateningly to the isolationists? Between them, they watered down several of the stronger Democratic proposals and shaped a new bill which eventually got the required vote.

But the experience with the isolationists made its mark on Foster Dulles. It left him in considerable awe of the diehard members of his party, and, in Nitze's opinion, "caused Foster to have an undue respect for the opinions of his fellow Republican senators. It was the strong group and he was an outsider, and he wanted to appease them. It was terribly important to have their respect. It affected his attitude toward them later."

But he liked the Senate, for he found it an extremely congenial place in which to be cold-shouldered, and he particularly enjoyed the respect he got from government servants, as well as the perks that went with the position. "They even cut your hair free of charge," he told his family. By the end of the session he was hooked, and indicated to Dewey that he was now willing for his name to go forward for the 1949 off-year election, if, that is, the governor failed to find "a more suitable" candidate. Dewey was well aware that candidates didn't grow on trees for this particular election, because the Democrat would be Herbert H. Lehman, a former governor, and he would be extremely hard to beat. He figured that only a respected public figure with clean political hands would have a chance of upsetting the tight state and city machine which Lehman headed.

The Republicans drafted a cadre of hardheaded, experienced, and efficient political experts to get the Dulles campaign rolling, and they included much of Dewey's own staff. Among them were Herbert Brownell, who looked after campaign strategy, James H. Hagerty to handle the press,* Gabriel Hauge to direct research, and Tom Stephens to head the advance men who would set up the statewide meetings. There was also a young lawyer along named Roderick L. O'Connor, who was drafted to get out the Roman Catholic vote, and Allen Dulles came in from Washington to work at headquarters.

*Brownell later became Attorney General under Eisenhower and Hagerty subsequently became Eisenhower's press secretary.

The campaign for the Senate seat in New York that autumn was far from being the cleanest in the history of such elections, and both sides took some nasty punches below the belt. Foster Dulles went into the fight with the intention of making it a high-minded campaign about major issues of national and international concern, but quickly discovered that that wasn't how you won an election in New York. He was soon trading low blows with his opponent.

Janet Dulles had entered the campaign at Foster's side with the glowing enthusiasm of one helping to bring back to New York the great leader she felt it deserved, but she soon started wincing as the mud began to fly.

"I think Foster was a little bit ill at ease to begin with," O'Connor said later (this was hardly surprising since he had never run for elective office before), "but the more he got into it the more he enjoyed it. . . . Mrs. Dulles didn't like it at all. She was very unhappy when the campaign got down in the gutter. She was, and she remained, very bitter about it."

There was a big ethnic vote to be garnered in the election. The Republicans tried to help it onto their side by strongly suggesting that Lehman was "soft on communism" and approved what the Soviets were doing to the Czechs and other satellite peoples in eastern Europe. The Democrats riposted by trying to turn away the Catholic vote from the GOP, hinting that Dulles was against popery and had disinherited his son, Avery, for becoming a Roman Catholic priest.

It is true that Avery's decision, eventually conveyed to his parents, had considerably distressed Janet Dulles and disappointed Foster; but if there was a gap in their relationship it was, at least as far as his father was concerned, much more physical than emotional. It was, of course, absurd to suggest that he had "cut off" his son for taking his vows.*

"It was pretty damn ridiculous, anyway," O'Connor said, "because when you take the vows Avery did, you certainly don't take all your worldly goods with you."

But the accusation stuck, and it could affect large blocks of votes, especially in New York City, where the GOP was weakest. After several conferences, and with Foster's agreement, it was decided that O'Connor should get father and son together and demonstrate to the elector-

*Avery took his vows in 1948, but was not ordained as a priest until June 1956.

ate that the slanders were gross and they were still a happy family. That wouldn't be as easy as it sounded, because Avery at that time was serving in a Jesuit seminary at Woodstock, New Jersey, and the rules of the order were strict.

However, O'Connor was a resourceful young man, and he dug out a family connection who was now a priest working with a convent school for girls on Staten Island. His name was Father Robert Gannon, and in addition to once having been head of Fordham University, he was an old friend of O'Connor's father.

"Gannon was a strong Republican in the Jesuit order," O'Connor said, "and he had been very active in politics in New York when he had been president of Fordham. . . . I put this proposition to him: 'Is there any way Avery could be brought to New York?' And he said: 'Tell the senator I'm sure we can work something out.' "

It was discovered that Avery was allowed out of his retreat for two weekends a year. After some diocesan maneuvering, one of the weekends was moved forward. He was brought to New York for a photographic session at the family house on 91st Street, and posed chummily with his father round the breakfast table. Then he returned to Woodstock and his meditations.

Avery was well aware of why he had been brought to New York. "I knew it was for political purposes," he said later. "But I was willing to serve because the kind of things that were being said had to be stopped."

As it turned out, the photographs probably didn't do anything at all to affect the campaign one way or another. James Hagerty, the Republican press spokesman, had carefully arranged for the father-and-son picture to go only to the metropolitan newspapers in New York, the idea being to appeal to the Italian and other Catholic voters in the city.

"We didn't want it to go upstate," O'Connor said, "to what's called the Bible Belt, but somehow the picture got swiped and went out to all the upstate weeklies, and probably in the end didn't gain us anything. Because I think there was a certain feeling upstate about the Catholic connection."

One of the other rumors spread about Foster during the campaign was that he was anti-Semitic. The charge was made by Lehman after a speech the Republican candidate gave during an Upper New York

State meeting (where they were probably as antipathetic to Jews as they were to Catholics) in which he said:

"If you could see the kind of people in New York City making up this bloc that is voting for my opponent, if you could see them with your own eyes, I know you would be out, every last man of you, on election day."

If it wasn't an anti-Semitic remark, it was certainly an élitist one, and his sister Eleanor must have shivered in uncomfortable reminiscence when she read it in the newspapers next morning. Lehman called it "a diabolical and deliberate insult to the people of New York," and probably got more votes out of it than Foster did. Not that he had an easy victory. When the votes came to be counted, it was seen that the Democrats had carried the state by only 200,000. To have come so close to his opponent was a considerable achievement for a newcomer. Moreover, Foster had learned a lot from his electoral battle.

"He changed in the four months of campaigning from a rather austere lawyer," O'Connor said later, "and he began to relish speechifying and shaking hands. It was quite a turning point in his career."

But was it? He had still lost. He was no longer a senator. He was no longer senior partner of Sullivan & Cromwell, having resigned when he went to the Senate. It seemed as if his life had lost its momentum and there was nothing steady in prospect.

He was sixty-two years old. It was not a great age for a statesman. But what good was a statesman without power, and what were his chances of getting it within the foreseeable future? The Democrats were entrenched for another three years—when he would be nearly sixty-five—and in the meantime were not likely to welcome him any more even as a bipartisan associate. He had said too many harsh things about President Truman during his campaign.

If he had been the kind of man to be daunted, John Foster Dulles would have been daunted now. But, of course, he wasn't that kind of man. He settled down to write a book* while he waited for the next opportunity for aggrandizement.

* *War or Peace?*

On the morning after the election, Roderick O'Connor's telephone rang. Allen Dulles was on the line. He asked the young lawyer if they could meet in the men's bar of the Roosevelt Hotel, and after they had ordered their drinks he wasted no words. He had been very impressed, he said, by O'Connor's enterprise and energy during the campaign, and he was just the type he was looking for.

"How would you like to join the CIA?" he asked.

O'Connor looked at him in some surprise. He knew what the CIA was, of course, but he hadn't realized that Allen Dulles was connected with it. He said that if a genuine offer was made to him, he would be glad to consider it. Allen told him to go back to his law firm and hang on for a month or so while his background was checked, but plan to join the Agency from that date forward.*

Not many people, even in government, knew that Allen Dulles was part of the new Central Intelligence Agency; at that time (1949) his name certainly did not figure on the roster of employees. According to the records, he had left the OSS in 1946 and come back to the United States to rejoin Sullivan & Cromwell, and from then until 1950 had severed all connection (except as a consultant) with U.S. intelligence. In fact, he was never really out of it—although he was not always on the government's payroll.

Those who remember Allen Dulles in the fall of 1949 have a picture in their minds of an amiable, pipe-smoking, gray-haired bon viveur who always seemed to be at the best New York and many Georgetown parties and who, from his hearty laugh and the kindly twinkle in his eye, gave the impression of being the easiest and most relaxed man in the room. He had the air of one who, having lived a full and often hazardous existence, was now tasting the luxury of placidity as a prosperous Wall Street lawyer, with nothing more than an exigent client to keep him awake at nights. He looked as if he was coasting, and enjoying it.

In fact, inside that complacent-seeming exterior was a man who was often as jumpy as a Mexican bean. As in Foster's case, things were not going as he had hoped. Allen too had calculated on Dewey's victory in the 1948 presidential election to ensure his future. He had been pretty well promised that, for his efforts on the candidate's behalf, he

*It worked out exactly as predicted. Six months later, Roderick O'Connor joined the CIA and was almost immediately posted to Germany.

would be rewarded with a prestigious new job as overall controller of the nation's intelligence machine. It would be, moreover, a machine designed and run by himself, with no interference from outside agencies of the government. But it had not happened. Dewey's defeat had shattered a dream for him, too.

Like his brother, Allen Dulles had by no means lost his hopes and ambitions in 1949—far from it—but in many ways the postwar world had disillusioned him.

It had all seemed so promising when he had moved out of Switzerland at the end of the war in Europe, in May 1945. He had every reason to believe that the promotion which he had missed a year earlier—to the post of OSS station chief in London, the plum job in the organization—would not now be denied him. He had certainly earned it. Had it been possible at that time to make public his wartime achievements, he would undoubtedly have been hailed as one of the great heroes of the clandestine campaign, with a record perhaps more remarkable than that of any other director of a secret intelligence service. It was not just that he had organized the SUNRISE operation in Italy, and "controlled" two of the most effective agents in Germany, Fritz Kolbe and Hans Gisevius. He had masterminded at least a dozen less important but nonetheless spectacular operations: everything from the suppression of a Communist takeover in northern Italy to the smuggling out of the secret diaries of Count Ciano, Mussolini's son-in-law; from persuading the U.S. government to back the Communist Tito instead of the right-wing Mihailovic in Yugoslavia to smuggling an OSS radio operator into SS military headquarters.

Even if the public did not know of his remarkable record, his colleagues did, and most of them agreed that he deserved a substantial reward. He would have been more than satisfied with London. Under David Bruce and his successor, J. Russell Forgan, the office had looked after the whole of the OSS organization in Europe, with every other station chief subordinate to it. In the new postwar setup that was being planned, the potential of the London post would be greater than ever, a logical stepping stone to the directorship of the organization when the ageing Donovan, who was under heavy pressure and couldn't go on forever, was eventually forced out.

Those were the days when everyone in the OSS was presuming that the organization would continue in peacetime, only in bigger and better form. They could not believe, after its wartime experience, that the United States would ever again be without an overall intelligence service. It is true that there were influences in the United States trying to sabotage such a peacetime organization, chief among them J. Edgar Hoover of the FBI, who feared a challenge to his own bureau, which he was anxious to expand beyond the American shores.* But no one thought President Truman would take them seriously.

So Allen Dulles, hearing that Forgan was resigning, waited for promotion to the post that would make him heir to the throne. To his stupefaction, and the considerable distress of many of his colleagues, Donovan announced instead that he was ending London's role as a control center for Europe, and that henceforth each station would be an autonomous organization reporting direct to Washington. Once more he flew out to explain personally to Allen why London would not be his, and offered him the job of German station chief instead. Privately, the OSS chief confided to friends that he had refrained from giving London to Allen, but had preferred to break up the European network instead, because he hadn't wanted to hurt his feelings and "he is such a damned poor administrator." But Allen and some of his intimates suspected that Donovan was becoming increasingly jealous of Allen Dulles's achievements in Switzerland, feared for his own place in the history of wartime intelligence, and in no sense wished Allen to be considered his heir apparent.

It wouldn't have mattered, anyway, as it turned out. President Truman was still walking in the dark that year and was extremely anxious not to bump into anything that needn't be there. If he could appease his critics in Congress, he was more than ready not only to remove the specter of a "New Deal Gestapo" but to wipe out the OSS as well. In the fall of 1945 he sent a curt letter to Donovan saying he was giving orders that its central organization should be run down, its satellite units hived off to other departments of the government.**

Some of the best brains in the OSS had already seen the writing on the wall and made haste to get themselves demobilized. Donovan took

*When Donovan submitted a blueprint for a postwar OSS to President Roosevelt in 1944, Hoover had his experts tamper with it and leaked the result to the Chicago *Tribune,* which condemned it as a plan to build a "New Deal Gestapo" for prying into private lives. The irony of the charges, coming from such a source, is obvious.

**Shortly afterwards the OSS was disbanded by Executive Order.

a job with the International War Crimes Tribunal at Nuremberg as an assistant prosecutor to Mr. Justice Jackson. Either because he was not a very good administrator himself, or through deliberate carelessness, he did Allen Dulles a last bad turn before he departed. He failed to have the OSS organization in Germany accepted as the intelligence arm of the occupation authority, but allowed it to become just another of several American intelligence units operating inside the conquered Reich. The head of the British SIS in Germany was made the director of Military Government in the British sector, with all the power that gave him to control intelligence activities. The Russians and the French had their secret services turned into an integral part of their occupation missions.

On the other hand, Allen Dulles, as head of the OSS German station, found he was in competition not with the secret services of other nations, but with rival bodies within the U.S. occupation forces. It would be untrue to say that he and his organization had no standing, because no body with Allen Dulles at its head would ever lack prestige or fail to win respect. But one considerable disadvantage he suffered was that he failed to win the full support of General Lucius Clay, the U.S. military governor, who remained impervious to his charms and made it clear that he preferred to rely on Army intelligence and the Document Center in Berlin rather than "those radicals" in the OSS.

Clay's opinion of the Dulles setup was not improved by a scandal in the Berlin section of the OSS, which broke some months after Allen took over. The temptations in the wrecked and semi-starving old German capital had proved too much for a small group of headquarters officers of the organization, who had gone into the black market in a big way. They amassed a fortune of nearly $1 million in gold, dollars, Swiss francs, and art treasures before they were uncovered by the military police.

"How the hell can you expect those guys to catch spies," General Clay asked, in derision, "when they can't smell the stink under their own noses?"

Allen Dulles blamed the incident on the fact that he had been scraping the bottom of the barrel for staff for his German operation, and it was inevitable that he would come up with some bad apples. Too many top-flight operatives had either gone home, been shipped to the Far East, or been taken over (at Donovan's suggestion) to work on the dossiers of Nazi war criminals for the forthcoming Nuremberg trials.

He had no doubts at all, however, about the integrity, skill, and dedication of the small group of operatives with whom he surrounded himself as the top of the German organization. He had brought in from Rumania as his second-in-command a dashing, self-confident young lawyer from Mississippi named Frank Wisner. Wisner had had considerable success running the OSS station in Bucharest and masterminding some tricky operations in the Balkans, especially after the Russian armies came in. During World War II he had played a key role in pinpointing the Ploesti oilfields of Rumania—on which the German war machine heavily relied—for the great raid which the U.S. Air Force laid on from Egypt. He had recruited a member of the German Embassy in Ankara as one of his agents. Later on a Russian spy who pitted his wits against him in Washington described Wisner as "too opinionated . . . too aggressive . . . too pompous," but added that "he had a sense of mission, and the power hunger that goes with it." He was a brave and highly capable young agent with only one fault: the bitter anti-communism which he had picked up from his encounters with the Russians in the Balkans was sometimes apt to cloud his judgment.

There were three peacetime newspapermen closely working with him. They were Richard Helms, a former United Press correspondent in Rome and Berlin; Andrew Berding, an ex-Associated Press correspondent in Rome; and John Oakes, a Rhodes scholar and ex-political writer for the Washington *Post*.*

There was also an attractive young woman whom Allen had brought into Germany with him and upon whom he relied heavily for advice and suggestions when it came to dealing with the Germans. She was an American of Swiss origin, Mrs. Emmy Rado, who knew the Dulles family well through her close association with the World Council of Churches. She dazzled and warmed everyone she met, including Allen, and, as Frank Wisner subsequently remarked, "She was a really shrewd cookie about what was going on in Germany, long before everyone else got off their white horse."

When Allen Dulles first moved into Germany, he saw as his principal mission something which, he believed, might well bring the Western Allies and the Russians together in common cause now that the war

*They were later to become, respectively, a director of the CIA, a press relations expert for John Foster Dulles, and editorial page editor of *The New York Times*.

was over: the rounding up of the big Nazis who had gone into hiding, the chasing down of hidden Nazi funds, the uncovering of stolen treasures which the Nazis had plundered from occupied Europe. He had no particular cause to love the Russians, who had not exactly treated him in comradely fashion while he had been operating in Switzerland. They had done their best to sabotage SUNRISE, and, by delaying its implementation, had, he believed, cost the Allies thousands of unnecessary lives. They had repeatedly refused any cooperation between their espionage networks in Switzerland and Germany and his own during critical phases of the war. At the same time, they had infiltrated disguised Communists into his organization—Noel Field and his family, for instance—and used the OSS to smuggle red agents into Germany.

But unlike some of his staff—in particular, Frank Wisner—he was among those who believed that wartime friendship could be kept alive by a common effort to solve the question of Germany. There were some powerful anti-reds strutting around in Germany in those days, especially in the higher ranks of the U.S. Army. This was the time when General Patton was proposing that he should raise and arm a couple of divisions of the Nazi SS "and lead them against the reds." When rebuked for disturbing U.S.-Russian relations by such talk, he replied: "What do you care about those goddamned bolshies? We're going to have to fight them sooner or later. Why not now while our army is intact and we can kick the Red Army back into Russia? We can do it with my Germans . . . they hate those red bastards."*

Allen was revolted by such sentiments. But, on the other hand, he was quickly disillusioned by the Russians. Like the statesmen at the postwar conference tables, he speedily came up against stony Russian hostility. As Eleanor had been in Austria, he was repeatedly repelled by examples of red callousness and brutality toward the defeated Germans. But this he could live with. After all, the Russians had suffered appallingly at German hands in the war, and their desire for revenge was understandable.

What riled him was the treatment his own men received whenever they moved into Russian-controlled areas. At this stage they were not on espionage missions against the Russians but on the hunt for Nazis,

*It was for such talk and some other rumbustious activities that Patton was sacked by Eisenhower on October 22, 1945. He died in a car crash two months later.

yet they were frequently savagely beaten by Soviet security goons and two of them never returned from errands into Prussia. Once Wisner announced that they had found a German general who was wanted for war crimes, and a team was sent to bring him in. It was ambushed on the way back, the Americans battered with rifle butts, the general snatched by the reds. As a result of this and other incidents, all Allied forces were banned from the Russian zone of Germany, though Red Army officers continued to move freely in the Allied zones where they picked up Germans they claimed were wanted Nazis. Allied officers suspected that they were simply hunting down leftwingers who happened to be anti-Communist.

In the months that Allen Dulles spent in Germany, he saw the One World conception of a postwar relationship with the Russians go sour, and he was soon a skeptic, and then a disbeliever in friendship between the wartime Allies. When his sister came to see him in Wiesbaden in 1946, she found that they shared a common despair over what was happening. He was cast down by a propaganda campaign that had been launched against him by Russian stooges in which he was dubbed a pro-Nazi, an anti-Semite, and chief villain in America's plots to get a separate peace with Germany. Since he had made his loathing of the Nazis plain years before World War II, and announced his support of the British and French decision to fight them long before it became fashionable in the United States, he took this charge particularly hard. After all, it was he who had played a leading role in persuading his brother, as the head of Sullivan & Cromwell, to break off all business ties with Germany. Now the Russians were trying to link his name with bankers who had financed Hitler. The fact that the charge was absurd made it no less hurtful.

Allen had encouraged Emmy Rado to bring into Germany a number of Socialist and left-of-center émigrés to balance the hard-line German Communists from Russia whom the Soviets were now pouring into Germany. Among her charges were William Hoegner, who later became minister-president of Bavaria, and Erich Ollenhauer, later president of the West German Social Democratic Party. But dozens of others who ventured to go back to their homes in parts of Germany under Russian control lived to rue the day—or died. The Russians had agreed that Germany's new leaders should be chosen from all parties, so long as they were not Nazi. But those non-Communists who submitted themselves to Russian control and showed signs of having popular appeal were quickly suppressed. They disappeared forever, or surfaced years later from red camps in Siberia.

"If I don't trust the Russians," Allen said, in an argument with his brother after he came back home, "it's because of what I have seen them do. You don't have any idea."

He admitted that the Russians had their grievances against the Americans. Patton was only one of the most blatant advocates of an immediate war on the Soviet Union, while they were still staunching their blood and licking their wounds. There was an unseemly scramble going on among the Allies to get their hands on German scientists and war specialists and profit from their knowledge of jet propulsion and rocketry, and nobody cared whether they were Nazis or not, so long as they had the know-how. But, on the other hand, the British had proof that red agents were sabotaging their ships in Hamburg, and were doing everything in their power to weaken the control of their zones and open them up to Communist infiltration.

By the time he was recalled to the United States, Allen was beginning to sympathize with Frank Wisner, who wanted to "forget the Nazis and get in there and find out what the Commies are up to instead."

On one of his last visits to Switzerland before the German surrender, Fritz Kolbe, Allen Dulles's favorite spy, had brought with him a proposition and a startling item of news. The proposition, as we have seen earlier, was that a group of anti-Nazi students and other elements, all of them left-wing but non-Communist, would stage a coup against the last vestiges of Hitlerite resistance in Berlin, take over the city, and hold it until a force of Anglo-American paratroops could be flown in to take over from them. This would have delivered the German capital into the hands of the West before the arrival of the Russian army, still battling on the outskirts of the city.

Allen Dulles had passed the suggestion on to SHAEF headquarters, where it was turned down flat as being contrary to the spirit of the wartime alliance. It was just as well, or World War II might have ended with the first clashes of World War III. Warned of the plan, the Red Army parachuted its own force into Berlin dressed in civilian clothes, with orders to put down ruthlessly any civilian rising, whether it was against Hitler or not. There were also indications (although these became known only later) that if any Allied force *had* arrived in Berlin before the Russians, the Soviet commanders, Marshals Koniev and Zhukov, planned to "drench" the Americans "by accident" with an artillery bombardment, "so that they will get a taste of the Red Army's lash."

But Kolbe's other information was more intriguing. For some time Allen had been feeding information to the U.S. Seventh Army, then poised to move into Germany, about Hitler's plans for a last-ditch stand in an Alpine redoubt in Bavaria. He went to Seventh Army Headquarters several times and briefed Colonel William W. Quinn, its G2 intelligence officer, about a Nazi plan for mustering a Werewolf Army to hinder and sabotage the Allies inside Germany. He told Quinn that one of the brains behind these Armageddon-type operations was a fanatically devoted Nazi intelligence officer named General Reinhard Gehlen, who was head of one of the arms of the Abwehr, the Fremde Heere Ost (FHO), which had agents throughout eastern Europe and specialized in military information about the Russian army. Allen's briefing was so thorough that he persuaded General Eisenhower at SHAEF headquarters that the end of the war in Europe would not come until the Allied armies had stormed and overcome a force of dedicated Nazis strongly entrenched in a mountain fortress close to the heart of Hitlerism, near Berchtesgaden.

Now Kolbe brought Allen the startling information that Gehlen had been dismissed by Hitler. The two men had parted after a flaming row, sparked mainly by the fact that the Führer did not like the information (accurate, as it turned out) that Gehlen was feeding him about the Russians. Gehlen was out—on the loose would be a more appropriate description of his condition, because he had left Hitler's headquarters at Zossen taking the staff and files of FHO with him. He was letting it be known through various pipelines that he was ready to come over to the Allies, and prepared to bring his files and experts with him.

From everybody's point of view, the news could not have come at a more confusing time. Allen was in the middle of the most frustrating moments of the SUNRISE operation, and he was being driven pretty well distracted by his attack of gout. The Seventh Army was on the move. Although he did pass on the information to Colonel Quinn, everyone seems to have been overtaken by the excitement of the advance into Germany and for the moment Gehlen got lost in the shuffle.

In any case, at that time no one thought it really important that among the German generals now ready to surrender themselves to the Allies —and there were plenty—was one who knew more about the Red Army than anyone among the British, French, or American intelligence services.

Of what value was such an expert in a world where all would be peace and light, the alliance would continue, and the armies of the West and Russia would be brothers-in-arms? No one cared a damn about General Gehlen; for the moment.

In the circumstances, it is hardly surprising that General Reinhard Gehlen had some considerable difficulty in selling himself to the Americans when he eventually did succeed in reaching their lines and surrendering. Gehlen himself and several of his biographers have told the story of how he became a prisoner of the U.S. Army, and it differs in details according to the writer. Even Gehlen has altered his own account over the years. What is certain is that he, two of his officers, and three girl members of his staff chose their own moment to give themselves up. First they buried fifty steel cases full of FHO files and documents; then they removed their insignia and badges of rank and slipped into the small Bavarian town of Elendsam, where Gehlen had friends. The war had been over for twelve days now, and the German army had surrendered. No one was looking for a German intelligence officer named Gehlen, but the U.S. Counter Intelligence Corps, charged with rounding up war criminals and SS men, was looking for some SS officers rumored to be hiding in the area. Gehlen and his group spent the Whitsun holidays with friends, then went to the town major of Elendsam, a young U.S. Army lieutenant, and gave themselves up.

Gehlen had no doubt that he would be received with the respect which he believed was due to his rank and special position. "In some ways," he wrote later, "I felt a grim humor in the situation that I—who after all was a Major General in an important position during the war —should now have to hand myself over to a young American lieutenant," but once it was realized who he was, he was confident that the red carpet would be rolled out for him. Was he not going to help the Americans save Europe from being overrun by the Red Army?

He had his first jolt when he was driven to a CIC detachment at the nearby town of Miesbach and turned over to Captain Marian E. Porter. The following dialogue took place:

"I am Head of the Section 'Foreign Armies East' at German Army Headquarters."

"You *were*, General."

"I have information of the highest importance to your Government."

"So have they all," Captain Porter said.

Dispassionately, he had Gehlen's name and number recorded, and then turned him over for preliminary interrogation to a young CIC sergeant named Victor de Guinzbourg. Gehlen was insulted, but, in fact, he did not know how lucky he was. De Guinzbourg looked over Gehlen—who was small in stature, drab in the uniform from which all his staff tabs had been ripped—and was still impressed. He did not agree with Porter that this was "just another Nazi." There was something about Gehlen's manner when he talked of "my importance to the Americans" which sounded genuine.

Under interrogation, Gehlen was wary with the sergeant, but did spell out his position, the nature of his job, and the fact that he had access to some important Wehrmacht intelligence records; but he did not say where they were hidden. De Guinzbourg wrote a long and careful report of the conversation and strongly recommended that Gehlen be interrogated in depth further along down the line.

After forty-eight hours, the general was shipped to the POW cage at Salzburg and no one took much notice of him there. The place swarmed with Wehrmacht officers of much higher rank. He was finally interrogated again, but when he explained that his specialty was Russian intelligence, the officer seemed to lose interest. He was plainly not enamored by the general's air of self-importance, and finally signed an order shipping him to Wiesbaden POW cage, on the grounds that he was a Gestapo general and deserved "special" (which meant rough) treatment. Four weeks had gone by since he had strolled into the town major's office at Elendsam and asked to be taken to "someone important," and look where he was now.

Luckily, events were still in his favor. Up in northern Germany, at Flensburg, where the Allies were working with the rump of the Nazi government under Admiral Doenitz, the name of Gehlen suddenly began floating on the air. Russian interrogators, questioning Nazi officers captured by the British, had found some members of the FHO and had begun working on them. When they realized that this was the unit which had specialized in penetration of eastern Europe and the Red Army, they demanded the files of the bureau. It was explained that they had gone south with General Gehlen. They at once demanded of the Allies that General Gehlen be found and that he and his documents be turned over to them immediately. Flensburg alerted SHAEF and asked what had happened to the general, and was he as important as the Russians made him sound?

Almost at the same time, back in the American zone, Colonel Quinn was reading through interrogation reports from the POW cages and his eye lighted—and lighted is right in both senses of the word—on the interrogation of General Reinhard Gehlen by Staff Sergeant Victor de Guinzbourg, CIC. As soon as he saw the German's name, memories of his briefings from Allen Dulles came back to him, and he reached for his telephone to alert his chief, Brigadier General Edwin L. Sibert, G2 of 12th Army Group. Sibert, an ex-military attaché and a professor of military science, had had several briefings himself from Allen Dulles during the last stages of the war, and he did not need to be told that Gehlen was important. But where was he? A search of the camps was organized and Gehlen finally run to earth at a moment when he was beginning to fear he would never get out of the POW cage alive. He had had an unpleasant time at Wiesbaden.

"The Americans were downright unfriendly," he said later, "and at times their attitude was such that I feared actual physical violence."

Sibert got him out and over to the more civilized POW cage at Augsburg, and it was there that he had his first talk with him. He was at once impressed by Gehlen. Allen Dulles had become disillusioned with the Russians because of their behavior in Germany since the end of the war, but Sibert had never had any illusions about them at all. He had always believed that Russians and Americans were not meant to be friends, and now he was convinced that only enmity lay ahead. Therefore, the more the United States knew about the Red Army the better. And Gehlen knew a lot.

The German seemed to realize that now was the moment to prove himself. As if sensing that Sibert shared his deep antipathy for the Russians, he expatiated on the knowledge of them and their armed forces which he and his staff at FHO had picked up. In this first conversation he forecast that Stalin would never allow Poland her independence, and that Czechoslovakia, Bulgaria, Hungary, and Rumania would be turned into Communist states. He predicted a rough time ahead for the Allies in Germany because, he said, the Russians still had their entire armed forces in being while the war-weary Allies were rapidly demobilizing. They would be pressed every minute of the day, because the Russians were ready to risk war in order to spread their influence over the whole of Germany, drive out the Allies, and turn the nation into a Communist state.

Sibert was impressed, and even more so when Gehlen told him that he could lead him to an enormous file of documents setting out in detail the battle order, tactics, and strategy of the Red Army. But first he proposed that the members of his staff, now in POW cages like himself, be rounded up and released with him. Then, and only then, would he be prepared to cooperate with the Americans, and lead them to his files.

On his own initiative, without informing his superiors ("I wanted to be sure of my man first"), Sibert had the other members of the FHO released. His officers went to work on them in various ways, hoping to prize out of them the secret hiding place of Gehlen's files, but with not much success. One young intelligence officer concentrated on one of the three girl members of the FHO staff and succeeded, after considerable resistance on her part, in winning her over to the extent that she went to bed with him. He discovered it was her first time, and it proved to be emotional in the extreme. But when, a week later, at the end of a passionate night together, he asked her about the files, she said firmly: "For that you will have to get General Gehlen's permission."

Sibert decided to allow the general to have his way. The FHO staff was brought together with their leader and assigned a sector in the Historical Research Center at Wiesbaden, where the U.S. occupation forces were headquartered. No one was allowed near them except Sibert and a few picked officers.

A few days after their arrival there, Gehlen led the American general to the place in the mountains where the FHO files had been buried, and watched while the GIs dug them up. Then he went over to one of the steel cases and stroked it with a gloved hand.

"Here," he said, "are the secrets of the Kremlin. If you use them properly, Stalin is doomed."

In the next few days, Gehlen settled down to writing a summary of
the treasures that the files contained. There were some tasty samples.
He included a pen portrait of Lavrent Pavlovich Beria, then head of
the Soviet Security Services, which appeared to have been written by
someone inside the Kremlin, describing him as a ruthlessly ambitious
careerist who would stop at nothing to oust Josef Stalin. Stalin was
described as being mortally afraid of him, and had recently appointed
him a field marshal as a gesture of appeasement.* Other items he gave
included a list of members of the U.S. Communist Party who, he
claimed, were working for the OSS and should be closely watched now
that the war was over; a series of reports from the British SIS office in
Switzerland giving their extremely uncomplimentary opinions of the
Americans in general and Allen Dulles in particular; and a long internal memorandum from Winston Churchill castigating the late President Roosevelt for his naïve attitude toward the Russians, and forecast-
ing that as a result of this "honeymoon madness" on Roosevelt's part,
the whole of eastern Europe, and perhaps Greece and Italy too, would
soon be "groaning under Stalin's heel, and who knows when France
may feel the jab of his blood-flecked spurs?"

All this was good enough to convince Sibert that he had a valuable
property on his hands, and to hell with the fact that he was a goddamned Nazi. He decided to alert his superiors. General Walter Bedell
Smith, Chief of Staff at Supreme Headquarters, was informed and told
that Sibert would like to put Gehlen and the FHO to work as an
intelligence unit working for the Americans. Bedell Smith agreed on
his own initiative, without consulting his chief, General Eisenhower,
on the grounds that Ike had forbidden fraternization with the Germans
and also could be compromised in his dealings with Marshal Zhukov,
the Soviet commander in Germany, if it became known he was using
German experts on Russia.

It was at this stage that Sibert called in Wild Bill Donovan. He also
alerted the War Department in Washington and had a message sent
to Allen Dulles, who had returned to the United States on a visit.
Donovan, the War Department, and Dulles all agreed on Gehlen's
value. But they agreed on another thing too. For the time being, it was

---

*Beria was subsequently executed·by the Soviets for anti-State activity, but only after
the death of Stalin.

vital to get the German general out of Germany. The Russians were after him.

Finding their repeated demands for the production of Gehlen and his files were being ignored by the Allies, the Red Army intelligence services had instituted their own search for him. As their knowledge of his activities improved, and they realized how much he knew about the Red Army, they became more and more anxious to lay their hands on him. At all costs they wanted him out of Allied control, or silenced. Some tipoffs were coming into Sibert's headquarters that Soviet agents were on their way to Wiesbaden with orders to kidnap the general or eliminate him. Shortly afterwards, Gehlen's car was hit by a bullet while it was traveling from his new hideout in U.S. headquarters in Wiesbaden.

It was indeed time to get him away.

So Gehlen and three members of his staff were smuggled aboard General Bedell Smith's private plane and flown to Washington, a nondescript crew dressed in ill-fitting civilian clothes.* They arrived on September 20, 1945.

Allen Dulles was looking forward to questioning the general. But in fact, September 20 was, for him, a day significant for another and more melancholy reason. On that day President Harry Truman signed an executive order disbanding the OSS.

*The first thing the general did when he arrived was ask to be taken to a good tailor.

CHAPTER FOURTEEN

Call to Battle

Harry Truman's executive order of September 20, 1945, chopped the OSS to pieces; except for the men and women who had soldiered in its service, few people mourned the massacre. Owing to the secrecy which still cloaked its wartime activities, the general public was, in any case, still ignorant of its achievements. Its clandestine triumphs remained clandestine.

Some of the severed limbs from the bleeding corpse were grafted onto other government bodies: the Strategic Services Unit, for instance, went to the War Department, and the Office of Research and Evaluation to State. But the blood content was not the same and no amount of artificial injections could prevent their ultimate rejection.

A new organization came into being, the Central Intelligence Group (CIG), which had a staff of 100 (including secretaries) in the summer of 1946 and managed to expand to 1,816 by the end of the year. But it was quantity, not quality. Some OSS veterans abroad were incorporated, notably James Angleton in Italy (who stayed on there) and Richard Helms in Germany, but most of the new recruits wouldn't have known a microdot from a flyspot. As CIG's director, Lieutenant General Hoyt S. Vandenberg, remarked, he had a budget and an establishment: "If I didn't fill all the slots, I knew I'd lose them."

What CIG lacked was know-how, enthusiasm, incentive—and talent.

Allen Dulles remained on the sidelines while these upheavals were taking place, as did his erstwhile assistant in Germany, Frank Wisner. It is true that Allen was frequently consulted by General Hoyt Vandenberg, whom he had known since childhood,* and both he and Wisner were members of a number of committees. Allen, for instance, sat in on several debriefings of General Gehlen, got to know him well, and was one of those who recommended that the general be returned to Germany, given a budget (of $3,500,000), and set up in business as the supplier of Russian and east European intelligence to the United States. But he was mortified when Gehlen's services were annexed not by the CIG but by the Army.

Both Allen and Wisner were back with their law firms, Allen once more at Sullivan & Cromwell, Wisner with Carter, Ledyard & Milburn. They met in downtown restaurants or at Long Island weekends to exchange rueful anecdotes about the chaos in Washington. Their attitude was wry rather than bitter. They knew it couldn't last. The situation with the Russians had shifted only too rapidly from wartime comradeship to peacetime antagonism. The icy winds of the cold war were beginning to blow across Europe and Asia, and, in the words of a Senate report:

"Recent events had aroused alarm over the growing belligerence of the Soviet Union and had revealed the United States' relative ignorance of Soviet military strength in relation to its own."

Vandenberg had shown Allen a request he had received from the White House asking him to coordinate the CIG with the intelligence services of the Army, Navy, and Air Force, "to produce the highest possible quality of intelligence on the USSR in the shortest possible time." Allen later remarked to Wisner, during a Washington weekend, that "they can get the information they want from Gehlen's boys, but how in Hades are they going to interpret it?"

He added that he didn't believe the Army would cooperate, anyway. Gehlen was General Clay's protégé now, and he doubted if he would let any other service near him and his data.

"I just hope they know what to do with it when they get it," he said.

Between 1945 and 1947, Allen Dulles's worst fears were realized. As the cold war got icier, and the need to know Soviet intentions became more urgent, especially once the Russians began tightening their grip on eastern Europe and making threatening gestures toward the West,

*He was the nephew of Senator Vandenberg, the Republican leader in the Senate and close friend of Foster Dulles.

the U.S. government had only a sort of pseudo-intelligence service to keep it informed as to what was going on. As Ray S. Cline, later a deputy director of the CIA, put it: "What passed for central intelligence machinery in this period was essentially a facade of centrality, covering up the usual departmental fragmentation and inefficiency."

Wild Bill Donovan had sent to President Roosevelt, in November 18, 1944, the blueprint of what he hoped would be a postwar development of the OSS. It was to be a sort of super intelligence machine under the direct control of the President, working independently of the Army, Navy, and Air Force intelligence services, to keep tabs for the nation on what was going on behind the scenes in the postwar world.

The project was killed by President Harry Truman, for economy reasons, and because he did not wish to be accused of setting up what one newspaper called "a peacetime Gestapo." He killed the OSS at the same time. It was not until a year later that he had reluctantly agreed to the creation of the CIG, and then it was an inadequate organization, which did not begin to meet the need for a really up-to-date and efficient central intelligence operation.

Allen Dulles and others argued eloquently for the creation of an entirely new intelligence organization, with rights, privileges, its own constitution, and funds; freedom to act without interference from the State Department, the Army, Navy, or Air Force departments; and direct access and responsibility to the President. Thanks to their persuasive arguments—and to Soviet Russia's increasing hostility—they succeeded in persuading both Truman and the Congress that the time had come to create such an organization. In July 1947, Congress passed the National Security Act, which established a National Security Council "to advise the President with respect to the integration of domestic, foreign and military policies," and to set up under the NSA "a Central Intelligence Agency with a Director of Central Intelligence, who shall be the head thereof. The Director shall be appointed by the President, by and with the advice and consent of the Senate, from among the commissioned officers of the armed services or from among individuals in civilian life."

A young lawyer who had served in the OSS, Lawrence Houston, drew up the legislation for that part of the Act concerning the CIA, working with the help of two other OSS veterans, John Warner and Allen Dulles. They incorporated large chunks of the blueprint which

Wild Bill Donovan had presented to Roosevelt in 1944, and the makeup of the new CIA was chiefly modeled on his original ideas. Walter Pforzheimer, legislative counsel of the CIG on Capitol Hill, then carefully and successfully steered the proposals through Senate and Congress.

The CIA was born. But who was to be its first head? There was no doubt as to who it would have been if Houston, Warner, Allen Dulles, and Walter Pforzheimer had had their way. Wild Bill Donovan was still around, still fighting fit, still brimming with ideas for a first-class intelligence organization.

Unfortunately, he and Harry Truman loathed each other. There were also rumors that the President had received an approach from the chief of the FBI, Edgar Hoover, who had showed him a secret report and strongly recommended that Donovan not be considered. Whatever the reason, Donovan did not get the call. Instead, an amiable and innocuous naval career man, Admiral Roscoe H. Hillenkoetter, was appointed as first director of the new CIA.

To Allen Dulles it was unsatisfactory, but at least it was a start.

If the Army had been unfriendly toward the old CIG, it was downright jealous of the CIA. One of the first moves Admiral Hillenkoetter made was to approach the Army and offer the cooperation of himself and his staff in the effort to coordinate intelligence about the USSR. He was rebuffed, being told that Soviet intelligence was the Army's affair and they had all the information they needed. As a Senate report put it later:

"The project [for coordinating Russian intelligence] was ridden with contention from the start. The military regarded the project as their own and did not expect or want CIG [or CIA] to review and process their raw intelligence materials for evaluation."

But if the CIA was frustrated by this snub, its members had their own back within the year, and Allen Dulles's suspicion that the Army's analysts just did not know how to handle the material Gehlen's unit was furnishing them came only too true. In 1948, almost as a direct result of military misinterpretation, the United States had the first of its big postwar "war scares."

In February 1948, the Communist coup in Czechoslovakia toppled the Beneš régime and brought in a ruthless Communist government in its stead. At the same time, Soviet sabotage in north German ports, through which the Allies shipped their supplies into Germany, suddenly increased. Serious strikes crippled Italy and France, all of them financed and directed by the Communists. The port of Marseilles, through which much of the U.S. food to feed starving Europe was shipped, came to a standstill, added to which heavy Russian military movements of troops and tanks were reported in Germany and Czechoslovakia.

Gehlen's unit reported the Soviet movements to U.S. Army intelligence in Germany. It also sent intercepted transcripts of messages from Moscow to European Communist leaders ordering them to start strikes and sabotage operations.

At the same time, the new CIA was active, and its headquarters in Washington was receiving its own information about these events, notably from James Angleton in Italy, Richard Helms in Germany, and Philip Horton in France.

But the way in which this raw information was interpreted by the Army and by the CIA was vastly different. The Army analysts sent their conclusions from Gehlen's reports straight through to General Clay. The CIA station chiefs reported to Admiral Hillenkoetter, and he called in a small group of ex-OSS experts, including Allen Dulles, who reported back to him with their conclusions on the data they had been given.

Now no one in Washington thought much of Admiral Hillenkoetter as the director of an intelligence organization, and he himself often wondered aloud why he had been given the job. He was a salt-water sailor, much more at home with ships than with spies. In addition, as an official report subsequently concluded, "he lacked the leverage of rank to deal effectively with the military." Or anyone else. The report described him as "more passive than active."

In the case of the 1948 situation, however, passiveness was a quality of sterling value. Hillenkoetter read through the assessments of his advisory panel and kept calm. The panel agreed that the Russians were getting restless, but recommended nothing more than watching them with a sleepless eye. In the case of the Italian and French Communist-fomented strikes, the panel recommended upping the Moscow ante and pumping more money into the pockets of the moderate political and union leaders than the Russians were handing out to the extremists.*

General Lucius D. Clay's reaction was almost exactly contrary. By this time Commander-in-Chief, European Command, General Clay read through the Gehlen Report, glanced over the opinions of his analysts, and reached for the panic button. The sound of marching men and revving bomber planes throbbed ominously in his ears. He sent an urgent message to Washington (to Lieutenant General Stephen J. Chamberlin, director of Intelligence, Army General Staff) reporting, in part:

> . . . I HAVE FELT A SUBTLE CHANGE IN THE SOVIET ATTITUDE WHICH I CANNOT DEFINE BUT WHICH NOW GIVES ME A FEELING THAT IT [WAR] MAY COME WITH DRAMATIC SUDDENNESS. . . .

General Chamberlin spread the word and the alarm was raised. As a later Senate report stated: "In March, 1948, near hysteria gripped the U.S. Government with the so-called 'war scare.'" The report placed the cause of the hysteria squarely on the shoulders of General Clay, whose cable had "precipitated" it. U.S. armed forces were put on the alert throughout the world, and Britain, France, and Italy were warned to get ready for the worst.

In fact, as soon became apparent, the Soviet government may have been flexing its muscles but was in no position to start a fight. The U.S. Army in Germany had badly misinterpreted Gehlen's information. Allen Dulles let it be known in Washington that the sooner his unit was taken away from the amateurs and given back to the professionals, the better.

The Central Intelligence Agency was in being at last, but Allen Dulles despaired of its future in the hands of the undynamic Hillenkoetter. Truman had repented his hasty decision to wipe out the OSS, but seemed to have no idea of what sort of organization to create in its place. He wanted an agency that would tell him what the Russians were going to do, and how to outwit them without having to mobilize

*It worked. Agency money swung the results of the Italian elections to the right. It also brought the Marseilles dock strike to an abrupt halt, allowing food for Europe to flow in once more.

the nation; but other than the fact that he didn't want to bring an American Gestapo into being, he had scant knowledge of what its size, shape, and nature should be.

What he was getting under the deprecating Hillenkoetter was, in Frank Wisner's words, "a bunch of old washerwomen exchanging gossip while they rinse through the dirty linen," and so long as CIA stayed that way Allen Dulles preferred to play no official role in its activities. He was, in any case, too plainly an avowed Republican for anyone in the administration to recommend him for the kind of prestigious position that his background and experience would merit. But he kept in close touch with the diminished and scattered members of the intelligence community, did some quiet recruiting, and made frequent trips to Europe.

He always had a good cover for these journeys. One of them, in 1947, for instance, was made as an expert adviser to the Herter Commission, an all-party group of congressmen and senators which visited Europe to do some fact finding over the validity of the Marshall Plan.* For others he used the excuse of contacting clients and associates of Sullivan & Cromwell in London, Paris, and West Germany, or accompanied his wife to Switzerland for one of Clover's continued consultations with her Jungian psychiatrist.

Paul Blum, his young emissary during the SUNRISE operations, was still working for the CIA's Swiss station, and Allen liked to drop into the bureau, now operating out of Zurich, to see how he and the staff were doing. One of Blum's operators, who remembered Allen Dulles's days of fame and glory with the OSS, invited him during one of these visits to a party which the U.S. consul in Zurich was giving for July 4.

"Well, he came to the party," he said, "and it was sad. This was only 1948, and yet no one knew who he was. Here was a great man who had done all these tremendous things in Switzerland—and he had to be introduced. I could see his wry expression as I took him round the room and said his name to all those blank faces."

But events were working in his favor and that of the intelligence community. General Clay's ham-handed treatment of the Gehlen reports and the war scare hysteria that had resulted played into the hands of the CIA. Not only Truman but many of the most thoughtful men

*He formed a close friendship with a young senator named Richard M. Nixon on this trip.

in government at that time decided that the proliferation of military espionage agencies, the lack of good analysis, and the need for a concerted and aggressive covert organization made it vital that the CIA should be given teeth, plus the money and priority to use them.

As George Kennan, at that time director of the State Department Planning Staff, put it later:

> . . . We were alarmed at the inroads of the Russian influence in Western Europe beyond the point where Russian troops had reached. And we were alarmed particularly over the situation in France and Italy. We felt that the Communists were using the very extensive funds that they had in hand to gain control of key elements of life in France and Italy, particularly the publishing companies, the press, the labor unions, student organizations, women's organizations and all sorts of front organizations of that sort, to gain control of them and use them as front organizations.

Kennan strongly recommended that to combat these red inroads in Europe, the CIA should be given "some facility for covert operations."

He added: "It ended up with the establishment within CIA of a branch, an office for activities of this nature, and one which employed a great many people."

The new branch was called the Office of Policy Coordination (OPC), and thanks to a little behind-the-scenes manipulation by Allen Dulles and some other OSS veterans, it did not develop quite as Kennan or the State Department had conceived it. For one thing, OPC, though supposed to be part of CIA, and pledged to keep the State Department informed of what it was doing, was soon working entirely independently. Or at least it was during the period when Admiral Hillenkoetter remained director of the Agency.

No one suggested that Allen Dulles should take over OPC, but he was consulted about who should be appointed to head it, and without hesitation he recommended his old assistant, Frank Wisner. Wisner, by this time bored with legal work, had taken a job as deputy to the Assistant Secretary of State for Occupied Areas. Like his ex-chief, he was keeping his hand in as an intelligence agent, and the position gave him a prime excuse for frequent visits to Germany and eastern Europe. Now he came back into the official world of espionage, and set out at once, with Allen Dulles's enthusiastic aid, to make OPC into an independent unit.

As a Senate report later put it:

> Responsibility for coordination with the State and Defense Departments rested with Frank G. Wisner, appointed Assistant Director of Policy Coordination on September 1, 1948 . . . [but] . . . that did not occur. Wisner quickly developed an institutional loyalty to OPC and its mission and drew on the web of New York law firm connections that existed in postwar Washington as well as his State Department ties to gain support for OPC's activities. . . . In this context, operational tasks, personnel, money and material tended to grow in relation to one another with little outside oversight.

Wisner's unit had set up 5 stations, employed 302 agents, and had a budget of $4,700,000 in 1949,* and from the start engaged in covert activities in many other places besides France and Italy. It was particularly interested in anti-Soviet moves in eastern Europe and espionage inside Russia, and established its main station inside Germany, where it immediately began negotiations to take over General Gehlen's operation from the U.S. Army.

Allen Dulles was consulted (though the State Department and Admiral Hillenkoetter were not) on all phases of OPC's development and expansion. Frank Wisner, like Allen, was a loyal Republican—though politically far to his right—and he shared Allen's conviction that Dewey would win the 1948 presidential election. He was aware that when the new régime came in, Allen had been promised the directorate of the CIA and that his brother, John Foster, would become Secretary of State, in which case he was more than willing to join the team.

In the meantime, he continued, as one CIA counsellor put it, "to fight like cats and dogs with anyone who tried to muscle in on OPC, and thumbed his nose at Hilly."

While he waited for the election results, Allen Dulles spent a considerable time and much travel working as a member of a three-man team which President Truman had appointed to report on the CIA, and

---

*By 1952 this had increased to 47 stations, a staff of 2,812 plus 3,142 contract personnel, and a budget of $84 million.

recommend changes. For Truman had at last decided that the present setup was incapable of coping with postwar intelligence problems. The other two members of the team were William H. Jackson, who had once written a wartime study of British intelligence, and Matthias Correa, who had worked for Secretary of the Navy James Vincent Forrestal. Both were lawyers, as seemed inevitable in anything connected with U.S. intelligence.

Correa, who had really been inducted to please Forrestal, played little part in the subsequent survey or in the writing of the report. Jackson, a hard-driving, hard-drinking man with some definite opinions on counter-espionage, concentrated on that aspect of CIA activities as well as its administrative restructuring. Allen Dulles went into the problems of clandestine collection of intelligence and covert operations. Their subsequent report, National Security Council Report No. 50 (NSC50), recommended some drastic changes which would reorganize many of the functional aspects of CIA.*

The report was submitted to President Truman before the election in November 1948. When Foster Dulles heard that Allen had handed it in, he called him up and pointed out that he had been foolish to do so. What if President Truman decided to implement the report and bring about the changes recommended? He would inevitably ask for Admiral Hillenkoetter's resignation and appoint a new director in his place—"and it won't be you," Foster said. "He knows where you stand."

So on Foster's advice, Allen sent in a formal request asking that Report NSC50 be put on one side and held for consideration until after the election, when (as they then thought) it would be Dewey's baby.

It became President Truman's orphan instead, and, as far as he was concerned, no longer a child in which he was very much interested. Reelection had brought him triumph but also problems. There were ominous stirrings in the Far East, where Chiang Kai-shek had been driven out of China and trouble was brewing in Korea. Stalin was making threatening faces at Tito's breakaway Communist régime in Yugoslavia. The Russians had exploded an atomic bomb in August 1949, and it was so far ahead of all predictions that someone must have

*The report is still restricted.

been betraying the West's fission secrets to the Soviets.*

It was no time for shaking up the CIA and creating chaos among its personnel, not, at least, until a strong new dynamic leadership could be found to revitalize the Agency. Report NSC50 was laid aside, and no one really studied it closely for a year.

Meanwhile, Allen Dulles remained in limbo, waiting, like his brother Foster, for something to turn up.

Eleanor had been loaned by the State Department to the National Production Agency, taking care that food supplies reached Europe under the Marshall Plan. She remembers it as a tranquil and satisfying period, both emotionally and professionally. She had bought herself a splendid small house in McLean, Virginia, with a pool within diving distance of her bedroom window. All the Dulles family were swimmers, and if they sometimes complained that the balmy Virginia breezes made the temperature of the water far too tepid—they liked to break the ice before diving in—nevertheless, Foster and Allen were regular bathers there. A dozen lengths apiece, a dry martini mixed with Foster's deft expertise, and they settled down to lunch with an appetite that the years had made no less hearty. Janet always came with Foster, but Clover was a more infrequent guest. She now had psychiatrists both in America and in Switzerland, and though they did not seem to make her less vague or restless, they had managed to spur new interests in her to fill the vacuum in her life.

She had taken up prison welfare and work in the black ghettos; while she still had the habit of wandering off without warning, nowadays Allen could guess that she would turn up at Attica or some Virginia prison farm, and come back enlivened by someone else's problem.

Mary Bancroft was still a friend of Allen Dulles, as she would continue to be until his death, but the intimacy they had achieved in wartime Switzerland had now gone out of their relationship. Mrs. Bancroft had turned her strong personality in other directions and lighted upon Henry M. Luce, president and editor-in-chief of *Time* magazine, whom she set out to "convert" from his right-wing ways to her more liberal philosophy. They met frequently in various parts of the world and kept up a running correspondence while they were

*Klaus Fuchs, a German-born scientist working for the British at Los Alamos, was subsequently arrested and convicted for this offense.

apart, and her letters were often as irritating as a bullfighter's banderillas. She waxed sarcastic in twitting Luce for his support of "that unassuming little blond Communist Tom Dewey," and for his eulogisms of Foster Dulles and the American way of life. She got more fun out of Luce's reactions to these barbs than she did from trying to prick Allen Dulles's more sophisticated hide.

Allen missed her lively company. His family life was fraying at the edges. His two daughters were no longer around, for both had now gone off and got married. He admired his son, Allen, who had grown into a strapping and charming young fellow, warm toward everyone except his own father. Between them, there seemed to be a gulf that no words or gestures could span. Allen Dulles was not really an affectionate man, and he distrusted emotions, yet he would have been prepared to expend both affection and emotion if he could have been sure of a response from his son. But he was not, and would not risk a rebuff. Meanwhile, his relations with Clover always hovered somewhere between light Noel Cowardish badinage and tears.

When Eleanor saw Allen together with his son, she blessed the fact that her own David had turned out so much better. He adored his mother. He was bright, sharp, ambitious, and fascinated with politics. She got him a job as a page in the Senate, and he reveled in his close contact with the lawmakers of the nation. She might have hesitated over the fact that his politics, even at fifteen, were staunch Republican, remembering with Maurois that "a young man under twenty-five who is not a Socialist has no heart, one above twenty-five who remains a Socialist has no head," but she loved, admired, and was proud of him and his winning ways.

Eleanor was busy, happy in her work, still determined to rise in the diplomatic world, and sorry for the hiatus in the careers of her brilliant brothers. As Allen put it, the prospects for both of them "weren't very bright." She longed to be able to help them. Instead, an old friend of Foster's decided to see what he could do.

One evening in the fall of 1949, shortly after John Foster Dulles had lost his bid to get back into the U.S. Senate, the telephone rang in the Washington home of a young State Department official named Lucius D. Battle. Battle was one of the bright hopefuls of the postwar era who had been picked by the new Secretary of State, Dean Acheson, to work with him as his special assistant, and it was well known in Washington that he had more influence than his position seemed to indicate.

That evening the telephone call came at an awkward moment, because Luke Battle and his wife were just on their way out to dinner, and they had reached the door when the bell rang.

"Don't answer it," his wife said.

He had already gone back and picked up the phone. Carl McCardle, Washington correspondent of the Philadelphia *Bulletin,* was on the line. Battle knew him as one of the newsmen through whom Foster Dulles had often leaked pronouncements during the big postwar conferences of a year or two back, and his antennae began to vibrate. Friends of Foster Dulles were not exactly friends of the administration at that moment. Around the White House they were still smoldering over some of the things Dulles and his political supporters had said about Truman during the recent Senate campaign. They felt that many of his charges were savagely unfair and had gone far beyond the normal donnybrook of political contests. Carl McCardle had given Foster Dulles's attacks a great deal of prominence in the *Bulletin,* and though it did not occur to Battle to bear any grudge against him for that, he saw no reason to be over-cordial or to waste too many words, especially as his wife was tugging at his sleeve telling him they would be late for dinner.

He asked what he could do for the reporter, and the conversation then went something like this:

MC CARDLE: John Foster Dulles is very worried that it might be thought that the recent Senate campaign would destroy his usefulness to the administration in the field of foreign affairs.

BATTLE: Well, Carl, I can see that he might be concerned. He has given the President a pretty nasty roughing up.

MC CARDLE: Well, he doesn't—he considers that was just the game of politics, and it ought to be forgotten. He has very much enjoyed his role advising in foreign affairs.

BATTLE: Carl, what are you trying to tell me?

MC CARDLE: I'm trying to tell you that John Foster Dulles wants to come back to work.

Those were the bare bones of the conversation, but McCardle managed to flesh it out into thirty minutes of variation on the single theme: John Foster Dulles was asking President Truman to tell him to come home, that all was forgiven.

As he and his wife finally drove off to their party, Luke Battle's first instinct was to laugh. The sheer effrontery of the approach was both risible and breathtaking. The idea of bringing back into the fold a man who had made it plain how much he despised his President, loathed his Secretary of State, and held all their policies in contempt was one that only a masochist could contemplate.

And yet, when Battle slept on it, he began to realize that there were advantages for the administration in the return of Foster Dulles, painful though the prospect might be. Truman's program was getting into a mess up on Capitol Hill because there had been a deterioration of bipartisanship since the last election. The State Department was deeply concerned over the lack of consensus for its policies, and Battle saw that Foster Dulles, respected by all Republicans for his views on foreign affairs, could probably help them push through projects which otherwise might get hopelessly mired down in controversy.

Next day, at the 9:30 A.M. meeting at the State Department, James Webb, the Under-Secretary, presided (Acheson was away on other business). After the conference was over, Battle went to him.

"Jim," he said, "I want to tell you that I've had a call from Carl McCardle, and John Foster Dulles would like to reassociate himself with the administration in some way."

Webb laughed and said: "That's the craziest idea I've ever heard in my life. President Truman would never buy it."

Battle mentioned it to Acheson when he returned, and he reacted more or less the same way. But by that time Battle had turned the idea over in his mind and become convinced that it ought to be followed up, for the administration's sake, and not because Foster Dulles was hanging around the door, cap in hand. But Acheson and Webb brushed his advocacy aside, and it lay dormant for a week or two. Acheson went off to a conference in Paris and took Battle with him.

It was while they were there that the Secretary received a TELACH cable from James Webb.* Foster Dulles had made another approach. He really wants the job, Battle thought, and felt a rather grudging

*Personal messages in code between the Secretary and his deputy were known as TELACH if they were sent to Acheson, and ACHTEL if they were sent by him.

admiration for the way in which such a stern and lofty figure was willing to humble himself in order to get back in. The TELACH revealed that by this time Webb had joined him in thinking that it might, after all, be a good thing for the administration. There had been a meeting at the State Department, Webb reported, and the general consensus had been that it might be helpful if Dulles were brought back in, as a kind of ambassador-at-large.

"I think it's an absolutely outrageous idea," Acheson said again.

And now Battle began to argue with him.

"I did my best to persuade the Secretary that it had more positive than negative elements," he said later. "I stressed that we really ought to do it. Finally, he gave in, and we sent an ACHTEL back to Webb saying that there was now no objection on Acheson's part, and to take it up with the President."

Webb got an appointment with the White House and put the proposition to the President. Harry Truman, who had been genuinely hurt by Foster Dulles's attacks on himself and his program, reacted with an angry: "What, that bastard? Not on your life."

It looked as if Foster had gone down on his knees in vain. But, in fact, his battle was half-won. In the Republican Party the powerful Senator Arthur Vandenberg, alarmed by the Soviet atomic explosion and developments in the Far East, where the situation in Korea was boiling up, was now in favor of closing ranks on foreign policy, and had begun pushing hard for Dulles's appointment. In the State Department Acheson, Webb, and Battle had been joined by Deputy Assistant Secretary Dean Rusk. It was now a question of winning over the President.

It took several months, and it was not until April 1950, that Truman finally gave way. But he made two conditions, just to cut Foster Dulles down to size—as he thought. One was that Senator Lehman, his erstwhile opponent in the New York senatorial race, who also considered he had been traduced by Dulles, must agree. Lehman was only too willing so long as he received Foster Dulles's assurance—which was given—that he would not be a candidate at the next New York election. The other was that Dulles should accept the post of mere consultant rather than the grander-sounding one of ambassador-at-large. Foster did not hesitate.

He was back, his sojourn in the wilderness ended. Luke Battle was later to say: "I regret that I was responsible for his return." For Foster's appointment as a consultant was to prove the turning point in his career, from which a fame would flow that few members of the Truman administration would remember with any pleasure.

CHAPTER FIFTEEN

The Gospel According to Luke

Everyone was wary of him at first. Several of the advisers at State, remembering only too well Foster's tendency to leak news to the press of the kind that would redound to his credit, made an attempt to keep top-secret documents from him.

"The question came up as to what sort of telegrams and messages and so forth should be shown to him," Luke Battle said, "and the first attitude was distrust, hesitation. The people who handled the telegrams were worried about it. But I argued that you couldn't have two classes of citizens in the building, and if you were going to have Foster there at all you were going to have to send him the daily summary— of all the incoming messages as well as those on which he was working. And that was the way it was done."

Battle had not expected any recognition from Foster Dulles of the part he had played in his restoration, but he was somewhat startled at the way Foster tried to elbow his way past him in his dealings with the Secretary. Battle had worked a special niche for himself in Dean Acheson's office. He was not only sentry at the gate but Acheson's third ear at almost all interviews which the Secretary conducted.

"Foster didn't like this at all," Battle said. "He didn't like to work through me, didn't see any reason for that young person there having anything to do with *him*. Well, I did have a relationship with Acheson that everybody in the building accepted and I sat in at all his meetings, and knew immediately what was going on. But I didn't press myself on Mr. Dulles, though with everybody else I walked into the room immediately. And if I didn't sit in on the meeting, I asked Acheson immediately afterwards what had happened, and what we had to follow up. This was my role."

Foster Dulles went to see the Secretary a couple of times and made it plain he didn't want Luke Battle around. So the assistant stayed out.

"Well, Acheson forgot to tell me what it was he said he would do, and a couple of things Dulles wanted to get done didn't get done because I didn't know about them. So finally I said to him one day, 'Mr. Dulles, I think it will work a great deal better if I am privy to your conversations with Mr. Acheson. If you have any reason to wish to see him alone, I have no objection, but if I know about it, then it will get done. If I don't know about it, it won't get done.' "

Foster took the hint. Except on rare occasions thereafter, he always indicated he would like Battle along.

"But it was a sort of wary relationship all through," Battle added.

And, of course, as they all ruefully discovered shortly after Foster came aboard, he hadn't changed a bit. They had thought that his months in the desert would have chastened him, and that from now on he would play the game like a member of the team. George F. Kennan was the first to find out that he still insisted on following his own set of rules.

By the time John Foster Dulles came into the State Department in 1950 as bipartisan consultant, the postwar world had evolved with convulsive rapidity. The Iron Curtain had slammed down in Europe. In Asia the red armies of Mao Tse-tung had driven Chiang Kai-shek, America's ally, out of mainland China with the remnants of his forces. There were rumblings of other Asian confrontations, the most potentially dangerous being in Korea. There the country was divided at the 38th Parallel between the Communist North Koreans and the pro-American South Koreans under the leadership of a proud and fiery character named Synghman Rhee. The soldiers from each side glared at each other across the 38th Parallel.

It seemed to strategists in both Washington and London that the sooner a peace treaty could be signed with Japan, just across the water from both China and Korea, the better could that palpitating mass of people be kept out of any coming Asiatic upheaval.

But what sort of peace? Thanks to General MacArthur, Japan had been under enlightened military occupation by U.S. (and token British,

Australian, and New Zealand) forces since its surrender in 1945, but, particularly with those countries whose armies and peoples had experienced the barbarism of the Japanese military in wartime, it would be a long time before they would be forgiven or their excesses forgotten. They had already made it plain in Sydney, Auckland, and Manila that they hoped to see a peace treaty signed that would remind the Japanese for generations to come of the monstrousness of their wartime behavior.

On the other hand, the United States badly needed Japan as a military base, and it was obvious that American troops, ships, and planes could not stay there much longer by right of subjugation. Some concessions would have to be made to secure Japanese acceptance and acquiescence.

George F. Kennan and his Policy Planning Staff drew up a paper proposing liberal changes to ease Japan from her status as a defeated enemy into a potential member of the family of free nations, "neutral on our side."

When he read the paper, John Foster Dulles went further. He added a memorandum for Dean Acheson which was short but sage. As Townsend Hoopes wrote later:

> It reflected two deeply held personal convictions: 1) that any attempt to impose vengeful terms on a defeated enemy was a self-destructive approach, and 2) that the intensity of the Cold War now made it imperative to align Japanese interests and assets with the coalition of the free nations. On the first point he was insisting that the world must finally learn and apply the tragic lesson of Versailles—that magnanimity and generosity were essential ingredients of any sane solution, on both moral and practical grounds. . . . On the second point, he was reflecting the growing view that the former Asian enemy must now become an ally.

When a friend asked Dulles how anyone could possibly forgive the Japanese for their appalling war crimes, the Bataan Death March, for instance, he replied: "Jesus teaches us that nothing is unforgivable."

It seemed to Dean Acheson that Dulles was the man for the job of bringing about a Japanese treaty that would be acceptable to all the parties, not simply because his views would gain him a rapport with the Japanese, but because his authority, his air of sincerity, and his sense of purposiveness could well be crucial in persuading Japan's ex-enemies—especially the xenophobic Australians, the New Zealanders, and the British—that they should accept a liberal treaty.

He set off on June 14, 1950, with a single assistant (John Allison) for an exploratory tour of the Far East. He made the journey to Japan by way of South Korea, for he wished to see and talk with President Synghman Rhee. Rhee, a fellow member of the World Council of Churches, was an old friend, and Foster Dulles had always seen qualities in this sly, ruthless Oriental dictator which had escaped other Occidental observers. Synghman Rhee and Chiang Kai-shek were, for him, Christian gentlemen of a very high order. Ambassador George V. Allen, at dinner with Foster Dulles, once ventured to criticize both of them for preventing free elections among their peoples, describing them as "not exactly paragons of the democratic process."

Foster leaned forward in his chair, his eyes blinking, and said:

"Well, I'll tell you this. No matter what you say about the president of Korea and the president of Nationalist China, those two gentlemen are the equivalent of the founders of the Church. They are Christian gentlemen who have suffered for their faith. They have been steadfast and have upheld the faith in a manner that puts them in the category of the leaders of the early Church."

Allen added that Dulles spoke as if he had "his own line to God," and that "he was getting his instructions from a very high source."

Foster Dulles spent four days with Rhee in South Korea and made several speeches and one full-scale address in the South Korean Parliament. President Rhee had expressed fears that war was coming between his country and his North Korean neighbors, and that when it came, America would not be willing to help. He complained that Dean Acheson had already threatened to cut off aid unless he allowed free elections—which he was not about to do.

Foster Dulles took it upon himself to reassure him. In his speech to the Korean Parliament on June 19, he declared:

"The American people welcome you as an equal partner in the great company of those who make up the free world, a world which commands vast moral and material power, and whose resolution is unswerving . . . I say to you: You are not alone. You will never be alone so long as you continue to play worthily your part in the great design of human freedom."

It was a surprisingly bold pronouncement for a bipartisan consultant, especially since the speech had not been cleared with Washington. But it took on an even greater significance the following Sunday (while Foster and Janet were sightseeing in Kyoto, Japan) when the North Koreans invaded South Korea, and seemed likely to score a speedy victory over Synghman Rhee's panicking troops.

Foster rushed back to Tokyo and, with Allison's help, wrote an urgent cable to Acheson recommending that if the South Koreans could not hold the attack, "we believe that United States force should be used," because not to do so "would start a disastrous chain of events leading most probably to world war."

Truman and Acheson, who had started out by being furious with Foster Dulles's Korean speech, now agreed with his assessment of the situation. It was time to show the Communists, the President decided, that armed invasion and the conquering of independent nations would be resisted by the democracies. With the wholehearted support of General MacArthur, Truman ordered in the troops, and, taking the opportunity presented by Russia's absence from the forum, stage-managed a United Nations vote giving America the full support, including military aid, of its members.

When Foster heard the news, while on the way back to the United States, he promptly told Allison that Truman was "the greatest President in history," and was "happy and buoyant" over the way things had turned out. His feelings about the Communists had been crystalizing during his months in the wilderness, and he was increasingly sure that only the active resistance of the democracies would henceforth prevent them from mopping up the small nations of the world.

The American and United Nations action in Korea marked the commencement of the process of "rolling them back."

It had been an exploratory journey, and the Japanese Peace Treaty negotiations still had some way to go; but it was nonetheless an extremely confident John Foster Dulles who arrived back in Washington in mid-July 1950. Before his departure, he had, as the only Republican among all these Democrats, adopted a low posture at State Department meetings, and seemed determined not to be too assertive about his views.

Now he appeared to be cloaked in a new authority, and those around him were immediately conscious of it. George Kennan particularly.

The director of the Policy Planning Staff was worried about Korea, and about Chinese reactions to what was going on there now that the American forces, under UN guidance, were involved.

At the Secretary of State's meeting on July 21, Kennan mentioned that the U.S. government had failed to make it clear that, once the North Korean invaders had been repelled, operations would cease at the 38th Parallel, the dividing line between North and South Korea. He pointed out that the Americans could get themselves into dangerous difficulties if they continued to advance up the Korean Peninsula, because once they were up there, mass armies—Chinese armies— could be used against them, and "we would be distinctly at a disadvantage."

Foster Dulles indicated, almost with a snort of derision, that he didn't agree with this at all. The North Koreans should be shown that invasion didn't pay.

A few days later, on July 25, a meeting at consultant level of the National Security Council was held at which both Kennan and Dulles were present. There had been a move in the United Nations to have the new Communist régime in China admitted to the organization; this had been strongly opposed by the United States, strongly supported by its Asiatic but more reluctantly by its European allies.

Now Kennan expressed the view that America should not be afraid of letting the Chinese Communists be admitted if the other countries wanted them. He didn't suggest that the United States should propose them or even vote for them, but he saw no reason why they should go against the major feeling that China ought to be there.

Foster Dulles spoke up at once, firmly rejecting this viewpoint. It would confuse the American people, it would dismay the Chinese Nationalists under Chiang Kai-shek, and it would weaken the President's program to strengthen American military defenses. An argument began in which Kennan stuck to his point, and Dulles led the opposition to it, gradually lining up Dean Acheson, Dean Rusk, and others behind him. The Secretary eventually decided that there would be no change in American attitude, and that any attempt to let the Chinese Communists into the United Nations would be vetoed. Kennan noted the glint of triumph in Foster's eyes.

All this had, of course, been discussed at a high-level conference in the strictest secrecy, each member speaking freely in the knowledge that he would not subsequently be reported in the press. But a few days later, there was a sequel. George Kennan wrote in his diary on July 28:

> A member of the Planning Staff dropped in to tell me that he had learned from one journalist, who had learned it from another journalist, that Mr. Dulles had said to journalist number two that while he used to think highly of George Kennan, he had now concluded that he was a very dangerous man. He was now advocating the admission of the Chinese Communists to the United Nations and a cessation of United States action at the 38th Parallel. This information had been passed to the member of the Planning Staff under such solemn grounds of secrecy and discretion that I could do nothing about it. It seemed to me to raise serious problems about the privacy of discussion among top officials in the Department in the presence of the political adviser of the Republican Party.

As Paul Nitze remarked: "Foster hasn't changed. He hasn't changed at all."

Later on, Luke Battle wondered "whether I had given birth to a monster" by bringing John Foster Dulles into the State Department in 1950, but that was after Foster went on to bigger things. In 1951, for all his continued tendency to leak the most confidential material, the administration was extremely thankful to have him around. In that year President Truman promoted him from consultant to ambassador-at-large, and told him to spend the whole time on bringing the Japanese Peace Treaty to fruition.

He did so, and it was a remarkable achievement, one which his brother Allen was quite right in later describing as "one of the most extraordinary things he did in his lifetime." His most bitter critics would probably say that it was the only achievement for which he should be remembered.

There were other people involved in drawing up the treaty, of course—George Kennan, Dean Rusk, Paul Nitze, and John Allison among them—but there seems little doubt that without Foster Dulles's "tremendous energy, ingenuity and great skill," as Allen described them, it would never have gone through. And not simply because, as the Republican adviser, he influenced its subsequent ratification in Congress by the GOP. It was his masterly handling of the other nations involved in the negotiations that pushed through the mild treaty which the United States (for strategical purposes) and Foster Dulles himself (for historical reasons) wanted.

The Japanese were all for it, of course, since it unshackled them, restored their independence, gave them a defense force of their own, and made no demands that they pay reparations for the damage and suffering they had wrought during the war. Foster Dulles became a popular figure in Japan as a result.

It was with Japan's former enemies that he needed to summon up his greatest skills as a negotiator and persuader. The French wanted $2 billion for the damage the Japanese had wreaked during the occupation of their Indo-Chinese colony. The Australians and New Zealanders wanted a fifty-year ban on all Japanese rearmament, plus a substantial money compensation for every one of their soldiers and citizens who had been in a Japanese prison camp, or died there. The British wanted control over future Japanese foreign policy and supervision of any alliances Japan might wish to initiate. The Philippines simply wanted to see Japan under continued subjugation and constantly reminded of the wartime outrages she had committed against harmless people.

All these demands were resisted, and all the nations were eventually brought round by Dulles's evident sincerity and the persuasiveness of his arguments, the most reluctant being the Philippines. President Quirino had lost his wife and daughter at the hands of the Japanese, and every government representative to whom the ambassador-at-large talked had suffered personally and seen the people suffering around him during the Japanese occupation. They told heart-rending tales. Now they wanted revenge—a permanent boot on Japan's neck, and, as some monetary compensation for the Philippine people, a reparations payment of $8 billion.

No mere eloquence was going to succeed here, so Foster Dulles concentrated on the long-range strategic need to conclude a reasonable treaty. Eventually President Quirino gave way with these words:

"I have no reason to do anything but hate the Japanese. But I've listened to you and what you've said, and after all we must remember that God put us both in the same ocean and we've got to get along with each other in the future."

Foster came back with a general agreement in his pocket, and roughed out a draft treaty in thirteen pages. It was subjected to some alterations when submitted to the interested parties, but its general principles and provisions remained the same. A last attempt was made by the Russians to wreck it, but this was deftly overcome by the skillful maneuvering of Dean Acheson, and the Japanese Peace Treaty was formally signed in the Opera House at San Francisco on September 4, 1951.

Almost everyone praised John Foster Dulles for the tireless efforts and the supreme craftsmanship which he had brought to the negotiations. By sheer force of personality he had won himself a place in the big league of international statesmen, and he would never again be looked upon as a mere bipartisan consultant.

He was well aware of this, and aware, too, of its significance for his future. When President Truman sent his enthusiastic congratulations and offered him, as a reward, the job of first postwar ambassador to Japan, Foster firmly turned him down. He was looking to bigger things. He felt, as he told Truman, that he could be more useful "at the powerhouse than at the end of the transmission line."

He meant a Republican powerhouse, of course, for already his eye was on the 1952 presidential elections, and this time—although he would never again make wild presumptions about the American voter —he was convinced the GOP really had a more than fifty-fifty chance of winning. His new reputation as a negotiator would ensure him a high place in any future Republican administration. Provided, that is, he did not get tainted through guilt-by-association with the less popular measures that the Truman régime had put through while he had been a member of the team.

From the moment the Japanese Peace Treaty was ratified by the U.S. Congress in January 1952, Foster deliberately set out to distance himself from any other decision which the Democrats had taken. He had in fact accompanied Dean Acheson to most of the big political conferences that had taken place in the postwar period, with the exception of the hiatus while he served as senator and his months in limbo thereafter. He had been associated with all the decisions made during that time. Since rejoining the State Department in 1950, he had backed the ratification of the Austrian Treaty, and he had strongly approved the use of American troops in Korea.

But now he set out to demonstrate that these had been decisions in which he had played no part. He had once declared Truman "the greatest President in history" for having intervened in Korea, but now the war was going badly. So he leaked to Carl McCardle a story that he had never really been in favor of intervention. He had once snorted at Kennan for expressing alarm at plans for crossing the 38th Parallel. Now the American army was over the line and in trouble, and Foster hinted to reporters that they should never have crossed it in the first place.

As the credit of the Truman administration dropped with both Congress and public in the winter and spring of 1952, Foster decided that the time had come for him to get out. One day he called Luke Battle on the telephone and asked him to come round to his office. There he handed him a sheet of paper and said: "I am going to resign. I want to show you my farewell press statement."

Battle looked at the paper and was first startled, then angry. He doesn't remember the exact wording, but the drift of the statement was that John Foster Dulles had been brought in by President Truman to negotiate the Japanese Peace Treaty. He had completed that. It was the only thing he had had anything to do with in the administration. He was leaving, having completed the task for which he had been summoned.

Battle "looked him straight in the eye," and said: "Mr. Dulles, this statement suffers from one fundamental defect."

"What is that?" asked Foster.

"It isn't true."

"What do you mean?" asked Foster, indignantly.

"Mr. Dulles," said Battle, "I went very much to bat to get you into this administration, and to have you participate in a great many things, and I have to say that in my presence you have participated in a whole series of important issues."

He then reminded him of them, one by one.

Foster had the grace to look uncomfortable, and agreed to alter the farewell statement to say that he had been called in *primarily* to handle the Japanese Peace Treaty.

"It helped a bit but it wasn't satisfactory," Battle said later. "What he was attempting to do was remove himself from responsibility for anything which had gone on in the régime—and he had been involved in all kinds of things."

Truman and Acheson both shrugged their shoulders and laughed when they heard about it. These things happen in politics, the President said. But Battle was shocked.

"I regretted having brought him in. He had turned out to be an extremely *devious* man, and I ended up with a low opinion of him. He was an intelligent man, and I'll have to admit that there was a first-rate mind there. But from then on I had absolutely no regard for him. More than that, I felt later on that thanks to me, a man had been foisted onto the government who was a disaster for the United States."

Unaware of having made an enemy, Foster Dulles departed for New York to have talks with Thomas E. Dewey and his brother Allen about the prospects for the 1952 election. By this time Harry Truman had announced that he would not be seeking reelection, so the Democratic candidate would be a dark horse. There was no obvious candidate on the horizon.

More than ever it looked as if this could be the GOP's election, so long as a strong and popular candidate could be discovered by the party and sold to the public. But who? The isolationists and the pro-National China lobby in Congress were drumming up the cause of Senator Robert Taft, who was a close friend of Foster Dulles. But that only made him acutely aware that Taft was, in fact, a stubborn and inflexible diehard with entrenched opinions which no amount of argument would change. He had no suppleness or give, and Foster doubted whether he could work with such a man as President. He also doubted whether Taft had the personality needed to win the hearts and the votes of the American people.

At one point during the Dewey-Foster-Allen conversations in New York, General Lucius Clay appeared. He had now retired from his command in Germany and gone into the financial world, a move which Allen, remembering Clay's "war scare" miscalculation of a few years back, considered good for the Army but not necessarily for the banks. Foster was not exactly Clay's greatest admirer, either. They had differed over how to handle the Berlin blockade by the Soviets in 1948,* and Foster considered him altogether too trigger-happy.

But Lucius Clay was a close friend of his former commander-in-chief, General of the Army Dwight D. Eisenhower, who, after an unhappy spell as president of Columbia University, had gone back to Europe as commander-in-chief of NATO. Clay pointed out that the times were tough, what with Soviet aggression in all parts of the world, and were likely to get tougher. What was needed at the top in the United States was a man whose appeal crossed party lines, and whose reputation made him admired and respected, even feared, abroad. He was for Dwight Eisenhower as the Republican candidate and the next President of the United States, the strong man the nation needed.

Both the Dulles brothers stayed noncommittal. In Allen's view, if a strong man was what the nation needed, Eisenhower did not exactly fit the bill. He agreed with Mary Bancroft, who described Ike as "a soldier who doesn't like or want war—doesn't need it for his 'performance.' . . . It's like a whore who believes in chastity." Whatever other qualities he might have, strong he was not.

Foster wondered whether Eisenhower was a real Republican. When he had sought Ike's help during his New York senatorial campaign (while Ike was still at Columbia), he had refused to back him on the grounds that, as a five-star general, he was in the Army for life and must remain "nonpolitical."

A few days later, however, Foster went out to his sister's house in McLean. Eleanor's son, David, was still working in the Senate and had now developed ambitions as a kingmaker.

"My son had thought Foster . . . should know some of these more important senators," Eleanor said later. "And Jim Duff had just been elected to the Senate, so David persuaded me to invite Duff out for dinner to McLean with Foster, and it worked out. They both came. Janet and Mrs. Duff. This was early in 1952. . . . It was good weather, we sat outside, we probably ate outside. Anyway, we sat outside and Foster and Jim Duff walked around the swimming pool, back and forth,

*Clay had wanted to drive a U.S. armored column through the Soviet defenses into the city—"a Clay pigeon put up to be shot at," as Allen termed it. On the advice of General Marshall and Foster Dulles, Truman settled for an airlift into the beleaguered city.

and you could hear what they said when they came this way, but not when they went that way. What they said was that Foster should go to NATO headquarters in France and persuade Eisenhower to run for President."

She added: "Now this doesn't fit in with anything that anybody else has said, except that Foster did go to Paris, he did see Eisenhower, and it was about that time that Eisenhower decided to run for President."

What had happened in between the meetings with Clay and Senator Duff was that Foster and Allen had got their heads together, and had come to the conclusion that Eisenhower was indeed the man they should back for the presidency. What did it matter if he was not the strong man everybody thought, so long as he was popular? Who wanted a strong man in the White House, anyway? Certainly not Foster. Much more important to find out how Eisenhower viewed the world, and whether he would buy the kind of foreign policy that both brothers now considered was needed to face up to the realities of the cold war.

Foster Dulles began to rough out a statement of his views on the world situation, and it is an interesting example of brotherly collaboration, because Allen was involved as a consultant on several occasions during the writing. Foster's own views of how to cope with what he viewed as a growing Soviet menace to the free world is immediately recognizable in one of the key statements in the document:

> There is one solution and only one: that is for the free world to develop the will and organize the means to retaliate *instantly* against open aggression by the Red armies, so that, if it occurred anywhere, we could and would strike back where it hurts, by means of our own choosing.

It was the first indication that his mind was working toward what would later become known as "massive retaliation."

But Allen's influence at this stage persuaded Foster to point out that such retaliations need not necessarily mean that the United States should go on relying on conventional forces and spending enormously on armaments. There were other means: *covert means.* The term was not used in the paper, but there were continual references to "freedom programs" for the captive peoples of eastern Europe, schemes to "put heavy new burdens on the jailers," and laudatory references to the CIA's pet projects, Radio Free Europe* and the Voice of America.

When the statement was finished, Foster handed it over to Lucius Clay, who took it with him to Paris to show Eisenhower. Shortly afterwards, Foster followed. He had two meetings (in May 1952) with the general at SHAPE headquarters at Fontainebleau, and came away by no means sure that Eisenhower was a convinced supporter of firmness in the face of Communist aggression, but aware that as a man he was charming, modest, and malleable. Add to that his reputation as the man who had won World War II, and he seemed just the candidate the Republicans needed.

But where would he, Foster, stand in the event of his adoption? Eisenhower had made it clear that, for his part, he was quite willing for Foster to draw up the foreign policy program of the party for the election. But, ever the good chairman, anxious as always to bring rivals together, he suggested that Foster might feel the need to talk to the other, pro-Taft, wing of the party and endeavor to secure its agreement. This was exactly what Foster did immediately after returning to Washington; he saw Robert Taft himself, informed him that he had decided to support Eisenhower's candidacy, and pleaded with him to abandon his own ambitions and join him. Taft made it clear that he was still in the running and could count on considerable party support, but he did make one remarkable concession to his friend. He told Foster that he would be agreeable if he wrote the foreign policy program of the party on behalf of both Eisenhower and himself.

A few days later, Foster announced publicly his support for Eisenhower's candidature. He had meanwhile been in touch with the Time-Life organization in New York, and two weeks later the paper he had prepared for Eisenhower's approval was published in *Life* Magazine under the title "A Policy of Boldness." It sharply attacked the Truman administration's handling of overseas affairs, particularly the Korean War, now in its most humiliating stage, and told the nation the time had come for a change. It was a blueprint of John Foster Dulles's very personal foreign policy program for the Republican Party.

The article caused a good deal of comment in political circles, and no one read it with more avid interest than Allen and Eleanor Dulles.

*Organized by Frank Wisner in 1949.

It had the feel of having been written by an up-and-comer, in tune with the mood of the country, confident that his time was coming, a winner's program if ever there was one. If that were so, both Allen and Eleanor sensed that rewards were coming for them too. Allen was now back in the CIA. Eleanor was preparing to go back to the State Department.

Could it be that a Dulles era was about to begin, with all that could mean for their own future roles in the running of the United States?

CHAPTER SIXTEEN

Beetle Juice

Allen Dulles came in from the wings and back on center stage in the fall of 1950.

One morning in late November of that year he was in his office at Sullivan & Cromwell when the telephone rang. General Walter Bedell Smith was on the other end of the line, and Allen did not need to be told why he was calling. The buzz had already reached him.

"Say," said the general, "you're the guy who wrote most of the Dulles-Jackson-Correa Report, aren't you?"

"I had some part in it," Allen replied modestly.

"I know what part you had in it," the general said. "Now don't you think it's time you gave up those lucrative legal pursuits of yours and got down here to tell us how to implement some of the changes you suggested?"

Allen said: "I'd have to clear up my desk here first."

"You do that," said Bedell Smith, "and report here Monday."

It was the Korean War which had brought the general into the CIA as its new director. Though there had been rumblings of approaching trouble long before the North Koreans finally attacked across the 38th Parallel, the actual advance had taken the United States completely by surprise, as had the strength and military expertise of the North Korean forces. This was principally due to the fact that the Far East commander, General of the Army Douglas MacArthur, ran his own intelligence services in the theater and wouldn't allow CIA in. His G2 arm had not only failed to predict the attack but grossly underestimated the North Koreans, whose army, MacArthur confidently stated, he could lick "with one arm tied behind my back." But this the public didn't know and Congress refused to recognize. They wanted to know why the CIA hadn't had agents inside North Korea signaling the enemy's moods and intentions, and put it down to the woeful state of the Agency.

Well, as Allen Dulles knew, the CIA was in a woeful state, even if it couldn't be blamed for Korea. The NSC50 report had made that quite clear. But what with one thing and another, it was not until the charges started flying around Washington that Truman at last decided to ask for Admiral Hillenkoetter's resignation and called General Walter Bedell Smith to take his place. At the same time he handed him the Dulles-Jackson-Correa Report and told him to use it as a blueprint for reorganizing the Agency and reshaping it to fit the times.

"Beetle" Smith, as he was called, told the President that he would have to hold his horses for a time while he had an ulcer operation, but that he would read the report through as soon as he regained consciousness. He then went into the hospital to have half his stomach cut away. That was in the summer of 1950; he did not take over his new job until the following October.

He was worth waiting for. Walter Bedell Smith was one of the more interesting and rewarding results of the American process. A poor boy who barely finished high school, and never got near West Point, he joined the Army from the Indiana National Guard and was commissioned in France in 1917 during World War I.* In World War II he rose to the rank of three-star general and served in Europe as General Eisenhower's Chief of Staff. Those who observed him at close quarters during that period—especially in the critical days before the D-Day landings in France—were aware that he was a much stronger character than his amiable chief, and that it was he who stiffened Ike's boldness and resolution during his worst moments of doubt. The war would not have gone so well in Europe without him.

In his postwar years Bedell Smith had served as ambassador to Moscow. He had come away with a deep suspicion of Marxist philosophy, a hatred of Soviet cruelty, deception, and hostility, and a contempt for any "parlor pinks," as he called them, in the United States who believed that communism was the salvation of the people. He was a rabid enemy of the Soviet system abroad and *any* form of socialism

---

*Which was where, the story had it, he had first met Allen Dulles—at the Sphynx, the famous Paris brothel.

at home, and he could see something subversive in the mildest liberal comments. He was once, for instance, reputed to have called Nelson D. Rockefeller a "red" for a lukewarm statement in favor of the unions.

But though charm was a quality that escaped him and though he had a temper, as one Agency official described it, "that only a mother could abide," those who watched him closely in war and peace never saw him penalize a man for his opinions, no matter how much he loathed them. But with those who made mistakes he could be ruthless.

"He was brutal, brutal," one CIA man said. "Every staff meeting was a squash court, and you never knew who was going to get hit next. He used to say that every officer had a right to one mistake—and you've just had yours."

Yet his qualities as an organizer, his remarkable percipience, his formidable memory, and his hard-driving determination to step on everyone and thrust all obstacles aside to achieve the task he had set himself were such that even his enemies were forced to admire him.

"It was fortunate for the CIA that it was Smith, not Dulles, who presided (1950–53) over the reorganization of the post-war raggletaggle that followed Truman's disbandment of the OSS," wrote Kim Philby later.*

> I fear that Dulles would have confounded confusion. But Smith was no chairman. He was the boss, and a boss of outstanding intellect and character. Many times I saw him read a long memorandum, toss it aside and, without pause for thought, paragraph by numbered paragraph, rip its guts out—real virtuoso stuff! With him, I had to do my homework; with Dulles, it was desirable, but not necessary.

He ripped the guts out of the NSC50 report and, to the consternation of those who knew about it, put in a call to London and asked an Englishman to become his deputy and take over control of all foreign intelligence operations of the CIA. The man to whom he put this extraordinary request was an old friend and wartime colleague, General (later Sir) Kenneth Strong, who had acted as Chief of the Intelligence Staff at Supreme Allied Headquarters during World War II under Eisenhower. A brilliant linguist and intelligence analyst, Strong was now head of the Joint Intelligence Bureau at the War Office in

*In a letter to the author.

London. Beetle Smith, with whom he had worked in happy collaboration from just before the D-Day invasion of France to the collapse of Germany, told Strong that they would remake the CIA together. It was a tempting prospect for Strong. He was well aware that the strengths and influences of British and American intelligence services were changing, and that his own would soon be in decline.

"Does it mean I would have to become an American citizen?" he asked.

"Yes, of course," said Smith, "but we can soon fix that up. We might even get you married to an American girl."*

There was a pause, and then Strong said: "I'm sorry. I don't think I could do that."

"Why not?" asked Smith. "I thought you liked Americans."

"Oh, I do. You're splendid chaps—absolutely splendid fellows. But I don't think I could ever stop being an Englishman." A pause. "Not at my age. I'm sorry, Beetle."

It was just as well, because it seems doubtful if President Truman and his advisers would have allowed even Beetle Smith to get away with such an appointment.

Rebuffed by his old friend, Smith then offered the post of deputy director to William H. Jackson, proving that, like some of his subordinates, he could sometimes make a cardinal error. He had given Jackson credit for producing the major part of NSC50, and had believed advisers who told him that Jackson was a first-rate intelligence officer. In fact, Jackson was a good administrator but lacked flair. It was Allen Dulles who had written the most important parts of the report, and no one questioned that he knew the espionage game backwards. Moreover, Jackson was supremely unaware of his own comparative dullness, and had a drinking problem. He quickly demonstrated that he was totally unsuitable for the job.

Beetle Smith set about remedying the situation as gently as possible so far as Jackson was concerned. After all, it was he who had persuaded him to give up a well-paying job (with J. H. Whitney, the New York stockbroking firm) and asked him aboard, and it was he who must suffer for the error. It took him some time to engineer Jackson's retire-

*Strong was a lifelong bachelor.

ment without hurting his feelings, but eventually "he left us," as one CIA agent unkindly put it, "from the rear end of the horse first, as he had come in."

Meanwhile, Smith reached for the telephone again and called Allen Dulles. Allen, who had been considerably jolted and offended at having been overlooked in favor of Jackson, whom he felt to be his inferior, nevertheless made no effort to play hard to get. Like his brother, he knew when and how to be humble; he badly wanted the job, and when he got it was the time to begin maneuvering. He accepted without any hesitation. Smith then assured him that if he would come in and just "shuffle papers around" for a time, he would get Jackson's job.

One of the main recommendations Allen had made in the NSC50 report was that the Office of Policy Guidance (OPC), the cover intelligence operation for which he had recommended Frank Wisner as assistant director more than two years earlier, should be brought under the CIA's control. It was supposed to be overseen by the State and Defense Departments, but under Wisner's direction it had become a successful intelligence unit on its own, operating on a secret budget with little or no superintendence. Admiral Hillenkoetter had strongly protested, in vain. Wisner was far too vigorous to be restrained by him.

Beetle Smith had the necessary muscle and recognized the wisdom of Allen's recommendation. Shortly after taking over at the CIA, he announced that OPC would be brought into the Agency and Wisner would henceforth report to him. Wisner was content with that since he was assured that, as deputy director of Plans, he would still be running covert operations and would be in complete charge of the far-flung intelligence service he had built up. He now had what the OPC called "back alley" operations going in Europe and Asia, all of them aimed at curtailing Communist advances. He had had particularly spectacular successes in Italy, where he had wrecked red hopes of winning the election by backing the Socialists and Christian Democrats while, at the same time, financing plots to denigrate the Communists by all means, fair and foul. He was working in close cooperation with General Gehlen's units in Germany. He was operating in Malaya, the Dutch East Indies, and sending agents into China.

Wisner had no qualms about Beetle's decision, and his satisfaction over working with the new CIA chief was certainly not diminished when he heard that Allen Dulles was coming back aboard. But that was where he got a shock. Once inside the Agency, Allen was by no means content to "shuffle papers" while waiting to step into Jackson's shoes. He needed a division and a title. He told Beetle Smith he would accept the post of deputy director of Plans.

"But what about Frank Wisner?" the director asked.

"Oh, he won't mind," said Allen. "We're friends. He's worked under me before."

It was all the same to Beetle as long as the Agency got itself organized. He sent Wisner word that he had been dropped a rung to component chief and that he was to report to the new deputy director of Plans, Allen Dulles.

"The two men were old and dear friends, but it caused a bit of feeling," an Agency man said. "Frank didn't make as much fuss as he did later, when someone stole his cook, but I think he was hurt. He'd done things for Allen while he'd been at OPC, and he didn't like what had happened."

Allen Dulles stayed for three months as deputy director of Plans, and spent most of that time catching up with what was in the dossiers. He was "shuffling the papers" after all, but to some effect. Beetle Smith had made it plain that he was going to get on with the job of reorganizing the structure of the Agency—which he proceeded to do with skill, effectiveness, and dispatch—while Allen oversaw all future foreign operations and meanwhile caught up with what had been happening. Both of them wanted to know, in particular, what Wisner and the OPC had achieved—and failed to achieve.

The credit balance was considerable. One of Wisner's early moves, as soon as he had turned OPC into a viable operation, with its own unvouchered funds, had been to make contact with General Gehlen at Pullach in Germany and form a link between the German's unit and his own. Gehlen was more than ready to be amenable to reasonable terms, for he was being kept on a starvation diet by the U.S. Army and in danger of having to cut down his operations. To raise funds he had spent the last $125,000 in his budget buying cocoa from the Army Post Exchange and selling it on the black market at quadruple prices. He had pleaded in vain for more.

Now Wisner came with an offer of enough money to bail him out and

273

more. In the late spring of 1949 the terms were finally settled, and the Gehlen unit became an operating arm of OPC. It began bringing in results almost at once. Gehlen triumphantly produced the plans and test-flight records of Russia's first jet plane, the Mig15. He followed these with a detailed account of Soviet plans to establish a quasi-military force in East Germany (contrary to the Potsdam agreement with the Allies), which would be camouflaged as a police unit, to be known as the Volkspolizei (VOPO); when the Allies had digested this, it would be followed in turn by a gradual conscription of young men into a People's Army.

Gehlen also turned over to OPC a complete list of his unit's "V" men in East Germany; henceforward, they would work for Wisner. They included several East Germans who were, ostensibly, members in good standing of the Communist Party. One of them was Kurt Heinz Wallesch, who was a member of the committee of the East German Party, a senior councilor in the administration of the city of Leipzig, and a close friend of General Timon Dudorov, the Soviet army's district commander; and another was Dr. Hans Jess, director of the East German railroad system. There were others in less prominent but no less important positions.

Gehlen's unit at Pullach had begun a systematic investigation of all German prisoners-of-war now beginning to return from prison camps in Russia. What had their experiences been like? What had they seen? Had they learned to speak Russian, Polish, Siberian dialects? Had they brought any souvenirs back?

When Wisner examined the results of this probe, he realized he had found a treasure trove of information about the Soviet Union. Most of the ex-prisoners had brought back scraps of paper—passes, vouchers, tickets, notepaper, and the like—which would be invaluable for use in forging fake papers and genuine-looking "pocket trash" for spies. There were maps of the regions where prisoners had seen tank factories, army barracks and headquarters, airfields and navy yards. Several men had worked in the mines in Siberia, and one reported that the pit where he had been employed to shift debris seemed different from the others; the workers in it wore gloves and protective clothing. He had brought back a souvenir, which Gehlen's interrogator took for examination.

It was a rock containing uranium. The location of the mine where

the prisoner had worked proved that the Soviets were no longer relying on Czechoslovakian mines alone for uranium supplies. They now
had a source in Siberia.

The Gehlen dossiers in the OPC files intrigued Allen Dulles so much
that he flew out to Germany to renew his acquaintance with the general. The years had done nothing to diminish Gehlen's peacock persona, and in thought, manner, and braggadocio he was as much, if not
more, of a Nazi as ever. Allen had no illusions about him. Later on, he
was asked how he could employ and consort with such a rascal.

"I don't know if he is a rascal," he replied. "There are few archbish-
ops in espionage. He's on our side and that's all that matters. Besides,
one needn't ask him to one's club."

But he was pleased with him, and promised him all the funds he
could use if he could help the CIA set up espionage agents in Soviet
Russia itself and get them into successful operations. This was now one
of his prime ambitions.

The Gehlen dossiers, however, were only part of Wisner's successful
operations. Besides the detailed accounts of how much he had paid,
and to whom, to swing the elections in Italy, there were the names of
soi-disant Communist trade union leaders in France who had accepted
bribes to break the great strikes there. Among those on the most-secret
list of OPC informants and collaborators was a monsignor at the Vatican, a member of the French cabinet, a Soviet military police chief in
Austria, and a girlfriend of one of Marshal Tito's chief aides.

Wisner was in process of raising small private armies of Russian
dissidents: Rumanian, Hungarian, Bulgarian, and Ukranian refugees
for possible future armed missions into their former homelands.* He
planned to add stations to Radio Free Europe for broadcasting more
anti-Communist propaganda into Russia's east European satellites.
Their role would change into that of channels of communication in the
event of uprisings, spontaneous or otherwise.

One thing Wisner never seemed to have lacked was ideas, and some
of them had been brilliantly successful. There was one that gave Allen
Dulles a certain quiet satisfaction. He had never quite got over the
embarrassment that Noel Field had caused him by concealing the fact
that he had been a card-carrying Communist from his student days,

---

*Some time in the mid-fifties, he hoped.

and had used both Dulles and the OSS in Switzerland as dupes during the last stages of World War II. It was the British SIS, still somewhat jealous of Allen's successes in Switzerland, which had called Wisner's attention to the fact that "Joe Stalin's man on Mr. Dulles' staff in Berne" had finally come into the open as a member of the Communist Party. They reported that he was flying to Czechoslovakia in May 1949, and planned to offer his services to the party machine there.

An idea bubbled in Frank Wisner's calculating mind after he had read through the British memorandum. Since Field had used his friend Allen as a dupe, why not reciprocate? It so happened that he had lately acquired an important agent who was a high official of the Polish Communist Party's security services in Warsaw. By the very nature of his job, he was in close touch with the KGB in Moscow and the security services of the other east European satellites. His name was Jose Swiatlo,* and Wisner now sent a message to him. He told Swiatlo to spread the word to his opposite numbers in Moscow, Prague, Budapest, Bucharest, Sofia, and East Berlin that Noel Field was an agent working for the CIA, sent on a special mission by his erstwhile wartime collaborator, Allen Dulles. Swiatlo should let it be known that all Field's old Communist friends, with whom he had worked in Spain, France, and Switzerland, were now back in eastern Europe and were suspected of being part of Field's network.

The scheme worked far beyond Wisner's calculations. It was an arctic moment in the cold war, with a psychopathically fearful Josef Stalin desperately afraid of his friends, collaborators, and allies. The word went out from Moscow. Field was arrested in Prague and taken to Budapest. There, a few days later, the Hungarian foreign minister, Laszlo Rajk, was charged with treason. Noel Field had helped to rescue him from a Vichy French prison camp during World War II, and they were old comrades. (Rajk was subsequently found guilty of working with Field and the CIA and executed.)

It was as if Field's arrest was the catalyst which released all the pent-up paranoia that now began to surge through the corridors of Soviet power in eastern Europe. The second great purge began, and no one was immune from it. Not only were friends of Field flung into jail and tortured, tried, and executed, but so were casual acquaint-

*Swiatlo defected to the United States in 1953 and is now a U.S. citizen living under another name.

ances, people whom he had once met on a street corner or seen in a camp he had visited. The dragnet was spread across all the satellite countries; first his friends were drawn in, then friends of his friends, then members of their staffs, their families, their neighbors. As the fever mounted, Swiatlo took the opportunity to pay off old scores by bringing in officials he disliked, or those who had done him a disservice. He personally arrested the First Secretary of the Polish Communist Party, Josef Gomulka.

Wisner exultantly reported that over 100,000 Communists were in jail, or had already been executed—the figure rose to 150,000 by the end of 1950—and "the comrades are merrily sticking knives in each others' backs and doing our dirty work for us." The names of Noel Field and Allen Dulles figured in the trials of all of them. It was a neat coup, though not one, perhaps, for the squeamish to think about. Allen Dulles, however, had long since acquired a strong enough stomach to contemplate it without nausea. As for Noel Field, he was certainly in no position to complain about what his fellow Communists and his fellow Americans between them had done to him. He was languishing incommunicado in a Budapest jail. On Wisner's advice, the State Department was not taking any serious steps to find out what had happened to him, either.*

If Allen Dulles still remembered that moment in Zürich in 1918, when a twelve-year-old Noel Field had pledged himself "to bring peace to the world," he must have reflected that he had achieved singularly little of his lifelong aim. But as a pawn in the game, he had certainly had his uses.

All these were Frank Wisner's successes, and Allen Dulles lifted his hat to his assistant for his remarkable performance in less than three years. But there had been failures, too, and one of them stuck out like a sore thumb.

In April 1950, in collaboration with the British SIS, Wisner had organized what was intended to be a *coup d'état* in one of the key

---

*Noel Field and his wife, Herta, who was arrested when she flew into eastern Europe to look for him, were released after the death of Stalin in 1954. They had been held in nearby cells in the same jail, unknown to each other, since 1949. When they learned the truth about Noel's arrest, they refused to return to the United States and turned in their passports, electing instead to stay on in Hungary. Noel Field died in Budapest in 1972.

countries of the Balkans. In the bitter and often bloody skirmishes, overt and clandestine, of the cold war, Greece had seen hundreds of her children kidnapped and taken into eastern Europe and her independence threatened, though she had finally been wrested from the hands of the Communists. Yugoslavia under Marshal Tito had broken away from Moscow's domination. One small and strategically important nation on the shores of the Mediterranean remained in Communist hands: Albania. Both Wisner and the British were convinced that the red-aligned dictator, Enver Hoxha, had only a tenuous hold on the loyalties of his fellow countrymen and that he could be removed by an uprising without much trouble, always provided that some help was forthcoming from outside.

An army of five hundred Albanian émigrés was recruited, armed, and trained in Greece, and sent across the border into Albania in April 1950. The émigrés and their CIA and SIS advisers had been assured that they would achieve complete surprise, and little or no resistance would be encountered. In any case, the Albanian troops were extremely poorly armed.

It was a wrong assessment if ever there was one. Not only did the invaders meet troops armed with machine guns, mortars, and artillery, but they were ambushed at exactly those points where they had been assured they would have a free passage. Two hundred men were slaughtered; 120 were captured and subsequently executed; only 180 men struggled back to Greece, where they angrily cried out:

"But they were waiting for us! They knew we were coming!"

How? Who had betrayed them?

The more Allen Dulles studied the dossier of the Albanian misadventure, the firmer became his conviction that it was not just tittle-tattle among the émigré troops which had tipped off the Hoxha régime to the operation. Playback comments from CIA agents in eastern Europe, and reports from the Gehlen unit, strongly indicated that it was Moscow which had masterminded the counterrevolution and routed the invaders. There was convincing evidence that the Soviet government had flown its own troops into Albania just before the Anglo-American invasion began, and had positioned them along the exact routes the invaders followed—routes which only the planners at the top knew about until sealed orders were broken at H-Hour.

Someone in London or Washington had obviously betrayed the

plans to Moscow, and it was probably Washington. There, the day-to-day planning of the operation had been concentrated on a Committee of Four representing the State Department, the British Foreign Office, the OPC, and the SIS. Robert Joyce, a Balkan expert, sat in for State; Earl Jellico, of the British Embassy, for the Foreign Office; Frank Lindsay, Wisner's deputy, for OPC; and Harold A. R. (Kim) Philby for the SIS.

A process of involved cross-checking enabled Allen Dulles to eliminate three names, but the fourth intrigued him. He called Wisner.

"Tell me something about Kim Philby," he said. "I've read his c.v. What's he like personally?"

"Kim? A great feller," said Wisner. "Never met a Limey easier to deal with. He's a real friend. Like to meet him socially?"

"Yes," said Allen Dulles.

"Good," said Wisner. "I'm giving a party."

Harold Adrian Russell Philby, known to everyone as Kim, had arrived in Washington from London in 1949 to act as liaison officer between the British and American intelligence services and coordinate their activities in various parts of the world. Those were the days when the British were still looked up to by the Americans as the masters of the intelligence game, though at the moment rather strapped for funds, and the policy on both sides was supposed to be complete openness and a mutual trust. In fact, neither the SIS nor the CIA ever told each other *everything.* The Americans, for instance, were extremely reticent about their dealings with the Gehlen unit, and the British kept silent about many of their activities in the Far East. But *en principe* they were partners. They continued to consult about mutual problems even when, late in 1949, a British scientist, Dr. Klaus Fuchs, was found to be passing American atomic secrets to the Russians, and a little later, when it became apparent that, among the personnel of the British Embassy in Washington, there had been an extremely active spy for Moscow who had reported on the most confidential discussions, including NATO secrets.

There were, in fact, three major Soviet spies of British nationality working against the Americans during the 1949–51 period. One was Donald Maclean, who had formerly worked in the British Embassy in Washington but had gone back to London to become head of the

American Department at the Foreign Office. The second was Guy Burgess, a gay and orgiastically inclined drunk who had been posted to Washington as an SIS official. The third was Kim Philby.

Maclean and Burgess need not concern us here. They slipped away before Allen Dulles had any contact with them. But Kim Philby he had a great deal to do with.

Philby, son of the great Arabist, Harry St. John Philby—friend and adviser of King ibn-Saud of Saudi Arabia—had been a Soviet spy since his college days, but had spent most of his life concealing that fact from his friends and colleagues. Not even his wife and children suspected that he was anything but a loyal Briton of slightly right-wing views, pro-Franco during the Spanish Civil War, pro-Chamberlain in the days before World War II when Britain was appeasing Hitler and the Nazis.

During World War II he had done first-class work as a member of the British intelligence services, and had been made an Officer of the Order of the British Empire for his brilliant campaign in tracking down Nazi spies in Spain and Portugal. Many of his friends thought that he should have been rewarded with a knighthood.

Now he was in Washington as liaison officer between the SIS and the CIA, and everyone agreed that he was a popular choice. He had arrived during the days when Admiral Hillenkoetter was still director of the Agency, and no one raised an eyebrow when he took a biggish house on Nebraska Avenue and started giving parties and receptions. His income was £2,000 a year ($8,000) and British expense allowances were scanty in those days. He had no private income, as the SIS knew. Yet no questions were asked, even when Guy Burgess moved in with him and the parties got much rougher and rowdier.*

In fact, in the cellar at Nebraska Avenue, Philby had encoding and photographic equipment, and after every important CIA and OPC meeting that he attended on behalf of the SIS, he made meticulous notes which he passed on to one or other of his Soviet "controllers" in the United States. It was in this way that he had conveyed to Moscow full details of the joint operation against Albania.

Almost at once he had formed a close liaison with Frank Wisner, who quickly became friendly and trusted him completely. That was not unexpected, since Philby had come to Washington strongly recom-

*Though Philby's wife, who didn't like him, complained about Burgess's drunkenness, and the neighbors complained about the noise.

mended by the new British intelligence chief, Major General Sir John Sinclair, and with a brilliant reputation from World War II. He had then made himself an expert on German intelligence systems, particularly the Gehlen unit, and this naturally interested Wisner greatly.

To begin with, the encounters were formal.

"There were major conferences which I attended both in Washington and London," Kim Philby wrote later,*

> formal affairs with several representatives on each side. AD [Allen Dulles] would open for their side, Sinclair for ours, with a load of generalities. Then the Wisners, Angletons, etc., would get to grips with matters of substance. When substances emerged, Sinclair's interventions were more frequent than AD's. Then I, as one of the two conference secretaries, would get together with my U.S. opposite number, draft the minutes and record the compromises reached. There was very little acrimony. Much of the agenda concerned what we called "war planning," stay-behind organisations, etc. Most of the people whose potentialities were earnestly discussed are now dead—of old age.

But later there were working conferences in Washington with only four or five participants and Philby was the lone Briton present.

"They would end by Wisner or whoever producing Bourbon from his office bar," Philby said, "after which we would debate the wisdom of again abandoning our wives for a regular-guy evening on the town."

But if Philby pretended to reciprocate Wisner's friendship, the feeling was, in fact, like most other emotions in his life, spurious.

"I should here declare an interest," he wrote to the author about Wisner.

> I never liked him. Our professional and social relations were always friendly, but there was a false note. I thought him pompous? self-opinionated? aggressive? too stout and too bald for his age? a shade too cordial towards the British liaison officer? Perhaps all of those things. Anyway, the feeling was always there on my side. So, as a friend, he fell short of bosom.

He added: "Wisner had a sense of mission, and the power-hunger that often goes with it. He was shrewd enough, with a sense of movement in the Corridors; drove himself hard, professionally and socially; drank heavily and regularly (but I never saw him drunk)."

*In a letter to the author.

281

They saw a lot of each other out of the office, at Philby's house on Nebraska Avenue, at Frank Wisner's home in the suburbs. And it was there that Allen Dulles made it plain that he too would like to begin seeing Philby socially. Thereafter they were always bumping into each other at parties. It did not arouse any suspicion on Philby's part, because Dulles was well known in Washington as a gregarious type ("he refueled himself on parties after an exhausting day at the office," one CIA man said) and they moved in the same circles.

Philby found in Allen Dulles qualities that were missing in Frank Wisner. He was "nicer." He didn't admire him as an intelligence expert, nor give him credit for having a keen mind. He writhed over his "compulsive resort to cliché" and groaned when he used a favorite phrase: "I can make an educated guess" (which usually meant "I don't know, but . . ."). Nor did he believe his fame as a wartime spymaster was altogether justified.

"All intelligence people who achieve fame or notoriety, *quorum pars minima fui,* are elevated to legendary status—by their own side," Philby commented in parenthesis, wryly. "Dulles did nothing to play down his legend; his unprofessional delight in cloak-and-dagger for its own sake was an endearing trait. It sank him, finally, in the Bay of Pigs."

But he seemed so obviously friendly (and pro-English, moreover) that Philby warmed to him.

"I visited his home a few times," Philby said. "There I met Clover, but she is no more than a blur in my memory; another gracious American hostess, perhaps more lively, less self-conscious than some. But it would be quite unfair of me to attempt an assessment on such vague recollections."

Usually, however, he would join Allen and two or three CIA colleagues for lunch or dinner in Washington at the Colony, La Salle, Mayflower, Shoreham, or other D.C. restaurants ("Harvey's was off-limits because of Hoover's addiction to the place; it is nice to have found out that he never paid for his meals"). Philby would often call at Allen's office in the late afternoon on business, "knowing that he would soon suggest drifting out to a friendly bar for a further round of shop-talk. In short, nothing eccentric or particularly worthy of note; a predictable pattern for a predictable person."

The Briton seemed to have no inkling that he was being cultivated for any other than social purposes. He was not particularly wary and he had no fear that this was a man capable of stripping off the cover which he had so carefully erected, like layers of coral, over his true mission and persona for so many years. For Philby it was Beetle Smith who had "a cold, fishy eye and a precision-tool brain," while Allen Dulles was "bumbling."

"Why did I call him 'bumbling'?" he commented.

> Well, it was the first adjective which occurred to me after our introductory meeting, and he gave me no cause for second thoughts. He had a habit of talking around a problem, not coming to grips with it. Sometimes, he seemed to be ruminating aloud—and pretty diffusedly at that; sometimes, when several of us were present, he would talk at random until we had all spoken, then mull and mumble over verbal formulae which might cover all views, however conflicting they might be. In short, he was the genial chairman.

He added:

> Your prodding has caused me to think more deeply than for many years about AD. I find recurring, with inexorable insistence, the adjective "lazy." Of course, AD was an active man, in the sense that he would talk shop late into the night, jump into aeroplanes, rush around sophisticated capitals and exotic landscapes. But did he ever apply his mind *hard* to a problem that did not engage his personal interest and inclination; or was he basically a line-of-least resistance man? . . . Personally, I liked him a lot. He was nice to have around: good, comfortable, predictable, pipe-sucking, whiskey-sipping company. A touch of Hannay, perhaps; definitely not Bond (detestable fellow!).

What Philby does not seem to have realized was that Allen was almost as good an actor as he was, that he too had built up a persona over the years, and that all was not as sunny, lighthearted, and easygoing inside as it seemed on the surface. There were, too, senior members of his staff to whom he listened carefully, even when it was only small talk between them, and the one to whom he paid most heed was his director of Counterintelligence, James Jesus Angleton. Angleton was Allen's antithesis, a cold fish, unsociable, introverted, relaxed only with Englishmen and his friends in the Israeli intelligence services, with whom he had close connections. But underneath his distant manner and snobbish air, he had an acute skill for sensing the phoney in men, and an unerring eye for the chinks in their armor. And at a late night session with Allen, he had once talked about Kim Philby. He described how, one day in London shortly after the war, they were on their way to a ceremony at Buckingham Palace where King George VI was to present an award to Philby for his wartime services. Perhaps Philby was disenchanted that it was only an OBE when, as many of his friends thought, he had really earned himself a knighthood. At any rate, he stopped just before they entered the yard of the Palace, and, turning to Angleton, said: "You know, what this country could do with is a good dose of socialism."

To Angleton, the remark rang bells.

"From that moment on, I've been wary of the fellow," he told Allen. "You know, he sounded like a Commie. I have a feeling in my bones about him."

Allen had remembered that comment, tucked it away in his mind, but never for a moment let Philby know that it had been made. He was always as amiable as ever, and as "bumbling," when he was in the Briton's presence. But what Philby should have known was that when he began "ruminating aloud—and pretty diffusedly at that," as Philby scornfully put it—it was time to beware of him. Both Allen and Foster indulged in this Dulles trait, and it was while they were doing so that it paid to be most suspicious and attentive. In the case of Allen, this was when he could be at his most dangerous; and in the case of Foster, it was when he could be at his most misleading, as many world statesmen subsequently discovered to their cost.

Four months after Allen Dulles returned to the official world of espionage, William Jackson at last resigned and he took over from him as deputy director of the CIA. (At the same time Frank Wisner slipped back into his old job as director of Plans.) Allen had mentioned his suspicions about Kim Philby to Beetle Smith, who had in turn discussed them with Jackson. And that was unfortunate. Just before leaving, Jackson sent out an instruction that in future Philby was to have certain information withheld from him and certain topics were not to be discussed at meetings where he was present.*

* Some friends of Jackson deny that he was responsible for the order, but as deputy director he should certainly have known that it had been made.

Allen Dulles, as soon as he took over, tried to remedy this mistake in tactics by restoring Kim Philby's "privileges," for the last thing he wished to do was alert the British officer to the fact that he was suspected. But it was too late; the damage was done. Philby was too smart not to discover what had happened, and he pressed one of his emergency buttons. Alerting his Soviet controller to what was going on, he urged immediate action. He made only one error of judgment. Convinced that his own cover was still complete, and that not even the fishy eye of Beetle Smith could see through him, he concluded that the ban on the British was general and that it was Maclean whom the CIA had rumbled. He urged his controller to get Maclean into safety behind the Iron Curtain before he was arrested, broken down under questioning, and implicated them all.

The controller went further than that. He engineered the departure to London of the other Soviet spy in Washington, Guy Burgess, and he and Donald Maclean slipped away to Moscow in June 1951.

Kim Philby breathed a sigh of relief. He had moved fast and saved the situation. Or so he thought. But his own situation was not entirely saved. As a CIA man said later: "Allen may not have caught him with his pants down, but he certainly found him with his zip undone."

There was not enough evidence to turn Philby over to the Justice Department for trial, thanks to Jackson's overhastiness, but there was quite enough to suggest that he was working for the Russians. In the circumstances, the CIA had no option but to hand him back to the British and suggest that they go to work on him. Beetle Smith signed a strongly worded letter to the SIS declaring Philby persona non grata with the Agency. He added, in a private note to his old friend in London, General Kenneth Strong: "I hope the bastard gets his. I know a couple of Albanian tribesmen who would like to have half an hour apiece with him."

But Kim Philby was not to be trapped that easily.* It was not until twelve years later that the British were at last able to turn up proof hard

---

*Though SIS interrogators in London tried. He was mercilessly grilled by one of the London bar's most ruthless barristers, but unlike Klaus Fuchs, who had crumpled under a similar interrogation, Philby gave nothing away. With the guile and suppleness acquired from years of perfecting his technique, he wriggled out of the net.

enough to arrest him as a Soviet spy. And by that time it was too late. One step ahead of the enemy, as usual, Kim Philby sailed from Beirut on the night of January 23, 1963, to safety inside the Soviet Union, still unaware of how close the "bumbling" Allen Dulles had come, in 1951, to putting him behind the bars of an American jail.

CHAPTER SEVENTEEN

All Aboard

In the spring of 1952, Mary Bancroft arrived in the United States on a visit from her home in Switzerland. She spent most of her time with her daughter, who was now married to one of the sons of Senator Robert Taft, and with her great admirer, Henry R. Luce; but she also managed to see her old beau, Allen, and her old protégée, Clover.

With the exception of Clover ("who still doesn't know Monday from Friday"), she found them all keyed up about the forthcoming presidential election. She was not exactly a Republican by inclination, but out of loyalty to her daughter's in-laws she was for Taft as the GOP nominee, and she twitted them unmercifully about their support for General Dwight Eisenhower. Luce "grew white with rage," and Allen was irritated when she told them that they didn't really have any faith in Eisenhower as a great leader, but were only on his side for what they could gain from his election. It was too uncomfortably close to the truth for them to accept it calmly.

Allen was taking no overt part in the election because by this time he was up to his neck in clandestine operations at CIA—and loving it. He brimmed over with professional high spirits as he hinted at some of the ploys Wisner's unit was now carrying out in eastern Europe. Physically, however, he had his ups and downs. He had periods when he was out on the tennis courts owned by his rich friends, the Belins, challenging and beating Bill Bundy, Jim Angleton, and Bob Amory, or other members of the Agency's top echelon bold enough to take him on. At others he would be back in carpet slippers, goutily hobbling into the office. His doctors urged him to go on a diet, but he was not willing to eschew his beloved good food and wine, and fought back at the gouty manifestations with colchicine and cortisone, which may have eased the pain but created devastating inner turbulence.

Joan had got divorced and Toddie was having a nervous *crise,* but as ever he weathered his daughters' upsets with light, good-humored sympathy, though he was always ready when they sought his help and advice. The offspring who was strappingly fit and never asked for advice or help at all—his son, Allen, Jr.—was the one he worried about. He had gone off to the Korean War as an officer in the Marines and was involved in the bitter fighting at Inchon, and that fact increased Allen Dulles's bitter feeling toward Truman at the way he had handled the Korean business. He didn't think much of General Douglas MacArthur either for the clumsy and often inept way he had conducted the war, but that he kept to himself, since MacArthur was a hero among the kind of people who were likely to vote for the GOP.

Allen's contribution to the Eisenhower campaign, both in the primaries and the runup to the election, was to provide fuel for Foster's speeches on foreign policy, which increasingly concentrated on the menace of communism in Europe and Asia. He briefed Foster on the CIA's program of stirring up unrest in the Soviet Union's European satellites, through sabotage, espionage, and propaganda, and helped inspire his brother's "liberation" policy, which figured increasingly in his campaign speeches.

The great red purge in eastern Europe, to which the CIA and Noel Field had made their contribution, was still going on, and Allen Dulles was not the only one in the Agency who drew conclusions from it that were not subsequently justified by events. He was convinced that Russia's empire was on the point of disintegration, and that a coordinated campaign, covertly through the CIA, overtly through the U.S. government (when Eisenhower was elected, of course), could roll the red armies back beyond the Russian frontiers through the spontaneous uprising of the captive satellite nations.

His enthusiasm infected Foster, and it was not simply because he was after the votes of the Czech, Hungarian, Polish, and Rumanian minorities in the big cities that Foster began preaching the possibility of "liberating" their relatives in Europe. His brother had convinced him that it was possible, and for the moment he believed it.

In fact, if Frank Wisner had told him the truth, Allen Dulles would have had to face the fact that the CIA was falling flat on its face with

288

regard to its liberation policy. All its efforts to infiltrate and shake up the Soviet Empire, as well as the Soviet Union itself, were failing, at a huge cost to the U.S. taxpayer.

"All of us were engaging in this quite tricky business of infiltration at this time," said Howard Roman, a CIA officer, later. "There were, for instance, the very complicated air drops into Russia itself. It was a terribly hard thing to do logistically and technically, and it caused us no end of headaches. You had to have airplanes, you had to have guys who were willing to do it. They might turn out to be Russian agents —they usually did."

The espionage, sabotage, and propaganda agents Frank Wisner's unit was using were recruited from among the homeless Russian and East European displaced persons who were still wandering around Germany. They were gathered into camps near Wiesbaden, where the CIA had taken over a former Nazi camp and part of the nearby airfield. Many of them were KGB spies, but the CIA usually found that out only when it was too late. Meantime, they put them all through a rigid training course.

"It cost an awful lot of money," Roman said. "They were trained to do everything under the sun: codes, radio, sabotage, armed combat, everything. It took a lot of money, a lot of people and a lot of effort. And it was pretty damned heart-breaking because when we sent the guys in, and then we heard from them again, we wondered—were they controlled or weren't they? Had they been caught or were they reporting back freely? Were they still loyal to us, or had they been Russian spies from the first, now feeding back to us what they knew we wanted to hear?"

He added:

"Allen loved this kind of thing. He thought it was exciting. When he heard that we'd been doing some pretty nasty things, and stirring up captive peoples to expect things that weren't going to happen, he justified it morally and in every other way, as the Presbyterian he was, as being for the sake of the country. He was never against the unclean side of intelligence, so long as he could convince himself, as he usually could, that it was being done for a cause."

The cause, in this case, was "liberation of the captive peoples," and Allen sold it to his brother, who in turn sold it to the American people. It was to prove a popular vote-getter, attuned to the mood of the times.

Senator Joseph McCarthy and his fellow demagogues were stirring up the fear of communism at home, Senator Knowland and his China Lobby supporters were sounding the tocsin against the aggressiveness of the Communists abroad, and here was John Foster Dulles, a solemn, solid, God-fearing man, assuring them that the red menace could be rolled back and the enslaved people set free; though exactly how he carefully did not say.

The Democrats fought back as best they could, if not always with expertise, against the charges that they were soft on communism at home and weak toward the Soviet menace overseas. President Truman feistily dubbed the GOP's red-baiters "a bunch of Nazis," and his foreign policy spokesmen sturdily insisted that they were just as hard-lined in their attitude to Russia as the Republicans were. (And that was true.) Perhaps the most reasonably argued opposition to Foster Dulles's promises of "liberation" was presented by the veteran Democratic statesman, W. Averell Harriman. On several occasions he debated the issue with Foster.

"I violently disagreed with his 'liberation policy,' " he said later. "I thought that he was playing domestic politics with international problems. I was gravely concerned that the eastern European nations would misinterpret it, and would think we could do something, that we could go in and help them free themselves. I had several debates, one face-to-face on TV. I said, 'Foster, if you follow this policy, you're going to have the deaths of some brave people on your conscience.' He defended it legalistically."

The CIA was taking Foster's speeches and and rebroadcasting them into eastern Europe from its tame propaganda service in Munich, Radio Free Europe, and that particularly worried Harriman.

"I do think the emphasis on 'liberation' and the way it was used in broadcasts from the United States did have an effect on people behind the Iron Curtain," he said later. "I saw a good many of the young men and women who came out after the Hungarian incident (we took in 30,000) and they all thought we were going to intervene and help them if they started something."

Harriman had been a close collaborator of Dwight Eisenhower during World War II, and afterwards he had kept up a warm friendship with both the general and his wife, Mamie. But friends and observers of both men soon became aware that Harriman had doubts about Ike's ability to make the transition from Army to statesmanship, feeling that his lack of experience in politics would severely handicap him in the White House. As the election neared, he found it impossible to keep silent about it and began making speeches and television appearances in which he did not mince words in suggesting that it was all wrong to have a general in the White House. He and Harry Truman soon became the most forthright critics of Ike's candidacy, roundly declaring that his election would be a calamity for the country, since he would make a disastrous president.

In deference to his old friend, he repeatedly praised Eisenhower's wartime service and stressed the fact that as a general he had no equal, but that the presidency needed altogether different qualifications. But his disclaimers failed to prevent a rift from developing between the two men.

From that time on, the atmosphere was cool between Harriman and Eisenhower. Instead of "Averell," Eisenhower took to calling him "Governor Harriman," and they met only at the annual governors' meetings. Though they made it up later on.

In the meantime, Harriman noticed with wry amusement that Foster Dulles seemed to have taken his cue from Eisenhower, and from being extremely affable now became "quite reserved" with him. But that may have been because Harriman's attacks had wounded him, too. One particular quotation he had made had momentarily shaken Foster. It came from a statesman Foster greatly admired, Secretary of State John Quincy Adams. In a July 4 address on America and her foreign relations which Adams made in 1821, he had strongly criticized proponents of U.S. "liberation crusades" abroad.

"Wherever the standard of freedom and independence has been or shall be unfurled," Adams declared, "there will her heart, her benedictions and her prayers be. But she goes not abroad in search of monsters to destroy. She is the well-wisher to the freedom and independence of all. She is the champion and vindicator only of her own."

It was advice Foster was not about to take, nor would he be grateful to the man who had passed it on.

Not that he or Ike needed to worry about what Harriman (or Adams) said about them. Both Eisenhower and the GOP won in a landslide vote, and a Republican President was back in office—with a Republican Senate and Congress—for the first time in twenty years.

291

*   *   *

There were quite a few members of the Republican Party who thought they would be, or ought to be, the President-elect's choice for Secretary of State. Henry R. Luce had hopes that he would get a call, and Mary Bancroft mocked him for thinking that putting Ike four times on the cover of *Time* magazine qualified him for a post in the cabinet. When the summons did not come, he picked up the telephone himself and suggested Thomas E. Dewey for the post, which startled Foster when he heard about it, for it was he (Foster) who had received all the heavy praise from *Time* for his foreign policy speeches during the campaign.

Others in the running for the job (according to themselves or their supporters) included Paul Hoffman, who had been Eisenhower's campaign manager, and Congressman Walter H. Judd, a right-wing member of the China Lobby with some steamy anti-Communist views. According to a statement he later made, he heard rumors that he might be up for Secretary of State or Assistant Secretary in charge of the Far East. He at once rang the President-elect and said:

"Ike, don't give me a job like that. I'm much too valuable to you in the House. I've got ten years' seniority there and I can help you with your administration. So don't do it. But I would like to say one thing. Can I make some suggestions as to whom you might put in? As far as Secretary of State is concerned, I would like to suggest John Foster Dulles."

Eisenhower (according to Judd) replied: "Well, he is being considered, but he's got a lot of opposition."

Judd asked what kind of opposition, and the President-elect responded that many of his advisers thought that Dulles was far too "anti-British—maybe not that strong, unsympathetic to the British maybe." At which Judd said: "That's one of the reasons I'm for him. We've had administrations where our State Department was an outpost of the British Foreign Office for altogether too long. It was particularly so under Mr. Acheson and the Rhodes Scholars boys, Fulbright and the rest of them. I know Mr. Dulles is not sympathetic to the British, but he'll have an American foreign policy, and that's one of the strongest reasons for his appointment, in my opinion."

This would imply that Eisenhower hesitated to begin with; but Foster never seems to have had any doubt from the start that it was he who would get the appointment. In early November, before the election, Eleanor telephoned him to tell him that she had been offered a new job. Her work in the Department of Commerce had come to an end because her boss had told her: "I know you're the best brain in this building, and I haven't any doubt that you could handle any job we gave you. But I warn you you're never going to get any further than your present position, and I'll tell you why. You're a woman, and I don't believe in women getting too high up. It bothers me." So she had begun to look for something else and had run into James W. Riddleberger, at that time head of the German section at the State Department. He knew her record in Austria, and he offered her a job in charge of the Berlin desk.

Eleanor always made a point of consulting her elder brother on all her professional decisions, even when, as in this case, she was sure the move would be a good one. Foster said: "Well, if you get back into the State Department before I get there, that's all right. If I am already there, under no circumstances will you get a job in the State Department."

So Eleanor called Riddleberger and accepted his offer, confident that her brother would soon be Secretary, but unworried about herself once he got there. When the official announcement was made she was already working at the Berlin desk. By the time Foster was confirmed by the Senate, she had flown to Berlin to see her new bailiwick and was not around for his swearing-in. Foster had a shock waiting for her when she got back.

At the CIA there was a buzz that changes were coming at the top, and that General Walter Bedell Smith would soon be resigning as director in order to accept a more important job at the White House. It seemed logical that now Dwight Eisenhower was President he would want his old Chief of Staff beside him to guide him and sustain him, as he had done so frequently during the worst moments in World War II. Beetle was making no secret of the fact that he wanted to go. He had done a splendid job of reconstructing and streamlining the CIA, and now that it was running smoothly he was bored with it. When he was bored his temper ran on an extremely short fuse, his ulcers acted up (they had come back to plague and agonize him), and he made life difficult for both himself and everyone around him. He needed new

293

fields in which to find achievement and distraction.

But who would step into his shoes? He confided to a friend and subordinate, Stuart Hedden, that he feared Allen Dulles would inevitably get the job, and confessed that in a rash moment he had even promised Allen to recommend him if and when he stepped out. He was regretting it now. After watching him at work over the past few months, he had decided that Allen was far too romantic about the practical business of espionage, too interested in the excitements of covert operations and too little concerned with the hard, painstaking, slogging research and analysis which was now the essence of the modern intelligence machine. Scornfully, he called him "The Great White Case Officer," and said he feared the CIA would start to run down if it came under Allen's direction.

But how could he be circumvented? Who was big enough to leapfrog him?

He was tempted to put forward the name of Lyman B. Kirkpatrick, Jr., whom he had made a deputy director of the Agency, with a brain that might have been tooled on the same lathe as his own. Kirkpatrick had a distinguished record from World War II, having been in the OSS in London and on the staffs of Bradley and Patton in Europe as intelligence adviser. He shared Beetle Smith's cold, precise view of intelligence, which for him was a science and certainly not a game.

The only trouble about Kirkpatrick was that he had two strikes against him. First, Allen Dulles did not like him, and would probably leave the Agency if he was appointed. He had never shared Beetle's regard for Kirkpatrick's talents and had several times tried to block his rise in the ranks of the CIA. As Kirkpatrick was later to write about his first big promotion:

"But I quite clearly understood that I was not a unanimous choice for the job by any means. Smith and Bill Jackson wanted to put me in the job, but Allen Dulles had another candidate, and I gather there had been rather a strenuous debate on the subject."

While Beetle did not consider Allen's departure would have been fatal to the Agency, he was well aware what the consequences would be. He had a host of friends and admirers in the CIA, and they were not only among the best brains but were also extremely loyal. They might well resign too, and that would be disastrous.

The other strike against Kirkpatrick seemed to be even more serious, though Beetle didn't consider it so. He had been stricken with polio in the summer of 1952 and was still recovering. When he came out of the hospital and back to work, he would be in a wheelchair, almost certainly for the rest of his life. Beetle had already assured him it didn't matter that his legs no longer worked, because "all I care about is your brains." But would others agree, particularly Congress, which would have to approve him?

Stuart Hedden was by no means as enthusiastic about Kirkpatrick as Beetle was, but he shared his suspicions of Allen Dulles, chiefly on political grounds. To most people Allen looked and sounded like a mild and amiable Tory; but to Hedden, whose ideological base stood somewhat to the right of Beetle and only slightly to the left of the John Birch Society, he was a bleeding-heart liberal whose apotheosis would mean the packing of the CIA with Socialists and Communists. He didn't suggest that Allen would do it deliberately, but that he was a sucker for the "parlor pink" approach.

Hedden too had a potential candidate for the directorship, and one, he thought, who would not only make an admirable chief but would also be accepted by Allen Dulles and his friends without too much fuss: his wartime chief in OSS, Wild Bill Donovan.

When Hedden approached Donovan with his proposition, and hinted that Beetle Smith would discreetly back it, the veteran leader of the OSS eagerly accepted the challenge. He would have liked to have had the post at the CIA when it came up in 1947 but had not really angled for it, because he and Harry Truman disliked each other and he knew the President had documentation about him from the FBI and would never have accepted him. But Eisenhower was a friend and wartime colleague who knew his record and had many times publicly expressed his admiration for it.

It was true that Donovan was seventy years old, but he was fighting fit. He had an additional reason for allowing his name to go forward. He felt that Allen Dulles should be edged out, because he still considered him a woefully inept administrator who would run the CIA into the ground.

"As a matter of fact, neither Allen *nor* Bill Donovan could administer two pins," said a CIA man who watched the in-fighting at this time. "And Donovan was certainly getting on in years. But Donovan had a mind which exploded all over the place, whether it was clandestine

295

collection, covert action, or analysis. Don't forget it was Bill, while he was in OSS, who established the R&A Branch [Research and Analysis], which brought together the greatest scholars in their subjects, economists like Charles Hitch and Émile Dupres, Russian experts like Geroid Robinson, China experts like John K. Fairbank, Japanese experts like Burton Faho, African experts like Ralph Bunche, historians like Conyers Read and Hajo Holborn, South American agents like Maurice Halperin, and German experts like Herbert Marcuse, and banged their brains together for the good of the nation's intelligence. Bill Donovan would have brought to the CIA the knowledge of certain aspects of the intelligence business that Allen Dulles may have seen and recognized, but never understood. It was a nuisance to him. He was just crazy about the operational side of the business, and that was all."

Allen Dulles was acutely aware of the intrigue that was going on in Beetle Smith's office, and he was furious with Beetle for reneging on his promise, but not too alarmed. He had already alerted his brother, and though Foster often appeared ponderous and heavy-handed, he could move swiftly when the occasion warranted it. It was no part of Foster's strategy as Secretary of State that anyone but Allen should take over as new director of the CIA, and he was confident he could fix that with the President. There was really no problem. He knew that Bill Donovan was not as fit as he made out, and, in any case, he had been out of the intelligence business for too long. As for Kirkpatrick, how could the CIA be run by a cripple in a wheelchair?

His concern was what to do with Bedell Smith once he left the CIA. He did not want him too close to President Eisenhower, where he might easily exercise the same strong influence over him as he had done in World War II. But what sort of a job could he be persuaded to accept, one that seemed prestigious and important but would keep him away from the White House? In the end he came up with the offer of the Under-Secretaryship in the State Department, and in a long session with Beetle pointed out to him that it would be a position of much more importance than seemed at first apparent. For one thing, he (Foster Dulles) envisaged his role as being that of a sort of Super-secretary of foreign policy, which would leave the Under-Secretary in practically complete charge of the State Department and its day-to-day affairs.

Beetle Smith was tempted and fell. It sounded to him remarkably like the job he had had as Ike's Chief of Staff in Europe, with everything of importance passing through his hands. A key job, in fact, and one of great influence. He was to be disillusioned—but not until later.

In the meantime, he went to the White House to tell Eisenhower he had taken the job with John Foster Dulles, but that he couldn't really stand by his promise to recommend his brother as his successor at the CIA. Anyway, wouldn't there be something almost incestuous, he inferred, in having Foster and Allen in two such intimately associated key positions? Ike told him not to worry. Foster had already been to see him and had reassured him about that, and he now proposed to send Allen Dulles's name forward for confirmation.

Stuart Hedden broke the bad news to Donovan. Beetle Smith went to see Lyman Kirkpatrick at the Institute of Physical Medicine and Rehabilitation at the New York Medical Center and told him that Allen Dulles had won out. Kirkpatrick took the blow well.*

One night in November 1952, while the in-fighting was still going on about Allen Dulles's appointment, his sister Eleanor had a bad dream in which Allen's son kept appearing, voicelessly crying for help. She was so disturbed that she got up early next morning, a Sunday, and drove through the deserted streets from her home in McLean, Virginia, to Allen's house in Georgetown.

It was only 6:00 A.M. when she got there, and since she had a key she opened the door without ringing and went right in. Allen was already up and came to the top of the stairs. He didn't seem surprised to see her.

He had had a message from Korea. Allen, Jr., lightly wounded in the hand during an enemy attack, had thereupon led a retaliatory charge on a machine-gun nest at the Chosen Reservoir and had been hit in the head. He had been evacuated to Japan, where he was in critical condition.

Allen had been offered immediate facilities for a flight to Japan for himself and his wife, but he couldn't leave for the moment. Clover was

*If he had cherished any revanchist feelings, they would have been satisfied in 1962, when he wrote the official report on the Bay of Pigs disaster and roundly condemned Allen Dulles's part in it. Kirkpatrick retired from the CIA in 1962 and in 1965 became professor of political science at Brown University. He also wrote a book called *The Real CIA* which is not as revealing as the title suggests.

in Switzerland for psychiatric sessions, and the CIA was trying to find out where she had gone for her Sunday outing, so they could pick her up and bring her back to Washington. Meanwhile, he was waiting and in great distress, for he had been warned of the gravity of his son's wound and the slim chance he had of surviving. Even so, Eleanor was surprised. He had always seemed so casual about his son.

"I don't think he'd given a great deal of thought to Allen's future," she said later, "until this thing came along and threatened to wipe it out."

Two days later, Allen and Clover reached Tokyo and hurried to their son's bedside. He was still in a deep coma. The bullet had lodged in his head within a hair's breadth of his brain, and it was touch and go whether it destroyed the body or the man. The doctors were puzzled how best to save both his life and his sanity.

It was a particularly lonely moment for Allen Dulles. The cord between Clover and her son had always been strongly attached, and a mere loss of consciousness on the part of one of them could not sever it. But in the case of the father there had been no rapport even when his son was up and about, so how could a connection be established now? It was two weeks before Allen, Jr., came out of his coma and the doctors could begin to fight for his survival. When Allen and Clover flew back to the United States, they carried with them the assurance of the doctors that Allen, Jr., would live, but that was as far as they could go, for the moment.

Allen had one consolation. The family had always complained that during the most critical moments in his married life—as, for instance, the birth of his children—he had never been on hand. At least Clover could not rebuke him this time for not being there.

It was some months later, at the beginning of February 1953, just before he was due to appear before the Senate to seek confirmation as director of the CIA, that Allen received another message from the Far East, this time to inform him that Allen, Jr., was being flown home.

He and Clover went down to Andrews Air Force Base to meet the incoming plane. Photographers had been alerted, and they were on hand as the boy, on a stretcher, was disembarked. Next day all the newspapers carried a picture of Allen Dulles leaning affectionately over his son and kissing his bandaged head. It did him no harm whatsoever at the subsequent confirmation hearings, where he won full approval for his short exposition of his version of how an intelligence organization should operate.

By the time Eleanor Dulles got back from Berlin the inauguration was over, both her brothers had been confirmed in their new jobs, and Foster was installed as Secretary at the State Department. She returned tremendously excited about the challenges and problems of Berlin and bubbling over with ideas for coping with them. For the first time since leaving Austria she felt as if she had found a job worth having.

On Saturday she got a telephone call from Foster asking her to come over to dinner, and she accepted with pleasure. It would be the first time she had been at her brother's home since the election campaign, and though she had spoken to him by telephone she had sensed a strain in their relationship, particularly with Janet, who had been cool.

It was during the campaign that Eleanor had fretted over the complete failure of Dwight Eisenhower and other Republican spokesmen to repudiate the outrageous attacks Senator McCarthy had been making on great men like General Marshall, and on solid, respectable members of the Foreign Service and State Department. She was disgusted.

Finally, she could stand it no longer, and in October 1952 she had called up her brother to tell him she was coming up to New York for dinner.

"He made a very fine martini," she said later. "I had one. Then he started to fill up my glass again, and I said: 'No, I don't need another one.' He looked at me sort of queerly and he said: 'You must have come over here for a serious purpose if you won't have two martinis.' I said: 'I have.' So then I said to him: 'I want you to know that I think this is an evil business that is going on. If the Republicans don't repudiate McCarthy, I'm going to vote the Democratic ticket.' Of course, one vote—you know how important that is!"

She went on:

"Well, he didn't look annoyed. Janet looked annoyed, but he looked amused. He asked me a few questions as to why I felt the way I did, and then we dropped the subject. And I'm sure he was more amused than anything else."

But he hadn't done anything about McCarthy's behavior, and she hadn't been asked round since. She suspected maybe Janet didn't like the way she bugged Foster, and dared to talk back to him.

Anyway, now all seemed to have been forgiven. She was back on the invited list, and since, like Foster, she loved good food and drink, she was glad that Janet ran a good table. Besides, she had much to tell her brother about Berlin.

She did not get the chance. One of the first things Foster said to her was: "I think I've solved the question of what you should do. I've talked to Harold Stassen, and he's ready to give you a job."

"But I have a job," she said.

He shook his head. "I don't think you can stay in the State Department. You go and see Stassen. He'd like to give you a job."

She was so astonished that all she could to say was: "That's very kind of you."

She went home, stunned, to spend a miserable weekend, all her hopes and plans for the future shattered.

On Monday she went to see Harold Stassen, who greeted her cordially and offered her a job looking after European refugees. She told him that hardly suited her talents, and couldn't she do something about the relationship between aid and East-West trade? He agreed at once. Then she asked: "Will I attend your staff meetings?"

Stassen looked surprised and said: "Oh, I don't think so."

That was all she wanted to know.

"I went back to the State Department and I wrote Stassen a letter," she said later, "and I said that my obligations to Jimmy Riddleberger and my Berlin job were such that I felt I couldn't give them up at the present time. I didn't say: 'You're giving me a job with a name and a salary but no power,' which was the case. I know the bureaucratic life, and I knew if I didn't go to staff meetings I'd be pushed around. I knew that under Stassen there was a great massacre going on, and he was cutting throats as fast as he could."

She had decided she was going to sit tight in the State Department and see what happened. About a week later Foster called and asked her what about the job with Stassen, and she told him that it hadn't worked out.

"He was quite annoyed really," she said later. "I don't mean he was angry, but he was just—well, he'd taken all this trouble and *why* hadn't it worked out? Things were supposed to work out. So I said to him: 'Well, it wasn't a job that was very serious. I realized he was trying to

300

accommodate you, and I've got a very interesting job here.' But he said: 'You can't stay here!' I was sort of taken aback by that, because I knew that I hadn't been bothering him, and I knew I was carrying on a perfectly legitimate job. So I finally said: 'Well, won't you give me a try?' He said: 'All right, I'll give you a month.' "

She didn't see him for a month. "But exactly thirty days later," she said, "on a Saturday at ten o'clock in the morning, he called me up and he said: "Eleanor, it's all right. I guess it's all right. Goodbye.' And that was that. And that was my Berlin job. But this is all kind of characteristic. He didn't want me out on the street, he didn't want to see me stranded, but he was terribly nervous of my being in the State Department."

She figured that in the month which had elapsed he had gained a little confidence, and decided that no one was going to accuse him of packing the government with relatives. In Eleanor's case, there was never any substance to it. It was for Allen that he had gone to work behind the scenes. She was ruefully aware that Foster would comfort her if she was sick, lend her money if she was broke, commiserate with her if she was miserable, but never go to bat for her in her professional career, though he knew she was as good as if not better than most men around State. Why? Because she was his sister—or because she was a woman?

Anyway, she had sat tight at the Berlin desk, and not even Foster had succeeded in prying her loose from her chair. Allen was now in charge of the most elaborate intelligence organization that the world has ever known. Foster was bringing the dogs of the State Department to heel and getting ready to go hunting.

In one way and another, all of them had made it. Grandfather Foster and Uncle Robert Lansing would have been proud of them.

CHAPTER EIGHTEEN

Bread and Circuses

A few days after the inauguration, in January 1953, George V. Allen, who was ambassador to Yugoslavia at the time, was having lunch at the Army and Navy Club in Washington when he got a call from the White House. It was Tom Stephens, the appointments secretary, to tell him he had an appointment with President Eisenhower at five o'clock that afternoon.

Allen was glad to hear it. Everybody around official Washington was telling him that he would be the new ambassador to India, and only the day before the Chief of Protocol had congratulated him on his new appointment, but so far he had received no official confirmation. He was due back at his post in a couple of days, and had no idea whether to tell his wife to start packing for the snows of Belgrade or the searing heat of New Delhi.

When George Allen reached the White House that afternoon he was, somewhat to his surprise, taken upstairs and told to wait in an anteroom. Presidents usually saw their ambassadors in the office. An aide explained that the President would be a little delayed because he was watching a TV show, but he would be right out.

When Eisenhower came out and saw Allen, he looked startled.

"Oh, it's you," he said.

"Yes, Mr. President," Allen said, "it's me."

"I was expecting the other George Allen," the President said, "the funny George Allen, the man who wrote the book *Presidents Who Have Known Me.*"

At that Ambassador Allen rose to his feet.

"I don't like to be here under false pretenses," he said, and got ready to go.

Eisenhower motioned him to sit down again.

"No, no, don't go," he said. "Just a minute." He picked up the telephone and spoke to someone in the next room: "Did I have an appointment with George Allen, the funny man George Allen?"

Allen could hear Tom Stephens's voice over the line explaining that he had an appointment with George V. Allen, his ambassador to Yugoslavia. At which the President said:

"Well, that other feller, I haven't seen hide or hair of him since the nomination convention last July. Yesterday I got word from someone that he was in town and would like to come and pay his respects. I said I'd get someone or other to fix an appointment some time. It was a surprise it was arranged so quickly, but I just saw George Allen on the blotter and thought that's who it was."

Ambassador Allen got the impression that all this was being said for his benefit. He was still uncomfortable when the President put down the telephone and turned and began to talk to him about Yugoslavia. He was still more uncomfortable forty-five minutes later when first Milton Eisenhower popped his head round the door, then Nelson Rockefeller, and no mention whatsoever had been made about India. Allen was acutely conscious of having overstayed his time, and had visions of a lengthening queue of officials with urgent papers gathering beyond the door.

"I think I should go," he said, finally.

"Oh, we haven't finished yet," said the President. "There's something else I wanted to see you about. Let's have a whiskey."

So they had a couple of highballs while the President asked about Trieste, Yugoslavia, and Tito. It was not until an hour and a half later that he was allowed to go. He still did not know whether or not he was being appointed to India.* He came away with the definite feeling that the whole rigmarole had been gone through to make him feel better over the President's error.

As far as American voters were concerned, Dwight David Eisenhower was one of the most popular Presidents in the history of the

---

*He received official notification next day.

United States, but succeeding generations have begun to realize that he was also one of the least effective, at a moment when his country was in dire need of decisive leadership. One of his more bitter critics, the American writer Paul Theroux, has written of his presidency:

> In 1952, after he'd won the war but lost the rest of his hair, impotent, inexperienced in politics, eater of crow and taker of orders, a bad golfer and not particularly sound in wind and limb, there was really no choice but to make him President of the United States, where he was to have a very different sort of congress to contend with.

Eisenhower's contemporaries were more understanding and constructive, but as they watched him struggling to make the change from general into statesman, they squirmed with uneasiness and shuddered at his lack of insight and courage. Inevitably, his old friends compared him with his predecessor, Harry Truman, especially in the matter of security and presidential prerogatives.

Truman had always been a doughty defender of the presidential office and went to battle against anyone in Congress who sought to weaken its powers of direction and decision. Once during his battles with McCarthy and the Senate, it was suggested that he should accept a watchdog over security and Averell Harriman was sent to try to persuade him to agree. His reply was:

"No, Averell, that's an invasion of the President's responsibility as an executive. My greatest responsibility while I'm in this chair is to protect the authority of the President. If Congress takes over the President's authority, the country will be chaotic. Each member of Congress represents specific districts or states, and I'm the only one who represents the country as a whole."

He was adamant. He refused to accept a watchdog, saying that giving way would only make it harder for the Presidents who followed him.

But now his successor was doing just that—giving way under pressure. Truman was by no means the only statesman in the nation who viewed Eisenhower's weakness with alarm and dismay, and those friends who had predicted that as a President he would be a disaster now felt all their worst fears were coming true. He did not have the understanding, nor the sense of responsibility, that the office required. As one of them said: "He just wasn't educated up to it."

In no way did John Foster Dulles consider Dwight Eisenhower's qualities of amiability, willingness to listen, anxiety to put his subordinates at ease, unwillingness to take difficult or unpopular decisions, made him a poor President. From his point of view, he could hardly have been better. One of the things which Foster had always admired about Britain was that nation's system of constitutional monarchy, with a sovereign who was a symbol of the unity of the people, who brought disparate elements together yet played only a passive role in the big decisions. That was hardly possible under the American system, but the very qualities which had made Ike such a success in World War II —keeping temperamental generals like Patton, Montgomery, and Bradley happy while fighting on the same front—seemed likely to benefit anyone with a strong personality and forthright opinions who would henceforth be working under his presidential command. It was the domineering and difficult generals who had always won Ike over in Europe, and it did not appear likely that he would behave any differently in peace. He thought the military staff system would work in the White House and he would still be the amenable chairman, which meant that he would be as malleable as he had been in wartime.

But malleable by whom?

The observers on the sidelines got an indication of how things would go very early in the administration when President Eisenhower, in his February 2 State of the Union Message to the Congress, made the extraordinary statement that since the "Red Chinese" had intervened in the Korean War, he felt no longer any need to "protect" them from an invasion by the Nationalist Chinese forces of Chiang Kai-shek. IKE READY TO UNLEASH CHIANG ON REDS said the headlines in the next day's newspapers.

Averell Harriman said later that he was "aghast" at the President's threat to "unleash" Chiang, not because he feared the Nationalist Chinese would invade—they were in no condition to do so—but because the speech made it plain that Eisenhower could be persuaded to use international affairs for domestic political reasons.

One of the pledges Foster Dulles had made to himself upon becoming Secretary of State was that he would never go against the will of Congress or swim against the tide of Senate opinion, and that the chief reason for the failure of the Truman administration's foreign policy had been its inability to win congressional goodwill. He was determined to seek and secure the friendship of the more powerful elements

305

in the Senate from the start, and was prepared to make gestures to gain their aid and influence. One of the most influential of them all was Senator William Knowland, a perfervid supporter of Chiang Kai-shek. The President's words, written into his speech by Foster, were a blatant gesture to win Knowland's approval.

"It seemed to me a tragically unwise thing to do," Averell Harriman said later. "Chiang could make difficult our relations with mainland China as time went on, and I thought this was the first and perhaps the worst mistake Foster Dulles made. I blame him for it rather than President Eisenhower because I assume that he was the one that advised it. He was in the difficult position of having to appease Senator Knowland, and I think he thought he could get goodwill with that. . . . He said he was going to get along with the Senate if he became Secretary of State. So this was one of the ways of doing it of which I heartily disapproved."

The incident sent a chill down the spines of quite a few other experienced students of government. What sort of a President had they got who would allow himself to be used for such a ploy? And what sort of a Secretary of State was the one who had suggested it?

Immediately after his appointment as Secretary of State, Foster called in two bright young men to act as his executive assistants. One of them was Rod O'Connor, who had been Foster's press aide during the abortive try for the Senate in 1949; the other was a young man with relatives high in the Republican Party, John W. Hanes, Jr. They both worked for the CIA and, until a few months before, had been together on covert operations in Germany with Frank Wisner's unit. They shared a common belief in the need to roll back the reds in Europe and root out the Communists and fellow travelers at home. It was Allen who arranged their transfer to State from the CIA.

They put their desks together within sight of the door of Foster's office and got down to the task assigned to them: that of changing the complexion of the State Department and Foreign Service and wiping what they considered was a politically pink Democratic expression off its features.

"Dulles started with the same suspicion of the system as Rod and I did," Hanes said later. "His was based on more knowledge, having worked down there on the Japanese Peace Treaty, but he was less politically motivated than Rod and I. We were very young and starry-eyed and very interested in the political side. I think he had much more knowledge of the basic immobility of the system and its tendency to preserve mediocrity and the status quo. His basic theory was not that because the Republicans had been out for twenty years, you ought to go out and reward Republicans by putting them in jobs, but, in fact, if the people had voted for a change they were entitled to a change. And that simply to change a President and a few top people around him would be to cheat the electorate."

But what sort of changes was Foster visualizing? To listen to or read through his speeches was to gain the impression that they would be radical and possibly earth-shaking. The Democrats under Acheson, he trumpeted, had been weak in confronting the postwar challenges of Stalinist Russia. He would make it his business to change all that. Captive peoples would be "liberated," Allies would close ranks behind the United States, or be faced with an "agonizing reappraisal" of what America was doing for them in the way of food and military aid. And the State Department itself must be reshaped, its discipline tightened, its staff willing to display "positive loyalty" in order to cope with the challenges that were coming.

Yet to those in the State Department of whose services he still had need (while he put his house in order) he had no hesitation in admitting that much of the fuss he was making was little more than window-dressing, meant not so much to frighten the Russians or give hope to the enslaved as to please members of Congress and impress the electorate.

On January 20, 1953, he came back to the State Department from the White House inaugural luncheon and called Paul Nitze into his office. Nitze had been Dean Acheson's Policy Planning chief, and was still around in his old job while the Republicans got themselves organized. Foster started gossiping about what he proposed to do.

"You know, Paul," he said, "I really don't disagree at all with the Acheson policies, or those policies you've worked on. I'm in general agreement with what you and Acheson have been trying to do. The one quarrel I have is the way in which Acheson has handled the Congress. I don't think he did it well and I think I can do it much better. But as far as policy is concerned, I have no quarrel with you."

Nitze looked at him with an owlish expression in his bright blue eyes, giving no hint of the cynical amusement these words aroused in him. To think of what Foster had said about those same policies during the campaign!

"As for the work you fellows have been doing on the Policy Planning Staff," the new Secretary went on, "I think that it is most important work. But I don't think it should be done in the State Department, but under the aegis of the National Security Council, because it is not the conduct of foreign affairs but national security policy. I think it is a most important part of foreign policy, even more important than the conduct of foreign affairs. In fact, what I propose to do is spend ninety percent of my time while I'm Secretary in the National Security Building, working with the NSC staff on national security policy."

He cleared his throat, was silent for a long moment, and then went on:

"One other point I ought to make clear right off the bat is that it would be impossible for me to continue you as director of the Policy Planning Staff. You were associated with the Acheson policies, and I can't have the same policy planner, because my public position has been that we are going to have a new foreign policy."

Nitze realized that what Foster was planning was a cosmetic job, which would keep the policy but get rid of the people who had conceived it. He said:

"Fine, what do you want me to do? I can disband the Policy Planning Staff today."

"Oh, no," said Foster, hastily. "I'm not quite sure that this idea I had in mind of spending ninety percent of my time at the Executive Office Building with the NSC people is going to work. For one thing"—pause —"it would mean I would have to turn over the whole conduct of foreign affairs to Beetle Smith."

Nitze said: "Foster, you know it just isn't going to work. You'll have to spend most of your time over here in the State Department running the show. It's a big organization, you can't turn it over to a deputy."

"You may be right," Foster said. "But I don't want you to disband the staff."

"But how about me?" Nitze asked. "You've just told me you don't want me."

"Well," Foster said, "I haven't got a successor for you yet. I'd like you and Beetle to see if you can't find an appropriate person to take your place."

"You want *my* choice for your new chief of Policy Planning?"

"That's right," said Foster.

The Americans called it a witch hunt, but it was Senator McCarthy who was really the witch, riding his broomstick over the White House, the State Department, and Capitol Hill, and terrorizing all those who sniffed the sour evil smell of his passing. He was at the height of his peculiar powers in 1953, and careers in Washington were crashing all around him as the frightened men in the corridors of American power turned upon each other and sacrificed their friends in an effort to appease him.

Foster Dulles should have been well aware of the banality of the senator from Wisconsin. His aide, John Hanes, knew McCarthy "well enough to call him Joe." In a way, he was a sort of family friend. When McCarthy had first come to Washington as a young senator, a friend from Wisconsin had asked Hanes's sister, June, and her husband, Henry McKnight, to look after him, and Hanes had seen a lot of him thereafter.

"McCarthy, he was pretty tough to take," Hanes said later. "To say that he was a rough diamond was a mistake only in the sense that he was never a diamond. He was rough. And June and Henry did dutifully have him out on several occasions, dutifully, I say, because they had been asked by their friends to do so. He would usually get drunk. He would fairly often get disorderly. He brought a succession of floozies out with him. If he didn't he was making passes at everybody in the house, including my sister."

There had come a time when McCarthy had been invited out to a fairly small dinner party, and brought a "floozie" with him.

"He disappeared upstairs and screwed her on June's guest-bed," Hanes said. "And, as June said, 'He didn't even take the damn counterpane off.' She put her foot down and said she would never have him in her house again."

But, of course, others did. There came a time when McCarthy could have "screwed" his "floozie" on the dining room table and the guests would have gone on eating their soufflé and pretending not to notice.

People in or connected with government were prepared to let him get away with anything, so long as they could continue to call him "Joe." He had ridden to fame, or rather notoriety, on the crest of postwar disillusionment with the way the world had shaped up after victory had been won. All the golden promises that had seemed possible of fulfillment in the euphoric period just after the war had failed, and everywhere things had gone sour. Half of Europe had gone Communist. So had China. From South America to Africa, America's motives were being questioned, her gifts sneered at, her flag booed.

How had it gone wrong? Why had wartime hopes turned rancid? Why were the Russians "winning"? Along had come Joseph McCarthy with the kind of answer that people wanted to hear: the Russians were "winning" because the American people had been too trusting, had believed what their so-called experts had told them, and those experts had been wrong. And not only wrong, but deliberately wrong—because they were secret Commies, eager to betray their own country in Moscow's cause. They had lied and cheated on behalf of the Kremlin, and they must be hunted out if America was to survive.

There was no doubt that McCarthy had responded to the mood of the country with his wild charges of treachery and deceit. A large portion of the population thought he was right. A minority thought he was a cheat and a liar and a traducer of reputations, but were afraid to say so.

One would have thought, however, that the exception would have been John Foster Dulles. As a pillar of the Church and an upstanding believer in Christian charity, a man of impeccable morals with a life-long reputation as an unsullied Republican and supporter of the American Way of Life, he seemed the ideal crusader capable of riding out and puncturing the gibbering monster and demonstrating that he was nothing but a bag of wind.

To the stupefaction of his friends, and some of his relatives, Foster gave signs of being just as craven as the others. He assembled the staff of the State Department and demanded of them "positive loyalty" in a tone of voice which seemed to infer that he believed McCarthy's charge that a large minority among them were secret Communists. McCarthy and members of the China Lobby had demanded the heads of certain Foreign Service officers—John Paton Davies and John Carter Vincent were the best known of them—who had forecast the rise of

Mao Tse-tung and the Chinese Communists and characterized Chiang Kai-shek as a corrupt leader who had no real hold on his people. They were secret tools of the reds, McCarthy charged, and had helped to lose China for America's faithful ally.

Foster could hardly agree with such absurd charges. The dossiers of Paton Davies and Vincent amply demonstrated that they were loyal Americans working in the best interests of their country, and pretty percipient observers of the Chinese scene, as it turned out. But the word was out that McCarthy was after them, and they had to go. Foster sacked them not, as McCarthy charged, for "treachery" and "willful deceit of the American people," but for "stupidity" and "incompetence" for having dared to forecast that Chiang was corrupt and the Communists would drive him out of China.

He allowed another McCarthy target, a distinguished Foreign Service expert, George Kennan, to retire from the State Department without even a letter of thanks or regret for his lifelong services to his country, and all because McCarthy had sneered at his judgment and called him a "Commie lover." He refused to ride in the same car or be photographed with Charles "Chip" Bohlen when that solid Foreign Service officer came under McCarthy's scrutiny during the confirmation hearings over his appointment as ambassador to Moscow. It may or may not have been significant that both these two professional diplomats had complained in the past about Foster Dulles's habit of leaking government secrets to the press.

"It looked to me as an outsider," Averell Harriman said later, "that he was sacrificing Foreign Service officers who had any connection, or were accused of having anything to do with communism. He was throwing them to the wolves. The most startling was the one which involved Chip Bohlen—the lack of support. There were certain people whose careers were destroyed for lack of support from the Secretary of State. I thought that they were unjustifiably criticized. Why he did this I don't know. I always thought that his mistake about Alger Hiss* made him feel that in order to protect himself he had to sacrifice others. But I still didn't admire it."

The appointment which shocked and shamed Allen and Eleanor

---

*An admirer of Alger Hiss, Foster had recommended him to head the Carnegie Foundation after World War II. Then, when Hiss was accused of perjury over his alleged Communist connections, he refused to testify in his favor.

Dulles when they heard about it was that of a certain Scott McLeod, who was brought into the State Department to organize a security service and police the private lives of its employees. McLeod had once been a muck-raking reporter on the staff of that peculiar New Hampshire newspaper, Loeb's Manchester *Union-Leader,* then an operative in the FBI, and latterly an assistant to Senator Styles Bridges, a Commie-hunter like McCarthy but lacking McCarthy's style, outrageousness, and bad breath.

McLeod was not so much a security officer, it turned out, as a sort of Pavlovian dog who salivated over certain trigger words like "Communist," "liberal," "freethinker," "homosexual," and "nymphomaniac," and he organized a squad of goons to root all such elements out of the State Department. Within a few weeks of his arrival he had shattered what morale was left in the Department after Foster Dulles's opening address to the staff. His operatives broke open desks, read private letters, listened in on conversations and telephones, and tailed employees after hours.

Anyone suspected of being a homosexual (in the case of males; McLeod didn't seem to have heard of lesbians) or promiscuity (in the case of females) was harried out of the Department. Those who refused to be harassed into resigning were posted to distant parts and deprived of promotion.

"You move them to western Australia and then you move them to South Africa and keep moving them around," said John Hanes. "They get the idea pretty soon and go away rather than go through these long and tortuous processes."

To Hanes, who was a close friend of McLeod (he called him "Scotty"), his fault was not that he was a scourge and a bully and a Nazi, but simply that he had the habit of talking too much.

"He had one of the most beautifully developed penchants for putting both feet into his mouth every time he opened it that I have ever seen in anybody," Hanes said later. "Some people are accident prone. Scotty was accident prone every time he opened his mouth. If there are 999 ways of saying something which is harmless and only one which isn't, he would infallibly light on that one. And much of Scotty's life was spent wondering why he was so miserable and picked on. Literally wondering, because so much of his intention in this kind of thing was good."

Hanes added:

"Now sure he was a conspirator by nature too. He loved conspiracies. He was deeply suspicious of many of the things in the State Department he did not understand, particularly the intellectuals. He knew shortly from his own records and investigations and his people what he had suspected viscerally—that there was a part of the Foreign Service that had been infiltrated by fairies, which made him suspicious. Because, as I say, Scotty had the essentially simple approach to a fairy that you will find in a cop who has never had the benefit of, let us say, courses in abnormal psychology at Yale, or some of the other things taught us of normality and abnormality. Scotty had a very black and white kind of approach—and this wasn't white."

To those veteran members of the State Department and Foreign Service who survived the McLeod purge, a picture comes back of what it was like as Hanes talks of his friend Scotty.

"He did not fit easily into the intellectual conversations of the Foreign Service," Hanes said. "They hated his guts. He cordially reciprocated. He could be as vindictive as anybody else. You could always simmer him down, but he'd get mad and in a temper and he'd fly off the handle, and he'd start off by doing something wrong and end up by doing something nasty. That was part of his foot in the mouth business."

One rising young man in the Foreign Service made an audible comment one day, in the hearing of one of McLeod's minions, about "the apish behavior of that jumped-up gumshoe." McLeod started digging into the young man's past and discovered a schoolboy homosexual episode. He sent his name through to the so-called Loyalty Committee which was investigating security cases in the Department, and the young man was called before them. He admitted that he had engaged in a schoolboy episode but asked the forgiveness of the committee. He was cleared of "disloyalty." This didn't satisfy McLeod, who wanted the man out. He began digging again. Soon his victim was before the committee once more, confessing that it hadn't been the only episode, and once more he was acquitted of "disloyalty."

Still McLeod wasn't appeased. A third time the young man appeared before the committee. This time he had come to the end of his tether. All his friends and relatives had been grilled by McLeod's goons. A permanent tail was assigned to him. His nerves were shredded.

313

"He broke down completely," said Eleanor Dulles later, "and told the committee: 'I was, I am, and I probably always will be a homosexual.' And he made an emotional spectacle of himself. Well, he was allowed to resign."

He was a friend of Eleanor Dulles, who admired his talents as a Foreign Service officer and believed he would go far. But she could not save him. And it was this and other cases which finally persuaded her to intercede with her brother.

"I talked to him about it and I criticized him once," she said later. "As I've said before, I didn't criticize him very often because you don't fight with a ton of bricks unless you are made of steel and know you've got good sound footing. I remember saying to Foster that it was a pity McLeod was there. He turned on me rather sharply and said: 'Do you know what you are talking about?' And I said: 'No, I don't,' and I didn't. I only knew the general run of things. He said: 'Well, you shouldn't believe hearsay evidence, and I think this man has ability.' Now I don't think he was very happy about the McLeod situation, but he was technically right. I didn't know what I was talking about, and he knew more than I. Except that I had an instinctive feeling McLeod wasn't a great hero."

But so far as Foster was concerned, he was doing a necessary job, not so much in digging up spies and security risks out of the Department as in appeasing McCarthy's insatiable hunger for victims and Congress's need to believe that a sense of order, discipline, and loyalty had come back to a service which the Democrats had turned into a nest of subversives. What Foster did not seem to realize, or deliberately chose to ignore, was that McCarthy was also gravely wounding the State Department's strong sense of *amour propre,* its pride in itself, its confidence in the right of its officials to judge and observe and then freely give their opinions. He humiliated them and inflicted them with a sense of inferiority from which, even today, they have never really recovered. Their strength was sapped and their ability to influence the government consequently diminished. Across the road, Allen Dulles was behaving impeccably and strongly resisting all similar McCarthyian attacks against individuals in the CIA; the Agency stayed loyal, united and self-confident, ready to move into any power vacuum created by the self-doubt which Foster had instigated at State.

Foster refused to sack McLeod, no matter how rough his excesses.

He agreed with John Hanes that: "Basically he was a bluff and hearty fellow. As I say, he was capable of saying the damndest things without half the time realizing it. He had a terrible temper and when he got mad he could do some very stupid things. He wasn't an evil man. He wasn't a brilliant man. He was a very hard working man. He did feel very strongly his responsibility to take the fire. Most of the things he did were under direct orders from our office, and most of them were with the knowledge and concurrence of the Secretary. Scotty felt that one of the parts of his job was that if anybody was going to get mud on his face, it ought to be him and not the Secretary. This didn't make him happy. Nobody likes to get his face wiped in the mud."

But it did secure him a good job when he left the Department. The qualities which broke the morale of the Foreign Service and put McLeod's name up beside Joseph McCarthy in Washington in 1953 were considered just the ones that America's allies should learn to know and love. At the suggestion of John Hanes, Foster signed the necessary papers and passed them to the White House, and Scott McLeod resigned as security officer to become U.S. ambassador to the Republic of Ireland.

There is only one episode in this murky story of Foster's relations with McCarthyism in which he emerges with any courage or credit. Ironically enough, it concerns his fight to prevent injustice to books rather than men. He was outraged when he discovered that McCarthy's two egregious young aides, Roy Cohn and David Schine, had been given the State Department's blessings in the summer of 1953 to go on a tour of U.S. embassies abroad. Their mission was to examine the kinds of books which figured on the shelves of the embassies and information offices, and to rip out and burn any of a "subversive" nature.

The idea that any book could be burned was anathema to Foster, and he displayed unusually fierce anger when he heard that a State Department official, Robert Johnston,* was already destroying volumes cited by Cohn and Shine. He demanded and got Johnston's resignation. When the two McCarthy aides came back to the United States, one of McLeod's assistants, Frances Knight, was photographed enthusiasti-

*Who had been president of Temple University and ought to have known better.

cally embracing the returned warriors against the written word, and was narrowly saved from being thrust into the outer darkness by the intervention of a mutual friend, Walter Robertson, head of the Far East Department.*

It was while he was still fuming over the depredations of Cohn and Schine that Foster received a message from Paris. It came from the U.S. ambassador, Douglas Dillon, but had actually been written by Benjamin Bradlee. Bradlee (now editor of the Washington *Post*) was at that time a counsellor in the embassy, and he was also a friend of the Associated Press correspondent in Paris, Theodore H. White. Among the books which Cohn and Schine had ordered consigned to the flames was White's book, *Thunder Out Of China.*

"[White] came to me and reported that his book had been banned," said Bradlee later, "and also said, almost with tears in his eyes, that the next day was the day that the Book of the Month Club was to discuss the possibility of accepting his next book, *Fire in the Ashes,* about the rebirth of Europe. The story of the banning of his book was on the front page of *The New York Times,* and Teddy White pointed out that it seemed unlikely that they could choose as Book of the Month one by an author who had been condemned as subversive by Cohn and Schine. Was there anything I could do about it?"

Bradlee at that time was "way down the totem pole," but he immediately went to bat for his friend. He got hold of all White's accreditations as a war correspondent, and then he sat down and wrote a cable.

"I signed it Dillon," he said, "because any kind of cable sent out had to be signed by the ambassador. It said that Theodore White had the confidence of fifteen ambassadors and twenty-two accreditations, and what a terribly bad name the American government was going to get if they let these two assholes ban his book. I took it up to Dillon and asked him if he would go along with it. Dillon crossed out the classification—I guess it was SECRET—and made it EYES ONLY SECRETARY OF STATE, which meant it went directly to Dulles. In fact, he made it rather stronger than I had."

The telegram went off. Twenty-four hours later the ban was rescinded on White's book.

"Now Dulles must have done it," Bradlee said. "It was very impres-

*Ms. Knight later replaced Mrs. Shipley as head of the U.S. Passport Office.

sive that he had Ambassador Dillon's backing. But Dulles, who is so often criticized—well, he kind of tossed Chip Bohlen to the wolves and was so often insensitive to personal issues—risked something to rescind Cohn and Schine. I guess they were still in Europe and about to make their invasion of Great Britain. But immediately after this, their mission was aborted and they were called back."

Unfortunately, none of the victims in the State Department had written a book. Not yet, anyway.

CHAPTER NINETEEN

Double Deals

Allen Dulles was having his own troubles with Senator McCarthy, but came out of the battle with rather more honorable bruises. He was well aware that the senator was gunning for the CIA, for he had several times proclaimed that it was a nest of lily-livered liberals who were soft on Communists. In the climate that prevailed in Washington at the time, Allen knew the Agency was vulnerable, for though the Communists who worked for OSS during and after World War II had long since been weeded out, several civilized souls with liberal ideas were still on the roster. McCarthy would undoubtedly have dubbed them Commies.

The first assault from McCarthy's office had come during the CIG days and was easily repulsed by the CIG's legislative counsel, Walter Pforzheimer, a rambunctious round man with a capacity to talk back to McCarthy in his own language when his dander was up.

Among the CIG employees at that time was a young woman analyst whose job was to translate and comment on articles in the Soviet press. She lived in a rooming house in Washington, a couple of doors away from a male analyst also employed in the Soviet section of the CIG.

"The girl had committed the heinous offense," Walter Pforzheimer said later, "of taking the Soviet newspapers *Pravda* and *Isvestia* home with her at night so she could keep up her Russian and knowledge of Russian contemporary affairs. And there was a guy in the next room of this boardinghouse who was also a Russian analyst. They used to speak Russian together because they knew the landlady was very conservative and saw spies under every bed, and, in their case, in them.

They thought talking Russian in her presence would drive her up the wall—which it did."

The landlady wrote to the FBI, which bugged the young woman's room, paid a stealthy and illegal visit and found the Russian newspapers, but could come up with nothing concrete. But Edgar Hoover, who somehow had never learned to love his rivals, thought the incident might cause them some inconvenience, and he tipped off McCarthy, who trumpeted it abroad that the CIG was employing Russian spies. Pforzheimer promptly went to work, gathered the facts, went into McCarthy's office, and blew the case out of the window.

The second case was equally absurd but rather more difficult to deal with. It concerned one of the bright young hopes of the Agency, William Bundy, who had been with the CIA as an analyst since 1951, but had just been made assistant to Robert Amory, a deputy director. Bundy had an impeccable background: son of Henry L. Stimson's Assistant Secretary of State; married to Dean Acheson's daughter; Yale; law school; an amiable but very proper Bostonian. He had already been through a security clearance, but his new job necessitated a more acute examination of his record, what was known as Atomic Energy Clearance, and this meant examination by a board which, for the first time, included a member of the FBI.

In Bundy's file was a fact that he had already revealed to Allen Dulles when he first joined the Agency in 1951, that he had contributed to the Defense Fund for Alger Hiss. Before becoming a CIA agent, Bundy had been a member of the same law firm as Alger's brother, Donald. It seemed to him not out of the way to write a couple of checks to help Alger fight the charges against him. The CIA considered he had been foolish to link his name, even so innocently, with a man involved in a treason case full of such strange ambiguities, but they accepted his explanation.

But by 1953 Alger Hiss had been sent to jail for perjury and his name was flaunted like a talisman of evil by every Commie-hunter in the country.

"And I am sure as everything that J. Edgar walked the file over to McCarthy's office the moment he got it," Bundy said later. "That's how charming a fellow he was."

It was a moment when McCarthy needed a headline in the newspapers to take attention away from his own affairs. One of his associates was in trouble. Dr. J. B. Matthews, a fire-eating new member of his research team, had made the astounding charge that among the Protestant clergy in the United States were five thousand active Soviet agents. It was the kind of statement McCarthy and his staff were always making at this time, and if Matthews had said five thousand Socialists, or Democrats, or members of B'nai Brith were Soviet agents, the comments around the country would have been: "That doesn't surprise me at all." But this was the Protestant Church Matthews was attacking, and every WASP in the country was roused.

"You can imagine what a scream that created on the floor of the Senate," said Walter Pforzheimer later. "All the Protestant senators rose up, seventy-five Protestant clergymen symbolically behind each one of them, and demanded Matthews's head. They told McCarthy this was a slur on the Church, and he'd have to get rid of the man who had made it. Joe said: 'If it's true, what the hell are you bothering about?' They said: 'We don't care if it's true or not—he's got to go.' The real guts of the Senate, who'd kept quiet about Joe's activities until now, they said: 'Joe—out!' meaning out with Matthews."

McCarthy had to face the fact that Matthews was going to have to resign, and that on the day it was announced all the newspapers would have it in big headlines. At least they would unless he could think up another bigger headline that would bury the embarrassing one. How about CIA HIRES PAL OF COMMIE SPY?

On the day of Matthews's resignation, Roy Cohn called Walter Pforzheimer and said:

"Walter, as legislative counsel for the CIA, I'm calling you first. We'd like William Bundy up here to testify before the [Un-American Activities] Committee at eleven o'clock. The son of a bitch has contributed to the Alger Hiss Defense Fund. He's up for a topmost, uppermost type clearance and he'll have access to every secret the nation possesses. The security of the United States is in danger. Get him up here."

That was at 9:15 in the morning.

"No man in CIA, while I am legislative counsel, is going to lay his life bare less than two hours after a guy like Joe McCarthy sends for him," Pforzheimer said. "Two hours to lay your life on the line to McCarthy, who would butcher you to death—that wasn't on, I decided.

I told Roy I'd have to check, that I hadn't seen Bill Bundy that day and I didn't know where he was. I said I'd have to call him back."

He hung up and alerted Allen Dulles. Allen called in Bundy and said: "Look, we simply must not have a confrontation on this in the form of a subpoena. So take the weekend off and get out of town as fast as possible."

Bundy took off and was playing golf with his father on the links in Boston that afternoon, when Cohn and then McCarthy began screaming for him.

Bundy began by being nervous about whether Allen Dulles would stand up for him. So did his wife, who hadn't forgotten how he had lost his nerve over signing her father's, Dean Acheson's, pro-British petition in 1940. Both she and Bill Bundy knew how Foster was cringing to the monster over at State. Would Allen begin making kowtows too?

"Allen's conduct in the affair was certainly a crucible in our relationship," Bundy said later. "And not only mine. I think it was terribly important for him from every standpoint. I thought he measured up. Of course, he wasn't alone. I had good friends in the Republican Party. It wasn't as though he had to take on the rest of the world for someone who had no friends at court. So it wasn't that Allen was the boy on the burning deck or anything like that. But that doesn't take away the fact that he stood up absolutely totally, and made it clear that under no circumstances was I going to appear in Congress and testify as to my loyalty to McCarthy. He went further than that. *Nobody* from the CIA was going to account for their loyalty to McCarthy."

Cohn and McCarthy tried every way they could to get Bundy up to Capitol Hill. When Bundy stayed hidden, they sent down subpoenas for Walter Pforzheimer and Bundy's secretary, and proposed to grill them about the way they had "spirited" Bundy away. Allen Dulles stood his ground.

"He established a principle," Bundy said. "And when other fellows around the government saw what he had done, they looked at each other and said: 'Why have we been letting those fellows from the State Department and the U.S. Information Office go up there to be roasted by McCarthy?' And in the end, nobody from the Executive Branch ever went before McCarthy again."

In fact, it didn't end as easily as the newspapers reported at the time.

Both Allen and Bundy had to pay for their defiance of the irascible McCarthy. All the time Bundy had stayed hidden, a lively correspondence had been going on between McCarthy and Allen Dulles. It came to a head on August 3, when McCarthy wrote to Allen:

> I note your refusal to give us any answers to our questions. Your insistence is extremely revealing. It would seem that the last man in the world who would try to protect and hide the facts about one of his top officer's association with, and contributions to, a convicted traitor would be the head of the CIA. I think it is necessary for me to call your attention to the tremendous damage you thereby do to this organization. That the matter cannot and will not rest here is, of course, obvious.

A few hours later, Roy Cohn learned that Bundy and his wife were planning to sail for Europe aboard the *Queen Mary,* and McCarthy was all for having them arrested on the dockside. Allen Dulles heard about the ploy, and scotched it with a quick note to the State Department (which had been asked to seize the Bundy passports) giving documentary proof that the young couple had booked a European trip many months ago, and that it was to be their annual holiday.

But McCarthy had pushed him into a corner. He was in no position to ignore the matter any longer, or to stave off a confrontation with stonewalling letters. Instead, he went to see Vice-President Richard Nixon, to ask him to intervene with McCarthy and persuade him to call off the subpoenas on Pforzheimer and Bundy's secretary. Nixon did so on condition that Bundy submitted himself to a new Civil Service security clearance board. Bundy was persuaded to accept, and lived to regret it.

"You got a real bunch of time-servers on this board," he said later, "and they were protecting their backsides every which way. And it became a very unpleasant inquiry as to why I was still having any dealings with Donald Hiss, and a lot of things extraneous to the original charges. And in the end they submitted one of the most bizarre reports ever rendered. They said: 'We can find no basis for questioning his loyalty or security,' but they still didn't think the Agency should have me. It was bad publicity for the CIA, they thought."

It took another eight months before he was finally in the clear. But through the painful hours of yet another board of inquiry, Bundy says he was sustained by Allen Dulles's faith in him. He never ordered him off the payroll. He allowed him access to the most secret papers.

"I never wavered in my feeling about him," Bundy said. "My wife and others close to me were critical of him for not immediately issuing a raking defense of me. But as those things went, it was a question whether you got the rhetoric or the results. In the end the results bore out the way he handled it."

Bundy added:

"I guess there was an element of tribal loyalty in the way Allen handled this, that he knew me, he knew my brother, a sort of fellow feeling—a feeling for the comradeship of the CIA but also a tribal feeling toward a set of people who were in law firms, entered government when the need was felt, could be invited back to the house. Anyway, he stood up to the fire."

Allen Dulles used to tell his sister that 1953 and 1954 were the good years at the CIA, when everything seemed to be going right and the Agency was his brother's strong right arm in helping to reshape the world and make it a place fit for free and decent people to live in.

No matter what expedients the brothers stooped to use to placate and appease demagogues and rabble-rousers at home, there was no doubt of their sincerity in the way in which they regarded their mission overseas. The blight of communism in Europe and Asia had replaced the scourge of Nazism and Japanese militarism, and it was America's duty to confront and overcome it. Since the advent of the atom bomb had made war unthinkable, even against a Stalinist tyranny which both of them equated with Hitlerism, and since the American people were, in any case, in no mood for any new war, the CIA in its new form could be the weapon with which the new crusade could be waged. It was the sword of Excalibur with which evil could be driven from the world. Or so Allen professed to believe.

The intelligence machine which Beetle Smith had overhauled during his period as director was now running smoothly, and, as Kim Philby later remarked, all Allen Dulles had to be careful about was that it didn't run away with him.

For the first time, the CIA now had a budget running at over half a billion dollars, and there was no one outside the Agency Allen needed to tell how the money was spent. Congress accepted his word for it that the funds were needed, and passed the appropriations with a wave of the hand. Beetle Smith had instituted a rule during his régime that all intelligence propositions submitted to him must be no longer than a single sheet of paper, and Allen continued the practice. Now he would read through a single-sheet suggestion for a covert operation abroad, budgeted at several millions of dollars, and sign the authorization with a flourish.

"Let's give it a try," he would say.

He was still not interested in the technical side of the Agency's activities, and never pretended to understand the work of the huge new scientific analysis section now in operation—studying all facets of Soviet life, weather, geology, economy, and military development— but he never stinted it of funds. When the experts came to him for money to build something or to experiment with a new plane, a new weapon, or a new listening device, he signed the appropriation without any hesitation.

But primarily he was interested in only two sides of intelligence. One was the old-fashioned business of getting information out of people, and in that he considered that he was still the most successful agent the world had ever known. Over the years he had built up a roster of friends and acquaintances in various parts of the world who had quite often become the leading men in their countries. His brother's close friend was Chancellor Adenauer of Germany, but Allen had cherished and nurtured Heinrich von Brentano, who was now Adenauer's right-hand man, and he told Allen what the Germans were planning long before the chancellor confided in Foster.

Allen used to boast in the Agency that he had friends or informants in every important cabinet in the Western and neutral world, all of whom kept him in touch with what was said and planned by their governments. From the director's own discretionary fund, he paid one member of the French cabinet $30,000 a year for himself, and, during the French Chamber's discussion of the European Defense Community project, handed him another $500,000 to distribute among his fellow members. Foster wanted the EDC bill passed by the French, because without them it would wither and die. Foster was strongly backing the project, which would, for the first time since the end of World War II, allow the Germans to rearm and join with the Western allies in a defensive force designed to deter or repel any invasion by the Russians and their satellites. The Germans would come under joint

—definitely not German—command, and Foster had guaranteed that the United States would see to it that the government in Bonn had no say in the disposition of any of their nationals in the force. But he had set his heart on seeing Germany inside the European community of nations as a full member, and he had promised his friend Adenauer that it would be done. Allen was putting the CIA's resources behind him to ensure that the French demonstrated their willingness to welcome the Germans back.*

But for the most part Allen didn't have to pay his informants, leaving that to his subordinates.

"His business was people," said one Agency man, "his face-to-face contact with them, and simply winning them over by his geniality and the American flag flying at his back and the President behind him."

The other intelligence activity which fascinated and absorbed him was covert operations. Thanks to the dedicated and fervent enthusiasm of Frank Wisner, this had now become the CIA's major activity and swallowed up most of the money. Covert operations had planes and secret airfields in Greece, Germany, England, and Japan. It had a cadre of American officers, on loan from the Army, trained in all branches of guerilla warfare, and hired mercenaries for them to lead. There were five thousand of them in camps around various parts of Germany, trained and armed to start a clandestine campaign.

Frank Wisner believed that one day these men would spearhead the forces of revolution that would free the world from the Communist yoke. He lived in hope that the day would not be long in coming, and meanwhile dispatched airplanes from Wiesbaden, northern Greece, and Hokkaido with agents aboard, whom he parachuted into Georgia, the Ukraine, Byelorussia, or Siberia to speed up the revolt. It did not lessen his perfervid belief in the "liberation" that he never heard from most of them again.

The clandestine operation which brought Allen Dulles most pleasure in 1953, and one which won Foster over to the efficacy of covert activities, was the overthrow of the red-inclined leader, Mossadeq, in Iran. The shah had fled in face of threats from Communist mobs. The oil wells in the south (hitherto under the control of Britain's Anglo-

*In this case, however, his bribes failed to win the day. The Chamber still voted the project down, and moved Foster to make his famous "agonizing reappraisal" speech, in which he roundly warned America's European allies to toe the line—or else.

Persian Oil Company) had been seized. The business of restoring them and of putting the shah back on his Peacock Throne and the oil back into the hands of Western oil-users, was handed over to an able Wisner aide named Kermit (Kim) Roosevelt, who, as head of the Middle East Department of the CIA, had once worked closely with the British agent-cum-Russian spy, Kim Philby. Philby knew something about politics in the Persian Gulf through his father, St. John Philby, who had been adviser to ibn-Saud of Saudi Arabia. He admired Kim Roosevelt's technique.

"Oddly enough, I dubbed him 'the quiet American' five years before Graham Greene wrote his book," Philby wrote later.* "He was a courteous, soft-spoken Easterner with impeccable social connections, well-educated rather than intellectual, pleasant and unassuming as host and guest. An equally nice wife. In fact, the last person you would expect to be up to the neck in dirty tricks."

It was Kim Roosevelt who arranged the shah's flight from Teheran when the mobs menaced him; at CIA expense the shah was established in Rome with his wife, Soraya, and told to hold himself ready to return to his country. While in Rome, Soraya received a visit from an American gynecologist who had been summoned from the United States by Kim Roosevelt. She had been trying for some time to produce a son and heir for the shah, and had failed to do so. The specialist put her on a course of injections and sent her down to Ischia for mudbaths. Soraya, a rough-tongued and earthy young woman who knew her future as the shah's consort was doomed if she didn't get pregnant quickly, kept badgering the gynecologist to explain to her why it wasn't happening.

"Four times a night," she said, "and twice every afternoon. Still I don't have a baby."

The gynecologist went into a complicated explanation of the fertility cycle, the waywardness of ovaries, and why it was difficult to make eggs drop at the right moment. She must just keep on trying and keep her husband "interested" in her.

"Doctor," said Soraya, "all I'm asking you to do is find something to break my eggs. I'll see the shah goes on making the omelettes."

The Iranian army was thoroughly bribed. The police force was fixed.

*In a letter to the author.

Some of Mossadeq's more powerful supporters were quietly spirited away, their throats slit, their bodies buried in the Elburz Mountains. Demonstrators were hired. A revolt was then organized and orchestrated by the CIA, and, with hardly a shot fired, the amiable and torpid Mossadeq, who had simply wanted to get the international oil cartel off his country's back, was easily toppled. Kim Roosevelt felt sorry for him and saw to it that when he came out of jail—he served a three-year term—he was given a comfortable pension to eke out his rapidly declining years.

When the shah and his queen returned from Rome, it was the CIA which distributed the baksheesh to beef up the cheering crowds that greeted them. Altogether it had been a triumphant operation by the Agency, and people began to believe that under the new director, the CIA could not only influence elections but actually change governments. Allen Dulles certainly had the magic touch, they decided.

Everyone was grateful to him except the Russians and the shah, the latter being described by Herbert Hoover, Jr., one of the agents involved in the operation, as "an ingrate by nature." The young monarch crisply pointed out that any favor the CIA had done him would be adequately paid for in oil. And anyway, what kind of gynecologists did they employ who couldn't tell his queen how to get pregnant?*

There were no such successes yet for Foster in 1953. The Korean War dragged on. The cold war with the Russians in Europe was frigid. And Foster was discovering that he could run into difficulties with members of the Congress who were not demagogues like McCarthy but ordinary, avidly interested men anxious to get the measure of the new Secretary, find out what he really knew about the condition of the world, and what ideas he had for ameliorating it.

One of the particular processes of government in the United States requires the Secretary of State to come once a year before the House Committee on Appropriations, when he is asked by the chairman to give a *tour d'horizon* of the political problems around the world. This is the foundation for subsequent hearings on appropriations for economic assistance, military assistance, and other budgetary items. Fos-

---

*The shah subsequently divorced Queen Soraya and married a young Iranian student, Fara Dibah, who speedily produced him a son. The CIA's doctors were not consulted.

ter's first appearance before the committee now came up, in February 1953.

Under Dean Acheson as Secretary the Policy Planning Staff, led by Paul Nitze, had always prepared an outline for him, noting points to be considered country by country and setting it out so that the Secretary himself could fill in details and thoughts wherever he thought fit. Nitze, who was still around at this point, believed it would help Foster to do a similar outline for him. The staff got down to work and the outline was sent in to the Secretary.

A couple of days later, Rod O'Connor came into Nitze's office and said: "Who asked you to send in that outline to the Secretary?"

"No one," said Nitze. "I thought the Secretary might find it useful. After all, he's the one who speaks. This is just a checklist for him."

O'Connor said sharply: "Don't ever send in a paper again unless the Secretary asks for it."

Nitze shrugged his shoulders. O'Connor might have worn a smile when he spoke, but Nitze understood how the "tight little group" around Foster was feeling at that time, "sort of in hostile territory, surrounded by ardent Democrats." He had tried to be helpful and had been rebuffed. Too bad.

A few days later, after Foster had done his dog and pony show for the House committee, he called Nitze into his office.

"Paul," he said, "you remember that outline of yours? I wish I'd used it. You know, I didn't understand one thing about this *tour d'horizon* business. I'd been told it was all completely off the record, but when I'd gotten through it was explained to me that it was only off the record for that day, and when the committee published its hearings they would start off with that testimony of mine. So it's only temporarily off the record. Now what I would like for you to do is get ahold of the secretary of the committee and ask him for a transcript of my talk, and then I'd like you to rewrite it in accordance with that outline of yours."

Nitze replied: "Mr. Secretary, you know these committees let you make corrections of grammar and sense and that sort of thing, but they don't let you make radical changes, because that puts out of gear the questions and the comments by members of the committee. It corrupts the record."

"Well, anyway," said Foster, "get ahold of that fellow and see what you can do. And do your best."

Nitze called up the clerk and asked him whether it would be possible to make more substantive corrections to the transcript than usual. The clerk said: "I don't give a goddamn if you scrap the whole thing and rewrite it from the beginning. This is the worst testimony that was ever given before the committee."

Burt Marshall, Nitze's assistant, took the transcript and sat up until three or four the next morning going through it.

"I was absolutely amazed," Marshall said later. "I couldn't believe my eyes. Molotov once said at a meeting with us that he had a procedural motion to make. He said: 'I propose we insert a *not* before every verb in the text.' You could have done that to Foster's testimony. I struck out whole parts of it and rewrote whole parts of it. The things he'd said! He goes around the world, and starts with Canada. He takes a few slams at Canada—their inferiority complex, their ambivalent attitude to the U.S.—but points out that it's a very important piece of real estate and should be humored along. Then he jumps to the United Kingdom. They have all their good days behind them and they don't really amount to much any more, and they're ultra sensitive, but they're important real estate, and should be kept sweet."

Country by country, he demolished them.

"He said France was the place where they have all those mistresses and sell dirty postcards," Marshall recalled, "but it's a damned important piece of real estate because it's got all those canals and highways leading directly to Germany. Then he's in Germany, and how those people have cut the throat of the world twice in a generation, but they're a really vital piece of real estate. Then he turns to the Scandinavians and how, through every important crisis, they got a free ride on other peoples' backs. The Italians: they've been an asset to their enemies in every war they've fought. The Middle East: full of Arabs, but also full of oil and air communications."

By the time he reached South America, Nitze recalled, taking up the story, Foster had really got into his stride.

"He talked about aid to South America and remarked: 'You know, aid is like opium. There are withdrawal pains when you remove it. I propose to cease all aid to South America. But I do want you to let me have a little leeway, to take care of the withdrawal pains.' "

As Nitze remarked, if the transcript had been published as Foster had delivered it, "it would have built up the Communist propaganda line for the next twenty-five years."

Nitze went over Marshall's revisions, then between them they put their heads together and rewrote the whole thing, including the congressmen's questions and comments. Then they sent it into the Secretary. He signed it, sent it off to the committee clerk, and never mentioned it again.

But even before that incident, Nitze had sensed that it would not be very long before Foster disembarrassed himself of his services.

The break came over a speech that President Eisenhower delivered —he called it "The Chance for Peace"—the following April, which not only resulted in Nitze's departure from the State Department but represented the one and only time the President challenged Foster's assessment of the world situation. He lost.

It was the death of Josef Stalin which brought matters to a head.

"Shortly after six o'clock on the morning of March 4 [1953]," President Eisenhower wrote later,

> Allen Dulles, the director of the Central Intelligence Agency, telephoned me to say that Stalin had suffered a stroke and that he was believed to be dying. Before eight o'clock I was in my office meeting with Foster Dulles, General Cutler, C. D. Jackson and Jim Hagerty to go over the draft of a possible statement which they had already started working on.

Foster was in his most uncommunicative mood. When the five men shortly afterwards moved into an emergency meeting of the National Security Council and he was asked what he thought should be the tenor of the statement, he was silent for a full minute (C. D. Jackson timed it on his watch), and then said: "I wonder whether we should make any statement at all."

The President suggested mildly that he didn't think that was very constructive. After all, Stalin had been one of the Big Three and Russia an Ally during World War II. Surely a word of sympathy . . . ?

What was troubling Foster Dulles was his discovery, only an hour or two before, that neither State nor the CIA had any contingency plans whatsoever for dealing with the death of Stalin. It would undoubtedly have a convulsive effect upon East-West relations and perhaps change the nature of the world, yet aside from some CIA assessments of certain of the Soviet dictator's possible successors, no one had produced any papers about what might be the repercussions and how to deal with them.

He needed time to think. Frank Wisner had rushed round to Allen's house on Highlands Avenue in the early hours of the morning, the moment he heard the news, to plead with him to dissuade both the Secretary and the President from any provocative statements. He was convinced that the Soviet satellites in Europe were in a volatile mood, and any rash talk from Washington could set a match to the fire.

And it was too early, Wisner insisted. If the satellite peoples rose up in revolt now, the Red Army would crush them. They were unarmed and not prepared. The CIA needed time to organize its clandestine forces and get arms dumps and commando forces ready to exploit the situation.

Allen had taken Wisner round to see his brother, who found the arguments of the covert operations expert persuasive. He agreed that any precipitate move could be fatal to whatever enterprise the CIA and the nation might undertake once Stalin was dead.

Foster told the President and the NSC that he would agree to the issuing of a statement on condition that nothing was said that would compromise future policy. He then took a hand in preparing a bromide text which he laced liberally with religious sentiments.

"At this moment in history," the statement read,

> when multitudes of Russians are anxiously concerned because of the illness of the Soviet ruler the thoughts of America go out to all the peoples of the USSR—the men and women, the boys and girls—in the villages, cities, farms and factories of their homeland.
>
> They are the children of the same God who is the Father of all peoples everywhere. And like all peoples, Russian millions share our longing for a friendly and peaceful world.
>
> Regardless of the identity of government personalities, the prayer of us Americans continues to be that the Almighty will watch over the people of that vast country and bring them, in His wisdom, opportunity to live their lives in a world where all men and women and children dwell in peace and comradeship.

331

As someone remarked later, it was Foster's message from on high that God had promised to look after the godless Russians.

Stalin died the next day. In his funeral oration his successor, Georgi M. Malenkov, made a call for new efforts to secure "peaceful coexistence," and reinforced this shortly afterwards with a plea for all nations to avoid the dangers of global war. It was a startling change from the menacing statements and actions that the Communists had lately been making in the world, and the President and some of his advisers were impressed. Eisenhower told his speech writer, Emmett John Hughes, that he felt an attempt should be made to meet the Russians halfway. Hughes warned him that Foster Dulles by no means shared this opinion. In a talk which Hughes had had with him the previous day, Foster had made it plain that what he thought should be done was not make gestures but act tougher. He had heard, for instance, that the Russians might be willing to persuade the Chinese to cease their intervention in the Korean War and accept a truce. He would be sorry if that happened.

"I don't think we can get much out of a Korean settlement," Foster Dulles had said, "until we have shown—before all Asia—our clear superiority by giving the Chinese one hell of a licking."

To which Eisenhower replied: "All right, then. If Mr. Dulles and all his sophisticated advisers really mean that they can *not* talk peace seriously, then I am in the wrong pew. For if it's *war* we should be talking about, I *know* the people to give me advice on that—and they're not in the State Department. Now either we cut out all this fooling around and make a serious bid for peace—or we forget the whole thing."

He agreed that the time had come to make a Big Speech as a gesture to the new Soviet régime. Foster was by no means enthusiastic when he heard about it, but Allen was a little warmer toward the idea and even proposed that the President might make two gestures: (1) suggest having the next meeting of the United Nations take place in Moscow, and (2) propose a joint Soviet-American aid program to provide economic assistance to Red China. It was agreed that Hughes and Paul Nitze would draft out the text of the speech between them.

But as the text began to be roughed out over the next few days, Foster grew increasingly hostile and Allen cooler and less enthusiastic.

"I grow less and less keen about this speech," Foster said, "because

I think there's some real danger of our just seeming to fall in with these Soviet overtures.* It's obvious that what they are doing is because of outside pressures, and I don't know anything better we can do than keep up those pressures."

He was extremely wary of Eisenhower's eagerness to talk, and deeply suspicious of the advice he was being given inside the White House.

Foster was planning to take Janet with him for a holiday on Duck Island, on Lake Ontario, where they would live in their log cabin, fend for themselves, fish, sail, chop wood, walk and talk. If Allen's way of recharging his batteries was to go out to parties and flirt with pretty women, Foster's was to play the pioneer and go back to the frontiers of the nation. But just before he left, he called Emmett Hughes in to see him and stressed to him the danger of "falling in with the Soviet scheme of things," and after he had flown north Hughes found a note he had left behind for him:

"Reference to ending of wars in Asia gives me a little concern lest it commit us to end the Chinese civil war and again to 'neutralize' Formosa."

Foster did not go so far as Senators Knowland, Bridges, and McCarthy, who had recently risen to drink a toast at the Nationalist Chinese Embassy and cried aloud: "Back to the mainland," but he was still ready to go quite a long way in backing that "Christian" gentleman, Chiang Kai-shek, and did not want the Korean War to end if it prevented the Chinese Communists from getting the licking he felt they so richly deserved.

"Damn it," said Nitze, after he had read the note, "if we mean peace, we mean *peace*—and not another civil war in China."

The atmosphere relaxed after Foster had departed for Duck Island. It was not exactly like a schoolroom after the teacher had slipped out, but everyone around the President acted easier and even Allen Dulles came round to say that if the speech could find a formula for ending the war in Korea, he was for it. He did not want any more American boys to suffer the fate of his son. For Allen Dulles, Jr., was up and about, but the bullet had glanced across the edge of his brain, and he would never be the same again.

*He was referring to the rumors, mentioned above, that the Russians might be willing to intervene with the Chinese.

The speech took shape more rapidly. On the Sunday morning before it was due to be delivered, a meeting was arranged at the White House to work over its final form. Paul Nitze was the first to arrive for the eleven o'clock meeting, but the White House attendants (who seemed to make a habit of it around this time) did a George V. Allen on him and gave him the wrong directions.

"I was told to take the elevator to the second floor and go straight ahead," said Nitze later. "So I go up alone and I walk into a room, and there is Eisenhower in his BVDs, almost stark naked. Mamie grinned but the President looked embarrassed, and tells me: 'No, you're in the wrong room, go up to that Oval Room in the far corner.' Apparently he had been delivering a speech to the Pan-American Union and had to wear a cutaway for that, and had been changing into something more relaxed."

The President had called in four advisers to discuss the speech with him: Emmett Hughes and Paul Nitze, who had drafted it; Milton Eisenhower, his brother; and Beetle Smith. Ike took the draft and began going through it word by word, until Beetle stopped him. Beetle too seemed to be looser and more relaxed—or as much as he ever could be—now that Foster was away, and there was an air of their wartime relationship as he said, firmly, "You know, this isn't the way to do it. Discuss the ideas in the speech. Discuss the ideas and see if there's anything you disagree with, and get them clarified, and then edit it. But it's impossible to edit a speech word by word at this late date."

"Okay, Beetle," the President said. Then he turned to Nitze.

"But Paul," he said, "I understand that Foster disagrees with this speech. What does he *disagree* about?"

Nitze said:

"What this speech proposes, among other things, is an armistice in Korea unconnected with any commitment by the Chinese that they would desist from any ambitions in Southeast Asia. Foster has always taken the position that a precondition for an armistice in Korea should be a commitment by the Chinese Communists that they would lay hands off Southeast Asia. Well, you can insist on that. But it means continuing the Korean War. And if you want to continue the Korean War, you can't do it concurrently with cutting the $5 billion out of the Defense budget, which you've just committed yourself to doing in your meeting with Senator Taft. Either you want an armistice or you want the war to go on. And you're not going to get an armistice if you insist the Chinese commit themselves, because they're not going to do it."

The President looked around the table.

"I agree with Paul," Beetle said. The others nodded.

"I guess I do too," the President said. "Let's get to work."

As Paul Nitze remarked later: "So the main issue, which I think was Foster's main difference with the speech, was decided against Foster in Foster's absence. He was furious about the whole thing, and tried to sabotage the effect afterwards."

President Eisenhower delivered his speech on "The Chance for Peace" before a meeting of the American Society of Newspaper Editors; his listeners were not alone in later acclaiming it as the best speech of his career. It was simple and effective, and it asked no more than reasonable commitments from the other side:

> Every gun that is fired, every warship launched, every rocket fired signifies, in the final sense, a theft from those who hunger and are not fed, those who are cold and are not clothed. The world in arms is not spending money alone. It is spending the sweat of its laborers, the genius of its scientists, the hopes of its children. The cost of one modern heavy bomber is this: a modern brick school in more than thirty cities. It is two electric power plants, each serving a town of sixty thousand population. It is two fine fully equipped hospitals. It is some fifty miles of concrete highway.

It seemed to be a turning point in history; the President went on:

> What is the Soviet Union ready to do? . . . A world that begins to witness the rebirth of trust among nations *can* find its way to a peace that is neither partial nor punitive. . . . The first great step along this way must be the conclusion of an honorable peace in Korea. . . . We seek throughout Asia as throughout the world a peace that is true and total. . . . This government is ready to ask its people to join with all nations in devoting a substantial percentage of the savings achieved by disarmament to a fund for world aid and reconstruction. . . . What is the Soviet Union ready to do?

The speech struck a chord around the world. Even *Pravda* and *Isvestia* printed it in full, and *The New York Times* called it "magnificent and deeply moving."

But such gestures need a follow-up if rhetoric, no matter how stirring, is to be turned into action. When the White House staff met next morning, purring with delight at the world reaction, their feeling was: Where do we go from here? They hoped that the cabinet meeting, called for two hours later, and dubbed a "special" meeting by the White House spokesman, would produce the answer. The press had been alerted that big decisions would be made.

To everyone's astonishment, President Eisenhower was not even *at* the meeting. He had left town in a hurry and was believed to be on a golf course in North Carolina. Vice-President Richard Nixon took the chair at the White House cabinet instead. He had spoken to Foster Dulles overnight, after the Secretary had come ashore at Henderson, New York, and got ready to return to Washington, where he was to talk to the Society of Newspaper Editors too.

Richard Nixon was a friend and admirer of John Foster Dulles. He had consulted him during the Alger Hiss case and had been delighted that he had testified against Hiss at his trial.

"I'm told by people in court that watched the jury, they concluded Hiss was more hurt by Dulles's testimony than even by the testimony with regard to the typewriter, the rug, and other things, because they believed Dulles," Nixon said later, and added that "he had a reputation for honesty no matter what people think of his views." Nixon added that he "cherished [his] relationship with him," and listened carefully when he gave advice, "because he knew a lot more about diplomacy and human nature, and he knew a lot more about the working of the Communist mind."

Whether Nixon took Foster's advice about the Eisenhower speech will never be known, but the extraordinary fact is that at the cabinet meeting he made absolutely no mention of it. It might just as well not have been given. The cabinet talked instead, under Nixon's guidance, about how to win the 1954 congressional elections. Emmett Hughes wrote in his diary that night: "I suppose a lot of people thought we spent this day in the White House talking about peace in the world."

As for Foster Dulles, he returned to Washington and quickly put Eisenhower's challenge for peace where he considered it belonged— on the back burner. He told the Society of Newspaper Editors that there was nothing new in it, and the government's policy would continue to be "so firm, so fair, so just that the Soviet leaders might find it expedient to live with these policies rather than live against them."

One of the actions Winston Churchill, the British Prime Minister, had urged on reading the text of Eisenhower's speech was a summit meeting to bring the new Soviet leaders together with the West to thrash out their differences and misunderstandings. Foster, who had never been enthusiastic about summits, preferring foreign ministers' conferences, where he could take the initiative, managed to fob that one off.

In any case, he made it clear that he preferred to meet the new leaders with the thumbscrew rather than the handclasp. He believed that pressure on the Russians while they were adjusting to the post-Stalin era would have a more lasting effect than overtures of amity, which, he was convinced, they would interpret as weakness. Even before becoming Secretary, he had made a point of visiting Chancellor Adenauer on every occasion he was in Germany, and the German leader, a hard-line anti-Communist, was to have an increasing influence on his thinking about Europe from now on. Adenauer had been even more antagonistic to Eisenhower's speech than Foster, because he was certain that a slackening of tension between the Soviet Union and the United States would mean less attention to West Germany—and less eagerness by America to press for the reunification of East and West Germany.

"I thought Foster gave in too much to Adenauer," Averell Harriman said later. "I was opposed to the idea Adenauer developed that the way to get the unification of Germany was to be stubborn about everything, and to refuse to accept the reality of the Soviet zone of Germany . . . I didn't think Foster's policies were wise at that time. He got too much involved in Adenauer's policies."

Chip Bohlen, that veteran of the Foreign Service, who was now watching the situation from his post as ambassador to Moscow, felt that Foster Dulles was being altogether "too rigid and inflexible" toward the Russians, and that a summit might have been "useful" and "we might have gotten a great deal out of it." He suspected the reason why the Secretary was against it was his unwillingness to see "the spectacle of the President of the United States shaking hands with the Russians," and the depressing effect this might have on the resistance movements in eastern Europe and Asia which he, along with his brother Allen and Frank Wisner, continued to believe were ready to throw off the Soviet yoke at a trumpet call from the West.

337

So the opportunity presented by Stalin's death was lost, and the President's initiative whittled away. Henry Cabot Lodge, back from a foreign tour some months later, reported: "I heard everywhere one major criticism—that promises of action in the foreign field don't seem to have been kept. There's just a widespread feeling of no follow-up to the sweeping declarations of last April."

It was the last time Dwight Eisenhower made a foreign policy declaration that did not have the wholehearted approval of Foster Dulles. And Paul Nitze was told that the time had come for him to clean out his desk and depart. But he had one consolation prize when he left. He had been quite right when he said that the United States could not continue the Korean War and cut $5 billion out of the Defense budget. So a Korean armistice was signed in July 1953—without the Chinese giving any commitment about Southeast Asia.

As it turned out, it was Beetle Smith who picked Nitze's successor. He brought down Robert Bowie, a professor at Harvard who had served with the U.S. occupation forces in Germany and had a reputation as a man of forthright and fearless opinions. In some ways, it was almost as if Beetle were appointing his alter ego, for they had much in common.

Beetle had discovered in the early days of the administration that his position in the hierarchy of the State Department, important as Foster had made it sound, was little more than a sinecure, to be measured in worth alongside that of the vice-presidency, only without the succession rights. Foster had tricked him. Or had he tricked himself?

As Under-Secretary of State, with Dulles himself concentrating on long-term foreign policy goals, he had imagined himself in charge, settling all the day-to-day problems of the Department and making all its important manifold decisions. It would be rather like being aboard an ocean liner, with John Foster Dulles playing host at the captain's table, glad-handing at the ship's dances, making little speeches, keeping the important passengers happy, while he would be staff captain giving out the orders to officers and crew, seeing the schedule was kept, and charting the course through fog, rain, and storm safely to port. It hadn't worked out that way.

One of the first things that happened, almost immediately after his own appointment, was that Foster made another. He brought in a businessman named Donald B. Lourie to be under-secretary in charge of Administration. A few days later, after a staff meeting, Beetle invited Lourie to have coffee with him in his office. He poured out his cup and then said: "Now, Lourie, I want you to be clear on just one thing. There's only one Under-Secretary in this Department. Do you understand?"

Lourie, who had been president of the board of Quaker Oats until his appointment and was as bland as his company's product, hastened to assure Beetle that he would keep a low profile and never presume to speak for State. In the event it did not matter. From the start Foster abandoned the idea of being Secretary by remote control, and never let Beetle get his hands near the wheel.

Foster had gathered around him a tight little staff of admiring aides: the trusty twosome, O'Connor and Hanes; a phalanx of Republican lawyers and diplomats like Herman Phleger, Livingstone Merchant; two sons-of-their-fathers, Douglas MacArthur, Jr., and Herbert Hoover, Jr.; and an ambitious young Foreign Service man, William Macomber. Phleger was legal adviser to the State Department and was always there to back up his chief with precedents to support his actions, and both he and Merchant were masters of the kind of courtroom prose that can *smother* an unpleasant truth in a mass of verbiage. MacArthur was so devoted to his master that he lived more in the office than he did at home, and once had to be ordered back to his wife "because your marriage front is crumbling."* Herbert Hoover, Jr., was cast in the image of his father, the former President, and had inherited the same overweening egotism and conviction that he knew best for everyone. His unwillingness to listen to arguments was perhaps in some measure due to the fact that he was partly deaf. William Macomber was also a workoholic but he had more reason than MacArthur for staying around the office, since he was in love with Foster's personal secretary, Phyllis Bernau. He eventually married her.

This proud and devoted staff formed a palace guard. They guarded the door jealously, and slowly closed it in Beetle's face. It was a time when the pains in his stomach were becoming so great that they increasingly sapped his energy, leaving him no strength to fight for precedence. So it was almost as a gesture of substitution that he had

---

*Foster had inadvertently hooked in on a telephone conversation in which Mrs. MacArthur raged at the tyranny of the State Department for overworking her husband.

brought in Robert (Bob) Bowie, who had Beetle's decisiveness in expressing his views (though they were more liberal-minded) and could not be overawed.

At his first interview with Foster, Bowie said that he thought the Secretary "ought to check with one or two people about me personally because I was aggressive in stating my views. I had worked for people like Clay and McCloy and Judge Patterson, all of whom welcomed a forceful statement of views, and I wanted it essentially known what he was getting. It wasn't interesting to me if he wanted someone more muted or someone who carried out orders. I said policy involved imprints of various views as forcefully as could be stated, and the only condition I accepted was that, as long as you were in government, you did not try to pursue your own views outside by means of leaks to the press. He could count on that. But I thought he really ought to check to see whether he was going to be comfortable with me."

Foster's eyes flicked sharply toward Bowie when the word "leaks" was mentioned, but then he said, well, he thought he could live with that. Bowie took over Nitze's desk and job as director of Policy Planning.

The last Democrat now left in Foster's immediate entourage was Nitze's assistant, Burt Marshall. For various reasons he was asked to stay on temporarily, and he remained a skeptic about the Secretary's abilities. Marshall's final experience of Foster's way with a tricky international situation came at the end of 1953, during his last days on the job.

The president of Panama was paying a state visit to the United States, and one of his engagements was to be an official visit to the State Department. Latin American Department experts went to Foster's office to brief him during a crowded twenty-minute interview.

"We told Foster he would have to be very careful," Mashall said later, "because we didn't want anything to go wrong. It was just the beginning of Panamanian agitation over the Canal, and we stressed that they were very sensitive over their independence. We said to him: 'This above all. Don't make any mention whatsoever about U.S. sovereignty in the Canal Zone. It is leased territory, and the Panamanians are most sensitive to the notion that the U.S. considers it as American territory. Keep off it. Don't get into the juridical question.' "

Then the president of Panama arrived and was shown into Foster's office. Foster went forward to him, grasped him by the hand, and said:

"What an honor it is to meet the president of the only country in the world which stands on both sides of American soil."

The Panamanian ambassador was doing the translation, and he swallowed. Then he translated:

"The Secretary says it is a great honor to meet the president of Panama."

CHAPTER TWENTY

Double Agents

Socially, the President mixed neither with his Secretary of State nor with the director of the CIA, for they had no intellectual or cultural rapport and no level of off-duty conversation in common. Dwight Eisenhower preferred the company of wartime soldiers who had now gone back into big business, and with whom he could play golf and reminisce about SHAEF, Algiers, London, and Paris. If he had a friend in the cabinet, it was George Humphrey, the Secretary of the Treasury, who talked Ike's language over the value of the dollar and the profligacy of government.

The President admired Foster and was a little frightened of him, sometimes referring to him as an Old Testament prophet, and those who attended meetings of the cabinet or the National Security Council noticed that his eyes sometimes glazed as Foster droned on about the need to be firm and resolute in the pursuit of the right policy. Allen he liked, for his sparkle, his perennial good humor, and that Ho-ho-ho laugh of his; but his tastes were too cultivated and he would have been uneasy having him home to eat with him and Mamie, especially if he brought that vague wife of his along, who never listened to what you were saying.

Foster's friends were still the solid, successful New York lawyers who made up the Eastern establishment of the Republican Party. A lot of them were sailors like himself, and some of the hardier ones he took on trips aboard his yacht on Lake Ontario, or challenged to dinghy races on Long Island Sound. He liked his friends tough, but he also liked them if they shared his love of good food and drink and the kind of conversation where, if one man speaks, the others listen and don't interrupt. If he could have chosen a regular companion with whom to spend his social evenings—in addition to Janet, of course—it would have been Chancellor Adenauer of Germany, for whom he now felt a genuine and deep affection.

"Dulles valued his friendship with Adenauer a lot," his aide, Rod O'Connor, said later. "He even went to the extent of writing him handwritten letters and sent him pictures and presents and that sort of thing. He was perfectly aware that the personal relationship had a great international advantage, but he also greatly admired and respected the old gentleman."

They had outlook and beliefs in common, and though one was a Presbyterian and the other a Roman Catholic, they had been weaned on the milk of the Word and could spend hours talking of religion and its power to make the world a better place. They saw each other much more than was necessary purely for political purposes, and Foster took pleasure in the fact that when he was away Adenauer missed and "needed" him.

"It got to the point where Adenauer would get increasingly upset and very suspicious if he hadn't been in touch with Dulles for a while," O'Connor said. "Then he had to have a personal contact with the Secretary to reassure him."

This was often handled by the CIA, and sometimes by Allen himself.

"Quite a number of messages went back and forth through that channel," O'Connor said. "Apparently Adenauer trusted the CIA more than he did his normal foreign policy channel."

If Foster or Allen couldn't get over, it was Eleanor who saw or wrote to Der Alte.

"Part of the personal relationship was through Eleanor, who, I think, was quite close to Adenauer," O'Connor said. "And again I think Adenauer thought it was almost a family relationship."

Foster's affection for the chancellor added a new facet to his relationship with his son, Avery, and not only completely reconciled him to Avery's conversion to Roman Catholicism but also made him realize that in Avery he had a bridge to many of the Catholic statesmen of the world. When he talked to Pineau or Pius XII or Diem, he often had Avery along, a sort of house Catholic to give the encounter an extra cachet.

He also had made a friend of Vice-President Richard Nixon, and often had him and his wife, Pat, over for a quiet dinner *à quatre*.

"What on earth do you talk about when you don't talk politics?" someone once asked Foster.

"Sport," he replied.

Once every few weeks, when the brothers were in Washington, Eleanor had them over with their wives to her house at McLean. Eleanor was on top of her form, reveling in the excitements of her work at the Berlin desk. Not only did it bring her close to Adenauer, but to Willy Brandt and many another West German politician. She had been in Berlin, and crossed into the eastern sector during the 1953 riots, when the citizens rose against their Communist rulers. She fumed when the Americans could do nothing, and came sadly to the realization that her brother's heady talk of "liberation" had been just a myth. But she felt she had to do something, so she rushed back to the United States and organized a food shipment program. Blocked from sending food parcels into the Soviet Zone, she had built up dumps in West Berlin, and the East Germans streamed across in their thousands to pick up the manna from the American heaven. She had organized the scheme in concert with Allen, and the CIA picked up the bill.

"I was not supposed or thought capable by the higher level people in the German section of having anything to do with policy," Eleanor said later. "But so far as the Berlin desk was concerned, little by little, like corals building a reef, I built a situation in Berlin. Nobody said: 'You can influence our policy on Berlin.' They just let me loose in a certain area, and I built up the situation."

It was a special position, and she was enjoying it. At home she kept a low profile and never bothered Foster about the problems of her job, but no one believed that, particularly the Germans. On anything below an Adenauer-Dulles level, they had taken to coming to her when they wanted something done—and eventually even Washington began to believe that she was one of the powers at State. She was still three rungs below the level she would have reached if she had been a man ("and that meant $3,000 less in salary, which I needed to keep my family"),* but for the first time she could look Department chiefs straight in the eye, ask for favors, and get them—things like schools and hospitals and halls for the people of Free Berlin.

*Her General Service rating varied between 14 and 16, and she had the personal title of "Minister."

They were heady days, and rarely had the brothers and sister been happier or closer. The only cloud in their clear blue sky was Allen's son, who would sometimes come out to McLean with his parents and flop morosely by the side of the pool. Allen, Jr.'s, scars had healed, but mentally he was walking wounded, and would always be so. He would sometimes turn to look at his father, his uncle, and his aunt with such evident contempt and dislike that they shuddered internally, and the sun went in. Allen often said to Clover: "I don't know what we're going to do with him."

Clover knew. Jungian therapy would do for her son what it had done for her—make life bearable for him again.

Allen now had a live-in Secret Service officer at the house he rented on Highlands Avenue. He roomed in the basement, handled the scrambler telephone, and vetted all comers. When Allen invited his colleagues from the Agency to bring their wives over for dinner, the officer sometimes helped to bring round the dry martinis, but was otherwise self-effacing (though there was one story later current that, on the side, he furnished a list of the guests to the FBI).

It was sometimes said that if you belonged to the Agency and didn't get asked to Allen's parties, you didn't really count, no matter how high-sounding your position. Those who did appear on the guestlist might seem to have absolutely no standing whatsoever, but if Allen had anything to do with it, their rise in the firmament of the CIA would not be long in coming.

On the whole, these favored guests came from the same professions, colleges, and family backgrounds, and had shared many common dangers in the Agency's service. Many of them, like Lawrence Houston, Frank Wisner, Tom Braden, and Kermit Roosevelt, were veterans of service in the OSS. Others like William Bundy, Robert Amory, and Tracy Barnes were lawyers, had been to the same universities, chased the same debutantes, married the same girls, and shared a tradition of service with the U.S. government. Their brains were burnished bright, their patriotism was high, their suspicion of the Soviets was fierce, their intake of alcohol was phenomenal (it sometimes made them talkative but rarely made them drunk), and their wives were usually blond and long-legged.

They had their rivalries with each other: Robert Amory, for instance, who was deputy director of Intelligence, clashed frequently with James Angleton, who specialized in counter-intelligence and counter-espionage, and Amory was sometimes to be heard in Georgetown drawing rooms loudly recounting the latest "hopeless ploy" of "our poor friend Jim." But at Highlands Avenue you would never have guessed that they loathed each other.

One of the things that Amory envied Angleton was the hugeness of his budget. Angleton supervised special activities in Europe, particularly in the south and southeast, where he paid off union leaders, Communist, Socialist, and Christian Democrat Party satraps, newspaper proprietors, film directors, and brothel keepers. He spent an awful lot of money to manipulate elections in Italy, and was sometimes asked by Allen why he insisted on keeping certain people—usually loudly anti-American—on the payroll.

"Because one day it may pay off," Angleton said. And it did, indeed it did.

Frank Wisner, a flush on his round cheeks, one hand round a highball, the other round the slim waist of his watchful wife, Polly, was always back from some outlandish spot or mission, like the tunnel the CIA was digging under the West Berlin border into East Berlin, or a boat trip across the Formosa Straits into China, or a mysterious rendezvous in Prague, or a bear-hunting safari through the Finnish forests along the Soviet frontier. He was the Cold Warrior par excellence and made no bones about it, fervently believing in the rightness of all the extraordinary and often merciless operations he superintended. As he talked of the day of liberation from bolshevism that was coming, a glint of fanaticism flashed in his eyes, and a ghost battalion of masked mercenaries seemed to be lining up behind him.

His two chief aides in his nefarious enterprises, who also turned up at Allen's parties whenever they were in Washington, were more urbane and sophisticated, and confined their conversation to music, sailing, and the charming of female company. But both were smooth and efficient operators, and one of them, Kim Roosevelt, was in the process of trying to change the control of the Persian Gulf, while the other, Richard Bissell, had even loftier and more grandiose plans.

The CIA had several big operations going on during 1953 to 1955, and the successful ones were destined to polish the reputation of Allen

Dulles as the supreme expert on covert actions. They persuaded people high in government in Washington, even Foster Dulles and President Eisenhower, that his Agency could remove régimes whose policies or ideologies were distasteful to the United States without involving any official intervention by the Americans, and that was a tempting prospect.

Kim Roosevelt in 1953 had been behind the overthrow of Mossadeq in Iran and the restoration of the shah, and, as we have seen, it was done with the minimum of fuss and the expenditure of not too much CIA money.

The following year, Tracy Barnes organized the coup to overthrow the Socialist-inclined dictator of Guatemala, Jacob Arbenz, and once more the operation went through without too much fuss. Arbenz had made the mistake of trying to expropriate lands in Guatemala owned by the big American corporation, the United Fruit Company, and that was rash of him, because United Fruit had some powerful friends in Washington and the Republican Party.* The Agency assembled a small air force piloted by CIA operatives, gathered together a band of mercenaries, and started a rebellion. Arbenz was denounced as a Soviet agent trying to infiltrate communism into Latin America, and replaced by a régime which promised to be pro-American in future and leave United Fruit alone.

The British had a grievance over this operation, too. The CIA's station chief in London approached his opposite number in SIS and persuaded him to ask the British government to waive the rights of free passage for their ships in areas adjoining the Guatemalan coast, in order to allow U.S. vessels (loaned to CIA by the Navy) to search any incoming vessels. The CIA produced "proof" that a Czech ship was on its way to deliver a load of Soviet arms to Arbenz, and the Americans needed to intercept her. She might try to disguise herself.

Anthony Eden, the British Foreign Secretary, reluctantly gave his consent, and brought other Commonwealth countries into line, in the cause, he said, of Anglo-American friendship.

*Foster Dulles had been United Fruit's legal counsel, Allen Dulles was a shareholder, General Robert Cutler, head of Eisenhower's National Security Council, was a director, Thomas G. ("The Cork") Corcoran was a paid consultant of the company while simultaneously working for the CIA, and Spruille Braden, Secretary for Latin American Affairs, later joined United Fruit as a director.

"It was a proud right which the British had never before given up even in wartime," Eden said later, "and the Americans never even said thank you. Or gave us a quid pro quo later, when we asked for one."

Worse than that, they bombed a British ship in harbor at Puerto Berrios, in Guatemala, in mistake for the Czech vessel—which, for all anyone knows, is still sailing the seas like some latterday *Flying Dutchman*—and it took years for the British to get compensation, since the B-24 that bombed the ship carried no markings and no one would acknowledge its identity.

There was one CIA operation which did not work out successfully, so naturally the Agency did not acknowledge having any part of it. Nor did Allen consult his brother before authorizing it, and that was a pity, because it might have saved the CIA a lot of money. This was the attempt by Saudi Arabia to wrest Buraimi Oasis, a fertile strip of well-watered land in the middle of the Arabian Desert, from the two countries that owned it, Oman and Abu Dhabi.

The Persian Gulf States of Abu Dhabi and Oman were under the postcolonial control of the British government, which supplied them with officers for their troops and financial advisers for their revenues. Saudi Arabia, on the other hand, thanks to the omnipresent U.S. oil consortium, Aramco, was under American influence. Moreover, its new king, Saud, and his brother, Prince Faisal, had long been on the payroll of the CIA, who had bailed them both out to the tune of several million dollars.

As some sort of recompense, they now proposed that if the Americans could bring Buraimi Oasis under Saudi control, any oil concessions found in the area (and the potentiality was great) would be assigned to Aramco.

Kim Roosevelt was assigned the task of arranging the annexation. First of all he filtered Saudi troops (transported in Aramco trucks) into the oasis, and, after several days of feasting, offered Saudi citizenship to the inhabitants and an air-conditioned Cadillac to the local sheikh if he would acknowledge Saudi sovereignty. The local sheikh, a shrewd character with a nose like an eagle's, named Prince Zaid (who is now one of the richest men in the world from Abu Dhabi oil revenues) was already on the British payroll and he immediately informed them of the Saudi approach. The Saudis were driven out by a force of British-led Omani Scouts.

Roosevelt then tried outright bribery. He offered 400 million rupees ($90 million) in CIA-Aramco-Saudi gold if Zaid would repudiate his brother, Sheikh Shakbut of Abu Dhabi, and cede the oasis to King Saud, "preventing the [British-controlled] Iraq Petroleum Company from operating in the disputed territories and leaving the field open to Aramco."

Zaid asked for a written guarantee, but it was not forthcoming. So Zaid once more told the British. They then took the dispute to an international court in Geneva, where the CIA immediately tried to bribe the arbitrators, but only succeeded in delaying the proceedings.*

It was an expensive failure, and no one mentioned it to Kim any more after the Saudis lost their case. He had tried his best. The blame lay with the British.

To Allen, and, more importantly, to Foster it was a last snap of the teeth from the dying lion that had once been the British Empire. Foster's first visit overseas after becoming Secretary had been to talk to President Nasser in Egypt and survey the situation in the Middle East, and the tour had convinced him that Britain's sun was setting there, as it had already done in India; the sooner an American solar system rose in its place the better.

He wanted Nasser's aid in fighting the threat of global communism, but had some difficulty persuading the Egyptian that Russia was more a menace to Egypt's future than British occupation at home and the Israeli army on the other side of the Suez Canal.

"How can I go to my people," Nasser asked Foster, "and tell them I am disregarding a killer with a pistol sixty miles from me at the Suez Canal to worry about somebody who is holding a knife a thousand miles away? . . . We've never had trouble with [the Soviet Union]. They have never attacked us. They have never had a base here, but the British have been here for seventy years."

Foster agreed that it was too long, and that Britain's time was over. One of the resolutions he took back from his Cairo meeting was that the British army would have to move its eighty thousand men from the Canal Zone of Egypt. Naturally, that would mean the British would eventually have to leave the Persian Gulf and other parts of the Middle

*At one point the Saudi member of the tribunal was accused of not being impartial. "What has that to do with this case?" he asked. "I am here to arbitrate, not to be impartial."

East where the Union Jack still flew. And a vacuum would be created. But what could be better for the Arabs than the arrival of the Americans to fill it? A few months later, when an Egyptian military delegation arrived in the United States in the hopes of purchasing arms, he saw them in a room from which, on one wall, hung a map of the world. All over Europe and Asia little Stars and Stripes had been stuck in where American troops or airfields were planted. Foster waved at the blank area of Egypt and the Gulf.

"What we need are some flags here," he told the Egyptians.

That would take time and negotiation. Meanwhile, Kim Roosevelt was encouraged to keep CIA money flowing to promote American influence among the sheikhs and emirs. He had already given $12 million to General Naguib, who, with Nasser, Sadat, and others, had led the Egyptian revolution and unseated King Farouk. But that money hadn't done much good. Nasser had usurped Naguib and put him under arrest. During a search of his house, the $12 million was discovered, and Nasser taxed him with it. Naguib claimed it had been a personal gift from President Eisenhower.

"Then we will build an American souvenir with it," Nasser cried. Part of the $12 million was used to build the famous Cairo Tower, which was known privately to Nasser, Sadat, and their intimates as the CIA Monument.

There were other lavish CIA payments. Another $12 million went to the queen mother of Jordan, in the hope that she would influence and manipulate her son, King Hussein (who was already being paid by the British).

But it was in Saudi Arabia that the CIA's seemingly inexhaustible secret funds were used most lavishly. This was before the days when Arabia became fat on the riches from her vast oilfields, and King Saud was a spendthrift king. He had an enormous appetite for virgins and small boys, and for the more sophisticated abilities of the dancing girls in Beirut and Cairo. He had talent scouts searching the Middle Eastern flesh markets and shipping him potential wives, concubines, and other kinds of playmates. He also had a fascination for intrigue, and a profound belief in the efficacy of bribery. There was no one anywhere who could not be bought, he believed, and he doled out fabulous amounts in the certainty that he had thus purchased the fealty of the friends of his enemies.

350

The CIA paid King Saud's enormous bills, eventually to the tune of nearly $40 million. Much of it found its way into the pockets of seedy and unscrupulous hangers-on, who encouraged the king to embark on dangerous and profitless schemes. CIA's money was better spent on the king's brother, Prince Faisal, who cost less and gave reliable information about tribal thinking in the Gulf. But what he never revealed either to Kim Roosevelt or, for that matter, to his brother, the King, was that while taking bribes from the CIA he was also acting as an unpaid agent for President Nasser of Egypt, whose beliefs in Arab nationalism he shared.

King Saud had ambitions to overthrow Nasser and assume the leadership of the Arab people, and he poured out money lavishly to courtiers and adventurers who promised to assassinate the Egyptian president. They were always thwarted, thanks to Faisal, who kept Cairo informed of the complots, just as he kept Nasser informed about all the CIA activities in the Middle East which Roosevelt and and his operatives confided to his brother.*

Foster was one of the few people in the American government who showed any wisdom over the handling of the Buraimi Oasis affair. At one point, when the British had made it plain that they would reject any Saudi claims, and by force, if necessary, Kim Roosevelt cabled Allen and asked him to enlist his brother's aid in influencing the British. Allen went to Foster to discuss with him whether it might be a good idea to contact Anthony Eden and persuade him to accept some sort of compromise ("a softer position") that would get the Americans off the hook—a sharing arrangement at the oasis, perhaps.

Foster didn't believe it would work. The Buraimi blow-up had got into the newspapers and Britain's *amour propre* was now involved. In any case, this was just after the Guatemala incident, and Eden was

---

*When King Saud was overthrown in 1964 and succeeded by Faisal, Nasser offered him forgiveness and exile in Egypt, where he subsequently arrived with a huge entourage of bejeweled whores and painted small boys. Nasser summoned him and said: "Brother Saud, why did you waste all that money on trying to kill me? Seven million pounds spent on those silly plots!" "Oh brother," Saud replied, "I have a confession to make. It was not seven million pounds but twelve million I spent—but never mind, it was all American money." He did not die poor, or without heirs. There were 106 sons and daughters. The sons received $1½ million apiece, the daughters $1 million.

certainly not likely to respond in kindly fashion to any more American requests for favors.

However, the CIA was faced with a disaster if something wasn't done. So Allen went to the White House to talk over the situation with Christian Herter, the President's assistant; he wondered whether the President might not intercede, in the name of old friendship, with the British Foreign Secretary. The President must stress, of course, that it was not really America's affair, and that he was only intervening as a friend of both sides in their mutual best interests.

A few days later Foster's assistant, William Macomber, came into his office with a copy of a telegram which the White House wanted sent to Saudi Arabia. It turned out that President Eisenhower had mentioned the matter to Anthony Eden, and this was a telegram directing the U.S. ambassador in Jidda to inform King Saud that the President had interceded on his behalf. Foster looked at it and said:

"You know, Bill, this telegram violates a basic principle of diplomacy. The principle is that you never commit the prestige of the Head of State unless you're sure he's going to succeed. Now I don't think the British are going to accede to our request and the Saudi's request with respect to Buraimi Oasis. I think the President's intercession is not going to be successful. Therefore this message is going to make King Saud feel happy for a little while and gratified, but the end result is going to be that the President of the United States, even though he's an awfully important fellow, doesn't deliver."

He looked at the telegram again.

"Maybe you ought to send the message anyway," he said, "because there isn't any rule in diplomacy that can't be broken. But it sort of bothers me, Bill, and I'll bet you anything that the people who drafted this telegram and the people who cleared it weren't aware that they were violating a principle. There are times when diplomatic principles should be violated, but when you violate them you ought to know you're violating them."

He seemed tempted to let the message go—just to make fools of the people at the White House. Then his sense of duty reasserted itself and he picked up his direct line to the President and began to talk to him. The message was not sent. It was just as well. Eden did not back down, and Saudi Arabia failed to get Buraimi. This was one time when the close liaison between the Secretary and his brother had not worked.

To his close assistants, Rod O'Connor and Johnny Hanes, it was not that Foster Dulles disliked Anthony Eden and the British, as some people were later to charge, but that he just thought neither Eden nor the country he represented counted any more.

"The Secretary was convinced," said Hanes later, "that the British throughout the world were a rapidly declining power. He was convinced they no longer had any basic will to meet big international responsibilities, that they were attempting to duck out all over the world, that they were trying to put as good a face on it as possible, but that you simply could not count on the British to carry on in any responsible way, or, indeed, form an effective bulwark with us against anything. . . . The Secretary had some extremely close British friends and by and large he liked the British, but he had absolutely no regard for them internationally. He felt that they were clumsy and inept, as opposed to their carefully nurtured reputation of being the opposite, and he really literally had no admiration for them."

At the beginning of the Eisenhower administration, Foster had been extremely meticulous in being friendly and deferential to both Prime Minister Churchill and Foreign Secretary Eden. The first time he met Churchill was at a conference in Bermuda in 1953, where he was shocked that Churchill looked so decrepit and doubted whether he would understand much of what was to be discussed. But he saw that Ike was on the warmest terms with his two wartime colleagues, "and I guess he was moving somewhat carefully," O'Connor noted.

But the more Foster dealt with Eden, the cooler and less enthusiastic he became. Ironically enough, the faults he found in the British statesman were exactly those which he himself was frequently accused of displaying—imprecision, evasiveness, and even mendaciousness.

"There's no doubt that when Dulles didn't want to be fully frank," O'Connor said later, "he would use his words very carefully, to move away from any area he didn't want to talk about. There's no doubt also that when he wanted he could talk a pretty good line in double-talk. And if he wasn't clear it was because he didn't want to be, that's for sure. . . . He could be less than candid, and I've seen him with ambassadors and ministers where there were areas he didn't want to discuss

353

and he went into a backwards bicycle trip. . . . But Dulles was really such a precise man that when he was not being precise, then people who knew him knew fairly quickly that they were being led around."

But imprecision was just what he found most exasperating in Eden, his lack of interest in the legal nature of a problem, his "professional diplomat" attitude in contrast with his (Foster's) own "pragmatic and practical" approach.

"They just weren't on the same beam," O'Connor said later. "Every time I saw Eden I always felt an overwhelming sense of personal vanity, and Dulles was just the opposite. Dulles may have had intellectual vanity but no personal vanity at all. He was plain as a stick. Just personalitywise, they weren't destined to work together. . . . You know, [Eden's] homburg and all the rest, and his rather languid air. A calculated lazy manner which is one of the upper class manifestations of the old English aristocracy. It wasn't Dulles's dish of tea."

These, O'Connor said later, were Foster's early and "superficial" feelings about Anthony Eden. But in the summer of 1954, at the height of the crisis over the French defeats by Ho Chi Minh's forces in Indochina, his antipathy hardened into something more concrete over Anthony Eden's behavior.

The Korean War had come to an end at Panmunjom in July 1953, but all was not quiet in Southeast Asia. In Indochina, the French were battling to hold on to their colonial empire, and getting the worst of it. Foster Dulles was not the only one in the Eisenhower administration nor was he the first Secretary of State to believe that if Indochina fell to the Communist forces and the French were driven out of Southeast Asia, the rest of America's friends and allies in the area would fall to the reds, one by one, like dominos. First the Philippines, then New Zealand and Australia, and finally the whole of the Western Pacific would be in danger. It was a grave threat to America's allies and to the United States themselves, Foster believed.

But what was to be done? In one of his more notorious speeches, Foster had seemed to be threatening the Communist powers with "massive retaliation" by the U.S. Air Force armed with hydrogen bombs should they try to upset the balance of postwar global power. But if ordinary people in the Western world cringed at the thought of such a threat, more thoughtful strategists were not much impressed by it. It sounded very much like a smokescreen to conceal the fact that the United States armed forces were in a dangerously thin condition. George Humphrey, Secretary of the Treasury, had not just cut $5 billion out of the Defense budget but was planning to lop off a further $7 billion. And no claim by Humphrey that henceforward the United States would get "a bigger bang for a buck" or Foster's brandishing of the hydrogen bomb could conceal the fact that the men, material, and means were just not there for fighting "brush fires" like Indochina and Korea. It was the big blaze or nothing.

On the other hand, the French were already fighting a "brush fire" in Indochina, and it was well within the capacity of the United States to help them. The only danger was that sentiment back in France, where people were heartily sick of the Indochinese war, was in favor of a settlement, especially after an important French army garrison was besieged and put in what looked like a hopeless position by the Communist forces at Dien Bien Phu. Plans were already being made for a peace conference at Geneva later in the year (1954).

This was the last thing Foster wanted to see happening. It would represent the most dangerous triumph for communism in Asia, he felt, and could have disastrous consequences. At a press conference which he gave in London on April 13, 1954, the following exchange took place:

> What would you regard as a reasonably satisfactory settlement of the Indochina situation?
>
> DULLES: The removal by the Chinese Communists of their apparent desire to extend the political system of Communism to South East Asia.
>
> That means a complete withdrawal of the Communists from Indochina?
>
> DULLES: That is what I would regard as a satisfactory solution.
>
> Is there any compromise that might be offered if that is not entirely satisfactory with the Communists?
>
> DULLES: I had not thought of any.

In the meantime, Foster had been in close conference with Admiral Arthur W. Radford, chairman of the Joint Chiefs of Staff, and Vice-President Nixon, both of whom were for strong measures in Indochina. Between them they had concocted a plan for breaking the Vietminh siege at Dien Bien Phu by a series of air strikes by U.S. planes flying off U.S. Navy carriers. The Secretary called a secret meeting at the State Department on April 3 to which leading members of the Senate and Congress were invited.*

Admiral Radford explained the plan for the air strikes to the assembled legislators. No one asked him if he was thinking of using atomic bombs, though that was certainly in his mind. As he said later, when asked if the U.S. Navy carrier force had atomic bombs aboard: "They did. But I never felt it was a question basically of atomic weapons. It would have been decided at the time on the basis of a specific military operation. If we'd gone in to break the siege at Dien Bien Phu with conventional bombs and been unsuccessful—it was a tough nut to crack—then the question would have come up. . . . If we'd used atomic bombs we'd have probably been successful."

He added, when asked if Foster would have been reluctant to see atomic bombs used, "I think Mr. Dulles, as I said, was a very realistic man."

What the legislators did ask was whether there was a danger of war with China (Radford said there was), and whether, if the bombing failed, ground troops might have to be used (he said that was possible). Finally, Lyndon Johnson asked the question which quickened Foster's interest and revealed the nub of the problem.

"Where do the British stand on this?"

It subsequently became clear that Congress would only go along with intervention in Indochina if aid to the French was a "combined" operation, with Britain and the Commonwealth countries, particularly Australia and New Zealand, involved.

"Mr. Dulles made a great effort to persuade some of our allies to come in," said Admiral Radford later.

Foster left for London on April 10, 1954, taking Admiral Radford with him, and he had talks with the British Foreign Secretary Eden both in London and in Paris. During the Paris talks Radford was present. He had been to see members of the French government and was angry about the defeatist attitude of the French, who seemed resigned to Dien Bien Phu's fall and to a French retreat from Indochina. He used some strong language and startled Eden by suggesting

*Present were Senators Knowland, Milliken, Johnson, Russell, and Clements, and Congressmen Joseph Martin, John McCormack, and J. P. Priest.

that a small atom bomb would soon settle the situation, but that the French were trying to make conditions for intervention by their allies. They wanted an assurance that, if bombing raids did turn the situation around, the French would be left to restore the situation, and "foreign" troops would stay out. Radford said he wasn't going to stand for that.

Foster intervened to tell the startled Eden that he would like a promise from the British government that they would join him in "united action" against the Communists in Indochina.

Now this is where accounts of what was decided differ, according to whether Foster Dulles and Admiral Radford are talking, or Eden. Radford said later:

"President Eisenhower said I frightened the British by my hard words or something. I don't know what they could have been. For my part, I think Eden was a rather weak sister. He gave us the impression in Paris—I'm sure Mr. Dulles thought so too—he gave us the impression that he was going to go along with us. When he went back to England and talked to Mr. Churchill, they backed out."

Foster came back to Washington on April 16 and immediately gave the impression to the President and his collaborators that Eden had pledged British support to the plan. But Eden afterwards denied this.

"I did no such thing," he said later. "In no way did I give him any promise or hint of a promise that we would support him in his rash adventure."

But Foster proceeded as if he had a British pledge in his pocket. He called a meeting of all British Commonwealth, French, and some Southeast Asian ambassadors for April 27 to discuss "united action" in Indochina (to be known as Operation Vulture). When Anthony Eden heard of the meeting he had just arrived at the British Embassy in Paris to have dinner with the ambassador, Sir Gladwyn Jebb (and Lady Jebb), the Sir John Hopes (Liza Hope was the daughter of Somerset Maugham), and the Joseph Alsops. He stayed long enough to drink a cocktail and eat a hurried snack, then flew back to London.

From there, after consulting with Churchill at Chequers, he sent an urgent cable to his ambassador in Washington, Sir Roger Makins, telling him that under no circumstances was he to go anywhere near the meeting.

"Dulles was trying to bulldoze me," Eden insisted later. "It was an outrageous ploy—trying to exploit Anglo-American friendship to get the war he wanted in Indochina. I made it crystal clear that we wanted no part of his dangerous enterprise."

The British ambassador maintained close and friendly relations with the Secretary of State, and he was embarrassed by the peremptory nature of Eden's telegram, which instructed him to mince no words in turning down the Dulles invitation. He picked up the telephone and called Foster at his home on 32nd Street, in Georgetown, to tell him as diplomatically as possible that the British would not be there.

It so happened that Eleanor was with Foster at the time, and they were in the hall together when Foster put down the telephone.

"He was standing by that table," she said later, "that table in front of the mirror, and he looked at me and he pounded the table like that and he said: 'Eden has double-crossed me. He lied to me!' He didn't swear but he used some strong expression which expressed real emotion, because normally he never revealed his reaction to an event except in very measured terms. And I think this was one of his great disappointments."

As it turned out, the French were making such difficulties about the terms for American support that it is doubtful if Operation Vulture would have gone forward, anyway.

"I was not ready to support the French at Dien Bien Phu or anywhere else," said Admiral Radford later, "unless we could make proper military arrangements with them. . . . Our negotiations fell down because the British wouldn't play, and Australia and New Zealand wouldn't play without the British. But if the British had gone along I still think we would have had considerable trouble with the French. We might have participated, broken the siege at Dien Bien Phu, and we should have been faced with making an agreement that would have permitted us to have some say in the operations in Indochina. The French had this terrific fear that we were trying to take Indochina away from them. . . . My feeling is that Mr. Dulles did everything in 1954 to help the French. He was blocked largely by the British. He might likely have been blocked later, if the British had agreed, by the French themselves. We didn't really get to the stage where we discussed the arrangements they would have insisted on."

So there was no U.S. bombing of Dien Bien Phu, and the French garrison surrendered to the Vietnamese. Radford was "sorry that the

President and Congress required an allied operation," but the critical moment had passed. The French called enemies and allies together to discuss peace terms at a conference in Geneva in the spring of 1954. To Foster, however, the French collapse was a tragedy that need not have happened, a golden opportunity missed to rid Southeast Asia of the Communist menace.

He believed that if the British had been forthcoming in their pledge to mount a joint operation in Indochina, then, all difficulties with the French notwithstanding, the situation could have been salutarily resolved and the course of Communist expansion in Asia halted. He blamed neither Eisenhower's doubts nor Congress's wisdom for thwarting him in his determination to involve the United States, but preferred to place the responsibility on the shoulders of the British Foreign Secretary. He went on maintaining that Eden had made him a promise. Eden insisted, with mounting irritation as the years went by, that Dulles had at best misheard him or at the worst deliberately misinterpreted what he had said.

In fact, there was already an antipathy between the two men which made them suspicious of each other, and an increasing tendency to read a significance into each other's statements that was not there. Anthony Eden had always been a vain man, proudly British, used to a prewar or wartime world where Great Britain's word was listened to and the pronouncements of its Foreign Secretaries were words of authority from on high. He was having some difficulty in adjusting himself to the realities of the postwar world, where ears in the Western world were now bent more toward the United States than Britain, and a Dulles monosyllable (or even his silence) could mean more than Eden's most eloquent perorations.

Eden was jealous of Foster Dulles and the power base from which he was working. It did not help his feelings that quite obviously Foster Dulles was not jealous of him, but merely angry when he and the British got in his way, or upset his plans.

But if Anthony Eden from now on got the cold shoulder from Foster Dulles, it was a Chinese at Geneva upon whom Foster Dulles literally turned his back.

By April 1954 the French had had enough of Indochina and were looking for an honorable, or even any, way out of the military and political dilemma in which they found themselves. A conference was convened at Geneva at which not only the French and Indochinese would be present to discuss a settlement, but also the major powers, including Britain, Russia, Communist China, and the United States, to guarantee any agreement. Foster Dulles was against U.S. participation in a conference that could only end in the capitulation of the French (and, by implication, the West) to the Communists, and he was reluctant to play any part in it. But Eden would be on hand for Britain, Molotov for Russian, Bidault for France, and Chou En-lai for Communist China. The United States could hardly not be there alongside its allies, and Foster Dulles could hardly not be present at the opening meetings. However, he was in no mood for diplomatic niceties or fraternization with the "enemy."

He came to Switzerland for the opening ceremony on April 26, 1954, and, like the other delegates, made a short speech expressing hope for a just and equitable settlement. During a break in the proceedings, the delegates moved into the reception hall and stood around talking with their own staffs or other delegates. Chou En-lai, the Communist Chinese deputy prime minister, had been one of the first to leave the main hall. He was standing with his group when Foster Dulles came into the reception room, followed by his entourage of officials. Chou En-lai was turned toward him and watched him approach.

"When Dulles came in," said U. Alexis Johnson, a member of the U.S. Delegation, later, "Chou moved over, obviously intending to shake hands with him. A number of photographers were around, and Dulles quite brusquely turned his back. This was neither a natural nor normal thing for Dulles to do. I'm sure he was thinking of the impression back there in the United States."

It was a moment when statesmen have to measure their actions and take the consequences. Quite obviously, the Chinese minister was making a gesture. The representatives of two great nations, and two different worlds, were meeting face to face on neutral ground, and the Chinese was holding out his hand. In some ways he may have had more to lose than Foster Dulles in doing so. Who would earn the more obloquy at home by shaking hands, the man who was the quintessential capitalist warmonger to the Chinese Communists, or the bloodstained Chinese red who, to the Americans, was the monster who had driven a beloved American ally out of his homeland?

It was a question that would never be answered. Foster Dulles was taking no chances. Chou En-lai held out his hand in full view of the world's press, cameramen, and all the delegates, and it stayed there, empty.

Johnson, a Chinese expert at the State Department, was only too well aware of the significance for Chou En-lai.

"[The incident] deeply wounded Chou over the years, and it deeply affected his attitude," he said later. "This was a loss of face and a deep wound as far as Chou En-lai was concerned. This had some effect and I could see it reflected through the rest of the Conference."

Foster seemed unworried by the fuss he had caused. He stayed on at the conference for a few days, but made it plain that neither he nor the Americans were interested in taking any part in it, and certainly would accept no responsibility for any settlement reached. Someone asked Carl McCardle, his press spokesman, whether the Secretary planned to have any contact at all with Chou En-lai during the proceedings, since it would be the first opportunity the Americans had had to exchange views with the new régime in China.

"Not unless their limos crash into each other leaving the hall," McCardle replied.

One suspects that Foster's brother Allen would have handled the encounter with more finesse. But it was Winston Churchill who remarked: "Foster Dulles is the only case I know of a bull who carries his china shop with him."

The conference went on without the Americans. Foster returned to the United States, and refused to go back to Geneva. Eventually, a new French government came to power and its premier, Pierre Mendès-France, pledged himself to end the war in Indochina and get out no matter what the cost. He pleaded with Foster to come back to Geneva and put the weight of American power behind him. Foster refused, but did consent to go to Paris and talk with the new premier. As a result, Beetle Smith was shipped to Geneva as a substitute, but with no power to make any decisions.

A Final Declaration was issued on July 21, 1954, bringing the war in Indochina to an end, dividing the country in two, and ending French influence in Hanoi and North Vietnam. The eventual fate of the whole of Indochina was to be decided in elections to be held two years hence, in July 1956, and certain agreements made for its protection.

The Declaration was to be signed by all the delegations. Molotov and Chou En-lai expressed their willingness to endorse it on behalf of Russia and China, and also to participate in a multilateral guarantee of the settlement. But then Beetle Smith rose to declare that the United States would not sign. He had received express instructions from Foster Dulles not to do so.

Immediately, Russia and China reversed their decision and re-treated. In the event, none of the participants signed the Final Declaration, but contented themselves with unilateral statements associating themselves (or, in one or two minor cases, disassociating themselves) from the agreements. The United States issued its own separate statement, "taking note" of the Declaration and agreements, and "viewing any renewal of the aggression in violation of the said agreements with grave concern and as seriously threatening international peace and security."

A unique opportunity had been lost of securing common accord for a defense of Indochinese independence and sovereignty. And though it was not recognized at the time, the U.S. declaration, with its pledge to view with grave concern "any renewal of aggression," was to be used, notably by President Kennedy,* as a reason to commit the United States to the defense of Vietnam in the years to come.

Far from keeping America aloof, the refusal to sign provided a future excuse for unilateral involvement.

*Who quoted the words of the Declaration in 1961 to justify U.S. action in Vietnam.

CHAPTER TWENTY-ONE

Spy in the Sky

It was a curiously effective relationship which Foster and Allen had now developed, and it made its mark not only upon the State Department and the CIA but upon the whole machinery of the administration.

Outwardly, they were meticulous in observing protocol and proclaiming to everyone in Washington that just because they were brothers did not mean that they breached the guidelines or used brotherly strategems to cook up things between them. Allen ostentatiously followed the rules whenever he communicated with the Secretary, and claimed no special position.

"I've been present when Allen and Foster were discussing a matter of concern, some official business in which they were both interested," said a CIA official later, "and their exchanges before other people tended to be rather formal and inconclusive. Allen was more informal, and I've heard him put a case forward pretty vigorously. But Foster was generally very reserved in what he chose to say. And I always had strong feelings their effective relationship was conducted over the telephone on occasion, or after or before dinner at brief meetings outside the office, with nobody else present."

If Allen still cherished the ambition to go one better than his more rigid brother, he now seemed to take pains to demonstrate that he had no such intention. Those who worked with the two men were impressed by his deference to his brother.

"I think there's no possibility of doubt in those years that Foster was the senior partner," said the same CIA official. "Now if you speculate why this was true, I've always felt that both the obvious elements were present in the relationship. First there was still the fact that Foster was the older brother and Allen had always looked up to him and been quite willing to accord him a kind of seniority, probably going back to their professional lives as lawyers. Second, I'm sure Allen was deeply convinced that, as director of CIA, he should not try to play too much of a role, an exaggerated role, in policymaking, that the Secretary of State was the senior policymaker in things having to do with external affairs. Therefore it was really his duty as a public servant and citizen to accord the Secretary of State that kind of deference and recognition of, in effect, his seniority. So I had the feeling that Allen, wholly aside from his personal attitudes to his brother formed in the course of their lifelong personal relationship, made a real effort, and, I think, a successful effort, to discipline himself on this matter."

But the dividends Allen earned from this act of fraternal obeisance were great. Never before or since has the CIA had more support from the State Department, or, because Secretary Dulles was so powerful, more freedom to infiltrate U.S. embassies, consulates, and the U.S. Information Agency offices in foreign countries. It had complete freedom to undertake projects of enormous tactical or strategical significance with little or no oversight of its expenditure or the nature of its activities. In 1954 the CIA had four hundred of its agents operating out of London alone, controlled not only by the local station chief but by a resident director, or senior representative, reporting directly back to Allen Dulles. Thirty-eight of the top members of the two main CIA organizations operating out of London, the OPC and OSO, had diplomatic passports and positions in the embassy hierarchy.*

In all parts of the world, and particularly in Germany, South America, and Southeast Asia, the Agency expanded and infiltrated every arm of U.S. government. During the early days of World War II, it was the FBI which had looked after South American intelligence, but then the OSS took it over, together with a number of the FBI operatives who had run the local stations for J. Edgar Hoover. Many of them had been passed on to the CIA, but not before a weeding-out process had been carried out first by Wild Bill Donovan, then by Beetle Smith, and finally by Allen, to uproot the agents who had been left behind by Hoover to keep him in touch with what his rivals were doing. The Act of 1947 had

---

*The OPC under Frank Wisner looked after covert organizations, the OSO under Richard Helms pursued more direct espionage and other esoteric activities.

set up the National Security Council to oversee operations in which the Agency's many arms were now engaged, but in the two years since Allen had been operating as director of the CIA, the Council had had no real control over the activities that he ordered and approved— manifold activities, which were protected from interference by Foster's brotherly wing.

In 1955, Allen was able to extend the CIA's kingdom to the stratosphere.

Immediately after the Thanksgiving holidays in 1954, Allen Dulles called a special meeting of the United States Intelligence Board (USIB)* to discuss some secret findings of a body called the Killian Committee (after James Ryan Killian) on the Threat of Surprise Attack. One of the subcommittees of this body, under the chairmanship of Edwin Land of Polaroid, had been charged with the task of discovering means of monitoring Soviet military activities, and had reached conclusions which were considered so confidential that they were not even included in the Killian Committee's report but transmitted verbally from Land to Allen Dulles, and from him to the members of the USIB. This was that the United States should immediately build a very high altitude reconnaissance aircraft capable of engaging in invulnerable overflights of the Soviet Union and equip it with special photographic equipment to record military preparations on the ground.

Allen indicated that he was all in favor of Land's proposal, and the Intelligence Board agreed with him. They then went across to the State Department to see Foster, and afterwards met with the President at the White House. On December 1, 1954, he gave presidential approval for the building of the plane and its equipment.

But who was to provide the money for the project? It would cost many millions of dollars to design and build such a revolutionary aircraft. It was urgently needed and must be ready to fly in less than a year. Yet its purpose, even its very existence, must be kept secret. How was that possible if Congress had to be approached to approve it and vote the money necessary to produce it?

Allen Dulles had the answer. He pointed out that the CIA had large

*Which consisted of the heads of the CIA, the State Department intelligence service, and the intelligence services of the Army, Navy, and Air Force.

reserve funds, including the director's Discretionary Fund, whose exact expenditures did not have to be spelled out to Congress. He was ready to finance the project.

His offer was accepted with relief. It seemed logical, at the same time, to hand over control of the production of the plane, and its operations once it was airborne, to the CIA.

Thus was U-2 born.

Richard Bissell, Jr., was appointed as controller of the project, with an Air Force general as his second-in-command.

Richard Bissell, Jr., was one of the rising stars of the CIA. A tall, amiable, cultivated man, with an interest in ornithology, sailing, and ecology—all pursuits that the top echelons of the Agency strongly approved—he had previously worked for the Marshall Plan in Germany and the Ford Foundation in Washington. He had known Allen Dulles since 1948, was a friend of Frank Wisner, and had first met Foster when Eleanor threw a party at McLean for her brothers, Vice-President Nixon, Bob Bowie, and other members of the administration.

He joined the Agency early in 1954 at Allen's invitation, and filled an anomalous position as assistant to the director until Wisner decided to give him a chance to make his mark, and put him in joint charge of the Guatemala operation with an Agency veteran, Tracy Barnes.

Aside from one British ship bombed by mistake at Puerto Berrios, the operation was considered a thumping success, and Bissell was ready for bigger things. U-2 was henceforth his baby. He went to work with a will, enlisting a photographic expert named Arthur Lundahl to build him a camera of hitherto unheard-of power and accuracy, and engaging the services of a brilliant aeronautical engineer named Kelly Johnson to create a plane for him that would fly at 80,000 feet. By the following summer he had an aircraft ready to fly.

It was a bizarre kind of bird which, as Ray Cline remarked later, "looked more like a kite built around a camera than an airplane." It flew higher than any plane had ever done at that time, well above the reach of any antiaircraft missile, and it had the ability both to fly fast and to hover. When he at last heard of its existence, General Curtis LeMay, head of Strategic Air Command, tried to take it over, but he was told "to keep his cotton-picking fingers off it" by Allen at a stormy meeting in Colorado Springs in the late spring of 1955. It was with great reluctance that LeMay finally agreed to release a number of pilots to Bissell, and to allow him to use SAC in case of emergency.

An air base had been built in a circular dried lake in Nevada, and it was there that all training and test flying was carried out, under conditions of the strictest secrecy.

"I was sitting in my office one day," Bissell said later, "when the phone rang and I was told that a U-2 on a training mission from Nevada which was to take it over eastern Tennessee and back had had a flameout. It had happened within the previous five minutes and the U-2 was going to make an emergency landing in Albuquerque."

It was just the sort of thing that could blow the whole project if it reached the newspapers.

"I called the base commander at Albuquerque," Bissell said, "and made arrangements with him to handle the crashlanding* for security. He got his troops out there just in time, screened off the area into which the pilot made a dead-stick landing, and no one ever found out what we were up to."

In the summer of 1955, the first U-2s and a squad of pilots and maintenance crews (all former Air Force personnel but now enrolled as "civilian" employees of the CIA) were moved to the USAF airbase at Lakenheath, in Norfolk, England. But almost immediately after they got there, permission to use British territory was abruptly withdrawn by the new Prime Minister, Anthony Eden. Britain's own intelligence services had just muddied relations with the Soviet Union by sending a frogman, Lionel (Buster) Crabbe, to spy on a Russian war vessel on a goodwill visit to Britain—the spy was later found drowned—and Eden was in no mood to be further embarrassed by becoming involved in American espionage activities.

Chancellor Adenauer had no such qualms, and after being let into the secret of the U-2s by Bissell and General Charles Cabell, Allen's second-in-command, he offered them the hospitality of German soil. They moved into a base at Wiesbaden.

They were now ready to go. Bissell alerted Allen, who in turn informed his brother. A meeting was held in the White House in the spring of 1956 at which Bissell laid out his plans for a number of flights

---

*In fact, the U-2 crashed each time it landed and fell on its wingtips, because the weight problem precluded normal landing gear.

over Russia. He was told to wait outside while the President discussed them with Allen, Foster, and his military secretary, General Andrew Goodpaster. Presently, Goodpaster came out and said to Bissell: "Well, you've been authorized to conduct overflights for two weeks."

"I hope that means fourteen days of good weather," Bissell said. "In other words, bad days don't count."

"It doesn't mean anything of the kind," Goodpaster said. "It means two weeks. You're free to go for two weeks."

Three days later the weathermen reported that conditions were good over central Russia. Bissell sent a signal to Wiesbaden authorizing the first flight.

"It took off from Wiesbaden and flew directly over Moscow," Bissell said later, "and it turned north and flew directly over Leningrad and then back down the Baltic coast. I went in first thing next morning, when Allen was in the office, and I said: 'Well, Allen, we're out and running.' He asked me where this flight had been laid out and I told him, and he was quite horrified. 'Isn't that too much of a risk the first time?' he asked, and I said: 'Well, the first time is probably the least risky.' About ten a.m. I got the one-word code message back that the mission was satisfactory. It was a very exciting moment."

Almost from the start, the U-2 operation was a phenomenal success. The new camera operated with formidable accuracy and such precision that they could even identify the makes of automobiles in the Kremlin parking lot and distinguish players on a football field. It also delineated missile silos, atomic plants, launching pads, and aircraft caches.

For the present (and for almost two years, in fact), the Russians did not have an antiaircraft missile capable of reaching the U-2's altitude.

"The limitation on their ground to air missiles," said Bissell, "was that their missiles were optimized for 60–65,000 feet, where they had perfect control, but they began to run out of control surface in the thinner air above that height, where we were. We believed that potentially they could possibly reach 70–81,000 feet, but we had luck with us."

For the Russians were aware of the overflights almost from the start, and after the fifth operation—in fact, the fourth and fifth, for they were flown simultaneously—a formal protest was made through diplomatic channels, though it was never made public either by the Russians or by the Eisenhower administration.

But after that the flights were stood down for some time, and it was several months before Bissell got a call from Allen Dulles telling him to resume them, but to clear each flight plan with the White House beforehand.

"This was the time when I saw Foster most frequently," Bissell said. "The routine was that Allen and I and General Cabell would meet with the Deputy Secretary of Defense and the chairman of the Joint Chiefs of Staff at a conference with the President in his office. Foster would almost invariably be there. I would make my request for overflights, indicate where we wanted to go, and then the meeting would break up. The President never made a decision at those meetings. He would go off to discuss things with Foster, and then Andy Goodpaster would notify me later what had been decided."

Bissell added:

"At its peak, we had three U-2 detachments overseas, one in Adana, Turkey, one outside Tokyo, Japan, and the other at Wiesbaden, and I boasted, not unrealistically, that within twenty-four hours' warning I could have a recce plane over any part of the earth's surface. That was my main job for the next two years."

What the Soviet Union never discovered (nor anyone else, for that matter, except the initiates) was that, despite Eden's ban on British involvement, the Royal Air Force and SIS soon became mixed up in the U-2 operation. Some higher members of the RAF command had, of course, had to be told about the U-2 when the unit had first arrived at Lakenheath, and the CIA still retained its amicable links with Britain's M16. The Americans decided that a convenient way to maximize their chances of getting permission for overflights—President Eisenhower and Foster Dulles were apt to be cautious—was to convert the exercise into a joint Anglo-American operation, but to do it on such terms that *either* the prime minister *or* the President could authorize a flight by either British or U.S. personnel. The last thing Bissell and his aides wanted was a system whereby *both* chiefs of state had to agree, the whole idea being to make it easier rather than harder to get permission to overfly.

The idea was accepted by the British government, and a number of RAF pilots were brought to the United States, trained on the U-2s in Nevada, and then became part of the U-2 operation in Turkey. Like their fellow fliers among the Americans, they "resigned" their commissions and became "civilians," though they stayed on the British rather than CIA payroll. On at least two occasions, Prime Minister Anthony Eden personally authorized overflights of Russian territory on specific missions, and for these operations only RAF pilots were used.

Very few people ever learned that the U-2 operation used RAF personnel, and Eden was desperately anxious that no word of British involvement should leak out when the U-2 story eventually broke in 1960. It didn't. The Russians used every word in the dictionary against the Americans for their "piratical" intrusions into Soviet air space, but they never learned that at least one in five of the pirates was British.

The CIA was now so big and its operations so widespread that not even Allen Dulles could keep track of them. He tried.

"Allen's habit was to reach down into his organization as far as he wanted to go," one of his senior officials said later. "He would pick up the telephone and call a case officer and ask about an operation, or even occasionally give instructions without going through the intermediate echelons. I contested this with Allen, and quite bitterly. Once he talked not to me, or to my deputy, Richard Helms, or to the division chief, but to someone at least another echelon down. I objected. I said he ought to have come to me. He turned on me, and said: 'I am not going to be walled off from anyone in this organization. Down to any level, down to the secretaries, I'm going to talk to anyone I want. The rules are that I have to have access to any sort of problem. And if I give instructions to any subordinate of yours, it's his duty to clear that with you, and it's up to you to make sure that your subordinates do that. But I'm going to have direct access, both for command and for information.'"

But the trouble with the Agency was that there was such a multiplicity of small activities going on at any given time that no one could keep account of them all, except, perhaps, the finance department, which had to pay for them—sometimes in weird and wonderful ways. And even the cashier sometimes didn't know why he had to arrange for half a million dollars in gold ingots to be airlifted to Mexico City, $2 million in assorted yen, Deutschmarks, and Danish Kronen to be sent to an agent in Singapore, and who were the owners of the safeboxes he regularly filled in a bank in the 16th arondissement in Paris, a private account in Zurich, a poste restante in Marseilles, and an American

Express office in Istanbul, among other places.

When he was head of clandestine activities, Richard Bissell tried to find a way of organizing them into programs, country by country. He said later:

"I wanted to arrange things so that, for a given country, you could say that, under these two or three headings, here are the propaganda activities the Agency is carrying on, here are the political liaison activities, here the political actions we are undertaking. It never worked out that way. The business of the CIA is hundreds of mostly small projects, having relatively little similarity to one another."

Until the U-2 came along, there was little doubt that the CIA's greatest success was the Berlin Tunnel, which the Agency dug into East Berlin to tap the telephone exchanges of the East German government and the Red Army. It was based on an idea of General Gehlen and developed and carried out by Frank Wisner in 1954,* and it paid off in a lavish amount of material about the social activities, thoughts, morals, intrigues, and sexual liaisons of prominent officials of the East German government, in addition, of course, to some invaluable military and political information.

The tunnel was built, at a cost of $4 million, from a bombed-out tract of ground in the Berlin suburb of Rudow for nearly 1,000 yards, under the East Berlin border, to end up under the local and trunk terminus of the East German telephone service. The work took four months and was "covered" by the construction, not many yards away, of a new U.S. Air Force radar station.

Experts flown in from the Bell Telephone Company plugged a CIA telephone exchange into the East German one, so that all calls from Communist Berlin, including long-distance calls to Moscow, Warsaw, Prague, Budapest, Bucharest, and Sofia, passed through the control of the CIA. The tunnel had an air-conditioning and heating unit, a recreation center and dormitory, and it was staffed with maintenance men and a twenty-four-hour duty roster of telephone tappers fluent in Russian, German, and all the satellite country languages.

They listened in to the Red Army headquarters at Pankow, the Soviet Embassy in East Berlin, all the East German ministries, and the private lines of most of the principal Soviet and East German leaders.

*Some accounts of CIA activities give Richard Bissell credit for operating the tunnel, but he was only marginally involved.

A wealth of recorded reports began to flow back to Washington for the attention of CIA analysts.

"I used to read the reams of intelligence reports that came back from this," Richard Bissell said later, "and I was tempted to issue a ration to the German station of the number of words they could transmit a month, because I was convinced that this flow of words into Washington was probably counter-productive. And it was too tempting to send in bits of political gossip from East Germany. Now the doctrine I soon encountered from the other side of the house, that is the intelligence analysts who take these raw reports and produce estimates for the daily report, was: 'Oh, we don't want any screening in the field. We want to decide what's relevant and what isn't, what's important and what isn't.' For them it was the old story of you never knew when a little piece will just fit in and complete a puzzle. We never did cut down."*

Elaborate precautions were taken to prevent the Russians and East Germans from learning that they were being overheard. There were even booster units sending power back into the lines, so that East German operators would not notice any diminution in strength and realize they were being tapped. The most publicized narrow escape from discovery that the CIA had was in the winter of 1955, when, as Allen Dulles subsequently recorded, there was a heavy snowstorm in Berlin. When someone walked over the ground near the tunnel, it was noticed that the heating plant down below had melted the snow above the tunnel, and an arrow of damp, wet bare ground was pointing across the otherwise snow-covered earth straight to the barbed wire fence and beyond the boundary into East Germany.

The alarm was sounded, and the heating turned off; luckily it snowed again that night and covered the telltale corridor of bare ground. The operators below worked in sweaters and overcoats until the weather got warmer.

There was another narrow escape when a conversation was monitored between a Red Army commander at Pankow and his wife in Moscow, during which she talked about her pregnancy. A general on the U.S. military staff in Berlin, on a trip home to Washington, was shown some of the reports of the Red Army conversations and read

*Around about this time the amount of information pouring in was so great that the CIA incinerator at FM-Holbird broke down for a time and documents had to be shredded or destroyed by hand.

As one of his last acts as Director, Allen Dulles shows President Kennedy over the Agency's new headquarters.   (*CIA photo.*)

Overleaf: Also in November of 1961, Dulles watches Kennedy depart in a helicopter. It was the day that marked the end of his intelligence career.

(*Photo courtesy of Mr. Walter L. Pforzheimer.*)

On March 21, 1968, Allen Dulles attends the dedication of a marble bas relief of himself on the wall of the main entrance to CIA headquarters. At left, Director of Central Intelligence Richard Helms and at right, CIA's Executive Director-Comptroller Col. L. K. White.

(Photo courtesy of Mr. Walter L. Pforzheimer.)

Mr. and Mrs. Allen W. Dulles in front of CIA headquarters on his last day in office, November 28, 1961.

(Photo courtesy of Mr. Walter L. Pforzheimer.)

President Kennedy awards Distinguished Service Medal of CIA to the retiring Director. (*CIA photo.*)

President Kennedy announced the resignation of Allen Dulles as Director of CIA and nominated John A. McCone to succeed him at a ceremony at the Naval War College, Newport, R.I., on September 28, 1961. Picture shows them leaving the ceremony. *(United Press International.)*

President Eisenhower speaking at the laying of the cornerstone for the new CIA headquarters building, Langley, Virginia, November 3, 1959. Director Dulles sits behind him. *(Photo courtesy of Mr. Walter L. Pforzheimer.)*

Allen Dulles (*left*) and Ray S. Cline (*right*), former Deputy Director of CIA, photographed during Allen's world tour, 1956.　(*CIA photo.*)

Top left: Robert Amory, former Deputy Director, Intelligence, CIA. (*Amory family photo.*)

Top right: General Walter Bedell Smith, Director of the CIA, 1950–1953, Ass't. Secretary of State, 1953–55. (*U.S. Army photo.*)

Bottom right: Walter L. Pforzheimer, former Legislative Counsel of the CIA. (*CIA photo.*)

Bottom left: Richard M. Bissell, Jr., former Deputy Director of Plans, CIA.

(*Bissell family photo.*)

John Foster Dulles was interred at Arlington National Cemetery on May 27, 1959. Here Dr. Russell P. Barnes, secretary of the World Council of Churches, presents an American flag from the casket to Mrs. Janet Dulles. Standing beside her are (*left to right*) John Dulles, eldest son; Mrs. (Lillias Dulles) Robert Hinshaw, daughter; Father Avery Dulles, S.J., son; and President and Mrs. Dwight D. Eisenhower. (*Wide World photo.*)

A meeting of the U.S. Intelligence Board, 1960. At the head of the table, pipe in mouth, Allen Dulles, Director of the CIA. (*CIA photo.*)

John Foster Dulles in Walter Reed Hospital just before his death, receiving an unexpected visit from Winston Churchill and President Eisenhower. The three statesmen are in the Presidential Suite at the hospital and the date is May 5, 1959. The picture over the mantlepiece is of Churchill painted by Eisenhower. Dulles died on May 24. *(Wide World photo.)*

Dulles and Clare Booth
Luce arriving in Rome,
October 1958, for the
funeral of Pope Pius XII.
Behind them is John
McCone, later (1961)
successor to Allen Dulles
at the CIA.
(*United Press International
photo.*)

Secretary of State John
Foster Dulles' last trip
abroad, to see
Chancellor Konrad
Adenauer in Bonn,
February 1959.
(*Wide World photo.*)

"Don't Be Afraid --- I Can Always Pull You Back"

Herblock's cartoon commentary in the *Washington Post* on Dulles' "brinkmanship" statement. (*From Herblock's Special for the Day, Simon and Schuster*, 1958.)

Janet and John Foster Dulles with two of their three children, Mrs. Lillias Hinshaw and Father Avery Dulles, S.J. (*United Press International photo.*)

Dulles confers with adviser Charles ("Chip") Bohlen while Eisenhower listens in at opening session of the Geneva Summit Conference, August 6, 1955.
(*Radio Time Hulton Picture Library photo.*)

Suez crisis. Prime Minister Eden greets Dulles at 10 Downing Street, August 15, 1956. (*Radio Times Hulton Picture Library photo.*)

Dulles confers with Prime Minister Churchill and Foreign Secretary Eden at 10 Downing Street, September 17, 1954.

(Radio Time Hulton Picture Library photo.)

Chancellor Adenauer paid his first official visit to Washington under the Eisenhower Administration on April 7, 1953. He is being greeted at the airport by Dulles and Vice-president Nixon.

(USDI National Park Service photo by Abbie Rowe.)

Geneva Conference on Indochina. *Left to right*: Dulles, French Foreign Minister Georges Bidault, French aide Jean Chauvel, British aide Lord Reading, U.S. Ass't. Secretary of State Walter Bedell Smith. April 1954.

(Associated Press photo.)

John Foster Dulles' official photograph as Secretary of State.
(*Whit Keith, Jr., photo.*)

the transcript of the commander's talk with his wife.

A few weeks later, back in Berlin, he was present at a joint ceremony at the Red Army memorial in the Western sector of the city to commemorate the fall of the then-German capital, and afterwards went on to a celebration with his Red Army confrères at which a more than adequate amount of vodka was drunk. At one point, the American general saw the Red Army commander, went across to him, and jovially remarked: "I hear you're going to be a father. I hope it's going to be a boy and will grow up to be a great soldier like you!"

The U.S. lieutenant who had tagged along with him as translator was about to launch into the Russian version of the general's remarks when the general realized what he had done. He swung himself around in a sort of wild twizzle, his vodka glass raised in the air, and knocked the translator flat on the ground. Then he stumbled down beside the discomfited lieutenant and whispered fiercely in his ear: "Don't translate that! Give him a bromide about Russo-American friendship."

The two men scrambled sheepishly to their feet, apologized to the grinning Russian, and drank a toast to mutual friendship. But the general duly reported his gaffe to the CIA that night, and everyone held their breath while urgent inquiries were made about whether the Red Army commander knew English. Finally they breathed again. He couldn't even speak German.

The Berlin Tunnel continued to operate without discovery for nine months, until its presence was finally revealed to the Russians by the British double agent, George Blake.* Soviet agents and East German police burst into the tunnel from the Communist side on April 22, 1956. But the inbuilt early warning systems had worked and the CIA had fled—leaving a coffee pot still percolating on one of the tables.

If the Berlin Tunnel was yet another triumph for Frank Wisner and his clandestine operators, both he and Allen Dulles were well aware that there was one area where all his efforts had been an inglorious failure. These were his attempts to penetrate the Soviet Union itself. It was true that the U-2 was now reporting back much information about Russian activities, but not even Lundahl's magic cameras could

*Blake was sentenced to thirty years in jail at the Old Bailey, London, in 1961 for treason. He escaped and reached Moscow, where he was awarded the Order of Lenin in 1970.

penetrate buildings or tunnels or reveal what was being said at meetings of the Party leaders. Nor, it seemed, could the agents whom Wisner continued to send in by parachute, submarine, or other covert means of entry into the USSR.

"I think the only really effective clandestine collection on Russia came from defectors," Richard Bissell said later. "I don't know that you would call that a failure. It was part of the duties of the clandestine service to receive and encourage defectors, and some extremely valuable ones came in. But I don't think clandestine collection is ever going to be a useful activity in a totalitarian society. The reason is only partly the difficulty of infiltrating agents into the country. The key difficulty is that even if you get an agent in place, in Russia, say—and supposing he's well trained, of Russian nationality and speaks the language fluently, and knows his way around—this agent will still have no way of acquiring information of much value. Where can he get it? Unless he's a high-up Russian, and he never was, he can only see as much as the ordinary Russian, which is hardly anything. The ordinary Russian isn't privy to what is said in the councils of State. He doesn't know the design of a warhead on an intercontinental ballistic missile. He doesn't know if there's an air base a hundred miles down the road."

Wisner had to face the fact that most of the Russians he did recruit and, at great trouble and expense, did successfully plant inside the Soviet Union—and there were very few genuine ones—came from relatively low walks of life and had no contacts worth a damn. They were never in a position to send back anything more interesting than what could be seen by the visiting newsman or tourist.

So most of the information about Russia came from the U-2 overflights,* from defectors, or from contacts with Soviet citizens, satellite citizens, or friends of Communist citizens in Third World countries. At CIA stations in most Western and neutral nations there was a suitably anonymous operator whose job it was to keep up a close contact with local left-wing elements, especially Communists, since they were often in touch with Soviet and East European diplomats, and sometimes in their pockets. The U.S. operator's job was to pick their brains for any information they managed to glean at the Soviet, Czech, Polish, or Hungarian embassies—for payment, of course.

*Or, later, from space satellites, which Bissell also pioneered.

Some Communist leaders in Europe were on the CIA's payroll without ever being asked to deliver any information at all. They were being held in hand for an emergency. And in 1956 an emergency came up.

In February 1956, Nikita Krushchev, the new First Secretary of the Soviet Communist Party, addressed a secret session of the 20th Party Congress in Moscow, and in a speech lasting nearly six hours gave the astonished delegates a blow-by-blow account of the bloodthirsty reign of the Soviet dictator, Josef Stalin. Only a few of the foreign Communist delegates to the Congress were invited to the secret session, and among them only two, Maurice Thorez of France and Palmiro Togliatti of Italy, came from Western countries.

The delegates were warned not to wash the Soviet Union's dirty linen in public by talking about the speech outside the conference hall, but soon rumors began to spread about the sensational charges and revelations Krushchev had made, first in the satellite nations and then in western Europe. Stories about the speech began to appear more and more frequently in reports from station chiefs in Europe, and Allen Dulles was finally aroused. He called a meeting of his clandestine chiefs (Frank Wisner, Richard Helms, Richard Bissell, James Angleton, and Cord Meyer among them) and told them he had talked the matter over with his brother, and Foster was most anxious that he and the President should see a full transcript of Krushchev's speech. It was up to them to get hold of it, somehow; he indicated that half a million dollars would not be too high a price to pay for it.

Wisner and Meyer had built up excellent contacts in eastern Europe, and the Gehlen unit in Germany had good information services in Prague and Warsaw. Between them, they managed to patchwork an account of the speech which no doubt contained some genuine passages but also had great gaps and obvious inventions.

It was left to James Jesus Angleton to produce the genuine article.

Angleton was the son of an American businessman who had run the subsidiary of the National Cash Register Company in Milan before World War II, and both father and son had fought with the OSS in Italy. Angleton *père* was a loudly outspoken anti-Communist who had played a prominent role in suppressing red attempts to take power in Rome and other places in Italy toward the end of the war. Angleton *fils* was a much subtler character, and the emotions he wore on his

sleeve were rarely genuine ones. For instance, though it emerged that he more than shared his father's antipathy to the Communists, he hobnobbed with them and exuded bland goodwill toward them in the days after Italy's liberation, and was an invited guest at the celebration which the Party gave for the return from exile in Moscow of their leader, Palmiro Togliatti.

Like some cardinal-diplomat from medieval Rome, Jim Angleton was willing to sup with the devil for the good of the Church. He kept up his connections with the Italian Communist Party long after the war, and went on subsidizing many of its leaders even when they were loudest in their denunciations of American imperialism. He continued to see Palmiro Togliatti while serving as OSS counter-intelligence officer in Rome in 1948,* and when he returned to Washington to work for the CIA he still kept up the connection. A sort of cautious rapport, a mutual admiration and respect, built up between the two men, like the murderer and his invigilator, though which was Raskolnikov and which the inspector depended upon one's ideological point of view.

Angleton knew something about Togliatti of which even his comrades in the Italian Party were unaware: that their leader had learned to loathe and despise Josef Stalin during his wartime years in Moscow, hated him for his brutalities, and cursed him for his betrayal of what he believed were the decent principles of communism. But he had kept his feelings to himself and muttered the curses under his breath during his exile in Moscow, well aware of what could happen even to faithful Party men who dared raise their voices. But once, like a penitent moved to confess to an outsider rather than his own parish priest, he had confided his feelings to Angleton, and Angleton had not betrayed him.

Who better to ask for a transcript of Krushchev's speech? Togliatti had been among those who had heard it delivered, and every word of its harsh denunciation of the evils of Stalinism must now be etched in his memory and engraved on his heart, justification at last of the hatred of the tyrant that he had cherished to his bosom for so long.

How much was paid by the CIA for the transcript of the Krushchev

*Where he also consolidated connections with the Israeli intelligence service, later known as Mossad.

speech is one of the secrets the Agency still keeps to itself, but if it was $750,000, as informed rumor has it, that is the amount of money by which Communist Party funds rose in Italy in the spring of 1956. But it was not for money that the transcript had been sold, but because Palmiro Togliatti decided that people should know that Communists, too, had abhorred the horrors of Stalinism, and that the Party so many of his fellow Italians feared had a human face behind the rigid mask of the Soviet dictator.*

Ironically enough, even when the speech came into CIA hands, it almost didn't get published. Ray Cline, a former deputy director of the Agency, has told the story of how Angleton and Frank Wisner, once they had it, decided that it should not be issued in its original form.

"To my amazement, Wisner and Angleton demurred," Cline wrote later.

> Once we had agreed that the text was authentic, their operational minds began thinking about feeding selected bits of the text to specific audiences on which they wanted to have an impact. They kept saying they wanted to "exploit" the story rather than simply let everybody read it. This was an example of the covert mind at work that, in this case, seemed excessively narrow and Byzantine. Jim Angleton much later admitted I was right, but that day he tried hard to keep his secret paper secret.

It was 1956, and the anti-Soviet rising in Poland and the rebellion in Hungary would happen later that year. Wisner and Angleton were building up propaganda and dissident forces ready for the great "rollback" of communism which Wisner in particular believed was now coming. The Krushchev speech, in carefully selected sections, would be volatile fuel with which to fan the flames once the fire began.

Cline was able to overcome their reluctance.

"I made what I thought was an eloquent plea to make the speech public," he wrote.

> I said that it would provide scholars and students interested in the Soviet Union invaluable insights into the real workings of Stalinist Russia. I also

*Some CIA sources say Mossad had an agent planted at the Moscow secret session, and that the Israeli intelligence service also provided Angleton with a copy of Krushchev's denunciation of Stalin. If so, it did not make Togliatti's price any the less worth paying.

said it was a rare opportunity to have all the critical things we had said for years about the Soviet dictatorship confirmed by the principal leader of the Soviet Politburo.

On June 2, 1956, Allen Dulles was in session with Cline. Suddenly he said: "Wisner says you think we ought to release the Krushchev speech."

Cline explained his reasons why he thought it should be done, and Dulles, "with a twinkle in his eye," said: "By golly, I am going to make a policy decision!"

He buzzed Wisner on his intercom and told him he was going to release the speech, and then telephoned Foster. Foster agreed. The speech was sent over to the State Department, which "leaked" it to *The New York Times.* They published the text of the speech in full in their issue of Monday, June 4, 1956.

CHAPTER TWENTY-TWO

Nile Boil

———————◆◆◆◆◆◆———————

Beetle Smith had long since resigned from the State Department,* in the bitter realization that he would never make anything of his position as Under-Secretary, that Foster Dulles had bureaucratically emasculated him. Foster was glad to see him go.

"I think on a number of occasions the Secretary felt he had a very inadequate vessel in Bedell Smith," John Hanes said later. "Bedell's knowledge of and sensitiveness to the nuances of politics, as opposed to how you run a war, was limited. As was his temper. If I'd had his stomach, my temper would have been even more limited, because this man the last ten years of his life never passed a comfortable minute. Every time he ate anything he was uncomfortable, vividly uncomfortable and painfully so. For the next six hours, until he got hungry again. I mean he was a physical wreck."

Foster sometimes used to remark to his relatives that it was a pity Beetle made it so obvious that he was feeling pain, and allowed it to influence his attitudes—and probably even his decisions. It went without saying that neither Foster himself nor his brother—nor Eleanor, for that matter—ever allowed pain to cloud or curdle their judgment. The doctor whom Foster and Eleanor shared once said that Foster was the only man he had ever known who insisted on walking normally when he was suffering from gout. Even Allen hobbled and put on carpet slippers. Foster went on wearing his "sensible" shoes and never showed a limp or let a whimper escape his lips.

"When you figure," said Eleanor later, "that he had had thromboid

*On October 1, 1954.

379

phlebitis, very bad eyes, malaria, a slipped disc, gout, diverticulitis, quite serious hay fever if he didn't watch it, and finally cancer, which is quite a complement of physical ills, it's amazing how he refused to let them limit his activities or cloud his brain. I think that enjoying food and drink and all the normal pleasures of life, he got about as much out of his body and his mind as he could possibly have done. He handled it in a logical way, just as a space man would handle his space engine or a jet pilot would handle his plane."

He was still father of the family, and they all came to him for domestic advice. He lent Eleanor money to pay medical bills (and was astonished when she paid it back). He commiserated with her when her son, David—whom he had once dubbed the hope of the Dulles family—failed to live up to his mother's ambitions for him. When Allen dropped out with a sudden bout of kidney stones, he stepped in to give away Eleanor's adopted daughter at her marriage. He took time out from a diplomatic trip to Germany in 1955 to stop off in Switzerland and visit Allen's son, Allen, Jr., who was now in a clinic there for treatment of his head injury. When he heard that Clover had begun writing a study of Jungian philosophy, he even offered to read it and give "an impartial" opinion; she, no doubt wisely, for he had not much in common with Jung, refused.*

On the whole, he was proud of his own sons and daughter, and sometimes remarked that they had "turned out better than Janet and I thought they might." It was true that he often complained about having to give a helping hand to "my impecunious son-in-law," but both Avery and John (now a professor of mining engineering) had chosen their own paths to follow and had surmounted all obstacles, and he admired them for that.

He was sixty-seven in 1955, and the first summit meeting of President Eisenhower's administration was coming up, two years after Churchill had originally asked for it and too late for the frail British premier, who had had a stroke and been forced to retire. In preparation for it, Foster had his doctor give him a thorough checkup and was pronounced in reasonably good shape, provided he gave up his after-dinner cigar. He could continue with his large strong dry martini

*She never even showed it to Allen.

before his weekend lunch, his glass of Overholt rye whiskey before dinner, his good wine and good food. He took no other exercise than a biweekly swim at Eleanor's house at McLean, the sailing on Lake Ontario, and the logcabin chores on Duck Island during the summer breaks, but for a man of his age he seemed remarkably fit.

He had accepted the summit at Geneva that summer because he believed the time was propitious for the United States and that, at long last, the Russians had seen the light and realized that the Americans meant business in the way they saw and wished to shape the world. He had long since given up the idea of "rolling back" Soviet hegemony in eastern Europe ("rollback" had, in any case, been mostly a domestic trigger word to catch ethnic votes), but he did believe that the firmness of purpose which he had displayed in shaping the foreign policy of the United States and its Western allies in Europe and in Asia through SEATO* had shown the Russians that they could advance no further.

It remained to shape the strategy and decide the tactics that would give President Eisenhower the best chance of scoring good results and showing the world the summit had been worth waiting for. Because Foster was determined on one thing. This would be the President's summit. There were rumors that Anthony Eden also had great hopes of it. It would be his first appearance at an international conference as prime minister of Great Britain, and he needed to show his countrymen that he had Churchillian qualities. This was his golden opportunity.

For who else among the Western delegates had a better chance of matching the skills of the Russian leaders, Krushchev and Bulganin? It would be President Eisenhower's first summit, but Anthony Eden had been attending them all through his long and eventful diplomatic career. He knew how to deal with totalitarian leaders. He had talked to Hitler and Mussolini and Stalin. He knew the form. He was Ike's wartime friend. In years of diplomacy, he was old enough to be Ike's father, and like a father he would guide and advise and save him from gaffes as he matched words and wits with the Soviet leaders.

*The South East Asia Treaty Organization, born in Manila on September 8, 1954, joined together eight nations—the United States, Great Britain, France, New Zealand, Australia, the Philippines, Thailand, and Pakistan—for mutual defense.

Or so he thought. It was a measure of Eden's physical and mental condition at that time that he sincerely believed Foster Dulles would let him get away with it.

"Now at the summit meeting it was quite interesting," one of Foster's aides said later. "Eden had just married his second wife, who was much younger.* She was coming into the meetings on the arms of a couple of attachés. There was quite a bit of posh and spit. Mr. Eden, I think, was quite interested in keeping this impression of glamour, as much to her as to the public. He was obviously taking sunbaths or a sunlamp every day, because throughout the entire conference he had a blooming vigorous tan. He was quite chagrined, I think, because he didn't come out of the conference as the outstanding diplomat."

There was never any chance, of course, that Foster would let him anywhere near the President in a way that could influence his judgment or affect his tactics. That was what the Secretary was there for, and his guard went up the moment Eden arrived to greet his wartime comrade.

So far as the actual conference was concerned, the cards had, in any case, been stacked against the British premier. The seating at the conference table was arranged so that the United Kingdom came first, then the USSR, then the United States, and then France.

"So the first rebuttal was always from us," Roderick O'Connor, Foster's aide, said. "And the British, if we had a proposal, they always came after. And that gave them much less of a position to predominate, you might say. And what they said was responded to by the Russians, so that the Russians were always knocking them down. And we were knocking the Russians down. From a purely press and public point of view, it put us at a considerable advantage."

The hardheaded Russians quickly got the feeling of the meeting and sensed that things had changed among their adversaries. Churchill was gone; no longer did the Americans show deference to the British and allow them to lead. The power no longer sat in the prime minister's chair (it had not for a long time, really, but under Churchill a pretense had been kept up) but resided in that of the President of the United States, and in the vigilant figure of his Secretary of State seated beside him.

*Clarissa Spencer Churchill was a niece of Winston Churchill.

"Actually, the Russians paid absolutely no attention to Eden whatsoever," Foster's aide said, "and in the coffee break Eden would be by
himself with his group, and the Russians were surrounding Eisenhower. (The French were off having tea.) Eden just wasn't getting any
play, nor did he end up getting much of a play in the press. . . . I came
away with the very strong impression that Eden was very disappointed
that he had not emerged as the star. He had been overwhelmed by
Eisenhower both on position and attention. The Russians treated the
British with calculated denigration, I would say. They obviously
wanted to deal directly with us, and that was quite a blow to Eden.
. . . I got the impression of a very piqued and chagrined man, on a
personal basis."

For Eisenhower, the Geneva Summit Conference was everything
that Foster had promised him. On the fourth day, he rose and read the
text of the speech Foster had written for him proposing an "Open
Skies" agreement, and he added in an aside to the Soviet Delegation:
"The United States will never take part in an aggressive war."

The Russians were obviously impressed.

"We believe that statement," Bulganin said.

With the possible exception of Anthony Eden, everyone had been
encouraged by the American performance and by the evident eagerness of the Russians to let bygones be bygones and change the nature
of East-West relations from deceit to frankness, from hostility to
friendship, from cold war to cooperation.

President Eisenhower returned home in triumph. A phrase began to
be heard in speeches and read in the newspapers: The Spirit of Geneva. There was a feeling of new hope in the world.

But, in fact, nothing had really changed. Even while the delegates
were toasting the new sense of honesty and openness in their relationship, a nice little intrigue was going on behind the scenes which would
soon make a mockery of the Spirit of Geneva.

When the United Kingdom agreed, in 1954, under strong American
pressure, to start withdrawing its garrison of eighty thousand troops
from the Suez Canal Zone of Egypt, Winston Churchill asked Foster
Dulles why he was so anxious that Britain should make this gesture to
the new Egyptian revolutionary government.

"Because," replied Foster, "it will restore Egyptian pride and strengthen the Egyptian position, so that she can in future play a leading role in the Middle East."

"Anything in which Egypt plays a leading role," replied the British premier sourly, "means trouble."

Trouble had indeed followed on the heels of the British withdrawal, and not just for the British. Foster Dulles had believed that he would get a quid pro quo from Nasser, the Egyptian leader, in return for his aid in ridding Egypt of the British army. He asked Nasser to make a gesture and align Egypt with Iraq, Turkey, and Pakistan in the so-called Bagdad Pact which the United Kingdom, with U.S. backing, had sponsored as a barrier against the encroachment of the Soviet Union into the Middle East.

But Nasser did not share Foster's anti-communism nor see the Russians as a threat to his people or the rest of the Arab world. He was more concerned with the stepping up of Israeli reprisal raids against Egypt, and the Zionist enemy just across the Canal. While the British were still garrisoned in Egypt, the Americans had refused Nasser's requests for arms for his forces because Churchill had intervened personally with Eisenhower and said: "You can't give them arms with which to kill British soldiers who fought shoulder to shoulder with you in the war."

"But now the British are going," Nasser said to the Americans. "If you give us arms, there won't be any British for us to kill."

There had still been no U.S. arms deal. In the 1954 mid-term elections in America the Republican congressional vote had been smaller; political experts put this down to resentment among the pro-Zionists at Foster Dulles's attempts to forge ties of friendship with Egypt at the expense of the Israelis. The British had delivered sixteen Centurion tanks to Cairo as part of a shipment the Egyptians had already paid for, but were holding back the rest as a carrot with which to tempt Nasser into the Bagdad Pact. Nasser had no taste for carrots. Instead, he had sent out buyers to shop for arms in Belgium, Switzerland, and Holland, with meager results.

Then, in April 1955, Nasser announced that he was going to the Conference of Unaligned Nations at Bandung, Indonesia, much to the disgust and annoyance of Foster Dulles. For one thing, he firmly believed that there was no such animal as an unaligned nation in the cold

war jungles of 1955, and that countries not for the United States were against it. For another, he knew that Chou En-lai, Mao Tse-tung's right-hand man, would be at Bandung as the representative of Red China.

He felt threatened by Red China at that moment. The Communists had just driven the Nationalist forces of Chiang Kai-shek out of the Tachen Islands and seemed to be making threats toward the offshore islands of Quemoy and Matsu and the Nationalist stronghold of Taiwan.* Senator Knowland was all for blockading the Chinese mainland immediately, though he didn't say how it was going to be done. Admiral Radford was reported to have proposed that Shanghai should be atom-bombed as a nuclear warning to Peking. Even President Eisenhower, on Foster's advice, when asked if the United States would be in favor of using tactical atomic bombs in Asia, replied: "Yes."

The idea that the Egyptian leader—whom he still regarded as an invaluable if temperamental protégé, the key to his Middle East policy —would soon be hobnobbing with an enemy of one of his favorite allies was anathema to Foster, and he urged the U.S. Embassy in Cairo to do everything they could to persuade Nasser to cancel his plans. The Egyptian leader, who almost invariably did exactly the opposite of what he was pressured to do, left for Bandung at once.

He stopped off en route at Rangoon for a meeting with India's leader, Jawaharlal Nehru, and the Burmese premier, U Nu. Chou En-lai was also there, and expressed a wish to have a private talk with Nasser. He waited patiently, smoking long Chinese cigarettes, when the Egyptian was late for the appointment. The two men got on famously. When they parted, Chou promised to speak to the Russians about Egypt's arms problems.

That was in April 1955. About a month later, at the Sudanese Embassy in Cairo, Nasser found himself next to the Russian ambassador, Daniel Solod, who told him he had been ordered by Moscow to ask for an audience. By the beginning of July a Soviet army officer, Colonel Nimoschenko, was having secret talks at a house in the Cairo suburb of Maadi with Egyptian army and air force officers, and a list of the arms the Egyptians wanted was being drawn up.

And then suddenly, on July 20, 1955, the Soviets switched. Nimos-

---

*In fact, as it turned out, they had no such plans.

chenko explained that the summit conference was in progress and the talks with the Americans were going well. Moscow was anxious that nothing should be done to disturb the atmosphere or sully "the Spirit of Geneva."

Therefore, the Russians were not going to supply the Egyptians with arms, after all. Instead, they would be provided—in strictest secrecy, of course—by one of Russia's satellites, Czechoslovakia.

On July 20, an Egyptian military delegation left for Prague.

That same day, Moshe Sharett, the Israeli prime minister, arrived in Geneva and had a talk with Foster Dulles. He brought him news from the Israeli intelligence service. They had information, he said, that the Egyptians were in process of buying arms from the Russians. Foster was alarmed, but incredulous.

A few hours later he saw Nikita Krushchev, the Soviet leader, and asked him point-blank whether he was planning to sell arms to Nasser. Krushchev gave him a comradely grin and assured him that the Soviet Union was not, and had no intention of, selling arms to the Egyptians.

Foster was relieved. Sharett had lied to him. It was just Israeli provocation, to blow the bridge he was trying to build with the Egyptians.

Allen Dulles was in Teheran when word reached him of what the Israelis were saying. He was on the Middle Eastern leg of a round-the-world trip to mend fences with his chiefs of station, and was making no secret about it. The Air Force had adapted a DC-6 cargo plane to carry passengers, and the party included Clover, Ray Cline, James Billington, a young Soviet specialist, and a doctor to watch Allen's uric acid count and keep down his gouty manifestations.

At each stopover there were meetings not only with the local CIA representatives but also with chiefs of state. His position in the Eisenhower hierarchy was well known, and everyone was anxious to do him honor.

But in addition to these public activities there were serious discussions going on behind the scenes, in safehouses and debugged rooms, with the less overt members of the Agency's network. In Teheran, Allen had summoned the Cairo station chief, John (Larry) Eichelberger, to see him and confided to him what Premier Sharett had told his brother Foster in Geneva. Was it true that the Egyptians were trying to do an arms deal with the Soviets?

Eichelberger pointed out that Henry Byroade, the U.S. ambassador in Cairo, had already reported such a rumor to Washington and had been chewed out by the Secretary for putting too much credence in it. Foster had been given the strongest assurances by the Soviet government that it was not supplying arms to Egypt, and that was that. Nasser was just trying to bluff the United States into letting him have guns, planes, and tanks.

"Do you trust what the Russians say?" Allen asked.

"No," said Eichelberger. "I'd rather trust the Gyppos than the Bolos."

He promised to get back to Cairo fast and check. The Dulles caravanserai lumbered on (as soon as Clover had got back from a trip to Ispahan) to Karachi and points east.

A few days after Eichelberger returned to the Egyptian capital, one of his agents came to see him in some excitement. The agent was an Egyptian subject whose cover was that of a contractor to the Egyptian armed forces. He had good connections with the general staff, and he produced indubitable proof in the form of telegrams and memoranda to show that an Egyptian army delegation was in Prague, and that the Czechs were preparing to ship arms to Egypt.

Knowing what had happened when Ambassador Byroade had reported similar bad news to the State Department, Eichelberger sent a crash message to the CIA in Washington and asked them to alert Allen Dulles, wherever he happened to be. The Agency picked him up in Delhi and told him what had happened. It was Allen who telephoned Foster and told him the worst. He suggested that Foster tell his ambassador to get over to Nasser at once and persuade him to cancel the deal.

But Foster had lost faith in Ambassador Byroade. Once one of the bright young hopes of the State Department, Hank Byroade had demoted himself from Assistant Secretary for Middle East affairs at Foster's special request in order to accept the Cairo mission, his assignment being to bring Nasser into the Western camp. But he had failed —as anyone else would have done, given the circumstances—and Foster did not tolerate failures.

So Allen suggested that CIA's own Middle East specialist, Kim Roosevelt, should be alerted and flown to Cairo without delay to twist Nasser's arm and make him see reason. He agreed. Foster did not need

to be reminded that it was Kim who had restored the situation in Iran. Perhaps his appearance in Egypt would scare Nasser as much as it had Mossadeq.

He summoned Kim Roosevelt to come and see him at the State Department and briefed him for his special mission. Outwardly the Secretary was keeping his cool, but his aides were aware that he was simmering with anger. Not so much against the Russians for lying to him—that, after all, was a big power ploy—but at Nasser's daring to defy him and go against his known wishes. He must be brought to heel.

It was Eichelberger, not Byroade, who was first informed that Kim Roosevelt was coming. He was told to let the Egyptians know that a special envoy was on his way.

The CIA man had no official contact with the Egyptian government, so he telephoned Mohammad Heikal, editor of the official government newspaper *al Ahram* and a close friend and collaborator of Gamal Abdel Nasser. It was three o'clock in the morning. Heikal thought Eichelberger was drunk when he came on the line and heard the CIA man begin to plead with him to persuade Nasser not to sign, that the Communists were dangerous characters, that he should recall what they did to Masaryk in Czechoslovakia, and that at all costs he must "keep his pants on" and do nothing until the envoy arrived from Washington.

Meantime, the Egyptian ambassador to the United States, Dr. Ahmed Hussein, who happened to be on holiday in Cairo, heard the news that Kim Roosevelt was on his way. He knew Kim to be a top CIA man, and he blanched. Rushing round to see Nasser, he warned him not to defy the Americans, and especially the CIA. The Agency's overthrow of Arbenz in Guatemala had taken place only the year before.

"Remember Guatemala, remember Guatemala," Dr. Hussein kept saying.

"To hell with Guatemala," retorted Nasser.

The Egyptian ambassador persisted: "How can I go back to Washington and meet Mr. Dulles?" he asked plaintively.

"You don't have to go back if you don't want to," Nasser replied, sharply.

He was now surrounded by so many panicky colleagues, fearful that the wrath of John Foster Dulles was about to descend upon the Egyp-

tian people, that he decided to demonstrate that neither the Secretary of State nor the CIA could frighten him. Just before Kim Roosevelt flew into Cairo, he appeared suddenly at an army photographic exhibition, and there he publicly announced that Egypt had signed an arms agreement with Czechoslovakia.

There, it was done, a fait accompli. Dulles was defied. Let the Americans do their worst.

Soon the local Cairene wits were remarking that there were more American envoys than garbage hawks hovering over the city. Kim Roosevelt came in and spent two days trying to impress on Nasser the heat of Foster Dulles's wrath and the need for him to renege on the deal with the Czechs before he got burned. At the same time Eric Johnston, the President's special representative, flew into town and got into the act. Then came a message from Washington that the Assistant Secretary of State, George V. Allen, was arriving in the next forty-eight hours. Rumor had it that he was bringing an ultimatum from the Secretary, threatening to stop all aid to Egypt, stop all trade, break off diplomatic relations, and blockade Egyptian ports to prevent arms ships arriving if Nasser did not cancel the deal.

Nasser called in Kim Roosevelt and told him brusquely and sharply that if Assistant Secretary Allen was indeed bringing such a message, he (Nasser) would have the chamberlain show him the door, call in the reporters, and announce that he was breaking off diplomatic relations with the United States.

In the middle of all these threats and counter-threats there was a diplomatic incident, and it concerned Ambassador Byroade.

Hank Byroade was by far the unhappiest man in Cairo at that time. It so happened that Paul Nitze, who had once been Foster's temporary director of Policy Planning, was staying with the ambassador in Cairo, and his heart bled for his old friend. He knew how hard Byroade had tried to bring the Egyptians and the Americans together, and he believed Foster's harsh criticisms of his envoy had been quite unjust.

Byroade was in a difficult position. Some time ago his marriage had run into difficulties, and while in Cairo he had met and been seen around a lot with a beautiful young Cairene from a well-known political family. Some weeks back, the police had raided the house of the

girl's brother-in-law and discovered Byroade and the girl there. The ambassador had explained who he was, and the police had phoned Nasser.

"Let them go," Nasser said.

It had later been explained to Byroade that the house had been raided because the girl's brother-in-law was suspected of being involved in a smuggling ring, and that it was quite fortuitous that the raid had happened on the day of his assignation. But Byroade quite reasonably found that hard to believe. He felt the Egyptians were trying to blackmail him, to put pressure on him to favor them in his reports to Washington.

In the midst of all the slowly mounting tension between Egypt and the United States—it was being carefully built up by Nasser's friend, Heikal, in *al Ahram*—a labor expert on the U.S. Embassy staff, Jim Finch, went down to the Suez Canal Zone to have a look at some work there. Apprehended as a spy, he was roughly manhandled by groups of Nasser activists and police and came back in extremely bad shape. His wife had hysterics when she saw how badly he had been beaten up. It did not improve the atmosphere around the embassy, and Byroade was angry at what had been done to his aide.

In an attempt to relieve the atmosphere, the amiable Dr. Hussein, still the Egyptian ambassador to Washington, and still on holiday in Cairo, decided to give a party and bring the contenders together. He was staying with his father-in-law, who had a house at Giza, in the shadow of the Pyramids, and that was where the party was held. Byroade, Roosevelt, and Johnston were the principal American guests, and Nasser had signaled his intention of attending.

By the time the Egyptian leader arrived, Hank Byroade had had a few drinks, and they had heightened rather than lowered his tense and desperate mood. Nasser asked for an orange juice and had just taken a sip when the American ambassador came over to him. Shaking with emotion, he stammered out: "Mr. Premier, one of my men was beaten nearly to death today in Suez."

Nasser replied mildly that he had heard of the incident, and wondered why the American had gone to Suez. Byroade replied that since he was the labor attaché, it was his job to study the labor movement.

"Unfortunately," said Nasser, "the man behaved suspiciously and people thought he was a spy."

Byroade's face darkened.

"He was no spy," he said, "and yet he was beaten!" He paused, drew in a gulp of breath, and then burst out: "I am sorry, I thought we were in a civilized country!"

Nasser looked around for an ashtray and stubbed out his cigarette. Then he turned to his aides and said: "Let's go."

Kim Roosevelt and Eric Johnston had been standing by, expressions of horror on their faces. Byroade had blown everything with his emotional outburst. Roosevelt hurried after the Egyptian leader and tried to persuade him to return, but was curtly brushed off.

That night the two special envoys sent a telegram strongly urging Dulles to recall his ambassador without delay. But before any action could be taken, George Allen arrived. Roosevelt and Johnston rushed to the airport to meet him and told him in the car on the way back to town that if he was indeed bringing an ultimatum to Nasser from Foster Dulles, he had better keep it in his pocket. The Egyptian leader was in a nasty mood, and anything might happen if he was provoked. George Allen said he would keep the Secretary's letter to himself for the time being.

But who was to take him to see Nasser? Protocol ordained that the ambassador should do the honors, but in the circumstances would Nasser deign to receive him?

Nasser would. The extraordinary truth was that he rather liked Byroade and sympathized with the trials he had experienced during his sojourn in Cairo. It was not Byroade's fault that the policies of the two nations were on a collision course, and nothing he could have done was capable of making the Egyptian leader change course.

Nasser greeted Byroade with such affection that the American had tears in his eyes and could hardly speak for emotion. But the premier's manner suddenly hardened when he turned to George Allen. He waited for the famous ultimatum to be presented, knowing quite well, even if the Americans didn't, that not a single gun had yet arrived from Czechoslovakia, and that it would be another ten days before the first ship docked at Alexandria. If the United States was actually going to start a blockade, what could Egypt do?

But the special envoy had taken the Roosevelt-Johnston warnings to heart, and instead of presenting the Secretary's letter, he talked. He

talked for two hours, although long before that he realized that it was going to do no good at all.

He went straight to the airport after leaving the Abdin Palace to fly back to the United States. Two hours after he left, a stern telegram arrived from Foster insisting that whatever else happened, he *must* present his letter.

But it was too late. Gamal Abdel Nasser had won. Round One, anyway.

CHAPTER TWENTY-THREE

Not Worth a Dam

Foster's relationship with Dwight Eisenhower, even after three years in office, had never really warmed up. In truth, the President was still a little uncomfortable with his Old Testament prophet and had no desire to include him in his intimate circle of friends. As for Foster, he looked upon the President with a mixture of affection and disdain, typical of the professional statesman for the languid amateur.

If Eisenhower had a personal friend in the cabinet, it was Secretary of the Treasury George Humphrey, at whose Thomasville, Georgia, plantation he often liked to foregather with his businessmen cronies to play golf and chew the rag. During the Czech arms crisis, Foster had to go down and deliver a message to the President at the plantation.

"We got there at night in an Air Force plane," said Louis W. Jefferson, Jr., who was Foster's security officer. "The Secret Service sent a White House car for us, and we rode out to the plantation and the Secretary talked to the President."

Neither the President nor George Humphrey asked Foster to stay the night. Instead, other arrangements had been made.

"When we left the plantation," said Jefferson, "we went to the Three Toms Inn, where the Secret Service put us up, a creaky bed sort of place. I remember him sitting on a creaking bed, literally squeaking away. I broke out the rye and had a drink with him. There was the President out at George Humphrey's plantation, but Dulles's relationship with the President was such that he'd simply reported to the President. I think maybe Mr. Dulles preferred it that way."

The fact had to be faced that Dwight Eisenhower's interest in foreign affairs was now minimal, and he was quite content to leave it all to

Foster. As for the presidency, for all its glamour he had begun to be bored with the chores that went with it, and he had alarmed the Republican Party (one of whose leaders had recently proclaimed: "I believe in God and Dwight Eisenhower") by hinting that maybe he shouldn't try for a second term in 1956. Although, of course, he changed his mind later.

In the fall of 1955, while the crisis in the Middle East was building, Eisenhower went on an extended golfing, fishing, and card-playing vacation with a bunch of male buddies at the Byers Peak Ranch in Colorado. He had a hamburger-and-onions lunch after a game on September 23 and afterwards complained of heartburn. He went on to spend the night with his mother-in-law in Denver and at 2:30 the following morning had a heart attack. It was not a massive thrombosis, but it certainly meant that the President would be in the political wings for some time while he recovered, and the Vice-President, Richard M. Nixon, would be in charge of affairs.

The first thing Nixon did when he heard the news was telephone Foster.

"Our relationship became very close at the time of Ike's heart attack," Nixon said later. "There had to be men on whom I could rely. The men I was particularly close to—Dulles was the first—were Dulles, Humphrey, Brownell, and Rogers . . . Dulles was the man who advised and guided me . . . to what I could do and the role I should play."

In practice, that meant instructing Allen that Nixon should be fully briefed in all the activities in which the CIA was engaged, and made familiar with its methods and techniques. Allen personally took the Vice-President on a tour of the Agency and into Virginia to the Farm for a show-off visit to the more esoteric training schemes and experiments that were going on there. He met the top-echelon brains of the CIA—Wisner, Angleton, Helms, Cline, Houston, and Robert Amory among them—and was given a thorough "no spit" briefing which made him an enthusiastic admirer of the Agency from that moment on. Henceforward he became absorbed in its activities, and, by the very nature of its setup, realized what an invaluable instrument it could be for furthering presidential policies, and ambitions.

It was, however, to Foster Dulles that he felt gratitude for the cooperation he was getting. The Vice-President relied heavily upon him for guidance during Eisenhower's absence in Denver.

"In fact, I would say that Dulles was really the general at that point," says Nixon. "We never did anything at that period without checking with Dulles."

Unfortunately, Foster did not check with anyone else. While the President was still convalescing in Denver, he gave an interview to reporters from the Time-Life organization during which he looked back on his reign as Secretary. In the course of it, he cited some of the tricky decisions he had taken in Asia in facing up to the challenge of communism.

"You have to take chances for peace, just as you have to take chances in war," he said. "Some say we were brought to the verge of war. Of course we were brought to the verge of war. The ability to get to the verge without getting into war is the necessary art. If you cannot master it, you inevitably get into war. If you try to run away from it, if you are scared to go to the brink, you are lost."

He added: "We walked to the brink and we looked it in the face. We took strong action."

It was a display of arrogance that was to cost Foster Dulles dearly. His critics hastened to point out that most of the crises he claimed to have solved by going "to the brink" just hadn't happened the way he said they had. The British Foreign Office denied statements he had made about certain events in which they had been involved. James Reston in *The New York Times* called him "a supreme expert" in the art of "diplomatic blundering," and added that "he doesn't stumble into booby traps: he digs them to size, studies them carefully, and then jumps."

"Brinkmanship" as a word for diplomatic recklessness would henceforth be associated with Foster's name. First had come his rebuff at the hands of the wily Egyptian, and now came evidence that when he got angry he took unacceptable risks. His prestige slumped. His credit was so low that early in 1956 even President Eisenhower had to be persuaded to issue a statement rebuking his critics and claiming that Foster was "the best Secretary [of State] I have ever known."

But Foster had a ploy up his sleeve. He was convinced that it would restore his standing by ending the uncertainty in the Middle East and bringing Gamal Abdel Nasser back into line. It had to do with the River Nile, on whose waters so much history had been written, and with a project known as the Aswan Dam.

For generations men had dreamed of turning the deserts of Egypt on either side of the River Nile into fertile pastures by feeding into them waters from the great river, and doing it by careful control, instead of by the arbitrary floodwaters that swirled down each year from the melting snows of the Ethiopian highlands. It meant building a dam, and the best site for the dam was at a place called Aswan. Only a lack of money had so far prevented it from being built, and by 1956 that obstacle seemed not so formidable as it had been in the past.

Eugene Black, president of the World Bank, had read a report from his experts and decided that the Aswan Dam was a feasible project. He was prepared to advance $200 million of the Bank's money, provided that the U.S. government would provide another $300 million and the British government $80 million. George Humphrey, the U.S. Secretary of the Treasury, was against it from the start. The way he saw it, the dam was just a British plot on the part of Anthony Eden to pull Britain's irons out of the Egyptian fire, with the help of America's hard-earned dollars.

Humphrey didn't believe the dam was going to work, anyway. One of his closest friends was Herbert Hoover, Jr., who had taken Beetle Smith's place on Foster Dulles's staff. Hoover, who, like his father, the former President Hoover, was an engineer and an expert on dams, maintained that there were not enough Egyptians in the Nile Valley nor was there enough industrial development in Egyptian towns to benefit from the irrigation waters and the huge number of kilowatts of electricity that the dam would develop.

But Foster was in favor of the dam. He argued eloquently for it over Humphrey's objections and against the tide of sentiment running in both the Senate and the Congress, where there was reluctance to subsidize a maverick Egyptian who had just thumbed his nose at the Americans and turned to the Russians for his arms. Foster maintained that a loan for such a project would demonstrate to the Egyptian people and the world that while the Russians were in Egypt as merchants of death, America was offering the means for growth and life.

In the speeches and statements made at this period Foster Dulles did not specify another, much more Machiavellian, reason he had for supporting the loan. He had already made it clear, in conversation with

Eugene Black, that American money would not be paid over or expertise made available until the Egyptians had promised to fulfill certain conditions. In the matter of repayment, for example, Nasser's government must pledge itself so to arrange its budget that regular repayments should be made, and World Bank and American financial experts would be on hand to see that they would be able to do so.

The Aswan Dam would take ten years to build. That would give the United States ten years of effective control over Egypt's financial affairs. In the circumstances, it seemed unlikely that Nasser would have much change left over to go spending on Russian arms, Czech arms, or arms from anywhere—except as and how the Americans so designated.

It was a stroke of genius on Foster's part. Though the Czech arms deal had been signed and the first deliveries begun, it was still not too late. As has since become known, Nasser was worried. He had been pushed into the deal with the Communists by U.S. procrastination and by Foster's failure to understand his temperament—that when he was bullied, he did the exact opposite of what was being demanded of him. But the truth was that both the Egyptian leader and his army generals would have preferred American and British arms. They all spoke and read English, and they had been trained on English instruction manuals by English instructors.

They were apprehensive about having to start all over again with strange weapons, instruction books in Russian and Czech, and the awkward and imprecise business of translating lectures and courses by Russian instructors into Arabic. They were also apprehensive about an influx of Russian Communist training personnel into Egypt. Nasser was by no means a Communist, and he feared ideologues from Moscow and Prague mixing with soldiers and the simple Egyptian fellaheen.

No, there was still time to turn him around, and backing the Aswan Dam was a brilliant way to do it—that plus an American hand on his moneybags.

Unfortunately, Foster made one mistake. He put his new Assistant Secretary of State, Herbert Hoover, Jr., in charge of the negotiations, principally because he assumed him to be an expert on projects of the nature of the Aswan Dam. What he did not seem to know was that

Hoover and George Humphrey had already decided that the Aswan Dam was a British ploy to gouge money out of the United States. In a joint statement which they made later, these remarks occur:

HUMPHREY: The first time I heard the particulars of the Aswan Dam was just after the President had his heart attack, before he returned. September 1955. He was back home but not available as far as all of us were concerned. This thing was whispered that there was going to be a request for a great amount of money coming from Britain. We were alerted to the fact that it might develop and we tried to find out something about it.

HOOVER: It originated in Britain.

HUMPHREY: It all started with Anthony Eden, as far as I know.

HOOVER: There was a combination of European manufacturers and contractors who wanted to supply all the equipment and they wanted us to pay for it.

HUMPHREY: British manufacturers.

HOOVER: And construction companies. (Aside) This may be pretty harsh. We can edit it.

The inquiries which the two friends had made had convinced them that the scheme would not really improve the lot of the Egyptian peasant, would prove to be an endless drain on the U.S. Treasury, and that the United States was being dragged into it because the British were blackmailing the Americans. It was a period when the United States was pressuring its allies to cut down on exports to the USSR and other Communist nations. Britain had a considerable trade with China and eastern Europe and was reluctant to curtail it, or abide by the list of banned exports that had been drawn up.

"There was a kind of threat from the British that if we didn't help," said Humphrey, "they were not going to abide by the strict list we had with the Russians."

Humphrey said later that the question came into the open for him at a cabinet meeting at Camp David in December 1955, the first since Eisenhower's heart attack. The President had come up from his Gettysburg farm. Foster spoke to him, then came over to Humphrey and said: "I've got something I want to talk to you about before the meeting."

"He had a cable from Eden," said Humphrey. "This cable was a very sharp cable, demanding—half-demanding, half-threatening—that if

we did not join them in this building of the Aswan Dam, they would no longer restrict their trade and the fat would be in the fire. It posed a very difficult problem. The President talked with us for just a minute and then we went to lunch. Foster brought it up at the meeting, and said it was inevitable that we do something about this. Nobody said anything. I don't think anybody had heard about it. I objected then strongly. The result of that was that the decision was put off for a day or two, to think about."

A few days later, Foster appointed Herbert Hoover, Jr., to go into the details with the British, and he and Humphrey went to talk to Sir Roger Makins (later Lord Sherfield), the British ambassador, and Lord Harcourt, financial secretary to the British Treasury.

The Humphrey-Hoover report of this meeting goes on:

HUMPHREY: At this first meeting it developed right away what I had feared all the time. In this partnership affair, we asked them how we would divide up. I remember Gene [Black] said it would cost $800 million to build the Dam.

HOOVER: That was the external exchange requirement, just the incoming money, not the local expenditures.

HUMPHREY: That was just our money. This was a proposal by them [the British] as a partnership affair with Britain. I asked what basis it would be on. It was just about what I thought. They'd take ten percent and we'd take ninety percent, and that was about the pattern.

HOOVER: I can interject here one little thing, George. Also at that point the British had told the Egyptians all about this, and their tongues were hanging out. So the Egyptians were in there pushing too.

HUMPHREY: Everybody was. Then we went on. Herb [Hoover] had innumerable meetings. I'd come once in a while. It went on for a long time. Foster went on the theory that we ought to do it to help our relations elsewhere. He thought that things were sufficiently serious, and he thought that it was not only a turning point in our relationships with Egypt but with Britain and our relations elsewhere. Foster very slowly and very gradually came to realize what we were up against.

What Foster had come to realize, in fact, was that he was up against George Humphrey—the only other member of the cabinet as strong

as he was. Moreover, in this case, the Treasury Secretary had all the cards (as well as the dollars) in his hands. He was the President's friend and they talked the same language when it came to money. He had powerful friends on Capitol Hill, and it was not difficult to mobilize them. Southern senators and congressmen were susceptible to suggestions that the desert made fertile by the waters of the dam would produce more Egyptian cotton, to compete with Southern cotton on the world market. Members with big Jewish constituencies were reminded that friends of Israel would be likely to resent such expensive favoritism toward their enemies. The anti-Communist lobby didn't need to be told that Nasser was playing around with the Russians.

Foster had said from the initial days of his incumbency that Acheson had failed in his foreign policy because he never listened to the voice of Congress, and that he would not make the same mistake. He heard the sound of raised voices now, and when they grew loud he decided to heed them. It had been a good ploy and it might have worked and brought the recalcitrant Nasser back into the fold. But if opinion was against him on the Hill, he did not feel that this was a cause worth fighting for. After all, what had Gamal Abdel Nasser done for him?

While all these maneuvers had been going on behind the scenes in Washington, Eugene Black of the World Bank and Hank Byroade, the U.S. ambassador, had been working on the Egyptians to persuade them to accept certain conditions in return for Anglo-American aid in building the dam. Nasser had turned and twisted like the wily eel he was to evade the financial net the Americans were trying to throw around him. But in July 1956, he finally gave way.

The indefatigable (and pro-American) Egyptian ambassador to Washington, Dr. Hussein, had returned to Cairo to explain to Nasser that opposition to the Aswan Dam project was building up rapidly in Congress, and that if he wanted it to go through it was now or never. To his astonishment, Nasser, who had procrastinated so adroitly, now instructed him to go back to the United States and gave him carte blanche to accept all Foster Dulles's conditions.

News that the ambassador was on his way back to sign the deal preceded him, and made headlines in all the newspapers. It also caused a turmoil in the State Department. Foster called an immediate meeting of his staff, and they went over the pros and cons of the loan for two

hours. Finally, as the Secretary listened without comment, all agreed that every clause would have to be fought bitterly through Congress and would cause such strife that, in the words of Robert Bowie, head of the Planning Staff, "on balance it just seemed that it wasn't worth the candle."

It was decided that it would be folly to go ahead and turn a promise into a signed commitment. In other words, no loan, even if it meant no Aswan Dam.

"On that part of it," Bowie said later, "I remember that we talked it out and I agreed with that conclusion. Then the second question was: How do we handle it? Now I remember here that I disagreed. I remember saying flatly: 'Well, if you tell him just like that it will be a slap in the face and it will likely cause some kind of a ruckus.' "

Bowie was all in favor of "negotiating the thing to death," as he put it, "so you don't ever say no but raise all sort of new problems and keep on delaying."

But Foster and the others didn't agree.

As Bowie put it:

"The others said: 'We have this fight on with Congress. If it looks like we're still going to back the dam, it's going to make it even more difficult to get through the foreign aid bill. Remember, we're still trying to get money through for Yugoslavia.' So the consensus was that we should go ahead and make the announcement right off, and that would take part of the weight of Congress off our necks and we'd have an easier job getting money for Yugoslavia. So it was decided to write this communiqué and hand it to Hussein when he came."

Foster had already decided that the Egyptian envoy must be met with a refusal, and he had telephoned President Eisenhower at Gettysburg to tell him so several days before (on July 13, 1956). If he had any regrets that the original plan had failed, he did not show them. Instead, he seemed to be looking forward to his meeting with Dr. Hussein and the publication of the communiqué. It would put Gamal Abdel Nasser in his place once and for all, and show him it did not pay to trifle with the power of the United States government.

The Egyptian ambassador was shown into Foster's office on the morning of July 19, 1956, accompanied by an aide. Herbert Hoover, Jr., and George V. Allen were also present, at least one of them a happy witness to the slaughter to come.

If Foster had any qualms about slapping down Dr. Hussein, whom he liked, who had worked hard for Egyptian-American rapprochement, they were quickly dissipated by a gaffe which the ambassador committed almost at the start. He announced that he had brought good news from Egypt and then added, skittishly, that he hoped the Americans weren't planning to renege on their promises about Aswan because (patting his pocket) if they did, he had here a promise from the Soviet government that they would finance and build the dam instead. It was not true, of course. The Soviet government had not even been approached about the dam.

For Foster's purpose, the envoy's remark was manna from heaven. One of his aides, John Hanes, once said he had only seen the Secretary lose his temper on two occasions, and both of them were artificial tantrums worked up to make an effect.

"One was with the Egyptian ambassador," Hanes said.

This was the occasion. Foster said:

"Mr. Ambassador, we are going to issue a statement. I am sorry, we are not going to help you with the Aswan Dam . . . We believe that anybody who builds the High Dam will earn the hatred of the Egyptian people, because the burden will be crushing . . . We don't want to be hated in Egypt, we are leaving this pleasure to the Soviet Union—if they really want to do it."

He then went on, with a sharpness which punctured Dr. Hussein like a toy balloon, to point out that the U.S. government did not accept ultimatums. He had been a good friend of President Nasser and the Egyptian people. He had done all he could to help the new régime. And how had he been repaid? With humiliation. This was the end of the road and he would tolerate it no longer. The whole world was watching the United States, especially small countries who wanted American aid, and he was determined to show them that this wasn't the way to play the game, and this was not the way to deal with the United States.

With that, Herbert Hoover, Jr., handed over to the crestfallen envoy a copy of the communiqué which was, at that moment, being issued to the press. It had been much harsher in tone a few hours earlier, but Robert Bowie had protested and had been allowed by Foster to rewrite it in milder terms.

"If you read that thing over again," Bowie said later, "you'll find that there is all sorts of palaver about our love for the Egyptian people and our hope of being able to cooperate in different ways, all that sort of stuff. So in that sense I suppose I had an effect in that the communiqué was as bland as possible. But of course there was no way to be bland. If you say what Foster had said to the Egyptian envoy, which was: *No, we're not going to do it, you're not credit-worthy,* it was bound to be incendiary."

Dr. Hussein scurried from the room to cable the bad news to his master. As one of Foster's aides remarked as he went by: "He looks as if he's had a kick in the pants."

But how was Nasser going to take it? If the jubilant Herbert Hoover, Jr., was not worrying about that, there is evidence that Foster may have been.

Normally, at the end of his working day at State, Foster went through the office in which Phyllis Bernau, his personal secretary, and William Macomber, his chief of staff, worked, and went straight on to the elevator. But on the day the decision was made, he changed his routine.

"I was working on papers . . ." Macomber said later, "and I didn't even notice that instead of walking out straight he had turned right and slumped himself down in this chair right in front of my desk. Of course when I spotted him sitting across from me I stood up, and he said: 'Sit down, Bill.' I sat down again. He said: 'Well, this has been quite a day.' I said: 'Yes, sir.' 'Well,' he said, 'I hope we did the right thing.' I've forgotten what I said; that I hoped so or something like that, and then he said again: 'Yes, I certainly hope we did the right thing.' Then he got up and left. But he never did that before, or after."

Gamal Abdel Nasser was on an official visit to President Tito of Yugoslavia when the news reached him. Jawaharlal Nehru was also there, and Nasser passed over the envoy's cable for the Indian leader to read.

"Those people, how arrogant they are," Nehru said.

The Indian and Egyptian presidents flew back together to Cairo from Brioni and arrived about midnight. All the foreign ambassadors accredited to Egypt were lined up to greet them, including Hank

Byroade, acute embarrassment on his face. Nasser passed him without any expression, but a few minutes later sent an aide to tell the American ambassador that he wanted to see him.

When the Egyptian and the American were alone together, Nasser said:

"You know, I've had a lot to do with the Russians, and I don't like the Russians. I've had a lot to do with your people, and basically I like your people. This action of Mr. Dulles is an action against me by a great power, and no great power can take action against me without taking into account the necessary consequences of it." He stabbed a finger into Byroade's chest. "And the necessary consequences are that you fellows are out to kill me. And all I can do is protect myself. I tell you this. I am not going to be killed."

Byroade did not have the courage to ask him what he was going to do, though he was shrewd enough to suspect, from Nasser's words, that one of the consequences of all this could well be that henceforward Russia would earn herself a foothold inside the Middle East.

Meantime, in the United States, Great Britain, and France, Foster Dulles was something of a hero, hailed as a brilliant statesman who had firmly put an upstart dictator in his place. *Time* Magazine had a caption in its issue that week saying: "Master Chessman Dulles made his finest move."

Bill Macomber underlined the phrase and sent the magazine in to Foster, who said to him later: "Bill, it's much too early to tell. We must wait and see what their reaction is."

But of all the guesses which had been made in the Department about what Nasser would do, none predicted that he would hit the Western allies where it hurt most, by taking over the Suez Canal.

On the night of July 26, 1956, British Prime Minister Anthony Eden was giving a dinner at 10 Downing Street for King Feisal of Iraq and his premier, Nuri Said. A messenger arrived from the Foreign Office with a note. Gamal Abdel Nasser had just made a speech in Manchia Square, Alexandria, Egypt, announcing that he was canceling immediately the Anglo-French concession and nationalizing the Suez Canal.

Eden was in no condition to absorb shocks of this kind. Physically, mentally, and politically, he was in a poor way. Some time back he had been operated on for trouble in the bile duct, and it had gone badly

wrong. Restorative surgery had somewhat alleviated the situation, but the experience seemed to have exacerbated his weaknesses. He had always had a sharp temper and now he was subject to fits of ungovernable rage. He had always been sensitive to criticism—and there was plenty around among his more diehard Tory colleagues at the moment —but now he just could not take it.

Unstable, seeing conspiracies everywhere, he had long since decided that Gamal Abdel Nasser was scheming the downfall of the British Empire (he still believed there was a British Empire), and that he was a tinpot dictator, a Nilotic Hitler, who must be removed from the scene before he set the Middle East afire.

The nationalization of the Suez Canal was the last straw. He did not smile when Nuri Said, attempting a joke to relieve the sudden tension, pointed to a bust of Benjamin Disraeli in the hall of No. 10 and said: "That's the old Jew who got you into all this trouble."*

Instead, he got rid of his Iraqi guests and called an emergency meeting at No. 10 of the inner cabinet, the Chiefs of Staff, a representative from the U.S. Embassy, and a French director of the Suez Canal Company.

"It was a deeply humiliating meeting," William Clark, Eden's press secretary, said later. "In effect, the prime minister said there had been an act of aggression against us and, while asking the Foreign Office to look into our legal remedies, he wished to respond forcefully and immediately. What could the Chiefs of Staff recommend? Their answer was ill-prepared but perfectly clear: we could do nothing immediately. It was suddenly obvious that Britain was armed to participate in a nuclear armageddon with the Soviet Union or in small colonial guerilla wars (e.g., against EOKA in Cyprus and against the Mau-Mau in Kenya) but had no capacity for this kind of emergency."

It was what Nasser was banking on. He had already had a survey made by his own military experts, who had told him that neither the British nor the French had the means of mounting a military expedition against him without at least a month of preparation. He had not declared the nationalization of the Canal until he was certain of that. And to make sure that, in the interim, hot heads would cool down, he

*Benjamin Disraeli, twice British prime minister (1868 and 1874–80), bought a large block of Suez Canal shares in 1875, thus giving Britain a controlling interest with the French in the waterway.

had been careful to stress in his declaration that he was not closing the Canal, only taking over the company, and that ships of all nations* would continue to pass through freely—so long as they paid their dues. Moreover, he announced that he was prepared to pay compensation to the Anglo-French shareholders of the Suez Canal Company.

There. Once they had got used to the idea, and once they realized that they couldn't immediately invade Egypt and usurp him, it would all settle down. It would all settle down, and he would have proved to the world that even Foster Dulles and the United States couldn't make a fool of him. He would still build the Aswan Dam out of the revenues from the Canal, under the supervision of absolutely nobody.

On the morning of July 27, a lawyer was shown into Anthony Eden's office with a report from the legal department of the Foreign Office. It stated that the situation had been examined from all angles and unless Nasser closed the Canal to shipping—which he was not proposing to do—the nationalization was quite legal.

Eden took the report, read it through, then tore it into pieces and flung it in the lawyer's face.

He now began orchestrating a campaign to prepare the British public for an invasion of Egypt and the restoration of the Canal into "the hands of its rightful owners." In a TV address to the nation he stressed that Britain could never allow the Canal to remain in the hands of "foreigners," since it was vital for the nation's oil supplies. His Chancellor of the Exchequer, Harold Macmillan, was meanwhile saying that he would rather pawn all the pictures in the National Gallery than be humiliated by Nasser, and told any dinner guest who happened to be listening that doing nothing would mean the end of the British Empire, and "Britain would become another Netherlands if it yielded." The Dutch ambassador, who heard the remark, luckily had a sense of humor.

Those who opposed the increasing belligerency of the prime minister and his inner clique were angrily called "weak sisters" by Eden. When news came from Washington that Foster Dulles was not at all pleased by the way events were going in Britain, and was sending Robert Murphy over to smooth things down, Eden lashed out and said

*Except those of the "enemy," Israel.

he would rather the Empire fell in one crash than be eaten away by mice.

But he was not really worried about the detestable Dulles. When it came to the crux, it was Eisenhower who was in charge of the United States, and Eisenhower would not let him down. After all, he was an old friend and comrade, and he knew about war. As Macmillan kept on saying, once Great Britain took action Ike would "lie doggo" and let them get on with it, and that was all they needed.

It was the costliest miscalculation the British had ever made.

CHAPTER TWENTY-FOUR

"A Very Sloppy Performance"

Everyone in London had got so worked up by this time that the Secretary's special envoy, Robert Murphy, telephoned to say that unless Foster came over himself and did some heavy persuading he couldn't answer for the consequences. Three-way conversations with the British and the French were getting nowhere because of the conspiratorial uncommunicativeness of the French, and because no British delegate knew what Anthony Eden was going to do or say next. Whitehall and the diplomatic salons were rife with rumors about the volcanic nature of the prime minister's choler, and the almost Pavlovian frothing at the mouth that occurred when the name of Nasser was mentioned to him.

A minister of state in the British cabinet, Anthony Nutting, was still metaphorically wiping the flecks of spittle out of his eyes after one encounter with Eden's growing fanaticism. He and advisers in the Foreign Office had concocted a memorandum suggesting that the best way to handle the Nasser situation was for Britain to make overtures to the leaders of the other Arab nations, in such a way that the Egyptian leader would be isolated. He was in the middle of dinner with Harold Stassen, an American expert at the three-way conversations, when he was summoned to the telephone, and it was Eden.

"What is all this poppycock you've sent me?" Eden demanded. "What's all this about isolating Nasser, or neutralizing him, as you call it? I want him destroyed, can't you understand? I want him removed, and if you and the Foreign Office don't agree, then you'd better come to the cabinet and explain why."

Nutting tried to calm him by saying that, before removing Nasser,

it might be as well to have an alternative leader to take his place, otherwise there would be chaos in Egypt.

"But I don't want an alternative," Eden shouted. "And I don't give a damn if there's anarchy and chaos in Egypt."

Two days after that incident, the well-known military expert, Captain Liddell-Hart, had come to see the prime minister at 10 Downing Street. Eden had asked him for an outline of how a military campaign should be fought in Egypt, and Liddell-Hart had written one for him —only to have it sent back, with curt demands for alterations, no less than four times. Finally, rather than do a fifth revision, he had sent in the original outline and decided to leave it at that. Eden summoned him and said:

"Captain Liddell-Hart, here I am at a critical moment in Britain's history, arranging matters which may mean the life and death of the British Empire. And what happens? I ask you to do a simple military chore for me, and it takes you five attempts—plus my vigilance amid all my worries—before you get it right."

"But sir," Liddell-Hart said, "it hasn't taken five attempts. That version, which you now say is just what you wanted, is the original version."

There was a moment's silence. Eden's handsome face went first pale and then red. He looked across at the long, languid shape of Captain Liddell-Hart, clad in a smart off-white summer outfit, then he reached out a hand, grasped one of the heavy, old-fashioned Downing Street inkwells, and flung it at his visitor. Another silence. Liddell-Hart looked down at the sickly blue stains spreading across his immaculate linen suiting, uncoiled himself, picked up a government-issue wastepaper basket, and jammed it over the prime minister's head before slowly walking out of the room.

Rumors of the prime minister's mood reached Washington. It was time, Foster decided, to cross the Atlantic and do some smoothing down.

His opinion of Eden's alertness was not improved at their first meeting after his arrival in London on August 1. William Macomber and Roderick O'Connor had flown over with him, and O'Connor remembers that almost immediately they went to a meeting at 10 Downing Street to discuss the problems created by Nasser's takeover. Anthony

Eden's first statement was to remind the Americans that what had happened was strictly illegal and breached the treaty Britain and France had signed, generations earlier, with the Bey of Egypt.

"Dulles asked to see the treaty," O'Connor said later. "Mr. Eden was taken very much by surprise and ordered his private secretary to find the treaty. It was half an hour before they got hold of a copy of it. And it was soon obvious, in the context, that neither Eden nor any of his staff had really read the darned thing."

O'Connor added:

"And Dulles was appalled. I remember he reacted very sharply to that. Well, it was a hell of a way to run a railroad. I remember it wasn't a very long document, a very slim one, easy to read. When Dulles got it he just gobbled it up. Well, that was a very sloppy performance. The British did not know what they were talking about. And I think this impression of Eden became the dominating impression in Dulles's mind. Eden wasn't doing his homework."

If that was the way Foster Dulles really felt, he concealed it well from Eden and his confrères in the next few days. One of the Englishmen with whom he really got on well was Lord Salisbury (known to his intimates as "Bobbety"), leader of the Tory Party in the House of Lords, son of a distinguished family of English statesmen, and a staunch supporter of the Eden line toward Nasser. Foster went to weekend with him at Hatfield House, the ancestral Salisbury home near London, and was taken by his host on a tour of the picture galleries from which long lines of famous family statesmen and their dames looked down in lofty disdain upon the ordinary mortal men below.

"Salisbury got to talking about Suez," said Rod O'Connor later, "and how it was just an impossible affront to the British. That this could be done by Nasser! Dulles's comment was that he then recognized for the first time, and was made suddenly keenly aware of, the emotionalism that the Suez situation created in the British. I think he was quite shocked and saddened that this had gripped hold of a man whom he regarded as having real intellectual ability. He sort of shook his head and said it was a human but painful thing to see."

Anthony Eden had contemplated the Secretary's arrival with absolutely no relish at all, but was surprised to find him forthcoming,

friendly, and sympathetic. Foster made it clear at once that he agreed with a statement the prime minister had made in the House of Commons in which he said that no settlement of the Egyptian crisis would be satisfactory that left the Suez Canal "in the unfettered control of a single power" which could then "exploit it purely for the purposes of national policy." The Secretary then went on to declare that ways must be found "to make Nasser disgorge."

This was the kind of language Eden wanted to hear from his American allies, and he began to feel that perhaps he had done Foster an injustice in the past. Pompous, rigid, pious, and blundering he might be, but when it came to the historical crunch he was showing himself understanding, helpful, and amenable.

That impression grew in Eden's mind the following day after a long conversation which the two men had alone. And this is where a mystery begins. Foster went to see the prime minister at 10 Downing Street on the morning of August 2, taking William Macomber with him. Macomber sat in the hall while the two men talked. When they came out, Foster introduced him to Eden, they walked together to the door, and the prime minister saw them into their car.

They were driving back to the U.S. Embassy when Foster said: "Anthony said a strange thing to me just a few minutes ago. Anthony said I'm going to go down in history as one of the great foreign ministers."

Macomber, remembering the cold relations between the men, and having in mind that they were right in the middle of the Suez crisis, thought this extraordinary and said so: "My gosh, it's strange he said that."

Foster again confirmed that he had said it, and they drove on through the traffic in silence. After a time, Foster said:

"You know, Bill, nobody knows and nobody's going to know really for at least twenty-five years, the reason being that all the returns aren't in. And for this same reason, nobody knows whether I'm doing a good job or a bad job as Secretary of State. This is a great comfort for me when people are certain I'm doing a bad job, and criticize me so severely. I realize that they don't really know and the returns aren't in. I take some comfort in that. I remember this, and it's comforting when people criticize me as severely as some people do. But it works both ways. And when you're excessively praised, you've got to discount that too. Because they don't know either. Your friends don't know either."

Macomber was fascinated that these comments could have been triggered off by Eden's praise, and realized that Foster was "sort of bemused by it."

But what had Foster said, pledged, or promised Anthony Eden to have spurred him into making such a fulsome statement? There is no official record and Foster does not appear to have told Macomber anything about his conversation with the prime minister except for the flattering remark. Eden, however, is quite clear about what was said.

He told Foster that he did not feel that a peaceful solution of the Suez crisis was possible, and that the only language Nasser understood was force. The British and French had already begun preparations to take back what belonged to them. The CIA station chief in London was trying to find out what those preparations were. Should Eden tell him —or should he tell Foster? Foster replied that he did not want to know. But, went on Eden, did Foster agree that what they were doing was right? Foster said he fully understood the Anglo-French point of view. The prime minister then said that neither the British nor the French governments would ask for the military help of the United States when they "took steps to restore the situation in Egypt," but would they be able to count on the moral support of the Americans? Foster replied that the British government could *always* count on the moral support *and* sympathy of the United States, and Anthony (Foster always called him Anthony) need have absolutely no qualms about that. Eden then said he thought the situation would come to a head some time in October—but was here interrupted by Foster, who told him firmly that he did not want to know anything about the Anglo-French plans. It would be better that way.

"So, of course," Eden said later, "one took great care not to inform him, officially or otherwise, when the time came."

He added:

"Perhaps that was a mistake. It might have been better if one had sent a message, a personal message, to Ike just before the balloon went up. I take the blame for that. I should have relied on the good sense and support of my old friend Ike. But I thought that he had been kept in touch with my conversation with his Secretary of State. Foster misled me."

Did Foster, in fact, inform the President of his talk with the prime minister? It would be fascinating to know. Because later on one of the

principal reasons given by his friends for Eisenhower's anger at his British and French allies was that they failed to let him know what they were going to do, and when.

Allen Dulles came back from his round-the-world tour at the height of the Suez crisis and immediately called a conference of his deputies, a Watch Tower meeting. He heard a roundup from the CIA's station chiefs in London, Paris, Tel Aviv, and Cairo, and was told that in London the SIS had suddenly crawled into its shell and was saying nothing. Tel Aviv reported that General Dayan was missing and was believed to be in France, where it was hardly likely that he was simply saying thank you to the French air force for flying two squadrons of manned Mystères into Israel. The senior members of the French cabinet, the Paris station chief reported, were doing what they always did in moments of national crisis or decision: they had retreated to the country to talk and plan in the tapestried halls of a moated château, with the drawbridge up. In Cairo, Gamal Abdel Nasser was relying on kismet and his luck. He had little else if the worst came to the worst. He had asked the Soviet Union for help in the event of an invasion, and had been told that Moscow was prepared to mobilize troops and announce maneuvers as a show of strength, but he mustn't expect anything more.

Allen told his deputies that his own source of information in the French cabinet was now insisting that agreement had been reached and plans made for a joint British-French-Israeli invasion of Egypt. He could understand the French and the Israelis collaborating with each other, since they were both fighting the Arabs;* but he found it hard to believe that the British would risk compromising their relations with their Arab protégés in Iraq, Jordan, and the Persian Gulf by teaming themselves up with the Israelis.

Richard Bissell produced U-2 pictures of British convoys assembling in Malta and Cyprus, and French ships taking on military supplies in Marseilles and Toulon, and dryly remarked that they were hardly there for a regatta.

At this Robert Amory interjected that Eden was now so mad at Nasser that he would team up with anyone who would help wipe him

---

*The French were at that time fighting the Algerian rebellion, which was being supported by Egyptian arms and propaganda.

413

out. Amory, an amiable, eloquent Harvard law professor, had some excellent contacts in high places in Britain, where he often visited the English branch of his family. A second cousin, Derek Heathcote Amory (later Viscount Amory), was a member of Eden's cabinet. He said he had heard that almost everyone on the British General Staff was dead against a military operation in Egypt, since they had not had adequate time to prepare, had few ships and slow ones, and a quite inadequate number of landing craft. Earl Mountbatten, the queen's uncle and First Sea Lord at the Admiralty, was rumored to have had a row with the prime minister over the paucity of equipment and the dangers of the adventure.

As for the Israelis (Amory went on), he had just had a message from his man in the U.S. Embassy in Tel Aviv who said:

"My Israeli chauffeur has been called up for military service. He has lost one leg and is C3 from the 1948 war. But he has still been called up, and I would say that this means the Israelis are serious and are calling up everything they've got. This time it isn't maneuvers or just standing still on the frontier."

James Angleton, chief of Counterintelligence and Counterespionage, listened to this with a smile of disbelief on his face. Angleton was known to his colleagues by this time as "No Knock" Angleton "because he was the man who would come into Allen's office through the bathroom door, he did not have to be announced." He was apt to regard other members of the Agency, with the possible exception of Frank Wisner, with a slight quiver of the nostrils, as if they brought an odor into the air that was not quite pleasant. He was considered by Allen to be the Agency's great expert on Israeli affairs because, over the years, he had increased and consolidated his close liaison with the Israeli intelligence apparatus, Mossad, which passed him useful information and sometimes participated in actions with his operatives. He now said:

"Amory's remark may sound alarming, but I think I can discount it. I've spent last evening and most of the early hours with my Israeli friends in Washington, and I can assure you that it's all part of maneuvers and is certainly not meant for any serious attack. There is nothing in it. I do not believe there is going to be an attack by the Israelis."

He spoke with such authority that Amory's information was discounted, for the moment, anyway. If "No Knock" said the Israelis were

not going to attack, then he had to be believed.

But Amory, who did not like Angleton and loathed his arrogant, self-confident air, checked back and was more than ever certain he was right.

That evening he got a call from Allen Dulles asking him if he would come to a meeting the following morning (October 27) to discuss with Foster a speech he was planning to make that night in Dallas. A survey of the world situation, it would be Foster's only formal participation in the election campaign, and it would include references to the Middle East. They assembled next day for a nine o'clock meeting, and copies of the speech were on the table to be gone through paragraph by paragraph as Foster read it aloud.

When they came to the part about the Middle East and Foster read: "We cannot guarantee a peaceful outcome . . . " the dozen or so present nodded their agreement, but Amory intervened.

"Mr. Secretary," he said, "if you say that and war breaks out twenty-four hours later, you will appear to all the world as *partie prise* to the Israeli aggression—and I'm positive the Israelis will attack the Sinai shortly after midnight tomorrow."

Allen looked flustered and said: "That's much stronger than the Watch Committee's conclusion yesterday."

To which Amory replied: "Okay. I'm sticking my neck out. I'm only a $16,000-a-year CIA official, but I'm prepared to lay my job on the line that there's a war coming tomorrow or the day after."

He was right. The Israelis moved into the Sinai Desert two days later. Fortunately, Foster had removed the offending references from his speech, and later thanked Amory for his intervention.

By the time Foster was ready to leave for Dallas, he could not have been in much doubt that Amory was right and there was going to be war in the Middle East. Nor can the President have been left in ignorance of what was happening, even though it is true that the conspirators hoped to the last to keep the U.S. government in the dark.

After leaving the State Department conference, and before taking the plane for Texas, Foster went on to a meeting of the National Security Council. When it was over Admiral Arleigh H. Burke, chief of U.S. Naval Operations, who had taken part in the discussions, buttonholed Foster in the corridor and said he would like to talk with him.

Admiral Burke had already informed Foster when the Middle East

crisis first erupted that he planned to keep his Mediterranean forces mobile, so that "nobody will get caught by surprise." Now he told the Secretary it was obvious that the British and French were about ready to go, and that he had signaled his ships to move in toward Egypt. He added that he was worried about British preparations for the action. He had gone one better than Robert Amory and had actually talked to Lord Mountbatten, the First Sea Lord at the British Admiralty in London, and had been told that everything was "in a hell of a mess" in Malta and in Cyprus, where war vessels and supply ships were assembled. Mountbatten said Eden and hard-line members of the cabinet had badgered and bothered the General Staff so much, and given and retracted so many orders, that now the moment had come to begin operations they just didn't have enough of the right ships and enough landing craft for a swift, incisive operation and landing in Egypt.

"The British can't do it," Burke told Foster. "The reason the British can't do it is because they're totally unprepared." He pointed out that they were mounting the operation from Malta, over 1,000 miles away, and they only had slow boats and a lack of landing vessels. He went on: "For God's sake, let's give them the craft. Give them ours. They're over there. They've got to make this thing successful."

Foster replied that he didn't think this would be proper. As if referring to some errant schoolboy who was reported to be masturbating in the toilet, he said primly that he didn't think the British should be doing it. "Maybe," replied Burke, "but we've got to supply them, I think."

"We can't," said Foster, firmly.

Admiral Burke took the matter to a formal meeting of the Joint Chiefs of Staff, and a report of their views and conclusions was sent to both the White House and the State Department. They began by tacitly accepting that an Anglo-French operation was going to take place. They would have been foolish not to, since their opposite numbers in the British General Staff had so informed them. The only thing they weren't sure about was whether the Israelis were included in the military plan or were simply exploiting the situation. The Joint Chiefs of Staff left it to the President to decide whether military assistance in the form of landing craft should be offered to the British. But they did express the feelings about the coming operation. In Admiral Burke's words: "The Joint Chiefs submitted their recommendation [to the

White House] that we should be a kindly observer on this occasion, and not put things in the way of the British."

So it was not exactly a surprise to the President when the invasion took place. Both the French and the Israelis kept their mouths shut, and so did Prime Minister Eden and most members of his cabinet; but practically every senior general, admiral, and air marshal in the British armed forces was keeping the U.S. Joint Chiefs informed of every move they were making.

On the other hand, there was a presidential election in progress in the United States, and it seems that Dwight Eisenhower's advisers—and Foster Dulles must have been one of them—considered that it would seriously hamper his chances of defeating Democratic candidate Adlai Stevenson if he were officially cognizant of the complots his British and French allies were engaged in, and appeared to be giving them his tacit approval.

In fact, there was never a chance that Eisenhower would lose the election. The American people believed in his sincerity as a President, and, more important in this instance, they respected his judgment as a military leader. He had no need of concealment. He could have spoken out, for or against it, as soon as he knew there was going to be a war in the Middle East, and the electorate would have given him their wholesale vote of approval. His later indignation was pure hypocrisy.

Early on the morning of October 31, 1956, a U-2 reconnaissance plane flying out of the United States air base at Adana, Turkey, passed over Egypt in the course of its sweep across the eastern Mediterranean. The U-2s did not have special instruments aboard and relied on celestial navigation; their normal practice when passing over a reconnaissance target on the ground below was to make a 270° turn and fly over it for a second time before going on to the next leg of the flight. The reason for this was to be certain that on each leg the pilot started from directly over his target once more, precisely by dead reckoning.

The U-2 on this mission had been instructed to fly over the principal military airport outside Cairo, and then take a 270° turn to the west and north and fly over it again in an easterly direction. He did so. When his photographs were developed, the experts in the photo-interpretation section rang their alarm bells. Ten minutes had elapsed between

417

the two sets of pictures taken over Cairo airfield. The first showed Egyptian military aircraft peacefully on the ground, the second planes, hangars, and installations burning fiercely. In the intervening ten minutes the Royal Air Force had been in and destroyed them.

The CIA telephotoed the pictures to the RAF and got a message back:

WARM THANKS FOR PIX. IT'S THE QUICKEST BOMB DAMAGE ASSESSMENT WE'VE EVER HAD.

The U.S. Chief of Naval Operations, Admiral Burke, telephoned Foster to tell him that the British and French had sailed and were on the way to Egypt. The Secretary seemed deeply distressed at the news and asked whether it wouldn't be possible to stop them.

"Mr. Secretary," replied Burke, "there is only one way we can stop them. We can stop them but we will have to blast hell out of them."

"Can't you stop them some other way?" Foster asked.

"No," said Burke. "If we're going to threaten, if we're going to turn on them, then you've got to be ready to shoot. I can't give these people orders to do something they can't do in the first place, no matter who gives them orders, to make a demand and then get laughed at. The only way you can stop them is to shoot. And we can do that. We can defeat them. The British, the French, and the Egyptians and the Israelis, the whole goddamn works of them we can knock off, if you want. But that's the only way we can do it."

While Foster went off to consult with his brother, with the NSC, and with the President, Burke flashed an order to Captain "Cat" Brown, commanding the U.S. naval force in the Mediterranean, telling him to be prepared for anything, "to have his bombs up, to be checked out, so as to be able to fight either another naval force or against land targets, and to make sure of all his targeting data."

Captain Brown signaled back:

"WHO'S THE ENEMY?"

"DON'T TAKE ANY GUFF FROM ANYBODY," Burke replied.

Burke said later that "I didn't know *who* the damned enemy was, because we were having the discussion, that was the basis of that."

As it turned out, the U.S. ships never did get the order to take action, and it was the verbal guns fired in the United Nations by Foster and Henry Cabot Lodge, the American ambassador to the UN, which

finally sank the British and the French. Burke suspected that Foster was distressed about the whole Suez fiasco.

"I knew he was unhappy about the British," Burke said later. "I was unhappy about the British too, but for a different reason. Unhappy because they were doing a job inadequately prepared and directed by somebody who apparently didn't know what the hell he was talking about. I later found out from Mountbatten that the British government gave the chiefs the order like that—snap. Without the time for preparation."

He added that he thought Foster was "just as wrong as hell about this Suez thing," but that he had "acted from a high sense of honor. He didn't stoop to things other people have done . . ."

Frank Wisner was furious with the British, French, and Israelis. By taking action in the Middle East at such a moment they were in danger of sabotaging the best chance the CIA had had since the war to overturn Soviet hegemony in eastern Europe. The people of the satellite nations were at last turning on their Russian masters and beginning to fight for their freedom. First the Poles had risen against shortages, restrictions, and the heavy hand of the secret police, and had sullenly accepted a temporary truce only when Krushchev had personally promised to look into their grievances.

Now it was Hungary's turn. There the revolution was in full flood. From his station in Munich, Wisner poured out propaganda to swell the stormy waters and breach the Soviet dams that contained them. And as the revolt increased in intensity and the anti-Soviet rebels took over in Budapest, he stepped up the signals, saying:

"Hold on. Your friends in the West are coming."

And he meant it. Wisner was in a highly excitable mood, filled with a heady euphoria at what was happening. All the hard work he had put into covert operations and anti-Soviet activity was now coming to fruition. The people were on the rise. His private armies were ready. He came into Allen Dulles's office and asked for permission to give them the signal to go—hoping it would not be long before Hungary was followed by East Germany, Czechoslovakia, and Poland in reestablishing democracy in eastern Europe.

To his unconcealed chagrin, the permission was not forthcoming. Allen listened with intense interest to the reports coming in from

Hungary, where anti-Soviet rebels had taken over the Hungarian capital. Wisner eloquently argued that they must be given aid and given
it urgently. He asked for an airlift to provide them with immediate
supplies of arms and trained reinforcements. Soon it would be too late.
There were reports from Rumania and Bulgaria that the red armies
were on the march, charged with suppressing the rebellion.

"We must act now," he kept saying. "How can they fight back at the
Soviet tanks with rifles and machine guns? We must give them anti-
tank weapons and expert cadres to lead them. Now now now. It must
be done now, before it is too late!"

Wisner's fellow members at these Watch Tower meetings, studying
Allen's face, got the feeling that to begin with he had been wholeheart-
edly in Wisner's camp, even if he prudently did not say so. In the first
flush of the Hungarian uprising, there was a glint in his eye and a halo
of euphoria around him, as if he too felt that this was the beginning
of the great anti-Communist crusade. But then, as the Anglo-French
operation at Suez got under way, and it became apparent that the
United States was going to block it, he began to give more and more
priority to the Egyptian affair. He was in close consultation with his
brother, both on the telephone and over at State, and their conversations conditioned his reactions. "How can anything be done about the
Russians, even if they suppress the revolt," he was soon asking, "when
our own allies are guilty of exactly similar acts of aggression?" Wisner
dragged back the old fighting words from the early days of Foster
Dulles's tenure at State: "What about 'liberation' and 'rollback'? And,
in any case, since the United States is now taking a stand against her
allies at Suez, have we not recovered the moral right to take a stand
against our enemies and come to the aid of the Hungarians in their
fight with the Russians?"

Allen tried gently to explain that it just wasn't in the cards. With a
presidential election on his hands, the Secretary just wasn't about to
advise the President to do anything. Except talk, of course. Speeches
in the United Nations condemning Soviet barbarism, and words of
encouragement to the "brave slave nations of eastern Europe" were
good for the ethnic vote. But action was dangerous. It could rebound
in the voting booths, and was to be strictly eschewed.

As it slowly sank into Wisner's head that nothing was going to
happen, that Soviet tanks were going to be allowed to grind down the

rebels in Budapest, that all his clandestine activity had been so much show, his mood changed. His euphoria ebbed away, to be replaced by alcohol. He began coming to the office with a high whiskey flush on his chubby face, and colleagues began to remark that they didn't like his tone of voice or the glint in his eyes.

One day, at a committee meeting, he suddenly lashed out that all of them around the table were "a bunch of goddamned Commies," and that they were betraying the American people. In subsequent days he stayed home, with his worried wife, and the bottle. Soon Polly Wisner was calling up anxiously to say that Frank kept taking out his revolver and talking to it. The rumor spread through the Agency that Frank was out gunning for someone, but no one was quite sure who it was. Maybe himself.

Allen passed the word to the Agency medical staff, which had handled this sort of emergency before. Arrangements were made for Frank Wisner's hospitalization.

Events in Egypt and Hungary had been running side by side. By the time the British and French armies had landed and occupied the Suez Canal Zone, Soviet tanks were rolling through the streets of Budapest in a savage suppression of the uprising. Unless the United States was prepared to intervene and risk a full-scale war with the Soviets, it was too late to help the Hungarians. No words of condemnation were likely to divert the Red Army from its task of putting down the revolution, and words were the only weapons that anyone was prepared to utilize. The presidential campaigners dug into their dictionaries for fighting epithets to make their revulsion at Soviet actions clear, but were ultra-careful to make sure that there were no threats of reprisal, and no rattling of swords.

On the other hand, the Anglo-French operation was much more susceptible to pressure. A resolution had been made in the United Nations Security Council condemning the British and French invasion of Egypt, but it had been vetoed by the two powers. Thereupon, Henry Cabot Lodge, the U.S. representative at the UN, had hurriedly—too hurriedly, some people were to say later—invoked a means of bringing the matter before the General Assembly at the UN, where a majority vote would prevail, terming the Anglo-French action a threat to world peace. A full dress debate was due to begin and Cabot Lodge was

polishing up a fighting speech for the occasion, spelling out exactly what he thought of the behavior of America's allies.

He never had a chance to deliver it. Foster Dulles, never one to miss a big occasion, and not over-fond of Cabot Lodge,* curtly informed him that he (Foster) would act as spokesman and "give a little more impetus" to the debate.

November 1, 1956, the day of the Assembly debate, was one of the worst flying days of the year. There were heavy fog and storms, commercial flights had been grounded, and, in the words of Carl McCardle, Foster's press spokesman, who traveled with him, "even the birds were down."

Foster had never had any fear of flying. He ordered the Air Force plane to take off, but they soon ran into heavy weather, and the pilot decided to stay over a clear space just north of Philadelphia and circle there until he got the signal that one of the fields had opened up. But all of them, Idlewild, La Guardia, Newark, were fogged in. While they cruised around, Foster and his legal adviser, Herman Phleger, paid no attention to conditions outside but concentrated on drafting a Cease-Fire Resolution, which would be put to the General Assembly vote, and the Anglo-French invasion brought to a halt. They had just about got it into shape when the pilot signaled that there was a hole in the cloud cover over Newark, and they buckled up their seat belts and dived in. Cars had been stationed at every available field, and they were rushed to the UN. They were late. The debate was already on its way. Sir Pierson Dickson, the British delegate, had just finished a long peroration justifying British actions when Foster and his party came in.

There was a strained moment as the two men eyed each other. Dickson was about to turn away abruptly when Foster held out his hand. Did Dickson remember a similar occasion, with Chou En-lai and Foster at opposite ends of a handshake, as he saw the Secretary's gesture? If so, his reaction was different. He shook hands with Foster. But, as the photographers crowded in for a shot, a British aide shouted: "Don't smile, sir!" and the expression went out of Dickson's good-humored face to become wooden as the cameras clicked.

Then Foster spoke. Read coldly years afterwards, it was far from being one of his better speeches. On the other hand, it was delivered

*Who had a habit of wasting Foster's time with "trivial matters," and, even worse, going over his head to talk directly with the President.

extemporaneously, it was spoken with feeling, and it made crystal clear to every delegate that the United States was determined to stop the British and French, and to do so urgently and with no ambiguity. When he sat down there was a scattered round of applause—but not from Sir Pierson Dickson, who had hurriedly left the Assembly chamber.

Herman Phleger noticed that Foster looked tired. It had been a long, hard day. He suggested that the Secretary should leave, go back to his quarters at the Waldorf Astoria, and get some sleep. But McCardle objected, pointing out that if the Secretary left, most of the other delegates might do so too. The vote was not in.

"We know that as long as you're sitting there," McCardle said, "the delegates on our side* won't dare to vote against the resolution, and without your presence they might, or abstain."

So Foster stayed on as delegate after delegate rose to speak. It was not until 1:00 A.M. that the vote finally came. It was all but unanimous, only New Zealand voting with the British and French against it.

Once more Phleger suggested the Secretary should leave, and once more McCardle intervened. He pointed out that Brosio, the Italian delegate, had only agreed to go along with the Cease-Fire Resolution providing the United States would agree to back a further resolution, this one condemning Soviet Russia for its actions in suppressing the Hungarian rising.

"So he stayed on," said McCardle. "There was some mix-up about his getting to the floor and speaking. He had to listen to about ten fulsome speeches until about three or four in the morning before he rose to make his speech. He was a very weary man, shoulders bent with fatigue, as he mounted the rostrum and in a hoarse voice and again spontaneously said the United States wanted to associate the United States with the Italian proposal."

This resolution was passed too, but it was after 5:00 A.M. when the delegation got back to the Waldorf Astoria. Foster drank an unusually large glass of Overholt whiskey before retiring to bed. Phleger again noticed that his chief looked abnormally tired, not himself by any means, though he did make it plain he wanted to be back at his office in Washington before noon the following day. *He should take the day off,*

---

*He meant by "our side" America's Western allies, many of whom were secretly in favor of the Anglo-French action. The "other side," consisting of neutral, Arab, and pro-Soviet nations, was automatically supporting the resolution.

Phleger thought. *This time it's really been too much for him.*

But they were off on schedule from La Guardia at 10:30 next morning.

The Russians made some loud and angry noises over the resolution condemning their action in Hungary, but otherwise took no notice of it. It certainly had no effect upon the brutality with which they now began hunting down all suspected anti-Communists in Hungary.

The British and French, too, were reluctant to obey the UN Resolution concerning their operations, especially when the cease-fire order was immediately followed by United States pressure to force them into an immediate evacuation of their troops from the Suez Canal. It would be a supreme humiliation for both Eden and Great Britain, and the prime minister, in alternating bursts of rage and tears, was all for holding on and brazening things out. So were some of his generals, especially those who had had previous experience in Egypt and were confident they could hold on to their gains, no matter what was brought against them.

But times were against them. Eden had lost the support of the bulk of his cabinet and most of the British people. Nasser had effectively blocked the Canal by sinking ships in it. The pipeline from Arabia to the Mediterranean had been blown up and Europe's lifeblood was pumping away on to Syrian Desert sands. Most of western Europe was already beginning to run desperately short of oil.

George Humphrey, the U.S. Secretary of the Treasury, added the final touch. The British had asked for a loan to tide them over the run on the pound which had begun once the operation ran into U.S. objections. But of course, said Humphrey. The Americans were always ready to help their old ally, no matter what folly she had committed. Of course there would be a loan—and supplies of oil, too, to relieve the shortage. Only one thing. First evacuate your troops, and do it at once.

Humphrey then twisted Eden's arm. The run on the pound would have quickly halted if the U.S. Treasury had announced that a billion-dollar credit was being granted, even if, later, it had to be approved by the Congress. But no announcement came. Harold Macmillan, the Chancellor of the Exchequer in Eden's government, telephoned to ask for a statement, but never managed to speak to Humphrey. The Secre-

tary of the Treasury later strenuously denied that an announcement was held back until the British agreed to evacuate.

"It's just ridiculous," he said later. "I didn't give them their money immediately because I didn't know where to get it. We told them we would get it. We looked everywhere to get it. And finally we did get it, out of half a dozen different sources. And then we gave them support for the pound."

But that was, of course, *after* the Anglo-French troops had begun pulling out of Egypt. Three unlikely partners—Gamal Abdel Nasser, the Soviet Union,* and John Foster Dulles—had made sure that the British lion had roared for positively the last time.

*As will be recalled, the Soviet Union said it would make all the appropriate noises in Egypt's support if Nasser got into trouble with the British, but refused to offer actual help. At the height of the Suez crisis, the Soviets threatened to bombard London and Paris if the Anglo-French did not withdraw. But though some people took this seriously, Nasser knew only too well that it was an empty threat.

CHAPTER TWENTY-FIVE

Spies in the Stratosphere

Considering the number of ills that afflicted their sturdy-looking bodies, the Dulles brothers and their sister kept awfully quiet about it when the bug struck or the pain came. It was as if they believed that ignoring a malady would persuade it to go away. And all of them had a horror of surgery.

Once in Germany, at the tail end of World War II, Eleanor went for a medical checkup and happened to mention to a young U.S. medic, who had noticed that one of her eyes bulged slightly, that she had heard it might be a sign of a tumor on the brain. She laughed when she said it. But a few days later, she had a fainting fit and when she recovered consciousness she was being loaded into an ambulance.

As they wheeled her into the military hospital at Munich, she took a look at the label which they had hung around her neck. It said: BRAIN TUMOR. OPERATE.

When they reached the ward and started to undress her, she resisted and said she would do it herself. The moment the nurse had gone, she slipped into the corridor, telephoned a friend in her unit, and told him to send a car for her. She then walked out of the hospital and did not come back. Thirty-two years later the brain tumor still showed no signs of giving her trouble.

Likewise, when Foster began feeling pain during the Suez crisis he ignored it, and it went away—for the time being. Back in Washington after the UN debate, he put in a full day's work at the office. That night, after dinner, he played a little backgammon with Janet and went to bed around ten o'clock. He was awakened by a terrible pain at midnight, waited until it had passed, then went to sleep again. But a few hours

later it was back again, and he telephoned Macomber.

"I've been taken ill, Bill," he said. "I want you to come over here. The doctors are coming and the ambulance is coming, and I want you to come and take charge until the Department opens. You can get in touch with Mr. Hoover. I don't know how ill I am, but come over. In the meantime, I want you to call Jim Hagerty [the President's press secretary] and explain to him what's happening, and get his advice as to how we should play this from the public relations angle."

It couldn't have happened at a worse time. The invasion was still going on in Suez. The presidential election campaign was in full swing.

"This was a Saturday and the voting for the presidency was next Tuesday," Macomber said later. "President Eisenhower had had his illnesses earlier and had recovered from them. Mr. Dulles thought that his going to the hospital at this particular moment would remind an awful lot of people of the President's earlier heart attack, and could possibly have an adverse effect on their willingness to vote for him."

When Macomber got to the house, the ambulance men were having a hard time trying to get Foster down from the first-floor bedroom.

"He's a big man and it's a winding staircase," said Macomber, "and they tried to carry him down and that didn't work worth a damn. He was in real pain at this point and he said: 'Let me get down.' And he just sat on the steps and eased himself down by sitting on one step at a time all the way down. They put him in the ambulance and I drove Mrs. Dulles in my car right behind it. I remember I was a little irritated because there was hardly a car on the street and the ambulance stopped at every red light. There wasn't a car left or right anywhere, and they just stopped. And then also—incredible—the driver got lost going out to Walter Reed. We finally got there but it wasn't the most professional performance you ever saw."

The doctors came in and took a number of tests. While they were consulting, Foster calmly and dispassionately discussed with Macomber the prospect before him: (a) It might be a temporary pain and he would be back on the job on Monday; (b) it would need an operation and as a result he would be out for three weeks or so, and that would mean taking certain steps which he enumerated; or (c) "I'll be completely taken out—in which case we've got a lot to do before they come for me." (He meant the morticians.)

The doctors had meanwhile come back and told him: "Mr. Secre-

427

tary, we're going to have to operate on you."

"All right," he said, "but how long before I can do business again?"

"Well, Mr. Secretary," one of the doctors replied, "we'll operate about ten or eleven this morning. And you should be able to do some business Monday afternoon for about twenty minutes."

Foster leaned back, closed his eyes for a moment, then said to Macomber: "All right. Now let's go over what you've got to do and the people you've got to get hold of."

The operation was a big one, and it was cancer. Herbert Hoover, Jr., was put in charge of the State Department and briefed on what Foster had been doing. It was agreed that until he was up and about again, the Secretary should be consulted only on urgent matters. So Hoover handled the rest of the Suez crisis, and must have got a certain amount of satisfaction out of dealing personally with an urgent request which reached him from the Egyptian government in the wake of the Anglo-French withdrawal. Gamal Abdel Nasser himself made an appeal to America for credits, food, and medical aid for the refugees from the fighting in the Canal area. Thousands of homes had been destroyed and there was much suffering. Hoover turned him down flat, without consulting his friend, Secretary Humphrey, or Foster.

But he did consult the Secretary of State on one matter. That was about a telephone call which President Eisenhower had received from Anthony Eden in London. Surrounded by the smoking ruins of his Middle East policy and his political career, Eden had asked Ike if he could come over and consult with him about the situation.

"Sure, Anthony," the President had said, "come on over and let's talk."

Hoover didn't think it was right, and Foster didn't either. He sent an urgent message to the President, rebuking him for making such a move without consulting him, and strongly suggesting he should uninvite the British prime minister. Eisenhower meekly did so.*

On the morning after the election, with Dwight D. Eisenhower sent back to the White House in a landslide vote of confidence, the President came over to Walter Reed to see his Secretary of State. There had been times when Ike was plainly bored with the presidency, but this was not one of them. To Macomber, who was present, it was clear that

---

*Eden was afterwards to say that this was the rebuff that wounded him most in the wake of the Suez débâcle.

he was enjoying having been reelected. He came into the Presidential Suite, which he had put at Foster's disposal, and sat down in a low chair, looking at Foster propped up on the pillows of his high bed.

"This was just a few days after Prime Minister Eden had been invited and then uninvited," Macomber said later. "The President knew it had not been the right thing to do at the time. He had originally thought it was a good idea and then Mr. Dulles had persuaded him it was not a good idea . . . It was obvious that the President, even though he was excited about just being reelected, was a little nervous about this meeting."

It seemed to Macomber that Ike needed to get one thing out of the way first before he went on to talk about the presidency, and that was to excuse himself over the Eden business. He said, in effect:

"Foster, I understand why you thought it was a bad idea, why it should have been called off, and as you know, it was called off. I quite agree, but I want to explain to you what I had in mind when I did it."

He then went into a long rigmarole about old friendships, wartime comradeship, ancient alliances, that sort of thing. Macomber will always remember Foster looking down at him while the President stumbled on. There was no expression on the Secretary's face. All Foster said was: "Well, Mr. President, I think it was right we called it off."

It was plain he wanted to pass on to other things, but the President persisted.

"After having asked him," he went on, and then: "You understand why I did it. I think he expected—"

Foster interrupted with a crisp: "I see!" in a tone to indicate that as far as he was concerned, the subject had been exhausted. Macomber said that later he told Foster he thought he had been "kind of mean to have been so stern on the morning after he'd been elected President of the United States." Altogether he found it "an interesting episode in their relationship."

So far as the public was concerned, the U.S. government professed to have known nothing about the Anglo-French plot over Suez, and that, of course, gave people the impression that the CIA had been caught napping. There were rebukes in Congress and in the newspapers. Allen Dulles bore them lightly, since everybody who was anybody knew the truth.

In fact, the Agency's reputation as an efficient instrument of intelligence-gathering on a worldwide scale had never been higher. The U-2s were still flying over the Communist heartlands and keeping a vigilant eye on Soviet and Chinese airfields and naval bases. The researchers and analysts were pouring out daily summaries of trends and developments in all parts of the world, and though they were not always correct—the Russians, for instance, tricked them for a time over whether they were concentrating on big bombers or missiles—they did give an invaluable picture of the evolving state of friends, enemies, and neutrals, politically, economically, socially.

The one lesson the Agency had not yet learned was that it could not, single-handedly, roll back the Soviet armies in eastern Europe, restore Chiang Kai-shek to mainland China, or keep Ho Chi Minh out of southern Vietnam, which would cost it (and the United States) much blood and suffering in the years to come. But for the moment, the CIA's reputation stood high. In Europe chiefs of state like Konrad Adenauer would still rather deal with the CIA than the U.S. Embassy in getting messages to and from Washington. And in Mexico there was an even more bizarre situation. There the United States had appointed an ambassador whom the president of Mexico, Ruiz Cortines, neither liked nor consulted. But he did like the CIA station chief, and they established a special relationship. Once a month, an unmarked black limousine would pick up the station chief and take him not to the Presidential Palace but to one of Cortines's many houses in the suburbs of Mexico City. There the president would be waiting and they would talk for two or three hours.

"Most of the things the president of Mexico wanted to communicate to Washington, what he thought really important, he would communicate in this fashion," said an ex-CIA official later. "And the station chief would send it on through CIA channels to the State Department. This was known to Foster Dulles, Herbert Hoover, Jr., and the Assistant Secretary for Latin American Affairs, but to no one else."

Some time later the U.S. ambassador was recalled and replaced by the man who had been Assistant Secretary for Latin American Affairs. He had therefore been cognizant of the arrangement between the CIA's station chief and the president, but he was cautioned to say nothing about it when he presented his credentials at the Presidential Palace. After he had been there for a month or so, President Cortines,

at one of his regular meetings with the station chief, said: "You know, I think your new ambassador is an excellent man, and I would like to set up a special relationship with him too."

So from that time on, the black unmarked limousine picked up both the station chief and the ambassador, and took them out to the suburbs of Mexico City to talk confidentially with the president.

The technical and electronic side of the Agency's activities was steadily expanding; more and more millions went into scientific research and development. Allen was still fascinated by gadgets, and he took great delight in playing around with the new miniature tape recorders, radios, and bugging devices that were now coming into the Agency. But he also willingly signed away millions of dollars for projects that he only vaguely understood when their sponsors in the Agency tried to explain them to him.

There was certainly no shortage of money in the CIA kitty. It was still the only department of government into which the beady eye of Secretary of the Treasury George Humphrey could not penetrate. Allen had established excellent relations on Capitol Hill, and got on extremely well with Clarence Cannon, in those days in charge of the Appropriations Committee of the House. He would go before the committee and submit himself to questions, answering easily, openly, fleshing out his narrative with fascinating little espionage anecdotes, and showing no sign of strain even when the session lasted three or four hours. And on several occasions, his appearance would end in the same way, with Chairman Cannon saying: "Mr. Dulles, I want to ask you one more question. Are you sure you have enough money?"

The U-2 had cost a fortune to develop, but its pioneer, Richard Bissell, saw well ahead of time that it would soon become outmoded and the next stage of extraterrestial surveillance would have to be developed. He went to Allen and said:

"I am very worried that the Russians are getting ahead of us in rocketry and space. In your capacity as head of psychological warfare, you ought to persuade the administration to do something about it. Because if, in two or three years, the Russians have a space rocket and we have nothing, that could have a shattering effect around the world."

This was several months before the Soviet Union put Sputnik into space in October 1957, and though there were rumors and hints from CIA sources that it was coming, no one had yet responded to it. Allen

suggested that Bissell go over and talk to the Air Force, who sent him on to Charles Wilson, the Secretary of Defense. The feeling around was that such things as space programs were "the kind of foolishness the Democrats indulge in, and we Republicans cut down on." So once more, Allen agreed to fund money for a space satellite out of CIA secret funds, and went to see the President about it. In February 1958, he called in Richard Bissell to see him. Edwin Land was already there. Allen said that the President had approved the development and operation of a reconnaissance satellite, and that Bissell would be in charge for the Agency and would have an Air Force officer as his co-director.

"He and I presided over something that was known as the Corona program," Bissell said later, "and we conducted it much as we had the building of the U-2. It so happened that the Air Force itself had a satellite reconnaissance program, and the first thing we did was announce that this was canceled. Of course, there were lots of wailings and gnashings of teeth and complaints that this was the Republican Party economizing where we could least afford it. The newspapers hit out at us. We couldn't of course tell anyone that the Air Force program was being replaced by a bigger one."

Bissell knew less about space rockets than he had about U-2s, and he and his aides learned the hard way.

"About a year later, flights of this system began," he said, "and one after another was a failure. It was a most heart-breaking business. If an airplane goes on a test flight and something malfunctions, and it gets back, the pilot can tell you about the malfunction, or you can look it over and find out. But in the case of a recce satellite, you fire the damn thing off and you've got some telemetry, and you never get it back. There is no pilot, of course, and you've got no hardware, you never see it again. So you have to infer from telemetry what went wrong. Then you make a fix, and if it fails again, you know you've inferred wrong. In the case of Corona, it went on and on. By April of 1960 there had been eleven flights, none successful. The first one in which both the satellite and the camera functioned perfectly and from which film was retrieved was No. 14 in August of 1960."

But from then on they were in business. The workhorse satellite proved to be a most remarkable instrument of reconnaissance. The in-built camera worked with fantastic precision.

"Any time I look at any of the photographs," Bissell said, "I am still

impressed. We took a picture of the U.S. Capitol Building and when we enlarged a triangle of it, we could see a small section where they were working on the dome. There was another taken over Butte, Montana, of a football game. You could see all the players, even if you couldn't see the ball itself. And remember that this was taken from a hundred miles up."

The satellite was ready to go. But for the moment, it was the U-2 recce plane on which the Agency still relied for its aerial surveillance over Russia and China. The Russians were reported to have developed a rocket capable of reaching the height at which the U-2 flew, and neither Allen nor Bissell could understand why the Soviets so far hadn't tried to shoot one down.

Until they did, they would hold their satellite wonder in reserve.

The doctors assured Foster that the operation had been successful and the cancer eliminated from his body, and the remarkable reserves which the Dulles family could muster when facing physical crisis came to his rescue. No doubt his recovery was speeded up by a discreet visit from Allen, who came to tell him that Thomas E. Dewey, their old New York friend and protégé, had been in touch. Did Allen know that during Foster's illness Ike had approached him to sound out whether he would be willing to take Foster's place in the event of his non-recovery? Dewey told Allen to assure Foster that he had refused even to contemplate the suggestion since "Foster is irreplaceable."

Eisenhower never mentioned the matter to Foster either during his illness or after he had returned to the State Department. The President, in George Allen's words, continued to "let Dulles conduct the foreign policy of the United States any way he wanted to"; and he added: "I never saw any friction between the two." But there was a difference. The President's euphoria over his reelection soon faded as the problems of office crowded in: desegregation at home (he was lukewarm about civil rights), the launching of Sputnik I in 1957, and the growing possibility of missile threats from Russia. He was beginning, his intimates suspected, to have a jaded feeling about the whole presidential business, and to suspect that he and Foster between them had made a mess of the Suez crisis, let the Russians into the Middle East, propped up an Egyptian demagogue, and endangered a darned good alliance with Europe.

With cool Gallic logic, the French had analyzed the Suez débâcle and drawn certain conclusions from it. Not that they had been wrong—which was neither the Gaullist nor the Quai d'Orsay view—but that their supposed ally, the United States, could not be relied upon in an emergency, and had let them down for dubiously moral reasons which had been, in truth, purely domestic and political. Therefore, the alliance was worthless and the sooner it was abandoned the better. Steps were already being taken to change the direction of French foreign policy, to turn away from the Atlantic and forge new and closer links in Europe with Germany and the members of the Common Market.

It might have been wise for the British to do the same thing, and embrace Europe for reasons of self-interest and self-protection. The history of the United Kingdom in the next two decades could have been different, and more hopeful, had it done so. But the British have always felt less easy fraternizing with their neighbors 21 miles across the English Channel than they do hobnobbing with their richer American cousins 3,000 miles across the Atlantic.

Moreover, the new prime minister, Harold Macmillan, who had succeeded Anthony Eden,* was half-American by birth, had been a close wartime collaborator with Dwight Eisenhower in Algiers, and shared the enthusiasm of his old mentor, Winston Churchill, for the "special relationship" with the United States. Ironically, Macmillan had been an even more fervent interventionist at the time of Suez than Eden, but had scurried for cover when he saw things going wrong and was safe on the sidelines by the time the tarring and feathering of his leader began. His hands had been scrubbed clean when Foster Dulles arrived in London in the summer of 1957 for a NATO conference, and the two men were able to embrace each other as if Suez had never come between them. By the end of the year, the "special relationship" seemed to be working once more, though it would become a progressively more unequal, and finally unreal, partnership as time went on.

In the meantime, Macmillan was careful not to chide Foster or Ike for hypocrisy over their stance at Suez. He did not do so even when they introduced into Congress, hard on the heels of Nasser's triumph, a resolution known as the Eisenhower Doctrine. It was supposed to "deter Communist aggression in the Middle East," but Foster pri-

*Eden resigned on the grounds of ill-health on January 9, 1957.

vately admitted that it was directed more against Nasserist expansion in the Arab countries than Soviet intrusions. The heart of the doctrine was that "overt armed aggression from any nation controlled by international Communism" would be met by "the armed forces of the United States." In the circumstances, some of America's allies thought that it sounded like a *mea culpa* for recent sins of omission.

In 1958, Nasserite propaganda looked as if it was about to suborn the Lebanese armed forces. In Jordan and Iraq, there was an incipient rebellion and an active one. In Bagdad the king and his prime minister, Nuri Said, were murdered and their bodies dragged through the streets, and the mob also killed the local CIA station chief, Eugene Burns.

Was this "overt armed aggression" from a "nation controlled by international Communism"? Or was it, as in the case of Suez, just another uprising of Arab nationalism? Foster went to the illuminated globe in his office at State and studied it in silence, whittling away at a pencil with his pocket knife, as he often did when he was mulling over a decision. Then he made up his mind, went to the White House, and told the President to implement the Eisenhower Doctrine. American interests were threatened and if the situation were allowed to deteriorate, the whole Middle East would collapse into chaos. What did chaos produce but communism? Therefore . . .

Once more Admiral Arleigh Burke was given orders and began flashing signals to the U.S. 6th Fleet in the Mediterranean. This time the orders were for the ships to steam hard for Lebanon, where they would land Marines at Beirut, the capital, and occupy the city. The mission was described as being vital and urgent, and the Marines went ashore in full battle gear, expecting to meet elements of the Soviet army, or, at least, some belligerent Egyptians. They found sunbathing Lebanese bathing beauties waiting to greet them instead.

The moment the Lebanese landing had been decided on, the President picked up the telephone and called London to tell Prime Minister Macmillan what he had ordered.

"You are doing a Suez on me!" Macmillan exclaimed.

The British premier later recalled that when he said that, "the President laughed." A hollow laugh, no doubt.

*   *   *

Frank Wisner was back from sick leave and in business as a covert operator again. He had been down to the CIA training farm in Virginia to update himself on Agency tricks and gadgets, small arms drill, booby-trapping and unarmed combat, and he loudly proclaimed himself fighting fit. But the Hungarian tragedy had left its mark on him; there were dark fatigue smudges under the eyes, a tendency to stutter, and the ice would sometimes shake in his liquor glass when his grip on it loosened.

His disappointment over the failure of the Hungarian revolution had not dissipated his hatred of communism in all its shapes and forms, nor his determination to harry it down anywhere it reared its Hydra head. Wisner had plenty of operations going. The emphasis in his section now had moved away from Europe and was beginning to concentrate on Asia. He had private armies operating in Laos and South Vietnam, where swashbuckling agents bustled around dispensing bribes, running arms and drugs, and manipulating politicians and princes. His biggest operation was in Taiwan, where, under the control of Station Chief Ray S. Cline, a U-2 base had been established and reconnaissance planes were flying over China, Tibet, and Manchuria in search of atom plants and missile bases. One of Cline's principal activities was the recruitment of Chinese espionage agents whom he parachuted back into China. He reported that several of them had begun to radio warnings that the Chinese Communists (or Chicoms, as the Agency dubbed them) were planning to move in on Quemoy and Matsu, the offshore islands under Chiang Kai-shek's control, which were between Taiwan and the mainland. Wisner informed Allen, who passed on to his brother the news that a confrontation was coming between the Chicoms and the Nationalists.

In the meantime, there was Indonesia. Wisner was able to point out to Allen that if President Nasser of Egypt was a tool of international communism, then so was President Sukarno of Indonesia. Sukarno had been a thorn in America's side for some time, and the wound was beginning to fester. He scornfully rejected American advice and resisted the pressure that went along with U.S. aid. He continually adopted the pro-Chicom line in his speeches and scoffed at the "mythological ambitions" of Chiang Kai-shek.

Inside the CIA it was well known that Foster loathed Sukarno and would not take it amiss if his régime was overturned. In briefing the

new U.S. ambassador to Indonesia, Hugh S. Cumming, Jr., he had told him:

"Hugh, I expect from you objective reporting. As a matter of our general policies, don't tie yourself irrevocably to a policy of preserving the unity of Indonesia. The important thing is that we help Indonesia to the extent that they will allow us to resist any outside influence, especially Communism. The preservation of unification of a country can have dangers, and I refer to China. The territorial integrity of China became a shibboleth. We finally got a territorially integrated China, but for whose benefit? The Communists."

Foster went on:

"Now this is something that cannot be in writing, but you should know where my mind is running. You may arrive at a different conclusion yourself when you've been there. But this is my own feeling: As between a territorially united Indonesia which is leaning and progressing toward Communism and a break-up of that country into geographical units, I prefer the latter, as furnishing a fulcrum which the United States could use to help them eliminate Communism in one place or another. And then, if they so wish, arrive back again at a united Indonesia."

In the circumstances, Wisner did not have much trouble persuading Allen to approve an anti-Sukarno operation, and with his usual flourish he signed the chit which would authorize his deputy to collect the $10 million that would be necessary to see the operation through. Ray Cline in Taiwan was ordered to detach a number of B-26 bombers and pilots from his China operations and tell them to stand by for an Indonesian operation. (The planes belonged to an ostensibly commercial airline, CAT, which was in reality CIA-financed. Its pilots were paid by the Agency at mercenary rates.) The object was to attack and provoke an uprising in the largest island of the Indonesian group, Sumatra, and to detach it from Sukarno's régime at Djakarta.

When the plans and dispositions had been made, Allen went to his brother Foster to tell him what was afoot and get his approval and that of the President. This was obtained with no difficulty at all, but the Secretary did suggest that Hugh S. Cumming, Jr., the ambassador in Djakarta, be advised that something was about to happen; he gave the task of informing him to Herbert Hoover, Jr., and Walter Robertson, chief of the Department's Far Eastern Bureau.

"I was called in and briefed on a very delicate matter," Cumming said later, "and was told that the Secretary himself had wanted me briefed on this matter, but only to the extent that I wanted myself to be briefed."

The ambassador listened for a time to what they were telling him, then held up his hand.

"I think that is enough," he said, before they could go into details.

The action against Sumatra was Wisner's first big operation since his return to the Agency, and it was a fizzle. The initial aim was to panic the pro-Sukarno troops on the island with a series of bombing and strafing raids on their camp by the CAT B-26s, but almost from the start something went wrong. On May 18, 1958, one of the planes was shot down by the Indonesian army and its pilot captured.

His name was Allen Pope, and all the Indonesians should have been able to find out about him was that he was a commercial pilot for CAT. There was a strict order that anyone flying for the CIA must refrain from carrying any indication whatsoever that they were working for the Agency. It was an order largely ignored by the pilots, who possessed a lively sense of self-preservation and realized that whereas a lone commercial pilot who had just bombed them might be killed out of hand by indignant troops, his life might well be saved if he was discovered to be working for the United States government. President Sukarno himself would want him preserved as living evidence of American iniquity.

Pope had plenty of evidence on him that he worked for the CIA. He was, of course, publicly disavowed by the U.S. government. But Ambassador Cumming (who must have been thankful he never heard the details of the operation) was called up by Walter Robertson and told to inform President Sukarno that, on the orders of the Secretary of State and President Eisenhower, 37,000 tons of rice and $1 million worth of arms were being sent immediately to Indonesia as part of America's foreign aid program. And could they please have their pilot back?

Sukarno took the aid but kept the pilot until 1962.

As for Frank Wisner, he withered on the vine. In 1959 he retired from the CIA on the grounds of ill-health, and in 1961 he committed suicide.

CHAPTER TWENTY-SIX

Final Call

One gets the feeling that by the end of 1958, the sixth year of his presidency, Dwight D. Eisenhower spent much of his time wishing that the world crises crowding in on him would go away, and his Secretary of State with them. He had had a cerebral spasm the year before which had caused malfunctions in his mental processes and difficulties in expressing himself, and though these had now been overcome, the attack, coming on top of the thrombosis and ileitis from which he also suffered, had left him lassitudinous and sapped of his mental vitality. He had lost his enthusiasm for political battles at home and cold war clashes abroad, and his aides at the White House who sometimes caught him with a faraway look in his eyes soon learned that what he was thinking about was golf.

On the other hand, illness seemed to have left Foster with a seething brain and a driving sense of energy, and he was zipping all over the globe, wherever trouble was stirring, often for the purpose of giving it a touch of heat that would bring it to the boil. The situation that was engaging his attention most closely toward the end of the year was in Asia, where the Chicoms had begun bombarding the offshore islands of Quemoy and Matsu. Chiang Kai-shek had asked for help, prophesying that at long last the Communists were making their move, and the capture of the islands would be the first stage of invading Taiwan.

Should the United States take action to prevent a Chicom occupation of the islands? None of America's allies, whether in Europe, Asia, or Australia, believed that they should. Britain produced a long and closely argued legal brief to prove that Quemoy and Matsu were, in fact, part of the offshore islands of the Chinese mainland and legiti-

mately belonged to the government in Peking; Chiang Kai-shek's troops had no right to be there in the first place. On the other hand, several members of the National Security Council and members of the Joint Chiefs of Staff believed that this would be the right moment to confront the Chicoms and curb their belligerency in Asia.

Before deciding how to advise the President, Foster arranged to fly to Taipeh for a conference with Chiang Kai-shek, but just before he was about to leave news came from Rome that Pope Pius XII had died. Foster was appointed by the President to lead the U.S. Delegation to the funeral, and he left in a USAF jet tanker plane* on October 17; he was accompanied by Clare Boothe Luce, former ambassadress to Rome and the Vatican; his secretary, Phyllis Bernau; his aide, Jerry Greene; a number of assistants; and, of course, Janet. The plane was only superficially adapted for passengers, and makeshift bunks and hammocks had been slung to allow them to sleep during the nine-hour overnight journey. In the early hours of the morning, Foster's bunk collapsed and he was flung to the floor of the plane, painfully wrenching his back. He already suffered from a slipped disc and was in acute discomfort, but he deliberately refrained from wakening anyone and stayed prone, silently suffering, until morning.

The pain was great by the time he reached Rome, but no one who watched him accompany the delegation into St. Peter's saw him limp.

He left Rome on Sunday, October 19, and flew to England for a two-hour stop, where he saw Foreign Secretary Selwyn Lloyd, who drove out to meet him at Brize Norton airfield in Oxfordshire. Lloyd stayed long enough to see Foster and Janet on their way again, then went back to London to write a note to the Secretary in which he said:

"As I saw the side door of the aeroplane close on Janet and yourself, I thought what a gallant couple you were and how little gratitude is sometimes shown to those who so much deserve it."

The plane landed next at Fairbanks, Alaska, and there a CIA operative was waiting for him with a message. The bombardment of Quemoy and Matsu by the Chicoms, which had temporarily ceased, had started up again with new intensity. It did not take Foster much time in Taiwan to make up his mind that the United States should take a stand. To some extent, he had been presented with a fait accompli. Ray Cline of

*There were no passenger jet planes in 1958.

the CIA had already drafted military "advisers" to the islands, and Admiral Arleigh Burke had begun ferrying supplies to the Chinese garrisons there. By the time Foster returned to Washington, Burke was waiting with a suggestion that U.S. naval air cover should be flown over the Straits to make the Chicoms even more aware of the American presence.

It took a great deal of argument to persuade him. Foster still smarted from the criticisms that had been made of his "brinkmanship" of a few years back, and he told his aides that he dreaded seeing a new headline in the newspapers: DULLES SAYS: ONCE MORE TO THE BRINK. He was acutely aware that all of his allies and the majority of the public in the United States were against risking war with the masses of Communist China for the sake of a couple of offshore islands.

"Well, eventually he was persuaded," said Admiral Burke later. "The President was a little reluctant."

He was indeed. He had great fears of the United States getting itself involved in an endless struggle with the Chicoms in the great land mass of China, and had visions of a new kind of Hundred Years' War, with no victory possible. But once he had made up his mind, Foster was persuasive.

"[The President] wasn't so eager to do this," said Burke, "but Mr. Dulles went over to my side on this thing, and he supported me to the President. And then we got permission to escort the landing ships we were lending the Nationalists with U.S. naval vessels to within three miles of Quemoy and Matsu. We did a lot of things outside the three-mile limit, and actually we did a lot of things inside the three-mile limit. And it all worked out. It worked just exactly the way we had predicted. We were there. If they wanted Quemoy and Matsu, [the Chicoms] were going to have to fight the 7th Fleet and the United States. And we were not going to tell them—not say a damn word—just do those things which would make it clear to them. And it worked."

It worked to the extent that, if the Chicoms ever did intend to take over the offshore islands in 1958, they backed off. The bombardment ceased. All was suddenly peaceful again in the Taiwan Straits.

It was the last time Foster took the world to the brink, and the risk had been genuine this time.

*   *   *

On October 23, 1958, BBC television showed an interview with Foster by William Clark, who had been Anthony Eden's press secretary during the Suez crisis, but was now back to being a working newsman. During the course of it Clark asked:

"You have been Secretary of State now for six pretty gruelling years, and you seem to be doing very well and look very healthy on it. Tell me, what is it that keeps you going? Is it faith, hope, or do you somehow enjoy all the pressures and the power that go with this great post?"

Foster replied:

"You know, I don't think anybody is a very good analyst of himself, and I have never psychoanalyzed myself. So I don't really know the answer to this. But I can say this, Mr. Clark: These are times of tremendous importance. Anybody who has a tradition, as exists in my family, of public service in the international field cannot but feel the challenge of these times. And when you have a President, one who himself knows a great deal about international affairs, problems of war and peace— if he says: 'I think you are the fellow to carry this job at this time,' I think one cannot but take satisfaction and do one's best to justify the faith that President Eisenhower puts in you. And I think it is that perhaps more than anything else that keeps me going."

He did not mention his twisted and still murderously painful back, nor did he reveal that his latest medical checkup had disclosed another physical ailment to which his flesh had become victim: diverticulitis, an inflammation of the digestive tract and lower bowel.

He looked as fit as ever when he got back to Washington, but he was acutely aware of the fact that things were going wrong, with the administration, with the world situation, with himself. He told his aides that he would be needing all the strength he could muster for the political crises which seemed to be looming—the Russians were beginning to murmur about the status of Berlin—and he was taking a few days off to visit his log cabin on Duck Island, in Lake Ontario. November seemed a strange time of the year to be visiting the mile-square rock in the middle of an icy expanse of water, but William Macomber, who knew his boss, suspected that he had received intimations of mortality and wanted to see the beloved scene of his childhood for the last time.

Foster and Janet were flown to Watertown in an Air Force plane and

there transferred to an amphibian for the flight to the islet. They had their dog Pepi with them. Foster had bought it in Paris for his wife and named it for a Dulles ancestor, Pepin le Bref. It did not get many walks through the woods on this visit. The weather was bad. Rainstorms scudded across the lake, and heavy winds battered the cabin, but it was cosy inside before the log fire; they sat quietly in front of it and read, only occasionally glancing through the windows at the lightning flashing in the sky.

A few days later the lighthouse keeper brought a message. Krushchev had made a speech about Berlin, and Foster was needed back in Washington. The amphibian plane flew in despite the weather and got them away. Janet said later that when they circled and passed over the island, Foster did not look down.

On Thanksgiving Day, 1958, Eleanor gave a last meal for her brothers and their families in the house at McLean. The Berlin situation was erupting, and they were all immersed in it, but they took time out for the celebration. Foster and Janet arrived from attending mass at St. Matthew's Cathedral and he remarked, with some asperity, that one of the churchmen he had met there had voted a few weeks before, at a meeting of the World Council of Churches, for the recognition of Communist China. He added, jokingly, that they should never have allowed him inside the cathedral.

It was a jolly lunch. Eleanor's son, David, and her daughter, Ann, were there and so were Allen and Clover, together with their son, Allen, Jr. Both David and Allen, Jr., if for different reasons, had tempers and temperaments that could flare like fireworks, but today they were on their best behavior. The three children served the dry martinis and canapes. Eleanor's two adoring servants from her Viennese days, Relli and Trudi, hovered in the background while Foster carved the turkey.

Then the telephone rang—a call, in turn, for each of them. Krushchev had sent a note on Berlin, calling for the freeing of the city from outside control. It was something that the allies would never stomach, and he knew it. The last big Berlin crisis was upon them.

They stayed long enough for coffee and brandy and a toast, then they hurried back to their offices: Foster to State, Allen to the CIA, Eleanor to her Berlin bureau. The crisis involved all of them. Foster

must make the policy that the allies would follow. Allen must reply to one of the charges which Krushchev had made, that the CIA had turned Berlin into "a springboard for intensive espionage, sabotage and other subversive activities." And Eleanor must approve the press release that would be put out later in the day about the attack on allied control of the city.

They were back at their desks by three o'clock, and they were never to eat together at the same table again.

The following day, leaving the Berlin situation to seethe for a while, Foster flew down to Mexico City for the inauguration of the new president, Adolfo López Mateos. His son, John, and his granddaughter, Edith, came in from Monterrey, where John was teaching at a college, to spend a few hours with him. John was shocked at his father's condition; he was obviously in great pain.

Foster came back to Washington and went into Walter Reed Hospital on December 6 for a rest and another checkup. He was out and on his way to Paris for a NATO meeting six days later. He gave no sign of distress to anyone who met him, and he talked firmly and rationally to his NATO partners—they agreed to stand firm on Berlin and resist Soviet threats—about future meetings. The next one would be at the end of January 1959.

But in the meantime, rumors spread about his condition. He returned from a holiday in Jamaica on January 13 to be asked by a reporter how he felt.

"Well, I am feeling good," he said. "I feel able to carry on. At any time I don't feel able to carry on, you will know it."

He was suffering badly from intestinal pain by now, but he had recovered confidence about himself. The doctors had informed him at the December checkup that they really had cleared up the cancer during the 1956 operation, and he need not worry. Two years had passed and it had not come back. All he had was diverticulitis—and a hernia which he would need to have operated on when he had time between conferences.

He did not lose his optimism on his way to Europe on January 30, even when he was sick on the plane. At his meeting with Konrad Adenauer in Bonn, he sipped barley water while the others ate. When his old friend, escorting him to the airport on his way home, asked him gently whether his cancer had returned, he reassured him.

"No," he told the German chancellor. "It is not cancer. It's diverticulitis, and they are going to clear it up."

But when he was about to board the plane, he turned to grasp Adenauer's hand for the last time, and said:

"I don't think I will be coming back."

Most of the staff, almost of a common accord, were at the airport to meet him as the plane from Bonn touched down. Normally, when he came back from a trip, he went straight to the office and did a day's work, but this time he beckoned to Douglas Dillon and William Macomber, his two special aides, and they drove off with him back to his home. When they got into the drawing room, he told the two men: "This thing's come back on me. I'm going to resign."

The two men argued with him. How could he be sure? Why didn't he wait for another checkup and the doctors' verdict? He shook his head. He was pretty sure it had come back, he said. He called in a secretary, dictated a resignation note, and had it sent over to the White House. But Eisenhower rejected it out of hand. He too told Foster to wait until he could go into the hospital and get the doctors' verdict.

He had dates with Willy Brandt, the mayor of Berlin, and Chancellor Pittermann of Austria on February 9, and he insisted on getting up from bed to keep them. He could no longer dress himself and Janet wanted to do it for him, but he wouldn't let her; his aide, Jerry Greene, did it instead. Then Eleanor helped him downstairs and they drove to the State Department for the session with Brandt at which they talked for nearly an hour about Berlin. After that Pittermann was shown in. Foster looked on the point of exhaustion, but rumors that the Russians were backing down on Berlin and were suggesting another summit meeting in the spring seemed to hearten him.

He took the elevator down to the lobby and waited while the security officer went to find his car. He usually stood around while it was brought, but this time he looked for a chair and lowered himself into it, gingerly. The car drew up, and he nodded to the receptionist and went out to join it. He never came back. Next day he entered Walter Reed for his hernia operation.

And now a strange thing happened. It had been a long time since Foster had been popular with press, public, or Congress. He had been

under some sort of attack ever since Suez. Senator Hubert Humphrey, spokesman for the Democrats, regularly dubbed him a disaster and called upon him to resign. Even the President grumbled that "people just don't like that personality of Foster's, while they do like me."

But when word spread that Foster had undergone an operation for hernia on February 13, 1959, and was likely to be out of the office for some time, a sort of spontaneous "Don't let Foster resign" movement started on the Hill. After the operation was over, and they were waiting for the results of the tests, Foster called in Macomber and asked him to go up to Congress "and talk to certain people and find out how long they thought he could, in effect, be an absentee Secretary of State. The word I brought back from my soundings was about six weeks, and they would cover up for him in Congress for that long."

Then the results came through and the doctors had to admit it. The cancer had come back. They couldn't say how long he had left, but his days were numbered.

The first thing Foster did was to call in Allen and have him send a CIA man over to see Konrad Adenauer and explain that he hadn't meant to mislead him, he hadn't realized his cancer had come back. Then he spoke to Macomber again.

"The only issue now," he said, "is whether I live long enough to go to the Geneva Summit Conference in May. In which case, if I'm well enough to do that, I'll probably live into the summer, but no longer. Six months is the longest."

He added that it might take only two or three months.

"The only issue now is that narrow margin," he said, "but it's an important margin. Because if I get the longer length of time, I'll be safe to go to Geneva."

News reached Congress that Foster had incurable cancer and might be out for some time—or permanently. Senator Lyndon Johnson immediately introduced a resolution in the Senate wishing the Secretary a speedy recovery and looking forward to his return. A groundswell of sympathy began to gather. At the end of six weeks, Macomber was summoned to the Hill by one of the leading Democrats, who said:

"Bill, that six weeks estimate was wrong. Please tell the Secretary we'd rather have him run the Geneva Conference from a bed in Walter Reed Hospital than put anyone else in there, and for him to hang on

there and not to worry about any problem about being an absentee Secretary."

Macomber took the message back. Foster looked pleased, but said: "Bill, I'm not going to do it. Either I'm going to be well by then, well enough to go to Geneva, or I'm going to resign. It's flattering. They think I can run this thing from a hospital bed better than the others, but I can't. But I'll always remember this." He was silent, his eyes closed, but when he opened them he went on: "I have found out that a man's accomplishments in life are the cumulative effect of his attention to detail. And you can't attend to detail of what's going on in Geneva from a hospital bed in Walter Reed. I'm going to be there or I'm going to resign."

It was clear, as the weeks passed, that he was not going to be there. His pain did not go away, and his strength was obviously dribbling away. Janet, Eleanor, and Clover hovered in the anteroom, occasionally tiptoeing in to see him, Janet in dry-eyed grief, Eleanor gripped by a profound sense of approaching loss, Clover as cheerful as a bird, full of hopeless optimism. One day Foster opened his eyes and said to Eleanor: "Don't you have a meeting in Berlin?" She nodded. "Then get over there and do your job. Don't hang around here waiting for me."

The President went to see him on April 13, and announced Foster's resignation three days later. Acting Secretary Christian Herter was appointed to his post a week later, and Foster was named Special Adviser to the President with a post in the cabinet. A month later, the CIA brought a message to Eleanor in Berlin telling her to get back fast. Her brother had pneumonia.

But he wasn't dead yet. He continued to dictate to his secretary every day about world affairs, preparing a dossier for his successor. He had long talks with his special aide, William Macomber. He wasn't very cheerful—about the world, that is. So far as his own condition was concerned, "He was just about as objective as if he were dealing with some Departmental problem. I never saw anguish. I never saw: *Why is this happening to me?*" But about the world he was pessimistic. He told Macomber that he felt appeasement was in the air, and he didn't see how anyone who succeeded him could continue to hold things together.

447

"I don't mean that as egotistically as it sounds," he added. "I don't think that even I could hold it together much longer. Because there is wishful thinking building up in the world, and that adds up to a tendency to appeasement. You see it in our allies and you see it at home. It's getting harder to mobilize people to take a stand."

He kept on talking about this, about the need to stand firm, and his doubts that people would. On Macomber's last meeting with him, he seemed to drop off and his aide got up to leave, but Foster called him back from the door. His eyes were wide open again.

"Bill," he said, "just remember this. If the United States is willing to go to war over Berlin, there won't be a war over Berlin."

They were his last coherent words. Faithful to his principles to the end, he passed into a coma. On the morning of Sunday, May 24, 1959, he went to the brink of his own personal crisis and looked it in the face. Just after dawn, in the presence of all his family, he died, in his seventy-second year. Janet Dulles looked down at him and said:

"My life is over too."

And walked out of the room.

His old friend from Paris, Jean Monnet, a frail, decrepit Winston Churchill, Prime Minister Macmillan, and scores of senators and congressmen had been to see him in Walter Reed. Now it seemed that the whole world wanted to come to his funeral.

President Eisenhower announced that it would be a state affair in Washington Cathedral, and immediately there was a domestic crisis. Allen objected.

"We're Presbyterians, and we've always gone to the Presbyterian church here," he said. "Why should we change? What would father think? Why can't we have a small, simple funeral?"

Eleanor and her sisters overruled him. Foster's body was moved to the Bethlehem Chapel of the cathedral and lay in state there, flanked by a guard of soldiers and sailors, draped in the American flag. All through the hot night a steady file of men, women, and children went past. It was a remarkable sight. A few weeks before, his name had been a synonym for intransigence, rigidity, inflexibility to the point of preferring armed conflict to concession. Now young men and women were weeping over his body.

On May 27 the streets were lined with great crowds of silent people

as the coffin passed by on its way to the cathedral, followed by heads of state and prime ministers and foreign ministers from almost every country in the world. Gromyko, the Soviet foreign minister, flew in from Geneva. President (formerly Chancellor) Konrad Adenauer, though eighty-three years of age, marched in the procession. So did Secretary of the Treasury George Humphrey, Foster's old rival in the cabinet, but he had heart palpitations on the way and had to be whisked off in a car. Dwight D. Eisenhower marched with tears dampening his cheeks. And every member of the Dulles family was there save one: a niece, Mary Park, who was at home having a baby. She named it Foster.

Another distinguished statesman in the funeral procession was Foster's predecessor, Dean Acheson. After the ceremony was over, he walked across the road to the house close to the cathedral where Luke Battle was living. It was a miserably hot day and Dean looked exhausted.

"Some fellow got up and read all of the Old Testament," he said, "and then somebody else, not to be outdone, read all of the New Testament. By that time I was so tired I could hardly bear it. The number of eulogies! You'd never believe it."

Battle handed him a drink and he sipped at it gratefully. Then he said:

"You know, Luke, the greatest mistake I made was not to die in office."

CHAPTER TWENTY-SEVEN

Nose in the Trough

It was all in the mind to begin with, because no one suggested that things need be any different for Allen or Eleanor now that Foster was dead. Christian Herter, the new Secretary, sent Eleanor to Berlin to help dedicate the new John Foster Dulles Allee, which the city government had named in Foster's honor, and it was appropriate that Eleanor should be there—but a nice gesture, just the same—since the street ran through the Congress Hall complex, for which she had raised the funds and secured U.S. backing. When she got back, Herter congratulated her on making a good speech and waving the American flag at a felicitous moment.

Christian Herter called in Allen to assure him that State would work as closely and, he hoped, as cordially with the CIA under his direction as it had done with Foster. But his Agency colleagues noticed that Allen seemed a little uncertain and lacked self-confidence when dealing with Herter. And it opened cracks.

"The moment they became aware of it," Richard Bissell said later, "deputy assistant secretaries and senior Foreign Service officers began to maneuver for greater independence between the two agencies, feeling they could afford to hold firmer to the positions they deemed proper for their own agencies. There were subtle differences of attitude as a result of this feeling that the widely presumed intimate connection at the top no longer existed. Perhaps because I was in the CIA, and it is presumed to be subordinate in respect of policy to the State Department, I had the feeling that down the line the people in State became readier to stand up to their positions, and the CIA people felt a little weakened."

The trouble was, of course, that both brother and sister felt orphaned. A father figure who had been more than a father to them, the really dominating influence in their lives, was no longer there to be feared, rebelled against, criticized, mocked, resented, admired, envied, adored, even hated sometimes, but always there to be leaned on, relied on, a Presence. If the choice had had to be made, they would have sacrificed their right arms to keep him alive and keep him there always as head of the family. They were weakened and made vulnerable because of his departure, and they knew it long before it was sensed in the corridors of Washington power. It unstabilized them.

In the months following Foster's death, they were not the only ones who suffered a sense of loss. Dwight Eisenhower might have been expected to get a certain sense of relief from the fact that his Old Testament prophet was no longer around, a heavy conscience nagging at him to keep his mind on affairs of State. Many was the time when his eyes had glazed over as Foster rumbled on about the iniquity of neutralism, the duties of power, the virtues of morality in international relations, only to be pulled from some dream of green fairways or cold beer or wartime adventures by the blaze of a pair of blue eyes dragging him back to unpleasant reality, like a naughty school boy. His aides suspected that he missed the old buzzard. An element had gone out of his life at the White House, leaving a gap that was not filled by his new Secretary of State. Christian Herter was amiable and conscientious but always seemed to be smiling through some dreadful pain,* whereas Foster had never made you feel conscious of his. In addition, after Foster's supreme self-confidence in the rightness of everything he did, Herter's very reasonableness and placability filled one with uncertainty. At least Foster had made one feel that a policy had been successful, even after it had failed. Now it sometimes seemed as if the administration was floating in limbo, and every man out there was desperately trying to think for himself. It was disturbing. For six years Foster had kept the President up there, like a king, above the fray. Now there was a danger that he might have to climb down into the battle.

The first of them to feel the draft from the winds of change was Eleanor. She came back from her gall-bladder operation in December

*Herter suffered badly from arthritis.

1959 to find that she had been eased out of her Berlin job and transferred to some nebulous position with State Department Intelligence under Hugh S. Cumming, Jr. She regretted having to leave the affairs of Berlin, because it had been exciting and she had made some close contacts with the Berliners which owed nothing at all to her brother. "I was never the horse as far as Berlin policy was concerned," she said later, "but I was often the thistle under the saddle, and I kept the horse active." She had, in fact, done a great deal for the people of Berlin and they were grateful to her.* But if State chose to think of her as her brother's shadow, she must grin and bear it and demonstrate, by doing her new job well, that she had no need of nepotism. All the same, it was hard. All her career in State had been dogged by difficulties created not by her abilities—which everyone admitted were high—but by first her sex and now her fraternal connections, both of which had hampered rather than helped her.

What was certain was that she was not going to resign. She was sixty-four and could have done with a few months of taking it easy after her operation, but almost immediately she was handed a monumental assignment: to travel to forty countries in Asia and Africa and make a study of Soviet aid. She was in a clapped-out old plane flying from Saigon to Pnom Penh, surrounded by chickens and squealing pigs, when pain and nausea bent her double.

In true Dulles fashion, she waited for it to pass and continued with her program. She sweated it out in Bangkok and Burma, then had another attack in Delhi. She weathered that one and pressed on to Nepal, where the pain poleaxed her. She was staying in the ambassador's house and managed to signal for help, but the telephone was out and it took a couple of hours for the Methodist missionary, the only doctor around, to reach the house.

"He felt around my stomach," she said later, "and grinned when I said I had one more interview to make, and then I had to get back to Delhi. 'I can feel the stones in there,' he said. 'But I'm only a simple doctor and I have no equipment. Forget about your interviews and get yourself Stateside and into a hospital fast. You need an operation.' I got him to give me painkillers and went on to Delhi."

The pain got worse, but she kept to her schedule, going on to

*They made her a Freewoman of the City, and she was a guest of honor at the Bicentennial Celebrations in Berlin in 1976.

Karachi, Teheran, Ankara, Cyprus, and Paris before finally taking a plane home. She was determined that no one could accuse her of being weak and female. Besides, what would Foster have thought if she had given up just because her body was giving her hell? Hadn't she always maintained that she was as tough as her brothers?

A week after her return, she went into a Boston clinic for an abdominal operation. But she was back at her desk in Washington and writing her report less than a month later.

In the middle of April 1960 (sources differ on the exact date; it was probably April 13 or 14) Allen Dulles went to a meeting at the White House with Christian Herter, Richard Bissell, Hugh S. Cumming, and President Eisenhower to discuss a projected U-2 mission over the Soviet Union.

In conversations they had had beforehand, Bissell had suggested to Allen that maybe they were beginning to push their luck so far as the U-2 was concerned. When he first launched it, Bissell had given it an effective life over hostile territory of about two years, and that was four years ago. Why hadn't the Soviets shot one down? They had long since been capable of doing so. The CIA had blueprints of one of their new missiles, which could home in on a target flying at 80,000 or more feet, the U-2's cruising height. Yet they still flew over regularly and brought back invaluable photographic information. The Russians knew all about them. Why were they unmolested? How many more flights dare they risk before someone in Siberia pressed a button and a U-2 exploded in space? Wasn't this the time to call a halt? In a month's time, the leaders of the four powers were due to meet in Paris for a summit which should not only settle East-West differences over Berlin but work out some sort of modus vivendi by which they could learn to live together in other parts of the world. A U-2 incident could sabotage the whole prospect.

But Allen did not agree. He had become fond of the U-2, and not simply because it had done a darned good job of reconnaissance. It had become something of a talisman for him—a sort of bellwether to tell him where East-West relations were standing. One of the most important Russians ever to defect to the United States had told him that the Red Army and Air Force had long since been in favor of shooting the U-2 out of the skies, since each time it passed untouched

453

was a humiliation, "like a trail of slime across a shining barrack floor." But they had been overruled by the Party strategists, who expressed no concern over what the U-2 photographs revealed. For why did they need to hide? In an East-West world kept at peace by the capability of mutual destruction, it was good for the Americans to have a regular photographic reminder of *some* of the weapons which the USSR had as their share of the balance of power.

On the other hand, this defector said, the U-2 was one of those spies they could grab any time they liked. It was just a question of choosing the right moment, and using it for the appropriate purpose or reprisal. But when the moment came, *en garde,* because there would be big trouble coming.

At the White House meeting the request for permission to run the U-2 was all but routine. President Eisenhower, as usual, listened while Bissell detailed the route it was proposed the plane should follow. It would take off from Adana, Turkey, fly over eastern and central Russia, taking in the Sverdlovsk missile base, then proceed more or less along the Urals, and finally land at a USAF base in Bodö, Norway. Weather had been bad over the central and northern part of Russia for some time, and Bissell asked for a two-week leeway to allow the weather to clear, and for permission to go any time after that.

Herter pointed out that the summit conference was due to begin in Paris in mid-May, and the President remarked that "we don't want to have that thing flying up there while the summit's on." It was agreed that that was too much of a risk.

As usual, Bissell and Cumming left at this point and Allen stayed behind with Herter, the President, and Andy Goodpaster, the military aide, to talk things over. When he came back to the Agency later in the afternoon, he called Bissell in and told him that permission had been given.

"But we have a cut-off date," he said. "We can go any time good weather comes up until two weeks before the summit opens in Paris." He looked at his calendar. "That gives us until May 2." He grinned, then said: "What about May Day?"

Bissell said he'd rather go before. How would Americans like a Russian spy plane overflying them on Independence Day? Allen laughed and said they would be so busy jamming the beaches and the

ballparks that no one would ever notice—and wouldn't that be the case with the Russians? Wouldn't they be celebrating and off guard? But Bissell continued to hope that the weather would clear before the end of the month, and he could give the order to go. It was not to be. The cloud cover persisted, and it was not until April 30 that the weathermen reported it was clear.

The U-2 took off from Adana the following morning, May 1, 1960, with a civilian pilot employed by the CIA, Gary Powers, in the cockpit. Allen was tickled when Bissell told him about it, and his loud Ho-ho-ho echoed down the corridors outside his office.

Neither he nor Bissell seemed to be particularly worried about the flight. There was nothing special about it. It was just another routine flight, like all the others. It does not seem to have occurred to Allen to wonder what his brother Foster's attitude would have been, given the fact that the most important summit meeting of the Eisenhower administration was just over two weeks away.

Later on, when the inquests began at the CIA over the May Day flight and its disastrous outcome, what Allen and Bissell tried to discover was not why the plane was shot down—it had to happen some time—but why the Soviet government handled the affair in the way it did.

Krushchev played cat-and-mouse with them in the first few days of the disaster. He inferred in his initial statements that the U-2 had simply been destroyed in the air and its pilot killed. Allen fell for the ploy. The Agency's cover story was released to the effect that the U-2 was merely a weather plane that had strayed off course into Russian territory. Then he was shown up as a liar and a fool when Krushchev revealed that the plane had been captured practically intact, was full of sophisticated espionage equipment, and its pilot was more than eager to admit that he had been on a mission for the CIA.

That bit they understood. It was all part of the game. If the Russians were able to make monkeys out of the CIA—and monkeys they certainly were—then they could hardly be blamed for squeezing the utmost propaganda value out of it. But why did they have to go on and involve the President? Why did Krushchev come all the way to Paris

for the summit meeting and then deliberately use the U-2 incident as an excuse for calling it off?

"I would have thought that, if they wanted, they could have got the maximum propaganda advantage out of shooting down the plane," Bissell said later. "They didn't need to break off the summit meeting. Indeed, I would have said that there might have been a way in which it could have been used for bargaining purposes at the summit, if they had played it quietly."

It was a misreading of the situation which, one suspects, Foster Dulles would never have made. Ever since the previous summer the Research and Analysis Division of the CIA had been reporting a toughening up of the Soviet attitude toward Berlin. Krushchev was in difficulties with the hard-line members of the Supreme Soviet, who were feeling threatened in eastern Europe and disturbed by stirrings of independence in China. It was no time for making concessions to the West, or for gathering around a table in front of the international press and trying to make a virtue out of intransigence.

A more percipient man than Eisenhower would have guessed that they would try to get out of the summit. A more experienced Secretary of State would have warned him that there were crises coming. A more alert director of Central Intelligence would have warned his deputies to stay away from all anti-Soviet provocations until the summit was over.

"I think it can be said with hindsight," Richard Bissell commented later, "that it was bad judgment to take such a risk as to send a U-2 on a mission as close as that in time to the summit. But it was the President's decision. He made it."

Foster Dulles must have been spinning in his grave. Here was a cold war situation after his own heart, and he was not there to deal with it. As everyone sadly realized later on, Foster would not just have vetoed the U-2 mission. He would also have vetoed the summit.

And this time he would have been right.

"The trouble was," said one of his old deputies at the Agency, "I think by 1960 Allen was beginning to run on three cylinders instead of four. There were so many things going on in the CIA now that he could not possibly keep up with all the details even if he jumped

channels and tried to find out down the line. The Agency was just beginning to go out of control, and Bissell, Angleton, Dick Helms, Tracy Barnes, and Bob Amory, these were the people who were doing most of the work now."*

It was true that Allen's role seemed to be changing. Once upon a time he had made a virtue of the United States's involvement in intelligence, and persuaded both the public and the media that the men who worked for him at the CIA were the heroic lifeguards of the nation's security, sleeplessly vigilant and active in the service of the nation. He had been a favorite on the lecture circuit and liked giving the graduation speech at girls' colleges. Each New Year's Day he gave a CIA party for the staff of the Columbia Broadcasting Service, for which the Agency would foot the bill and Allen would play the genial host. William Paley, head of CBS, was, of course, a good friend of the CIA and often gave the Agency access to the system's files and correspondents, assuring them that they were performing a patriotic duty in giving aid and information.

"Allen would get them [the CBS staff] to a dinner at the Alibi Club in Washington, a favorite place of his," William Bundy said later, "and it was a terribly nice party. There would be about twenty-five of us all told, about fifteen of them from CBS. We had a CIA man next to each CBS, and there was general table conversation, very useful in giving the feeling of Allen's thinking without giving them secret material, and at the same time extracting their views and thoughts—he was particularly good at this. Later critics like David Schoenbrun and correspondents like Eric Sevareid would be there, and it was a very warm and relaxed occasion."

But now these public relations efforts were growing less frequent, because, though the Agency was much more active, there was little Allen could talk about, much less boast about. The climate was changing. Stories were coming back from Asia about what the CIA was doing in Vietnam and Laos, and no one liked what they heard. Could it be true, as it was rumored in certain restricted circles in Washington, that the CIA in Southeast Asia was actually *running heroin* and using it as a

*Bissell was head of the directorate of Plans and Tracy Barnes was his chief assistant. They were mainly concerned with covert operations. Angleton was still chief of Counterintelligence and Counterespionage. Richard Helms was chief of Operations, responsible (until he succeeded him) to Bissell. Robert Amory was still deputy director.

currency for paying for covert operations in Saigon, Pnom Phen, and Vientiane? It sounded like a hark back to the beginning of the century, when the British had used opium in China to buy their way in and make the mandarins rich and the masses supine as they tightened their colonial grip on the country. Yet the skeptics who protested that Americans—even American intelligence agents—could never stoop so low were confounded. It was only too true. The CIA was spreading drugs and corruption through Asia, and the stench of evil was beginning to cling to the Agency's name.

At home in the United States peoples' attitudes had begun to turn against the Republican Party and the principles it stood for. The gungho anti-communism of the early Dulles years was beginning to seep away in the twilight of the Eisenhower administration, and the President had lost prestige over the U-2 affair. Despite his clownish and boorish behavior in Paris, there was little disposition to blame Krushchev or the Russians for breaking off the summit,* and a tendency instead to whisper that a CIA conspiracy had sabotaged the most promising international conference of the decade.

Whether he was slowing down or not, Allen still liked to be involved in, or in close touch with, the more bizarre operations in which the Agency was engaged. He would turn up at the CIA training farm in Virginia to watch recruits performing and sit in on the polygraph (lie detector) tests to which they and all Agency operators were subjected at regular intervals. He was particularly shocked when one pretty girl operative displayed obvious signs of being a lesbian, and asked why she was still in the service when male homosexuals were dismissed, once they were discovered.

"Because no one blackmails lesbians," said the unit officer crisply. "Anyway, it means she never falls in love with the guys she's working on."

"But what if she suddenly meets the right man and becomes normal?" Allen asked. "A pretty girl like that—she can't remain a lesbian all her life."

Once his enthusiasm had been for the CIA's production of gadgetry: bugs, flashless pistols, exploding candles, miniature radios and tape

*The fact that the Soviet government had launched a space satellite to overfly Europe and the United States on the same day that Krushchev complained of the U-2's intrusions into Russia was largely ignored by both the media and the public.

recorders. But now he was interested in the more sinister Agency experiments in mind-bending drugs, portable phials of lethal viruses, and esoteric poisons that killed without trace. Allen's sense of humor was touched when he learned that the unit working on these noxious enterprises was called the Health Alteration Committee (directed by Dr. Sidney Gottlieb and Boris Pash), and he added to his collection of CIA curios a noiseless gun which the committee had produced for firing darts smeared with LSD, germs, or venom at enemy agents or foreign personalities whose existence the CIA was finding embarrassing.

Richard Bissell was meticulous in briefing Allen in all the operations in which he was engaged. Bissell had now succeeded Frank Wisner as deputy director of Plans, which meant that he was in charge of all clandestine operations; and though he was no less zealous in promoting them, he was a much blander personality and rather more cynical than his predecessor.

Quite a few years had passed since he had scored his first success by helping overthrow the Jacob Arbenz régime in Guatemala and substituting one more amenable to the directors of United Fruit. Since that time Bissell had thought a great deal about the efficacy of such operations, and had begun to be dubious about the results they were likely to achieve.

It was not that he was morally against clandestine operations or the Agency's sponsorship of movements to overthrow Communist régimes. But he had begun to wonder whether they were worth while in the long run for the welfare of the United States.

"Guatemala was a complete success in the sense that the tactical objective was achieved," he said later. "It was done more or less on time and on budget. But all you could hope to do in a paramilitary operation like Guatemala was to place in power a friendly individual. Whether, having placed a friendly political leader in power and having got rid of Communist influences, you can then turn the situation around in the country concerned is open to question. We got Arbenz out. We substituted Armas. But I think most people would argue that from the day he was installed nobody has been able to make much of a success of Guatemala."

To Allen Dulles the CIA was still the knight in shining armor riding the white charger of the United States to the rescue of the ideologically

459

oppressed, and he was all in favor of covert actions in all parts of the globe. But Bissell had begun to wonder whether there weren't better ways of securing enduring results for the good of the nation. At the same time that his left hand was involved in all kinds of plots and conspiracies to overturn régimes or their leaders, his right hand was engaged in much gentler and more subtle means of subversion.

"One of our most successful functions," he said later, "was to maintain contact with individuals or groups in various countries who were out of office. In France we had very good contacts with the Socialists. I think this was true in Spain with the anti-Franco groups. I made it a part of my responsibilities to see that the Agency all over the world was in close contact with the developing opposition. In the Third World, for instance, one was always being surprised by *coups d'états* launched, very often, by officers of the rank of major or captain or below. We kept in close contact with the likely upstarts."

He added:

"I think some of our most successful operations were our subventions of youth organizations and labor organizations. They had a much longer term effect upon our relations, and for the good, than any of our covert actions. The most covert actions could do, I had begun to realize, was achieve the immediate power objective. But what happened after that, whether the country you turned over remained a dependable friend and a dependable ally, had really nothing to do with it."

So what good were they?

It was ironic that these thoughts were going through Bissell's head in 1960, when there was already well developed at the CIA a program, of which he had charge, for overthrowing by force the régime of Fidel Castro in Cuba.

Toward the end of September 1960, Allen Dulles was called to the White House for a meeting between the President and the National Security Council. The last months of the Eisenhower régime were upon them, and the President was in a curious mood.

Like a man approaching execution, the knowledge that only a short time remained for him as the chief magistrate of the most powerful nation in the world seemed to have remarkably concentrated his mind. Once upon a time he had groaned under the burdens of office and

longed to be free of its responsibilities. Now he seemed acutely aware of what he was about to lose, of the obscurity that was looming, and he was engaged in a flurry of activity designed to remind everybody that he was there and in charge.

The President had just come back from a session of the United Nations and while in New York had had his first and only meeting with Gamal Abdel Nasser of Egypt. It had done wonders for his ego. Dwight D. Eisenhower had always been one of Nasser's military heroes—he put him up there with Alanbrooke, Montgomery, Rommel, and Patton —and he had gone personally to the President's suite at the Waldorf Astoria to thank him for the action he had taken during the Suez crisis.

"By taking that position," the Egyptian said, "you put your principles before your friends."

He went on to tell the President that though he felt John F. Kennedy was a more youthful and liberal candidate, he would, if he had a vote, have given it to Richard M. Nixon in the forthcoming election because Nixon had been Ike's Vice-President, "and Egypt could feel nothing but gratitude toward both men for the position they took in 1956."

It was a pity, the President seemed to suggest, that the leaders of other small nations couldn't be as recognizant of the United States's power and influence and goodwill. Everybody was aware that Fidel Castro had also come to the United Nations meeting and was throwing his weight around in New York—especially in Harlem—making snide remarks about the racial and social policies of the United States. But since steps were already being taken to remedy the Cuban situation, the political leader against whom the President expressed the most lively dislike was not Castro but an African named Patrice Lumumba.

Lumumba was a hotheaded black politician who had already upset a number of applecarts, including those of the United States, during the transition of the Belgian Congo from a white colony into a black African republic.

"Rarely has a government proved in so short a time its lack of ability to govern," wrote President Eisenhower later.

Within two days of the independence ceremonies, tribal disturbances began. These reached alarming proportions four days later when troops of the Forces Publique, a Belgian-led constabulary of twenty-five thousand, revolted against their white officers. To pacify the troops, the

461

Lumumba government promoted all native personnel one grade and dismissed all the Belgians. . . . Now began a long series of riots, alarms, and rebellious outbreaks that should not have surprised the world but did, to say the least, cause both dismay and disgust.

The CIA was helping the Belgians to promote a breakaway province in Katanga, with a dissident black politician named Moise Tshombe as its leader, and thus assure the Western world of steady shipments of the minerals that were in rich supply in Katangese (and internationally owned) mines. But the Lumumba presence threatened the Western investment in Katanga, and CIA reports indicated that, in Eisenhower's words, "a Soviet ship with trucks and technicians had arrived in the Congo in the latter part of August, and it was estimated that two hundred Soviet technicians, in addition to some aircrews, were in the Congo without United Nations authority . . . military personnel prepared to engage in military activities in support of Lumumba," who was, the President was now convinced, "a Soviet tool."

To the National Security Council meeting at the White House, the President showed a pugnacity that was unusual in a normally sunny and equable personality. There was something about Lumumba which bugged him. It was true that the Congolese leader was a nervy, unbalanced character, who had an instinctive suspicion of Americans and a leaning toward communism, and it was also true that he was xenophobic, irreverent about American Presidents, and determined to bring Congolese mineral assets under Congolese, rather than outside, control. But when a member of the National Security Council suggested that, like all other African leaders so far, he was probably ready for a deal, provided the money was right, the President showed no desire for such a peaceful solution to the Congolese problem. He wanted Lumumba out. Who would rid him of this turbulent black?

"It was perfectly clear to me," said Richard Bissell later, "reading some of the cables and also some of the minutes of at least one special group meeting, that Eisenhower certainly wanted Lumumba got out of the way. Put on a great deal of pressure to have it done."

Normally (if that is the word) a request for the assassination of a foreign leader would have been left in the hands of Richard Bissell. But Bissell was away on holiday, yachting peacefully off Connecticut, so Allen told the President that he would personally see to the affair and

would put Richard Helms in charge of the details. A few days later Helms produced a blueprint for the "elimination."

A CIA employee was called back from Leopoldville, the Congolese capital, and there found Bronson Tweedy, head of the African division of the CIA, waiting for him with a "first aid kit," as it was jocularly called. There were rubber gloves, a phial of lethal fever germs, a portable electric toothbrush complete with batteries, and three tubes of toothpaste. The tubes of toothpaste were to be impregnated with the germs and somehow introduced into Lumumba's toilet requisites. He had nice bright teeth and it was presumed that he liked to keep them well scrubbed.

The CIA operative returned to his post with the assassination kit, and Allen waited for news that the hated Lumumba had been taken ill. Nothing happened. Lumumba still continued to intrigue with the Communists, make a mockery of the United Nations, and threaten the uncertain tenure of the West in the Congo. Why didn't he succumb to the deadly dose the Agency had prepared for him?

But it seemed that Lumumba was not so keen on dental hygiene after all. Around the Agency, where Lumumba was known as "Prissy," some wit remarked that "Prissy obviously believes halitosis is better than no breath at all."

It was not until several weeks later that a more effective CIA puppet came on the scene in the shape of Joseph Mobuto, and he took over power and captured the maverick Patrice Lumumba. Lumumba died shortly afterwards "while trying to escape," but whether Mobuto did the deed at the behest of the CIA or from more personal motives is one of those mysteries time is not likely to elucidate.

At least President Eisenhower had the satisfaction of knowing that his black African gadfly did not survive the end of his administration. Lumumbo died, in fact, on January 17, 1961, three days before the President handed over his office to John F. Kennedy.

On the other hand, the fate of Fidel Castro, on which Eisenhower, Foster, and Allen had been working since 1959, would have to be dealt with by the incoming President.

CHAPTER TWENTY-EIGHT

Siempre Fidel

—◆—

Fidel Castro did not wrest power from the Cuban dictator, Fulgencio Batista, until January 1, 1959, but even before that his guerilla activities in the mountains of the Sierra Maestra had aroused the ire of several members of the Joint Chiefs of Staff in Washington, and at least one of them was all for having him and his rebel band snuffed out.

The United States has had a military, naval, and air force base at Guantanamo, on the island of Cuba, since the days of the Spanish-American war, and though it is nowadays sealed off from the rest of the island by the Castrist régime, under Batista U.S. troops often made trips to other parts of Cuba. It was on one of these outings, in 1958, that a group of Marines, on their way back in a Cuban bus from a bathe in Guantanamo Bay, were held up and taken hostage by Castro guerillas.

When word reached Washington, the doughty Admiral Arleigh A. Burke, chief of U.S. Naval Operations, stormed in to see Foster Dulles and demanded the right to send a platoon of Marines into the mountains and "get 'em." He told the Secretary that he realized there would be a fight and some Marines might get killed, but at least it would demonstrate to Castro that he wouldn't monkey around with Americans.

Foster had vetoed the suggestion. Batista's situation was already precarious and the Secretary had no wish to embarrass him. Instead, discreet contacts were made and the missing Marines quietly ransomed. At the same time, efforts were made to persuade the dictator to liberalize his régime, end corruption, and institute reforms that

would take some of the revolutionary wind out of Castro's sails.* But it was no use. The winds of change were blowing too hard, and Castro came to power a few months later. He immediately set about cleaning up corruption and crime in the island, and inevitably clashed with U.S. interests, which had until now regarded Cuba as a sort of American colony, an offshore nest of gambling joints, brothels, bathing beaches, and sugar plantations there to be exploited by American dollars.

The revolution was conducted with a ruthlessness that shocked Cubans and Americans alike. Not only were the casinos closed down, the gangsters and prostitutes deported, but legitimate U.S. businesses were taken over, and the process of socialization begun with little if any talk of compensation. To the President, to his Secretary, and to the director of the CIA, it was an affront not to be borne. Castro was behaving like Nasser, only this time it was not British but American vital interests that were threatened.

In the spring of 1960, Richard Bissell was called in to see Allen Dulles and told that Foster and the President had talked it over and decided that action must be taken. A project had been agreed upon, Allen said, and he had presidential authorization to carry it out.

"The project was to seek to overthrow, or at least to promote sabotage and revolutionary activity against, Castro in Cuba," said Richard Bissell later. "The project, as it was originally conceived, was to evolve in the selection, recruitment and training of a key group of about twenty to thirty young Cubans. They would be trained in sabotage, communications, guerilla and jungle war activities, and the notion was that they would then train a considerably larger group—up to about two hundred Cubans."

These two hundred men would then be infiltrated into Cuba, in small groups, to make contact with anti-Castro dissidents inside the country. The idea was that they would link together, be supplied from the U.S. mainland, and "constitute a true underground network within the island."

This was decided upon in March 1960, but things moved slowly. In August, Bissell flew down to Panama and saw a camp being prepared

---

*Batista was brought to the United States on an official visit, and lauded by some sections of the press.

for twenty or thirty potential guerillas, but they didn't move in until a week or two later.

"Then, in the early autumn, September or October," Bissell said, "events were moving fairly rapidly in Cuba. Castro was consolidating his position, and our original plan was way behind its time-table. There didn't seem to be time to keep to the original plan and have a large group trained by this initial cadre of young Cubans. So the larger group was formed and established at La Finca,* in Guatemala, and there the training was conducted entirely by Americans."

But by the end of October, Bissell had to let Allen know that the original plan wasn't going to work out. For one thing, there just didn't seem to be any anti-Castro dissidents inside Cuba with whom infiltrators could link up. The idea was that the CIA's Cubans would land and beef up and inspire the anti-Castro underground. But when the infiltrators got there, they discovered that the underground didn't exist.

"I think that every team we sent in was picked up within a few days," said Bissell. "Part of the reason was that the Cubans were totally insecure and hadn't the most rudimentary notion of security. Part of the problem was the political exiles in Miami, who all claimed large and organized followings on the island. Well, they may have had vague sympathizers on the island, but they had no way of communicating with them securely, no command or control over them, and therefore there were no internal underground cells to which we could send supplies, or with which we could establish communications. It was a mess."

By this time the presidential election was reaching its climax in the United States. John F. Kennedy, who knew nothing about what was going on, campaigned loudly for the Cuban vote in Miami by attacking Castro and promising U.S. help in bringing his socialistic régime to an end. Richard M. Nixon, who had been Eisenhower's liaison with the CIA throughout the planning, and knew every detail, said nothing. He had been informed by Allen that the original plan would have to be abandoned, and that the concept was shifting to a project not of infiltration but of invasion.

"And that concept crystalized in January 1961," said Bissell, "and the notion was that a spot would be chosen where, by reason of the

*Ironically enough, La Finca means "The Farm," which is also the name the CIA gives to its covert operations training camp in Virginia.

terrain, a small landing force could establish a beachhead on the Cuban shore and hold it."

Though he has never said so, one suspects that by this time Richard Bissell was beginning to have great doubts about the viability of the Cuban enterprise.

"It had become a very complex undertaking," he commented later, "complex at the Washington end as well as in the training camps. I was commander of this operation, and I tried to keep Allen and Cabell* informed, but I didn't keep them well *enough* informed, and Allen used to be quite irritated with me on occasion for not keeping him briefed almost from hour to hour."

It was the Cuban element of the operation that was causing him the worst of his worries.

"A General Council of Cuban political leaders had been formed," he said, "and they were very quarrelsome. Several of the more liberal, or left-wing, elements of the anti-Castro movement refused to join the Council, so that we had to merge it with another, larger so-called Political Council. They were constantly fighting and it took the full time of several people to keep them sorted out."

Early in January they came up with a manifesto which they planned to distribute to the Cuban populace when the landings took place, and a copy of it reached Bissell.

"I took one look at it," he said, "and I told them: 'If this piece is published, it will kill any counterrevolution.' It was much too reactionary. It promised to return all seized property, even that which had been given to the peasants from the big landlords. I said: 'You can't have your group issuing a manifesto like this, saying that you're going to return all the sugar plantations and everything else. It's got to be a very much more liberal document.' I'm glad to say the State Department agreed with this, but we had to go through hoops negotiating them into writing a more attractive, sexier political manifesto."

One of the reasons it was difficult was because it was hard to get hold of the Cuban leaders. All of them wanted to go down to Guatemala to visit the training camps and show themselves off to the men there, because if the operation were successful, these were the troops whose

*General Charles P. Cabell, of the U.S. Air Force, was deputy to Allen Dulles at the CIA.

influence would count in the new Cuba and they wanted to insinuate themselves. They might have saved themselves the journey. With almost no exception, the Cuban exile leaders were intensely unpopular with the men, who once or twice threatened to throw them into the swamps outside their camps.

It was in this atmosphere that Bissell learned that Allen had fully briefed the new President on the operation. John F. Kennedy had immediately called a meeting of the Joint Chiefs of Staff and brought them up to date with what the CIA had been doing, and had Allen detail the various developments in the plan from what had begun as an underground infiltration into the present program for an outright invasion. The Joint Chiefs of Staff then decided that they would make their own evaluation, and appointed "three officers of clover rank"* to go down to inspect the camps and examine the plan of operations.

Somewhat to his surprise, no doubt, Bissell learned that the report the Joint Chiefs of Staff received from their emissaries was one of complete approval. The next step was to have the President's endorsement of the preceding administration's decision, and this came with little hesitation from Kennedy. He was in a feisty mood. At the same time that he was going over the Cuban plans he was approving Green Beret operations in Southeast Asia, and sustaining the belief, which he had voiced during the election campaign, that this was the era of the "little wars" and that the United States should be prepared to fight them where and when they cropped up.

In the case of the operation against Cuba, Bissell now got presidential permission to press on with all dispatch. From this moment on the three Army majors were permanently attached to his operational headquarters (which were in some old buildings beyond the Reflecting Pool in Washington), and they were kept closely informed of how things were going. They reported weekly to the regular meetings of the Joint Chiefs of Staff.

"And then," said Bissell, "there began a series of policy meetings at the White House, and I would go along with Allen, and quite often with Cabell and a Marine major who was my military deputy."

The President would be there, together with Dean Rusk (Secretary of State), Robert McNamara (Secretary of Defense), Robert Kennedy

*Major.

(the Attorney General), Paul Nitze (who was back in government as a policy planning expert), and Adolphe A. Berle (who had been brought in as a special adviser to the President). At other times William Bundy was there, also as a special adviser.

The least enthusiastic member of these White House discussion groups was Dean Rusk.

"I was always aware that Dean didn't like the operation at all," Bissell said later.

At the first meeting, Bissell outlined the operational plan and described how the Cuban exiles would land and secure a beachhead close to a town named Trinidad, on the southern shore of the island some 350 miles from Havana. Rusk objected at once. He said that attempting a landing near a big town like Trinidad would inevitably attract a great deal of publicity, and that wasn't what they wanted, was it? He was not enthusiastic about the operation at all, but if it did have to take place, wouldn't a more obscure landing place be better, so that it would look more like a genuine guerilla operation?

He then looked across at Allen and asked him whether he really thought the landing would ignite a revolt in Cuba against Castro. Allen turned the question over to Bissell. William Bundy, who was present on this occasion, said later:

"I would say that Allen and, *a fortiori*, Dick Bissell were much more honest in their staff recommendations and advice than I thought the people in the Pentagon, the generals, were. Bissell said that you just couldn't tell whether this thing would ignite a real revolt. 'We have reports it will,' he said, 'but how can you possibly tell?' He was very cautious in his words. He promised nothing."

Rusk thought this all the more reason to act quietly. His point was accepted and the meeting adjourned while Bissell consulted his planners and a new landing beach was found.

It was in this way that they came up with the Bay of Pigs.

By this time Bissell must have been getting really concerned and confused. The Cuban operation wasn't what he had started out with at all. What had begun as a series of infiltrations, for producing long-term results, had been transformed into a *coup de main,* and all the hawks in the Pentagon and the cabinet were expecting miracles from it. Hadn't the CIA overturned Mossadeq in Iran? Wasn't Bissell the

man who had helped mastermind the Guatemala operation and saved South America from the Communists? Bobby Kennedy, who was one of the most rapacious of the hawks, sounded as if he were inwardly rubbing his hands in glee at a prospect of an imminent weekend in old-style Havana. As for Castro, he wouldn't be around; the CIA would have taken care of him.

In the circumstances, it was difficult for Bissell to explain that Cuba was very different from Iran, and that Fidel Castro was a much more challenging proposition than Jacob Arbenz. Did he have premonitions of disaster? No, but neither did he feel like Henry the Fifth on the night before Agincourt. He could only caution and warn his listeners not to expect too much, and not to believe that a wave of revolt would flame through the Cuban countryside the moment the guerillas hit the beach at the Bay of Pigs.

As for Allen, "He had turned the whole thing over to Dick Bissell three quarters of the time," as William Bundy said later. "I had the feeling that by then he was slowing down a little. Thinking about it, after the whole thing was over, I came to the conclusion that he hadn't been quite the man I had known. All through, he hadn't been as much on top of the operation as I had expected."

Allen was afterwards to tell Dean Rusk that he never had much faith in the Bay of Pigs operation, and had serious doubts about its outcome, "but the terrible thing was that he never once mentioned those doubts during the cabinet meetings," Rusk said.

In fact, Rusk had never really trusted Allen, not since the days when Rusk had been head of the Rockefeller Foundation and Allen had come to him one time and said: "I hear the members of the Foundation keep diaries about the important people they see and talk with in the course of their travels. Can the CIA have copies of their diaries?"

Rusk told him that under no circumstances would he allow this, since it would seriously compromise the relations of the Foundation and its fellows with foreign governments and personalities. Allen said he accepted that and went away.

"But then I found the CIA had started reading the Foundation's mail," Rusk said, "to find out what our members were writing, anyway."*

---

*It was part of a widespread mail-opening operation which the CIA began in the mid-fifties.

Now he had no faith in him, and was worried by his silence as the Bay of Pigs discussions went on. Rusk was more doubtful than ever about the whole Cuban venture. The men from the Pentagon were full of bright and breezy optimism, but there was something in Bissell's manner that filled him with apprehension.

All the same, when President Kennedy called the famous meeting at the White House on April 4, 1961, and asked all members around the table to raise their hands if they were in favor of the Bay of Pigs invasion, Dean Rusk's hand was up there with the rest of them—"but without any enthusiasm," as he said later. The President nodded at Bissell. The operation was on.

The silence that followed the decision was broken by Allen Dulles. He pointed out that he had a long-standing engagement to speak in Puerto Rico and dine with the governor afterwards. Should he go? It was decided it would alert people if he did not keep his engagement, and he was told not to cancel it.

He left for Puerto Rico the next morning, and that was his last contact with the Bay of Pigs invasion. He was still in Puerto Rico and out of touch with his commanders when disaster struck the whole sorry enterprise.

There have been plenty of inquests on the Bay of Pigs débâcle; this narrative does not propose to include another, except insofar as it affects the life and career of Allen Dulles. The sick prime minister of a dying Empire had brought about the disaster at Suez, but the Bay of Pigs proved that you could be the young and energetic President of the most powerful nation in the world and still engage in an act of gross military ineptitude and tragic political folly. Unhappily, the men in government in Washington did not learn the lesson from it, and Vietnam was one result.

John F. Kennedy has since been praised for so publicly taking the blame for the Bay of Pigs, but it is difficult to see what alternative he had. Dean Rusk said, as the bad news came in, "There's enough blame to go all around," and stressed the need to protect the President from international obloquy. But it would have been a shabby act of cowardice, and ineffective, anyway, had Kennedy tried to avoid admitting full responsibility. After all, he had presided at all the discussions, and from the moment the Joint Chiefs of Staff gave the operation their

approval, he had given it his full presidential backing. In saying *mea culpa* to the world he displayed the only stroke of political wisdom in the whole unhappy affair.

But behind the scenes, it was upon Allen Dulles's head that the guilt was heaped. In the inevitable inquiry which followed the failure of the mission, it might have been expected that some of the culpability (and contumely) would have been laid at the door of the Joint Chiefs of Staff and the generals in the Pentagon who had so enthusiastically backed the operation. It was under their influence that it gradually changed its nature and its objectives. Robert Kennedy, the Attorney General, might also have received a not unfair share of the blame for his repeated interferences in the planning and his hawkish eagerness to see the Castrist forces wiped out and the leader forced to eat crow.

The inquiry was put into the hands of the inspector general of the CIA, who was at that time Lyman B. Kirkpatrick, Jr. His regard for Allen Dulles had always been lukewarm and he seemed to believe (with good reason) that his own career in the Agency had been hindered rather than helped by Allen's attitude toward him. One presumes that he allowed no personal feelings to enter into his assessment of the Bay of Pigs operation and Allen's part in it; nonetheless he placed the blame for its failure fairly and squarely on Allen's shoulders and incisively criticized him and the CIA management for the way they had handled the whole affair.*

Curiously enough, Allen had always regarded Kirkpatrick as one of his prize pupils at the CIA and believed that he had enormously helped rather than hindered his career.

"I know he had very hurt feelings when the inspector general's report was shown to him," said one of his collaborators later. "It was very critical of him and of the CIA management of the whole thing. And he felt badly done by. He felt that he had helped Kirkpatrick's career and had been one of his mentors at the Agency. In fact, he often said that if Kirkpatrick hadn't been in a wheelchair, he would have seen that he bypassed Dick Helms and people like that and took over one of the top jobs, like director of Plans. And I think Dulles felt—well, Dulles was a great man for personal loyalty, and I think he felt this was a personal and disloyal exhibition on Kirkpatrick's part."

*The report has never been published.

Allen had offered his resignation to the President the moment it was obvious that the Bay of Pigs had failed, and it had been refused. Now he was expected to offer it again, but this time he stayed put. He thought other people should be resigning before he did, and made it clear that he was thinking of one person in particular, Robert Kennedy.*But it was Robert Kennedy, in fact, who was pushing the President to get rid of *him*.

It was eventually arranged that Allen should stay on until the CIA's grand new building complex at Langley, Virginia—which was the fulfillment of one of Allen's ambitions for the Agency—was officially opened. On September 28, 1961, he accompanied Kennedy to a graduation ceremony at the Naval War College at Newport, Rhode Island, and there heard the President announce that he was nominating John A. McCone to take his place.

It was only two years before that John Foster, Allen, and Eleanor Dulles had run the foreign policy of the United States among them. Now only "little sister" was left in government—and how long would she last?

Early in 1962, Eleanor Dulles got a call from the Secretary of State's office asking her to come in and see him that afternoon. It was a Wednesday and she was due to leave on Friday for a long trip around South America, as part of her study of Communist aid to foreign nations. For a wildly optimistic moment she thought that maybe Dean Rusk was going to put her back on the German desk. She had heard from friends in Bonn, backed by a personal message from Adenauer, that she was missed and the Berliners weren't doing so well in Washington without her. But when she went in and faced the Secretary, she saw from his expression that there wasn't a hope.

"The White House has asked me to get rid of you," Rusk said.

There was a strong rumor in the State Department that Robert Kennedy had been going through the lists "looking for political taint," hunting down dedicated Republicans rather as Hanes and O'Connor had flushed out Democrats in Foster's day. He had also been heard to say that "he didn't want any more of the Dulles family around." So

*One high CIA member later remarked: "Where Castro and Cuba were concerned, Bobby Kennedy went further than Henry the Second, and everybody covered up for him."

Eleanor wasn't surprised. All the same, she thought it was a bit rough; it wasn't as if hers had been a political appointment. She was far from owing her job to Foster. And she didn't want to go.

"It was silly, I suppose," she said later. "I was sixty-six years old, and a lot of my friends asked why I should want to go on working. Well, I had psychological and financial reasons. My job at State was a valuable thing to cling to. Besides, I had debts. I had put two children through college, and I needed a salary."

There was a job in Europe which was very inconspicuous, and she had the qualifications for it. It was very low profile stuff, and she wouldn't be around Washington any more. The Kennedys wouldn't know she existed, and it would give her two interesting years while she waited for her pension. Could she take it?

"No," said Rusk, and added that the White House didn't want her taking any more jobs or going on any more missions abroad. She knew too many people. He went on: "I have to say that legally you have a right to stay on for another two years—here in Washington."

"Yes," said Eleanor, "but you know what that means. As soon as it's known that the White House wants to get rid of me, my usefulness would be reduced to zero."

Rusk nodded in agreement.

"Well, then," she said, "can I take my annual leave and go out and look for another job?"

"You do that," said Rusk, greatly relieved.

So Eleanor Dulles emptied her desk and left the State Department for good. She had served there for fifteen years, and for another five years in other departments of government. It seemed hard that she was departing so shabbily, just because one brother had been a Republican Secretary of State and the other had been responsible for the Bay of Pigs.

CHAPTER TWENTY-NINE

Such Other Functions

In the fall of 1962 Howard Roman, an ex-CIA employee who had left the Agency to write a novel, had a call from one of his former bosses.

"You aren't going to make any money with fiction and stuff like that," Roman was told. "How about collaborating with Allen Dulles on some of his book projects?"

It seemed that Allen's friends at the CIA were worrying about him in his enforced retirement, afraid he would begin to fret and crumple now that his long career in intelligence had ended under such a cloud. They had encouraged him to begin writing his reminiscences, but it hadn't worked out. For a lawyer who had spent several years writing briefs, it turned out that he was unable to set down his thoughts on paper with any vitality or clarity. In any case, as he said himself, he lacked the "residual energy." One attempt at collaboration (with Charles Murphy of *Fortune* magazine) had ended in an agreement to go their separate ways with the work unfinished. Now the Encyclopaedia Britannica had asked Allen to write a long piece for them on Intelligence, and Cass Canfield at *Harper's* had suggested he might like to expand it, once it was finished, into a book.

Would Roman take on the job of getting Allen's thoughts down in publishable form?

The result was an association that lasted through the twilight of Allen's life and resulted in four books: two edited volumes of espionage adventures, with prefaces by Allen; a handbook on espionage called *The Craft of Intelligence;* and the story of his famous wartime exploit, Operation SUNRISE, which he called *The Secret Surrender.*

Roman was much younger than Allen and their stations in the CIA hierarchy had been far apart, but their paths had crossed frequently over the years, mostly in Switzerland and in Germany, where Roman had worked for Frank Wisner as case officer for infiltrations into Russia and eastern Europe. In Switzerland, Clover Dulles and Roman's first wife had used the same Jungian therapist. When Roman's wife had to be sent for a time to a sanitarium, it was the same one to which Allen and Clover later took their wounded son, Allen, Jr., for treatment. And Allen was aware that Roman knew all about his long liaison with Mary Bancroft.

They would meet for work every day at 9:30 in the morning and continue until noon, when they would adjourn for a dry martini and a lunch, usually *à trois* with Clover, cooked by the superb Guatamelan mistress of the Q Street kitchen, Natalia. During working hours it was hard to get consecutive thoughts out of Allen. He was always mislaying papers and would rant around the house, shouting: "Clover, where the hell is that book I had last night?" or: "Clover, what in heaven's name have you done with those papers I left on my desk?"

Clover would never bother to answer, because she knew that in the end he would find what he was looking for. He used these searches as a distraction, to take the pressure off his mind and save him from having to think hard and concentrate on names, dates, and times which he was finding it hard to remember; and he no longer had access to the director's file room at the Agency, which would have enabled him to check. He frequently groaned from the pain in his gouty foot.

But over lunch he would instantly become the urbane and civilized man of the world that everyone knew, full of good stories about spies he had known, exploits in which he had participated, coups that had, or had not quite, come off. Clover listened with the slightly glazed look and distant, indulgent smile of one who had heard all of them before but didn't mind the repetition. Anyway, they were superb stories and well worth telling again. But one day the three of them were sitting around the table when Allen happened to say: "Remember that day at Ascona, on Lake Maggiore, when I sent you out with Frau Waibel on the lake?"

It was the climactic moment of Operation SUNRISE, when the German envoys were coming, and Allen had wanted to get Clover out of the way. At the mention of it, an expression as if from some great pain

passed over Clover's delicate face, then sheer rage took its place.

"Well, you would never have believed it," Roman said later. "It started a great fight all over again, and they wrangled bitterly over what he had done to her, how she had been kept out on the lake getting sunburned, and how she had never forgiven him for it. Then all the terrible things he had ever done to her came tumbling out. It went on and on and I couldn't stop them. I was very embarrassed. It was a real family spat—and all those years later. I realized then how unhappy Clover really was, all the resentments she'd kept to herself, how she'd hated what he had done to her. And I now knew why I'd heard that they'd almost got divorced a couple of times."

One afternoon in November 1963 they were working in Allen's study when the telephone rang, and Roman could tell that it was someone from the CIA at the other end of the line. Allen's words were mostly monotones. There was no expression on his face. All he said when he put down the telephone was: "Let's call it a day, shall we, Howard? The President's been shot in Dallas."

Not long afterwards President Johnson appointed the Warren Commission to look into the background to the assassination, and it was announced that Allen Dulles would be a member of the panel. Thereafter, he was in increasing telephonic contact with the CIA and several high officers of the Agency came round to see him. One day Dean Rusk asked him to come over to the State Department. When he got there, Rusk explained to him that following the President's death he had asked the CIA to make the closest possible inquiry into whether any foreign government could have been involved in the assassination. Did Allen have anything to tell him about that? Allen said he had not.

"I didn't know at that time," Rusk said later, "that the Agency had been involved in assassination plots against the heads of foreign governments, but the CIA didn't tell me anything about them. When I testified before the Warren Commission, I made essentially two points: (1) that we had no evidence of the involvement of a foreign government; and, as an afterthought (2) that I doubted that any foreign government had any motivation to be involved in the Kennedy assassination. I could not have made the second point had I known about our own plots against Castro. But no one who did know tugged my coat-tails to tell me about the plots and let me take that into account in my testimony. I find that unforgivable. I would never have testified on the

477

second point to the Warren Commission had I known. The President [Lyndon B. Johnson] would have had to decide whether I should inform the Warren Commission about the plots; no one can know what the President's decision would have been."

Rusk had no way of knowing at the time whether Allen Dulles knew about the plots.

"One can surmise that he must have," said Rusk, "but I am unwilling to make that allegation without some evidence—which I do not have."

The evidence, however, is now there, for most of the senior members of the CIA involved in assassination plans and discussions have confirmed that the director of the Agency was as much in the know as they were. In the circumstances it seems extraordinary that Allen, as a member of the Warren Commission, did not privately advise the Secretary of State that there were certain areas he should avoid when he was giving his evidence. But then, Rusk was not alone in being kept in ignorance. Allen did not tell his fellow members of the Commission what he knew, either, and they wrote their report ignorant of the fact that sitting among them was someone who, had he confided in them, might have altered the whole trend of their findings.

In 1965 two books were due out about the Bay of Pigs, one by Arthur Schlesinger and the other by Ted Sorensen, and extracts appeared in the magazines blaming the CIA for the débâcle. Allen called John Fischer, the editor of *Harper's,* and told him he would like to write a rebuttal to the charges. A young staff writer, Willie Morris, was sent down to Washington to help him whip an article into shape.

To Morris the former head of the CIA was a legendary figure, and like President Kennedy, he suspected he would find it "hard to operate with legendary figures." He was afraid he might prove to be "as cold and rigorous as his brother John Foster had been—a Calvinistic specter to me when he was Secretary of State." But he had a pleasant surprise awaiting him.

"From the moment we sat down to our twelve-hour work days in a study overlooking a sedate walled-in terrace I knew I was in the presence of a courtly and civilized man," Morris wrote later,

a little precious at first on the arcane calling which had obsessed him since his OSS days in Berne, but still an easy man to be with, curious and

478

feeling about his fellow creatures, a casual and entertaining host, and—
best of all—an engrossing raconteur, especially with stories about spies.

But, like Howard Roman, Morris found it hard to pin Allen down to
facts and dates, or to get him to remember details. Clover had gone
up to Watertown with her daughter, Joan, to stay with Eleanor, and
halfway through the consultations Allen flew up to Lake Ontario to
join them. Morris followed shortly afterwards, and almost immediately
ran into difficulties with both Eleanor and Joan. The more they heard
about the project, the less they liked it. They kept listening in on the
dialogue between the two men, and when they got Allen alone they
beseeched him in fierce whispers to call it off.

"Allen finally decided not to issue the article," Eleanor said later,
"and Willy blames me for it. I didn't want it issued. I still don't want
it issued, because Allen had already begun to lose his command over
his memory and ideas. If it were ever to be printed, it would not be
a credit to him, because it was from a man who had lost about thirty
percent of his faculties. I think it would have been unfair to make a
document out of a man who was seriously going downhill."

Willy Morris went back to New York, richer for some stories of
wartime derring-do against evil Nazis and extravagant Italians, but
poorer for the loss of an article about one of America's saddest and
silliest humiliations. In the course of a few frustrating weeks he had
come to realize that Allen Dulles, for all his easy smile and flow of
conversation, was old and weary.

Around this time, Allen and Howard Roman finished the draft of
The Secret Surrender and it was decided that it ought to be read by as
many as possible of the protagonists concerned before it was sent to
press, since this would be the first time that the full story, in all its
Byzantine detail, would be told of how the Nazi army's surrender in
Italy had been arranged.

"We'll have a monster proof reading rally," Allen said, aroused
suddenly from his increasing languor. "And what's more, we'll have it
at the scene of the crime!"

Publishers were consulted and it was all arranged. Invitations were
sent out for a Monster Proof Reading Rally at Ascona, on Lake Maggiore, where Operation SUNRISE had reached its climax.

Allen and Clover traveled to the rendezvous by boat via England,

where he stopped off to greet his old friends, Rebecca West and Barbara Ward, with whom he had long exchanged confidences. Then the two of them went on by train to Kreuzling, near Lake Constance, where Allen, Jr., was a patient at the sanitarium. Allen had already made arrangements so that his wounded son would never again want for financial help, but he grieved that Allen, Jr., seemed prepared to spend the rest of his existence sunk in a sloth of melancholia in a Swiss institution. He made a tentative suggestion that he might like to try the outside world again, at which his son gave him a look of absolute hatred and lashed out:

"Never! I'm never coming home to you, ever!"

They left him to his misery and went on to Ascona, and at once Allen's spirits rose again. For they were there and waiting to greet him: General Lyman Lemnitzer and General Terence Airey, the American and the Englishman who had liaised between him and army headquarters during the delicate moments of SUNRISE, both of them this time with their wives; Major Max Waibel, the amiable Swiss intelligence man, and his chubby hausfrau wife; the elegant German-American, Gero von Schulz Gaevernitz, who had arranged all the secret meetings between the Nazi and Allied generals; and General Karl Wolff himself, once commander-in-chief of the SS forces in Italy, now commonplace in civilian clothes, his complexion pasty from a stretch in Spandau for war crimes.

Only Wally was missing. The cheery Czech radio operator, who had risked his life by hiding inside SS headquarters in Italy and keeping radio contact between Allen Dulles and the Nazi commander, had gone back to Prague after the war. Like many another Czech who had fought in the West, he was rounded up when the Communists took power in Prague, and what the Nazis could not achieve the reds succeeded in doing. He had died in a Czech concentration camp sometime in 1948–49.

They drank a toast to his memory. And then the monster proof reading rally began, there beside the lake where, twenty years earlier, it had all happened and a mighty army's unconditional surrender had been fixed. There was no doubt who had been the hero of the occasion.

There was a sparkle in the eyes of all of them as they listened to the narrative of their fantastic adventure. And, as the story was retold, Allen Dulles seemed to grow younger; he was back in the heyday of

his career, the gay Lothario with a mission, dexterously balancing the fate of a nation in his hands with all the insouciance of a master juggler. It was SUNRISE again, and no longer the sunset of his life and career.

In 1967, President Johnson sent Allen down to the Deep South on a one-man mission. Civil rights workers had been murdered in Mississippi, and Allen was asked to look around and report on the climate of Southern opinion. It was not really his kind of thing. Compared with Germany or Russia, for example, the Deep South was terra incognita; in addition to which, he was physically rundown. As he hobbled through the thick heat of a Mississippi summer, his left foot throbbing with a painful attack of gout, his sensibilities were assailed by the unpleasant stench of racial hatred in the air.

When he got back home to Q Street, in Georgetown, he had the first of his strokes. It affected his eyes and he could no longer read. A few months later he seemed to recover both his sight and his spirits, but the stroke had slowed him down and an air of lassitude clung to him. He no longer had any will to work, and would sit around his study, sometimes in a dressing gown, always in bedroom slippers to ease the throb in his feet, his mind turned inward to the past.

The second stroke took away his lateral and peripheral vision, so that from now on if anyone stood on his left side he could not see them, and this caused him considerable annoyance when he discovered that there was someone there. He still continued to enjoy his food and wine, which did no good whatsoever to his gout.

There were four more strokes, and the doctors marveled that none of them killed him, only nudged him further and further down the hill. One of them was particularly unpleasant and put him into Walter Reed Hospital with a paralyzed throat, so that he was temporarily unable to swallow and had to be fed intravenously.

"Lord," he sighed croakily through cracked lips, when Howard Roman came to see him, "what I wouldn't do for a nice glass of beer."

Instead, Clover floated into the room, scarves and delicate perfume trailing behind her, and prattled cheerfully about how she had really found religion at last, and how marvelously it was changing her life.

He was up and about again after that stroke, too. And it wasn't until the night of December 24, 1968, with all his friends gathered to greet him at the party down below, that the flu virus crept into his bedroom

481

at Q Street and made him vulnerable for the final blow. He died of a bout of pneumonia a little over a month later—on January 29, 1969. By that time he had made it plain to everybody who came to see him that he would be glad to be going. For the past few years, life really hadn't been much fun any more.

He had asked to be cremated, but there was, of course, a memorial service for him and it took place at Georgetown Presbyterian Church on February 1. Almost everybody who mattered in the world of espionage and intelligence was there, as well as the diplomatic community and all his friends. Even the KGB sent a representative and a wreath, and the word went round that Kim Philby had got a message through from Moscow regretting that circumstances beyond his control prevented him from being there to salute the memory of his erstwhile associate.

The minister of Georgetown Presbyterian Church, the Reverend Russell C. Stroup, was a simple, honest, and sincere man who normally spoke from his pulpit in direct and unsentimental words, totally devoid of rhetoric. But on this occasion he seemed to have decided on something different from his normal prose and delivery; to the surprise of many of the assembled mourners who knew him well, he launched himself into quite a peroration in Allen's memory.

"It is as a splendid watchman that many of us saw him," he said, reading from the script before him, "a famous and trusted figure in clear outline on the American ramparts, seeing that the nation could not be surprised in its sleep or be overcome in the night. . . . It fell to Allen Dulles to perfect a new kind of protection, to further develop the Central Intelligence Agency, to inspire its people with conscience and meaning along with the techniques and intellectual discipline that the nation demands in our modern world. . . . The furious rhetoric of our times allied with the pervading cynicism has made many of us lose sight of the issues that really matter. With Allen Dulles what counted always were the central elements of the liberal tradition, liberty under law, conscience, the sovereignty of principle."

As one of the local flock whispered to his wife: "I didn't know Stroup had it in him."

In fact, he didn't. The previous night he had received a telephone call to inform him that a script was being sent for him to read for his

address from the pulpit on the morrow. Stroup pointed out that he was not in the habit of reading other people's messages, and always wrote his own.

"Ah yes," said the voice, "but this is a special occasion. The address has been written by the CIA."

It had indeed. It came from the pen of James Jesus Angleton, chief of Counterintelligence and Counterespionage, the man who had once unveiled the famous Krushchev speech to the world, and now seized a choice occasion to laud the virtues of Allen Dulles and the CIA.

Allen would have appreciated that. One could almost hear his great laugh again, Ho-ho-ho, ringing out in limbo.

Envoi

In the late summer of 1976 one son, two daughters, and twenty-six grandsons and granddaughters of the Dulles family gathered around Eleanor's log cabin on her island in Lake Ontario, at Henderson, New York, for a farewell singsong and barbecue before they scattered back to their homes, their jobs, or their colleges.

They came every year to spend their vacation with the woman who had now become matriarch of the Dulles clan, the last one to know what it had been like when three members of the family had shaped the destinies of the nation. There was now no one else to remember. Not only Foster and Allen were gone but their wives too. Janet Dulles had meant what she said, that day at Walter Reed, when she had looked down at Foster's lifeless form and declared: "My life is over too." In the intervening years before she, too, died she had made it clear that she couldn't wait to join her beloved husband, and hanging around had been a weary tedium. Clover had substituted religion for Allen and seemed happier, in consequence, but now she was dead. Only Eleanor was still there, as vibrant and forward-looking as ever, and this family get-together was the high point of her year. These children made her happy and kept her young. Though she was eighty-one years old now, she still swam with them before breakfast in the icy waters of the lake, she still beat them in the dinghy races round the isles, she still organized games and discussions which kept them absorbed once darkness had fallen. This year she had arranged a mock presidential election, and it had been won by Allen III, son of Allen's daughter,

484

Toddy. He was the charmer of the brood and he had stood in the Communist cause.

The young people slopped around in bare feet and frayed shorts and the girls didn't do anything about their hair or the boys their beards. They called themselves "The Poor Whites of Henderson." Yet they were a good-looking lot, and as she glanced at their eager, sun-bronzed faces shining in the firelight, Eleanor felt a pang.

She should have been happy, knowing that they were all gathered here tonight as a demonstration of their admiration and affection for her, come to salute the oldest and most distinguished member of their clan. But she was aware that there was something missing from the occasion, both tangible and intangible. For one thing, her own son was not there. For years she had pinned her hopes on David's future, saved, worked, and scraped for it, because she believed, as Foster had once predicted, that he was the one who would carry on the Dulles tradition and take the next generation of the family into the corridors of political power. It hadn't worked out that way. Though a lawyer like Foster and Allen, David had long since lost his taste for politics, or even for power. He blamed his mother for his broken marriage and the loss of his children. Nowadays, he refused to see or talk to her—and that was hard to bear.

Allen's son, Allen, Jr., was here corporeally, but in spirit he was far away, hiding beyond the glint of the firelight, nursing his private sorrows. From him there was nothing to be hoped, and one wondered which had wounded him more crucially, the Chinese bullet in his brain or the image of his father in his mind. He had come out of the clinic in Switzerland as soon as he had heard that his father was dead, and announced that he did not propose to return. But if Allen's death had released him from something, it was impossible to guess what.

Foster's sons: they were otherwise engaged, the one with the Church, the other with rock formations in Mexico. None of them now seemed likely to follow in their father's, their uncle's, or their aunt's footsteps and make some sort of family benchmark in Washington. It was too late. And what gave Eleanor a pang was the fear that the Dulles tradition, having skipped one generation, might now be in danger of skipping another.

She passed her eyes quickly over the avid faces of the young folk before her. Was there a new Foster, a new Allen, even a new Eleanor somewhere among them? Was there one of these healthy and hopeful girls and boys prepared, able, and willing to snatch up the family banner?

APPENDIX:

Letters from a Spy

So far as is known, H. A. R. (Kim) Philby is the most successful spy for the Russians ever to have penetrated the British intelligence network. Son of the famous Arab scholar and explorer, Harry St. John Philby, Kim was recruited into the Communist Party during his college days at Cambridge but went underground shortly after joining the Soviet espionage services in the 1930s. Thereafter he posed as a vaguely right-wing sympathizer with Fascist causes, backed the Franco cause in Spain, and joined the Anglo-German Fellowship, which advocated closer ties with Nazi Germany. Just before World War II began he joined the SIS (Special Intelligence Service) in London, where his promotion was rapid. He was in charge of the Iberian desk covering Spain and Portugal, and later, when British experts cracked the Abwehr code, was in control of reading the traffic sent out from the Berlin headquarters of the German intelligence system and deciding what reactions should be made to its messages. When Canaris and other Abwehr leaders indicated that they were joining dissident Nazi generals to revolt against Hitler, and asked for Allied help, Philby is believed to have turned the information aside in order to save his Soviet masters from being confronted with the possibility of a separate peace between the United States, Great Britain, and Germany.

He worked as liaison officer between the British SIS and the CIA in Washington, D.C., after the war, and was in close, almost daily contact with Allen Dulles and other senior members of the Agency. It is for this reason that I thought of contacting him when I began the research for this book. Philby has relatives living in London who visit him regularly in Moscow, and there are several old members of the SIS who, despite

the circumstances, still maintain a vague contact with him. It was through both elements that I put out feelers, indicating that I would like to go to Moscow and talk with Philby if he would see me. After some time, news came back that he did not like personal encounters but that he *might*—and the word was stressed—be willing to answer questions. Accordingly I wrote to him on October 18, 1976, and enclosed the following questions which I thought he might be prepared to study and answer:

1. When did you first meet Allen Dulles, and in what circumstances? How did he strike you, as a person, as a professional, during your first encounter?

2. Did you change your mind about him during your subsequent association? If so, why?

3. Among some of Allen Dulles' writings, I have found a half-finished sketch of you in which he says that "in some ways, in temperament, in his attitude to people, his love of womankind and good living, he is not unlike myself." I find this a surprising comparison, especially as you yourself, in your book, refer to him as "the bumbling Dulles." How do you feel about it?

4. Incidentally, could you tell me *why* you refer to Allen Dulles as "bumbling"? Was there a particular incident which stimulated this observation?

5. Some people say that Frank Wisner (who had charge of covert operations for many years at CIA) was the postwar cloak-and-dagger projection of Allen's persona, and that he relived his own WW2 adventures through the younger man's Cold War operations. Did you know Wisner and work with him? Do you have an explanation for why he killed himself?

6. Did you know any other members of Allen Dulles' circle: for instance, Amory, Cord Meyer, Walter Pforzheimer, Lawrence Houston, etc. etc.?

7. Did you ever meet John Foster Dulles, and if so, in what circumstances?

8. I believe you were in the Middle East around the time of the Iranian oil crisis (1952–4) and the Suez crisis (1956). Did you ever run into Schwarzkopf, Herbert Hoover Jr, Kim Roosevelt, etc., and could you tell me how and when?

9. I believe you saw a lot of General Walter Bedell Smith. He had, indeed, as you say in your book, a beady eye and a formidable

memory. But would you say he was an efficient head of the CIA? Do you believe he was deliberately maneuvered out to make way for Allen by John Foster Dulles? When and how often did you meet him and in what circumstances?

10. As an intelligence operation, how did you view the CIA? Efficient? How did it compare with the SIS?

It was not until nearly two months later, when I had just about given up, that the letter arrived which is printed in the Acknowledgments at the beginning of this book. I immediately airmailed Philby a copy of my biography of the late Charles A. Lindbergh, and on February 10, 1977, the following letter arrived from Moscow:

Dear Mr. Mosley,
It was very kind of you to send me *Lindbergh,* for which many thanks. I have postponed reading it, because I can only justify the indulgence by first earning it! Perhaps a lingering bourgeois prejudice?
I have not answered your questions one by one, nor in the order given. Some of them can only be tackled by reference to others, so my comments form a general answer to the questionnaire as a whole. If there are any obscurities, I shall be happy to clarify, if I can. I have already told you, in my first letter, of my vast areas of ignorance.
I hope I have not been too deprecatory about AD [Allen Dulles]. Personally, I liked him a lot. He was nice to have around: good, comfortable, predictable, pipe-sucking, whisky-sipping company. A touch of Hannay, perhaps; definitely not Bond (detestable fellow!).
Thank you again for your book, which I shall now pick up.
Yours sincerely, H. A. R. Philby.

Enclosed was a sheet of paper covered single-spaced on both sides and headed "Herewith my Comments in Detail":

1. I was indeed startled by your extract from the "half-finished sketch" of myself by AD. But, as the characteristics given are all private, the remarks have little significance. Any two men, however conflicting their politics, might fall in love with, say, Betty Grable or bouil-labaisse. "Attitudes to people" has the imprecision so characteristic of Dulles; just as "love of womankind" illustrates his compulsive resort to cliché. "I can make an educated guess" was another of his favorites, meaning "I don't know, but."

2. I first met Dulles in 1950, when he became DDI to Bedell Smith, and met him frequently for a year, professionally and socially. I had

489

known him much earlier by reputation, from his days in Switzerland where he acquired his legend. (All intelligence people who achieve fame or notoriety, quorum pars minima fui, are elevated to legendary status—by their own side.) Dulles did nothing to play down his legend; his unprofessional delight in cloak-and-dagger for its own sake was an endearing trait. It sank him finally, in the Bay of Pigs.

3. Actually the Dulles legend was conceived on the wrong side of the blanket. In Bern, he virtually put up a brass plate, which attracted an awful lot of eager salesmen; there had to be some nuggets among the dross. Of course, he deserves credit for having recognised the nuggets when he saw them, and for encouraging, by financial liberality which the British could not match, the offer of more. Equally, he would have deserved censure if he had not. Perhaps his most impressive personal triumph was to rise above his detractors in Britain, often prove them wrong, and nurse no bitterness. He retained his Anglophilia, so far as I know to the end.

4. Why did I call him "bumbling"? Well, it was the first adjective which occurred to me after our introductory meeting, and he gave me no cause for second thoughts. He had a habit of talking round a problem, not coming to grips with it. Sometimes, he seemed to be ruminating aloud—and pretty diffusedly at that; sometimes, when several of us were present, he would talk at random until we had all spoken, then mull and mumble over verbal formulae which might cover all views, however conflicting they might be. In short, he was the genial chairman.

5. I cannot resist comparison with Eisenhower, surely one of the least impressive of Presidents. A comfortable figurehead, no doubt, but one dares not think what he would have made of OVERLORD [D-Day, 1944] without Morgan, Bedell Smith and Co. to hold his hand. It was fortunate for the CIA that it was Smith, not Dulles, who presided (1950–53) over the reorganisation of the post-war raggle-taggle that followed Truman's disbandment of the OSS. I fear that Dulles would have confounded confusion. But Smith was no chairman. He was the boss, and a boss of outstanding intellect and character. Many times I saw him read a long memorandum, toss it aside and, without pause for thought, paragraph by numbered paragraph, rip its guts out—real virtuoso stuff! With him, I had to do my homework; with Dulles, it was desirable, but not necessary. What Smith would have done with the Agency, once he had streamlined it, is another matter. He might have got bored with it. Anyway, the organisation he handed over to Dulles *was* streamlined. The

genial chairman could take it over and let it run. But I am not surprised that in the end it ran away with him. (It may be that the contrast between Smith and Dulles coloured my assessment of the latter. Perhaps.)

6. I think it probable that Smith was deliberately removed at the insistence of JFD, understandably. JFD was a strong personality with views as narrow as a small-gauge railway. There could have been major political and personality clashes between him and Smith. The neatest way out was by replacing Smith by AD, thus ensuring that JFD had a controlling interest in CIA and that CIA could get what it wanted (within reason) from the State Dept. Between them they could assuredly fix chairman Eisenhower when need arose. Of course, this is an "educated guess." I hope you agree that it is plausible.

7. I knew and worked closely with [Frank] Wisner (1949–51). I should here declare an interest; I never liked him. Our professional and social relations were always friendly, but there was a false note. I thought him pompous? self-opinionated? aggressive? too stout and too bald for his age? a shade too cordial towards the British liaison officer? Perhaps all of those things. Anyway, the feeling was always there on my side. So, as a friend, he fell short of bosom.

8. Wisner had a sense of mission, and the power-hunger that often goes with it. He was shrewd enough, with a sense of movement in the Corridors; drove himself hard, professionally and socially; drank heavily and regularly (but I never saw him drunk). I am not sure I understand the suggestion that he was "the post-war cloak-and-dagger projection of AD's persona." Wisner began his operations before Dulles became DDI, long before he became Director. If the suggestion simply means that Dulles delighted in the covert operations which Wisner directed, it is certainly valid. They were both romantics, and a couple of easy successes (Iran and Guatemala) went to their heads.

9. Why did Wisner kill himself? I can only offer hearsay. When I was in the Middle East, I heard he had suffered a nervous breakdown, due to overwork, frustration and possibly to some instability (perhaps the aggressiveness mentioned in para 7 covered some inadequacy); it was *rumored* that drink contributed. After his suicide, a mutual friend, who knew him well, told me that the real crunch came from CIA's failure to help the Hungarian counter-revolution. He had devoted time, thought and nervous energy to the recruitment of paramilitary units from E. European emigres, and JFD's

491

failure even to try to honour his election promises of "rolling back" Communism was too much for him. After E. Germany and Poland, Hungary was the last straw. Si non e vero . . . (but I deprecate long-range psychology; I myself have not seldom been a guinea-pig!)

10. I first met Kim Roosevelt in Washington, where he was in charge of Wisner's Middle East Department. Oddly enough, I dubbed him "the quiet American" five years before Graham Greene wrote his book. He was a courteous, soft-spoken Easterner with impeccable social connections, well-educated rather than intellectual, pleasant and unassuming as host and guest. An equally nice wife. In fact, the last person you would expect to be up to the neck in dirty tricks.

11. I was in London during the Iranian crisis and had no contact with Kim at that time (though I met him several times in the Middle East thereafter; he was PRO to some U.S. oil company, Gulf?—but maintained his CIA link). However, his investment in the overthrow of Mossadegh has been amply documented, by himself among others. What is not so generally known is that the British were also heavily involved, and felt some resentment when the Americans a) blew the affair and b) grabbed all the credit.

12. Your last question, about relative efficiencies, would require a book to answer, not to mention encyclopaedic knowledge which I do not possess! Here a few inadequate lines must suffice. About the war years, there can be little argument. Apart from isolated successes, OSS lagged far behind SIS in every field, spending much more money to much less effect. In the first post-war period, roughly up to 1950, the Americans still lagged, except perhaps in research and analysis, largely because there was no agreement in the U.S. as to what sort of peacetime organisation was necessary, desirable and politically feasible. Increasingly since 1950, the growth in scale of the two organisations has been so unequal that comparisons are impossible. It may be that, in terms of cost-effectiveness, the British still have the edge; e.g., the huge expenditure of CIA in SE Asia was money wasted. Yet the British are dwarfed. Which is more "efficient"—Harrods or the post-office-cum-general store in Nether Wallop? Of course, I exaggerate.

13. Any more questions?

I found the reply a typical example of the Kim Philby method, amusingly written, full of a sort of worldly contempt for Dulles and the CIA, with many of its statements meant to influence or deceive; anyone

reading it should bear in mind that, like all his letters, it must have been carefully vetted by his superiors at the KGB in Moscow before being sent. But the invitation to send more questions was too good to miss, and I wrote him again on February 20, 1977, asking whether he had known any other members of the Dulles family, how he had worked with Frank Wisner and other colleagues at the CIA, and what he knew about General Gehlen and his organization. I also asked him whether he had had any dealings with General Sir Kenneth Strong, the British intelligence chief who had been a close friend of Beetle Smith, and made the observation that I, too, had never felt that President Dwight D. Eisenhower had been one of the great Presidents of the United States. He wrote back to me on April 6, 1977, as follows:

Dear Mr. Mosley,
Once again I must apologise for the long delay in replying, and this time to thank you for your kind comments on my first contribution. I hope the tongue was not too deep in your cheek. I have not got around to *Lindbergh* yet, but next month I go to the Crimea for what I hope is a well-deserved holiday, and he will be in my luggage.

I cannot be very helpful about your second batch of questions. To the best of my knowledge, I never met Eleanor D. and I do not know what attitude AD adopted at the time of the landings in Lebanon. But the local CIA man, whom I knew well, was dumbfounded by the intervention. More important was the dismay of Ambassador Rob McClintock, who jumped into a launch to intercept the fleet. Luckily for the USA, "trouble-shooter" (whatever that may mean) Bob Murphy was with the navy, and between them Bob and Rob persuaded the Admiral that the use of his sledge-hammer was quite unnecessary and potentially calamitous.

This, though unhelpful in itself, brings me to a point which may be of interest to you. It is quite impossible to make sense of the Lebanese enterprise except on the assumption that JFD really believed that a red [sic] takeover in the Middle East might be imminent. Yet I never met a single American Embassy official in Beirut, Damascus or Aleppo—Ambassador, Service Attaché, Consul, CIA man or run-of-the-mill Secretary —who gave the slightest credence to a red threat in either Lebanon or Syria. (Oddly enough, the British were jumpier than their American cousins; perhaps the Suez misadventure had unbalanced them.) The point, of course, is that JFD seems to have ignored the evidence provided by his officials on the spot, and this must have been deliberate. Why? Did he *need* something evil to combat, as the Puritans needed sin?

After all your researches, you must know him pretty well by now. May I suggest, with respect, that it is worth addressing yourself to this question. Long-range psychology again!

AD was certainly gregarious. But was he a gadabout? We know that he had a "love of womankind and good living," but perhaps the gadding about was another legend; he may have enjoyed a reputation for naughtiness. My own social contacts with him were mildly convivial, but stopped well short of the naughty.

I visited his home a few times. There I met Clover, but she is no more than a blur in my memory; another gracious American hostess, perhaps more lively, less self-conscious than some. But it would be quite unfair of me to attempt an assessment on such vague recollections. Otherwise, I would meet AD, usually with two or three colleagues, for lunch or dinner at the usual Washington eating places, the Colony, La Salle, Mayflower, Shoreham, etc. (Harvey's was off-limits because of Hoover's addiction to the place; it is nice to have found out that he never paid for his meals). I would often call at AD's office late in the afternoon on business, knowing that he would soon suggest drifting out to a friendly bar for a further round of shop-talk. In short, nothing eccentric or particularly worthy of note; a predictable pattern for a predictable person.

I knew about the Gehlen unit from the summer of 1943 onwards. It was the anti-Soviet section of the poor old Abwehr, and the British were reading the great majority of its signals. It seemed to be no better than the other sections of the Abwehr (on which I had been continuously engaged since 1941), which means that it was very bad indeed. No exaggeration, no joke. So I was undismayed when CIA took it over. It would be inadmissibly indiscreet of me to offer a valid comment on your Tat for Tat theory;* perhaps it has much going for it. Or should it be Tit for Tit? And were you asking for that one?

Conferences. There were major conferences which I attended both in Washington and London, formal affairs with several representatives on each side. AD would open for their side, Sinclair for ours, with a load of generalities; then the Wisners, Angletons, etc. would get to grips with matters of substance. When substance emerged, Sinclair's interventions were more frequent than AD's. Then I, as one of the two conference secretaries, would get together with my U.S. opposite number, draft the

---

*I had suggested in my letter that the whole business of intelligence rivalry by all the powers in Germany after the war was a futile game of Tat for Tat—or "If you hire those people, I'm going to hire these."

minutes and record the compromises reached. There was very little acrimony. Much of the agenda concerned what we called "war planning," stay-behind organisations, etc. Most of the people whose potentialities we earnestly discussed are now dead—of old age.

The working conferences in Washington with four or five participants, myself being alone on the British side, were more satisfactory, but they covered such a wide range that it is impossible to identify any single flavour: anything from a major operational planning session to MI5's fury at a bunch of CIA Poles arriving at Blackbushe [England] without prior notification. The meetings were informal and amicable; perhaps my own detachment from Anglo-American squabbles had something to do with it. They would end by Wisner or whoever producing Bourbon from his office bar, after which we would debate the wisdom of again abandoning our wives for a regular-guy evening on the town.

Yes, I knew Kenneth Strong,* first in Frankfurt, then in London, but only on a professional basis. I found his nickname, "the chinless wonder," seriously misleading. But, for all my respect, I find it impossible to believe that it ever occurred to Beetle to offer him the Deputy-Directorship—except in jest. Even if it were constitutional (which I doubt), the appointment of a foreigner would have raised a horrific storm in D.C. Surely someone as shrewd as Beetle would never have contemplated putting himself in the path of such a cyclone.

One last point, not in your questi nnaire. Your prodding has caused me to think more deeply than for many years about AD. I find recurring, with inexorable insistence, the adjective "lazy." Of course, AD was an active man, in the sense that he would talk shop late into the night, jump into aeroplanes, rush around sophisticated capitals and exotic landscapes. But did he ever apply his mind *hard* to a problem that did not engage his personal interest and inclination; or was he basically a line-of-least-resistance man? Your researches may already have undermined my allegation, in which case I withdraw it. If not, I put it to you that Dulles enjoyed what he did and did what he enjoyed, no less, no more. Quite enough, you may retort, for a nice guy. Yes, but not for the post he held.

I am gratified that you share my view of Ike. Now I can abandon my earlier reserve and call him an idle, ignorant, ungenerous old fraud. No wonder poor Mamie hit the bottle, long before the Summersby non-

*In charge of intelligence at SHAEF under Eisenhower during World War II, later head of combined intelligence for the British in London.

event. And how characteristic of Ike the none-ness of the event! . . . With best wishes for your book and yourself, Sincerely, H.A.R.Philby.

There was one further letter from him. I wrote back to thank him for his letter and hoped it was not too impertinent to suggest that it was about time he got down to writing a book about his espionage activities to fill in the gaps left by the one he wrote after he fled to Moscow in 1963, which had many obvious holes in it. On May 25, 1977, he replied:

> Dear Mr. Mosley,
> I am glad my notes have been of some help to you, and you may certainly quote them if you really think they deserve to be so honoured. It is good to hear that you propose a serious study of the Brotherhood.* . . . Of all bad books, I find that a bad book on the "nether world" is the most difficult to finish!
> I do not consider your comment on my book "impertinent." On the contrary, I know very well that it is highly pertinent. An awful lot had to be omitted, not only for reasons of state. I have been writing pretty assiduously to fill in the gaps. But when, or even if, the material will ever be published is another matter, depending on lots of things happening on both sides of the fence.
> Your *Lindbergh* gave me great pleasure in the Crimea. Before reading it, I knew only the obvious things about him, so that the book was full of interest from beginning to end. It seems to be what the lit. crits. so often call "the definitive word," and I shall certainly return to it. . . . I wish you a great success. Yours sincerely, H.A.R. Philby.

There is a postscript to this correspondence. Shortly after the last letter was received, I sent Kim Philby a copy of one of my books called *ON BORROWED TIME: How World War II Began.* It is a closely documented account of how the follies of British and French statesmen in the 1930s, and in particular the blind optimism of Prime Minister Neville Chamberlain in 1938, precipitated the world into a disastrous war which might otherwise have been avoided. It also contained a detailed indictment of how Soviet cynicism helped Adolf Hitler to make his initial conquests even more devastating than they might otherwise have been.

*I take it he means a book about the CIA, though he may also mean one about the Dulles brothers.

496

Some time passed, and then, on August 27, 1977, Philby wrote me again from Moscow:

> I feel dreadfully ashamed at not having acknowledged earlier the receipt of your 'On Borrowed Time.' So much kindness in return for so little effort!
>
> But what a splendid petard you put under the whole lot! It reminded me of having puked, some twenty years ago, over the biography of NC [Neville Chamberlain] by [Sir] Keith Feiling; so I dusted off my copy and had another look at it. At the end of the preface I found the following judgment: '(NC) was at once the most loyal of men and the most outspoken critic of unreality.' And that from a man of KF's eminence!
>
> Well, every chapter of your book blows the last six words to smithereens. If ever a man lived in cloud-cuckoo land, it was NC. As for loyalty, it was a pity he was loyal to Beck rather than to Beneš.* Not that he wouldn't have wriggled off the Polish hook, if Beck had given him the ghost of a chance.
>
> Of course, as you show very persuasively, NC was not alone in his folly. The only two men who rose slightly in my estimation after reading your book were Daladier (rather surprisingly) and poor old Sir William [later Lord] Strang.
>
> You may accuse me of folly, but I do feel fairly confident that the present helmsmen are more realistic than the characters in your book. They have more to be realistic about! So many thanks again for a wonderful read. Yours sincerely, Kim Philby.

There is no mention at all in his letter of my condemnation of the Soviets for the way they truckled to the Nazis, and for the infamous manner in which they treated the Poles after they were divided up between Germany and Russia in 1939. But perhaps that was too much to expect.

*Colonel Josef Beck was the Polish leader with whom Chamberlain signed a military aid pact in 1939. Edouard Beneš was president of Czechoslovakia, whom Britain and France left to the mercy of the Nazis in 1938.

Source Notes

Anyone who was a foreign correspondent during the 1940s and 1950s, as I was, inevitably encountered John Foster Dulles at some point in his assignments, and I have memories of talking with him or sitting in on his press conferences in London, Paris, Bonn, Geneva, Manila, Tokyo, Bangkok, New York, San Francisco, and, of course, Washington. The first time I ever met him informally was at a small reception at Claridge's Hotel in London after a Foreign Ministers' Conference. It was that drab postwar period in Britain when liquor was in extremely short supply, and everyone in sight was helping him- or herself liberally to the whiskey and gin that had been laid on by the government hospitality office for the occasion. Everyone, that is, except John Foster Dulles, who did not seem to be drinking. Then suddenly across the room came Mrs. Janet Dulles, dressed in a little black number and the kind of evening hat that only American matrons wore in those days, and carrying in her hand what seemed to be a leather flask. That was, indeed, what it was, and it contained a large measure of Overholt whiskey, his favorite evening tipple, but unobtainable in London. Foster had brought it along with him and Janet had fetched some of it from their room.

A glass was found, the whiskey was poured, a small measure of water added, then Foster Dulles dipped a large forefinger in it, put the finger in his mouth, and licked it. For the first time a smile broke like a rising sun over his somewhat dour features.

"Now," he said, warmth coming into his voice, "what was I saying about the German problem . . . ?"

He had suddenly become a human being.

Allen Welsh Dulles I saw less of, because, although he traveled just as much as his older brother, he was more apt to be a will-o'-the-wisp and inclined to confine his public appearances to social occasions inside the United States. I did once run into him at a party in Berlin in the early fifties and again in Cairo

499

a couple of years later. In between the two occasions I had written a biography of Orde Wingate, the eccentric British general who trained Jewish guerillas in Palestine before World War II, and helped Israel win independence, and I was pleasantly impressed when he came across and showed that he not only remembered me from the first occasion but had also read the book. We were talking animatedly about Arab-Israeli problems when a long-legged Swedish blonde passed by, showed all her teeth in a large smile, and said: "Why, Allen Dulles!" He was off in her direction like a shot, and I never got physically close to him again.

Eleanor Dulles I did not meet until I began researches for this book, but I have spent many hours with her since, and readers of the narrative will have gathered that of all the Dulles clan, she is the one that I admire. She is an indomitable old lady, as sharp as a razor despite her eighty-two years, and with a large heart and a warm sense of humanity which often seemed to have been missing in her brothers. Born two generations later, what a mark she would have made in this age of sexual equality!

This study of the Dulles brothers and sister is based, as are all my books, on research into all the background documents I could uncover, plus personal interviews with their surviving contemporaries. Both the John Foster Dulles Papers and the Allen Welsh Dulles Papers are in the archives of their old university, Princeton, though some of the Foster Dulles documents are un-available during alterations and enlargements that are being made, and several of the more interesting portions of the Allen Dulles documents were extracted by the CIA before being released to his old college. Nevertheless, I am more than grateful to Mr. Alexander P. Clark, Curator of Manuscripts at Princeton, and Ms. Agnes Sherman, in charge of Rare Books and Special Collections, for going out of their way to dig out most of the papers for which I asked, and for making the invaluable Oral Histories recorded by Foster's fellow states-men, of all nationalities, available to me. At the same time, I would like to express my thanks to Mr. Lawrence Reid Houston, former general counsel of the CIA, for making the Allen Welsh Dulles Papers available to me.

For much of the background of CIA operative procedure during Allen Dulles's day I owe thanks to Walter Pforzheimer, former legislative counsel and later archivist at the Agency. I shall long remember my first visit to Pforzheimer's home in Washington, where some signed personal portraits by the late President Eisenhower hang on the walls, side by side with silk-screen paintings made in prison by the famous Russian spy, Colonel Abel, and the first aerial portraits of the Soviet missiles in Cuba taken by a CIA U-2.

But it is upstairs that Pforzheimer's collection of intelligence documents becomes important. You pass through an aperture guarded by a thick steel electrified door into a library filled with books and papers dealing with espio-

nage from the days of Walsingham, Elizabeth I's secret agent, to the early 1970s, and taking in George Washington's letters on the value of intelligence in between. There are the curiosa of espionage here too, such as Mata Hari's passport and some exotic pictures of the lady in performance; but the value of the Pforzheimer collection is its files and records of espionage activity, both by the CIA and by its rival (and enemy) organizations in other countries. Not only has Pforzheimer read everything in the room; he also has an encyclopedic memory of everything he has ever seen, experienced, or heard of in a long and distinguished career in intelligence. There is nothing he doesn't know about every activity in which the CIA has been involved since its formation in 1947, even if he isn't always willing to talk about it. He has my thanks for answering *some* if not all of my many questions about the days when Allen Dulles was in charge.

Among those who have talked to me at length about both brothers during my researches are Mr. Robert Bowie, now back in Washington but formerly a professor at Harvard, and once a foreign policy adviser and member of the National Security Council in the Eisenhower administration; Mr. Paul Nitze, foreign policy adviser in the Truman, Eisenhower, Kennedy, and now the Carter administrations, and his assistant, Mr. Burt Marshall; Mr. Dean Rusk, Secretary of State in the Kennedy years, before that a frequent collaborator with Foster Dulles, and now a professor at the University of Georgia at Athens; Mr. Richard Bissell, Jr., once the director of Plans at the CIA, now a consultant in Connecticut; Mr. Robert Amory, once deputy director of the CIA, now general counsel at the National Gallery of Art in Washington, D.C.; Mr. William Bundy, formerly of the CIA, later a foreign policy adviser in the Kennedy and Johnson administrations, and now editor of *Foreign Affairs;* his younger brother, McGeorge Bundy, who filled similar jobs in Washington and is now head of the Ford Foundation; Mr. Lucius D. Battle, former aide to Dean Acheson, ex-ambassador, now senior vice-president of COMSAT (Communications Satellite Corporation); Mr. Benjamin Bradlee, executive editor of the Washington *Post;* Mr. Cord Meyer, a CIA and OSS veteran and former London station chief of the Agency; Mr. Rodney Dennys, formerly of the British SIS and now Somerset Herald of Arms at the Royal College of Arms in London; Mr. Mohammad Heikal, former adviser to the late President Nasser of Egypt and ex-editor of *al Ahram,* Cairo; Mr. Christopher Dobson, writer and expert on Middle Eastern affairs; Mr. Lawrence Reid Houston and his wife, Jean; Mr. Howard Roman, ex-CIA; the late Earl of Avon (Sir Anthony Eden) and Lady Clarissa Avon; Father Avery Dulles of the Catholic University of America in Washington, D.C.; and Mr. Alger Hiss.

I should also like to thank the following who allowed me to use their documents and recollections of the brothers, particularly Foster: Admiral Arleigh

A. Burke; Ambassador W. R. Macomber and his wife, the former Phyllis Bernau; Herr Willy Brandt; Mr. Roderick O'Connor; Mr. John Hanes, Jr.; Mr. Abba Eban; Monsieur Couve de Murville; the late Mr. Charles (Chip) Bohlen; Professor George Kennan; Senator Jacob Javits; the relatives of Monsieur Christian Pineau; the late Mr. Sam Pope Brewer; the late Herr Heinrich Brentano; Monsieur Charles Lucet; the late General Charles Cabelile; Mr. H. A. R. (Kim) Philby; and others whose names will appear in the text.

Particularly in the case of Allen Dulles and the CIA, not all sources have been cited by name. But in almost every case one of the people mentioned above—and sometimes several of them—has provided the information. There follows a detailed source list, chapter by chapter.

PROLOGUE *The Man Upstairs* Several sources are responsible for the account of the Christmas Eve party which ended with Allen Dulles's removal to hospital, and the account was built up with the help of several of the guests and of those who came in afterwards, including Lawrence Reid Houston, Walter Pforzheimer, Howard Roman, and Eleanor Lansing Dulles.

CHAPTER ONE *Cradle Marks* The account of the early days of the Dulles family in Watertown and Henderson, New York, comes from papers and letters in the John Foster Dulles and Allen Welsh Dulles Papers at Princeton University; from the Oral Histories by Allen, Eleanor, Lillias (Hinshaw) Dulles, and Margaret (Edwards) Dulles at Princeton; from an Oral History by Eleanor Dulles in the archives of Columbia University; and from conversations with Eleanor Dulles.

The story of Allen's club foot comes from sources close to the family.

CHAPTER TWO *Breaking Out* The background to Foster's early manhood, courtship, marriage, and career is to be found in the Princeton Papers, and it has been filled in by conversations with Eleanor Dulles. Allen's sojourn in India is described in letters in the Allen Dulles Papers, and has been supported by the writings of the late Sam Higginbotham, who ran a farming school near Allahabad, and the late Mrs. Pandit Nehru. See also Sam Higginbotham, *Farmer. An Autobiography* (New York: Scribner's, 1949).

Background to the activities of Secretary of State Robert Lansing, his relations with Wilson, his clashes with William Jennings Bryan, and his underhand dealings with the World War I blockade in general and the *Lusitania* sinking in particular, is to be found in the Lansing Papers in the National Archives. The best account of the skulduggery involved is undoubtedly given in *The Sinking of the Lusitania* by Colin Simpson (London: Longman's, 1972).

Eleanor Dulles's account of her first journey to Europe in World War I comes from talks with Eleanor Dulles.

CHAPTER THREE *Trio Abroad* Allen Dulles's adventures in Switzerland during World War I have been pieced together from many of his old letters, his writings, and some of the lectures he gave to new recruits at the CIA. References to his mistake over Vladimir Ilich Lenin were often included in his speeches as a cautionary tale, though it changed slightly in detail over the years. The description of Minister Stovall comes from Robert Murphy's account (he was a file clerk there at the time) in his book, *Diplomat Among Warriors* (New York: Doubleday, 1964). The details concerning Consul McNally and Dr. Herbert Field come from British intelligence records.

Eleanor Dulles's experiences in Paris and the Western Front in 1918 come from her letters home, her Oral History at Columbia University, and conversations with her. After her meeting with her two brothers in Paris, the narrative is based on the Foster Dulles Papers at Princeton, Allen Dulles's and Eleanor's Oral Histories, and conversations with Eleanor.

CHAPTER FOUR *Foster Father* Once more the background to the early postwar years, to Allen's career at State and his marriage to Clover, to Eleanor's first experiences as a working girl, and to Foster's career at Sullivan & Cromwell come from the Princeton Papers, plus the recollections of Eleanor and two Sullivan & Cromwell partners, Arthur Dean and Eustace Seligman.

The comment from Supreme Court Justice William O. Douglas comes from Vol. I of his autobiography, *Go East Young Man* (New York: Random House, 1974).

Allen's career at Sullivan & Cromwell is based on recollections of former S&C associates, the Allen Welsh Dulles Papers, and some veteran members of CIG and CIA.

For Foster's relationship with his children, several members of the Dulles family have provided background, notably Father Avery Dulles, S.J., his second son, and Eleanor. Avery also talked at length about his decision to join the Roman Catholic Church and what it meant to his parents.

CHAPTER FIVE *Mixed Marriage* Eleanor Dulles talked very frankly about her relationships with her parents, her brothers, and her emotional involvement with, and marriage to, David Blondheim. Though she was quite obviously hurt at the hesitancy which both of their families exhibited when the couple decided to wed, and must have inveighed at the time against the rigid prejudices of Orthodox Jews and Presbyterian WASPS, time has mellowed her; nowadays

she speaks of the difficulties she and her husband encountered without rancor or resentment. But no one who talks to her about David Blondheim, or looks over her shoulder as she goes over his precious scholarly works, can doubt the depth of her love for him, and the sorrow she still feels at his death.

Details of S&C's German connections come from recollections of some of the firm's veteran members, from the Princeton Papers, and from notes and letters written by Allen Dulles. The description of Eleanor's trip to Germany with Nancy Wertheimer comes from her Oral History at Columbia University. The critical meeting at S&C which ended with the decision to close down the firm's offices in Germany is described in notes made by Allen at the time, in the recollections of Robert Amory, to whom he later gave an account of the meeting, and in records kept by one of the partners, Eustace Seligman.

Father Avery Dulles, in conversations with the author, described how his father's and Allen's views diverged as World War II began to loom in Europe. Foster's letter to Charles A. Lindbergh is in the Princeton Papers.

CHAPTER SIX *Enter Wild Bill* For descriptions of the Republican Convention of 1940 I have gone to contemporary newspaper accounts, together with Thomas E. Dewey's Oral History in the Foster Dulles Papers and the recollections of Eleanor and Father Avery Dulles, made during conversations with the author. William Bundy, whose father-in-law was Dean Acheson, gave the author details of the "Letter to the *Times*" incident, when Allen reneged on his promise to sign.

The account of Eleanor's life with David Blondheim, his suicide, and the posthumous birth of her son has been pieced together from recollections in the family. The tragedy was hushed up and written records are hard to find. David Blondheim's sister died in 1977 (she left a small amount of money in trust for Eleanor's son), and Blondheim's son by his first marriage came from Israel but arrived too late in Baltimore for the funeral. He did, however, meet Eleanor for the first time and they have established a family link.

There is a note in Allen's papers about his meeting with Donovan. The background on Donovan himself is based on several contemporary accounts, and on conversations with some of his old colleagues, including Walter Pforzheimer. The quotation from Allen's account of Donovan's visit to Britain comes from his book, *The Craft of Intelligence* (New York: Harper & Row, 1963).

Donovan's speech on his return is quoted from contemporary newspaper accounts, and the comment by Allen Dulles is from *The Craft of Intelligence*. The account of the COI's rivalry with the FBI is based on many sources, including *Baker Street Irregular* by Bickham Sweet-Escott (London: Methuen,

1965), from which the quotation, "There's plenty of noise on the landing," is taken.

CHAPTER SEVEN *"Pontificating American!"* The description of Foster's trip to London in July 1942 is based on documents in the Princeton Papers, the recollections of the late Earl of Avon in conversation with the author, and the *Diaries of Sir Alexander Cadogan,* edited by David Dilks, (London: Cassell, 1971).

Allen Dulles's comment on Donovan's "blueprint" for the OSS is taken from *The Craft of Intelligence.* Charles Lindbergh's overtures to the new organization are described in Leonard Mosley's *Lindbergh* (New York: Doubleday, 1976). Bickham Sweet-Escott in *Baker Street Irregular* provides some details of the OSS's struggles with U.S. government officials, notably Mrs. Shipley.

The account of the FBI's watch on Eleanor Dulles and Michael "X" comes from a confidential source, as do the details of Allen's marital relations with Clover. His journey to Switzerland in 1942 is described in his account of his wartime mission, *The Secret Surrender* (New York: Harper & Row, 1966). Noel Field's journey into Switzerland was recounted in letters he sent back to the Unitarian Service Committee in New York. See also *The Man Who Disappeared: The Strange History of Noel Field,* by Flora Lewis (London: George Barker, 1965).

CHAPTER EIGHT *Swiss Role* The description of Allen Dulles's first period in Berne as station chief there in 1942 comes from the OSS Papers in the National Archives, and from his own account in *The Secret Surrender.* There are one thousand boxes of OSS material in the Archives, and I should like to thank my old friend John E. Taylor, a senior archivist there, for helping me to find my way through them. British views of the OSS operation and of Allen Dulles come from confidential British sources. Allen Dulles himself has described some of the doubts he felt about German peace overtures in his book *Germany's Underground* (New York: Macmillan, 1947). The Casablanca anecdote surfaced after the war in captured German letters, but although a good story, has never been thoroughly authenticated.

Kurt Grimm, like many another agent in Switzerland at the time, also had connections with the Soviet spy operating there, Lucy (alias Rudolf Loesser). So did the aristocratic Hans Berndt Gisevius, who not only fed information to Allen Dulles but also had good relations with the Swiss police and with at least two members of the Soviet spy organization, the Rote Drei Ring. These were Lucy and Georges Blum (alias Long).

Allen Dulles told the story of his spying housekeeper in *The Secret Surrender.* The book also mentioned Mrs. Wally Castelbarco, and her friends in the Italian Resistance, but the account of her association with Allen Dulles is based

on OSS reports and on conversations with old OSS colleagues.

The transcript of Prince von Hohenlohe's talks with Allen Dulles in 1943, made in a report to the Gestapo, was seized by the Soviet government after the war and subsequently "leaked" to two Communist-inclined propagandists in Britain who used it in a pamphlet attacking U.S. intrigues with the Nazis. Its origin does not necessarily make the document untrue, and it certainly sounds like the kind of report that von Hohenlohe would have turned in to his Nazi masters. Allen Dulles may well have said all the things the anti-American pamphlet charged him with saying, since he was playing a double game at the time.

Details of Noel Field's Communist associations come from CIA documents on the activities of Communist Party members and Soviet espionage agents in Switzerland during World War II (the Trepper Papers, for instance), and these have been confirmed from British SIS sources.

CHAPTER NINE *Dumbarton Acorns* The account of Foster's journey to Washington in March 1944, after he had suffered an attack of thromboid phlebitis, was reported in the newspaper at the time, but the details come from the Princeton Papers, from Thomas E. Dewey's Oral History, from Eleanor's account, and from Father Avery Dulles. Details of FDR's conference with him are to be found in the Roosevelt Papers at Hyde Park, New York.

Allen Dulles never revealed the real name of Fritz Kolbe, the German official who brought him so much invaluable information during World War II, and always referred to him as "George Wood." His true identity surfaced after the war. Many of the details of Allen's dealings with Kolbe come from *The Secret Surrender* and *Germany's Underground,* and the story of British skepticism about him from SIS sources, including one of its ex-members, Kim Philby, who mentions him in *My Silent War* (London: McGibbon & Kee, 1968), from which these quotations are taken. Allen's telegram to Donovan about Kolbe is taken from *The Secret Surrender.*

The quotation from Donovan at the end of the chapter is taken from notes made by Allen Dulles, and afterwards repeated to OSS colleagues in Washington.

CHAPTER TEN *Frustration* Foster Dulles's attitude toward Germany as the war drew to an end was reported by his sister, Eleanor, who was surprised at its rigidity, though, of course, he grew more supple later. Dewey made his remark about Foster's "high-mindedness" in his Oral History in the Princeton Papers. Eleanor Dulles described her own experiences in the State Department at this period in conversations with the author.

Details of Allen Dulles's association with Mary Bancroft come from various

sources. Eleanor Dulles owed her a particular debt of gratitude for interrupting her work with the OSS to look after Eleanor's son and daughter after she had "lost" them in 1944–45 while she went on her mission to Austria. The quotation from one of Mary Bancroft's letters comes from the biography of Henry Luce by W. A. Swanberg, *Luce and His Empire* (New York: Scribner's, 1972).

Noel Field's attempt to deceive the OSS over Communist émigrés was described in an OSS report by the analyst who saw through him, Arthur Schlesinger, Jr., who wrote about it later in *The Age of Roosevelt*, Vol. IV (Boston: Houghton, Mifflin, 1962). The Communist record of Field's adopted daughter, Erika Gläser, was dug up by OSS and CIA investigators, and appears in the Trepper Documents about Soviet espionage activities in Switzerland in World War II, and in the OSS Documents in the National Archives.

CHAPTER ELEVEN *Sunrise* The story of the SUNRISE operation is almost entirely based on accounts given by Allen Dulles in *The Secret Surrender* and in a number of speeches he made and articles he wrote later. But certain details have been added and come from others involved, such as Colonel Eugen Dollmann, Paul Blum of the OSS, General Karl Wolff, Major General Terence Airey, and Allen's German-American assistant, Gero von Gaevernitz. The details of Clover's uncomfortable day on the lake come from Howard Roman, who heard the full story from Allen *and* Clover. Von Gaevernitz later described Allen's struggle with gout in all its painful details.

CHAPTER TWELVE *"Lucky Rear"* The description of Foster's habit of leaking information at San Francisco comes from a member of the delegation who asks that he not be named. (Students of history will probably not have much trouble in guessing who it was.) Foster Dulles told the story to his family of his cool attitude toward Secretary Byrnes. His different regard for Secretary Marshall, especially during their first meeting in Berlin, was described to the author by his sister, Eleanor. At the Moscow Conference, it was Ambassador H. Freeman Matthews who described Foster's incorrigible habit of leaking his point of view to the press. Mark Clark's ill-temper and jealousy over Austrian problems was later described, no doubt with a certain mischievous humor, by Foster to his sister.

Paul Nitze, a Democrat and State Department adviser, told the author about Foster's leaks to the press at the Palais Rose Conference. He also kept his eye on Foster's demeanor around the conference tables, and was deeply impressed by his powers of concentration. Foster's own observations were recorded in his book, *War or Peace?* (New York: Macmillan, 1950), from which these quotations come.

It was Eleanor Dulles who described his gradual recruitment to the cause of anti-communism after the launching of the Marshall Plan. She is also partly responsible for the details of Foster's 1948 fight to get Israel admitted to the United Nations, but the Israeli statesman, Abba Eban, tells most of the story in his Oral History in the Princeton Papers.

Father Avery Dulles described to the author his trip to London to meet his father at the Foreign Ministers' Conference there, and how his decision to become a Roman Catholic came about. Eleanor's mission to Austria, and the family and other problems it involved, was described by her in a series of conversations.

CHAPTER THIRTEEN *Thwarted* McGeorge Bundy, now president of the Ford Foundation, gave the author details of how Dewey and his staff reacted to his defeat in the 1948 presidential election. Foster's appointment to the U.S. Senate the following year is described in Thomas E. Dewey's Oral History in the Princeton Papers. But it was Paul Nitze who noticed how the opposition of diehard Republicans in the Senate affected Foster's attitude toward them.

The account of the senatorial campaign later that year has been drawn from several sources, including the Oral History by Roderick O'Connor (later Foster's aide at State) in the Princeton Papers, contemporary newspaper accounts, and conversations with Father Avery Dulles. O'Connor's description of how Allen invited him to join the CIA is also in his Oral History.

Background to the description of Allen's state of mind at this time comes from family sources and memories of old colleagues at S&C. His relations with Donovan in the last days of the OSS and his early days in the CIA have been described to me by several members of the CIA, including Mr. Walter Pforzheimer, Mr. Cord Meyer, and Mr. Howard Roman. The advent, as an adjunct of the CIA, of the Gehlen organization and its subsequent activities has been documented in *The General Was a Spy,* by Heinz Höhne and Herman Zolling (New York: Coward, McCann, 1971) and in Gehlen's own *Memoirs of General Reinhard Gehlen* (London: Collins, 1972). Additional details come from British sources in the SIS, and from Mr. Sefton Delmer, the British correspondent who first revealed that Gehlen was working for the Allies.

CHAPTER FOURTEEN *Call to Battle* The background to the account of the demise of the OSS and the emergence first of CIG and then of the CIA comes from several sources. An outline history is to be found in the Final Report of Senate Select Committee's Study of U.S. Foreign and Military Intelligence (Vols. 1–IV); Walter Pforzheimer, legislative counsel to both the CIG and the CIA, and later the CIA's chief archivist, painstakingly took the author through the early days of both organizations. General Hoyt Vandenberg's remark about his

budget and establishment comes from the Senate Report, and so does the quotation from the White House's request for joint intelligence coordination between CIG and the armed forces. The background to Allen Dulles's activities, and those of his colleague, Frank Wisner, during this interim period, was provided by Pforzheimer, Eleanor Dulles, and the Princeton Papers. Pforzheimer also described the part played by Lawrence Houston, Allen Dulles, John Warner, and himself in getting the CIA established and working. The quotation setting out the army's jealousy of the new organization comes from the Senate Report (Vol. I), and so does the description of the "false war scare" in 1948, although Pforzheimer filled in other details.

The description of Allen Dulles's trip to Europe with an all-party group of congressmen in 1947 was given the author by Howard Roman. The quotation from George Kennan comes from the Senate Report (Vol. I). Walter Pforzheimer and others supplemented the Senate Report of how OPC came into being, and how Wisner began to operate it; Pforzheimer also filled in details not provided by the Senate Report of the Dulles-Jackson-Correa commission to reform the CIA.

The conversation between Luke Battle and Carl McCardle was described to the author by Mr. Battle, as was his reaction to it. He also gave the author a blow-by-blow account of how Foster Dulles was eventually brought back into the State Department as an adviser to Dean Acheson.

CHAPTER FIFTEEN *The Gospel According to Luke* The account of Foster Dulles's activities in the State Department under Dean Acheson comes from several sources: conversations with Luke Battle, George Kennan's Oral History in the Princeton Papers, John Allison's Oral History, George V. Allen's Oral History, Allen Dulles's Oral History (all in the Princeton Papers), and talks with Eleanor Dulles. The quotation from Townsend Hoopes on the Japanese Peace Treaty comes from his book, *The Devil and John Foster Dulles* (Boston: Atlantic, Little, Brown, 1973).

The Dewey-Foster Dulles-Allen Dulles conversations in New York over the 1952 election are described in Dewey's Oral History, and Foster's trip to Paris to see Dwight D. Eisenhower is dealt with by Louis L. Gerson in *John Foster Dulles* (New York: Cooper Square Publications, 1967). Foster's reaction to Eisenhower as a presidential candidate was described by Eleanor Dulles. His article in *Life,* "A Policy of Boldness," appeared in the issue of May 19, 1952.

CHAPTER SIXTEEN *Beetle Juice* The description of how Allen Dulles came back officially into U.S. intelligence is based on several sources: Walter Pforzheimer, Lawrence Houston, Robert Amory, and Ray S. Cline. The portrait of General Walter Bedell Smith is based on the author's own encounters with

him, and on many other sources. Walter Pforzheimer, one of his greatest admirers, is responsible for the description: "he was brutal, brutal . . ."

The quotation from H. A. R. (Kim) Philby about both Smith and Allen Dulles comes from letters to the author. Smith's attempt to recruit General Strong and his error in switching to Jackson were described by a CIA source who does not wish to be identified. The same source described Frank Wisner's discomfiture at being replaced as deputy director of Plans by Allen Dulles.

The description of the CIA's German operations under Wisner in cooperation with Gehlen come from several sources, including Gehlen's memoirs, conversations with CIA officials, and a former chief aide of Wisner, Howard Roman.

The Wisner operation to "blow" Noel Field to the Soviets is one of the black secrets of the CIA, and the source of the information about it (British, incidentally) does not wish to be identified. The background to the Philby involvement in the Albanian operation is also confidential.

Background to Philby comes from the author's own knowledge of him, from various British sources formerly close to him, and from FBI documents. The quotations from Philby are contained in his letters to the author. (See Appendix: Letters from a Spy.)

CHAPTER SEVENTEEN *All Aboard* The domestic background of the Dulles clan at the time of the 1952 election comes from close members of the family, and Allen's contributions to the campaign from his friends and associates at the CIA. The Agency's attempts to penetrate the Soviet Union were described to the author by Howard Roman, who worked in close cooperation with both Wisner and Allen Dulles.

Averell Harriman's remarks about Foster Dulles's "liberation policy" were made in his Oral History in the Princeton Papers, as were his criticisms of Dwight D. Eisenhower.

Henry R. Luce's hopes of getting a job with the Eisenhower administration are described by Mary Bancroft in *Luce and His Empire.* Walter Judd's comments come from his Oral History in the Princeton Papers.

For the background to the jockeying for position that preceded General Bedell Smith's departure from the CIA and Allen Dulles's apotheosis, I have gone to several sources, including Walter Pforzheimer, Howard Roman, Stuart Hedden, and Kim Philby, and I have also consulted *The Real CIA* by Lyman B. Kirkpatrick, Jr. (New York: Macmillan, 1968). The quotations concerning Wild Bill Donovan's rivalry with Allen Dulles come from Walter Pforzheimer.

The details of Allen Dulles, Jr.'s, war wound in Korea and his parents' dash to his side were given to the author by Eleanor Dulles. She also described her

visit to Foster Dulles after the election, their discussion of McCarthy, and her subsequent fight to hold on to her job at State.

CHAPTER EIGHTEEN *Bread and Circuses* George V. Allen's story of his strange visit to the White House to see President Eisenhower is told in his Oral History in the Princeton Papers. The description of Eisenhower by Paul Theroux comes from a review of Kay Summersby Morgan's book, *Past Forgetting: My Love Affair with Dwight D. Eisenhower,* which he wrote for the *New Statesman* (London), January 21, 1977. W. Averell Harriman's remarks come from his Oral History in the Princeton Papers.

John Hanes, Jr.'s, description of his work at the State Department as assistant, with Roderick O'Connor, to Foster Dulles comes from his Oral History in the Princeton Papers. Paul Nitze's conversation with Foster after the inauguration was recalled by Nitze in a conversation with the author.

John Hanes, Jr.'s, account of his (and his sister's) encounters with McCarthy come from his Oral History at Princeton. For the background to McCarthy's so-called anti-Communist campaign against the State Department, and Foster Dulles's reaction to it, I have relied on many sources, including *The Eisenhower Years* by Richard H. Rovere (New York: Farrar, Straus and Cudahy, 1956), *The China Hands* by E. J. Kahn, Jr. (New York: Viking, 1972), *Men Against McCarthy* by Richard M. Fried (New York: Columbia University Press, 1976), and my own observations at the time as a correspondent. I also talked at length with Alger Hiss about his experiences with McCarthy and his association with Foster Dulles.

For background to the activities of Scott McLeod, several people were consulted, including Eleanor Dulles, and I have also used the Oral Histories of John Hanes, Jr., Roderick O'Connor, and several other ex-State Department members in the Princeton Papers.

The story of the Cohn-Schine book-burning expedition to Europe, and how it affected Theodore H. White, was told to the author by Benjamin Bradlee, executive editor of the Washington *Post.*

CHAPTER NINETEEN *Double Deals* Allen Dulles's most important brush with McCarthy involved both Walter Pforzheimer, the CIA's legislative counsel at the time, and William Bundy, the target of McCarthy's attack. Both Pforzheimer and Bundy recalled to the author how they were involved and what happened to them. The letters exchanged between McCarthy and Allen Dulles during the subsequent confrontation come from a source that does not wish to be identified.

Several members and ex-members of the CIA have helped construct the method by which Allen Dulles ran the Agency and built up his contacts during

the early years of the Eisenhower administration. Howard Roman is responsible for the "his business was people" quotation. Kim Philby, in letters to the author, described some of Allen's right-hand men, including Kim Roosevelt.

The description of the relations between Foster Dulles and Eisenhower's adviser, Emmett John Hughes, is based on Hughes's Oral History in the Princeton Papers and his book, *The Ordeal of Power* (New York: Atheneum, 1962). Paul Nitze's clash with Roderick O'Connor, and Foster's maladroit appearance before the House Committee on Appropriations, were described to the author by Nitze and his assistant, Burt Marshall, who were of course closely involved in trying to retrieve the disaster.

The statement issued by the National Security Council after the death of Josef Stalin, and Foster Dulles's part in it, is based on the version given by President Eisenhower in *Mandate for Change* by Dwight D. Eisenhower (New York: Doubleday, 1963). The presidential conferences which subsequently took place in connection with Eisenhower's planned speech are quoted from *The Ordeal of Power,* and from conversations the author had with Paul Nitze. The text of the President's speech is taken from contemporary reports.

For background to the sequel I have gone to contemporary reports, the Oral History of Richard M. Nixon in the Princeton Papers, conversations with the late Charles (Chip) Bohlen, and to a contemporary newspaper report of a statement by Henry Cabot Lodge.

General Walter Bedell Smith's encounter with Donold B. Laurie is described by Roderick O'Connor in his Oral History in the Princeton Papers. Descriptions of life on Foster Dulles's staff at State are based on conversations with several ex-members, and on the Oral Histories of O'Connor, John Hanes, Jr., Herman Phleger, Livingstone Merchant, Douglas MacArthur, Jr., Herbert Hoover, Jr., William Macomber, and Foster's principal secretary, Phyllis Bernau (later Mrs. William Macomber) in the Princeton Papers.

Foster's encounter with the president of Panama was described to the author by Burt Marshall, who was present.

CHAPTER TWENTY *Double Agents* The relationship that Foster Dulles, in particular, and his brother and sister generally, maintained with Chancellor Adenauer of Germany is described in the Oral History of the German foreign minister, Heinrich von Brentano, in the Princeton Papers, and in Roderick O'Connor's Oral History. Eleanor Dulles told the author about her own relationships at State. Details of Allen's domestic problems come from family sources. His relationships at the CIA and the rivalries among members of his senior staff were described by several Agency members and ex-members who would prefer not to be identified.

There is much literature on the Guatemalan operation, but this account principally relies on the author's conversations with Richard Bissell, Jr., who led the operation; conversations with the late Lord Avon; a report by Ray S. Cline, who was CIA's London station chief at the time; and an interesting book about the operations of the United Fruit Company in Guatemala—*An American Company: The Tragedy of United Fruit,* by Thomas McCann, edited by Henry Scammell (New York: Crown Publishers, 1976).

For details of the Buraimi Oasis imbroglio, the author has used his own researches in the Persian Gulf and at the Foreign Office Library, London (see Leonard Mosley, *Power Play: Oil in the Middle East* [New York: Random House, 1973]), reports of the International Court proceedings at Geneva, and conversations with aides of Sheikh Zaid of Abu Dhabi, whom the CIA attempted to bribe. President Nasser's remarks to Foster Dulles during his Cairo visit about this time are quoted from tape recordings of Nasser's friend and adviser, Mohammad Heikal, made available to the author.

Foster Dulles's oblique involvement with the Buraimi affair is described by Ambassador William Macomber in his Oral History in the Princeton Papers.

Foster's attitude to the British in general and Anthony Eden in particular are described in detail in Roderick O'Connor's and John Hanes, Jr.'s Oral Histories in the Princeton Papers. His "massive retaliation" threat and his London press conference on April 13, 1954, when he gave his views on the Chinese Communists, both come from contemporary newspaper reports. Admiral Radford's remarks about bombing Indochina come from his Oral History in the Princeton Papers.

There are two different versions of what the British promised (or didn't promise) over intervention in Indochina in 1954. The Dulles thesis that Anthony Eden promised British aid is based on his own report to President Eisenhower and Admiral Radford's confirmation of this in his Oral History in the Princeton Papers. On the other hand, Anthony Eden strenuously denied this in conversations with the author, and Winston Churchill's documents tend to confirm that no definite promise was given. Eleanor Dulles recalled her brother's stupefaction at the British "double cross" in a conversation with the author.

The incident in which Foster Dulles snubbed Chou En-lai at the Geneva Conference of 1954 is described by Ambassador U. Alexis Johnson in his Oral History in the Princeton Papers.

CHAPTER TWENTY-ONE *Spy in the Sky* The Agency official quoted in the account of the relationship between Foster and Allen is Richard Bissell, Jr., who worked closely with both of them. The description of Agency activities at this

time comes from discussions with several ex-officials, and from details given in the Senate and House hearings (Foreign and Military Intelligence: Final Report, Vols. I–IV).

The account of the U-2 operation is backed by a thorough reading of all reports, but most of the details come from a long series of discussions with the man who organized it, Richard Bissell, Jr. So do the descriptions of various Agency operational methods and payment routines. The Berlin Tunnel operation has been widely publicized in many accounts, and the details are here supplemented by conversations with Richard Bissell, Jr., who was closely concerned with it. The account of how heating apparatus melted the snow and almost revealed the tunnel's presence to the Communists has, of course, been told before by Allen Dulles himself in his book, *The Craft of Intelligence.* The story of the U.S. general's gaffe at a Berlin party was told by a CIA source who does not wish to be named. Confirmation that the defecting spy, George Blake, betrayed the tunnel to the Russians comes from the SIS in London.

There have been many educated guesses of how the CIA obtained its copy of the Krushchev speech, and nearly all of them have given James Jesus Angleton credit for being mainly responsible for this considerable coup. But most accounts have suggested that because Angleton had built up an intimate association with the Israeli intelligence service, Mossad, the copy of the speech must have come from them as a quid pro quo (they infiltrated an Israeli agent, posing as a Communist delegate, into the famous meeting, etc.). The Togliatti connection has always been missed until now.

Ray S. Cline's book, *Secrets, Spies and Scholars* (Washington, D.C.: Acropolis Books, 1976) is the source for the description of the discussion at CIA over whether the Krushchev speech should be released. Cline, a former deputy director of the Agency, was involved in the discussion with Allen Dulles and Angleton.

CHAPTER TWENTY-TWO *Nile Boil* The quotation about General Walter Bedell Smith's state of health comes from John W. Hanes, Jr.'s, Oral History in the Princeton Papers. Eleanor Dulles discussed Foster's state of health at this time. Clover Dulles's work on a Jungian philosophical study was mentioned by a member of her family.

Background to the summit conference comes from discussions with many people involved, including the late Lord Avon (Sir Anthony Eden), and the quotations from Roderick O'Connor's description in his Oral History in the Princeton Papers. He accompanied his chief to the conference.

Churchill's remark about the Egyptians was repeated to the author by Lord Avon.

Admiral Radford's proposal that Shanghai should be atom-bombed was reported in the press at the time.

The description of President Nasser's journey to Rangoon was given by his adviser, Mohammad Heikal. Allen Dulles's round-the-world journey is described by Ray Cline in *Secrets, Spies and Scholars.*

The activities and conversations of Henry Byroade, Larry Eichelberger, etc., in Cairo come from various sources, including tape recordings made by Mohammad Heikal, who acted as go-between for both the Americans and President Nasser on several occasions. The tapes were made available to the author.

CHAPTER TWENTY-THREE *Not Worth a Dam* Louis Jefferson, Jr.'s, description of Foster's journey to Georgia to see the President, and of his general relations with Eisenhower, is taken from his Oral History in the Princeton Papers. Jefferson was Foster's security officer at State.

Richard Milhous Nixon's account of what happened following the President's first coronary attack comes from his Oral History in the Princeton Papers. How he was briefed by the CIA was described by a confidential source.

Foster Dulles gave the interview on "Brinkmanship," as it came to be known, to James Shepley of Time-Life, and it was published in *Life* magazine on January 16, 1956.

The transcript of the conversations between Secretary of the Treasury George Humphrey and Herbert Hoover, Jr., is to be found in the Princeton Papers. The day-to-day moves in the matter of the Aswan Dam offer (and withdrawal) were described to the author by Professor Robert Bowie, Foster's foreign police adviser at the time, and it is also dealt with at some length by Ambassador William R. Macomber in his Oral History in the Princeton Papers. The incidents in Cairo following the U.S. withdrawal of the offer are based on several sources, including tapes of conversations recorded by Nasser's friend and adviser, Mohammad Heikal, and made available to the author.

The account of Eden's behavior when he heard that Nasser had nationalized the Canal was described by his press counsellor, Mr. William Clark, in an article in *The Observer* (London), on October 3, 1976.

CHAPTER TWENTY-FOUR *"A Very Sloppy Performance"* Eden's clash with the late Captain Liddell-Hart is described by Liddell-Hart in conversations at the Royal Society of Literature, London. The quotations from the resigning British minister, Mr. Anthony Nutting, are taken from his book on the Suez incident, *No End of a Lesson* (London: Constable, 1967). Foster's encounter with Lord Salisbury is told in Roderick O'Connor's Oral History in the Prince-

ton Papers. The description of Foster's visit to Prime Minister Eden at 10 Downing Street, and his strange remarks thereafter, come from Ambassador William Macomber's Oral History in the Princeton Papers. Macomber accompanied his chief to Downing Street and talked to him afterwards. Eden's version of what took place was given the author during a long talk with him in Wiltshire in the summer of 1976, shortly before he died. He strongly insisted that Foster had appeared to give his agreement, if not his approval, to the Suez operation.

Background for the description of the Watch Tower meeting after Allen's return from his world tour, and of the clash between Robert Amory and James Angleton, comes from several CIA sources, and many of the details were filled in by several members, including Richard Bissell, Jr., and Amory. Robert Amory furnished details of the subsequent meeting with Foster to discuss his foreign policy speech. The description of the meeting between Foster and Admiral Arleigh Burke and the conversations that took place are in Burke's Oral History in the Princeton Papers.

In several talks over many hours, Mr. Richard Bissell, Jr., described in detail his organization of the U-2 operation, and of the fortuitous circumstances in which the plane photographed the before and after of the RAF raid on Cairo.

Frank Wisner vented his anger over America's failure to take action in Hungary at a Watch Tower meeting at the CIA, and the account here is an amalgam of the versions of several senior members of the Agency who were present.

The UN meeting at which a cease-fire was ordered at Suez was reported fully by the newspapers at the time, but this account is backed by descriptions and details in the Oral Histories of Carl McCardle and Herman Phleger in the Princeton Papers. Both of them accompanied Foster to New York. The author was also present as a correspondent.

The description of Secretary of the Treasury George Humphrey's squeeze on the British pound sterling is based on British banking reports.

CHAPTER TWENTY-FIVE *Spies in the Stratosphere* Eleanor Dulles told the author of her "brain tumor" misadventure during World War II, and she also filled in details of Foster's illness during the Suez crisis. The fullest account of Foster's attack and hospitalization is given by Ambassador William Macomber in his Oral History in the Princeton Papers; the Papers also fill in the background to the canceled Eden visit to Eisenhower.

Richard Bissell, Jr., told the author of the relations between the Mexican president and the local CIA station chief, and he also described his experiences in the building of the CIA's first space satellites.

Background to the description of the Lebanese crisis and American landings

there comes from several sources, including the Oral History in the Princeton Papers by Mr. Camille Chamoun, the Lebanese president, Admiral Arleigh Burke's Oral History, Mr. Kim Philby's letters, and Mr. Harold Macmillan's book, *Riding the Storm* (London: Macmillan, 1971), from which the exchange between him and President Eisenhower is taken.

The description of Frank Wisner's Indonesian operation comes from Ambassador Hugh S. Cumming, Jr., and is to be found in the Princeton Papers.

CHAPTER TWENTY-SIX *Final Call* Miss Phyllis Bernau (later Mrs. William Macomber), who was Foster's principal private secretary, describes the collapse of Foster's bunk during the transatlantic flight in her Oral History in the Princeton Papers. Mr. Selwyn Lloyd, at that time Foreign Secretary in the British government, has given an account of Foster's plane stopover at Brize Norton.

Background to the account of the Quemoy-Matsu crisis comes from contemporary newspaper reports and from Admiral Arleigh Burke's Oral History in the Princeton Papers. Foster Dulles's remarks to William Clark were made in a BBC interview during his stopover at Brize Norton and broadcast later.

Foster's last trip to Duck Island with Janet is described in Eleanor Lansing Dulles's book, *The Last Year* (New York: Harcourt, Brace, Jovanovich, 1963), and more details were given in conversations with the author. She also described the Thanksgiving Day dinner, Foster's hospitalization, and his pledge to Adenauer. Foster's last day was also carefully recorded by Ambassador William Macomber, and it is from his account in the Princeton Papers that I have taken many details.

The account of the funeral is based on eyewitness descriptions and contemporary newspaper reports. Dean Acheson's remarks about the service were made to Mr. Lucius D. Battle, who repeated them to the author.

CHAPTER TWENTY-SEVEN *Nose in the Trough* Richard Bissell, Jr., described to the author the results at the CIA of Foster's death, and its impact on Allen Dulles. Eleanor's illness while touring the world for the State Department was recounted by her during conversations with the author. Richard Bissell gave the detailed account of the White House meeting to plan the U-2 flight over Russia. He, Howard Roman, Walter Pforzheimer, Lawrence Houston, and Robert Amory talked about Allen's fascination with gadgetry.

The description of the Alibi Club celebration for CBS comes from a conversation with Mr. William Bundy.

Richard Bissell talked to the author about various phases of CIA activities abroad. Mohammad Heikal described the meeting with President Nasser.

Background to the Lumumba assassination discussions comes from conver-

sations with Richard Bissell, Jr., and from reports at the Senate hearings (Foreign and Military Intelligence: Final Report, Vols. I–IV). Eisenhower's remarks about Lumumba come from Vol. II of his autobiography, *Waging Peace* (New York: Doubleday, 1965).

CHAPTER TWENTY-EIGHT *Siempre Fidel* The kidnapping of U.S. sailors at Guantanamo Bay is recalled by Admiral Arleigh Burke in his Oral History in the Princeton Papers.

The background to the organization of the Bay of Pigs operation comes from various sources, chief of which are Richard Bissell, Jr., William Bundy, and Dean Rusk, all of whom were involved in it. I have of course also read all the available documents, contemporary newspaper reports, and Cuban accounts of the operation.

The CIA's mail-opening operation at the Ford Foundation was described to the author by Dean Rusk.

The Kirkpatrick Report on the Bay of Pigs operation is still restricted, but the tone of its condemnation of Allen Dulles is known throughout the Agency.

Eleanor Dulles's last dealings with Dean Rusk at State were described to the author both by Eleanor and by Dean Rusk.

CHAPTER TWENTY-NINE *Such Other Functions* Allen's life after his retirement was described to the author by Eleanor and by Howard Roman, who collaborated with him on his books. Dean Rusk described to the author his experiences before the Warren Commission. Willie Morris, in an article in the Washington *Star,* told of his attempt to collaborate with Allen on an article for Harper's about the Bay of Pigs, and Eleanor also gave the author her version.

Howard Roman described Allen's visit to Ascona, Switzerland, to relive the drama of Operation SUNRISE. Allen's subsequent mission for President Johnson to the South, his illnesses, and final hospitalization were described by many of his friends, colleagues, and collaborators, including Lawrence Houston, Howard Roman, Robert Amory, and, of course, Eleanor Dulles. Details of the funeral oration come from contemporary newspaper accounts, and the source of its authorship from a confidential informant.

Envoi Details for the description of the summer party at Henderson, New York, come from Eleanor Dulles and close friends of the family.

Index

Abdulla, King of Transjordan, 71
Abu Dhabi, 348
Abwehr, 5, 134, 135*n*, 148, 494
Acheson, Dean, 103–104, 195, 196, 248, 250–251, 253–257, 261, 263, 307, 321, 328, 400, 449
Adams, John Quincy, 291
Adenauer, Konrad, 7, 324, 325, 337, 343, 430, 444–446, 449
Airey, Terence S., 179, 480
Albania, 278–279
Alexander, Sir Harold, 184, 187
Allen, George V., 256, 302–303, 389, 391, 401
Allison, John, 256, 257, 259
Alsop, Joseph, 357
Alsop, Mrs. Joseph, 357
America First campaign, 99–100, 111
Amory, Derek Heathcote, 414
Amory, Robert, 287, 319, 345–346, 394, 413–415, 457
Angleton, James Jesus, 237, 241, 283–284, 287, 346, 375–377, 394, 414, 457, 483
Anti-Semitism, 88–91
Aramco, 348–349
Arbenz, Jacob, 347, 388, 459, 470
Arkel, Gerhard van, 172
Astor, Lady, 202
Aswan Dam, 395–403, 406
Atlantic Charter, 117, 120

Attlee, Clement, 119
Avery, Janet, 26, 28–31. *See also* Dulles, Janet (Mrs. John Foster)

B2H2 Resolution, 120*n*
Badoglio, Pietro, 144
Bagdad Pact, 384
Bancroft, Mary, 170–171, 173, 180–181, 184, 210, 247–248, 264, 287, 292, 476
Bandung Conference, 384–385
Bank of International Settlements, The (Eleanor Dulles), 93*n*
Barnes, Tracy, 345, 347, 366, 457
Baruch, Bernard, 19, 43, 56, 154, 190
Baszna, Elyesa, 160–161
Batista, Fulgencio, 464–465
Battle, Lucius D., 248–252, 262–263, 449
Bay of Pigs, 8, 282, 297, 469–473
Beck, Josef, 497
Belgian Congo, 461–463
Beneš, Edouard, 45, 48, 497
Bennett, Sir Courtney, 37
Berding, Andrew, 226
Bergson, Henri, 26, 99
Beria, Lavrent Pavlovich, 235
Berlin, 5, 195, 201, 293, 299–301, 344, 451–452
Berlin crisis (1958), 443–445, 448
Berlin Tunnel, 371–373

Bernadotte, Count Folk, 200, 201
Bernadotte Plan, 200, 201
Bernau, Phyllis, 339, 403, 440
Beveridge, William Henry, 69
Bevin, Ernest, 191, 195–199
Bezanson, Anne, 66
Bidault, Georges, 191, 197, 360
Bielaski, Bruce, 38
Billington, James, 386
Bissell, Richard, Jr., 346, 366–372, 374–375, 413, 431–433, 450, 453–457, 459, 460, 462, 465–471
Black, Eugene, 396, 397, 400
Blake, George, 373
Bliss, Woods, 42
Blondheim, David, 70, 85–88, 93–95, 104–105
Blum, Paul, 176–177, 243
"Boer War, The: A History" (Allen Dulles), 15–17, 65
Bohlen, Charles (Chip), 193–195, 311, 317, 337
Bowie, Robert, 338, 340, 401–403
Braden, Spruille, 347n
Braden, Tom, 345
Bradlee, Benjamin, 316
Bradley, Omar, 171
Brandt, Willy, 344, 445
Brentano, Heinrich von, 324
Bridges, Styles, 312
Brinkmanship, 395, 441
British Security Commission (BSC), 114
Brown, "Cat," 418
Brownell, Herbert, 218
Bruce, David, 114, 137, 164, 165, 223
Bruening, Heinrich, 114
Brugmann, Hans, 205
Bryan, William Jennings, 35–37
Bulganin, Nikolai, 381, 383
Bunche, Ralph, 296
Bundy, McGeorge, 215–216
Bundy, William, 104, 287, 319–323, 345, 457, 469, 470
Bundy, Mrs. William, 319, 321, 322
Buraimi Oasis, 348–353

Burgess, Guy, 280, 285
Burke, Arleigh, 415–416, 418, 419, 435, 441, 464
Burlingham, C. C., 103
Burns, Eugene, 435
Byrnes, James R., 191
Byroade, Henry, 387, 389–391, 400, 403

Cabell, Charles, 367, 369, 467
Cadogan, Sir Alexander, 120
Cambon, Jules, 61
Campione, 142–143
Canaris, Admiral, 134
Canfield, Cass, 475
Cannon, Clarence, 431
Carnegie, Andrew, 19
Carnegie Endowment for International Peace, 190
Casablanca Conference (1943), 134–135
Castelbarco, Mrs. Wally, 143–144, 176, 177, 183–184
Castro, Fidel, 460, 461, 463–466, 470
Central Intelligence Agency, see CIA
Central Intelligence Group (CIG), 237–240, 318, 319
Century Group, 103
Chamberlain, Neville, 496–497
Chamberlin, Stephen J., 242
"Chance for Peace" speech, 332–336
Chiang Kai-shek, 246, 254, 256, 258, 305, 306, 311, 333, 436, 439–440
China Lobby, 290
Chou En-lai, 360–362, 385, 422
Churchill, Clarissa Spencer, 382n
Churchill, Sir Winston, 109, 117, 118, 134, 137, 163, 180, 235, 337, 353, 357, 361, 380, 382–384, 434, 448
CIA (Central Intelligence Agency): in Albania, 278–279; under Bedell Smith, 268–273; Berlin crisis (1958), 443–444; Berlin Tunnel, 371–373; budget, 5, 323–324, 431; Buraimi Oasis affair, 348–353; in

Congo, 462–463; in Cuba, 460, 465–472; Dulles becomes director, 293–297; early association of Dulles with, 240–246; formation of, 239–240; in Guatemala, 347–348, 366, 388, 459, 470; Hungarian uprising, 419–421; in Indonesia, 437–438; in Iran, 325–327, 347, 388, 492; Krushchev speech transcript and, 375–378; in Lebanon, 493; liberation policy, 288–290; McCarthyism and, 318–322; mail-opening operation, 470; NSC50 report, 246, 269–272; OPC, 244–245, 272–277, 364; size, 364, 370; U-2 flights, 365–370, 430, 431, 453–456, 458; in Vietnam, 457–458

Ciano, Count Galeazzo, 139, 144, 223

Clark, Mark, 193, 194, 204, 207

Clark, William, 405, 442

Clay, Lucius D., 193, 225, 238, 242, 243, 263–264, 266

Clemenceau, Georges, 55, 56, 88

Clements, 356n

Cline, Ray S., 239, 366, 377–378, 386, 394, 436, 437, 440

Cohen, Ben, 193, 200

Cohn, Roy, 315–317, 320–322

Commission for a Just and Durable Peace, 116

Committee to Win the War by Aiding the Allies, 103

Condor Legion, 109

Conference on Arms Traffic (1925), 71

Coolidge, Calvin, 72, 75

Corcoran, Thomas G. ("The Cork"), 347n

Corona program, 432

Correa, Matthias, 246

Cowgill, Felix Henry, 158

Crabbe, Lionel (Buster), 367

Craft of Intelligence, The (Allen Dulles and Howard Roman), 475

Cuba, 8, 282, 297, 460, 464–473

Cumming, Hugh S., Jr., 437–438, 452–454

Cummings, Wilbur, 76

Cutler, Robert, 330, 347n

Czechoslovakia, 48, 145, 146

Daladier, Édouard, 497

Dalton, Baron Hugh, 69

Dansey, Claud, 132–133, 157–159

Davies, John Paton, 310–311

Davis, Dixie, 206

Davis, John W., 19

Dawes Plan, 59, 75

Dayan, Moshe, 413

Denniston, Alastair, 158

Dewey, Thomas E., 100, 101, 103, 106, 107, 121, 150–154, 166, 189, 213, 215, 216–218, 222–223, 292, 433

Dickson, Sir Pierson, 422, 423

Dien Bien Phu, 355, 356, 358

Dillon, Douglas, 316, 445

Disarmament Conference (1926), 71

Dollmann, Eugen, 175

Donovan, William J. (Wild Bill), 108–113, 121–124, 131, 133, 139, 157, 161, 164–165, 223–225, 235, 239, 240, 295–297

Douglas, William O., 76

Dudorov, Timon, 274

Duff, Jim, 264

Dulles, Allen, III (grandson of Allen), 484

Dulles, Allen Macy (father), 13, 17, 18, 21, 24, 26, 87, 93

Dulles, Allen Macy, Jr. (son of Allen), 72, 126, 248, 288, 297–298, 333, 345, 380, 443, 476, 480, 485

Dulles, Allen Welsh: as author, 9, 475–476, 478–481; Bay of Pigs, 8, 282, 297, 469–473; birth, 13; "Chance for Peace" speech and, 332–333; as chief of OSS in Germany, 224–229; childhood, 14–17, 21–23; children of, 72, 248, 288,

297–298, 345; CIA and, *see* CIA; as
COI staff member, 113–114; courtship, 64–66; death, 482; Donovan,
relationship with, 108–111, 113;
education, 26–27; Egyptian arms
deal, 386–387; Eleanor, relationship with, 15; Field and, 49, 73n,
130, 147–148, 172, 275–277;
finances, 38, 73, 77; in Foreign Service, 38–39, 45–49, 62, 71–72, 76;
funeral, 482–483; health, 13–14,
18, 150, 180, 184, 186, 187, 287–
288, 481–482; John Foster, relationship with, 7, 23–24, 450–451;
Kolbe, relationship with, 156–157,
159–163; law career, 76–79; marriage, 66; Nazism, attitude towards,
88–92, 95–99; 1940 election, 101–
102; 1948 election, 215–216, 222–
223; 1952 election, 263–266, 287,
288; Nixon and, 243n; Operation
SUNRISE, 179–188, 223, 227, 230,
476, 479–481; personality of, 6, 15,
17, 92–93; Philby, relationship
with, 279, 282–286, 489–491, 494–
495; power of, 5–6; religion and,
41; resignation from CIA, 9, 473;
Soviets, attitude towards, 227–229;
Stalin's death and, 331; Suez crisis,
413, 415, 420; travels, early, 32–34;
on Warren Commission, 9, 477–
478; wife, relationship with, 73–74,
125–126, 169, 180–183, 476–477;
women, relationships with, 33, 48,
60–61, 74, 125, 169–171; in World
War I, 45–49; in World War II, 99–
100, 103, 126–149, 154–165, 169–
188, 210, 223, 229–230
Dulles, Ann (daughter of Eleanor),
106, 204–206, 210, 380, 443
Dulles, Avery (son of John Foster),
54, 82–83, 95–98, 104, 168, 202–
204, 219, 343, 380
Dulles, Clover (Mrs. Allen), 3–4, 9,
11–12, 72, 76, 78, 93, 95, 102, 104,
125–126, 169, 180–183, 243, 247,

282, 287, 297–298, 342, 345, 380,
386, 387, 443, 447, 476–477, 479,
481, 484, 494
Dulles, Clover Todd (daughter of
Allen), 72, 288
Dulles, David (son of Eleanor), 104–
106, 204–206, 210, 248, 264, 380,
443, 485
Dulles, Edith (granddaughter of John
Foster), 444
Dulles, Edith Foster (mother), 13, 16,
17–19
Dulles, Eleanor Lansing, 7, 37, 192,
194, 198, 221, 228, 264–267, 358,
484–486; Adenauer, relationship
with, 343; Allen, relationship with,
15; Berlin crisis (1958), 443–444; at
Berlin desk, 5, 293, 299–301, 344,
451–452; Blondheim, relationship
with, 70, 85–88, 93–95, 104–105;
childhood, 14–17, 19–23; children
of, 104, 106, 204–206, 210, 248,
380, 443, 485; doctorate thesis, 69–
70, 84; education, 40; FBI surveillance of, 123–125; finances, 84,
208; on German Committee, 167–
168; health, 19, 150, 426, 451–453;
industry, work in, 66–69; on Janet
Dulles, 29, 30; John Foster, relationship with, 23–24, 93–94, 106,
299–301, 451; marriage, 94; at National Production Agency, 247; Nazism, attitude towards, 89–90; 1940
election, 101, 104, 106; personality, 92; religion and, 41; resignation from State, 473–474; Roosevelt, F.D., attitude towards,
167–168; as teacher, 69; at Versailles Conference, 58–60; in
Vienna, 205–213; in World War I,
41–42, 50–54; in World War II,
204–210
Dulles, Janet (Mrs. John Foster), 31–
32, 43, 54–55, 57, 59, 67, 74, 81–
83, 87, 94, 96, 104, 152, 153, 169,
203, 214–216, 219, 247, 257, 299,

333, 440, 442–443, 445, 447, 448, 484

Dulles, Joan (daughter of Allen), 72, 138*n,* 206, 210, 288, 479

Dulles, John (son of John Foster), 54, 81, 168, 203, 380, 444

Dulles, John Foster: Adenauer, relationship with, 324, 325, 337, 343, 444–446; "agonizing reappraisal" speech, 325*n;* aides at State, 306, 339–340; Allen, relationship with, 7, 23–24, 363–364, 450–451; as ambassador-at-large, 259; Aswan Dam, 395–403; attempts to join Truman Administration, 248–252; Austrian Treaty, 261; becomes Secretary of State, 292–293; Berlin crisis (1958), 443–445, 448; as bipartisan consultant at State, 254–259; birth, 18; brinkmanship, 395, 441; Buraimi Oasis affair, 351–353; "Chance for Peace" speech and, 332–336; childhood, 14–16, 19, 21–23; children of, 54, 80–83, 202–204, 219–220, 343, 380; Chou En-lai and, 360–361; college experiences, 24–26; Congress and, 305–307; courtship, 28–30; Cuba and, 464–465; Dawes Plan, 75; death, 7, 448; Eden, relationship with, 353–354, 357–359, 382, 410, 411; education, 24, 29; Egyptian arms deal, 349–350, 383–389, 391–392; Eisenhower, relationship with, 305–306, 332–336, 342, 393, 429, 433; Eisenhower Doctrine, 434–435; Eleanor, relationship with, 23–24, 93–94, 106, 299–301, 451; European Defense Community project, 324–325; finances, 31, 63, 73; funeral, 7, 448–449; health, 31, 150, 152, 379–380, 426–428, 433, 442, 444–448; Hiss case, 311, 336; Indochina and, 354–360; Indonesia and, 436–438; Israel and, 200–202; Japanese Peace Treaty

negotiations, 255–257, 259–261; Korea and, 256–257, 261, 332–334; law career, 29–31, 63, 75–76, 79–80; Lebanon and, 435, 493; liberation policy, 288–291; McCarthyism and, 310–311, 314–317; marriage, 31; Marshall, relationship with, 192–193, 199; Marshall Plan and, 198–199; massive retaliation, 265, 354–355; Nazism, attitude towards, 88–92, 95–99; 1940 election, 101–102, 107; 1944 election, 150–154; 1948 election, 214–215; 1952 election, 263–266, 288–291; Nixon, relationship with, 336, 343–344, 394–395; personality, 92–93; postwar conferences, 190–198; Quemoy and Matsu, 439–441; religion and, 40; reorganization of State, 307–309; Roosevelt, F. D., attitude towards, 166–167; as senator, 216–221; Soviets, attitude towards, 198, 199, 337; Stalin's death and, 330–331; Suez crisis, 406, 409–412, 415, 416, 418, 419, 422, 423, 425; summit meeting (1955), 380–383; *tour d'horizon* before Congress (1953), 327–330; U-2 operation, 367, 369; at Versailles Conference, 56–59, 61–62; wife, relationship with, 31–32, 54–55, 59, 67; in World War I, 42–43, 54; in World War II, 99–100, 111, 113, 116, 117, 119, 120

Dulles, Lilias (daughter of John Foster), 54, 81–82, 168

Dulles, Margaret (sister), 14, 21, 67

Dulles, Nataline (sister), 14, 17, 21, 87

Dumbarton Oaks Conference (1944), 151

Dupres, Émile, 296

Eban, Abba, 201

Economic Consequences of the Peace, The (Keynes), 59

Eden, Sir Anthony, 119–120, 347–348, 351–359, 367, 369, 370, 381–383, 396, 398, 404–414, 416, 417, 424, 428, 429, 434
Eden, Clarissa, 30–31
Edwards, Deane, 67
Egypt, 349–350, 383–389, 391–392, 395–425, 428–429, 433–434, 461
Ehrenburg, Ilya, 6
Eichelberger, John (Larry), 386–388
Eisenhower, Dwight D., 7, 230, 235, 264–266, 287, 290–293, 295, 296, 299, 302–306, 330–338, 342, 352, 353, 357, 365, 368, 369, 381–383, 393, 394, 398–400, 407, 412, 413, 415–417, 427–429, 432–434, 438, 439, 441, 445–448, 451, 453–456, 458, 460–463, 490, 495
Eisenhower, Mamie, 290, 334
Eisenhower, Milton, 303, 334
Eisenhower Doctrine, 434–435
Ely, Henrietta, 41–42
Erhard, Jacob, 204
European Defense Community project, 324–325

Faho, Burton, 296
Fairbank, John K., 296
Faisal, Prince, 348, 351
Farouk, King of Egypt, 350
FBI (Federal Bureau of Investigation), 112, 114, 123–124, 364
Federal Council of Churches, 151
Feisal, King of Iraq, 71, 404, 435
Field, Herbert, 47, 48–49, 129
Field, Herta, 130, 148, 277n
Field, Nina, 49
Field, Noel, 49, 73n, 129–130, 147–148, 171–172, 227, 275–277
Finch, Jim, 390
Fischer, John, 478
Forgan, J. Russell, 223, 224
Forzane, Jacqueline, 60
Foster, John Watson (grandfather), 16, 18, 22, 31, 79, 301
Fourteen Points, 56

Frank, Karl, 114
French Franc, The (Eleanor Dulles), 70, 84
Fuchs, Klaus, 247n, 279, 285n

Gaevernitz, Gero von Schulz, 138, 171, 174, 181, 186, 480
Gannon, Robert, 220
Gaunt, Alex, 37–38, 40, 71
Gehlen, Reinhard, 230–236, 238, 240–242, 273–275, 371
Giraud, Henri, 144
Gisevius, Hans Berndt, 138–140, 148, 162–164, 203
Gläser, Erika, 148, 172
Goebbels, Joseph, 89
Goldberg, Arthur, 114
Gomulka, Josef, 277
Goodpaster, Andrew, 368, 369, 454
Gottlieb, Sidney, 459
Green, Edward, 76
Greene, Jerry, 440, 445
Grimm, Kurt, 136–137
Gromyko, Andrei, 449
Grubelli, Countess de, 141–143
Guatemala, 347–348, 366, 388, 459, 470
Guinzburg, Victor de, 232, 233

Hagerty, James H., 218, 220, 330, 427
Haile Selassie, Emperor of Ethiopia, 109
Halperin, Maurice, 296
Hanes, John W., Jr., 306–307, 309, 312–313, 315, 339, 353, 379, 402
Harcourt, Lord, 399
Harding, Warren G., 72
Harriman, W. Averell, 290–291, 304–306, 311, 337
Hauge, Gabriel, 218
Hedden, Stuart, 294, 295, 297
Heikal, Mohammad, 388, 390
Helms, Richard, 226, 237, 241, 364n, 370, 375, 394, 457, 463

Herter, Christian, 8, 352, 447, 450, 451, 453, 454, 456
Herter Commission, 243
Herzog, Helene, 33, 48
Higginbotham, Sam, 32
Hillenkoetter, Roscoe H., 240, 241, 243–245, 269, 272, 280
Himmler, Heinrich, 145, 147, 148, 176, 179, 180
Hinshaw, Edward, 82
Hiss, Alger, 311, 319, 336
Hitch, Charles, 296
Hitler, Adolf, 69, 88, 90, 95, 96, 137–139, 145, 146, 163, 179, 230, 496
Hobhouse, Leonard, 69
Hoegner, William, 228
Hofer, Franz, 185
Hoffman, Paul, 292
Hohenlohe, Prince Egon, 145–147
Holborn, Hajo, 296
Hoopes, Townsend, 255
Hoover, J. Edgar, 112, 114, 123–124, 224, 240, 319, 364
Hoover, Herbert, 339, 396
Hoover, Herbert, Jr., 327, 396–399, 401–403, 428, 429, 437
Hope, Sir John, 357
Hope, Liza, 357
Horton, Philip, 241
House, Edward, 56, 57
Houston, Jeanie, 4, 9, 10–12
Houston, Lawrence Reid, 4, 9–11, 239, 345, 394
Hoxha, Enver, 278
Hughes, Charles Evans, 75
Hughes, Emmett John, 332, 333, 336
Hull, Cordell, 151–153
Humphrey, George, 342, 355, 393, 396–400, 424–425, 431, 446, 449
Hungary, 419–421, 423, 424
Hunt, Jim, 10–11
Hussein, Ahmed, 388, 390, 400–402
Hussein, King of Jordan, 350

Indochina, 354–362
Indonesia, 436–438

Iran, 325–327, 347, 388, 492
Iran, Shah of, 325–327, 347
Iraq, 413, 435
Israel, 199–202, 413–417

Jackson, C. D., 330
Jackson, William H., 246, 271–272, 284
Japanese Peace Treaty, 255–257, 259–261
Jaritzky, Alfred, 63, 75
Jebb, Sir Gladwyn, 357
Jebb, Lady, 357
Jefferson, Louis W., Jr., 393
Jellico, Earl, 279
Jess, Hans, 274
Johnson, Kelly, 366
Johnson, Lyndon B., 356, 446, 477, 478
Johnson, U. Alexis, 360, 361
Johnston, Eric, 389–391
Johnston, Robert, 315
Jordan, 350, 413, 435
Joyce, Robert, 279
Judd, Walter H., 292
Jung, C. G., 170

Kemal Ataturk, 71
Kennan, George F., 244, 254, 255, 257–259, 311
Kennedy, John F., 7, 8, 362, 466, 468, 471–473, 477
Kennedy, Robert F., 8, 9, 468, 470, 472, 473
Keynes, John Maynard, 56, 58–59, 75, 84
Khrushchev, Nikita, 8, 375, 381, 386, 419, 443, 455–456
Killian, James Ryan, 365
Killian Committee, 365
Kingsbury, Susan, 40, 66
Kirkpatrick, Lyman B., Jr., 294–296, 472
Knatchbull-Hugessen, Sir Hugh, 160–161
Knight, Frances, 315–316

Knowland, William, 290, 306, 356n, 385
Kolbe, Fritz, 154–164, 171, 223, 229, 230
Koniev, Ivan, 230
Korea, 256–259, 261, 268, 332–335, 338

Lamont, Thomas, 59, 63
Land, Edwin, 365, 432
Lansing, Eleanor, 20, 37, 57
Lansing, Robert M., 20, 35–38, 40, 42, 43, 55–57, 79, 214, 301
Laski, Harold, 69
League of Nations, 151
Leahy, William, 123
Lebanon, 435, 493
Lehman, Herbert H., 108, 218, 220–221, 251
LeMay, Curtis, 366–367
Lemnitzer, Lyman L., 179, 480
Lend-Lease Act, 110n
Lenin, V. I., 45, 46–48
Leslie, Edge, 133
Liddell-Hart, Basil, 409
Lindbergh, Charles A., 99, 121–122
Lindsay, Frank, 279
Lloyd, Selwyn, 440
Lloyd George, David, 55, 56
Lodge, Henry Cabot, 338, 418, 421–422
London Conference (1945), 191
López Mateos, Adolfo, 444
Lothian, Lord, 205
Lourie, Donald B., 339
Luce, Clare Boothe, 440
Luce, Henry R., 171, 247–248, 287, 292
Ludendorff, Erich, 53
Lumumba, Patrice, 461–463
Lundahl, Arthur, 366
Lusitania, 36–37

MacArthur, Douglas, 254, 257, 268, 288, 339

McCardle, Carl, 249–250, 262, 361, 422, 423
McCarthy, Joseph, 290, 299, 309–311, 314, 318–322
McClintock, Rob, 493
McCloy, John J., 90
McCone, John A., 473
McCormack, John, 356n
McKnight, Henry, 309
McKnight, June, 309
MacLean, Donald, 279–280, 285
McLeod, Scott, 312–315
Macmillan, Sir Harold, 406, 407, 424, 434, 435, 448
McNally, James C., 46–47, 48
McNamara, Robert, 468
Macomber, William, 25, 339, 352, 403, 409, 411–412, 427–429, 442, 445–448
Makins, Sir Roger, 357, 399
Malenkov, Georgi M., 332
Mao Tse-tung, 254, 311
Marcuse, Herbert, 296
Marne, Battle of the, 50, 51, 53
Marshall, Burt, 329–330, 340
Marshall, George C., 191–194, 197–201, 299
Marshall Plan, 198–199, 212
Martin, Joseph, 356n
Masaryk, Jan, 45, 48
Massive retaliation, 265, 354–355
Matsu, island of, 436, 439–441
Matthew, H. Freeman, 193n
Matthews, J. B., 320
Mayer, Gerald, 156n
Mendès-France, Pierre, 361
Merchant, Livingstone, 339
Merz, Charles, 103n, 104
Meyer, Cord, 375
Mihailovic, Draja, 144, 223
Milliken, Eugene D., 356n
Mobuto, Joseph, 463
Molden, Fritz, 137–138
Molotov, V. M., 151, 191, 197, 329, 360, 362

Monnet, Jean, 56, 75, 448
Morgenthau, Henry, 167, 168
Morley, Felix, 69
Morris, Willie, 478–479
Moscow Conference (1947), 192–195, 197–198
Mossad, 376*n*, 377*n*, 414
Mossadeq, Mohammed, 325, 327, 347, 492
Mountbatten, Earl, 414, 416, 419
Murphy, Charles, 475
Murphy, Jimmy, 122, 123
Murphy, Robert, 44, 193, 406, 408, 493
Mussolini, Benito, 139

Naguib, Mohammed, 350
Nasser, Gamal Abdel, 349–351, 384–392, 395–397, 400–406, 408, 410–413, 424, 425, 428, 461
National Security Act of 1947, 239
National Security Council, 239, 365
National Security Council Report No. 50, 246, 269–272
Nazism, 88–92, 95–99
Nehru, Jawaharlal, 34, 385, 403
Nehru, Motilal, 34
Nehru, Vijaya Lakshmi, 34
Nevins, Allen, 72
Niebuhr, Reinhold, 116
Nimoschenko, Colonel, 385–386
Nitze, Paul, 195, 196, 217, 218, 259, 307–309, 328–330, 332–335, 338, 389, 469
Nixon, Pat, 344
Nixon, Richard M., 243*n*, 322, 336, 343–344, 355, 394–395, 461, 466
North Atlantic Treaty Organization (NATO), 217–218
Norton, Philip, 172
Nu, U, 385
Nutting, Anthony, 408

Oakes, John, 226
O'Brien, John Lord, 109

O'Connor, Roderick L., 218–221, 306–307, 328, 339, 343, 353, 354, 382, 409–411
Office of Coordinator of Information (COI), 111–114, 121
Office of Policy Coordination (OPC), 244–245, 272–277, 364
Office of Strategic Services (OSS), 112, 121–123, 131, 132, 141, 143, 157, 159, 160, 164, 222–229, 236, 237, 239
Office of War Information (OWI), 113*n*
Ollenhauer, Erich, 228
Oman, 348
Operation JEDBURGH, 164
Operation Overlord, 160
Operation SUNRISE, 179–188, 223, 227, 230, 476, 479–481
Operation Vulture, 357–38

Palais Rose Conference (1949), 195–196, 199
Palestine, 200
Paley, William, 457
Park, Mary, 449
Parri, Feruccio, 143–144, 176–178, 183–184
Pash, Boris, 459
Patton, George S., 227, 229
Pearson, Drew, 153
Peenemünde, island of, 137, 165
Penfield, Frederic, 39
Pforzheimer, Walter, 240, 318–322
Philby, H. A. R. (Kim), 134, 158–159, 270, 279–286, 323, 326, 482, 487–497
Philby, Harry St. John, 280, 326, 487
Philippines, 260
Phleger, Herman, 339, 422, 423
Pierce, Henry Hill, 63, 75
Pittermann, 445
Pius XII, Pope, 440
Pope, Allen, 438
Porter, Marian E., 232

Powers, Gary, 455
Presidential election: 1940, 101–102, 104, 106, 107; 1944, 150–154; 1948, 213–216, 222–223; 1952, 263–266, 287, 288–291; 1956, 417
Priest, J. P., 356n
Pulitz, Baron Wolfgang zu, 114

Quemoy, island of, 436, 439–441
Quinn, William W., 230, 233
Quirino, Elpidio, 260

Radford, Arthur W., 355–358, 385
Radio Free Europe, 266, 275
Rado, Emmy, 226, 228
Rajk, Laszlo, 276
Rappard, William, 138
Read, Conyers, 296
Reston, James (Scotty), 196, 395
Rhee, Synghman, 254, 256
Riddleberger, James W., 293, 300
Robertson, Walter, 316, 437, 438
Robinson, Geroid, 296
Robson, 69
Rockefeller, Nelson D., 270, 303
Rockefeller Foundation, 190
Roman, Howard, 12, 289, 475–477, 479, 481
Romulo, Carlos, 215
Roosevelt, Eleanor, 200, 214
Roosevelt, Franklin D., 90, 100, 101, 103, 107–111, 117, 121–122, 134, 150, 153, 154, 163, 166–168, 180, 189, 190, 239
Roosevelt, Kermit (Kim), 326–327, 345–351, 387–391, 492
Rowley, 69
Rublee, George, 104
Ruiz Cortines, Adolfo, 430
Rundstedt, Karl, 173
Rusk, Dean, 200, 251, 258, 259, 468–471, 473–474, 477–478
Russell, Richard B., 356n

Sadat, Anwar el, 350
Said, Nuri, 404, 405, 435

Salisbury, Lord, 410
San Francisco Conference, 190–191
Saud, King, 348–352
Saudi Arabia, 348–353
Schellenberg, Walter, 145, 172
Schine, David, 315–317
Schlesinger, Arthur, Jr., 172, 478
Schoenbrun, David, 215, 457
Schuman, Robert, 195
Schuschnigg, Kurt von, 136
Schweinitz, Viktor von, 185, 187
Secret Surrender, The (Allen Dulles and Howard Roman), 475, 479
Seligman, Eustace, 76, 91
Sevareid, Eric, 457
Seymour, Charles, 61
Shertok (Sharett), Moshe, 201, 386
Sherwood, Robert, 113n
Shipley, Ruth, 122, 127, 169, 205
Shurtleff, Mrs. Ernest, 50–52
Sibert, Edwin L., 233–236
Sinclair, Sir John, 281, 494
SIS (Special Intelligence Service), 5, 159, 160, 277–279, 285, 347, 369, 413, 487, 492
Six Pillars of Peace, The (John Foster Dulles), 120, 151
Smith, Nicol, 122–123
Smith, Walter Bedell, 60–61, 193, 194, 235, 268–273, 283–285, 293–297, 308, 309, 323, 324, 334, 361, 362, 379, 490–491, 495
Solod, Daniel, 385
Solz, Adam von Trott zu, 138, 148
Soraya, Queen, 326, 327
Sorensen, Ted, 478
South East Asia Treaty Organization (SEATO), 381
Space satellites, 374n, 432, 433
Sputnik, 431, 433
Stalin, Josef, 151, 180, 186, 188, 199, 234, 235, 246, 276, 330–332, 375–377
Stassen, Harold, 300, 408
State Department, 112, 122–123, 167–168, 204, 307–317, 473–474

Stauffenberg, Count Claus Schenk von, 163
Stephens, Tom, 218, 302, 303
Stephenson, William, 114
Stettinius, Edward, 190, 206
Stevens, Will, 21
Stevenson, Adlai, 190, 191, 416
Stimson, Henry L., 71
Stovall, Pleasant Alexander, 44, 47
Strang, Sir William, 497
Strong, Sir Kenneth, 270–271, 285, 495
Stroup, Russell C., 482–483
Suez crisis, 404–425, 428–429, 433–434, 461
Sukarno, Achmed, 436–438
Sullivan & Cromwell, 29, 30, 43, 63, 75–77, 88, 89, 91, 92, 190
Sweet-Escott, Bickham, 122–123
Swiatlo, Jose, 276, 277

Taft, Robert A., 101, 217, 263, 266, 287
Taft, William Howard, 19
Taiwan, 436
Tawney, 69
Thatcher, Thomas, 103
Theroux, Paul, 304
Thorez, Maurice, 375
Thyssen, Fritz, 88
Tito, Marshal, 144, 223, 246, 278
Todd, Clover, 64–66. *See also* Dulles, Clover (Mrs. Allen)
Togliatti, Palmiro, 375–377
Toscanini, Arturo, 144
Toynbee, Arnold, 119*n*
Treviranus, Gottfried, 114
Truman, Harry S., 184–188, 189, 191, 213–215, 224, 236, 237, 239, 240, 242, 243, 245, 246, 249–251, 257, 259, 261, 263, 295, 304
Tshombe, Moise, 462
Tweedy, Bronson, 463

U-2 flights, 365–370, 373, 374, 430, 431, 453–456, 458

Union Theological Seminary, 190
United Fruit Company, 347
United Nations, 151–154, 190–191, 199–201
United States Intelligence Board (USIB), 365
Usmiani, Antonio, 176–178, 183

Vanden Huyvel, Count, 132–133, 135
Vandenberg, Arthur H., 154, 190, 198–199, 217–218, 238*n*, 251
Vandenberg, Hoyt S., 237–238
Versailles Conference, 55–62
Victor, Royall, 63, 75
Victor Emmanuel, King of Italy, 144
Vietinghoff, Heinrich von, 185*n*, 187
Vincent, John Carter, 310–311
Vishinski, Andrei, 194, 195
Voice of America, 266

Wagner, Robert F., 216
Waibel, Frau, 181–182, 480
Waibel, Max, 173–175, 181, 182, 185–187, 480
Wallesch, Kurt Heinz, 274
War, Peace and Change (John Foster Dulles), 97–98
War Industries Board, 43
War or Peace? (John Foster Dulles), 197, 221
Ward, Barbara, 119*n*, 480
Wardlaw-Milne, Sir John, 118
Warner, John, 239
Warren Commission, 9, 477–478
Webb, Beatrice, 69
Webb, James, 250, 251
Webb, Sidney, 69
Weizmann, Chaim, 71
Wenner, Sturmbannführer, 178, 185, 187
Wertheimer, Nancy, 89
West, Rebecca, 125, 480
Westemar, 69
White, Theodore H., 316
White, William Allen, 103

Willkie, Wendell, 102, 107, 108, 111
Wilson, Charles, 432
Wilson, Hugh, 39
Wilson, Woodrow, 34–36, 55–59, 61–62, 117
Winant, John G., 119
Wisner, Frank, 226–229, 237–238, 244, 245, 266n, 272–273, 275–282, 284, 288, 325, 331, 337, 345, 346, 366, 371, 373–375, 377, 378, 394, 414, 419–421, 436–438, 491–492

Wisner, Polly, 346, 421
Wolff, Karl, 175–182, 185–187, 480
World Council of Churches, 96, 97, 148

Young Plan, 59

Zaid, Prince, 348–349
Zhukov, Georgi, 230, 235
Zimmer, Guido, 175